D1562199

Madness Transformed

Madness Transformed

A Reading of Ovid's Metamorphoses

Lee Fratantuono

LEXINGTON BOOKS
Lanham • Boulder • New York • Toronto • Plymouth, UK

Published by Lexington Books
A wholly owned subsidiary of The Rowman & Littlefield Publishing Group, Inc.
4501 Forbes Boulevard, Suite 200, Lanham, Maryland 20706
www.lexingtonbooks.com

Estover Road, Plymouth PL6 7PY, United Kingdom

British Library Cataloguing in Publication Information Available

Library of Congress Cataloging-in-Publication Data

Fratantuono, Lee, 1973–
  Madness transformed : a reading of Ovid's Metamorphoses / Lee Fratantuono.
    p. cm.
  Includes bibliographical references and index.
  ISBN 978-0-7391-2943-2 (cloth : alk. paper) — ISBN 978-0-7391-2944-9 (pbk. : alk.
paper)
  1. Ovid, 43 B.C.–17 or 18 A.D. Metamorphoses. 2. Fables, Latin—History and
criticism. I. Title.
  PA6519.M9F73 2011
  873'.01—dc22   2011007081

♾™ The paper used in this publication meets the minimum requirements of American
National Standard for Information Sciences—Permanence of Paper for Printed Library
Materials, ANSI/NISO Z39.48-1992.

Printed in the United States of America

For Ann Batchelder

A gift in return

Contents

Preface and Acknowledgments

In the spring of 1996, immediately after the close of the academic semester at Boston College, I sat down to read Ovid's *Metamorphoses* in a fortnight marathon. I had read Virgil's *Aeneid* in a similar fashion over the Christmas holidays with what I at the time thought to be a measure of success in my efforts to achieve something approximating an understanding of what the poet was trying to accomplish with a long and difficult epic. Seth Benardete recommended such rapid reading of the whole forest, as it were, before analyzing individual trees (especially the more beautiful ones), and his method has remained dear to me over the past several years since his untimely death in November of 2001. As with my previous work on Virgil, many an Ovidian idea was first vetted during long conversations with Professor Benardete in Waverly. If I have anything worthwhile to say on Ovid, it is because I was trained in how to read classical texts closely by Seth Benardete. The pain of loss engendered by his premature passing does not fade with the years. Harvey Mansfield has written that Professor Benardete was the "most learned man alive" at the time of his passing, a judgment Seth would have found embarrassing. But I cannot refrain from calling him the most generous.

I did not have as much success with Ovid's *Metamorphoses* in that spring of 1996 as I had seemed to have with my winter Virgiliana. My sense of comfort with the *Aeneid* was fleeting, in any case; thoughts recorded in notebooks from that winter would seem surprisingly misguided a year or so later. But Ovid was an enigma to me before, during, and long after my first complete reading of his fifteen-book masterpiece. Indeed, after that spring investigation I did not return to the *Metamorphoses* in anything approaching a sustained study for many years. Ovid haunted me, more so even than my beloved Virgil, but I was certain I could not seek to come to terms with his work until I had studied Virgil ever more intimately. For surely, I thought, the key to understanding Ovid lies at least partly (if not foundationally) in understanding his great forebear and immortal poetic rival. Ovid's *Metamorphoses* cannot be appreciated apart from Virgil's *Aeneid* or without reference to its magisterial epic predecessor. The *Metamorphoses* is both *hommage* and challenge to the *Aeneid*. After years of study of both poems, I am more convinced now than I was in college and graduate school that both Ovid and Virgil would have been in essential agreement on the nature of the Augustan principate. Different in both temperament and reaction to a shared problem, Rome's two Augustan epicists have more in common than not

I shall state my case plainly from the start: I believe Ovid shared largely the same views as Virgil about the Augustan regime. *Madness Unchained* (Lexington Books, 2007) sought to provide an *explication de texte* for Virgil's *Aeneid* that could be used with profit by any reader of the poem (Latinist or Latin-less, of any level of sophistication in the study of Latin literature). *Madness Transformed: A Reading of Ovid's Metamorphoses* is a sequel to that work, with the same intent and hope: to provide a comprehensive introduction to and guide through a densely engaging epic. The present volume, then, like its predecessor, seeks to proceed book by book, metamorphosis by metamorphosis, through Ovid's grand spectacle, all towards a goal of trying to understand what the master poet was seeking to convey to his contemporary audience in Augustan Rome about the nature of the profound changes that had come over the city and empire.

Madness Unchained is one of many introductions to the *Aeneid* that are available to readers of the poem of all levels of scholarly understanding. There are comparatively fewer such works on the *Metamorphoses*, which I take to reflect the seemingly disparate mass of material that confronts and occasionally confounds readers of the epic. I assumed before commencing serious study of Ovid's masterpiece that his epic exhibited a carefully wrought, elaborate unity of design. The more time I spend with the poem, the more convinced I am of the truth of this prior assumption. I complained in *Madness Unchained* that Virgil suffered from pernicious excerpting. The same is true for the *Metamorphoses*, perhaps even more so than for the *Aeneid*. This book assumes that readers will take the time to study all fifteen books of Ovid's work, and is intended to be read in linear fashion, though of course readers looking for commentary on individual passages may avail themselves of the index to guide them—with the caveat that some threads of argumentation on individual scenes do presume one has read previous chapters. It might be good to admit that I also assume familiarity with the threads of argument from *Madness Unchained*; it would have added to the bulk of an already long book to restate old arguments in detail.

In general, with few exceptions I have not been able to take into account work on Ovid published after May of 2010.

After work is finished on my forthcoming commentary on *Aeneid* 5, it is my intention to add the *ultima manus* to the work I began with *Madness Unchained* and analyze Lucan's sequel to both Virgil and Ovid, the ten (not unfinished) books of the *Pharsalia* or *Bellum Civile*. Only in Lucan's verse exposition of Rome's madness under Nero do the themes first explicated by Virgil reach maturity and terrible fulfillment: madness triumphant.

As ever, I have the pleasant task of acknowledging the help and support provided by a number of friends and colleagues at Wesleyan and elsewhere. At my home institution, Dan Vogt, Margaret Fête, Sean Kay, Mike Flamm, Alison Lovell, Conrad Kent, David Caplan, Bob Olmstead, Mike Esler, Patricia Demarco, Marty Hipsky, Richard Spall and Katie Hervert have long been sources of strength and encouragement in both pleasant and difficult circumstances. At Holy Cross, my *alma mater*, Blaise Nagy, Thomas Martin, John D.B. Hamilton and Kenneth Happe have all remained good friends and classical colleagues.

At Fordham, Robert Penella has been a great aid in my work. So also Richard Thomas at Harvard, Shadi Bartsch and Sarah Nooter at Chicago, Michael C. J. Putnam of Brown, Stephen Harrison at Corpus Christi, Oxford, Michael McOsker and Paolo Asso at Michigan, Holly Sypniewski at Millsaps College, Emily Allen-Hornblower and Serena Connolly at Rutgers, Alden Smith at Baylor, Mary McHugh at Gustavus Adolphus College, Tyler Travillian at Boston University, and especially Professor Carl Deroux at the Université Libre de Bruxelles. I am grateful to Dr. Nicholas Horsfall for his unfailingly generous approach to questions Virgilian.

Johanna Braff of the Graduate Center of the City University of New York has been an insightful and astute collaborator on Ovidiana.

The University of Dallas has been a second home to me for almost a decade now, and offered me hospitality during part of the process of completing this book. The friendship and camaraderie offered by Stephen Maddux, David Sweet, Karl Maurer, Scott Dupree, Bainard Cowan, David Pope, Laura Baugh, Ivan and Laura Eidt, and Alexandra Wilhelmsen was a wonderful sustaining help in the completion of this volume. It is a special privilege to work in Carpenter Hall with Professor Grace Starry West, whose work on women in the *Aeneid* is foundational to my own research. Professor West hired me in 2001 to serve as visiting assistant professor, thus offering me not only the model of her classics work, but also a first academic post.

Donald Lateiner, my colleague in classics at Wesleyan, is as comfortable with Ovid as with Homer, Herodotus, Thucydides, Lysias, Cicero and Apuleius. Few of the modern generations of classicists can claim the same, and I hope he finds this book of some use. So also my former classmate and fellow Ovidian Matt McGowan, now of Fordham, my former classmate and fellow Virgilian Timothy Joseph of Holy Cross, and Bridget Buchholz, my junior colleague at Wesleyan during the last stages of completing this book.

My classics student Cynthia Ruth Susalla has been a consistently dutiful and impressively skillful assistant to my work; so also Katie McGarr and, at the University of Dallas, Rebekah Wallace, student of classics and French, who was instrumental in preparing the manuscript for publication.

The editorial staff at Lexington Books is to be commended once again for careful attention to another unusual project that has taken longer to produce than first expected. I am especially grateful to my acquisitions editor, Jana Wilson for her careful help and assistance.

At Wesleyan, besides my duties as a classics professor, for some years now I have been honored to advise and support the work of the Delta Upsilon chapter of the Delta Delta Delta sorority together with my colleague and friend, biochemist Dan Vogt. The senior sisters of the class of 2010 have been helpful in numerous ways throughout the production of this book, and I gratefully acknowledge the help they have consistently provided. The service and example of the pursuit of excellence the sisters of Tri-Delta have exhibited to me is both edifying and appreciated.

This volume is offered in gratitude to Professor Ann Batchelder. Professor Batchelder taught me ancient Greek at the College of the Holy Cross in three remarkable semesters of grammar, Homer (*Iliad*), and Sophocles (*Ajax, Philoctetes*) from the spring of 1992 through the fall of 1993. Professor Batchelder taught far more than the mechanics of how to read Greek with proficiency. She instilled in us a love of the Greek language and poetry, and offered an example of intense rigor tempered by admirable compassion. Some ideas considered in these pages were inspired by the wonderful discussions Professor Batchelder moderated in our myth class in the spring of 1992. If I have accomplished anything in the classroom, it is thanks to the example of Professor Batchelder, *optima magistra*.

Lee Fratantuono
William Francis Whitlock Professor of Latin
Ohio Wesleyan University
Delaware, Ohio
11 November, 2010
Martinmas

Ad Lectorem

The Latin text of Ovid that has been printed in this volume is an eclectic one. The text of Ovid's *Metamorphoses* is not nearly as stably established as that of Virgil's *Aeneid*. Most readers of the poem will now use Tarrant's Oxford Classical Text of 2004, which marks a significant improvement indeed over Anderson's 1977 Teubner. The text in both the Loeb and the Budé is out of date, despite the efforts of G. P. Goold to do triage on the former. Tarrant's text is the base for the new Fondazione Lorenzo Valla *Metamorphoses*; unpublished drafts of Tarrant's work provide the text for Hill's four-volume translation and commentary.

I have tried to alert the reader to some of the more interesting textual problems in the epic. A few have great significance for the meaning of a passage and for investigation of Ovid's views on critical points; one of the most intriguing comes during the apotheosis of Romulus in Book 14.

The *Metamorphoses* is "complete" (cf. the *Fasti*), though it would seem to lack the exiled poet's *ultima manus*. There are passages in the epic where we seem to have a double recension of the text that may preserve alternate views of the poet; there are sections were scribal interpolation seems likely. Despite the good labors of a number of textual critics, some *cruces* remain that are unlikely to be satisfactorily solved absent new evidence.

I have not done any textual work on the *Metamorphoses*, and the extent of my textual notes is to point the reader to some of the problems, and to appraise various solutions. For novice readers of the epic, it does well to remember that our classical texts were not handed down to us on golden tablets, but are the result of a not so exact science, textual criticism. Recommended introductory reading on the problem of editing the *Metamorphoses* is Tarrant's important *Classical Philology* article, "Editing Ovid's *Metamorphoses*: Problems and Possibilities" (*CPh* 77, 1982, pp. 342-360).

Introduction

The present volume was conceived as a sequel to *Madness Unchained: A Reading of Virgil's* Aeneid.[1] That work attempted to provide an *explication de texte* for the twelve books of Virgil's epic. This examination of Ovid's *Metamorphoses* has the same goal, and rests on the same basic presumption as its predecessor: a reader will study all fifteen books of the epic, in the order in which they appear in the text as we have received it.[2] If Virgil's *Aeneid* has suffered from excerption, Ovid's epic has fared far worse; the very nature of his poem, with its large number of individual stories more or less loosely linked together, would seem to invite abridgement and selection. We can be sure that this sort of picking and choosing of stories and passages would have been anathema to the poet, who no doubt expected his audience would be attentive to his entire work.

In numerous cases, a particular myth or story is best known (or even, essentially, only known) because of the version extant in Ovid's poem. This is a testimony to Ovid's poetic genius, but it also plays a part in obscuring consideration of the larger whole. Ovid's poem is difficult for undergraduate courses in Latin or classical literature in translation to read *in toto*, and this is unfortunate in terms of seeking to come to terms with Ovid's epic as it was intended to be read, integrally and in the order of its books, not abridged or rearranged. Virgil's *Aeneid* has suffered because too many monographs, classes, and scholars have prejudiced the first half of the epic at the expense of what Virgil himself terms his *maius opus* (this is beginning to change, but it took far too long and much remains to be done).

In the case of Ovid, the epic *Metamorphoses* suffered not only from pernicious excerpting, but also because too few have examined such things as the significance of the midpoint of the epic, why the poem seems to be composed not only of halves, but, more importantly, of thirds, and how these divisions offer commentary on the works Ovid is channeling and the ideas he is studying through a rereading of his predecessors. Indeed, every page of Ovid is an exercise in rereading Homer, Virgil, Callimachus and Ennius.[3]

As with Virgil, so with Ovid I make the recommendation for students to read the epic at least once straight through and at a reasonably rapid pace, so as to gain a sense of the whole.[4]

I have resisted the temptation to provide outlines of the stories contained in each book of the poem. This decision was the most difficult to reach in the process of composing this book. Two considerations ultimately swayed me. First, such divisions are readily available elsewhere. Second, and more importantly, I think such divisions ultimately contribute to exactly the sort of excerpting that Ovid's work has suffered. The result is what some will consider a dense book, for which I can only say that Ovid's is a dense and difficult poem. For the same reason, it has seemed better to provide more rather than less in the way of summary of the epic's individual episodes and scenes; it seems unfair to discuss every story in the poem with the expectation that the reader knows the details already, and, further, such summary—rather in the manner of translation— forces both commentator and audience to take as much of the poem into account as possible.

This book, like its predecessor, tries then to do two (if not more) things at one time; I can only hope the union is blessed.[5] It tries to provide an introduction to the *Metamorphoses* that is accessible to students of the poem of any level. Some reviewers of *Madness Unchained* felt that book was of greatest use to advanced undergraduates and graduate students; others felt it was inaccessible to students. I have not hesitated to cite literature in languages other than English; in the case of Ovid, even more so than Virgil, most of the foundational and best work is in German and Italian.

The present study offers a highly idiosyncratic reading of Ovid's epic, which is, of course, but one view among many. I have tried to be fair to opposing views in the bibliographical notes, which are deliberately dense—I want readers to be aware of the problems in the poem that have occasioned the most debate.[6] In working on this book, it was curious to see how much of the poem has been gone over countless times, in contrast to those (often quite significant) sections and stories that remain largely unconsidered. I have been necessarily selective in my citations, but I have tried to give some sense of what has been done on the epic's various problems, as well as what remains to be done (a vast amount). Moving from a book on the *Aeneid* to one on the *Metamorphoses* is an exercise in seeing how very little we really know about Ovid's masterpiece.

But I have learned much from my predecessors, though far more from commentaries than from monographs. Special mention can be made of Brooks Otis' *Ovid as an Epic Poet* (Cambridge, 1966; second edition, 1970).[7] For its time, this was a groundbreaking work that treated Ovid with a seriousness previous literary critics had eschewed. There are places where Otis displays a skilled capacity for understanding his poet, and passages where a blithe comment seems rather to miss Ovid's point. Still, for the student of the epic Otis remains a solid, valuable guide. Late in the process of working on this book, Sarah Nooter invited me to review Andrew Feldherr's new Princeton monograph on the epic, *Playing Gods*. I can only say that I regret not having had time to explore the book more thoroughly before completing my own work; it is a fine addition to the bibliography (which, mercifully, has not yet become as overwhelming as the Virgilian). Joseph Solodow's monograph on the epic is one of the best available studies of the poem, with sensible commentary on many key passages. Karl Galinsky's foundational book has aged well. I remain cautiously optimistic that certain unfortunate trends in psychoanalytic and (un?)critically theoretical scholarship will prove ephemeral. My students assure me every semester that it is very boring indeed to learn that a poem is, after all, about writing poems and other such meta-considerations.

A trend in recent classical scholarship has been the production of collections of essays, companions, guides and introductions to particular works, genres, and themes in classical literature. I lament that many of these volumes are woefully overpriced. The origin of these collections was the exemplary 1990 *Oxford Readings in Vergil's Aeneid*, edited by Stephen Harrison. That volume gathered valuable papers on Virgil in one convenient place. For Ovid, there is now not only *Oxford Readings*, but also *Cambridge Companion*, as well as Blackwell's and Brill's companions. Perusal of any of these volumes gives a good idea of the state of Ovidian scholarship at the turn of the millennium. The 1973 collection of essays edited by J. W. Binns (London: Routledge), *Ovid and His Influence*, remains invaluable. The essay there by E. J. Kenney on Ovid's style is the best study of that important (and vast) topic.

I first read the *Metamorphoses* straight through in English translation in the summer after my first year of undergraduate work.[8] It was, to borrow a sentiment from W. S. Anderson, an experience of a "poem to be enjoyed." Ovid's poem has a delight that is difficult to put precisely into words. My students tend to prefer Ovid to Virgil in classics courses in translation (for the Latin classes, my experience tends to be the reverse). But, as one student once noted, it is difficult to find any scholarship on Ovid's epic that seeks to explicate the work as a *whole*, not as a series of more or less loosely connected stories. Indeed, some scholars would hold that the work lacks unity of theme beyond the tenuous connection of "metamorphosis." It is interesting (and unfortunate) to note that much scholarship on the *Metamorphoses* can be summed up in two ways: 1) the poem is "fun," and 2) the poem is subversive and critical of the Augustan regime. I do not deny the first consideration, though I think we can move past that superficial observation; the *Metamorphoses*, rather in the manner of Lucretius' epic, uses delightful verse to charm the reader into pondering difficult truths and timeless problems. As for the second view, *tot homines, tot sententiae* aside, I simply do not see this poem as being anti-Augustan.

According to the poet's own *Tristia* 1.7.11 ff., when Ovid left Rome he burned the text of the *Metamorphoses*.[9] I suspect he was more interested in duplicating Virgil's desire to do the same with the *Aeneid* than in truly consigning the work to the flames. By A.D. 8 the poem was in circulation in Rome. He probably wrote the poem in tandem with the *Fasti* during his last years in the capital; it is not clear why the one poem is finished and the other only half done. At *Tristia* 2.549-552, Ovid claims he finished the *Fasti*; it is clear that he returned to it after c. A.D. 14, adjusting the first book to the new political reality in Rome under Tiberius. Indeed, most of what we know about Ovid comes from the *Tristia*, in particular *Tristia* 4.10, and we must be careful about ascribing too much credence to the poet's own elegy as a source of biography. Both the *Metamorphoses* and the *Fasti* begin with Chaos.[10]

But why an epic on transformations? Poems about metamorphosis most probably arose in the third century B.C., in the Hellenistic Age; we know of an *Ornithogonia* by Boeus or Boeo, a work in two books that dealt with the metamorphoses of human beings into birds; the Latin poet Macer adapted this work for a Latin readership. Macer was a friend of Ovid who wrote a Trojan epic (cf. *Epistulae ex Ponto* 4.16.6), which was perhaps a sequel to the *Iliad*. Nicander of Colophon (fl. c. 135 B.C.) wrote a *Heteroeumena*, a hexameter poem in perhaps four or five books. Our knowledge of these works comes almost exclusively from the *Metamorphoses* of Antoninus Liberalis, a prose work of paraphrases from perhaps the second century A.D. There was a *Metamorphoses* of Parthenius of Nicaea, but we cannot say much about it with certainty. But, as befits a universal history, Ovid had a full range of literary sources, which he plundered with aplomb: Homer lurks on every page, as does Virgil, Ennius, Lucretius, the tragedians of both Greece and Rome, Catullus, Herodotus, Callimachus and Apollonius of Rhodes, as well as the mythographers.[11] The notes in this volume can only begin to scratch the surface of the sources at play in almost every verse of this epic.

On the question of sources, I try to show in these pages that Ovid primarily considered himself a successor to Virgil, and that the *Metamorphoses* is principally a response to the *Aeneid*. Indeed, structurally Virgil's epic is the poem with the greatest influence on Ovid's, which at times is another *Aeneid*, and not only when Ovid is describing the same subject matter as Virgil.

Besides the poet's vast *Vorleben*, we might offer a few words on his afterlife. Here, too, we can only glimpse a vast whole. As the notes make clear, in my judgment the French have most drunk in the spirit of Ovid; from the French Middle Ages to the Renaissance and Baroque, Ovid's work was reinvented and reimaged with glorious success. Because Shakespeare and Milton are comparatively familiar to anglophone audiences, I have refrained from adding to an already long book by extensive notes on the influence of the *Metamorphoses* on those poets. I have noted more of Ovidian-inspired music than the visual arts for the same reason; Titian is far better known than Lully.

What is certain is that Ovid decided to write what is essentially a universal history, an epic that ostensibly proceeds from the creation of the world to his own time. In the progress of that history, Rome is the culmination of human (and divine) endeavors; Rome is the *domina rerum* and *caput* over the world. And Rome's history ends, of course, in the Age of Augustus; Augustus is the *praeses*, the *pater* and *rector* over both Rome and, by extension, the world. Augustus' father is Julius Caesar, and he was made a god, we learn in *Metamorphoses* 15, so that the great Augustus might have a divine lineage. And, someday, Augustus will become a god, though—following a common enough convention—Ovid prays that the day of *that* metamorphosis may be long delayed.

In Ovid's time, Augustus had already more or less secured his succession in the person of Tiberius, and that succession is noted in the closing movements of the epic. Whatever the feelings of the *princeps* about the choice, the fact remained that there was a destined successor, someone who could assume the reins of state. This had been one of the main concerns of Virgil's epic, written almost a quarter of a century earlier, in the wake of the sudden death of Marcellus, at a time when the succession question was a very real problem indeed. I find no clear evidence in Ovid's epic for what he thought about Tiberius. The point—a significant one for the regime—was that Augustus had an adopted heir. By the time Ovid was writing the *Metamorphoses*, Augustus was already an old man (by Roman standards), well into his sixties. But he had proven remarkably resilient, despite apparent hypochondria and bouts of real ill health. Ovid himself would prove less hardy than the *princeps*.

It is an attractive idea to imagine that Ovid chose the subject of metamorphosis as a paradigm for that was happening in Rome, in the wake of what must have seemed a transformation of the Republic. Metamorphosis becomes the unifying link between the ages, as Ovid proceeds through his universal history. One of the few constants in that history is transformation. Part of the idea behind the "perpetual song" that Ovid purports to sing is that just as Caesar became a god, and Augustus after him, so subsequent successors to Augustus will also become kings. Ovid suppresses much mention of the Republic, but he also decries monarchy. Romulus is swiftly made king, though he has a Sabine colleague, Tatius; Romulus bestows laws that are *non regia*, and only becomes a king after he dies and is deified as Quirinus. He is a father and protector, then, but not a monarch; he becomes a god, but he is never a despot or tyrant. There is and there is not a Republic, then, in Ovid's vision; Caesar must be stabbed to death so he can become a god, and though Octavian will rightly practice *pietas* and avenge his adoptive father, there is the wonderfully ambiguous comment that, after all, the conspirators did Octavian a favor by granting his father immortality as a new god. Ovid neatly deflects some of the problems between monarchy and republicanism by making his Romulus a king (and, implicitly, his Caesar and Augustus) *after* they have been deified. It is always easier to assuage autocratic tendencies with the consolation that one will become not just a king, but also a god—*post mortem*, of course. The business about praying that such a metamorphosis comes late has special resonance, then; on the one hand it means that one does not wish to see the death of the beloved ruler, while on the other hand, in terms of Ovid's presentation of monarchy it also means that one is delaying the onset of kingship. The longer the *princeps* stays alive, the longer he also waits to be king and god. On this point I think both Ovid and Horace were in fundamental agreement; there is much of Horace, c. 1.2 in Ovid's *Metamorphoses*, and in some ways Ovid's epic is a grand recreation of the world of that ode. I suspect that at least one source of Ovid's motivation to write an epic about transformation was Horace's Augustan ode about the different possible divine disguises the *princeps* might take.[12]

And, further, metamorphosis also comes as a question of genre. The present epic is Ovid's only surviving hexameter work; he spent most of his life writing elegiac couplets (which he did so well as to nearly kill the genre). In the proper places in the commentary, the present study will consider the genre question as it pertains to Ovid's epic (though I reveal my prejudice from the beginning in insisting that it is, after all, an epic). And not just an epic, but a serious one, an epic that aspires to do far more than merely entertain and delight its audience.

For *Madness Unchained*, I chose as title the image from Jupiter's speech to his daughter Venus, where *Furor* is envisioned in fetters: *A.* 1.294-296 *Furor inpius intus / saeva sedens super arma et centum vinctus aenis / post tergum nodis fremet horridus ore cruento.* Some reviewers have noted that I failed to show how "madness" is a unifying theme in the *Aeneid.* I drew a connection between the Homeric wrath of Achilles and the *furor* of Juno, which in the last movements of the *Aeneid* is handed over to Aeneas, who, at last, becomes Achilles by the slaughter of the "other" Achilles, Turnus. In my view, this transference of *furor*, especially after we were told by Jupiter that Madness would be chained (presumably forever), is the unifying theme of Virgil's epic. The madness that we were assured would be chained in seething indignation is released in the last lines of the poem. For Ovid's epic, then, coming as it does in the wake of Virgil's (even if chronologically it deals with events far before the commencement of Virgil's post-Trojan War narrative), Madness is an entity that is alive and well, reigning supreme, as it were, in the person of Virgil's Aeneas and the shattering image that the last lines of the *Aeneid* left to its audience. That is the scene that Ovid takes as his starting point, merely by virtue of the fact that he is writing the next epic after Virgil's in the long course of Latin literature.

In Ovid, I would argue that madness is reexamined and found to be not the province of this or that god or hero, but of the entirety of the universe. It is not a major unifying theme *per se* the way it was in the *Aeneid*, but its presence permeates the epic. Madness has been transformed, if you will, from something that can be studied in the way Achilles' wrath or Juno's anger can be analyzed, to something that is a universal constant and might infect any of us at any time— mortal or immortal. Where Virgil was concerned with the Homeric wrath of Achilles and its redemption at the end of the *Iliad*, in Ovid the madness is the possession of everyone. Virgil's vision was more terrifying than Homer's, in that for him the madness of a goddess was inherited by the would-be father of Rome. In Ovid, at points in the epic it can seem that nearly everyone is mad. And, unlike the *Iliad* with Achilles and the *Aeneid* with Juno, there is no clear resolution of the madness in Ovid, no easily definable redemption that might mark this epic with the same effect as Achilles' meeting with Priam or Juno's with Jupiter. One is left at the end of the *Metamorphoses* with the sense that chaos could erupt again, with little warning, though admittedly the Roman section of the poem has a serenity the earlier movements of the epic do not. This relative peace is a mark of the influence of Augustus, the new Aeneas, as it were, who is a man of peace once war has been put aside. It is significant that, in contrast to Virgil's vision, there is very little hint in Ovid of the military conflicts by which Augustus came to power. There is some, but it is muted. Like Ovid's Romulus, Augustus was a man of both war and peace, and by Ovid's day, peace was being underscored more than martial victories.

The *Metamorphoses* is rooted in the experience of its author's previous works. The *Amores* may have appeared (or at least the work started) as early as 25 B.C.; it was originally a five-book collection of love elegies that was eventually edited to the three-book version we now possess. That edition was published c. 16 B.C.[13] The collection of verse epistles known as the *Heroides* survives, as does the *Ars Amatoria* in three books and the *Remedia Amoris*. There was also a *Medea*, famously lost, and a poem on cosmetics, the *Medicamina Femineae Faciei*. From around A.D. 1 (perhaps not until 3), Ovid was immersed in the *Metamorphoses* and the *Fasti*; he was no Virgil in terms of laboring over every line, but had no problem churning out verses in quantity. He completed his works with astonishing rapidity. Ovid also completed a translation of Aratus' *Phaenomena* into Latin; only two tiny fragments survive of a work we should love to have. There is no clear evidence that the *Metamorphoses* was revised during the time in Tomis (unlike the *Fasti*). There is also no clear evidence of how the *Metamorphoses* was published, of who was entrusted with the task of seeing the work through to release.

In A.D. 8, the poet was exiled to Tomis (in the same year Julia Minor was also relegated). The mystery of the *carmen* (probably the *Ars Amatoria*, which, however, was not suppressed) and the *error* behind his banishment has never been satisfactorily solved. The period of exile produced the *Tristia* and the *Epistulae ex Ponto*, as well as the *Ibis*; no poetry or pleading, however, could reverse the sentence, and Ovid died in exile in A.D. 17, early in the reign of Tiberius. Born on 20 March, 43 B.C. (at Sulmo), Ovid was some sixty years old when he died, in the same year as Livy. It was the end of the Augustan Age. Literature had already begun to undergo a transformation at Rome, and under Tiberius the literary arts would see something of an eclipse, only to experience a revival under Nero. Ovid may have suffered relegation and personal failure in his relationship with both Augustus and Tiberius, but he succeeded in being the most prolific surviving author of his age.

Ovid's poem does not, in my view, express criticism of Augustus.[14] There is probably more, in fact, on Augustus in the *Aeneid* than in the *Metamorphoses*, simply because by its very nature there is so much in Ovid that has, frankly, nothing to do with Rome and Ovid's own day. But Augustus is the summit of the *Metamorphoses*, its climax and zenith; he is the lord on earth who presides like a Jupiter over the days of Ovid's composition of the work. The comparison—which Ovid makes explicit in the closing movements of the epic—is deliberate. For both Virgil and Ovid, Jupiter is essentially the god who is one with what we might call "fate" or "destiny." He represents accession to fate, a yielding to the dictates of destiny. His methods may not always be beyond question, but the end result of obeying his will is to see the coming of order and the estab-

xxii   INTRODUCTION

lishment of peace. He has no successor, of course, because he is immortal and has no need of one (in fact, he spends time seeking to avoid having any son who might challenge his authority). He is not really omnipotent, because he professes to yield to fate. He is the perfect immortal avatar for Augustus, who, alas, needs a successor because he is all too mortal. I think that both Virgil and Ovid would have argued that Rome was better off under Augustus than under Caesar. In the *Metamorphoses*, there is something of this topic in the depiction of Apollo and Bacchus; the former is an avatar of the young Octavian (who grows into the Jovian image), while the latter has something in common with Antony, and also his patron, Caesar. And, further, in imitation of Virgil's *Aeneid*, Ovid also addresses the divine rivalry between those opposing goddesses, Venus and Diana. In Ovid's vision, as in Virgil's, there is no doubt about which goddess is victorious by the end of the epic.

Ovid's main concerns, I shall argue in this reading of the epic, are philosophical and not political *per se*. I argue in these pages that Ovid (like Virgil) would have been fundamentally in agreement with the Lucretian (i.e., Epicurean view) of the afterlife—simply put, there is none. This is by no means a settled question. But in my view, the key bookends of Ovid's epic come in Books 2 and 14, where Ovid introduces a simile from Lucretius about the melting of a leaden pellet through the air. In Book 2, the simile comes amid a story of one of many divine amours, and is easily dismissed as being without significance. But in Book 14, we see the same image used to describe the apotheosis of Romulus—a most un-Lucretian idea indeed. Lucretius would have nothing to do with immortality and divine metamorphosis, and I think Ovid would have been in substantial agreement. This skepticism is used by Ovid in the closing lines of the epic to temper his statements about the immortality of the poem and the poet. Especially after his exile, Ovid had just cause to worry about his fame and the survival of his works (and it may well be a testimony to Augustus' literary sensitivity that so much of Ovid's poetry survived, even the material composed post-exile). At the end of the epic, Ovid will announce that he will indeed live—the last word of the poem is the haunting first person singular, present indicative active *vivam*—if the sayings of the bards have something of truth to them. It is a conditioned statement of immortality; it is less bold than Horace's claims at the end of his three books of *carmina*. I suspect that Horace's division of his *carmina* into three books was an inspiration for Ovid's division of his poem into three sections, where the Ceres-Proserpina story dominates the close of the first third, the Orpheus-Eurydice story the close of the second third, and Pythagoras and all that the close of the last third. The eschatology of the *Metamorphoses* is at the very heart of Ovid's poetic concerns. There is a movement in the epic from an evocation of a traditional world of the Homeric underworld, to an exploration of Orphism, to a mockery of Pythagorean views. Throughout, the spirit of Lucretius broods over all.

The *Metamorphoses*, I suspect, was written in tandem with the *Fasti* because the former was meant to address concerns more philosophical than political, while the latter poem (an elegiac epic in the truest sense) was meant to address the Augustan regime *per se*. There has been a tremendous amount of work done in recent years on intertextuality, especially the close examination of stories Ovid tells in both of his long works. The issues raised by this cross-pollination are discussed *passim* in my commentary, though in my experience more often than not the fact that Ovid tells a story in both poems does not have much bearing on the overall interpretation of the *Metamorphoses*.

It is perhaps always the case that a poet seeks to surpass the accomplishments of his predecessors. In the case of Ovid, I argue in these pages that the main rival is Virgil, the author of what became, essentially overnight, the classic of classics in Rome. I argue that the philosophical and political judgments of the two men were not terribly different, and that the principal means by which Ovid sought to surpass his predecessor was in his decision to tell the same story as Virgil on a more global stage. I would also argue that the young poet Lucan conceived the idea in his tender years that he might rival both Virgil and Ovid, and for his choice he went in the opposite direction: he wanted to tell the same story through not a global prism, but a highly specific one: the civil war between Caesar and Pompey. Where Ovid sought the macrocosm of a universal history to retell Virgil's story, Lucan chose the microcosm of one of the Roman civil wars. Where the nephew of Seneca stood on the question of Lucretius is another matter, for another book. Neither Virgil nor Ovid lived long enough to see what would become of the principate Augustus had spent so much labor seeking to perfect. In his short life, Lucan did see the progress of madness, and the *Pharsalia* can be understood as the third volume in a trilogy authored, ultimately, by *Furor*.

Notes

1. The present book does more or less assume familiarity with its predecessor, just as the *Metamorphoses* assumes familiarity with the *Aeneid* (and so much else besides).

2. Most undergraduate Latin students in the United States probably use Anderson's commentaries; the fact that the first volume appeared in 1972 on Books 6-10, and the second a quarter century later on Books 1-5, has somewhat prejudiced study of the epic. Aris & Phillips is to be commended for offering Hill's complete *Metamorphoses*; there are still, however, relatively few choices for anglophone Latin classes. Cambridge has begun releasing commentaries on the later books of the epic that are especially exemplary.

3. Ovid's debt to Ennius remains an area of potentially profitable investigation where more work needs to be done, especially with respect to Ovid's depiction of Romulus' apotheosis.

4. Students at Ohio Wesleyan University read the *Metamorphoses* straight through in a marathon performance in the spring of 2005 under the direction of my colleague Don Lateiner.

5. For a convenient introduction to Ovid, I recommend Sara Mack's *Ovid* (New Haven: Yale University Press, 1988, a sober and sensible appraisal of a difficult poet), and Kenney's notes in the Cambridge history of Latin literature; Holzberg's *Ovid: Dichter und Werk* (Munich, 1997) is a wonderful primer (and now available in a Cornell University Press English translation, 2002). Philip Hardie has a fine chapter on "Narrative Epic" in S. J. Harrison's exemplary Blackwell companion to Latin literature. In approach I prefer not to divide Latin epics into didactic and narrative categories; both Lucretius and Manilius have a narrative, too, and, in the case of Virgil, Ovid, and Lucan (the three great Latin narrative epicists), I think Lucretius is the foundational epic.

6. Regrettably, too few scholars have attempted a complete reading of the epic, one that takes the reader through every passage. This is in part because some scholars would argue that the work lacks a deliberate structure, especially on the micro-level. I do not pretend that every transformation is in the order it is in for some grand reason, though, more often than not, there is evidence of the poet's deep concern about the organization of his material. Still, because of the lack of studies of the poem as a unitary whole, with coherence and a purposeful, serious narrative, the conclusions reached in these pages are rather more idiosyncratic and speculative than those found in *Madness Unchained*.

7. I note that because of the exigencies of travel, my references to Otis are always from the first edition, which is, I believe, easier to find than the second.

8. The first translation I read was Horace Gregory's; Ovid has, in my view, been better served by English translators than Virgil. The Oxford World's Classics version by Melville is exemplary, with fine notes by Kenney, and can be recommended without reserve. Golding's classic translation, a masterpiece of English literature in its own right, is now available in Penguin. The Loeb edition of Ovid is a mixed bag. Goold labored to "update" the entire collection, but the Library's Ovid is looking ever duller. The Budé *Metamorphoses*, while out of date textually, has a fine translation by Lafaye. An Ovid encyclopedia, after the fashion of the two Virgilian ones, is a desideratum.

9. For biographical work on the poet, the article in the *Oxford Classical Dictionary* (3rd ed.) is a good start.

10. *Fasti* 1.103 *me Chaos antiqui (nam sum res prisca) vocabant* (says Janus).

11. I refer throughout to "Pseudo-Apollodorus" when discussing the problem that is the *Bibliotheca*. That work was ascribed to Apollodorus, as in, Apollodorus the Athenian, a second-century B.C. polymath. The *Bibliotheca* dates to either the first- or second-century A.D. The Loeb edition in two volumes is valuable for the fine annotations of Frazer; there is an Oxford World's Classics translation with good notes. Among other mythographers, I note the excellent Budé edition of the first Vatican mythographer, with ample notes after the fashion of most recent volumes in that series. For Parthenius' *Erotika Pathemata*, Lightfoot's full Oxford edition is magisterial; my teacher Jacob Stern has a very useful translation with notes of Palaephatus.

12. The influence of Horace on Ovid's *Metamorphoses* is a worthwhile subject for further investigation; much work remains to be done. I have the suspicion that the division of Ovid's epic into thirds may have been influenced by the structure of Horace's three books of *carmina*. This is most obvious, of course, in comparison of c. 3.30 and the end of *M*. 15.

13. For anglophone students, the Oxford and Penguin series have fine editions of the amatory and exilic poetry; the notes to the Penguins are especially full for that collection. There are also Penguin translations of the *Heroides* and the *Fasti*. The OCT has Kenney's critical edition of the love poetry, and Owen's old exile poems (with some useful fragments); Bristol Phoenix has reprinted the classic editions of Palmer's *Heroides* and Ellis' *Ibis*. For the *Heroides*, Dörrie's text remains standard; for the *Fasti*, the Alton-Wormell-Courtney Teubner. The Cambridge green and yellow collection has Kenney's commentary on the double epistles of the heroines, and a selection of *Heroides* by Knox. McKeown's edition of *Amores* 1-3 (awaiting the commentary on Book 3) is essential for the close study of that work. There is now a large Cambridge edition of *Ars Amatoria* 3 (ed. Gibson), along with the still useful briefer commentaries of Adrian Hollis on *Ars* 1 and *Metamorphoses* 8. The chapter notes make fuller mention of *Metamorphoses* commentaries; anglophone students must realize that close study of the *Metamorphoses* demands access to Bömer's magisterial multi-volume commentary (1969-1986), as well as, now, the Fondazione Lorenzo Valla Italian edition, with superb notes. The German commentary of Haupt-Korn-Ehwald-von Albrecht (last edition, 1966) still has much of value to commend it. There has been much recent work on the *Fasti*; the Budé edition is especially good, and note the commentaries of Green on Book 1 (Brill), Fantham on 4 (Cambridge), and Littlewood on 6 (Oxford); Bömer still reigns here, too, and Frazer remains a classic of the classics. In general, the British reviews of the more recent Budé Ovid volumes have been unduly harsh. The Budé of Antoninus Liberalis is indispensable.

14. The opposing view can be found *passim* in the scholarly tradition on Ovid. If there is criticism of the *princeps*, it comes mostly in the fact that there is surprisingly little about him in this epic. Again, Ovid's concerns are more philosophical than political.

At the end of the *Aeneid*, the wrath of Juno was handed over to Aeneas, the progenitor of Rome. In the *Metamorphoses*, we now see the madness everywhere, since Rome is, after all, the mistress of nations and lord of the earth.

Chapter I

Into New Bodies

Ovid opens his epic with four densely packed verses that offer a stunning response to the eleven lines that opened the *Aeneid* of his poetic predecessor Virgil:

> In nova fert animus mutatas dicere formas
> corpora. Di, coeptis (nam vos mutastis et illas)
> adspirate meis primaque ab origine mundi
> ad mea perpetuum deducite tempora carmen. (1.1-4)

> *The mind compels me to speak of forms changed into new*
> *bodies. O gods, breathe on that which I have begun (for*
> *you have also changed those forms), and from the first*
> *origin of the world down to my times lead forth an unending song.*

Few passages of Latin poetry accomplish so much in so economical a scope of verses; these are among the most allusive lines in all the Latin epic tradition.[1] The very brevity of Ovid's proem contrasts splendidly with the great length of his epic.[2]

From the very start, Ovid performs a neat verbal trick. *In nova*, "into new [bodies]," also reminds the reader or listener of the verb *innova*, "make new." The poet offers an imperative challenge to the audience, to innovate (i.e., to imitate him). And there is much that is indeed new for the Roman epic tradition in the first lines of the *Metamorphoses*, especially by comparison to the *Aeneid* that predates it by a quarter century. Instead of arms and the man, Ovid will speak of forms and bodies. Instead of a Muse, Ovid invokes all the immortals: his theme is implicitly greater than Virgil's because it encompasses a much wider field of material, and so more divine assistance is required. The immortals have themselves changed forms (besides causing the transformation of others), and so they are suitable patrons to inspire an epic of transformation. Ovid's epic will provide a continuous narrative that stretches from the creation of the world down to the Augustan Age, without interruption. Both in time and in space Ovid's epic will surpass the scope of Virgil's.

And so before addressing other concerns, we may consider that what is "new," then, is the existence of the poet's work in the wake of its immediate predecessor in Latin epic. Every change recorded in the poem renders new that which had existed before; this would seem to be an epic of novelty. Just how "new" Ovid's universe will be, of course, remains open to judgment as we proceed through the epic.

Virgil's *Aeneid* has a longer introduction than Ovid's poem, but no conclusion *per se*. Ovid's *Metamorphoses* has a brief, indeed breezy opening, with a formal close at the end of Book XV that contrasts with the abrupt end of Virgil's poem. Virgil boldly challenged Homer; Ovid will challenge Virgil (and, by implication, Homer as well) by writing a global epic that embraces (at least in theory) all things, since one could argue that mutability is among the few immutable universal constants.

Ovid calls upon the gods to breathe on his work; the *animus*, however, is what compels the poet to tell his tale. *Animus* is connected to the Greek word for "wind," but it also signifies the rational mind, the intellect, as opposed to the *corpora* or "bodies" of which it will sing. The *animus* can sing of the *corpora* and not *vice versa*. Ovid states explicitly that the gods have changed their forms (a recurring theme in many of the stories he is about to relate). What may well remain unchanging in Ovid's vision is this *animus* and, of course, the *carmen* whose composition it has compelled: once published, a poem is, after all, more or less fixed and immutable.[3]

A significant textual problem vexes these already difficult opening lines. *Illas* (in agreement with *formas*) should perhaps be corrected to *illa*, in agreement with *coeptis*.[4] The gods changed Ovid's beginnings from his hitherto preferred elegiac meter to the dactylic hexameter of epic poetry. The gods are suitable for breathing on the poet's work because they inspired the change of meter (and thus of theme). Of course *illa* could also be taken to refer back to the *corpora*, though the word order and meter point to *coeptis* as the likely referent. The allusion to the change in poetic meter and theme is attractive, though one does lament the lack of manuscript support for *illa*. In any case, the divine agency behind the metamorphoses of which Ovid will sing is beyond question: if *illa* is the correct reading, the crucial conjunction *et* indicates the gods changed beginnings as well as the forms.

One reason to favor the transmitted reading *illas* is Ovid's declaration that the *animus* compelled his poetic subject. If instead we prefer to read *illa* (with *corpora*), Ovid would seem to credit the gods with his change of song (or at least of the metrical medium in which he would dress his subject). Divine intervention to change the poet's song is what we find at the beginning of the *Amores*, where Cupid forced the would-be writer of epic to choose less lofty matter for composition:

Arma gravi numero violentaque bella parabam
edere, materia conveniente modis.
par erat inferior versus—risisse Cupido

dicitur atque unum surripuisse pedem. (*Amores* 1.1.1-4)

I was about to sing of arms and violent wars in
grave measure, with the subject matter befitting the meter.
The second verse was equal—Cupid is said to have
laughed and, what is more, to have snatched away a foot.[5]

No grand epic in dactylic hexameter for Ovid then, but rather the elegiac couplets of amatory verse.[6] Now, with his *Metamorphoses*, the poet would return to
what he had first envisioned—an epic—but the subject matter would not, it
would seem, be arms and battles. Virgil had already done that in the *Aeneid*.
But, as we shall see, while the announced theme of the *Metamorphoses* would
indeed be new, the finished epic will also include what the opening lines of the
Amores had declared to be the poet's first intention, complete with a new telling
of the voyage of Aeneas; this time, Cupid would not interfere with the poet's
plan, even if the spirit of Ovid's earlier work would infuse his often martial epic.
Ovid understood that the main theme of the *Aeneid* was not, ultimately, war and
battle, but rather Aeneas' erotic conquest of Lavinia after he triumphed in his
rivalry against Turnus. The poet of amatory verse has been well trained for the
task at hand. In a nice touch, later in this book we shall see how Cupid can fell
the great god Apollo.

But what is this *animus* that inspired Ovid's subject? As aforementioned, it
is the rational mind, perhaps the poet's own. In a brilliant nod to Virgil, the
word's connection to the Greek for "wind" reminds us of the wind god Aeolus
whose service to Juno started the action of the *Aeneid* by diverting Aeneas to
Carthage in the poem's first dramatic scene (1.50-123). The "wind" here is the
poet's mind, which compels him to analyze the changes that have marked human (and divine) history since creation, right down to the changes that Augustus
has wrought in Ovid's Rome. The poet here takes responsibility for his own
work; as we shall see, he is in a sense like Phaethon, the child of the sun god
whose misadventures will end this first book and dominate the first half of the
second.

Further, if we read *et illas*, Ovid's emphasis is on how the immortals have
themselves also changed their forms, which will yield interesting results as we
study the poem in the light of the contemporary historical realities of Augustan
Rome.

In the proem to the *Aeneid*, Virgil highlights the wrath of Juno (the quelling
of which will be a major theme of his epic). Juno's harassment of Aeneas invited the poet's accusing question whether the gods are possessed of such tremendous anger: *tantaene animis caelestibus irae* (1.11). Readers of the *Aeneid*
are thus conditioned to expect divine anger; Ovid's brief proem presents a more
neutral view of the gods. They changed forms, both their own and those of others; the reasons for these changes (let alone the results) are, as yet, unexplained.
The gods of the short introduction to the *Metamorphoses* are left without charac-

terization; there will be time enough for that as we advance through the poem.

Ovid's epic will be perpetual from creation to his own time; the gods are called upon to lead down (*deducite*) the song.[7] *Perpetuum* points as much to the enduring fame of the work as to the poem's unending narrative thread from creation to Augustus. *Deducite* is packed with metaphors; lurking images from the launching of ships and the leading of armies point to comparison with the first (Odyssean) and second (Iliadic) halves of the *Aeneid*. And, most especially, the collocation of *deducite* with *carmen* points to Apollo's intervention in Virgil's sixth eclogue and the weaving metaphor implicit in *deducite*:

> cum canerem reges et proelia, Cynthius aurem
> vellit et admonuit, "Pastorem, Tityre, pinguis
> pascere oportet ovis, **deductum** dicere **carmen**." (3-5)

> *When I was wont to sing of kings and battles, the Cynthian*
> *plucked my ear and admonished me "It is fitting, O Tityrus, for*
> *a shepherd to pasture fat sheep, but to sing a finely-spun song."*

The scene is reminiscent of that at the beginning of Ovid's *Amores*. In both the sixth eclogue and the preface to Ovid's amatory verse, a clear distinction is made between long epic verse and the shorter artistic compositions of the sort associated with Callimachus. But both the *Aeneid* and the *Metamorphoses* make no such division of genres and styles. There is much that is Homeric about both Latin epics, and much that is Callimachean; the seemingly discordant dichotomy between archaic epic and Alexandrian miniature is blended into a harmonious whole (as indeed may well have been the case for Callimachus' *Aetia*; we cannot be certain). In the proem to the *Metamorphoses*, Ovid prays that the gods may grant what Apollo ordered Tityrus to do in the sixth eclogue, and what he himself had done in previous poetic works: the *Metamorphoses* is thus viewed as a seamless part of the poet's *œuvre*. At the same time, *perpetuum* points strongly not only to the expected immortality of the work, but also to the unity of design that marks the seemingly disparate scenes that combine to create one coherent narrative. It is possible that what most distinguished Ovid's *Metamorphoses* from Callimachus' *Aetia* was narrative unity, besides any consideration of the political significance of Ovid's work in the context of Augustan Rome.

In addition to an allusion to the sixth eclogue, Ovid's proem also nods to Virgil's *Georgics* in its mention of *coeptis*. The word recalls Virgil's appeal to Octavian to nod favorably on his poetic beginnings: *da facilem cursum, atque audacibus adnue coeptis* ("Grant a smooth course, and, what is more, smile on my audacious undertaking"). Octavian, the Augustus of Ovid's day, is thus at the beginning and, as we shall see, the end of the *Metamorphoses*. By this additional allusion, Ovid provides a reminiscence of all three of his predecessor's poetic works, a marvelous tribute to the poet whose spirit imbues his successor's *magnum opus*.

We have noted that Ovid makes no explicit characterization of the immortals in his brief proem. Their existence is taken for granted, as in Virgil's *Aeneid*; in both works the gods will be active participants. Augustus is destined to be one of those gods. And yet in Ovid's ascription of responsibility for his song to the *animus* there is a strong emphasis on Stoic belief. Seneca would famously assert (*Epistulae* 65.24) that just as god rules on earth, so the *animus* rules in man (*quem in hoc mundo locum deus obtinet, hunc in homine animus*).

Virgil makes no explicit statement in the *Aeneid* regarding the immortality of his work. The closest he comes to one is in the remarkable address he makes to his dead young heroes Nisus and Euryalus (9.446-449). Ovid may well have borrowed the image of the *deductum carmen* from Horace, who closes his three books of odes (c. 3.30.13-14 *Exegi monumentum*) with a grandiose statement of his work's immortality. There, Horace declared that he had been the first to "lead down an Aeolian song into Italian measures" (*princeps Aeolium carmen ad Italos deduxisse modos*). The emphasis on the work's immortality points to its unchanging character; unlike the forms changed into new bodies, the poetic achievement is immortal precisely because it is not subject to change. Horace had considered Virgil to be one half of his soul (c. 1.3.5-8); Ovid does not neglect to include Horace in an epic proem that necessarily gives its most prominent attention to Virgil, his epic predecessor.

There is a hint in these first four lines that Ovid views his *Metamorphoses* as a continuation of one of the projects of the *Aeneid*, namely to provide a poetic analysis of the new regime in power in Rome. The *Metamorphoses* is a response to the *Aeneid*, benefitting from the existence of its venerable predecessor even as it labors to surpass it. As the opening lines of the *Aeneid* spoke of Aeneas and the Trojan founding of the future Rome, so the opening lines of the *Metamorphoses* speak of the contemporary times of Ovid's Augustan Rome. The *new* in Ovid will include a starting point from the present, in studied opposition to Virgil's commencement from the past.[8] The times are Ovid's own (4 *mea*) because as poet he will explicate them in undying verse. Virgil was concerned with the future of the Augustan regime and what would become of the Rome the new *princeps* had so transformed; Ovid's epic, with the benefit of an additional quarter century of time to observe Augustus, would share with Virgil's the same constraint that all poems concerned with history share: a lack of ability to predict what would come after the poet's own days. Augustus is the end of history precisely because the future is unknown. Ovid had the advantage of some twenty-five years beyond the death of Virgil in which to see that Rome would not slip back into its oft-repeated cycle of civil strife, though the future of city and empire remained no less uncertain, especially given the numerous difficulties Augustus faced in his succession plans in that quarter century between the release of the two epics.

We may well imagine that Ovid smiled on completion of his exceedingly brief proem, knowing well that it would stagger his learned audience. After launching his daring commencement, the poet proceeds at once to his story, with an account of the creation of the world.[9]

The first "character" in Ovid's narrative is chaos (1.7), which we might do well to capitalize. Chaos preceded the sea, the lands, and the sky.[10] Chaos is described as a rough and unorganized "mass" (1.8 *rudis indigestaque* **moles**), which echoes Virgil's description of the labor it took to found the Roman race:

> tantae **molis** erat Romanam condere gentem. (*Aeneid* 1.33)
>
> *So great a struggle it was to found the Roman race.*

Ovid's subject is the creation of the entire universe, not just one city (even the world's capital); the key word *moles* had described the whole mess of an effort to found Rome, starting in the immediate aftermath of Troy's fall. In Ovid, it fittingly describes the disordered mess that existed before the creation of order.[11] There was no systematic arrangement of the component elements of nature, but rather

> . . . congestaque eodem
> non bene iunctarum discordia semina rerum. (1.8-9)
>
> *. . . heaped up in one place,*
> *the discordant seeds of things not well joined together.*

The *semina* or "seeds" of things remind us of Lucretius' atoms, thus offering a nod to yet another of the poet's predecessors and confusing the issue of the poet's philosophical allegiances: Epicureanism *versus* Stoicism. Further, the mention of discord, the Greek Eris, points to the tradition that Strife inaugurated the whole mess of the conflict at Troy, the epic battle whose traditions underpin the story of Rome's eventual founding. Discord fittingly finds its place at the beginning of Ovid's epic, just as it stands at the head of Troy lore; as for Lucretius, Ovid's description of the *semina* signals agreement with the foundational assumption of Epicurean physics: the atoms are the elements of nature.

Despite the disordered, chaotic mess of primordial nature, there was a real unity:

> unus erat toto naturae vultus in orbe (1.6)
>
> *There was one face of nature in the whole orb.*

A mess, to be sure, but one mess stood forth everywhere; discordant, yes, but still one. By the use of the key word *moles* to describe this union of warring elements, the poet points both to the reality of Augustan Rome and his own poem, which becomes a metaphor for the city and empire. Under Augustus, unity had been achieved, despite the clash of, for example, republican values with the reality of the empire that was being birthed with every passing constitutional crisis or question regarding the imperial succession. As we shall see, Ovid's poem will provide a perfect ring to link the chaos that marks the beginning of creation with the establishment of the Augustan principate with which the poem ends, besides the poet's own commentary on the chaotic and yet unified nature of his own work. We may also see in the primordial chaos a metaphor for the Republic.

The first two immortals Ovid mentions by name are the sun and moon, Titan and Phoebe (1.10-11), which points us to the twins Apollo and Diana.[12] Both deities were of immense significance to the Augustan regime.[13] Neither deity, we might assume, as yet existed in the earliest days; such was the chaos that defined the universe that while there was land and sea, no one could stand or swim (1.15-16), since everything was always in flux and nothing kept its own form (17 *nulli sua forma manebat*). Indeed, there is no creation of the immortals in Ovid's cosmogony; their existence is later taken for granted (20), when one of them decides to put the chaotic mess in order.

For now, opposites war with each other. Here, the battle of cold with hot and wet with dry is viewed as an implicitly negative condition of the universe before the coming of order.[14] And yet Ovid would have known well that in Hippocratic medicine, opposites cure opposites.[15] In the primordial chaos, discordant elements were fighting "in one body" (18 *corpore in uno*). Ovid thus introduces into his narrative two crucial terms from his proem: forms and bodies. In the beginning there was one body, i.e., chaos, itself a jumble of elements in strife; nothing retained its own form. The irony that Ovid will unveil through his epic is that in the end, even after fifteen books of metamorphoses, the same primeval reality will remain: there will be one body (i.e., Rome), and nothing therein will retain its own form for long.

Ovid is somewhat vague about how chaos was resolved:

hanc deus et melior litem natura diremit. (1.21)

A god and a better nature disturbed this dispute.

The poet could not have done better to advance his creation story more splendidly; he will underscore the anonymity of the responsible divine party (1.32, *quisquis fuit ille deorum*). As for the mysterious god's action, *dirimere* is not a common verb, and its more usual meaning is not to "disturb" *per se*, but to divide or separate something out.[16] The verb might well have been used in this normal sense with *chaos* as its object (and, indeed, it describes well what the god actually does at 22-31), but instead we have *lis*, a legal dispute or quarrel. It is as if Ovid considers the warring primordial elements to be legally savvy, with the ability to press cases and seek redress. Some god, and "better nature," ended the legal wrangling. The passage owes something to Virgil's account of Neptune's quelling of the storm at the beginning of the *Aeneid* (1.142-56), with the simile of the man (Augustus?) who could resolve quarrels. There is also a reminiscence of the god Augustus who created leisure for Tityrus at the beginning of Virgil's first eclogue (1.6 *O Meliboee, deus nobis haec otia fecit*). In Ovid's creation narrative, there are echoes of Augustus' reordering of the Republic with its legally savvy, discordant elements. *Natura* forms a hendiadys with *deus*; nature is "better" (*melior*) because it has ended strife and brought peace. Ovid's epic, then, would seem to open with eminently Augustan ideas about the settlement of chaos. We might also see a shade of Stoicism in triumph over Epicureanism here as well.[17] In this case, there would be echoes of the same theme we find in Virgil's account in *Aeneid* 8 of the great Stoic hero Hercules, who (as a type of Augustus), triumphed over Cacus.[18]

The presence of a divine element in Ovid's creation myth is a challenge to the creation lore Virgil offered in the sixth eclogue (31-40), in the song of Silenus.[19] If anything, Silenus' song was eminently Lucretian; he sang of the great void (31 *magnum per inane*) that saw the coming together of the seeds of things and the eventual organization of the globe of the earth, the sea, and living things. But there is no god in the opening of Silenus' song; there is, in fact, nothing that would disturb Lucretius. He proceeds to the stones Pyrrha threw and the reign of Saturn (41), along with other mythological subjects of a decidedly unscientific nature.[20] But his foundational creation story is devoid of divine agency. Again, if Ovid's chaos is the Republic, then his *deus* is Augustus. The political realities of his day were of greater concern to him than arguments between philosophical schools.

Ovid takes care in describing the god's organizing actions at some length (34-75) in part because the universe now being set in order will be the stage on which he will produce his drama. The first hint that all may not be well in the new order is, appropriately enough, the ravaging power of the winds, which reminds us again of the storm caused by Aeolus' release of their blasts (at Juno's behest) that bedeviled Aeneas' fleet:

> his quoque non passim mundi fabricator habendum
> aera permisit; vix nunc obsistitur illis,
> cum sua quisque regat diverso flamina tractu,
> quin lanient mundum; tanta est discordia fratrum. (1.57-60)

> *To these also the creator of the world did not give the*
> *air to be possessed without limit; scarcely now are they resisted,*
> *though each one rules his blasts in his own region,*
> *lest they rip apart the world; so great is the discord of the brothers.*

The Stoic world of Ovid's creation (like that of Virgil's storm in *Aeneid* 1) needs a divine power to keep order lest the forces of destruction ruin everything in their path. In the "discord of the brothers," we may see a faint allusion to Romulus and Remus and the civil strife that stands forth from the very outset of Roman history (and cf. 145 below).[21] The echoing of the beginning of the *Aeneid* helps to underscore Ovid's point that in the actions of the seemingly benevolent Stoic god who established order from chaos we are to see the work of Augustus in the settlement of the disorder that marked the Roman Republic in the closing years of the first century B.C.

Above the winds, the mysterious creator of order places the weightless ether (1.67-68), in lines that the commentators have long noted are reminiscent of Lucretius (*De Rerum Natura* 5.495-501). The passage has evoked some scholarly debate.[22] After all, in Virgil's account of the winds (*A.* 1.61), Jupiter controls them not with the light ether, but with a mass of mountains. Scholars have argued that Virgil describes divine control over the winds by means of a Lucretian passage that is thus subversively echoed; Ovid's passage also evokes Lucretius (and with just as much subversion as Virgil's, since Lucretius would never have approved of any *deus* bringing order to his atoms). As we shall see, it is overly simplistic to ascribe subversive, anti-Lucretian sentiments either to Virgil or Ovid (especially the former); both poets are deeply imbued with the spirit of their distant, republican predecessor, and both are more fundamentally in agreement with his principles than not. Both Virgil and Ovid enjoyed the ease with which gods could be inserted into their epics without question, as essential characters in the drama, given the mythological nature of their subject matter. In another generation Lucan would compose a very different sort of poem.

The universe that has now been set in order is inhabited with fish, animals, and birds (1.74-75), but before these terrestrial creatures are noted, Ovid first describes how the stars began to appear (69-73), lights in the sky that had previously been obscured by the darkness of chaos. The passage reminds us of the opening of the first georgic (1.32-42), where Virgil wonders where in the heavens the star of the deified Augustus will ultimately find its place. The relatively obscure origins of the *princeps* (cf. Ovid's 70 *caligine caeca*) have given way to the expectation that Augustus will reign forever as a divine light, a new god in the heavens. Ovid attributes the creation of man either to the divine action of the god who established universal order (i.e., the god created man in his own image), or because the earth still possessed some seeds from the heavenly ether (i.e., the home of the immortals and thus the wellspring of divinity), seeds that the Titan Prometheus (1.82 *satus Iapeto*) fashioned into men after the image of the gods. The Golden Age (1.89-112) that marks the earliest history of the organized world offers a challenge to Virgil's *Eclogues* and *Georgics*; in Ovid one of the main emphases is the perpetual spring (107-120).[23] In the so-called Messianic Eclogue, Virgil announced the coming of a new Golden Age during the consulship of Pollio (4.4-17); Ovid sings of the original *aurea saecula*. A hallmark of that Golden Age was nature's ready offering of her fruits without labor; there was no need then for the lessons offered by the *Georgics*.

The basic division of the ages is twofold: pre- and post-Jovian (1.113-114; cf. Virgil, *Georgics* 1.125 and Tibullus 1.3.35-50). If Ovid is challenging the *Eclogues* and *Georgics*, what are we to make of his response to the *Aeneid*? The events of Virgil's *Aeneid* match Ovid's description of the Iron Age (1.127-150). *Pudor* fled in the actions of Dido (129); *fraudes* and *dolus* ruled the scene of the fall of Troy and the stratagem of the wooden horse (130). Sea voyages were now commonplace (132-134), while the division of lands Ovid mentions (135-136) reminds us of the debates over how to assign territory in Italy to the Trojans and

Turnus' Rutulians. War was a regular occurrence (141-143). Most strikingly, *piety* itself lay vanquished (149 *victa iacet pietas*). This hallmark of a ferrous age may point to the end of the *Aeneid* and Aeneas' decision to slay Turnus. Certainly the lack of affection between brothers (145) Ovid mentions also echoes with the fraternal murder that began Roman history.

Ovid next describes the attempt of the giants Otus and Ephialtes (whom he does not name) to climb Olympus by piling Pelion on Ossa, only to fall victim to Jupiter's thunderbolts. Once destroyed, Ovid notes that the warm blood of the dead giants was animated by their mother the earth and given human form. As one might expect (1.162), the children born from this violent blood are as vicious and sanguinary as the giants who sired them. If one were to place the complicated events of Greek and Roman mythology on a timeline, we might expect to find episodes like this gigantomachy before the events of the Trojan War and the founding of Rome. By placing the attempted scaling and invasion of Olympus last in his queue of declining events, Ovid equates the action of the rebellious giants and the birth of their bloody descendants with events after the narrative of the *Aeneid* (which was clearly signaled by 149 *pietas*). It is as if the end of the *Aeneid* signaled to Ovid the beginning of a dramatically worse period in human history.

The birth of these violent children introduces the first narrative in the poem where one of the familiar Olympian deities will be a character. Jupiter summons a divine council in the wake of a particularly heinous crime committed by one of these giant-born mortals. In the *Aeneid*, Jupiter is supremely calm (especially in contrast to his daughter Venus and wife Juno). Jupiter is firmly planted on the side of that mysterious force we know as Fate; he does not seek to countermand its dictates or to rail against destiny. He is a master of tact and diplomacy: in the first book of the *Aeneid*, he calms Venus with a speech that unfolds the future greatness of the Roman descendants of her son Aeneas, while in the last book of the poem, he makes his wife happy with a speech that details how the future Rome will be Italian, not Trojan (a detail he conveniently omitted from the address to his daughter; we can imagine what her reaction would have been). In Ovid, the first appearance of Jupiter is not tranquil; he groans in anger (164-166) as he sees the criminal behavior of mortal men. Ovid could not have made clearer his intention to equate the past (the world of mythology) with the present (Augustan Rome):

> hac iter [i.e., the Milky Way] est superis ad magni tecta Tonantis
> regalemque domum: dextra laevaque deorum
> atria nobilium valvis celebrantur apertis.
> plebs habitat diversa locis: hac parte potentes
> caelicolae clarique suos posuere Penates;
> hic locus est, quem, si verbis audacia detur,
> haud timeam magni dixisse Palatia caeli. (1.170-176)

By this route there is a path for the gods to the dwelling of the great Thunderer

and his royal dwelling: on the right and on the left the courtyards of the more
noble deities are crowded with their doors thrown wide open.
The plebeians dwell apart in their own places: in this part the
powerful and famous heaven-dwellers have set up their Penates:
this is the place, which, if boldness were to be given to my words,
I would scarcely fear to name the Palatine Hill of the great heaven.

Ovid did not name the deity who established order out of chaos, but the earth, seas, and stars (180 *terram, mare, sidera*) all tremble as Jupiter shakes his divine locks; the triple mention of the three zones of creation reminds us of the sea, lands and sky at, e.g., 1.5 and the 22-23; whoever created the current order (conveniently left unspecified), it is Jupiter who now rules all, by a process of accession Ovid leaves undescribed. In a nice touch, Jupiter is indignant as he recounts the sins of man (181 *ora indignantia*), a strikingly strong adjective that echoes the last line of the *Aeneid*, where Turnus' life flees to the shadows with a groan (cf. Jupiter's *ingemit* at 164). Again, there is a marked continuity between the two epics, and here Ovid associates Jupiter with the defeated Turnus, whose Italian side arguably won the Latin war, since the new foundation of Rome was destined to be Italian, not Trojan (cf. *Aeneid* 12.832-837). In that climactic revelation of the *Aeneid*, Jupiter urged Juno to let go of the madness (832 *summitte furorem*) that she had conceived in vain (*inceptum frustra*); her madness was vainly conceived because the goddess was destined to win that which would make her happy (841 *laetata*): Rome would not be Trojan. Ovid's reading of the *Aeneid* in these early movements of the *Metamorphoses* points to Aeneas' slaying of Turnus as an act that destroyed *pietas* and marked a precipitous decline in the history of the ages; Jupiter is now in sympathy with the victim (i.e., Turnus) of such deplorable behavior. At the very least, he is in the position of the defeated Turnus, indignant at the violent behavior of another. Ironically, Turnus had asserted to Aeneas that it was the gods he feared and Jupiter who was his enemy (894-895); now it is Jupiter who experiences indignation.

Jupiter complains that his anxiety for the world now rivals the fear he felt during the gigantomachy (182-184). Interestingly, Jupiter observes that his opponent then sprang from "one body" (185-186 *ab uno / corpore et ex una pendebat origine bellum*), language that reminds us of the primordial state of chaos at the beginning of the epic (cf. 6 *unus . . . vultus*). It would seem that the organization of the universe has not been without perils; there was no crime in the original chaos. Jupiter's plan is to destroy the human race and give over the earth to the nymphs, fauns, satyrs and other forest-dwelling demigods (192-193); here we have an idyllic wish to return to a pastoral Golden Age. All of this anger is centered on the attack made on Jupiter by the vicious Arcadian Lycaon, whose lupine nature is signified by his name.[24]

Lycaon stands at the beginning of the accounts of mortal myths and metamorphoses for Ovid, and appropriately so; his wolf-like qualities remind us of Romulus, Remus, and the she-wolf that suckled the founders of Rome.[25] In Ly-

caon we see the birth of the Romans in perverse glory; no triumphant scene of
the she-wolf as in Jupiter's first speech in the *Aeneid* (1.275-277), but rather a
tale of attempted murder and cannibalism. Here, the wolf is a symbol only of
violence: the ages have indeed declined since the narrative at the beginning of
Virgil's epic. The immortals are incensed with anger as they hear of Lycaon's
attack on Jupiter; Ovid compares them to a contemporary Roman throng in the
poem's first simile, an extraordinary comparison that reveals much of the poet's
intention in crafting his epic:

> . . . sic, cum manus impia saevit
> sanguine Caesareo Romanum exstinguere nomen,
> attonitum tantae subito[26] terrore ruinae
> humanum genus est totusque perhorruit orbis;
> nec tibi grata minus pietas, Auguste, tuorum
> quam fuit illa Iovi . . . (1.200-205)

> . . . *just as, when an impious band raged to*
> *extinguish the Roman name by Caesarean blood,*
> *the human race was struck suddenly by the terror of so great a ruin,*
> *and the whole world trembled much;*
> *nor was the piety of your subjects less pleasing, Augustus,*
> *than was that of Jove's to him . . .*

Once again, Ovid is interested in paralleling Virgil closely.[27] The present passage contains a famous ambiguity: does Ovid refer to the assassination of Julius
Caesar or to some attempted assassination of Augustus? A similar ambiguity
occurs in Jupiter's speech to Venus at the outset of the *Aeneid* (1.286-290),
where the coming of some great Julius is foretold. Ovid makes an explicit comparison between Augustus and Jupiter that would seem to rule out taking the
"Caesarian blood" to refer to the Ides of March. Still, despite the fact that we
must read an attempted assassination of Augustus in these lines, Caesar's ghost
from 44 B.C. also lurks, however allusively.[28] *Pietas* lies in avenging the cruel
acts of another; the immortals are full of rage against Lycaon, just as Augustus'
citizens were ready to punish the malefactors who sought to kill him (and, of
course, for those who prefer to read Julius here, the same thirst for vengeance
more or less applies).

Ovid probably refers here to the mysterious events of 23 B.C.[29] The year
was of the greatest significance for the clarification of Augustus' power (indeed,
Ovid makes the establishment of order in a chaotic universe a metaphor for the
ever more clearly defined nature of the Augustan principate), and was probably
the year of a conspiracy against his life. The threat to the *princeps* from Fannius
Caepio and (especially) the consular Varro Murena is most extensively recorded
in Dio's history (54.3.2-4; note also Velleius 2.91.2).[30] 23 B.C. was the year of
both Augustus' proconsular *imperium* and his tribunician *potestas*; certainly the
climate in Rome would have been favorable toward those who wanted to abolish

what they saw as a permanent threat to republican government. Tiberius was prosecutor in the trial of the conspirators (*in absentia*); Ovid's passage may well be at attempt to curry favor with both Augustus and Tiberius.

Ovid did not invent the story of the madly violent Lycaon.[31] When Jupiter descends to earth to investigate rumors of widespread violence, he flies over Lycaeus and Cyllene (1.217), cult sites for himself and his son Mercury that had been founded by Lycaon.[32] Virgil had briefly mentioned Lycaon at *Georgics* 1.138 as the progenitor of Arctos, in a passage that outlines how with the decline of the ages man began to set sail (using such constellations as *Ursa maior*); Ovid once again seeks to best his poetic predecessor by taking the briefest mention of a figure with a richly complex lore and expanding the story to suit his purposes. Ovid's Lycaon seeks to kill Jupiter under cover of night, but first he slays a Molossian hostage and tries to serve the cooked corpse as a meal to the god, all as part of an attempt to test the divinity of the guest all his subjects recognize. Jupiter destroys Lycaon's house with a thunderbolt; the king flees into the wilderness, where he is transformed into a wolf (1.232-239). Again, in a Roman context it is of the greatest significance that the first transformation in the poem of a mortal man is into a *wolf*, the animal that more than any other symbolizes the city.

Jupiter announces the punishment of Lycaon, but also declares that all humanity will suffer destruction since the evil he found in Lycaon's Arcadian abode is hardly unique. At this, the other immortals (despite fundamental agreement with Jupiter's plans) worry about the fate of the world; who will provide incense for their altars (1.248-249)? Jupiter, for his part, announces that there will be a rebirth of the human race, albeit a very different sort of people (251-252 *subolemque priori / dissimilem populo*). Strikingly, Jupiter and his fellow gods seem to have forgotten his avowed plan (192-195) to hand over the world to semi-divine pastoral creatures. Such an idea would not accord with the reality of human mytho-history, of course, which begs the question of why Jupiter mentioned such an idea, if only to have it completely ignored so quickly? The detail—which seems to be original to Ovid—strongly evokes the world of Virgil's pastoral poetry, absent the political themes that infuse both the *Eclogues* and the *Georgics*. In the announcement of the creation of a new race of men, there is an echo of the similar declaration at the end of the *Aeneid* concerning the forthcoming amalgam of Trojans and Italians, in which the Italian will be the dominant strain. And so Ovid masterfully links the new beginning with which the *Aeneid* ends with the beginning of the same epic, where the fragile ships that carried the Trojan exiles were devastated by a sudden storm sent by Juno and Aeolus. That storm—a recurring image in the early movements of Ovid's epic—will now be recalled yet again, though this time with Neptune as helpful destroyer rather than savior (274-275).

Jupiter decides to destroy the world by water and not fire (1.253-261).[33] Jupiter is fearful that a conflagration might ruin heaven as well as earth, and also mindful of a prophecy that one day fire would indeed wreak total havoc in the universe (another principle of Stoic cosmology); the story of Phaethon with which the present books ends and the next one begins will provide a ring with his decision here to use water and not flames. Ovid's flood is reminiscent of the storm that opens *Aeneid* 1, but it is more indebted to Horace (c. 1.2) than to Virgil.[34] Excluding the introductory, dedicatory ode to Maecenas, the poem is the first in Horace's collection of lyrics. It opens with a cry of "enough" (1.2.1 *satis*); Jupiter has punished the wickedness of the world more than sufficiently through past disasters. Horace asks whom the people will be able to call upon in a time of disaster for the state? In the end, he invokes Augustus, praying that he will remain on earth and enter heaven late:

> serus in caelum redeas diuque
> laetus intersis populo Quirini,
> neve te nostris vitiis iniquum
> ocior aura
>
> tollat . . . (1.2.45-49)

> *Late may you return to the heaven,*
> *and for a long time may you be present for the people of Quirinus,*
> *and may you not, as one made guilty by our vices,*
> *a swifter breeze*
>
> *raise up.*

Horace describes the past destruction of the earth by the flood at some length, in language Ovid imitates (e.g., the fish caught in the lofty elm at 1.2.9 and the fisherman angling in an elm tree at *Metamorphoses* 1.296). Indeed, as we enter the narrative of the flood we might wonder where Ovid's kindly *deus* is, the god who established the order that is now to see the terrible destruction of the *sanctius animal*, man (1.76).

In Ovid, the flood is a terrible perversion of the Golden Age: now the wolf swims with the sheep, both victims of the same deluge. Ironically, the rebirth of Rome in Augustan propaganda came as a result of Augustus' *naval* victory at Actium; water will now destroy the human race. Ovid lavishes poetic skill on the description of the flood, which is filled with nice touches such as the farmer who tries to escape in his curved boat (1.293 *cumba . . . adunca*), where *cumba* is a fitting choice of word for "boat," since it is the technical term for Charon's underworld vessel.

It would seem the destruction is complete; only the salvation of the devoted married couple Deucalion and Pyrrha spares the human race.[35] Here, there is learned humor: Jupiter had decided to spare the world an attack from his thunderbolts, out of fear that the whole universe might go up in flames; now Pyrrha, whose name in Greek means "fire," will be the mother of a reborn race of men.[36] The implication is that the new generation will not match Jupiter's expectation of improvement in humanity; the subsequent metamorphoses Ovid recalls will show that the children of fire are indeed worse than their predecessors. The rebirth of the human race comes at Mount Parnassus (1.316-317), where the skiff carrying Deucalion and Pyrrha alights. The Delphic oracle was there; Themis is its guardian in these days before Apollo enters the narrative. Themis was a Titaness, a daughter of Gaea and Uranus (Hesiod, *Theogony* 132); an interesting feature of the early sections of Ovid's epic is the unexplained presence of the different generations of the immortals. Ovid makes no attempt to disentangle where the gods came from or how the Olympian order came to be. Allusions to canonical versions of the battles of the gods are few (cf. 1.113 *Saturno tenebrosa in Tartara misso*, of the collapse of the Golden Age). Ovid focuses his attention on setting up the world as we know it as quickly as possible, with little or no attention paid to any of the traditional lore we find in, e.g., Hesiod's *Theogony*.

Deucalion, the son of Prometheus, and his cousin Pyrrha (the daughter of Epimetheus) are presented in seemingly flattering terms. There was no man "better" than Deucalion (1.322 *melior*), a description that reminds us of the "better nature" that gave order to the universe (21), an appropriate echo as the human race is about to experience renewal. There is humor, too: there is no man better than Deucalion, no one more loving of what is right (322), and no woman more fearful of the gods than Pyrrha (323), precisely because they are the only ones on earth, with no competition for thus rather empty comparatives. Indeed, Ovid will not describe any period in subsequent human history that is decidedly "better" than that which preceded the flood.

The stones that Deucalion and Pyrrha throw behind themselves to rejuvenate the mortal race constitute technically the third creation of men Ovid describes. The original creation (1.76-88) was due either to the independent divine action of the *fabricator mundi* or the demiurge's use of divine ethereal seeds left mixed in the earth. The second creation (156-62) was the action of the earth after the destruction of Otus and Ephialtes; these were the children of blood. There is no indication in Ovid of what happened to the original humans, or how they link to the blood-born mortals. Presumably they coexisted; perhaps the first group eventually died out. Both of these, in any case, were destroyed by the time of the flood, with the exception of Deucalion and Pyrrha. All subsequent mortals are from the race of stone (399-415).

In this third creation—which enjoys the lengthiest description of the three—Ovid returns to the question of *formae* and *corpora* from his proem. The stones take on "form" after they are thrown:

ponere duritiem coepere suumque rigorem
mollirique mora mollitaque ducere formam. (1.401-402)

They began to put aside their hardness and rigor,
and they grew soft with a delay, and, once softened, they took on form.

A part of the stones was transformed into body, and another into bone:

> quae tamen ex illis aliquo pars umida suco
> et terrena fuit, versa est in corporis usum;
> quod solidum est flectique nequit, mutatur in ossa. (1.407-409)

That part of them, however, which was wet with some moisture
and earthy, was turned into the use of body;
what was solid and was unable to be bent was changed into bones.

We might think Ovid is using his two key terms rather loosely in this passage. The stones obviously had *formae* before they were thrown; the proem speaks of forms changed into new bodies, which describes exactly what has happened here. Bones (not to mention the veins Ovid mentions at 410) are obviously constituent parts of human bodies. Ovid compares the birth of men from rocks to the work of a sculptor who fashions a human figure from a block of stone (405-406); the point, then, is that the *forma hominis* was concealed in the rock and merely had to be freed by divine power. The rock was then transformed into a new body (*in corporis usum*).

So that we do not lose sight of the fact that Ovid's principal concern is the transformation that overtook Rome, Deucalion and Pyrrha are described as practicing the eminently Roman custom of veiling their heads at the order of the goddess-oracle (1.382 *velate caput*; 398 *velantque caput*). Man's origins may be divine, but the earth is credited with the animal life that now appeared (1.416-417). Ovid describes this process in a lengthy passage (416-437) that focuses our attention on Egypt. The new animal life is born from the favorable union of heat and moisture. Moisture is abundant in light of the recent flood; the new animal life that appears is the result of a marvelous spontaneous generation:

> sic ubi deseruit madidos septemfluus agros
> Nilus et antiquo recens exarsit sidere limus,
> plurima cultores versis animalia glaebis
> inveniunt et in his quaedam modo coepta per ipsum[37]
> nascendi spatium, quaedam imperfecta suisque
> trunca vident numeris, et eodem in corpore saepe
> altera pars vivit, rudis est pars altera tellus. (1.423-429)

Just as when the sevenfold Nile has deserted its wet banks
and the fresh muck has been thoroughly heated by the ancient star,
farmers find many animals once the globs of earth have been overturned
and in these lumps they see some that have just now begun the process of birth,
and others that are yet imperfect, truncated as to their limbs,
and in the same body often
one part is alive, while the other part is still unfinished earth.

Divine power found the forms of men in rock; the earth finds the same forms in the muck and mire of the post-diluvian world. Any mention of Egypt in the years after Actium might have recalled the struggle of Octavian against Antony and Cleopatra. Some of the animals that are born of earth are the old, familiar; others are new monsters (436-437), among them the terrible Python. The Egypt simile is heavily indebted to Lucretius (cf. *De Rerum Natura* 6.712-734) and his method of explication of natural phenomena. But the historical context is important to keep in focus here. Ovid does not say that the new population of animals was born exclusively in Egypt, but his simile offers the only localization of the wondrous process of spontaneous generation that now repopulates the animal kingdom: Egypt. New monsters are born, among them the Python. And it will be Apollo, that is, Augustus, who will slay the monster, just as Octavian defeated the (barbarian) forces of Antony and Cleopatra (replete with their animal-headed deities).[38] Apollo slays the Python for the benefit of man; the huge serpent had been a terror to the newly born rock-people (1.438-440).[39] The Pythian games are established to honor Apollo's victory; the reward for the victors in the contests there is an oaken crown (448-449), which reminds us of the civic crown won by Romans who saved a fellow citizen's life in battle. The oak was necessary because (at least in Ovid's world) the laurel had not yet been invented (and cf. 1.563, where the laurel is ordered to keep watch over the civic crown).[40] This first post-diluvian story is a glorious moment for the Olympians; Apollo's victory and the establishment of the games occupy a mere fourteen lines, however, of brief description. Ovid will reserve lengthier treatment and lavish poetic skill on less glorious divine exploits and pursuits. The noble laurel is about to be the subject of a less than heroic tale for the archer god.

The laurel had been highlighted by Virgil in his poetic account of the arrival of the Trojans in Latium (*Aeneid* 7.59-80). There had been a laurel tree that Latinus found when he was setting up his capital city in central Italy; Latinus named his people the Laurentes from the laurel he dedicated to Apollo. Bees were seen to alight at the summit of the sacred tree; bards sang that the portent of the bees announced the arrival of a foreign man who would take power. Soon after, Latinus' daughter Lavinia was engaging in religious rites when her hair caught fire in another ominous sign that was taken to portend both her great fame and the war she would bring to Latium. The laurel, then, connects us once again to Rome's founding and to the important place of Apollo in the Augustan pantheon. Ovid now presents the etiology of the laurel's significance to Apollo through his elaborate narrative of Apollo's love for Daphne.[41] As will be the case with many of the individual stories in the *Metamorphoses*, Ovid's version became the canonical one for posterity.

But the preexisting tradition is of paramount importance in explicating what the Augustan poet has done with the available material. For Ovid, the most important account of Apollo's infatuation with Daphne was probably Parthenius', (*Erotica Pathemata* 15), where Daphne is the daughter not of the river god

Peneus, but rather of Amyclas of Laconia; elsewhere she is the daughter of Ladon in Arcadia. In Parthenius' version, Daphne is a virgin huntress like Artemis;
she is loved by Leucippus (= "White Horse"), who disguises himself as a girl to
join her coterie.[42] His true gender is uncovered by her (genuinely) female companions in a fateful bath; they attack him with their spears. Apollo then pursues
Daphne, and she is saved after a prayer to Zeus, who transforms her into a laurel.[43]

In Ovid's refashioning of the story, Cupid stands on Parnassus to attack
Apollo with his amorous shafts (1.467); the location is significant not only as the
locus of the Delphic oracle, but also as the place where Deucalion and Pyrrha
had found refuge from the flood (316-317). The first scene of "love" in the
Metamorphoses will come at the same place where the human race was reborn,
namely Parnassus, Apollo's mountain. Cupid is angry because Apollo, fresh
from his victory over the Python, had mocked the boy god for his playing with a
bow and arrows.[44] After Daphne is struck by a leaden shaft, she delights in the
world of Apollo's sister Diana (474-477), fleeing marriage and preferring the
hunt to a husband (a reversal of the Parthenian Daphne, who was already a huntress when Leucippus fell in love with her). In his depiction of the huntress
Daphne, Ovid presents the first account in the *Metamorphoses* of an image that
greatly appealed to him (judging by its frequent reappearances): the Diana-like
girl who encounters serious difficulties because of her virginal lifestyle.[45]

Again, the influence of Virgil can be discerned. In the first book of the
Aeneid (314-324), Aeneas' mother Venus appeared to him in the guise of a huntress. In the same first book, Cupid and Venus effected Dido's hopeless infatuation with Aeneas (657-722). In Ovid, Daphne's virginal status as a devotee of
Diana will be preserved. In Virgil, Venus' Diana-disguise has a comic air of
playacting about it; the capricious goddess of love is given to playful frivolity
and a lighthearted air. Here, in his description of Apollo's pursuit of the virgin
huntress Daphne, Ovid offers the first sustained comic romp in his epic. The
archer god who vanquished the Python as a favor to mortals, who established the
Pythian games to commemorate his victory, is now depicted pathetically as urging Daphne to run more slowly so as not to harm her legs on the brambles, with
a promise that he in turn will moderate his own pace (1.508-511). Cupid's influence has destroyed Apollo's dignity; the arrows of the boy god are indeed
sharper than Apollo's, because they can render the great deity of the Augustan
program a hapless fool in pursuit of an unattainable love.[46] The Ovidian context
for Cupid's action is far less serious than the Virgilian; there will be a lasting
consequence to the shooting of Apollo and Daphne, but it will be nothing other
than Apollo's assumption of the laurel as his particular tree. There is no comparison with the severity of the consequences of the actions of Venus and Cupid
in *Aeneid* 1. But Apollo is a far more significant target than Aeneas, especially
given his importance in Augustan religion. And, while Diana is absent from the
narrative, Ovid offers a conflict between the divine siblings; the goddess of the
hunt would not want Apollo to win a virgin who had chosen the forest over men.

In any case, Diana wins in the sense that Daphne's virginity is preserved; the laurel becomes an eternal symbol of that purity. Daphne asked her father Peneus to preserve her virginity, just as Jupiter had agreed to preserve his daughter Diana's (485-488); the request will be granted, in that Daphne does not suffer rape.[47]

The *Aeneid* is in some sense an erotic epic that is centered on Aeneas' conquest of Lavinia. But Virgil does not reveal the victory to his audience; while we know that Aeneas has defeated Turnus and won his future bride, we are left with no triumphant nuptial scene. On the contrary, the two great heterosexual passions of the *Aeneid* both end in disaster: Aeneas' affair with Dido, and Turnus' infatuation with Camilla that leads him to abandon his best chance at winning the war in Latium in his mad rage after her death. Love would seem to have negative consequences in Virgil; in this the poet was no doubt influenced by Lucretius and his famous attack on the power of passion at the end of *De Rerum Natura* 4. In Ovid, love reduces even one of the greatest of the immortals to the status of a mere animal:

> ut canis in vacuo leporem cum Gallicus arvo
> vidit, et hic praedam pedibus petit, ille salutem;
> alter inhaesuro similis iam iamque tenere
> sperat et extento stringit vestigia rostro,
> alter in ambiguo est, an sit comprensus, et ipsis
> morsibus eripitur tangentiaque ora relinquit:
> sic deus et virgo est hic spe celer, illa timore. (1.533-539)

> *As when a Gallic hound has seen a hare in an empty*
> *field, and this one seeks a prize with its feet, safety that one;*
> *the hound, like to one about to grab on, hopes now,*
> *now to grasp him and grazes his tracks with his extended muzzle;*
> *the hare is in doubt whether he has already been captured, and*
> *is snatched from the very jaws and leaves behind the mouth that touches him:*
> *so are the god and the virgin, the one swift with hope, the other with fear.*

The simile is based on Virgil's comparison of Aeneas' pursuit of Turnus to that of a hunter's dog chasing a deer (*Aeneid* 12.746-757); the Virgilian parallel of Aeneas and Turnus may account for the masculine sex of the two animals in the simile. One of the final similes of the *Aeneid* has been transformed into one of the first in the *Metamorphoses*. In place of Aeneas we have Apollo, and in Turnus' stead, Daphne; just as Turnus' side in the Latin war will ultimately know the victory of an *Italian* Rome, so Daphne will be immortalized with some of the highest honors Rome can offer. In the final analysis, both Aeneas and Apollo come off as something less than their respective quarries.

One might also argue that the erotic pursuit of Lavinia is part of the destruction that befalls Aeneas. The affair with Dido led to the terrible, lasting enmity between Rome and Carthage; the winning of Lavinia from Turnus might have

been bloodless, but in the end (and besides the many other casualties of the
Latin war), Aeneas was unable to spare his opponent (admittedly because of the
death of Pallas). Erato presides over the second half of the *Aeneid* (7.37-45),
precisely because the *Aeneid* is focused on the erotic element of Aeneas' quest.
Effectively (however anachronistically), Ovid underscores his point and the
connection of the Apollo and Daphne episode to the omnipresent Augustan regime by Apollo's decrees to the newly created laurel:

> postibus Augustis eadem fidissima custos
> ante fores stabis mediamque tuebere quercum (1.562-563)

> *On Augustus' doorposts will you likewise stand*
> *as a most faithful guardian, and you will watch over the oak in the middle.*

The reference is to the events of 27 B.C., when Octavian was awarded the title
Augustus by the Senate and given the perpetual use of the civic crown on the
door of his Palatine residence; a laurel was also affixed there, in commemoration of his victories.

Why did Ovid relocate the Daphne story from Arcadia to Thessaly?[48] Ovid
underscores the innocence of Daphne by removing her from Arcadia, which had
previously been associated with the ante-diluvian horror of Lycaon. The poet
also wanted to reserve Arcadia as the scene for the climactic story of Syrinx
(1.689 ff.) that would end his set of divine amours. Why did he relocate Daphne
from Laconia? As we have noted, in that version of the lore Daphne is pursued
by Leucippus, who disguises himself as a girl and is eventually discovered by
Daphne's companions. Here we can only say that Ovid wanted the story near the
Delphic oracle, in Thessaly, to underscore the connection of the story to the
archer god who played a role in all versions of the Daphne myth.

Apollo may be the key divinity in the Augustan pantheon, but Jupiter is his
father and superior. Ovid now proceeds to show how Jupiter, too, has been overcome by infatuation; this time, there is no Cupid to justify the amorous pursuit.
After the transformation of Daphne, the rivers visited Peneus to offer their respect and condolences (1.568-587); Inachus stayed away in grief for the loss of
his Argolid daughter Io, who had gone missing.[49] The Io story marks a decline
past even the degradation Apollo had suffered when he fell prey to Cupid's arrows; this time there is not only no excuse that can be offered for the god's behavior, but also a ravished, tormented victim.

In the Latin poetic tradition, the lost *Io* of Catullus' contemporary Calvus
would have been most influential on Ovid. Ovid had already shown an interest
in the story in the *Heroides* (14.86-109), where Hypermestra briefly recalls the
tale to her husband Lynceus.[50] But the lore is old; Herodotus uses it at the beginning of his *Histories* as one of several examples of the origins of the conflict
between East and West (a concern of Augustan propaganda as well). The story
figures prominently in the pseudo-Aeschlyean *Prometheus Bound*.[51] In Herodo-

tus, Io's importance cannot be exaggerated; she is the first cause listed of any conflict between East and West, a victim of the mutual kidnappings of women (1.1.1.-1.5.2).[52] She was abducted by Phoenician merchants who had come to Argos to trade; later, the Greeks returned the favor by stealing Europa and Medea. Herodotus notes that men of sense do not make much over such abductions; the loss of Europa and of Medea did not cause a tremendous stir in Asia, while the loss of Helen, of course, caused the Trojan War. In Ovid's vision, the image of Io as eventual Isis (see on 1.747 below) evokes the image of Cleopatra and Octavian's own East-West struggle.

Rivers mark the progression from the Nile (1.423-424) to the fathers of Daphne and Io; the story of Io will bring us back to the Nile and Egypt. Io does not travel far in her flight from Jupiter before she is caught and raped (598-600); we do well to remember that in Ovid's history we are still early on in the post-diluvian period, when presumably men were of a better stock than their predecessors; Daphne and Io may be imagined to be especially honorable women. In any case, Jupiter snatches away Io's modesty (600 *rapuitque pudorem*); her flight was unsuccessful.[53] Juno is at once introduced for the first time in the poem. The goddess knows all too well the tricks of her husband, and grows suspicious when she sees how the skies have darkened (so as to conceal Jupiter's rape).[54] Jupiter hastily transforms Io into a lovely heifer (whose beauty even Juno must concede); the vengeful, sadistic goddess seeks it as a present. Jupiter had snatched away Io's *pudor*, and now *pudor* urges him to surrender the girl to Juno (618). *Pudor* is conquered by the seemingly omnipotent *Amor* (619); we are perhaps reminded of how *pietas* and Astraea all fled the earth in the days before the flood (149-150). Jupiter had destroyed the earth's population because of its wickedness; since the repopulation of the earth, the immortals have been the criminals.

There is a clever trick in the Io story; Jupiter is infatuated with a girl who will soon have cow's eyes, in a nice nod to the traditional Homeric epithet of ox-eyed Hera.[55]

Io is entrusted to the care of the hundred-eyed Argus, Juno's faithful watchman. Ovid has great fun depicting the pathetic Io, who can only scratch out the (mercifully few) letters of her name in the dirt, so as to signal her identity to her hapless father Inachus (1.645-663). Jupiter can stand the captivity of his former lover no longer; he at once calls Mercury to assist him in freeing Io by slaying Argus (669-670). Here, too, there is a mockery of the serious use of the same scene in the *Aeneid*; there, Jupiter had summoned Mercury to warn Aeneas to leave his lover Dido and proceed to his Roman destiny. Here, Mercury is enjoined to save Jupiter's lover.

Mercury arrives playing his pipes and imitating a shepherd; the scene as Argus receives him is a virtual parody of the world of Virgil's *Eclogues*. The lulling to sleep of Argus by Mercury owes something to Virgil's description of Sleep's efforts with Palinurus. Argus struggles to stay awake and assists in his own doom by asking Mercury how his pipes came to be invented; the question opens the door to a story within a story (the first of many in the *Metamorphoses*): the tale of Syrinx.[56]

Syrinx returns us to the world of Daphne. She was an Arcadian, and, like the Arcadian Daphne, a devotee of Diana. Like Virgil's Venus in disguise, Syrinx was mistaken for Diana (1.696-698). The return to Arcadia also brings us back full circle to Lycaon and his crimes; Pan sees the virgin huntress returning from Mount Lycaeus. Syrinx runs to the streams of Ladon, the sometime father of Daphne, thus further reinforcing the ring composition wherein Ovid has brilliantly changed the story of Arcadian Daphne into his own (Thessalian) creation, and reminded us of the change by balancing her tale with that of the Arcadian Syrinx, who seeks salvation at Ladon.[57] Thus all versions of the Daphne lore are brought together in Ovid's one *carmen perpetuum*. Syrinx beseeches her sister nymphs to save her; she is at once changed into a set of reeds that produce a beautiful sound when the wind blows through them. And so just as Apollo has his laurel, now Pan has his pipes. And, in part, the humor of the episode derives from the fact that Argus was lulled to sleep by a story that is essentially a doublet of one the audience has already heard—Apollo and Daphne.

This last part of the Syrinx story is not directly told by Mercury to Argus; the watchman has at last fallen completely asleep. Sleep did not directly murder Palinurus, who was hurled overboard and, as Aeneas would learn in the underworld, made it successfully to the Italian coast (only to be killed by natives there). Mercury decapitates Argus as soon as sleep overtakes all his eyes. Juno sets the eyes of the beheaded guard on the tail of her peacock (1.722-723, a good example of Ovid's delight in offering brief metamorphoses amid lengthier stories). The angry goddess then summons a Fury (another echo of her actions in the *Aeneid*) and seeks to punish Io for the loss of Argus. The Nile is the last place where the hapless heifer seeks refuge in her lengthy flight.

In a marvelous nod to the end of the *Aeneid*, Jupiter approaches his wife and urges her to lay aside all fear for any future illicit amours from her husband (1.733-738). Io had begged for release; we might compare Venus' pleas with her father for the safety of her son and his Trojans. Ovid underscores the comic nature of the parody by having Jupiter swear solemnly by the Styx that he will keep a word the audience knows will be broken all too soon (737). Io is transformed back into a mortal girl; she is venerated as the goddess Isis by linen-wearing priests (747). She has a son, Epaphus (from the Greek for "to touch"); it is believed that he was Jupiter's son, though the paternity is not definitively settled. Here we have another commentary on the events of the *Aeneid*. In his speech to his daughter Venus in *Aeneid* 1, there had been no mention of the fact that the future Rome would *not* be Trojan; only Jupiter's wife Juno would receive the climactic revelation that Rome would be Italian. Here, Juno is assured that her philanderer of a husband would abstain from future peccadilloes. Yet, at once, Io is transformed into the Egyptian goddess Isis, complete with a son who may or may not be Jupiter's. As with the Virgilian treatment of Venus, we are forced to conclude that Juno would not be happy with the revelations that her rival would become a goddess and mother. And, besides, there are the shades of Cleopatra here; the beautiful Daphne was transformed into a tree, however honored in Roman religion. Io is changed into a foreign goddess.

Io's son Epaphus has a friend, Phaethon. The ambiguity over Epaphus' parentage provides a link to the dramatic story of another son of dubious parentage. Epaphus is in a better state than Phaethon, precisely because his mother is a goddess and he shares her temples with her; Phaethon's mother has no such divine status or cult (there is an implicit note here that Jupiter's paramour has a higher status than Sol's). The tale provides a cliffhanger ending to the first book of the *Metamorphoses*, and, as commentators have long noted, offers the reader the lengthiest single story in the entire epic.[58] The scene unobtrusively changes to Ethiopia, south of Egypt and the home of Phaethon's stepfather Merops (1.763). Phaethon's mother Clymene urges her son to visit his father the Sun to inquire as to his paternity, *if the mind compels him* (775 *si modo fert animus*), a brilliant ring to close the first book. The mind, of course, is as much Ovid's as the youth's; he has decided to embark on a lengthy tale whose prolegomena echo the end of the first *Aeneid*. There, Dido and her court sat rapt and ready to hear the dramatic tale of the night Troy fell, itself the longest single story in Virgil's epic. Here, the audience is left just as transfixed by anticipation of the coming drama. In a sense the story of Phaethon also returns us to Apollo; while Apollo and Sol (= the Greek Helios) are separate enough deities in Ovid, the link of Apollo with the sun does not permit exclusion of shades of the famous god in the lengthy episode that is about to commence, especially after the stories of Apollo and Jupiter we have just heard. The question of divine paternity is a comic enough result of the frequent escapades of the immortals. Thus far we have only heard of Apollo's infatuation with Daphne, for which we may blame Cupid; now we hear of Sol's relationship with Clymene, which, if we keep Phoebus Apollo in mind, underscores the philandering nature of that god.

In Virgil, Elysium is located under the Eridanus, where Phaethon's sisters will weep themselves into poplar trees that drip amber (*Aeneid* 6.659; *Metamorphoses* 2.340-366). From Elysium come the reborn souls of future Roman worthies. We may wonder if the comic tone of many of the passages of the immortals' amorous adventures is about to be transformed into a more serious enterprise, for which the comic served as preface. Jupiter had avoided destroying the world by fire because he feared a conflagration that would engulf the entire universe; Phaethon's actions in pursuit of the truth of his parentage will threaten the fiery destruction of the world. Given the structural parallels between the *Aeneid* and the *Metamorphoses*, we may connect Phaethon's ill-fated adventure with the story of the night Troy fell. That terrible night of fire and devastation led to a dawn of new beginning for the nascent Rome; as we shall see in Ovid, the narrow escape from destruction the world experiences in consequence of Phaethon will simply lead to exactly what happened before the boy's fateful chariot ride: *nothing new* in a poem of innovation. The call to innovation of the poem's proem, while fulfilled well enough in certain regards, will prove unanswerable in others.[59]

The *Aeneid* moved from the watery destruction of Juno's storm to the fires that consumed Troy; the *Metamorphoses*, with its grander scale and wider scope of interest, moves from the disaster of the great flood to Phaethon's near global conflagration. Phaethon rushes eastward to find the sun; he passes Ethiopia and the Indies (1.778-779) before his journey (and the book) end. His mother had urged this journey on him, *if his mind compelled him* to pursue it; in this evocation of the beginning of the book, Phaethon becomes another Ovid, about to embark on a mad quest. The madness of that journey comes from a number of considerations: the daunting task of addressing the transformations of the entire world down to his own time and the complex changes that had come about in Augustan Rome, and the poetic challenge of rivaling Virgil (and, by implication, Homer). And, in a sense, we are reminded also of Augustus, chasing the ghost of his adoptive father Julius Caesar, besides trying to forge a new political reality in Rome out of the still simmering ashes of the Republic. In a marvelous touch, the dramatic ending of Ovid's first book of changes, in its anticipation of a fateful chariot ride, calls to mind the simile with which Virgil ended the first georgic: the runaway chariot that is a symbol of the runaway Republic (512-514).

It is curious that the first book of the *Metamorphoses* has twenty-six verses more than the first book of the *Aeneid*: essentially the same number of years as elapsed between the death of Virgil and Ovid's exile.[60] It is yet another indication of Ovid's response to and continuation of the Virgilian program.

As we have noted, Phaethon's story is the longest individual metamorphosis in Ovid. Virgil had briefly sketched an image of Rome's chariot, out of control in headlong rush. It will now be left to his successor to flesh out that image, as the master poet lavishes his utmost attention on the impetuous boy of the sun and his fiery ride.

Notes

1. On the first book, standard (German) commentary is found in Bömer (Vol. 1 on Books 1-3); most useful for anglophone students is Anderson (Vol. 1 of an unfinished three on Books 1-5); note also Lee. There is now also the Italian commentary in the Fondazione Lorenzo Valla/Arnoldo Mondadori series under the general editorship of Alessandro Barchiesi; the first volume covers Books 1-2 of the poem (with lengthy general introduction). Luigi Galasso has produced a lengthy commentary on the entire poem (Turin, 2000) for the *Biblioteca della Pléiade* series.

2. Ovid's epic has three books more than Virgil's; scholars divide the books of the *Aeneid* into various equally valid arrangements (1-6, 7-12; 1-4, 5-8, etc., 1-3, 4-6, etc.). As we shall see, Ovid arranges his epic in response to Virgil's; this first book of the poem has neat parallels to *Aeneid* 1, even if they cannot be pushed too far.

3. This possible theme of the immutability of poetry may have held special significance to Ovid, the poet who saw the first, five-book edition of his *Amores* republished in a shorter version.

4. See further Kenney, E. J., "Ovidius Prooemians," in *PCPhS* 22 (1976), pp. 46-53, Relihan, J.C., "Ovid *Metamorphoses* I, 1-4 and Fulgentius' *Mythologiae*" in *The American Journal of Philology* 105 (1984), pp. 87-90, and Kovacs, "Ovid, *Metamorphoses* 1.2" in *The Classical Quarterly* N. S. 37.2 (1987), pp. 458-465.

5. The choice of *arma* as the first word of Ovid's first poem in the *Amores* illustrates well the profound influence of Virgil on the poet; on the pervasive echoes best now is Thomas, Richard, "Ovid's Reception of Virgil," in Knox, ed., *A Companion to Ovid*, Leiden: Brill, 2009, pp. 294-307.

6. On this passage note McKeown ad loc., and Otis, *Ovid as an Epic Poet*, Oxford, 1966 (second edition, 1970), pp. 13-14.

7. The bibliography on the *deductum carmen/carmen perpetuum* is immense. See especially Hofmann, H., "Ovid's *Metamorphoses*: *Carmen Perpetuum, Carmen Deductum*" in Cairns, F., ed., *Papers of the Liverpool Latin Seminar V, 1985*, Liverpool: Francis Cairns Ltd., 1986, pp. 223-241, and also Steiner, Grundy, "Ovid's *Carmen Perpetuum*," in *Transactions of the American Philological Association* 89 (1958), pp. 218-236, and Wheeler, Stephen G., *A Discourse of Wonders: Audience and Performance in Ovid's* Metamorphoses, Philadelphia: The University of Pennsylvania Press, 1999, pp. 118-122.

8. For reflections on the force of *mea tempora*, note Feeney, D.C., "*Mea tempora*: Patterning of Time in the *Metamorphoses*" in Barchiesi, A., et al., eds., *Ovidian Transformations: Essays on the Metamorphoses and Its Reception*, Cambridge: Cambridge Philological Society, 1999, pp. 13-30.

9. See further Robbins, Frank Egleston, "The Creation Story in Ovid *Met.* I," in *Classical Philology* 8.4 (1913), pp. 401-313, and Wheeler, Stephen M., "*Imago mundi*: Another View of the Creation in Ovid's *Metamorphoses*," in *The American Journal of Philology* 116.1 (1995), pp. 95-121 (together with "Correction: Another View . . . , in 116.2).

10. Ovid opens his account of creation with mention of how Chaos predated the *sea* ("ante mare . . . ") precisely to recall the opening of Virgil's *Aeneid* and its marine setting: his poem will have temporal precedence over Virgil's.

11. The word is a favorite of Virgil's, who uses it to describe, e.g., the bulk of the Cyclops (*A.* 3.656), a siege engine (*A.* 5.439), the mass of waves kicked up by storms (*A.*

1.134, 5.790), or a throng of people (*A.* 12.575); the word thus often has violent connotations.

12. The "Titan" is Hyperion, the father of Helios, the sun (*pace* Lee, who opts for Helios); for an Augustan audience, however, the most important image is Apollo's. "Titan" is regularly used in Ovid to refer to the sun. For the distinction in Latin poetry between Apollo and the Sun, note Fontenrose, Joseph E., "Apollo and Sol in the Latin Poets of the First Century B.C.," in *Transactions of the American Philological Association* 70 (1939), pp. 53-62, and the same author's "Apollo and the Sun-God in Ovid," in *The American Journal of Philology* 61.4 (1940), pp. 429-444.

13. Essential reading now is Miller, John F., *Apollo, Augustus, and the Poets*, Cambridge, 2009, and Green, C. M. C., *Roman Religion and the Cult of Diana at Aricia*, Cambridge, 2006.

14. See further Lloyd, G. E. R., "The Hot and the Cold, the Dry and the Wet" in *The Journal of Hellenic Studies* 84 (1964), pp. 92-106. Ovid borrowed mention of the primordial existence of these elements from Greek philosophy, e.g., Anaxagoras, frs. 4, 12.

15. See, e.g., Pinault, Jody Rubin, *Hippocratic Lives and Legends*, Leiden: Brill, 1992, pp. 50-11, on Hippocrates' alleged use of fire to quell a plague.

16. Cf. Lucretius, *De Rerum Natura* 6.1075.

17. Note Hill ad 21.

18. See further Galinsky, G. Karl, "The Hercules-Cacus Episode in *Aeneid* VIII," in *The American Journal of Philology* 87.1 (1966), pp. 18-51, and George, Edward, *Aeneid VIII and the Aitia of Callimachus*, Leiden: Brill, 1974, pp. 43-70.

19. In a sense, Ovid's *Metamorphoses* also fills in the song of Iopas that entertained the guests at Dido's court (*Aeneid* 1.743), which sang of the origins of men and beasts. But that, too, was an eminently Lucretian song.

20. Ovid reverses the order of Virgil's songs. As we shall see below, in Ovid the flood follows the Golden Age (as indeed it logically must); in Virgil, the *Saturnia regna* come after Pyrrha's stones. Virgil was concerned with the idea that after the punishing flood, there should be some explicit improvement in the human condition; Ovid offers no such consolation.

21. See further Bömer, and Anderson, ad 60.

22. Note especially Wheeler, Stephen M., "Ovid's Use of Lucretius in *Metamorphoses* 1.67-68," in *The Classical Quarterly* N. S. 45.1 (1995), pp. 200-203.

23. West, M. L., *The East Face of Helicon: West Asiatic Elements in Greek Poetry and Myth*, Oxford, 1997, pp. 314-315.

24. For Arcadia as the origin of pastoral poetry and the development of human civilization, note Fabre-Serris, Jacqueline, *Rome, l'Arcadie et la mer des Argonautes: Essai sur la naissance d'une mythologie des origines en Occident. Mythes, imaginaires, religion*, Villeneuve d'Ascq: Presses universitaires du Septentrion, 2008.

25. On Lycaon see further Haarberg, Jon M., "Lycaon's Impious and Ovid's Rhetorical Strategy: A Note on the Lycaon Episode in *met.* 1," in *Symbolae Osloenses* 58.1 (1983), pp. 111-115, Detienne, Marcel, "La Table de Lycaon," in *Modern Language Notes* 106.4 (1991: French Issue: Cultural Representations of Food), pp. 742-750, and Bechard, Dean Philip, *Paul Outside the Walls: A Study of Luke's Socio-Geographical Universalism in Acts 14: 8-20*, (*Analecta Biblica* 143), Roma: Editrice Pontificio Istituto Biblico, 2000, pp. 280-291.

26. *Tantae subito*: Tarrant conjectures *tanto subitae*, with substantially the same meaning.

27. On this simile, and especially its connection to the subsequent narrative of the flood, note Boyd, Barbara Weiden, "*Non hortamine longo*: An Ovidian 'Correction' of Virgil," in *The American Journal of Philology* 111.1 (1990), pp. 82-85. On Ovidian similes in general see Owen, S. G., "Ovid's Use of the Simile," in *The Classical Review* 45.3 (1931), pp. 97-106.

28. Hill ad 201 is unhelpful in claiming a reference to Julius' murder is "obvious" and that "there is no merit" in attempts to read an attack on Augustus into the passage. Conversely, Anderson considers it "wrong" to see an allusion to Julius; neither commentator seems willing to let Ovid evoke both Julius *and* Augustus, in imitation of Virgil.

29. See further McDermott, William C., "Varro Murena," in *Transactions of the American Philological Association* 72 (1941), pp. 255-265.

30. Macrobius, *Saturnalia* 1.11.21, describes how Caepio was helped by a faithful slave in escaping from Rome as far as Naples.

31. Bechard, *op. cit.*, conveniently gathers the extant testimonia (p. 282 n. 145); the story is probably Hesiodic in origin.

32. Pausanias 8.2.3; Hyginus, *Fabulae* 225.

33. On Ovid's flood note principally West, M. L., "The Flood Myth in Ovid, Lucian, and Nonnus," in López Férez, J.A., ed., *Mitos en la literature griega helenística e imperial*, Madrid, 2004, pp. 245-259 (a 1995 article significantly delayed); also Ryder, T. T. B., "Ovid, the Flood, and Ararat," in *Greece & Rome*, Second Series 14.2 (1967), pp. 126-129, Fletcher, K. F. B., "Ovidian Correction of the Biblical Flood?" in *Classical Philology* 105 (2010), pp. 209-213, and, more generally, Dundes, Alan, ed., *The Flood Myth*, Berkeley-Los Angeles: The University of California Press, 1988 (a collection of twenty-five essays), and Lambert, W. G., and Millard, A. R., *Atra-Hasis: The Babylonian Story of the Flood*, Oxford, 1969; also the classic article of Frazer, James George, "Ancient Stories of a Great Flood," in *The Journal of the Royal Anthropological Institute of Great Britain and Ireland*, 46 (1916), pp. 231-283, and the useful collection of Martínez, Florentino García, and Luttikhuizen, Gerard P., eds., *Interpretations of the Flood*, Leiden-Boston-Köln: Brill, 1999.

34. On Horace's ode see further Nisbet and Hubbard, and West, ad loc., as well as Nussbaum, Gerald, "A Postscript on Horace, *Carm.* 1.2," in *The American Journal of Philology* 82.4 (1961), pp. 406-417, and Womble, Hilburn, "Horace, *Carmina* 1.2." in *The American Journal of Philology* 91.1 (1970), pp. 1-30.

35. Ovid may have been especially influenced by the Hesiodic *Catalogue of Women* in his emphasis on Deucalion and Pyrrha; see further Clay, Jenny Strauss, *Hesiod's Cosmos*, Cambridge, 2003, pp. 167-168. Besides Ovid the fullest extant account is Pseudo-Apollodorus, *Library* 1.7.2. Virgil briefly mentions Deucalion (without his wife) at *Georgics* 1.62-63.

36. Horace mentions Pyrrha (c. 1.2.6), but not Deucalion; aware of the significance of her name, he begins his ode by saying that Jupiter has terrified the earth enough with snow, hail, and thunderbolts (1.2.2-4 *rubente / dextera sacras iaculatus arces / terruit urbem*), an ascending tricolon of destruction that culminates with fire. He then names Pyrrha (1.2.5-6 *terruit gentis, grave ne rediret / saeculum Pyrrhae nova monstra questae*), thus inaugurating his account of the flood with a neat linkage between doom by fire and doom by water; the fiery image returns, of course, at c. 1.5.

37. Tarrant prints 426 . . . *et in his quaedam perfecta per ipsum / nascendi spatium, quaedam modo coepta suisque / trunca vident numeris* (conjectured by van Leeuwen), which gives easier (better?) sense. But there is something attractive about the idea of some organisms just now being born, and others having been birthed imperfectly.

28 CHAPTER I

38. Cf. Virgil, *Aeneid* 8.696-713. In Virgil's depiction of the shield of Aeneas, the mourning Nile opens its lap for the defeated Antony and Cleopatra (711-713), a passage that Ovid may have had in mind here.

39. Essential reading is Fontenrose, Joseph E., *Python: A Study of Delphic Myth and Its Origins*, Berkeley-Los Angeles, The University of California Press, 1959.

40. Still useful is the classic article of Ogle, M. B., "Laurel in Ancient Religion and Folk-lore," in *The American Journal of Philology* 31.3 (1910), pp. 287-311.

41. See further Magnus, H., "Ovids Metamorphosen in doppelter Fassung," in *Hermes* 40 (1905), pp. 200-201, Parry, Hugh, "Ovid's *Metamorphoses*: Violence in a Pastoral Landscape," in *Transactions of the American Philological Association* 95 (1964), pp. 268-282, Stirrup, Barbara E., "Techniques of Rape: Variety of Wit in Ovid's *Metamorphoses*," in *Greece & Rome*, Second Series 24.2 (1977), pp. 170-184, Nicoll, W. S. M., "Cupid, Apollo, and Daphne (Ovid., *Met.* 1.452 ff.," in *The Classical Quarterly*, N. S. 30.1 (1980), pp. 174-182, Knox, Peter E., "In Pursuit of Daphne," in *Transactions of the American Philological Association* 120 (1990), pp. 183-202 and 385-386, Hollis, A. S., "Ovid's *Metamorphoses* 1.445 ff.: Apollo, Daphne, and the Pythian Crown," in *Zeitschrift für Papyrologie und Epigraphik* 112 (1996), pp. 69-73, Murgatroyd, P., "Plotting in Ovidian Rape Narratives," in *Eranos* 98 (2000), pp. 75-92, and Bittrich, Ursula, *Aphrodite und Eros in der antiken Tragödie*, Berlin: Walter de Gruyter, 2005, pp. 129 ff.. For comparison to the story of Vertumnus and Pomona in *Metamorphoses* 14, note the good treatment by Myers, K. Sara, *Ovid's Causes: Comos and Aetiology in the* Metamorphoses, Ann Arbor: The University of Michigan Press, 1994, pp. 114-121. For the *Nachleben* of the story, note Barnard, Mary E., *The Myth of Apollo and Daphne from Ovid to Quevedo: Love, Agon, and the Grotesque* (Duke Monographs in Medieval and Renaissance Studies, 8), Durham, North Carolina: Duke University Press, 1987, Martin, H. M., "The Apollo and Daphne Myth as Treated by Lope de Vega and Calderón," in *Hispanic Review* 1.2 (1933), pp. 149-160, Hesse, Everett W., "The Two Versions of Calderón's *El laurel de Apolo*," in *Hispanic Review* 14.3 (1946), pp. 213-234, Barnard, Mary E., "Myth in Quevedo: The Serious and the Burlesque in the Apollo and Daphne Poems," in *Hispanic Review* 52.4 (1984), pp. 499-522, and Huot, Sylvia, "The Daisy and the Laurel: Myths of Desire and Creativity in the Poetry of Jean Froissart," in *Yale French Studies* 80 (Contexts: Style and Values in Medieval Art and Literature), 1991, pp. 240-251. The myth held extraordinary fascination for the visual arts, on which see Reid, Jane, *The Oxford Guide to Classical Mythology in the Arts, 1300-1900s*, Oxford, 1993, pp. 325-335.

42. Froissart describes his Daphne as a maiden of Diana: *Dane si fu une pucelle, / (De Dÿane estoit damoiselle), / Que Phebus enama* (*L'Espinette amoreuse* 1572-1574 Fourrier).

43. An interesting example of the incomplete nature of the poem and the poet's method of composition can be seen in the variations of the Daphne story that exist within the text as we have received it. Lines 544 ff. show a marvelous variety in the codices ("mirifice variant codd."—Tarrant) that depict Tellus, the earth, and Peneus as alternate objects of Daphne's pleas for rescue. As Anderson notes ad loc., Ovid does not say which deity, if either, answered the prayer (though he opts for Tellus, given the earthly nature of the rescue). Did Diana save her favorite, and, in the process, offer an eternal tree to her beloved brother? It is regrettable that (as Goold notes in the preface to Miller's revised Loeb), the examples of alternate versions of certain passages are never terribly significant, which somewhat hampers exploration of the idea that there were two versions of the

epic. Of course in Ovid's version it would make no sense for Jupiter to be Daphne's savior, given his own proclivities.

44. And while there are abundant comic elements in the Apollo and Daphne story, the source of Apollo's love was the deadly serious cause of the "savage anger" of Cupid (1.453 *saeva Cupidinis ira*), which echoes the extraordinary threefold repetition of forms of *saevus* at the end of *Aeneid* 11 (896, 901, 910), where the savage power of Jupiter demands that Turnus abandon the ambush that might well have destroyed Aeneas and won him the victory in Italy, all because of the news of the death of the Diana-like Camilla.

45. The theme was of intense interest for Virgil as well as Ovid. In the *Aeneid*, the image of the virgin huntress provides a connection and comparison between Dido and Camilla. The former is no true huntress, though she playacts one (as does Venus). The latter is an authentic devotee of Diana, who enters the war in Latium to her doom (she would have done better to stay in the forest). Camilla is ultimately killed by the double intervention of Jupiter and Apollo, who are (not coincidentally, I would argue) the two culprits in the culture of divine rape in *Metamorphoses* 1. Virgil's Camilla ultimately becomes a symbol of the pristine purity of primitive Italy, a protomartyr for the new (non-Trojan) establishment in Latium that will give rise to the future Rome. That rôle is made all the more intriguing if my speculation is correct that Virgil's Camilla reflects a preexisting tradition of a lycanthrope, a tradition Ovid would have known; associations with the Romulean she-wolf are of particular interest. As we shall see, the Daphne story—Ovid's first introduction of the image of the virgin huntress—will be echoed in subsequent similar tales, most notably his depiction of Atalanta in Books 8 and 10 (who is modeled step by step after Virgil's Camilla).

46. Apollo complains to Daphne that while he is the patron of medicine, alas, his own skills cannot cure his wound of love (1.521-524). The passage owes something to Virgil's depiction of Aeneas' serious wound and how the Apollonian healer Iapyx could not cure it, thus forcing Venus (the goddess of love) to save her son (*A.* 12.391 ff.).

47. See further Tissol, Garth, *The Face of Nature: Wit, Narrative, and Cosmic Origins in Ovid's* Metamorphoses, Princeton, 1997, pp. 138-139.

48. On Ovid's source use in the Daphne story, see Otis, *op. cit.*, pp. 350-353.

49. For the different traditions of Ios in ancient Greece, see Mitchell, Lynette G., "Euboean Io," in *The Classical Quarterly*, N. S. 51.2 (2001), pp. 339-352.

50. And at *Ars Amatoria* 1.323, Pasiphaë wishes that she might be a Europa or an Io.

51. On the often underappreciated importance of the Io episode in the *Prometheus*, note especially White, Stephen, "Io's World: Intimations of Theodicy in *Prometheus Bound*," in *The Journal of Hellenic Studies* 121 (2001), pp. 107-140.

52. Good analysis of Herodotus' proem can be found in Bravo, Benedetto, and Wecowski, Marek, "The Hedgehog and the Fox: Form and Meaning in the Prologue of Herodotus," in *The Journal of Hellenic Studies* 124 (2004), pp. 143-164.

53. Io fled through Lerana and Lyrcea before Jupiter decided to cease her flight by darkening the sky (1.597-598); the mention of Lerna is ominous because of the famous Hydra that Hercules slew.

54. Juno has scientific concerns here; she recognizes that the sudden dark was not caused by river mists or natural fog (1.603-604), and that therefore there must be a supernatural origin.

55. Note Griffiths, J. Gwyn, "Lycophron on Io and Isis," in *The Classical Quarterly*, N. S. 36.2 (1986), pp. 472-477.

56. Best here is Murgatroyd, P., "Ovid's Syrinx," in *The Classical Quarterly*, N. S. 51.2 (2001), pp. 620-623; note also Konstan, David, "The Death of Argus, Or What Stories Do: Audience Response in Ancient Fiction and Theory," in *Helios* 18 (1991), pp. 17-18, and, with caution, Solodow, Joseph, B., *The World of Ovid's* Metamorphoses, Chapel Hill-London: The University of North Carolina Press, 1988, pp. 21-22 (*pace* Solodow, while Ovid evokes the world of the *Eclogues* in this short scene, 1.679 is not much of an echo of *Eclogues* 1.79).

57. In another nice touch, at the waters of Ladon Ovid has Syrinx invoke her "liquid sisters" (704 *liquidas orasse sorores*) to save her from Pan's advances, precisely because Ladon is not her father but Daphne's. Syrinx is a hamadryad (690), not a water nymph, though the connections are close enough to allow them to be called sisters. Daphne embraced the Diana-like lifestyle after she was struck by Cupid's blunted shaft; Syrinx was apparently always devoted to the goddess, which may be underscored by Ovid's having her call on her sisters—even if water nymphs are not forest huntresses (and even if Diana herself invoked her father to preserve her virginity).

58. The bibliography on this perennially popular Ovidian character and his *Vor/Nachleben* is considerable. See especially Otis, *op. cit.*, pp. 108-116, Galinsky, G. Karl, *Ovid's* Metamorphoses: *An Introduction to the Basic Aspects*, Berkeley-Los Angeles, 1975, pp. 49-52, Diggle, J., *Euripides Phaethon*, Cambridge, 1970, Reckford, Kenneth J., "Phaethon, Hippolytus, and Aphrodite," in *Transactions of the American Philological Association* 103 (1972), pp. 405-432, Nagy, Gregory, "Phaethon, Sappho's Phaon, and the White Rock of Leukas," in *Harvard Studies in Classical Philology* 77 (1973), pp. 137-177, Bass, R. C., "Some Aspects of the Structure of the Phaethon Episode in Ovid's *Metamorphoses*," in *The Classical Quarterly*, N. S. 27.2 (1977), pp. 402-408, Nethercut, William R., "*Aeneid* 5.105: The Horses of Phaethon, in *The American Journal of Philology* 107.1 (1986), pp. 102-108, and Knox, Peter E., "Phaethon in Ovid and Nonnus," in *The Classical Quarterly*, N. S. 38 (1988), pp. 536-551. For the intertextual connections of the episode with both Virgil and Homer, see especially Papaioannou, Sophia, *Redesigning Achilles: "Recycling" the Epic Cycle in the "Little Iliad*," Berlin: Walter de Gruyter, 2007, pp. 271-272 (with Bömer ad loc., pp. 220-341). Donald Lateiner creatively suggests to me that Phaethon straddles books just as he straddles different regions of the universe.

59. Phaethon's actions are also reminiscent of the giants' attempts to scale Olympus; the boy "conceives the ether in his mind" (1.777 *concipit aethera mente*).

60. 19 B.C. and A.D. 8; we cannot be sure when the *Metamorphoses* was "finished" before the exile, or exactly when the *Aeneid* was published after Virgil's death.

Chapter II

The Palace of the Sun

The second book of the *Metamorphoses*, the fourth longest in the epic, opens with an elaborate description of the sun god's palace.[1] The previous book had ended like its counterpart in Virgil's *Aeneid*, with the promise of a dramatic epic within an epic that would end in fiery destruction. But Ovid expands the parameters of comparison to Virgil with his ecphrastic attention to Sol's palace. The principal inspiration for the opening of *Metamorphoses* 2 is the beginning of *Aeneid* 6, where Aeneas arrives at Apollo's temple at Cumae, with its beautifully decorated doors (6.9-34). Sol and Apollo are both associated with the sun, thus reinforcing the parallel. Virgil had located Eridanus under Elysium; Ovid remembered his predecessor well and turned his Phaethon epic into a reminiscence of Virgil's underworld drama.[2]

The doors of the Sun's palace have reliefs carved by Mulciber (2.5-18). The seas, lands and sky are depicted; it is as if we are repeating the story of the ordering of chaos from the previous book. The sea is decorated with numerous marine gods, first among them the singing Triton (8 *Tritona canorum*), which reminds us of the story of Misenus' fatal contest with the sea divinity at A. 6.162-174). Misenus offers a parallel to Phaethon in that both ill-fated young men sought to rise above their mortal station. Vulcan's decoration of the doors (the mortal Daedalus could not have fashioned these heavenly haunts) calls to mind the same god's work on the shield of Aeneas, where the sea was the scene of the victory at Actium (A. 8.671-677).[3] This parallel, together with the poet's wish to forge a neat connection with the preceding book by evocation of the flood, may offer explanation for the prominent place of the ocean on the Sun's doors. Further, the emphasis on the sea reminds us of the unfinished work from Daedalus' Apollonian doors: the death of Icarus, whose body plunged into the waters of the sea that would bear his name (A. 6.30-33). Ovid will complete Daedalus' work by not shying away from the fiery fall of Phaethon, whose end parallels that of Icarus.[4] Together, both young men provide examples of doom from the two great elements of water and fire that conspire to destroy humanity.[5] If Phaethon had been able to read the sixth *Aeneid*, he would never have entered his father's palace.[6]

The underworld connection will be underscored by the sun god's binding Stygian oath (2.45-46, 101) to grant whatever his son desires.

Phaethon enters his father's palace; the purpose of the visit is to question the veracity of his divine parentage, while in Virgil Aeneas visits the underworld to consult the ghost of his father Anchises (who, according to the principles of Lucretian eschatology, would no longer exist). Sol is dressed in purple, the standard color for royalty, though in Virgil the color is often associated with the premature death of young heroes (so Marcellus at A. 6.884, Euryalus at 9.435, Camilla at 11.819); later, Aurora will open her "purple doors" (2.113 *purpureas fores*) as Phaethon prepares for his ride. The sun is attended by a youthful allegory of Spring (besides the other seasons), in another recollection of the first book, where the Golden Age was characterized by perpetual vernal weather (27). Sol immediately identifies Phaethon as his son (34); Phaethon responds by addressing the sun as *pater*, wondering if he is able to use that title. The scene reminds us of Lucretius' Iphigenia, about to be sacrificed even though she was able to address Agamemnon as "father" (*De Rerum Natura* 1.94). Phaethon's authentic status as the son of a god will not save him. And, in line with the theme of the Augustan succession, in Phaethon's visit to his father we are reminded of Aeneas visiting Anchises, with likely negative connotations for the Trojan hero.

The sun offers Phaethon any proof he desires for his father's identity; the boy at once asks for the day's control of the solar chariot, at which the god immediately repents of his oath (2.44-56). Sol offers a sustained argument regarding his special prerogative to steer the car:

> plus etiam, quam quod superis contingere possit,
> nescius adfectas; placeat sibi quisque licebit,
> non tamen ignifero quisquam consistere in axe
> me valet excepto; vasti quoque rector Olympi,
> qui fera terribili iaculatur fulmina dextra,
> non agat hos currus: et quid Iove maius habemus? (2.57-62)

> *More indeed, than what is possible for immortals to attain,*
> *are you unknowingly essaying; though each god is permitted to do what pleases*
>   *him,*
> *nevertheless not a one is able to stand on the fire-bearing axle*
> *except for me; even the ruler of vast Olympus,*
> *who throws fierce thunderbolts with his terrible right hand,*
> *may not drive this car; and what do we have that is greater than Jove?*

If we recall the out of control chariot that Virgil used as an image of the runaway Republic at the close of the first georgic, interesting light may be shone on the present passage. The gods are not able to control the sun's chariot; only Sol can hope to succeed at the task. Jupiter himself cannot manage it, and there is no one greater than he. If we draw a parallel between the sun (whom we associate with Apollo) and Augustus, who certainly conveyed the notion to the Roman state that he alone could manage its affairs with tranquil security, then in the speech to Phaethon there may be a hint of the succession crisis that bedeviled the *princeps*. In Phaethon's death, especially with Ovid's evocation of the world of *Aeneid* 6, the motif is highlighted. The loss of Marcellus (and its significance to the Augustan regime) is evoked by the poet in his depiction of Phaethon's failure. Even the sun's true offspring cannot hope to do his father's task; how much less any adoptive offspring.

There are no peaceful groves or cities of the gods that await the hapless youth, but rather treacherous ambushes from dangerous zodiacal monsters (76-78), which Sol proceeds to name.[7] Of course the sun would not travel through all the signs of the zodiac in one diurnal ride; part of the black humor of the sun's enumeration of Taurus, Sagittarius, Leo, Scorpio, and Cancer (all out of order) is to presage the boy's out of control flight across the heavens. The bull of Taurus was generally thought of as the bull in whose guise Jupiter abducted Europa. Once the sun's chariot is out of control and off the ecliptic, the first constellation to be impacted is the Great Bear (2.171-172 *Triones*): Ovid subtly presages two of the other stories forthcoming in the present book, and he mentions the bull first because it will be the last story in the present book.

We know that Phaethon will not listen to his father; his fate is settled. In Ovid's Phaethon we see something of Virgil's Pallas. Both young men are doomed to die after embarking on dangerous missions; both men are even mixed in origin (Phaethon of divine father and mortal mother, Pallas of Arcadian father and Sabellan mother, and thus ineligible to be the "foreign" king Etruria demands).[8] In striking contrast to Sol's treatment of his son, however, Evander does not try to keep Pallas from going off to war; he will instead upbraid Aeneas for not safeguarding his son. Lucifer is the last celestial being to make way before Phaethon as he embarks on his ride (2.115); when Pallas departed with Aeneas and Achates to fight in the Italian war, the young man was compared to the Morning Star upon its rising (*A.* 8.589-591); here Lucifer's setting presages the end of Phaethon.

But the most dramatic parallel between Ovid's Phaethon and Virgil's Pallas is the significant shared name of the Arcadian hero's horse with that of one of the sun god's steeds: Aethon, the "Blazing One" (*A.* 11.89, *Met.* 2.153). In Virgil, Aethon grieves for its dead master as it marches in the hero's funeral procession. In Ovid, the sun's chariot is a four-horse car, driven by Pyrois (whose name reminds us of fire), Eous (i.e., "Eastern," not only because of the sun's oriental rising, but because *A.* 11, the book of Pallas' funeral, opens with mention of Eous), and Aethon and Phlegon, whose names in conjunction evoke Phlegethon, the underworld river of fire—an appropriate image for Phaethon's imminent fate.[9] And, in a nice touch, once Phaethon realizes how much trouble his recklessness has brought him, he blanches (180 *palluit*) in terror, thus becoming true to the etymological identity of his Virgilian predecessor (Pallas/pallor). Ovid may well have invented the equine names; in any case, Phaethon does not know them and thus cannot call on them to moderate their course (192); there is an evocation here of the familiar epic topos of the hero's devoted horse (Homer's Achilles; Virgil's Mezentius and Pallas). Sol's steeds will engage in no mourning for Phaethon, whom they do not know. The horses of the sun go especially out of control once Phaethon drops the reins (200 *lora remisit*): Virgil's charioteer held on to them, though in vain (*G.* 1.513 *frustra retinacula tendens*).

The ride does not go on for long before the chariot becomes the terrible fulfillment of Virgil's image of the Republican car careening out of control (2.161-166).[10] The horses realize the weight of the driver is atypical; the chariot is compared to a ship that is unstable because it is too light. The idea of comparing the sun's out of control car to a ship greatly appealed to Ovid; he devotes two similes to the idea (163-166, 184-186), possibly influenced by Horace's memorable ode on the ship (of state), c. 1.14. In another wonderful nod to Virgil that emphasizes the theme of Augustus and the succession, Phaethon is terrified by the Scorpion the sun had warned him to avoid (83):

> est locus, in geminos ubi bracchia concavat arcus
> Scorpius et cauda flexisque utrimque lacertis
> porrigit in spatium signorum membra duorum:
> hunc puer ut nigri madidum sudore veneni
> vulnera curvata minitantem cuspide vidit,
> mentis inops gelida formidine lora remisit. (2.195-200)

> *There is a place where the Scorpion curves its claws*
> *into twin bows and, with its tail and arms bent on either side,*
> *he stretches his limbs into the space of two constellations:*
> *as the boy saw that beast dripping with the sweat of black venom*
> *and threatening injury with his curved tail,*
> *bereft of mind on account of chill fear he let go the reins.*

The passage is a terrible inversion of Virgil, *Georgics* 1.34-35, where the constellation Scorpio is envisioned as making way for the soon to be deified Octavian:

> . . . ipse tibi iam bracchia contrahit ardens
> Scorpios et caeli iusta plus parte reliquit.

> *. . . already now for you the burning Scorpion*
> *contracts its arms and leaves behind a more than just part of the heaven.*

Ovid's passage is an exact reversal of Virgil; the accommodating Scorpion that was willing to make way for Octavian has been transformed into the monster that menaces the terrified Phaethon. Ovid notes that Luna, the moon, was amazed at how low her brother's chariot was driving; again, the divine twins whose cults were so important to the Augustan regime are highlighted (208-209). Ovid bests Virgil in that his predecessor was concerned principally with the problem of the Augustan succession insofar as the *princeps* lacked a suitable heir; Ovid is concerned with that theme as well, but for him the greater concern is whether anyone would be able to assume the Augustan mantle. For Ovid, Augustus has the same problem as Sol—no one can guide the chariot of state as well as he, and even he has immense difficulty. Of course by Ovid's day the succession question had taken on far greater importance than in the early years of the Augustan regime that nurtured Virgil's epic verse.

Mountains are the first parts of the world that experience the heat of the falling sun as Phaethon dips too low in the heavens; Ovid offers an impressive catalogue of famous peaks, his second in the epic (2.217-226; at 1.577-585 a much abbreviated catalogue of rivers comes to pay respects to Daphne's bereft father Peneus, while both are mere prelude to the forthcoming expansive catalogue of fountains and rivers rendered dry by the scorching heat). The Ethiopians are permanently darkened by the sun's irregular course; the etiology takes on particular significance for Phaethon since his stepfather Merops was Ethiopian.[11]

Ovid proceeds to lavish attention on a long list of bodies of water mourned by presumably homeless nymphs (2.238-259). The rivers of Book 1 were polite mourners who came to visit one of their own after the loss of his daughter; the rivers enumerated now have a far more serious cause for lament. The Nile is given the most attention with three lines that describe how the sun dried its seven mouths (254-256). The expansive listing of the world's rivers, all jumbled together with no attention to geographical order, evokes the dream of Rome's expansion in the Augustan Age; the last river Ovid mentions is, of course, Rome's own Tiber (259), the river to which power over all had been promised (*promissa potentia*).[12] Dolphins and seals are mentioned in their marine suffering, thus providing another link to the flood narrative, where those mammals had free rein over a watery world (cf. 2.266-268 and 1.300, 302-303; the rare mention of seals confirms the echo). Peneus, the bereft father of *Metamorphoses* 1, is now one of the main river victims of Phaethon's flight (243).

Tellus, the earth goddess, makes a lengthy appeal to Jupiter to save the universe from Phaethon's fires (2.272-300). She enumerates the three zones of creation familiar from Book 1: her own region of the lands, Neptune's seas, and Jupiter's own heavens. She is explicit in her fear; "ancient chaos" (299 *chaos antiquum*) is due to return if Phaethon is not stopped. It is as if the poet had imagined Rome under the leadership of some future mad emperor, poised to destroy the world by virtue of the powerful office for which his talents are not suited. Jupiter listens to his ancient mother; he destroys Phaethon with a thunderbolt that smashes the sun's chariot and sends the boy hurtling down to earth like some supposed fallen star:

volvitur in praeceps longoque per aera tractu
fertur, ut interdum de caelo stella sereno
etsi non cecidit, potuit cecidisse videri. (2.320-322)

He is hurled headlong, and is borne aloft through the air
in a long trail, as sometimes from a serene sky a star,

even if it did not fall, was able to seem to have fallen.

This is the fourth simile in Ovid's miniature Phaethon epic, where the multipli-
cation of similes serves to highlight the epic nature of this, his poem's longest
individual story. Phaethon is compared to a comet that seems to fall through the
sky even if scientifically we know it has not really fallen. Here we have a terrible inversion of the auspicious sign of the falling star of 44 B.C. The scientific
humor by which Ovid seems to deflate the pathos of the scene—the star seems
to have fallen, even if it did not—underscores the connection of this simile with
the important place of the comet image in Augustan mythology. In 44, the year
of Caesar's assassination, the young Octavian encouraged the view that a comet
visible for seven days even in the daylight (cf. Phaethon's daytime ride) symbolized the apotheosized Julius, now welcomed among the gods. It is possible that
Virgil alludes to the famous comet in his scene with the portent of Acestes'
flaming arrow during the Sicilian games in memory of Anchises (*A.* 5.522-
528).[13] Phaethon is no Caesar, and so the highly significant image is appropriately undercut by Ovid's detail that no star really falls from the sky, whatever
the heavens seem to show.

  Phaethon, as the commentators have noted, is the only figure in the *Metamorphoses* who is accorded the title of *auriga*, "charioteer" (2.312, 327), and
only in the context of his death. The driver of the sun's runaway car, the terrible
fulfillment of the image Virgil conceived at the end of the first georgic, is in
some sense the only charioteer in Ovid's poem who matters for the poet's program.

  Phaethon's body falls into the Eridanus (the modern Po), where Naiads provide him with burial (having apparently no bitterness over how he once threatened to dry up all the world's rivers).[14] The dead Phaethon is mourned by his
mother Clymene and his sisters, the Heliades or daughters of the sun.[15] The sisters prolong their mourning for four months (2.344-346), until finally they are
transformed into trees (Ovid does not specify who or what was responsible for
this metamorphosis) that still cry. The heat of the sun (appropriately enough,
given the cause of their lament) dries the tears and—the science of course cannot be investigated too closely here—the dried product is electron or amber
(364-365), which becomes a gift for Latin brides, sent by the thoughtful river:
366 *nuribus mittit gestanda Latinis*). There is a humorous reminiscence here of
the familiar topos of how the youthful dead should have proceeded not to the
grave but to their marriage; Phaethon's death and his sisters' self-destructive
lament will, nevertheless, furnish attractive amber for newlywed Roman girls.
The passage nicely recalls Phaethon's pleas to his mother (1.762-764), where he
begged for a proof of his paternity by his life, his stepfather Merops', and the
"wedding torches of his sisters" (*taedasque sororum*).[16] Phaethon's loss deprives
not only him but also his sisters of marriage; there are hints in the story that the
sun god's son (notwithstanding his innocence) must be destroyed because he is
akin to those who would overthrow the Olympian order.

And Silenus, as we have noted, sang of the metamorphosis of the Heliades (Virgil, *Eclogues* 6.62-63 *tum canit Phaethontiadas musco circumdat amarae / corticis atque solo proceras erigit alnos*); as we shall continue to see, Ovid neatly follows the song of Silenus at various points in his epic.[17] This is to be expected, since the sixth eclogue is a programmatic poem that announces the Callimachean ideal of the *deductum carmen*. In important ways, the *Metamorphoses* is an epic expansion of the vision of the sixth eclogue, undertaken in the context of the *Georgics* and the *Aeneid* that followed the pastoral song.

There is further humor in Ovid's inclusion at this juncture of the metamorphosis of Cycnus, the swan.[18] The story was known to Virgil (*A.* 10.185-197), who alluded to it during his catalogue of Etruscan allies who came to support Aeneas during the Latin war. In Virgil, Cinyras, a Ligurian leader, is followed at once by Cupavo, who wears swan feathers on his helmet. The feathers are a sign of his father Cycnus' fate: Cycnus had been transformed into a swan after the Muse took pity on him as he mourned his beloved Phaethon (Virgil does not make explicit whether they were relatives or homosexual lovers). His son Cupavo now drives the huge vessel "Centaur" down river with a few companions to aid Aeneas.[19]

In Ovid, Cycnus and Phaethon are maternal relatives (2.368), and he is explicitly identified as a Ligurian monarch. His transformation into a swan is not credited to any particular deity; it is just as mysterious as the fate of the Heliades. Virgil had ascribed Cycnus' transformation to the Muse; Ovid quietly ignores that tradition, since there are, as yet, no Muses in his poem. The mention of the swan reminds us of 2.252-253 *et quae Maeonias celebrabant carmine ripas / flumineae volucres, medio caluere Caystro*, from the catalogue of rivers scorched by the sun's low-flying chariot.[20] The swans are an image of the poet's own work; Phaethon's ride threatened the very existence of poetry.

In the *Aeneid*, divine arguments are serious, but Jupiter always manages to quell disputes and pacify both his daughter Venus and his wife Juno. In the *Metamorphoses*, divine disagreements are more common and often seem to be veiled in comic dress. And so after the death of Phaethon Ovid presents the image of a sun god who is weary of his daily task and ready for retirement (2.381-393). The gods once again gather and seek to dissuade Sol from plunging the earth into darkness. The subject is serious; if Phoebus refuses his duty, the world will be bereft of life-giving light. But the flippant atmosphere demands that the crisis be averted quickly and without serious problem; the sun resumes his course, choosing to blame his horses for the loss of Phaethon (398-400).

Jupiter, in any case, has worries of his own. In a device Ovid will exploit again later at an important juncture in the poem, Jupiter decides to travel to earth to inspect the damage from Phaethon's ride; the topos will reappear in Book 5, when Pluto decides to inspect possible damage to his kingdom and is struck by Cupid's shafts. Jupiter's journey takes him to Arcadia, which returns us to the world of Lycaon and the god's previous Arcadian sojourn, thus providing a neat ring with that pre-diluvian atmosphere of wickedness. As we have noted, there is, ironically, nothing really new in Ovid's poem of novelty (even the worsening of behavior was presaged by the original decline of the ages); the Jupiter we knew as Io's pursuer will now find another paramour, in another return to the theme of the virgin huntress: the story of Callisto.[21]

The lore surrounding Callisto's rape and double transformation (bear, star) is only briefly alluded to by Virgil (*Georgics* 1.138, *Aeneid* 1.744-746).[22] It forms part of the implicit background to the astronomical lore of which Iopas sings at Dido's court. But nowhere does Virgil tell the huntress' tale in anything remotely approaching Ovidian detail. Iopas' song preceded Aeneas' account of the night Troy fell, for which the end of *Aeneid* 1 provided a cliffhanger similar to Ovid's presentation of the Phaethon story. Ovid has reversed the Virgilian order and expanded the brief mention of Callisto's star associations into a full-blown account. The scene of Lycaon's vicious cruelty, which had engendered the watery destruction of the world, will now be transformed into a scene of Jovian violence, as the god ravishes a descendant of Lycaon, whose ultimate fate will be banishment from the water. Jupiter borrows a trick from his daughter Venus (in Virgil's *Aeneid*); he disguises himself as Diana (2.425) to fool Callisto. Jupiter does not waste much time with idle conversation; soon enough his preliminary kisses—more than Diana-like as they were—give way to rape. Interestingly, Ovid does not detail any transformation from goddess to god; we are left to assume that Jupiter has abandoned his huntress guise and resumed his usual form.

Callisto's subsequent pregnancy leads to the betrayal of the rape to Diana and her coterie (2.441-465). In Virgil, Camilla had left the world of Diana and the forest to pursue battle, but this active abandonment of the goddess' venues did not sever her ties to her patroness; Diana loved her still and interceded on her behalf. Callisto, the unwilling victim of Jupiter's rape, is expelled from the goddess' presence precisely because of her lack of virginity; Diana does not bother to inquire as to the reason for the maiden's pregnancy. Ovid labels Callisto's situation with the pejorative *culpa*, "fault":

> vix oculos attolit humo nec, ut ante solebat,
> iuncta deae lateri nec toto est agmine prima,
> sed silet et laesi dat signa rubore pudoris;
> et, nisi quod virgo est, poterat sentire Diana
> mille notis culpam: nymphae sensisse feruntur. (2.448-452)

> *Scarcely did she raise her eyes from the ground, nor, as she*
> *was accustomed to do before, did she join herself to the goddess' side,*
> *nor was she first in the throng. She is silent and gives indication by a blush*
> *of her wounded sense of shame and, but for the fact she was a virgin, Diana*
> *would have been able to sense the fault with its thousand signs; the nymphs are said*
> *to have sensed it.*

Is Ovid having a humorous moment with the idea that not all of Diana's companions are so virginal? At any rate, the virgin goddess of the hunt has the greatest innocence of the entire sorority. From the viewpoint of the goddess and her sisters (including Callisto), the ravished maiden's predicament is indeed a *culpa*, if what matters before all else to Diana is biological virginity. The nymphs are said to have sensed Callisto's condition long before the pregnancy was unveiled at a riverbank; Juno, for her part, knew of her husband's philandering as well but put off punishment (466-467). The reason for her calm reaction is not given (Ovid in fact says there was no cause for delay—468 *causa morae nulla est*); if anything, we have here a subtle reversal of rôles for Jupiter and Juno—the stereotypically angry goddess here bides her time before seeking her revenge. Her patience will soon enough give way to her customary wrath (470 *saevam cum lumine mentem*), not coincidentally after Callisto gives birth to a son, Arcas. The goddess turns her rival into a she-bear (478-481).[23] In a subtle note, Jupiter is not nearly as concerned about Callisto's fate as he had been about Io's; the transformed girl feels that the god is ungrateful for the charms he enjoyed by virtue of his rape (488 *ingratumque Iovem, nequeat cum dicere, sentit*). Callisto's father Lycaon had been changed into a wolf; his daughter remains terrified of wild bears and wolves, despite belonging now among them (493-495). She is, indeed, a "Lycaonian parent" (496 *Lycaoniae . . . parentis*), whose identity is unknown to her son as he grows to the age of fifteen, when, a hunter like his absent mother, he encounters the she-bear that, in a sense, bore him.

   In the *Fasti*, Ovid has Callisto swear an oath to Diana that she will remain virginal (2.155-162); this detail may have been in Ovid's mind for the Callisto of the *Metamorphoses*, in which case the idea of Callisto's guilt makes more sense. In contrast, Virgil's Camilla is vowed to Diana by her father Metabus; the infant Camilla had no say in her destiny, though, ironically, she remains faithful to Diana. In an echo of the Camilla story, Ovid's Callisto is described as a soldier of Phoebe (2.415 *miles Phoebes*); her battles are with animals on the hunt. This detail makes it all the more interesting that the transformed Callisto is so afraid of bears and even wolves. Part of the explanation lies in the reversal of hunter and hunted; some of it may lurk in anthropomorphic lore about shape shifting, where here the she-bear is imagined as unable to come to terms with her human *vs.* animal forms; if in her folkloric origins Virgil's Camilla was indeed a lycanthrope (who found salvation through death), then in Ovid's Callisto we see a reversal of the same process—the human has been transformed into an animal, and death will not redeem her humanity.

   Arcas is ready to kill his mother, when at last Jupiter intervenes and snatches away both his victim and his child and, together with the living pair, the very crime he had committed (505 *nefas*). The word is deliciously ambiguous; it probably refers to Jupiter's rape, which has now been transformed into a major constellation, but it can also be taken of Arcas' unintentional matricide. The god's lover and his illegitimate son are now eternal stars by another metamorphosis; Jupiter's action seals forever the bear-like nature of the mother and her son. At the beginning of *Tristia* 4.3, the exiled Ovid invokes the Bear stars to gaze down on Rome to see if his wife pays heed to his memory or not; the Bear does not ever dip into the ocean and is thus a reliable witness to myriad mortal acts (like the sun whose chariot was at the center of the myth that immediately preceded hers).

We have noted that Ovid modeled his Phaethon story after the anticipated tale of Troy's fall that links *Aeneid* 1 and 2, and that the story of Callisto was alluded to in the song of Iopas that preceded Aeneas' long account of the destruction of his city and the wanderings that brought him to Dido's court at Carthage. At the end of *Aeneid* 2, Virgil depicted his hero Aeneas as he saved his father Anchises and son Ascanius, lifting the one and guiding the other by the hand. Aeneas' wife Creusa, the mother of his son, was lost in the turmoil of the conquered city. Jupiter's behavior has come full circle here with the story of Io; indeed, it has grown worse.

As for his sister and wife Juno, she reacts to the news of her rival's catasterism with the same attitude that is familiar to us from the opening of the *Aeneid*; the emphasis is on how she has been offended (2.518 *laedere*, 527 *laesae*; cf. *Aeneid* 1.8 *laeso*, which Ovid echoes). She demands that Oceanus and Tethys not allow the new constellations to dip into the ocean's waters; we are reminded of how she did not want Aeneas' Trojans to seek rest in Italy. The marine gods grant her request, and so another etiology is offered, this time for why the Bear never sets in the northern hemisphere. Jupiter was involved in the destruction of Callisto, just as in Virgil he is responsible (with Apollo) for the death of the huntress Camilla; while Callisto is honored with a star (and was spared death at her son's hands), both mother and child are most remembered now for their eternal prohibition from rest thanks to Juno's success in securing some measure of revenge.

In the *Fasti*, before the account of Callisto and her son, Ovid announces the praise of Augustus as *pater patriae* on the Nones of February (2.119-148), right before the coming of spring (149-152). The occasion commemorated by the entry is the bestowal of the title *pater patriae* on Augustus, which came in 2 B.C., in the year of his thirteeth consulship (see further Schilling ad loc.). Romulus is unfavorably compared to Augustus; the former was a rapist, the latter a champion and guardian of chaste marriage (139). Romulus admitted the guilty into a grove of asylum; Augustus repelled the *nefas* (140): the *princeps* is like Diana, unwilling to admit Callisto into her coterie; by implication in light of the *Metamorphoses*, Augustus would not have honored Callisto and Arcas by taking away *nefas* and installing it in the heavens. Phaethon was a reckless youth whose actions merited Jovian thunder and a driving out of heaven; now the sky god honors his bastard by raising him to the same glory of the stars that awaits Augustus. In a brilliant touch, Ovid ended his praise of Augustus' glory with mention of another of Jupiter's loves, another rival of whom Juno had complained at the beginning of the *Aeneid*, the Trojan prince Ganymede, the water bearer who was sometimes equated with Aquarius:

iam puer Idaeus media tenus eminet alvo
et liquidas mixto nectare fundit aquas.
en etiam, siquis Borean horrere solebat,
gaudeat: a Zephyris mollior aura venit. (*Fasti* 2.145-148)

Already the Idaean boy stands forth down to the waist
and pours liquid waters mixed with nectar.
Now indeed, if anyone was accustomed to shrink from the north wind,
let him rejoice: a softer breeze comes from the Zephyr.

The astrological occurrence of Aquarius made mention of Juno's rival possible;
the allusion anticipates how Callisto and her son will not dip into the northern
waters. And, in a subversive sense, the emphasis on Augustus' moral program is
undercut by ending the passage with an evocation of one of Jupiter's homosexual amours, a love that aroused Juno's anger (*Aeneid* 1.26-28).

Juno leaves the scene of her partial victory over Callisto and Arcas in her
peacock-driven chariot (2.531-532). Her sacred birds are adorned with Argus'
eyes in a linkage to the story of Jupiter's affair with Io. Ovid contemporizes the
change in the peacock's feathers with the alteration of the raven's feathers from
white to black, thereby segueing into his next set of stories: the loquacious raven
and the equally garrulous crow.[24] The story of these two birds will introduce a
complicated set of interlocked tales that provide background to the major development toward which Ovid is moving, the coming of the god Dionysus.

The raven is no longer white because it was a tattletale. Ovid proceeds to relate briefly the story of Coronis, a maiden of Larissa in Thessaly (cf. Pseudo-
Apollodorus 3.118 and Hyginus, *Fabulae* 202; the story is as old as Hesiod).[25]
Here the poet was no doubt principally inspired by the *Hecale* of Callimachus,
where Coronis' involvement with Ischys, the driver of horses, is betrayed to her
lover Apollo by a raven. Ovid is not entirely clear as to the nature of the god's
relationship with Coronis; she was pleasing to him, we are told, so long as she
was either chaste or undetected (2.544 *dum vel casta fuit vel inobservata*)—a
typically Ovidian antithesis or weighted alternative. The raven rushes to report
Coronis' adultery to Apollo (545 *adulterium*); the charge, especially in a Roman
legal context, would seem to indicate the god's relationship with the girl was
something different from the divine escapades we have just witnessed with Jupiter (Io, Callisto). Indeed, we do well to remember that Apollo's infatuation with
Daphne was not his own doing (cf. Jupiter's pursuits), but rather the work of
Cupid; here, Apollo is most certainly not like Jupiter in his relationship with
Coronis, but rather something akin to a Roman husband with a concern for mor-
als.

The crow comes upon the raven in flight, and warns its fellow bird of how
its black color belies its own baleful fate:

invenies nocuisse fidem. (2.552)

You will find that faith harmed me.

The Latin is ambiguous; it could also mean that the raven will learn that the
crow harmed faith or trust (depending on one's point of view). The bird proceeds to tell the story of Pallas' raising of Erichthonius (cf. other versions at
Pseudo-Apollodorus 3.14.6 and Hyg. *Fabulae* 116). Ovid assumes audience
familiarity with the background of the tale, which the mythographers supply:
Pallas was pursued by an amorous Vulcan, whose semen stained her leg. After
cleaning herself with wool, the goddess threw the cloth to the ground, where the
earth animated the divine seed and gave birth to Erichthonius. The embarrassed
goddess took the baby and entrusted it in a box to the three daughters of the
Athenian monarch Cecrops. Ovid politely passes over the details of the boy's
origins and begins his crow's story with the entrusting of the baby-box to the
three sisters (2.552-556). In a familiar folktale device, the women are charged
not to look in the box. Two of the sisters, Pandrosos and Herse, are faithful to
Minerva's dictates, while the third, Aglauros, opens the chest and finds a baby
and a serpent (558-561). The crow reports the whole affair to Minerva, and is
duly punished for having seen a secret the goddess did not wish to see revealed.[26] Aglauros is the guilty party (other accounts do not single her out from
her sisters), and she will be the victim of the ultimate punishment that provides a
climax to the whole story.

The crow, for its part, true to its garrulous nature, does not wait for any response from the raven but proceeds to explain how it never intended to be Minerva's favorite bird, but was chosen for the task unwillingly. The crow's story
may well be an Ovidian invention; allegedly she was once Corone, the daughter
of Coroneus. Ovid here is playing with the Greek word for "crow" and engaging
in learned wordplay for his audience's amusement. Corone was pursued by Neptune; she fled his amorous advances but grew tired and seemed to have no aid at
hand to which to make appeal; at last Minerva decided to intervene to save a
fellow virgin (2.572-580). Corone is transformed into a bird, the crow; unlike
Callisto, she is blameless because her virginity was preserved (588 *inculpata*),
and so she is a fitting companion for the virgin goddess of weaving and war.
And, besides, since Ovid is dealing in this section with primitive tales of Athens,
it is fitting that the city's patroness, Minerva, be at the center of the drama.
Corone is incensed that because of her divulging the secret of Erichthonius, she
has been placed behind the owl Nyctimene (598-595), which begs yet another
story from the ever talkative bird. In Corone's version of events, Nyctimene was
changed into an owl after having an incestuous affair with her father; in Hyginus
(*Fabulae* 204), she was the victim and not the aggressor.

The raven, in any case, spurns the crow's advice; if the story of Nyctimene
had been falsely related, the raven may have detected the lie and mistrusted the
whining, mendacious bird. The raven proceeds to report Coronis' infidelity to
Apollo, who at once fires a shaft and slays his lover (2.598-605). In a nice touch,
the god's laurel falls from his brow as he gives way to anger (600 *laurea de-*

lapsa est), a reminder of his previous pursuit of Daphne; the laurel almost seems to protest the god's emotional attachment to another by declining to remain on his head. In a bit of learned humor, Ovid has Coronis as Apollo's second love partly because her name evokes the idea of a crown such as that which his laurel provided—small wonder the laurel falls as Apollo slays his second beloved in anger.

Alas, the raven did not know everything; as she dies, Coronis reveals that she is pregnant (presumably with the god's child, for all Apollo knows), and that Apollo is slaying two in one. The god immediately seeks to cure the fatal chest wound by which he slew his *quondam* lover; the master of healing is unable to reverse the action of his deadly arrow. In a simile, the god is reduced to an animal state once again (2.621-625) as he utters groans that are like those of a heifer when it sees its calf about to be slain by a hammer blow to the head.[27] In the story of his infatuation with Daphne, Apollo was compared to a hound pursuing a rabbit (1.533-539). Now the god is emasculated; he is a heifer whose child has been violently slain; the irony, of course, is that he committed the murder of Coronis—the force of the simile is that he is watching the death of his unborn child. The god snatches away the infant and entrusts him to the Centaur Chiron; as for the raven, he is banished from the company of white birds (628-632).[28] The raven had hoped for the reward of a tongue that was not false (631 *non falsae praemia linguae*); despite the bird's (unknowingly incomplete) honesty, there will be no reward but rather punishment. Ovid is concerned in this book with the notion of falsehood; Bömer well compares this passage to 2.37 *falsa . . . sub imagine*, of the matter of Phaethon's paternity. And, at the book's end, Jupiter will assume the false guise of a bull to abduct Europa, just as Daedalus had fashioned a false bull for Minos' wife to gratify her unholy passion. The topos will return frequently in the epic, notably when in the next book we consider Ovid's depiction of Dionysus and Pentheus. Falsehood as a theme has special resonance in an Augustan era, with its inherent conflict between republican and monarchical modes of government.

We are now immersed in a rapid progression of stories; as we move from Phaethon to Callisto and a series of brief tales within tales, there is a shade of Virgil's progression from the unitary *Aeneid* 2 with the hero's recounting of the night Troy fell to the diverse miniature episodes of *Aeneid* 3. The first half of this book is unified in the story of Phaethon; the second half is disorganized in comparison, yet links back to the divine amours that preceded Phaethon at the end of Book 1. The myths Ovid has so far recounted have been Greek, and his setting the whole world (especially in its creation and destruction by the flood). Through his mention of Ericthonius and Cecrops, Ovid has introduced us to primitive Athens. The love theme will predominate in *Metamorphoses* 3-4, in neat imitation of Virgil's advance from the episodic narratives of *Aeneid* 3 to the love affair of Dido and Aeneas in 4. But Ovid's main point thus far, so early in his poem, is on the fragility of the order that was established in the first book and has been threatened with destruction twice. Frequent anachronistic allusions to Rome remind us of the real focal point of the poet's attention and concern, namely the world Augustus now rules.

Chiron is raising Apollo's baby (who is not yet identified as the healer god Asclepius); his daughter Ocyroe rushes to him, a child gifted with prophecy (like Apollo).[29] Her sudden bursting forth into announcements of future fates enables the poet to incorporate several more myths into his repertoire: Chiron is immortal, but will yearn to die once infected with the Hydra's blood, living in agony until the Fates release him (2.649-654).[30] The baby Asclepius will be so skilled as to raise the dead, until the gods kill him in anger, only to see him restored to life and deified.

The reference to Asclepius' future resurrection of one fortunate soul against divine will is a brief allusion to a story Ovid will tell at greater length much later in the poem: the raising of Hippolytus at the behest of Diana. The story appealed to Ovid; besides its prominence in the *Metamorphoses*, he tells it at *Fasti* 6.745-762 (where see Schilling ad loc., and Littlewood), as part of his discussion of the rising of Ophicuhus, i.e., Asclepius; *Heroides* 4 presents Phaedra's complaint to Hippolytus. Serpents figure throughout the Asclepius story (cf. the serpent Aglauros saw with Erichtonius in Minerva's chest; the creature was sacred to the goddess and its mention also anticipates the Chiron/Asclepius lore, with its own serpent imagery).

In the *Fasti*, Asclepius is killed after Pluto and the Fate Clotho complain about his resurrections; Jupiter restores the healer to life and sets him among the stars after Apollo objects to the death of his son. We shall return later to this lore; Ovid was no doubt inspired throughout by Virgil, *Aeneid* 7.761-782, where "Virbius," the "twice man," comes to aid the forces of Turnus against Aeneas. In Virgil's vision, after Asclepius' death (Virgil does not recount the healer's own restoration), Diana hides Hippolytus in her sacred grove at Aricia; his name is changed to Virbius (ironic, since it rather gives away the secret). He somehow has a son (strange enough given the chastity he once exhibited that led to his doom); Hippolytus' son Virbius (more playing on the meaning of "twice man") is the fighter who aids Turnus.

Hippolytus had been slain by horses, and Chiron is a Centaur; his daughter Ocyroe senses herself undergoing an equine metamorphosis as she tells of Asclepius and the rest (2.657-675).[31] Horses were prohibited from Diana's grove at Aricia because of the part they played in killing her favorite; ironically, now Ocyroe is transformed into a mare. Ovid may be original in linking Ocyroe to Asclepius lore; Ocyroe's story was previously told by Euripides in his lost *Melanippe Sapiens* (named after another of Chiron's daughters). The equine link may have appealed to our poet; Ovid does not offer a reason for the transformation, though Jupiter is named as the responsible party (677-768). We may speculate that her prophecies were potentially dangerous and that the god felt a need to silence her.

Chiron now begs Apollo for help given his daughter's plight; Ovid observes that the god would not have been able to rescind his father Jupiter's wishes, even if he had been present—thus announcing another transition by mentioning the god's pursuit of the pastoral life in Elis and Messenia; it is as if Apollo needed a vacation after his episodes with both Daphne and Coronis. The detail will serve to introduce the main story Ovid wishes to segue to next, that of Mercury and Battus.[32]

The god of the Augustan program was thinking of love (2.683 *dumque amor est curae*), presumably the loss of the two women he has already suffered in the poet's narrative, or possibly some new interest. Distracted, his cattle wander off, thus made ripe for Mercury's abduction in an Ovidian nod to the *Homeric Hymn to Hermes*. The only witness to the crime is one Battus. The character appears elsewhere in the *Metamorphoses* of Antoninus Liberalis (23), a Greek mythographer of unknown date (certainly between A.D. 100 and 300); he may have taken the character from Ovid, who also mentions the untrustworthy Battus at *Ibis* 585 *ut laesus lingua Battus ab ipse sua*. Battus is the hired hand of Neleus, the father of Nestor; slowly, Ovid is already preparing for the climactic set of stories from Greek mythology, the Troy cycle (the mention of Chiron has already paved the way for Achilles). Mercury is not unfair; he offers a prize cow from the flock to buy Battus's silence; the servant agrees to keep silent, and indicates that a nearby rock will sooner tell the tale (691-697). Mercury anticipates Battus' inevitable untrustworthiness (Ovid is ringing back to the raven and the crow, again with a hint of the decline of the ages—the birds did not agree to be silent). The god disguises himself and offers Battus a bull and its mate to reveal word of the herd, whose location the chatterbox discloses; in punishment Battus is transformed by the god into stony flint (705-707). He will forever remain as a marker of the spot where he proved himself unfaithful to his word to the god.

Apollo has been forgotten for the moment; Ovid does not bother to recount the familiar story of how the archer god uncovered the theft of his cattle by the infant Mercury (and, in fact, Ovid's Mercury—who has already made a memorable appearance in the epic as Argus' slayer at 1.668-721—is of course fully grown).[33] Mercury had told Argus of Pan's pursuit of Syrinx; now the god of trickery and thieves will be the subject of his own story, and it will be another tale of divine love, thus reinforcing the theme that, in an important sense, nothing is new in Ovid's world.

Mercury was an important figure for the Augustan poets. In Ovid's vision, as the narrative has unfolded, we might expect Mercury to be the deity who would bring change to the pattern of decline we have thus far seen (where Jupiter is the principal culprit, and Apollo tarnished but not nearly as guilty as his divine sire). At Horace, c. 1.2.41-44, Octavian is envisioned as a possible Mercury in human guise:

sive mutata iuvenem figura
ales in terris imitaris almae
filius Maiae, patiens vocari
Caesaris ultor

> or if with figure having been changed you
> imitate the youth, winged on land, who was
> the son of gentle Maia, willing to be called
> the avenger of Caesar.[34]

And at c. 1.10, Horace devotes an entire ode to the celebration of the various attributes of the god.[35] Of course these Augustan images of the god do not fault Mercury for the theft of Apollo's cattle (that defining episode of the divine infancy is taken as a sign of precocious cleverness).

As if to echo Horace, Ovid's Mercury is the *ales* (2.714) or winged figure that hovers over the Munychian fields of the Lyceum, where Aristotle taught; the (Athenian) girls are preparing to participate in a celebration in honor of Pallas Athena (709-713). The audience can anticipate the degradation of the noble Horatian image; Ovid's Mercury is entranced by the beauty of the girls he now spies. Prominent among them is Herse, whose beauty is said to exceed that of the other girls as much as the Morning Star shines more magnificently than other stars, or as much as Phoebe, that is, Diana, surpasses Lucifer (722-725). We are reminded of Callisto with her Diana-like companions, or Daphne, who preferred the forest; the scene is now redolent with the air of the huntress goddess. Mercury is agape at Herse's beauty; he is named the son of Jove (726 *natus Iove*: cf. 744 *pater est mihi Iuppiter ipse*; Mercury himself underscores his Jovian descent) deliberately so that we might remember Jupiter's own recent behavior. And, in line with the succession motif of Phaethon and the sun and the problem of Augustus' own house and who would replace him, we are now presented with another son of Jupiter who, despite our high hopes, appears dangerously close to following his father's dark path; Ovid begins to multiply similes (716-719, 727-729) to offer another anticipation of epic action (as he did with Phaethon). And the mention of Herse brings us back in a ring to the story of Pallas' Erichthonius, with its own undertones of the scandals of the gods and, in some cases, the vain attempts of the immortals to conceal them.

Horace imagined Octavian as Mercury in disguise; Ovid's Mercury does not present any hidden identity as he descends to earth, for which the poet claims the god's trust in his handsome appearance (2.731). Yet the god devotes close attention to his appearance (he is already somewhat emasculated by his infatuation); the wand by which he conducts the souls of the dead, a feature of Horace's reverential depiction of the god (c. 1.10.17-19), is now reduced to a mere ornament to enhance the god's attractiveness.

In a clever detail, the home where Herse, Pandrosos, and Aglauros dwell is decorated with tortoise-shell (2.737 *testudine*), which reminds us of the tortoise-shell that Hermes converted into a lyre (cf. the opening of the *Homeric Hymn*). Aglauros detects the presence of the god as he seeks Herse's bedroom and ultimately demands a heavy weight of gold as the price of her favor. Minerva sees the whole affair and is filled with anger that the girl who had uncovered the

Erichthonian scandal should now be blessed as the sister-in-law of Mercury, wealthy and favored by a god. Minerva visits the home of Invidia—the personification of the envy that in a sense (and an ironic one at that) both she and Aglauros share in common.

Ovid's magnificent *tour de force* description of the House of Invidia or Envy is the first of what will be several similar lavish allegorical scenes in the epic. We have moved again into stories of love, this time with sisters active in the romance; Ovid has manipulated the Virgilian Dido and Aeneas romance, where Mercury was merely Jupiter's messenger to warn Aeneas off from his fateful affair with Carthage's queen. Here, no Rumor is personified (Ovid will try to challenge Virgil on that count later), but rather Envy; nonetheless, the passage is modeled on Virgil's depiction of the jealousy that was rife among Dido's suitors in the wake of her lust for Aeneas.[36] And we are drawn yet deeper into Ovid's vision, as we forget about Mercury and Aglauros (just as we had left Apollo) and return to Minerva.

Minerva enters the threshold of the home of Envy and turns away at once from the terrible sight of the monstrous allegory that sits feasting on snake flesh (2.766 ff.); Ovid once again introduces the recurring imagery of the serpent (he may have been inspired by the importance of the snake image in *Aeneid* 2). The goddess does not enter the dwelling; further, she turns her face away from the horrific imagery that confronts her (770). Envy rises and slowly advances toward the goddess; she is at once filled with resentment of Minerva's beautiful appearance and fine armament (770-774). The groans Envy now utters draw the face of the goddess.[37] Minerva is forced to look at the wretched, foul hag long enough to give her command: Aglauros is to be Envy's target. As with the divine manipulation of Dido in the *Aeneid*, we are left with the impression that Envy's task will not be terribly difficult given Aglauros' disposition. The sluggish witch rises to her duty, and

> quacumque ingreditur, florentia proterit arva
> exuritque herbas et summa cacumina (?) carpit
> adflatuque suo populos urbesque domosque
> polluit . . . (2.791-794)

> *wherever she advanced, she trampled on flowering fields*
> *and dried up the grass, and plucked (destroyed?) the topmost parts (?),*
> *and with her breath both cities and peoples*
> *did she pollute . . .*

Cacumina poses a particularly interesting (and vexing) textual crux; *papavera*, "poppies," has better manuscript support and would seem (so Anderson *et al.*) to evoke the Livian image of Tarquin, silently striking the heads off of poppies as a sign of how to handle enemies (*Ab Urbe Condita* 1.54.6), a reading Tarrant (who prefers *cacumina*, though with reservations; he wonders if the true reading remains quite unknown) thinks might have been inspired by *Eclogues* 2.47

summa papavera carpens, describing the pleasant action of a Naiad.[38] The Livian image has its attractions, though Invidia's action does not parallel Tarquin's; an evocation of the lovely Virgilian passage might provide a nice antithesis here, though doubts remain. The verb *carpere* presents problems of its own. It often means "to pluck," i.e., in delicate action, in contrast to *proterere* and *exurere*, though it can also mean "to destroy" and imply strong action. *Carpere* is a key verb in Ovid's depiction of Envy; at 781 *carpitque et carpitur una* "she gnaws and is at the same time gnawed" (by her envious feelings). The tricolon of actions would seem to demand a floral/grass- or tree-related noun as object. Envy tramples the flowers, thoroughly dries out the grass, and then, we would think, performs an even more destructive act (for *carpere* in this sense of "consume completely or destroy" cf. the many poetic examples gathered at Lewis and Short B.1.b.ß). We might also expect that all three of her actions involve that which is beneath her (which favors *papavera* over *cacumina*); it is also possible that like Virgil's Rumor, she grows larger by advancing (and, here, seeing the beautiful countryside). In any case, the crux remains as a good reminder of the imperfect state of our knowledge of the text.

Envy carries out her slow, wasting work on Aglauros; the Cecropian girl is compared to ice that melts fitfully under an "uncertain sun" (2.808 *incerta . . . sole*), and to a pile of grass that has been set on fire. She knows not how to cure her suffering; she thinks of telling her father of Herse's divine affair (shades of the tattletale theme). Finally, determined to impede her sister's pleasure, Aglauros sits outside the doors, ready to exclude Mercury in a nice version of a *paraclausithyron* in which the jealous party will wait to try to prevent the happy couple from uniting. Aglauros swears that she will not move until Mercury leaves, and the god more or less obliges her by transforming her into a statue with the very wand by which he normally conducts souls to the underworld (815-832). Mercury was the psychopomp; his destruction of Argus fit with his usual rôle of conveying souls to the underworld. Here his presence brings death to Aglauros. And, we might observe, in Invidia's assault on the daughter of Cecrops there is a faint hint of Athens' fall from prominence.[39]

Interestingly, Mercury immediately leaves Athens; his punishment of Aglauros is not followed by reunion with Herse. It is as if the god is taunting Aglauros to leave the doorway now that he has departed; by *not* visiting Herse, there is also a hint of the irrationality of Aglauros's jealousy: Mercury does not think all that much of her sister anyway. Thus Mercury's love affair has neither a happy nor a baleful ending for the mortal girl; we do not hear of her again, and no child is mentioned. Instead, Ovid rushes to describe how the messenger god is needed by Jupiter; his father does not summon him to Olympus, but when Mercury returns home there is a task awaiting him. Jupiter is once again enamored of a potential rival to Juno: the maiden Europa.[40]

The story of Europa is a doublet, in some ways, of Io's; Ovid linked the two tales together in his *Fasti* (5.605-624), where he observes that the bull that rises on the eve of the Ides of May was thought to be Jupiter's disguise by which he abducted Europa, or else Io's heifer.[41] Ovid's elaborate rings now return to the last love story of Book 1; that story had been preceded by the first "romantic" narrative in the poem, that of Apollo and Daphne; Europa's abduction will introduce two books that are largely devoted to tales of ill-fated love. At the end of Book 1, Ovid provided a cliffhanger ending in the journey of Phaethon to his father's palace; at the end of the present book, Europa will literally ride into the next on the back of the amorous sky god, to introduce two books of doomed amours. Ovid plays a clever trick in having Phaethon and Europa frame his second book, with the former unable to control a god's chariot, and the latter carried off on the back of a god who knows how to conduct his passenger safely on a dangerous voyage.

Horace's treatment of Europa was no doubt an influence on Ovid (c. 3.27).[42] In Horace, when Europa has arrived in Crete on Jupiter's taurine back, she complains to her now absent father Agenor that piety has been conquered by madness: *pietas . . . / victa furore* (c. 3.27.35-36). In other words, the madness of Jupiter has managed to defeat Europa's sense of duty (she should not have abandoned her father, who, in Ovid, will soon send his son Cadmus to hunt for his lost child).

Thus far, Ovid has highlighted divine peccadilloes through the amorous misadventures of Jupiter with Io and Callisto. Apollo, as we have noted, is treated differently. His escapade with Daphne was not of his own doing, and Ovid explicitly noted that it was his first love (thus the story is replete with examples of the god's inexperience with women, and the conclusion, with its non-consummation of the desired union and the virginal symbol of the laurel, helps to connect Apollo to his celibate twin sister). The second Apollonian amour was Coronis, who was killed for infidelity—mortal infidelity, we might note, not divine; there is no mention that Apollo was unfaithful to Coronis. After that episode, Apollo was left tending flocks and seemingly in recovery from his two disastrous encounters with love. Mercury has also been treated with comparative respect; his one affair was presented with none of the overt violence of Jupiter, and, of course, thus far he has had only that one affair (by alluding to Mercury's theft of Apollo's cattle right before the Aglauros story, Ovid underscores the god's youth—the story was canonically part of his infancy narrative). Jupiter, in contrast, has been guilty of outright violence and explicit rape, besides his growing catalogue of partners. Ironically, it had been Jupiter who called for the destruction of humanity by the waters of the deluge. Arguably, Jupiter's affair with Io resulted in the imposition of the goddess Isis on the world and, in turn, Rome; if we press the connection between Isis and Cleopatra, we can trace a deleterious impact on Rome from the god's romantic escapade. We might also note that his rape of the *Arcadian* Callisto is especially deplorable given the sacred place of Arcadia in the origins of Rome. For Io, we may compare Jupiter's orders to Aeneas that he abandon Dido, another dangerous girl with Eastern associations; his Ovidian dalliance with Io brought an Egyptian goddess to Rome.[43] We might note that of Jupiter's attachments, no one dies *per se* (Callisto suffers catasterism); of Apollo's, one has become a tree and the other, Coronis, was killed. The women involved with the sky god have thus far been accorded "better" treatment, in some sense, than the Apollonian amours, though Daphne, Apollo's first love, in her virginal purity has been transformed into the tree that stood at the center of Latinus' palace in Virgil's vision of primitive Italy.

If we compare the gods of the *Metamorphoses* to those of the *Aeneid*, thus far Ovid's Jupiter has done the worst harm; his anger once destroyed the human race. In the *Aeneid*, while Juno was ultimately victorious in securing the Italian future of Rome, her anger and nearly uncontrolled wrath caused immense suffering. In Ovid her rage has, thus far, seemed justified, even if we might pity her hapless female victims; her husband has been the clearly guilty culprit and source of trouble.[44] The next two books of the epic will continue to explore the theme of divine amours, but will provide a ring back to the flood (and Jupiter's decision to destroy humanity): Ovid will examine the Virgilian problem of divine anger. At the heart of this question is the matter of Rome's suffering and why the city has endured so much sanguinary civil strife. The question haunted both Virgil and Ovid; by choosing as his canvas the entire world, Ovid has a more expansive area in which to explore his predecessor's shared concern.

As Ovid prepares to continue his subject matter and transition to a more explicit examination of the question of divine anger, he makes clear that Jupiter could not be more undignified as he pursues Agenor's daughter Europa. He assumes the disguise of a bull (2.846-851), since *amor* conflicts with the majesty his office should require:

> non bene conveniunt nec in una sede morantur
> maiestas et amor . . . (2.846-847)

> *Those two things do not go well together, nor do they tarry in one place majesty and love . . .* [45]

Jupiter mingles with a herd of cattle, the most beautiful bull one could imagine, snow-white and seemingly gentle (851-853; 859), with strong muscles and dewlaps[46] hanging in front. The book opened with an evocation of Daedalus' doors on the temple of Apollo at Cumae; it closes with the terrible image of the artificial bull that Daedalus had created for Minos' wife; that, too, had appeared on the temple doors (*A*. 6.24-26).[47] Ovid provides another cliffhanger of a book ending; Jupiter manages to delay his seizing of his prize long enough to coax the girl into mounting him and letting him lure her to the water's edge; she playfully puts garlands on his horns (867-868) in a gesture that anticipates his victory as if with a winner's wreath. The bull finally carries Europa off into the Mediterranean, leaving us in anticipation of how Ovid will continue the story. Daedalus had escaped Crete; Ovid will change the itinerary of that story, as it were, by having Jupiter ride from Sidon to Crete (his sacred island) as the next book opens (3.1-2). Callisto had been a follower of Diana. Europa, who is treated with less violence and considerably more fawning courtship than the huntress, is accompanied by Tyrian maidens (2.845), the only hint of a coterie: there is something of Homer's Nausicaa in Ovid's presentation of Europa.

Why is Ovid's Europa the victim of less overt brutality than his Callisto? Indeed, why does she suffer significantly less than Io? In Horace she bemoans her fate, only to be chided for her shortsighted whining by Venus—who is described as perfidious in her laughter at the poor girl. But in Ovid, there is nothing in Europa's story that approaches the suffering of her two rivals for Jove's unwanted affection. Part of the answer for this change in treatment may be found in a study of the respective fates of the three women. The affair with Callisto has the least lasting impact. Io is transformed into the goddess Isis, with dark associations for an Augustan Rome that had demonized Cleopatra. Europa's abduction will lead to the founding of Thebes by her brother Cadmus. Of the three women, Jupiter shows the most concern for Io, who is correspondingly rewarded with the greatest honors of the triad. Callisto, despite the relative lack of significance of her son Arcas, is both saved from death and immortalized as a constellation—a step (or several) below divinity, however. In contrast, Ovid does not bother to give Europa her own *Nachleben*, despite the monumental significance of the girl in inaugurating the Theban cycle. Rather, the poet dispenses with her with unexpected rapidity as Book 3 opens; the cliffhanger with which the present book ends is proven to be a red herring. There is a decline, then, in the treatment of these women, if they are compared in light of their ultimate fates. It is as if Europa is carried off and then discarded, however lasting her name will be. The casual nature of the liaison, however, will not prevent the train of events that leads to the birth of the great god Dionysus and the madness that his worship will inspire; the terrible consummation of the young god's wrath will provide the dramatic conclusion to the poem's next book.

Europa's story also introduces an element of geographical concern, for which Ovid paved the way in his elaborate enumeration of the mountains and rivers now endangered by Phaethon's fiery ride. Europa conveys Jupiter from Phoenician Sidon to Crete; in this regard she also paves the way for the introduction to Rome of the ecstatic rites associated with the East; in her origins Europa reminds us of Dido—Europe's eponym is a Carthaginian girl.[48] Again, Jupiter's dalliance will have long lasting consequences for Rome and carries with it ominous associations for an Augustan audience. Juno, for her part, remains ignorant of the Europa affair; Mercury fulfilled his task of keeping Jupiter's secret. The associations of the Phoenician Europa with Dido allow us to see Ovid's manipulation of another scene from Virgil; in *Aeneid* 4 Mercury's Jovian mission had been to end Aeneas' affair with a Phoenician girl. Now, Mercury has been charged with concealing Jupiter's dalliance with a girl from the same land. It is as if the world has experienced precipitous decline in the quarter century since Virgil composed his epic vision.

The end of *Metamorphoses* 2 links back to its beginning, which in its turn echoed the beginning of *Aeneid* 6. In Virgil, the artwork on Apollo's doors moved from the embarrassing story of Pasiphaë's love for a bull to the poignant tale of Icarus; as we have seen is his wont, Ovid has reversed Virgil's order, and the inversion serves a point.[49] Ovid dispensed with the theme of a lost youth, albeit at great length, as preface to a series of episodes highlighting less than heroic divine deeds. He has transformed Virgil's brief allusion to Minos' wife into another example of divine misbehavior. All of this serves as prolegomena to his consideration of the theme of the anger of the immortals, which will take shape in the coming book. Virgil dwelled on the loss of a boy as part of his concern over the Augustan succession; his Icarus paved the way for Marcellus. Ovid bests Virgil in not only returning to the same theme as his predecessor, but in exploring on a wider scale the question of divine behavior.

There is another point to consider. Daedalus was an artist; his work opens Virgil's underworld. In Elysium, Anchises tells his son that others will work in bronze and marble, but the Roman is to rule the peoples with *imperium*, to practice peace under the guardianship of lawful custom, to spare the subjected and beat down the proud (*A.* 6.847-853). In other words, let the Greeks have Daedalus; the Romans will have other concerns. We have seen very little of the practice of these Roman admonitions in the works of either gods or men thus far in Ovid's admittedly pre-Roman mythological world. In a clear nod to Augustan religion, the deities Apollo and Mercury, though not without tarnish (especially the former), have been depicted without terribly serious harm to their (august) images.[50] But we are very far from any fulfillment of Anchises' imperative to his *Roman* son, the progenitor of the Julian line and the fated hero who would save his household gods from Greek flames. Ovid will, in time, address all of the major themes of the sixth *Aeneid*; as we shall see, in an important sense the main concern of the *Metamorphoses* is to make a response to Virgil's underworld book and the philosophical problems it poses.

Ovid's Europa story links with his Phaethon epyllion in evoking the beginning of Virgil's underworld narrative. And, too, there is a brilliant reminiscence and manipulation of Horace's Europa ode. In Horace, Europa wonders if her abduction had been a dream:

. . . vigilansne ploro
turpe commissum, an vitiis carentem
ludit imago,

vana quae porta fugiens eburna
somnium ducit? (c. 3.27.38-42)

. . . *awake, do I mourn*
a crime I committed, or does an image
deceive one who is lacking any vice,

an empty image that brings a dream as
it flees from the ivory gate?

We think at once of the end of *Aeneid* 6 and the Gates of Sleep (893-901), where father Anchises sends out his son Aeneas by the Ivory Gate of false dreams. Ovid evokes the end of *Aeneid* 6, just as he had recalled its opening, by closing his book with Europa, who in the most recent Latin poetic treatment of her myth had wondered if her abduction had been a false dream sent from the underworld via the Ivory Gate. The effect is intricate, artistic and highly allusive, very much in the Ovidian style; just as the poet has crafted stories within stories, so there are allusive echoes within allusive echoes, and Ovid shows himself to be a most excellent student of the works of his predecessors. At the beginning of Horace's Europa ode, the poet asks that ill omens may terrify the impious traveler—there is, of course, no such fright awaiting Jupiter as he rides on with his stolen prize. In Horace, Europa is an image of a somewhat reckless girl who willingly takes the first step towards a journey she cannot discern; Horace's Galatea is advised to be cautious about sea journeys, remembering the mythological example of the ill-fated Sidonian girl. She is, of course, in one sense the most willing of the Jovian paramours we have met, though through neither fault nor even knowledge of her own. Like many of the characters in the epic, she will disappear, her fate left unexplored and unknown once she has served her narrative purpose.

And, in another allusive connection between the Europa story and the themes Ovid had raised at the beginning of the book with its evocation of Daedalus' doors from Virgil, we might note that Europa is traditionally the mother of *Minos* (as well as Sarpedon and Rhadmanthus; see further Pseudo-Apollodorus 3.1.1).[51] The stage is being set for other parts of the universal history Ovid's poem is unfolding.

Ovid will now indulge in a leisurely and at times seemingly casual approach as he advances his investigations and unveils his vision yet further. Without hurry or any easily discernible sense of clear direction, he will lavish attention on story after story, most of them concerned with some sort of ill-fated love. We are moving in roughly chronological order through the world's history, however, and so the next two books are fittingly centered on Theban lore, the greatest cycle of mythological drama before the Trojan War.

And so with Europa we ride on Jupiter's back out of another book. The sky god will continue, as we might expect, with his familiar sexual exploits, this time in a liaison with Europa's niece, Cadmus' daughter Semele. Jupiter's Theban amour will give birth not to a constellation or semi-divine hero, but rather to a new god whose worship will inspire a madness of a sort the world has not yet seen.

Notes

1. The only individual scholarly commentary to treat this book is that of Moore-Blunt, J. J., *A Commentary on Ovid, Metamorphoses II*, Vithoorn, 1977. For literary criticism, useful is Keith, A., *The Play of Fictions: Studies in Ovid's Metamorphoses Book 2*, Ann Arbor: The University of Michigan Press, 1992.

2. Cf. *Aeneid* 6.659 and *Metamorphoses* 2.340-366. In terms of numbers of lines, the first three books of the *Met.* more or less mirror those of the *Aen.* in relative lengths.

3. And, besides, the sun's chariot is, like Aeneas' shield, the work of Vulcan (2.106).

4. See further Bömer, *Kommentar* I-III, p. 76; Ovid will address the Icarus story himself at 8.183-235.

5. Ovid linked the stories of Phaethon and Deucalion at *Fasti* 4.793-794 (where see Fantham): *vix equidem credo: sunt qui Phaethonta referri / credant et nimias Deucalionis aquas*. Ovid apparently composed the two poems in tandem, and the *Fasti* passage confirms that he had these two stories in mind together as a pair.

6. On Ovid's Phaethon and its connection to his later account of Daedalus, note Wise, V.M., "Flight Myths in Ovid's *Metamorphoses*," in *Ramus* 6 (1977), pp. 44-59.

7. The Sun's detail about the palaces Phaethon will not see is reminiscent of the Sibyl's injunction to Aeneas that there is no time to look at the pictures on the doors of Apollo's temple (A. 6.33-41). Further, Aeneas' visit to his father is preceded by all the niceties of reverential liturgy; Ovid depicts Phaethon arriving at this father's palace so quickly to underscore the boy's reckless impetuosity.

8. *A.* 8.510-511.

9. The names of the horses are presumably original to Ovid; elsewhere only Hyginus names them, and he ascribes them to Ovid. Aethon's association with Hector (Homer, *Iliad* 8.185) only underscores its baleful correspondences.

10. For a different approach to the out of control chariot, note Zissos, Paul Andrew, and Gildenhard, Ingo, "Problems of Time in *Metamorphoses* 2," in Hardie, Philip R., et al., *Ovidian Transformations: Essays on the* Metamorphoses *and Its Reception*, Cambridge: Cambridge Philological Society, 1999, pp. 31-47.

11. "Another" Phaethon is named at Hesiod, *Theogony* 984-991 (where see West), a son of the Dawn and Cephalus, who was abducted by Aphrodite and made a custodian of one of her shrines; for a valiant attempt to unite him to his more famous namesake, note van der Sluijs, Marinus A., "On the Wings of Love," in *Journal of Ancient Near Eastern Religions* 8.2 (2008), pp. 219-251.

12. Not a "patriotic Virgilian flourish" (so Hill ad 258-259) to conclude his catalogue, but rather a terrible marker of how the destruction caused by Phaethon's ride threatens the very existence of the empire's capital.

13. The image recurs throughout the *Aeneid*; we shall revisit it in Ovid as well. Useful now on this popular subject is Williams, Mary Frances, "The *Sidus Iulium*: The Divinity of Men and the Golden Age in Virgil's *Aeneid*," in *Leeds International Classical Studies* 2.1 (2003), pp. 1-29, with extensive citations of the relevant bibliography.

14. Ovid did not mention the Po in his enumeration of the rivers Phaethon threatened.

15. The theme of the mourning mother is addressed by Fantham, Elaine, "*Mater Dolorosa*," in *Hermathena* 177-178 (2004-2005), pp. 113-124, while the *Nachleben* of

Ovid's story is exhaustively studied by the 1995 Fordham dissertation of Luciana Cuppo Csaki.

16. On this brief scene note Kruschwitz, Peter, "Phaethon, Clymene und Merops: zu Ov. met. 1, 762-764," in *GB* 24 (2005), pp. 151-154. In a typically Ovidian irony, Phaethon's sisters will never see marriage, but Roman girls will have amber jewels because of their tears. For an argument that the amber presents envisaged for Roman girls do not refer to necklaces, but rather to jewels meant to be rubbed in the hands to emit a pleasing fragrance, see Watson, Pat, "Balls of Crystal and Amber: Fact or Fantasy?," in *LCM* 17 (1992), pp. 23-27.

17. On the Virgilian passage note Huyck, Jefferds, "Vergil's *Phaethontiadas*," in *Harvard Studies in Classical Philology* 91 (1987), pp. 217-228.

18. Surprisingly little has been written on both Virgil's and Ovid's Cycnus; see Harrison on the *A.* 10 passage. Detailed Eridanus lore concerning the river of amber and swans can be found at Capovilla, G., "Le *Heliades* di Eschilo: Problemi sull'Eridanus, sugli Hyperboreoi, su Kyknos e Phaethon," in *RIL* 88 (1955), pp. 415-482; note also Debiasi, Andrea, *Esiodo e l'occidente*, Roma: L'Erma di Bretschneider, 2008, pp. 159-160. A different (and more studied) Cycnus, a figure from cyclic epic, will be highlighted in *Metamorphoses* 12.

19. In Virgil, the bird associations of the Ligurian are recalled at 11.700 ff., where Camilla's slaying of the Ligurian son of Aunus (presumably one of Cinyras or Cupavo's men) is compared to the action of a raptor that slays a hapless dove.

20. On this passage see Hinds, Stephen, *The Metamorphoses of Persephone: Ovid and the Self-Conscious Muse*, Cambridge, 1987, p. 149 n. 65.

21. On Callisto and her son Arcas, see Otis, *op. cit.*, pp. 116 ff., and 350 ff. (sources), Wall, Kathleen, *The Callisto Myth from Ovid to Atwood: Initiation and Rape in Literature*, Kingston-Montreal: McGill's-Queen's University Press, 1988 (along with the 1984 Manitoba thesis of Kathleen Geminder, "Callisto: The Recurrence and Variations of Her Myth from Ovid to Atwood"), O'Bryhim, Shawn, "Ovid's Version of Callisto's Punishment," in *Hermes* 118.1 (1990), pp. 75-80, and Johnson, W. R., "The Rapes of Callisto," in *The Classical Journal* 92.1 (1996-1997), pp. 9-24. Elsewhere Ovid relates the essentials of the story at *Fasti* 2.153-192; it is impossible to prove precedence for either of the accounts. On the entire second half of this book, note Keith, A. M., *The Play of Fictions: Studies in Ovid's Metamorphoses Book 2*, Ann Arbor: The University of Michigan Press, 1992. For a brilliant argument that places the Callisto story in the preface to Fulgentius' *Mitologiae*, see Relihan, Joel C., "Fulgentius, *Mitologiae* 1.20-21," in *The American Journal of Philology* 109.2 (1988), pp. 229-230. On the general theme of the hunt as locus for rape, note Heath, John, "Diana's Understanding of Ovid's *Metamorphoses*," in *The Classical Journal* 86.3 (1991), pp. 233-243. Virgil's Venus decided to imitate Diana right after hearing her father Jupiter talk about the Romulean she-wolf (*A.* 1.275); Virgil compares her to the lupine Harpalyce (315-317), the "Snatcher She-Wolf." Any violence in Diana's world is an attack on the very heart of Roman religion, where the wolf is sacred as the creature that nourished the founding (and foundling) twins. At *Fasti* 6.235-236 (where see Littlewood), Diana is said to chase away Lycaon, that is, Arcas (the "Bear Ward"), so that Callisto need not fear; the sentiment would seem to indicate that Diana resumed her loving concern for her former devotee, and that she wished to exclude Arcas from his mother. Note also Curran, L. C., "Rape and Rape Victims in the *Metamorphoses*," in *Arethusa* 11 (1978), pp. 213-241, which rather seems to state the obvious regarding Ovidian attitudes toward violence against women. In reading Ovid's rapes it should not be forgotten that rape (and the threat thereof) played a signifi-

cant rôle both in Rome's earliest history and in the traditions surrounding the establishment of the Republic. Jupiter's actions (appropriately enough) befit the behavior of the
monarch Romulus (himself reared by a wolf), not the spirit that gave birth to the Republic
by expelling a tyrant. The whole subject has led to flights of fancy for some critics; it is
best to stay grounded in consideration of the Roman historical context: the Sabine women
and Lucretia.

22. Cf. Propertius c. 2.28.23-24 *Callisto Arcadios erraverat ursa per agros: / haec
nocturna suo sidere vela regit.* Manilius briefly mentions the story at *Astronomica* 2.29
and 3.359, besides the expected frequent references he makes to Helice (i.e., *Ursa
maior*).

23. Callisto pitiably pleads as she is changed into a bear; for a study of how Ovid
(and Virgil) connect the language of supplication with doom, see Anderson, William S.,
"The Suppliant's Voice and Gesture in Ovid's *Metamorphoses*," in *Illinois Classical
Studies* 18 (1993), pp. 165-177.

24. On the episodes of this book after Callisto, note Gildenhard, Ingo, and Zissos,
Andrew, "Ovid's 'Hecale': Deconstructing Athens in the *Metamorphoses*," in *The Journal of Roman Studies* 94 (2004), pp. 47-72, and (for the important influence of Philodemus), Henrichs, Albert, "Die Kekropidensage im PHerc. 243. Von Kallimachos zu
Ovid," in *Cronache Ercolanesi* 13 (1983), pp. 33-43. For the Callimachean antecedent of
the raven and crow stories in the *Hecale*, besides Hollis ad loc. note Lloyd-Jones, Hugh,
and Rea, John, "Callimachus, Fragments 260-261), in *Harvard Studies in Classical Philology* 72 (1968), pp. 125-145; useful on Coronis is Burgess, Jonathan Seth, "Coronis
Aflame: The Gender of Mortality," in *Classical Philology* 96.3 (2001), pp. 214-227.
Elsewhere Ovid briefly mentions the nymph Coronis as the mother of Asclepius (*Fasti*
1.291-292). See further Galinsky, *op. cit.*, pp. 143-145.

25. For Chaucer's version of the Apollo-Coronis myth, see Fumo, Jamie C., "Thinking Upon the Crow: The "Manciple's Tale" and Ovidian Mythography," in *The Chaucer
Review* 38.4 (2004), pp. 355-375.

26. On Aglauros note Wimmel, Walter, "Aglauros in Ovids Metamorphosen," in
Hermes 90.3 (1962), pp. 326-333. The story of the three sisters and Minerva's injunction
not to look inside a closed container is an etiology for the secret rites of the Arrephoria in
Athenian religion. See further Pausanias 1.27.3, Burkert, W., "Kekropidensage und Arrephoria," in *Hermes* 94 (1966), pp. 1-25, and Simon, Erika, *Festivals of Attica: An Ar-
chaeological Commentary*, Madison: The University of Wisconsin Press, 2002, pp. 39-
46. "Pandrosos" and "Herse" both mean "dew," and the rituals of the Arrephoria may
have been designed to represent the need of Athena's olive for nourishing dew. At
Pseudo-Apollodorus 3.14.6 the three sisters are driven mad by Athena's anger and hurl
themselves down from the Acropolis; so also Pausanias 1.18.2. Apollodorus also notes a
version where the serpent in Athena's box killed the sisters. Hyginus (*Fabulae* 166) has
them throw themselves into the sea. The extant fragments of the *Hecale* do not reveal the
sisters' fates. Ovid is of course manipulating the audience; in his presentation of the Ce-
cropidae he is alluding to some of the most solemn rites of Athenian religion, but with a
focus on the embarrassing situation of Athena after Hephaestus' attempted rape.

27. For this scene of repentance and others like it, note Fulkerson, Laurel, "Apollo,
paenitentia, and Ovid's *Metamorphoses*," in *Mnemosyne* 59.3 (2006), pp. 388-402.
Ovid's Apollo gives in to violent anger over the report of Coronis' infidelity, but the
point of contrast with his fellow male divinities is his faithfulness to his love.

28. Ovid's account of the raven should be compared with his "other" Apollonian raven story, *Fasti* 2.243-266. There, the raven is sent on a mission by Apollo to gather wa-

ter for a Jovian festival; the bird tarries to wait for fruit to ripen on a tree, only to seize a snake and lie to the god that the serpent delayed his return by blocking the pure spring water. Apollo punishes the lying raven; constellations are formed by the bird, the snake, and the water bowl. See further Newlands, Carole E., "Ovid's Ravenous Raven," in *The Classical Journal* 86.3 (1991), pp. 244-255. In contrast, the raven in the *Metamorphoses* does not lie; perhaps significantly (as scholars have noted), the raven myth in the *Fasti* is the only one in which Apollo takes a direct part. We may have another example here of the poet recycling material in his simultaneous composition of two long works. At Manilius, *Astronomica* 1.417 the raven is mentioned as sacred to Apollo; at 1.783-784, in a passage modeled after Virgil's catalogue of Rome's future heroes from *Aeneid* 6, Manilius mentions Marcus Valerius Corvinus (*et commilitio volucris Corvinus adeptus / et spolia et nomen, qui gestat in alite Phoebum*), where Apollo is imagined to lurk inside the raven that aided Corvinus in his struggle against the Gaul.

29. Chiron figures prominently in the proem to the *Ars Amatoria* for his tutelage of Achilles; see further Hollis ad loc. and McLaughlin, J., "Vengeance with a Twist: Another Look at the Prooemium to Ovid's *Ars Amatoria*," in *Maia* 31 (1979), pp. 269-271.

30. Ovid gives a version of Chiron's end at *Fasti* 5.379-414, where the centaur is pictured in a delightful scene with the young Achilles and with Hercules, which is spoiled by his accidental wounding from one of the latter's Hydra-stained arrows. Chiron is unable to cure the fatal wound; in nine days he dies and is transformed into the constellation Centaurus. The version in the *Metamorphoses* is not contradictory, but the emphasis in Ocyroe's prayer is how her father will long to die, while in the *Fasti* there is no hint of this longing and the centaur does not seem to have much choice in the matter. See further Brookes, Ian, "The Death of Chiron: Ovid, *Fasti* 5.379-414," *The Classical Quarterly* 44 (1994), pp. 444-450, and Boyd, Barbara Weiden, "Arms and the Man: Wordplay and the Catasterism of Chiron in Ovid *Fasti* 5," in *The American Journal of Philology* 122.1 (2001), pp. 67-80.

31. Ovid's Chiron/Ocyroe exchange may have been based on Homer's *Iliad* 19 and Achilles with his horse; so Heath, John, "Prophetic Horses, Bridled Nymphs: Ovid's Metamorphosis of Ocyroe," in *Latomus* 53 (1994), pp. 340-353.

32. For a good example of Ovid's tight internal composition, note Castellani, Victor, "Two Divine Scandals: Ovid *Met.* 2.680 ff. and 4.171 ff. and his Sources," in *Transactions of the American Philological Association* 110 (1980), pp. 37-50. Anderson takes an excessively hard line against Mercury in this section, especially in light of Battus' fate and the god's alleged cruelty—Ovid will move to that theme with a vengeance soon enough. On the contrary, Ovid has thus far been careful to depict both Mercury and Apollo in a very different light from their father; if there is a divine villain in the early movements of the *Metamorphoses*, it is Jupiter.

33. On Ovid's characterization of the two gods note Fredericks, B. R., "Divine Wit vs. Divine Folly: Mercury and Apollo in "Metamorphoses" 1-2," in *The Classical Journal* 72.3 (1977), pp. 244-249.

34. On this theme see Miller, Paul Allen, "Horace, Mercury, and Augustus, Or the Poetic Ego of Odes 1-3," in *The American Journal of Philology* 112.3 (1991), pp. 365-388.

35. For a creative metaliterary reading of c. 1.10, which connects the Mercury image with the poet, see Houghton, L. B. T., "Horace, Odes I,10: A Very Literary Hymn," in *Latomus* 66.3 (2007), pp. 636-461; on the ode's borrowings from Alcaeus note Putnam, Michael C. J., "*Mercuri, facunde nepos Atlantis*," in *Classical Philology* 69 (1974), pp. 215-217.

36. See further Dickie, Matthew W., "Ovid, *Metamorphoses* 2.760-764," in *The American Journal of Philology* 96.4 (1975), pp. 378-390. For the possible connection of Invidia with the end of the first georgic, which would neatly ring the Phaethon and Invidia episodes of this book, see Kaster, Robert A., "Invidia and the End of *Georgics* 1," in *Phoenix* 56.3/4 (2002), pp. 275-295.

37. So I interpret 774, one of the more textually vexed lines in the poem, reading *ingemuit vultumque deae ad suspiria duxit*, as opposed to Housman's *una ac* for *deae ad* (so Tarrant, *inter al.*); Anderson prefers *ima ad* (which has good manuscript authority). Ovid then proceeds to describe Envy's appearance in detail and we, with the goddess Minerva, are forced to view the disgusting visage.

38. Tarrant may well be right to adduce the bucolic passage, especially since it comes after mention of Amyntas' jealousy (39 *invidit stultus Amyntas*). Paolo Asso wonders if a lacuna lurks (*fortasse recte*).

39. Ovid of course is not concerned with strict chronological exactitude in his mythological epic; cf. Pseudo-Apollodorus 3.14.5, where Deucalion's flood is situated in the reign of Cecrops' son. Pausanias 8.2.2-3 opines that Lycaon and Cecrops were contemporaries (he notes that Cecrops was the first to identify Zeus as the supreme lord, in contrast to his Arcadian counterpart). Cecrops was sometimes identified with Aquarius (Pseudo-Hyginus, *Astronomica* 2.28; cf. Manilius, *Astronomica* 5.487 = Ganymede). Ovid will revisit the lore of early Athens and the diverse fortunes of its inhabitants later.

40. The story appealed to Horace (c. 3.27), and was the subject of a Hellenistic epyllion by Moschus (besides the usual treatment in the mythographers Pseudo-Apollodorus and Hyginus). See further Landolfi, Luciano, "Europa: Da Mosco a Ovidio," in *BStudLat* 24.2 (1994), pp. 500-526, Létoublon, Françoise, "Le mythe d'Europe dans la littérature romaine au début de l'empire," in Tar, Ibolya, et al., eds., *Klassizismus und Modernität*, Szeged: Szegedi Tudománygegyetem, 2007, pp. 34-50, Reeves, Bridget T., "A Sleight of Hand: The Opening of Ovid's *Met.* II, 833 ff.," in *Latomus* 66.1 (2007), pp. 110-113, and the 2004 McMaster dissertation of Reeves, Bridget T., "The Rape of Europa in Ancient Literature." As with Apollo and Daphne and so much else in Ovid, the story was a favorite in the visual arts; on Titian's famous painting, see Stone, Donald Jr., "The Source of Titian's Rape of Europa," in *The Art Bulletin* 54.1 (1972), pp. 47-49, and Eaton, A. W., "Where Ethics and Aesthetics Meet: Titian's Rape of Europa," in *Hypatia* 18.4 (Women, Art, and Aesthetics), 2003, pp. 159-188. Manilius, who would have been working on his didactic *Astronomica* at the same time as Ovid labored on the *Metamorphoses* and *Fasti*, mentions the story at 2.489-491 and 4.681-685. For Lucian's treatment, note Baldwin, B., "Lucian and Europa: Variations on a Theme," in *AClass* 23 (1980), pp. 115-119. Europa is Phoenix's daughter at Homer, *Iliad* 14.321.

41. See further Reeves, Bridget T., and Murgatroyd, Paul, "Europa in Ovid's *Fasti*," in Deroux, C., ed., *Studies in Latin Literature and Roman History XII*, Bruxelles: Editions Latomus, 2005, pp. 230-233.

42. On this difficult ode see Nisbet and Rudd, Williams, and West ad loc., Wilson, Alice E., "The Path of Indirection: Horace's *Odes* 3.27 and 1.7," in *The Classical World* 63.2 (1969), pp. 44-46, Berres, Thomas, "Zur Europaode des Horaz (c. 3,27)," in *Hermes* 102.1 (1974), pp. 58-86, Bradshaw, Arnold, "Horace and the Therapeutic Myth: Odes 3,7; 3,11, and 3,27," in *Hermes* 106.1 (1978), pp. 156-176, Clay, Jenny Strauss, "*Providus Auspex*: Horace, Ode 3.27," in *The Classical Journal* 88.2 (1992-1993), pp. 167-177, and especially Harrison, Stephen J., "A Tragic Europa? Horace, Odes 3.27," in *Hermes* 116.4 (1988), pp. 427-434. In Horace, Venus orders Europa to cease her complaints, arguing that the girl should be pleased that she is the wife of the unconquered

Jove (c. 3.27.73 *uxor invicti Iovis esse nescis*), and that she should learn to bear her great fortune, namely that of giving her name to a continent (74-76 *mitte singultos, bene ferre magnam / disce fortunam: tua sectus orbis / nomina ducet.* In other words, Europa should bear her fortune the way Jupiter bore her; there are shades of how the Hellespont yoked East and West, and the Herodotean theme of an abducted (eastern) girl is prominent, as in the Io story. Venus is accompanied by her son Cupid with his unstrung bow (does he plan to wound Europa?). Most significant, though, is that Venus laughs "treacherously" at the abducted girl (67 *perfidum ridens Venus*)—Horace knows that she is a rape victim, eponymous heroine of Europe or not. For an interesting synthesis of Europa in the visual and literary arts, note Lapp, Catherine Lecomte, "Grues, étoiles, et taureaux: images de navigation antique," in *AC* 72 (2003), pp. 1-23 (with illustrations).

43. See Plutarch, *Antony* 26 for the Athenian reception of Antony and Cleopatra, with the celebration of Egypt's queen as both Isis and Venus. See further Brenk, Frederick E., "Antony-Osiris, Cleopatra-Isis," in Stadter, Philip A., ed., *Plutarch and the Historical Tradition*, London-New York: Routledge, 1992, pp. 159-182 (with illustrations).

44. In Virgil's vision, we can perhaps assume that it had always been fated that Rome would be Italian; Jupiter would presumably have known this crucial detail, though he chose to reveal it only at the end of the epic, and only to his wife (thus creating for Virgil a marvelous "twist" ending). The other alternative is to imagine that Jupiter has some control over certain aspects of fate and rewards Juno's persistent *furor* with the generous grant that Rome will not be Trojan. In either case, a main theme of the epic is the suffering divine anger causes mortals (Juno), besides divine neglect in the matter of resolving situations quickly to spare further harm (Jupiter).

45. On this passage see Galinsky, *op. cit.*, pp. 162 ff.

46. *Palearia*, "dewlaps," is not a common word; it appears once in Virgil (*Georgics* 3.53), of the full dewlaps (hanging from chin to legs) that are to be found on a desirable cow. Europa is no Pasiphaë, but she is struck by the beauty of the Jovian bull nonetheless.

47. The evocation of the stories on Apollo's temple doors from Virgil in turn also recalls Catullus' treatment of the same story of Theseus and Ariadne in c. 64, his miniature epic in the Alexandrian style; Virgil had introduced the imagery in part to remind the audience of the theme of Aeneas' abandonment of Dido (cf. Theseus' leaving Ariadne on Naxos).

48. Ovid may also have had in mind the connection between the image of Europa, conveyed on the bull, and the bull's hide that marked out the territory of Dido's settlement in north Africa (*Aeneid* 1.365-368).

49. Ovid links Europa and Pasiphaë together at *Heroides* 4.55-58, where Phaedra recounts to Hippolytus the origins of Greek disasters in love. Propertius also links the two women, at c. 2.28.52 *vobiscum Europe nec proba Pasiphaë*, where the poet admonishes Persephone that there are many beautiful women in the underworld, and so she should spare Cynthia.

50. On the difficulties of depicting Apollo in an Augustan context, note Gosling, Anne, "Political Apollo: From Callimachus to the Augustans," in *Mnemosyne* 45.4 (1992), pp. 501-512, and Wickkiser, Bronwen, "Augustus, Apollo, and an Ailing Rome: Images of Augustus as a Healer of State," in Deroux, C., ed., *Studies in Latin Literature and Roman History XII*, Bruxelles: Editions Latomus, 2005, pp. 267-289. For an interesting examination of the problem that uses Apollo's seemingly degrading pursuit of Daphne as starting point, see Francese, Christopher, "Daphne, Honor, and Aetiological

Action in Ovid's *Metamorphoses*," in *The Classical World* 97.2 (2003-2004), pp. 153-157.

    51. Also Pausanias 7.4.1 *et al.*

Chapter III

And Now the God Confessed

The second book of Ovid's epic opened with a boy who had traveled to his father's palace in search of an identity; the third book opens with another son on another journey.[1] Europa's brother Cadmus is sent out to find his sister (3.3-5); Agenor tells him not to come home until and unless he locates Europa.[2] Ovid defies audience expectation by removing Europa from his narrative without further comment; her brother Cadmus now takes center stage as the poet begins his account of Theban lore, the most important cycle of Greek myths before the era of the Trojan War. Cadmus fails in his mission; the poet observes that it is difficult to uncover Jupiter's tricks.[3] Significantly, it is Apollo who helps in the young hero's moment of crisis; Cadmus consults the oracle at Delphi and is given instruction about where he should settle, now that he is an exile from Sidon (7 ff.).[4] The oracle foretells of a portentous cow that will lead the way to the site of the future Boeotia (appropriately named from the animal's Greek and Latin name). The passage is reminiscent of Aeneas' visit to Buthrotum and the prophecy of Helenus, where the seer announces both the portent of the white sow and its thirty offspring that will mark the Trojan arrival in Italy, and the supportive presence of Apollo (*A*. 3.389-393).

Ovid is in some sense rehearsing for his own rendition of *Aeneid* lore, though in Thebes (as with Dido's Carthage) we have a Phoenician prelude to Rome. Cadmus leaves the site of the Delphic oracle and immediately encounters the fated heifer. The poet is in a hurry here to advance the story of his miniature doublet of Aeneas' wanderings.[5] But Cadmus is not only reminiscent of Aeneas, but also of Dido, his countrywoman; both were Sidonian, and both went into exile because of the cruel behavior of a relative. Dido would found the mighty city of Carthage; Cadmus founds the storied settlement of Thebes. Both figures inaugurate towns that will know serious misfortune. We noted that in Book 2, Ovid developed the theme of falsehood. Falsehood appears in the very first line of Book 3: *iamque deus posita fallacis imagine tauri*. The false image Ovid develops in the opening movement of his Theban cycle is how Cadmus reminds us of Aeneas; this correspondence will not do for a Phoenician (read: Carthaginian) hero. And so the miniature *Aeneid* Ovid traces in his foundation story of Thebes is also a false *Aeneid*; the Sidonian Cadmus can never be a true Aeneas. The Cadmus lore will stretch into the fourth book of the poem (the influence of Virgil's *Aeneid* on Ovidian book division can be discerned here).

Ovid's Theban cycle was of course eclipsed by the great *Thebaid* of Statius, which had enormous influence on later versions of the story, such as the twelfth century Old French *Roman de Thèbes* and even the lengthy late twelfth century *romans d'aventures* of Hue de Rotolande, *Ipomedon* and *Protheselaus*; Ovidian influence, however, can still be found in these medieval treatments of the lore.[6]

Ovid's Theban saga begins with the great dragon Cadmus' men encounter as the guardian of a spring where they had sought water for Jovian libations (3.26 ff.). Apollo had aided the Sidonian hero; Jupiter is now introduced into the narrative as a baleful figure, since the pious Thebans had gone to search for water to use in rituals to honor the sky god. The serpent's attack on Cadmus' men is reminiscent of the Minervan snakes that slew Laocoon and his sons (*A.* 2.199-227). Unlike Virgil's serpents, there is no divine responsibility for the monster that slays Cadmus' men; instead we have the familiar image of a hero who must win a victory to secure his fame. Cadmus will travel alone in search of his lost companions, and he must do battle with the beast that declared war on his people. Cadmus could not find his sister Europa; he will discover the grim fate of his men, but will of course not be able to lead them home.

The description of the combat of Cadmus and the dragon is vintage Ovid, with narrative excitement and dramatic surprise (3.50-94); the poet pauses to develop a scene of high adventure. A chorus in Euripides' *Phoenissae* (638-689) may have inspired Ovid's account. In Euripides' version the serpent was Ares', and Cadmus destroyed it with a stone; Ovid's version of the snake's death is more elaborate.[7] The stone is ineffectual against the monster; Ovid is directly challenging his tragic antecedent. Cadmus must fight with javelin and spear thrust. Ironically, in Ovid's account the serpent will be forced against an oak tree (3.91 *quercus*); Cadmus drives his spear through neck and wood. The oak was sacred to Jove, in whose honor the whole expedition to the cave and spring had been undertaken. In Cadmus' spear thrust against Jupiter's tree, there is a subtle hint of revenge for the god's abduction of his sister. Cadmus will pay a heavy price for his attack on Jupiter; the loss of his men to the serpent is but the beginning of his woes, and none of his current actions secure any sort of immunity for himself or his line from dire punishments.

Minerva had sent the serpents that slew Laocoon and his sons. In Theban lore, Pallas Athena had directed Cadmus' sowing of the serpents' teeth, whence would arise something of a population for the hero's nascent city. The men who are born from the dragon's teeth are, appropriately enough, fully armed and ready for battle; Cadmus assumes he will have to fight them:

territus hoste novo Cadmus capere arma parabat:
'ne cape!' de populo, quem terra creaverat, unus
exclamat, 'nec te civilibus insere bellis!' (3.115-117)

Terrified by the new enemy, Cadmus prepared to take up arms:

'Do not take them up!' did one exclaim, from the people the earth
had created, 'And do not insert yourself into a civil war!'

Any mention of civil war carries special resonance with a Roman audience. The martial youths begin to slay each other until only five are left; one of these, Echion, puts down his weapons at Pallas' bidding. The five make peace with each other and join Cadmus; together, they advance to the founding of Thebes, which, like Rome, was thus born out of civil strife. The speed with which the future city of Thebes is founded contrasts greatly with Virgil's development of the theme of Rome's founding; there is an ominous note, too, in the mysterious prediction that Cadmus will himself be transformed into a serpent (3.98 *et tu spectabere serpens*). No credit is given for the author of the prophecy, let alone reason for why Cadmus should suffer a serpentine fate. It is likely that here we may detect a Jovian punishment for the insult to his oak and, more generally, the impetuosity of the young hero in going forth to search for his lost sister, herself mysteriously vanished in Jovian abduction. Cadmus will soon recede into the background, his story only to be concluded in the next book.

Thebes will, of course, know tremendous suffering, pain that befits its origins in internecine strife. For the appearance of the dragon warriors, Ovid uses a magnificent image from the world of Roman theater, when he compares the gradual appearance of the tooth-born soldiers to the raising of the curtains on a stage:

sic, ubi tolluntur festis aulaea theatris,
surgere signa solent primumque ostendere vultus,
cetera paulatim, placidoque educta tenore
tota patent imoque pedes in margine ponunt. (3.111-113)

As when on festivals the curtains are raised in theaters,
and figures are accustomed to rise up and, first, to show their faces,
the rest little by little, and, led forth in peaceful tenor
the whole appears, and they place their feet on the lowest edge.

The poet leaves no doubt that the drama of Thebes is a Roman tragedy, a rehearsal, in fact, for the civil conflict that will stand at the very center of Roman identity.[8] The words of the soldier to Cadmus are well taken; no outsider should interfere in civil war. Further, there is an emphasis on the notion that Cadmus is not the father of these men, five of whom will survive to be his companions in city founding. Cadmus will marry (3.131-133); his wife Harmonia is identified allusively and not named, since a name such as hers would spoil the ominous undertones that accompany Thebes' founding (most notably Ovid's Herodotean admonition at 3.135-137 that no man may be called blessed until after his death—and Cadmus' misery will be most acutely felt in the fates of his descendants, the children of his union with "Harmony").[9]

Ovid notes that Cadmus' (unnamed) wife was the daughter of Mars and

Venus; again, the Roman connection is underscored. For Cadmus, all the troubles of Thebes can perhaps be traced to the offense Jupiter suffered at the hands of the son of Agenor. The trivial nature of the offense provides further grist for Ovid's mill: he continues to present Jupiter in the worst possible light (while Apollo's brief appearance at the beginning of the book was another example of Ovid's respectful treatment of Augustus' patron). In a sense, the attacks on Jupiter reflect a railing against monarchy, however; Jupiter's Olympian rule can be equated with anti-Republican sentiment. It is as if Augustus is being urged to follow the Apollonian example, not the Jovian (even if we cannot make an argument that Apollo somehow symbolizes Republican virtues).

And, further, the simile of the stage curtain provides dramatic foreshadowing of what will soon unfold in the poet's ongoing narrative; the climactic figure for the third book will be the Theban-born Dionysus. Before his appearance, however, the terrible fate of one of Cadmus' descendants must be told in painful detail—the violent end of his grandson Actaeon.[10]

The story of Actaeon provided a rich lore for Ovid to appropriate for his own purposes. This victim of Artemis had been the subject of a lost play of Aeschylus, the *Toxotides*; Callimachus knew the story (*Hymnus ad lavacrum Palladis* 106).[11] The usual account is that the hapless grandson of Cadmus chanced upon the goddess while she was bathing; Hyginus knows a version in which he tried to rape her.[12] The goddess always transforms the intruder to her bath into a deer; Gregory Nagy has demonstrated that in Stesichorus' version, too (where it might seem the goddess merely threw a deerskin over the hunter— cf. Pausanias 9.2.3), there was an actual metamorphosis. An old story, then, for Ovid to retell as the first fate of one of Cadmus' line.

Actaeon's fate reintroduces a familiar theme from earlier in the epic: the virgin huntress and her sylvan haunts. Actaeon is like Callisto in that he will be transformed into a hapless animal (though hapless on better grounds than Callisto's bear, who arguably might have been fiercer). But here it is the huntress goddess who will effect the transformation; no Jupiter will invade her grove to attempt the seduction of one of her favorites. Her violent reaction to Actaeon's accidental stumbling upon her bath will offer both her fellow immortals and Ovid's audience a chance to reflect upon the (excessive?) wrath of the offended goddess. Her anger will seem less objectionable, of course, if we recall Jupiter's prior invasion of the purity of her forest world.

The story begins with a reminiscence of Ovid's tale of Apollo and Daphne:

Prima nepos inter tot res tibi, Cadme secundas
causa fuit luctus . . . (3.138-139)

The first cause of grief for you amid so many favorable things,
Cadmus, was your grandson . . .

We may cf. 1.452 *Primus amor Phoebi Daphne Peneia*; the ordinal number in both cases introduces a tale involving one of the divine twins. The present story will be the first in which Diana will appear as a central character. In her brother's tale, the infatuated Apollo pursued Daphne; in the present story, his sister will instigate the pursuit of Actaeon by his own hunting dogs: the mistress of animals will incite the violent death of a stag by the hounds' jaws. It had been noon when Cadmus set out to find his lost companions (3.50), and it will be noon (appropriately enough, given the scene of Diana's bath at the height of the day) when Actaeon's tragedy unfolds (144-145).

Before Ovid even commences Actaeon's story, he absolves the youth of guilt (141-142 *at bene si quaeras, Fortunae crimen in illo, / non scelus invenies: quod enim scelus error habebat?*). The innocence of Actaeon in Ovid's version of the story serves to underscore a possible reason behind Diana's anger, namely Jupiter's invasion of her world in his rape of Callisto. Then, of course, the goddess had taken no time to inquire of Callisto as to the cause of her pregnancy; unwilling participant though she may have been, Callisto was punished for her loss of virginity. Ovid does not indicate whether Diana ever learned the story behind Callisto's pregnancy; what matters is the audience's knowledge. In other versions of the story, Actaeon had been an Orion-like member of Diana's inner circle; Ovid suppresses that detail to underscore the unwanted intrusion of this male figure into the forest.

But why did Ovid not follow the tradition that Actaeon was an attempted rapist? One answer lies in the human behavior the poet has thus far presented in his epic. Lycaon has been the wickedest of men, and Jupiter ultimately punished his evil with the flood. Since then, with a sense of supreme irony, Jupiter himself has engaged in wicked behavior. Cadmus went in search of his sister (who had been abducted by the criminal Jupiter); the Theban progenitor came off as an innocent victim (especially in the threat of his ultimate serpentine fate). Now his grandson is innocent, the victim of the expectation of violence Jupiter introduced into the forest by his rape of Callisto, as well as Diana's even more fearsome protection of the sanctity of her groves.

The scene of Actaeon's doom mirrors that of his grandfather's hapless men at the dragon spring. Another cave appears, this time in the valley of Gargaphie (3.156—the name was borrowed from Herodotus 9.25).[13] The grotto is seemingly perfect; the only hint of trouble—and a faint one at that—comes from the presence of pumice and tufa (159-160), which reveals its volcanic origins. This pleasant locale provides the locus for Diana's midday bath; a brief catalogue of her nymphs as they attend to her (169-172) will be turned soon enough into the massive and terrible listing of the hounds that devour Actaeon. As the commentators have noted, the names of Diana's nymphs all evoke water imagery; water, after all, is central both to the goddess' bath and Actaeon's punishment.

Fortune had been blamed for Actaeon's doom; Ovid notes that the "fates" led him to Diana's grove (3.176 *sic illum fata ferebant*). As with his grandfather, so with Actaeon there is no succor or hope for salvation; the line of Cadmus is cursed, a sentiment that would have appealed to a Roman audience given its

Phoenician origins. Indeed, Diana's wrath against Actaeon can be seen as an expression of the native Italian goddess' anger against a hunter who is essentially Carthaginian (again, from a Roman viewpoint). Indeed, as Actaeon enters Diana's grove Ovid echoes a Carthaginian scene from the *Aeneid*. Diana's nymphs are the first to see the interloper, and they rush to ring their mistress and conceal her nudity with their own bodies:

> inplevere nemus circumfusaeque Dianam
> corporibus texere suis; tamen altior illis
> ipsa dea est colloque tenus supereminet omnis. (3.180-182)

> *They filled the grove* [with their howls], *and having poured themselves around Diana*
> *they covered her with their own bodies; nevertheless, taller than the rest*
> *is the very goddess, and she stood head and shoulders above them all.*

The image is borrowed from Virgil's description of Dido's entrance with her retinue into the palace of Juno at Carthage (*A.* 1.496-504), where the Sidonian queen was compared to Diana and her assembly as she stood above them all. The comparison serves to underscore the *Carthaginian* undertone of the entire Theban cycle in Ovid; these are the children of Sidon, and Rome's native deities are hostile to them, notwithstanding the individual innocence of a Cadmus or an Actaeon. Virgil's image of a nascent Carthage at peace has been replaced with the sylvan locus of an act of terrible violence against a blameless hunter.

Diana's face grows red with rage at Actaeon's stumbling upon her bath (3.183-185). Her color is compared to the purple dawn (185 *purpureae Aurorae*), another mention of the color that often signals the premature death of the young (a sort of perversion of its usual association with royalty).[14] The goddess would have shot Actaeon with her arrows, had they been close at hand; instead she throws water at him from a bathing vessel. The waters are said to be "avenging" (190 *ultricibus*), since they will demand deadly payment for Actaeon having raped the goddess visually, however unwillingly. (Ovid does not even indicate up to this point that Actaeon had done anything other than enter the grove; no verb has described his gaze).

The water sprinkled over the hunter effects his transformation into a timid deer (3.194-199). Actaeon flees the grove, and his first indication of how he has been transformed is the speed with which he is able to escape. Fortune and fate had led Actaeon to the place of his transformation, but now the poet introduces an interesting detail into the narrative, as Actaeon wonders about what he should do:

> quid faciat? repetatne domum et regalia tecta
> an lateat silvis? pudor hoc, timor inpedit illud.
> dum dubitat, videre canes . . . (3.204-206)

What should he do? Should he seek his home and his royal dwelling
or should he hide in the forest? Shame hinders the one course, fear the other.
While he hesitates, the hounds see him . . .

The implication is that the tremendous speed of the stag, which Ovid has already emphasized, might well have saved Actaeon's life. He hesitates, however understandably, and in the brief compass of that crucial delay, he is seen by the hounds. The unnecessary detail serves to absolve Diana from a certain degree of guilt; she may be to blame for the prince's transformation, but his hesitation in flight left him as prey to the dogs.[15]

Up to this point in the narrative, the poet has been sympathetic to Actaeon and ready to absolve him from guilt. Now, just before the mock heroic catalogue of almost forty dogs that pursue the doomed deer, Ovid's sympathy for the doomed Theban youth is somewhat eclipsed. And, interestingly, in the catalogue of Greek names of Actaeon's dogs, we encounter Harpyia and her two pups (215), and Harpalos (221-222), a black dog with a white splotch on his forehead; both animals may remind us of Virgil's Thracian Harpalyce (*A.* 1.316-317), to whom the disguised Venus was compared. Similarly we meet Lycisce and her Cyprian brother (220); the name = "she-wolf," and may evoke the same Harpalyce lore as the other two dogs. These hounds are now working in Diana's service, simply because they are doing what their canine and lupine natures demand. Actaeon's own companions are part of the problem; they stir on the hounds to do their deadly work (242-246), with a pathetic note about how they complain that lazy Actaeon is off somewhere and missing the drama (246 *nec capere oblatae segnem spectacula praedae*).

The falsehood image remains at the forefront of Ovid's concerns; the hounds slay their own master under the fake image of a deer (250 *dilacerant falsi dominum sub imagine cervi*). We can discern an Ovidian reading of Virgil's Diana simile in his description of Dido; the Carthaginian queen was a false Diana, just as Aeneas' mother Venus was a false Diana in her huntress costume. The hounds, for their part, have done what hunting gods are supposed to do; Actaeon's death will contrast greatly with that of Pentheus at the end of the book, whose own mother and aunts imagine he is a wild boar ripe for slaughter.

We have observed that Jupiter's rape of Callisto may have impacted the attitude of Diana towards Actaeon. Ovid may have been aware that in at least one version of the Actaeon story, Zeus was to blame for the death. In a papyrus fragment of twenty-one hexameters that describes the immediate aftermath of Actaeon's death (*P. Oxy.* 2509), a goddess (Athena? Artemis?) visits Chiron and announces that Zeus and Semele will have a son, the god Dionysus. The goddess tells Chiron that Actaeon's dogs will go about for a while with Dionysus, only later to return to him. The goddess removes the dogs' madness, and they mourn for the master they killed. In Pausanias (9.2.3), we find a version of the Actaeon story where the Theban youth is killed because he was attracted to Zeus' love Semele, Dionysus' mother.[16] According to Pausanias, this was the subject of

Stesichorus' aforementioned poem. In this account—which may lie behind the passage in *P. Oxy.* 2509—Actaeon must be killed so that a rival may be eliminated before the advent of the great god; the madness that Dionysus inspires is so profound that it destroys even before his birth. Actaeon is torn apart in a manner similar to that of his cousin, Pentheus, whose terrible fate will provide a climax to the end of this book of Dionysian madness and violence.[17] And in the death scenes of these two cousins we see again the marked decline of the ages, as violence and madness grow worse with the passing stories.

Diana's anger was only satiated with the death of Actaeon (3.251-252 *nec nisi finita per plurima vulnera vita / ira pharetratae fertur satiata Dianae*).[18] Diana's wrath caused a debate among the immortals over the question of whether her anger in the matter of Actaeon's inadvertent voyeurism had been justified:

> Rumor in ambiguo est; aliis violentior aequo
> visa dea est, alii laudant dignamque severa
> virginitate vocant: pars invenit utraque causas. (3.253-255)
>
> *Rumor was in doubt; for some, the goddess seemed more violent*
> *than was just, while others praised her and said she acted in a manner worthy*
> *of her severe virginity; either faction found evidence.*

The passage is a brilliant commentary by the poet on the different versions of the story, which he and his audience would have known. Ovid could have expected that his readers would have known of Zeus' traditional part in Actaeon's demise.

If Ovid were interested in portraying Jupiter negatively, we might wonder why he followed the Callimachean version of the story in which Actaeon was punished for seeing Artemis naked (= the canonical version, no small thanks to Ovid). The very fact that we cannot disentangle the different threads of the tale (for example, when, if ever, was there a shift in blame) illustrates an important lesson for students of Greek mythology. Often, the discordant details of a myth tradition are not so mutually incompatible. Ovid's readers knew that Actaeon was a *quondam* suitor of Semele. Zeus has stayed in the background thus far in *Metamorphoses* 3; he will make his appearance soon enough in the drama of his affair with Semele. Actaeon's death may have been instigated by Zeus and Artemis, but the hero's pride (cf. 3.204-205, where the hero is too ashamed to return home) was a contributing factor in his death (at *Bacchae* 337 he thinks he is a better hunter than Artemis; in Ovid his pride cause him to indulge in a fatal pause in flight). Thus is the poet able to nod to seemingly diverse traditions in one coherent narrative. *All* versions agree that Actaeon was ripped apart by his hounds, and that salient fact more than satisfies the offended modesty of a goddess or the jealous rival for the love of a Theban princess. It is possible that we are to imagine Diana as an unwitting tool for the real source of the reason why

Actaeon had to die—Jupiter (as in Pausanias' account). And, in a ring for this book, both Actaeon and his cousin Pentheus will die after seeing forbidden, private female activities.

We have not heard of Juno for some time; Jupiter had engaged his son Mercury in trying to conceal his dalliance with Europa from his wife. Juno expresses no opinion in the debate over Diana's actions; she neither praises nor blames the huntress (3.256). This neutrality might seem odd given that Ovid expressly indicates that Juno rejoiced in the suffering of Agenor's house (257-258), but the goddess is entirely focused on Jupiter's actions (and rightly so). Suddenly, with no narrative introduction or anticipation, we learn that Semele is pregnant by Jupiter.[19] It is as if Ovid wants us to imagine that during the previous long episode, Jupiter has been occupied with his sexual union with Semele.[20] Some critics here, as with the Callisto narrative, find fault with Juno for her recurring habit of taking vengeance for her husband's peccadilloes on his (implicitly innocent) paramours; such analysis fails to take into account that Juno is rather powerless in the matter of directly attacking Jupiter. Semele is very different from Callisto; Juno finds fault with her in interesting lines that are textually vexed:

concipit—id derat—manifestaque crimina pleno
fert utero et mater, quod vix mihi contigit, uno
de Iove vult fieri: tanta est fiducia formae. (3.268-270)

She has conceived—this had been absent—and she bears manifest
her crimes in a full womb, and she wishes that which has scarcely befallen me,
to become a mother from Jove alone: so great is her trust in her beauty.

Besides a clever play on the different meanings of his crucial noun *forma*, Ovid here introduces the idea (admittedly from Juno's perspective) that Semele enjoys being the paramour of a god. We are very far from the world of Callisto's forest rape. The textual problem here is *uno*, the universally accepted correction for the manuscript *uni*, which would refer back to Juno (dative in agreement with *mihi*). Juno knows that she is not unique in having had children from Jupiter; she seems here to be saying that Semele hopes that her pregnancy will mark a change in the supreme god, that henceforth he will be faithful to her and perhaps allow her to supplant Juno.

The seemingly exaggerated fears Juno expresses here make greater sense if we consider the powerful destiny of the child Semele is carrying; unlike Callisto's Arcas or even the deified Io's Epaphus, *this* child will become one of the Olympians. Part of Juno's planned revenge for her husband's latest affair is that she will orchestrate her rival's death at Jupiter's own hands; this allows Ovid's narrative a clever bit of learned humor, if we imagine his audience's awareness that Jove was in some versions of the myth the instigator of Actaeon's death because of the latter's infatuation with Semele. In Ovid he escapes direct blame for the hunter's death; Juno will see to it that he is responsible for Semele's. The

poet will also contrast the direct (however unwilling) part Jupiter plays in Semele's end with the indirect (though willing) rôle Diana played in Actaeon's.[21]

"What indeed have I gained through so many arguments?" (3.262 *profeci
quid enim totiens per iurgia?*), Juno asks rhetorically; the answer, for those who
have read the twelfth *Aeneid*, is that she has profited very much. Aeneas, however, escaped Juno's wrath; he was immune from any vengeance she might have
wished to take on an individual Trojan. Aeneas had not personally offended
Juno (unlike the impact of the judgment of Paris or rape of Ganymede of which
she complains in the opening of the *Aeneid*); here, Jupiter's affair with Semele
stirs an angry desire to see the woman herself punished (263 *ipsa, ipsam*). Of
course previous Jovian paramours had suffered grievously; Semele's particular
fault (besides being yet another in a long queue) seems to be the pride she takes
in her status (again, at least from Juno's point of view)—though we should note
that Ovid does not reveal anything approaching the violence Callisto endured,
and we should recall the fact that Europa escaped punishment.

To accomplish her attack on Semele, Juno assumes the guise of an old
woman, the Epidaurian nurse Beroe (3.273-278).[22] The passage is a reworking
of *Aeneid* 5.604 ff., where Juno sends Iris in the guise of Beroe, the wife of
Tmarian Doryclus. Geographical differences aside, Ovid was inspired by the
Virgilian Beroe's successful instigation of the burning of the Trojan fleet in Sicily. Semele will suffer a fiery death, just as Juno had intended for Aeneas' ships;
a divinely sent rain had spared the vessels, thereby adding to Juno's bitterness at
her ineffectual attacks. Ovid's Beroe also owes something to Virgil's Calybe,
the Junonian priestess in whose guise the Fury Allecto stirs Turnus to war
against the Trojans (*A.* 7.406 ff.). Semele speaks of Jupiter to her nurse Beroe;
Ovid here manipulates his amatory advice to male lovers to seek colloquy with a
beloved's hairdresser or attendant, since they will be privy to the secrets of the
girl's heart. Beroe plants the seed of doubt in Semele's mind over Jupiter's true
identity; here Ovid returns to the theme of Phaethon's paternity (another example of the recurring topos of falsehood). The fiery fate of Semele also links back
to the similar fate of Coronis, killed by the action of a divine lover.

Interestingly, Beroe's advice is not for Semele to ask Jupiter for proof of his
identity *per se*; she states that it is not enough for Semele's lover merely to *be*
Jupiter (3.283 *nec tamen esse Iovem satis est*). As a token of his love (a *pignus
amoris*), he should appear to Semele just as he would appear to Juno. The suggestion hearkens back to Juno's comments about how Semele essentially expected to replace her in Jupiter's affections. Juno plays on Semele's probable
prideful tendencies; this girl is a very different Jovian love from the previous.
From this point in the story, we return in an elaborate ring to the Phaethon narrative: Semele asks Jupiter for a present *sine nomine* (288), and Jupiter of course
assents without thinking. Sol had promised anything to his son by the inviolable
oath of the Styx; Jupiter utters the same rash oath. Both Juno and Jupiter use the
solemn future imperative of religious and legal gravity (285 *rogato*, 290 *sunto*);
the language foretells the serious outcome of Semele's situation: she will be the

mother of an Olympian, whose life will be rescued from the flames that destroy his mother's mortal life. Phaethon's fatal request had little lasting impact on the world; Jupiter's affair with Semele will introduce a powerful and dangerous new force to the universe.

Semele's wish is granted, and despite the valiant (?) attempt of Jupiter to lessen the impact of his glorious, thunder-filled appearance by choosing weaker bolts of lightning from the Cyclops' armory, the hapless girl is burnt to a crisp. The infant in her womb is snatched up, however, and sowed into Jupiter's own thigh—if, Ovid observes, such a story can be believed (3.311 *si credere dignum est*). Jupiter completes the pregnancy and hands over the child to Semele's sister Ino; from her the young god is entrusted to the nymphs of Nysa in India (312-315). The suspension of belief the story calls for includes how we are to imagine that Juno did not notice the pregnancy or delivery; the hiding of the child is reminiscent of traditional stories of Jupiter's own secret upbringing on Crete, safe from his father's wrath.

The new god may be hidden away, but his spirit has already impacted the earth and the heavens. After the birth of the thus far nameless immortal, Ovid shifts his scene to Olympus and a drunken Jupiter (3.316 ff.). The mood is light-hearted as Jupiter and Juno enjoy a joke-filled moment (319-320 *agitasse remissos / cum Iunone iocos*; cf. 332 *de lite iocosa*) that hinges on comparison of the relative pleasure for men and women in sexual union. Thus Bacchus' first dramatic accomplishment, it would seem, is beneficial; we are more than surprised to see the divine couple at peace in a carefree scene of relaxation. Jupiter is convinced that women enjoy the greater delight in sex; Juno (perhaps not surprisingly) denies this assertion. Recourse is made to Teiresias, since he, it is observed, has experienced "either Venus" (323 *Venus huic erat utraque nota*).

This is a transition scene, then, which serves to introduce Teiresias to the narrative; Ovid sets up an anticipation of learning how Teiresias was both male and female. We might wonder why the famous blind seer enters the epic at this juncture. In Ovid's account, Teiresias will side with Jupiter against Juno and be blinded as a punishment; his gift of prophecy will be granted as compensation from Jupiter. But another version had Teiresias punished for essentially the same "crime" as that of Actaeon: he had seen Athena bathe.[23] The story is most familiar from Callimachus' fifth hymn "On the Bath of Pallas" (where see Bulloch), which ad 56 ff. details how the nymph Chariclo bathed one day near Hippocrene on Helicon with Athena, only to have the hunter Teiresias stumble upon them with his horses.[24] Chariclo at once reproaches Athena—is this what the goddess' friendship means? Athena, for her part, recounts the story of Actaeon, with the point that Teiresias has escaped relatively unscathed. Nonetheless she grants him avian knowledge and a staff as recompense for his blindness.

Ovid suppresses all mention of this story, though his audience would have known the lore well. Indeed, Ovid's Teiresias will serve as a device for the lengthy story of Narcissus and Echo, which will begin with Narcissus' mother asking the prophet for word of her son's future; the mirror image that is central to that tale (Narcissus' reflection in water) is an image of the double nature of Teiresias (and cf. his experience of both sexes and the link that can be made between that and Narcissus' implicit homosexuality). There is a Teiresias we shall know from Ovid's narrative, and a Teiresias we know from the preexisting tradition. *That* Teiresias was another Actaeon—the story that dominated the beginning of this book. Not surprisingly, Ovid does not repeat the same (Theban) story; he instead highlights the tradition that Teiresias intervened in a divine dispute. We could not have expected Jupiter and Juno to remain at peace for long. Further, the snake imagery and gender transformation story in the background credentials for Teiresias' job as arbiter of sexual pleasure recall not only Cadmus, but also look forward to the bisexual undertones in the forthcoming Narcissus narrative. Ovid, the poet of so much amatory verse, has thus far in the *Metamorphoses* studied "love" principally through the prism of its perversion at the hands of culpable gods such as Jupiter; as we have noted, there has been a real dearth of happy couples in the epic. The stories of love we are about to explore will not change that reality.

Ovid's story that Teiresias was struck blind for taking sides in a divine dispute is known to Pseudo-Apollodorus (3.6.7) as an alternate to the Athena bathing scene; he attributes this version to Hesiod. In Ovid's narrative, Teiresias was a suitable judge for the sex debate between Jupiter and Juno because he had been transformed into a woman after disturbing two copulating snakes (3.324 ff.).[25] After seven years as a woman, he came upon the same snakes, struck them again with his staff, and was changed back into a man. The story was known before Ovid, though no great literary account survives.[26] Teiresias, the *quondam* woman, sides with Jupiter and is blinded by Juno; some say (334 *fertur*) that she took the matter too seriously and went beyond justice—a return to the theme of the anger of the immortals. Jupiter consoles Teiresias with the gift of prophecy, and the seer goes forth to provide irreproachable answers to those who come to him in search of knowledge of the future. One of these, the nymph Liriope, is the ill-fated mother of Narcissus (342-346).[27] Her name means "Lily-Face," and the seemingly trivial detail about her flower-like beauty already looks forward to the flower metamorphosis that awaits her son.

Once again, Ovid has defied expectation. We expected to hear more of the great god Dionysus; instead, we have not even learned his name. Ovid has instead returned in a ring to the Actaeon theme, and he will create yet another ring when he finally does address Semele's son in the story of Pentheus: at the beginning of Book 2, Phaethon had inquired after his identity as the son of a god, and toward the close of Book 3, Pentheus will suffer a terrible fate for questioning the legitimacy of Dionysus' divinity. The stage will then be set for a long journey back to Cadmus, the beginning of the whole Theban cycle.

Narcissus' mother is the victim of rape; the river Cephisus had ravished Liriope (3.344 *vim tulit*).[28] Narcissus is sixteen when we meet him; Ovid describes the liminal state of his age:

... poteratque puer iuvenisque videri:
multi illum iuvenes, multae cupiere puellae;
sed fuit in tenera tam dura superbia forma,
nulli illum iuvenes, nullae tetigerae puellae. (3.352-355)

He was able to appear as a boy and as a youth:
many youths desired him, as did many girls;
but there was in his tender form a stubborn pride,
and no youths touched him, nor any girls.

Ovid adds the detail that Narcissus is a deer hunter; he is engaged in this pursuit when he is spied by the nymph Echo.

With Ovid's description of Narcissus' liminal age and his vain desirability to many, we may compare Virgil's Camilla and Ovid's own Atalanta (*Metamorphoses* 8.317 ff.), herself modeled after Virgil's huntress. Atalanta will be described as looking both boyish and girlish; Camilla is appealing both to the youths of Latium and their mothers (i.e., as a prospective daughter-in-law). Neither woman is fated to have luck in love. But Ovid is most evoking Catullus' celebrated epithalamium (c. 62), *Vesper adest*, with its theme of how a virgin is desirable before her marriage, not after (39-48). In Catullus' lyric, a chorus of girls compares a maiden to a flower in a closed garden, untouched and unplucked; Narcissus, of course, will be transformed into a flower. Narcissus is a hunter (like Camilla and Atalanta); he thus evokes Diana's sylvan world yet again, and in his ambiguous sexuality he underscores the connection to the virgin goddess. Like most of the tragic figures from Diana's world, there is a separation from the other members of one's coterie; too little attention has been paid by critics of this story to the existence of Narcissus' fellow hunters.

A nymph is infatuated with Narcissus; her name, Echo, tells her story most briefly and effectively.[29] In Ovid's account, Juno had caused Echo's speech pattern as a punishment for how the nymph had provided cover for Jupiter's escapades with other nymphs by engaging Juno in endless chatter (3.359-369).[30] She is unable to express any original ideas to Narcissus; she pursues him in frustrated longing. He, for his part, was separated from his "faithful throng of companions" (379 *forte puer comitum seductus ab agmine fido*), a significant detail: Narcissus has a coterie, just as if he were a huntress nymph of Diana or, for that matter, Actaeon with his friends. The falsehood theme returns as Narcissus engages in fruitless exchanges with the echoing nymph (385 *perstat et alternae deceptus imagine vocis*). "He persists, and is deceived by the image of an alternate voice." The passage has not attracted much notice, despite its intrigue; because Echo can only repeat Narcissus' last words, she is, in a sense, subsumed into his identity. But it seems strange to say that the youth is deceived by the image of another's voice, when in fact there *is* another voice. The *imago* no doubt foreshadows Narcissus' own fate; his search for the source of the voice will lead to his mirror image.[31] In the end, while Narcissus will be destroyed by the self-love that keeps him transfixed to the pool, Echo will be ruined by her inability to give up her obsession with Narcissus; both are joined in a common infatuation.

Echo soon enough comes forth to throw herself at Narcissus (3.387 ff.). Here Ovid reverses the established pattern; this time, the woman will be the aggressor in the sylvan setting for would-be romance. The gender reversal was signaled by Teiresias' experience of both sexes, and by Jupiter's conviction that women have the greatest pleasure in sex. Here, Echo seems to confirm Jupiter's belief; she is desperate for union with Narcissus, who for his part shuns her for reasons Ovid does not make clear (his separation from his friends was also left unexplained, though he is searching for them when Echo begins her fruitless conversation with him).

Narcissus has been dismissed as "a cold egoist" (Anderson) for his behavior here; the fact that he had companions—whom he was seeking out when Echo made her move—complicates the question of his personality. Spurned and rejected, Echo retreats into isolation in the forest; she wastes away with constant grief and longing for Narcissus, and eventually only her voice and the stones that were once her bones remain (393-401). No explanation is given for the petrification; ironically, the only thing that remains of her is the one attribute that Juno had, in a sense, taken away. There seems to be no particular connection between Echo's being turned into a rock and the similar fates of Battus and Aglauros.

In Narcissus, then, we have a male figure that lives in the forest as if he were some Diana-like nymph; he has no interest in Echo, and apparently no interest in many others of both genders (3.402-405). Finally, some rejected suitor prays that Narcissus, too, may understand what it is like to suffer an unrequited love. The goddess Rhamnusia, i.e., Nemesis, hears the just prayer (406 *precibus . . . iustis*). With the mention of Rhamnusia—not a common goddess in Latin poetry—we return to evocations of Catullus, who famously inserted mention of the goddess in his version of the Protesilaus and Laodamia story at c. 68.73 ff., and perhaps in his Peleus and Thetis epyllion.[32] Rhamnusia will be the goddess who oversees Narcissus' destruction; part of the reason for his doom is the inappropriateness of having a male in Diana's world. Like Hippolytus or Orion, men who would seek the forest for a solitary life with Diana are doomed. Only Apollo, the goddess' twin brother, is allowed some latitude in that regard. Rhamnusia had been established by Catullus as a goddess with concerns in amatory affairs; she is willing to hear complaints about this proud youth.

Narcissus is soon to be another victim of a sort of forest violence; Ovid emphasizes that the pool where he will soon see his reflection was of pristine, indeed virginal purity: no shepherds, nanny goats, birds or animals ever came to drink of it. Narcissus will be punished for his rejection of suitors; he had deceived them (403 *luserat*) into thinking that he was a potential romantic partner by virtue of his handsome appearance.[33] His arrival at the pool comes when he has grown tired of the day's hunting (413 *studio venandi lassus*), thus ringing the story with emphases on his Diana-like pursuits. As he satiates his thirst, he is captured by the image he sees; 3.416 *visae correptus imagine formae* echoes back to 385 *alternae deceptus imagine vocis.* Not sound, this time, but a visual image will interest Narcissus; this time, there is no question the image is "real"—it is nothing less than the viewer himself.

Narcissus falls in love with his image, which bears the beauty of Bacchus (appropriate for the Theban lore in which the poet is immersed, especially in light of the god's forthcoming epiphany) or Apollo, the huntress' brother. He seeks to kiss his mirror image, but the font is deceptive (3.427 *fallaci . . . fonti,* with yet more of the deception motif, and cf. 439 *mendacem . . . formam* and 454 *fallis*) because it seems to offer the chance to embrace the beloved. He has made a mistake—an *error* (431, 447)—the same word Ovid used to absolve Actaeon of guilt (142). The emphasis on the image as a shadow (417, 434 *umbra*) presages his death. Ovid addresses the credulous youth (432-436), precisely to highlight how he is utterly lost in his trance-like state. The grove is dark and shady (438; cf. 412) so as to underscore that the weak sunlight hinders full knowledge and understanding.[34]

Narcissus is the victim of Rhamnusia, but his madness does not last forever: he will recognize himself, despite his transfixed state. Ovid was explicit: this is a type of madness, and a novel one, the poet had said of the voice of Tiresias' prophecy (3.349-350 . . . *exitus illam / resque probat letique genus novitasque furoris*).[35] The Theban seer had experienced life as a woman, and Narcissus is the first mention of a homosexual love in the poem. His realization of the object of his madness ends the cycle of falsehood:

iste ego sum: sensi, nec me mea fallit imago. (3.463)

I am that one: I have sensed it, and my image does not deceive me.

Narcissus had sworn to Echo that she would not have an "abundance" of him (391 *copia nostri*), while now the hungry youth is insatiable despite having an abundance of himself (466 *inopem me copia fecit*)—a typical Ovidian antithesis.[36] There may be a subtle comment on the homoeroticism implicit in Narcissus' tale; the lover who desires his own sex has, in a sense, of abundance of himself. Narcissus had rejected lovers of both sexes, but his final choice of himself remains homoerotic, previous repulsions of suitors notwithstanding.

Echo had partly turned to stone; Aglauros was petrified for her envy of Herse (2.819-832). That envy had consumed her like ice eaten away by weak sunlight (2.805-809). Narcissus is eaten away like wax that melts before a weak flame, or like the morning frost that disappears under a tepid sun (3.486-490). The images are striking and connect to each other; Narcissus is consumed with envy of himself that cannot be satiated. We do well to remember that this is the first extended story in the epic that does not involve any immortals as major characters; this is the first account of a love between two essentially mortal beings. Narcissus has adopted the traits of the forest nymphs so often raped and abused; his ambiguous looks and homoerotic attachment to himself underscore his emasculation. Given the Jovian example—not only his treatment of affairs, but also the poor marital harmony on Olympus—the pursuit of the celibate forest life, however "narcissistic," might seem understandable.

But Ovid underscores the ultimate pointlessness of the self-centered example of Narcissus: there will be no children, no progeny. Small wonder, then, that the youth's struck breast is compared to fruits that appear to be of mixed color when not yet ripe (482-485)—this fruit will wither on the vine without successful harvest (491 *et neque iam color est mixto candore rubenti*). The fruit does not reach ripeness, but instead dies on the vine, as it were.[37] Echo sees the end, and, despite her anger, she mourns (494 ff.). Narcissus dies and continues to gaze at himself in the Styx; he is lamented by his naiad sisters, and by dryads— the latter a good reminder that Narcissus was part of the forest world, which encouraged its own strange blend of isolation mingled with (celibate) companionship. A funeral is prepared, but there is no body; instead there is a narcissus, a yellow flower with white petals.[38]

Teiresias had correctly foretold Narcissus' fate; most people acknowledged him as a true prophet, while Pentheus, the son of dragon-tooth Echion and Cadmus' daughter Agave, cursed him as a fraud.[39] Teiresias now introduces the final movement of the book by summarizing Pentheus' terrible fate (3.515-525).[40] This has been the long anticipated climax of Ovid's Theban cycle; the founding of a city was dispensed with quickly at the beginning of this book, while now the poet begins his account of the appearance of a new god, one who will inspire savage madness. Pentheus refuses to acknowledge the god; we might consider the theme of how the behavior Jupiter has thus far exhibited has not lent itself to devout worship. His affair with Semele has resulted in the most serious consequence of any of his dalliances thus far in the poem. The land of Sidon, for a Roman audience the birthplace of Carthage, has delivered a dangerous god whose worship inspires madness. And this god is a son of Jupiter; the violence he will now inspire will make the divine wrath we have seen thus far in the epic seem mild in comparison.[41]

Liber adest (3.528): the god is at hand, and in his epiphany a scene of madness commences without further delay.[42] A crowd rushes forth, just as another will do so at the climax of the terrible drama. Pentheus' question would inspire the poet Lucan a generation later:

'Quis furor, anguigenae, proles Mavortia, vestras
attonuit mentes?' (3.531-532)

'*What madness, snake-born ones, Mars' children, has
struck your minds?*'

Lucan would ask the question, *quis furor*, what madness, at the beginning of his *Pharsalia* (1.8), when he wondered how his fellow citizens could be so hungry for civil war. Indeed, Pentheus sounds almost like a traditional Roman as he asks his fellow Thebans how they could possibly admit the worship of Bacchus, with its strange instruments and magical frauds (534 *magicae fraudes*), not to mention its emphasis on women's voices (536 *femineae voces*) and other elements that should repel a hardy warrior race.[43] The passage has affinities with the complaints of the native Italians in the *Aeneid* about the introduction of Trojan customs and the worship of the Great Mother Cybele from Phrygia to Italy; in Virgil's vision, such Eastern practices were part of the Trojan identity that would be suppressed in a future Italian Rome. There is something, too, of Lucretius' great vision of the worship of Cybele (*De Rerum Natura* 2.598 ff.).[44] That worship, eminently Trojan in its origins and thus presumably suitable for Roman consumption, was treated with considerable caution in practice (and in the Augustan regime, with a veritable reworking of the goddess into a more "acceptable" image), even if the Roman reception of the goddess and her devotees was far more welcoming than the Athenian.[45] It is also important to note that in his lengthy narrative of the Theban lore, Ovid refrains from the anachronistic mentions of the Augustan Age that we have previously encountered. Cadmus' Thebes has too much of a connection with Dido's Carthage to permit that.

Ovid addresses the question of Cybele's entry into Rome at *Fasti* 4.181-186 and 249-260.[46] In his vision of the goddess' reception, there is nothing of the galliambic horror we find in Catullus c. 63, but rather a reverential, dignified entry of the Trojan mother into Rome. In A.D. 3 Augustus himself restored the Roman temple of Cybele (*Res Gestae* 19), which had been destroyed by fire in 111 B.C. In the *Metamorphoses*, Pentheus rails against his fellow Thebans who have embraced the worship of Bacchus, in language that evokes the *Aeneid* and the journey of the Trojans to Italy, but, more importantly, the Italian mindset of protest against ecstatic Eastern cults. Pentheus, a scion of Thebes, sounds like a traditional Italian, urging that the primitive spirit of the snake that had slain so many of Cadmus' men to defend its spring (3.544-546) might live on in the fierce, masculine Theban heart.[47] Pentheus insults Bacchus by describing him in language that Virgil's Iarbas or Numanus Remulus would use to insult Aeneas:

quem neque bella iuvant nec tela nec usus equorum,
sed madidus murra crinis mollesque coronae
purpuraque et pictis intextum vestibus aurum (3.554-556)

[Bacchus,] *whom wars do not please, nor weapons and the use of horses,*
but locks wet with myrrh and soft garlands
and purple and gold woven into embroidered robes.

Ovid has cast Pentheus into the rôle of a Turnus or native Italian from Virgil's *Aeneid*; despite his Sidonian (Carthaginian) associations, here Pentheus speaks in language that evokes the spirit of primitive Italy, the spirit that Juno's wrath would ultimately see triumph in the settlement of Rome. The fact that Bacchus is the son of Juno's rival Semele adds to the drama; Juno was on the side of the Italians, and though she plays no part in the forthcoming destruction of Pentheus, she is opposed to Semele and, by implication, her son (whom she would have been happy to see burned up in his mother's womb). In a foreshadowing of an important forthcoming narrative, Pentheus evokes the example of Acrisius of Argos, who is said to have shut up his city against a false god (559-560; the story is obscure and otherwise unknown).

Pentheus orders Bacchus' arrest; his counselors seek to dissuade him, which only increases his rage. Cadmus makes a subtle appearance here, as Pentheus' "grandfather" (3.564 *avus*); the character has returned to the epic. The party that is sent out to apprehend Bacchus returns with a mysterious worshipper of the god, one "Acoetes" (582), an Etruscan devotee. Pentheus' men are bloody (572 *cruentati*); we can assume they have abused their captive. The passage is vexed; shades of Virgil's Sinon lurk, though there are no overt lies in what this prisoner relates.[48] It is possible (if not likely) that this is Bacchus in disguise; in Virgil, Acoetes is the name of Pallas' arms-bearer and guardian, who watches over the dead body of the slain hero.[49] Ovid's Acoetes is asked to tell how he became a follower of the new god. He tells a lengthy story of how he was an impoverished fisherman who decided to try his fortunes abroad; he set sail for Delos with a company of men, only to arrive at Chios (582 ff.).

The presence of several men points to a problem in the narrative; it seems odd that this poor angler, whose father had left him so little as an inheritance, managed to become the apparent leader (622 *pars hic mihi maxima iuris*) of a fully staffed ship. Acoetes tells how his crew came upon a handsome young man of ambiguous gender, a youth with a girl's beauty (607 *virginea puerum ducit per litora forma*). The crew wishes to abduct the handsome youth; Acoetes protests the decision and tries to bar the attempted kidnapping. The whole story is a retelling of the narrative of the Tyrrhenian (i.e., Etruscan) pirates who tried to abduct Dionysus in the *Homeric Hymn* (7).[50] The story was famous; Philostratus the Elder (*Imagines* 1.19) describes at great length a Greek painting depicting the whole episode.[51] Dionysus' association with tragedy is exploited in many of the literary and visual depictions of his mythology.

The theme of falsehood continues in the lengthy episode of the Etruscan sailors, as does the theme of madness (3.641 *quis te furor*, 650 *fraudem*, 655 *fallitis*); there is a triple deceit in the tale, if we consider the lying sailors, the disguised youth who conceals his divine identity, and, possibly, the god who may lurk in Acoetes' own person. There is a wonderful irony in having Bacchus himself tell the Homeric story of the attempted pirate abduction.[52] The sailors promise to convey the young man where he wishes; he names Naxos. Acoetes follows course for the island, only to be forced away from the sacred island at the last moment by his wicked crew. The young man protests and asks what glory is to be found in having so many delude a single boy (654-655). The audience knows the rest; the swift ship is stopped in mid-course and transformed into an exotic, Indian panorama: ivy and grape clusters appear on the sails.

Grapes are everywhere, as are savage animals from the East: tigers, lynxes and panthers. Ovid notes that the animals were not really there, but rather empty images of the beasts (668 *simulacraque inania*), hallucinations and mirages caused by the god of the vine. The crewmembers are transformed into dolphins (671-686).

The metamorphosis into dolphins was actually an act of mercy on the part of the god; Ovid notes that either through madness or fear, the men had begun to throw themselves overboard (3.670-671 *sive hoc insania fecit / sive timor*). If they were mad, it was because of Bacchus' bewitching; if driven by fear, the god is to blame for the terror. Acoetes is the only one left on the ship; Bacchus orders him to sail to Naxos, and upon arrival the sole survivor becomes a Bacchic reveler (688-691). Acoetes was frightened and chill with fear because of what he had seen happen to his crew; he was also "scarcely himself" (689 *vixque meum*): a change had been wrought in him too, however less dramatic than the metamorphosis of his dolphin companions.

Acoetes' tale (especially if Acoetes is the god in disguise) is designed to present a positive image of the deity; as in the Homeric tradition, the Etruscan sailors are a despicable lot whose fate is well merited. They are, of course, the very Maeonians who in the Virgilian tradition had allied with Aeneas against Turnus. The lengthy story only serves to enrage Pentheus; once it is over he orders that Acoetes be enclosed in prison and face a torturous demise (3.692-695). We are not surprised when the Bacchic servant is mysteriously delivered from his chains; Ovid notes that the doors of the jail flew open of their own accord, and that the chains fell from the prisoner's body of their own accord as well (699 *sponte sua*, 700 *sponte sua*): again, the power of the god is clear, whether we accept that Acoetes is Bacchus or not. Acoetes disappears from both Pentheus' prison and Ovid's narrative; he has served his purpose to admonish the god's cousin to accept the new divinity in his family.

Pentheus does not accept the divinity of Bacchus, or, if he were to confess the godhead, he does not approve of the type of cult Bacchus engenders. The story Acoetes tells only serves to enrage Pentheus precisely because it presents a positive, indeed merciful god who demands worship. Significantly, there is also the matter of the attempted homosexual rape of Bacchus by the Etruscan sailors that Ovid makes implicit in his story. Indeed, the detail may be original to Ovid. Ovid was concerned with the question of why the Romans accepted Cybele's worship, given the nature of her ecstatic worship; the case of Bacchus is a similar one and offers a parallel to the matter of the Magna Mater.[53] Bacchus is made admirable in Acoetes' story in part because he was rescued from a would-be homosexual rape; Acoetes, that is, "Bedmate," becomes a telling name: in Virgil's *Aeneid*, it was the name of Pallas' guardian, who slept in his tent; Virgil's Pallas evokes Homer's Patroclus and his relationship with Achilles.

In an important sense, Ovid's Pentheus is doomed because he rashly and inappropriately tries to introduce Roman sentiments into his Theban context; Pentheus' echoing of the criticisms of the Trojans from various indignant characters in the *Aeneid* may be admirable from a Roman point of view, but remains tragically inappropriate given his time and place. Significantly, both Jupiter and Juno are presumably unconcerned with his fate because the former is more devoted to his divine son, while the latter is angry at all of the children of Europa's family.

Ovid's Pentheus is a Greek tragedy in Roman dress, a retelling of Euripides' *Bacchae* in Latin hexameters. As the third book hastens to its close, Ovid sets the stage for a savage climax: the slaughter of the blasphemous Pentheus:

> monte fero medio est, cingentibus ultima silvis,
> purus ab arboribus, spectabilis undique, campus (3.708-709)

> *At almost the middle of the mountain, its edge girt with forest,*
> *free from trees, able to be seen from all sides, a plain*

Campus is the emphatic word with which the ecphrasis ends; there is suspense in the Latin as the picture is described. This plain, midway up the mountain, will be the scene for Pentheus' terrible death. The previous victims of the god had suffered a comparatively mild fate; mercifully, the god had transformed them into dolphins and spared their lives.[54] There was something comic, even, in the fate of the wicked sailors; they had done so much wrong (especially in Ovid's version, as they countenanced abducting a young man for rape and plunder). The scene about to unfold has nothing of the lighthearted air of that shipboard punishment.

Falsehood has been the theme for some time now, indeed the central theme of Ovid's Theban cycle. Thebes is no Rome; Thebes is not even Carthage, despite the clear associations the poet has made with the foundation legends of both cities. The falsehood began when Jupiter assumed the guise of a bull to abduct Europa; he had carried his quarry over the seas as the drama of Thebes began, while the Etruscan sailors were stopped in their attempt to abduct Bacchus and convey him over the waters. Jupiter had disguised himself not only to seduce would-be paramours, but also to test the story of Lycaon's wickedness; there has been no clear reason for Bacchus' hiding of his divinity.[55] The falsehood now would be to assume that all is playful and easily forgiven in Bacchus' world. It is true that Pentheus has been a blasphemous sort, contemptuous of the divinity of the young god. And there is a serious difference between scorning the son of a god in the manner of Turnus' rejection of Aeneas' prerogatives, and the sort of anger we see Pentheus display toward the new deity.

But new he is, and, in Pentheus' view, a danger to his people. His death—notwithstanding his own admitted wrongdoings—illustrates the point well. Pentheus' eyes may be profane as he sees the Bacchic rites (3.710), but his mother Agave is insane (711 *insano cursu*) as she rushes on her son and calls her sisters Ino and Autonoe to aid her in destroying him. The Etruscan sailors had thought they had seen wild animals on the deck of their ship; the Theban women think Pentheus is a wild boar (714-715). The god has deluded them; whatever Pentheus' vices, Bacchus has inspired madness in these women of Cadmus' house. The throng is insane as it rushes at its prey (715-716 *ruit omnis in unum / turba furens*). Both Actaeon and his cousin had seen a group of women engaged in private activity; both cousins are destroyed for seeing secrets, with the animals of Actaeon's death now terribly perverted into the very women who raised their victim.[56] We might also note that Jupiter has been absent from the destruction of Europa's relatives and their descendants; he has, for now, receded from center stage.

Pentheus repents all too late of his wrongdoings. He speaks words now that are less violent; he admits that he was wrong about Bacchus and he damns himself for his actions (3.717-718). He is in terror as his relatives advance on him. Actaeon had also stumbled upon a sacred site, and he had been literally transformed into an animal; his own hunting hounds pursued him to rip him to pieces. Pentheus undergoes no such transformation; just as Acoetes had said that he was scarcely himself, so the Theban women have been deluded into thinking that Pentheus is a boar. Autonoe, Pentheus' aunt, was Actaeon's own mother; appropriately, Pentheus invokes his cousin's shade as he begs for mercy. Ovid effectively silences those who would question the savagery of Bacchic frenzy in horrifically damning verse as he described Autonoe's response:

> illa, quis Actaeon, nescit dextramque precanti
> abstulit, Inoo lacerata est altera raptu. (3.721-722)

> *She does not know who Actaeon is, and the right hand from the one praying*
> *does she rip off, and the other hand is torn away by Ino's theft.*

Previously Ovid had introduced the idea of a suppliant who cannot raise up any hands to invoke divine mercy, since the hands had been transformed into an animal's body part; Pentheus' hands are rent away by his aunts' attack. There is also an effective bit of humor in the name "Autonoe," since under the influence of Bacchus she will hardly act according to her own mind. The pathetic invocation of Actaeon returns us in a tight ring to the book's first lengthy story; significantly, no gods will debate whether this act of divinely inspired rending is excessive in the way Diana's action was analyzed.

Perhaps if Pentheus had had his hands, he might have offered successful prayers to his mother Agave (so Ovid seems sarcastically to opine); when Agave sees the bloody stumps, she conceives the idea to tear off his head (725-728). The decapitation happens with great speed: 3.726 *avulsumque caput*, follows right on mention of Agave's shaking the hair of her own head in the air as she tosses her neck back; Ovid effectively shocks us with the tearing off of Pentheus' head by his own mother. Ovid describes the vicious dismemberment in a powerful simile:

> non citius frondes autumni frigore tactas

iamque male haerentes alta rapit arbore ventus,
quam sunt membra viri manibus direpta nefandis. (3.729-731)

Not so quickly does the wind snatch away from a lofty tree
the leaves touched by autumn chill that now cling weakly,
as were the limbs of the man snatched away by unspeakably wicked hands.

Nefandis leaves no doubt for the conclusion of the story; Pentheus' killers bear hands that are unspeakable in their wickedness. And, too, there is something terribly *civil* about the destruction of Pentheus; we have moved from the hounds of Actaeon to the female relatives of Pentheus. These women are destroying their own nephew and son; Bacchus' arrival in Thebes has brought the worst sort of internecine strife. Bacchus himself, of course, is involved in the destruction of his own relatives; the Etruscan sailors had been foreign strangers, while Pentheus is a cousin of the god.

The beautiful image of the loss of the leaves in the first chill of autumn is borrowed from Virgil (*Aeneid* 6.309-310). There, the image of the fallen leaves (and that of birds flying south to escape winter's chill) had been used to memorable effect to describe the throng of souls waiting to cross the Styx; the coming of winter is an image of death. As with the death of Phaethon and Ovid's evocation of the Virgilian doors of Apollo's temple at Cumae, so now in the Pentheus narrative do we find a major echo from Virgil's underworld narrative: as we have noted, Phaethon and Pentheus complete a ring whose theme is the questioning of identity.

First among the souls in Virgil's underworld was the only recently lost sailor Palinurus, Aeneas' helmsman. He proceeded to tell Aeneas of how he had successfully navigated the waters to Italy after having been lost overboard from Aeneas' flagship; upon reaching land, he had been savagely murdered by native inhabitants.[57] Palinurus is one of many souls in the underworld; Ovid's black humor implicitly compares the many parts of Pentheus' lacerated body to the throng of souls waiting at the shores of the Styx. His death may well have been caused by his own stubborn, arrogant refusal to accept the *fait accompli* of Bacchus' entry into the Olympian pantheon. In his doom he evokes the seemingly fruitless rebellion of a Turnus or Numanus Remulus against the new order. In the twelfth *Aeneid* Juno, of course, helped to show how anger and mad fury could accomplish much. The admission of Bacchus into Olympus—like the reception of Cybele at Rome—cannot be questioned. But the nature of the worship can be, and discomfort with the latent tendency towards ecstatic violence can be understood as reasonable for the ideal of sober, rational Romans. Jupiter's affair with Europa has led to a world where mothers can rip apart their sons with a seal of divine approbation; the world has indeed gone mad, and it may require the rage of a Juno to help restore sanity to a Jovian world lost in frenzy.[58]

Ismenis (i.e., Theban) had been the descriptive adjective for Crocale, one of the nymphs who attended Diana at her fateful bath before Actaeon had interrupted the noonday relaxation (3.169). Now Theban women (733 *Ismenides*) are warned by the example of Pentheus' doom, and they worship Bacchus with incense and the keeping of sacred altars. The daughters of Thebes are thus now envisioned as dutiful devotees of the new god. There is a clear hint that the worship was engendered by a healthy amount of fear in the wake of Pentheus' fate. "Ismene" had been the name of a Naiad nymph associated with a celebrated Boeotian fountain; "Ismenid Crocale" had been more learned than the other nymphs of Diana (*doctior illis*), a nod to the Greek meaning of "knowledge" for the name Ismene. Now, the Ismenides are said to worship Bacchus because—out of fear for their self-preservation—they are learned enough to know how to surrender to the inevitable, and more intelligent, as we shall see, than their Minyad counterparts whose story will soon commence.

The third book of the *Metamorphoses* ends quietly, and, in notable contrast to the previous two, there is no anticipation of what will follow (though we still wonder what will become of Cadmus, destined to become a serpent).[59] We might well assume that the worship of Bacchus is now not only assured, but also free from challenge and insult. Ovid will soon defy any such expectations, as new challenges emerge to the mad frenzy that Bacchus has brought to Boeotia. Along the way, as the Theban saga advances, the recurring theme of love will return in abundance, with a number of stories that continue to cast that emotion in a negative light. For now, Cadmus' children are immersed in the mad adoration of a god who inspires terror by the example of maternal dismemberment. Juno—ever the patroness of the splendor of primitive Italy—will soon enough return to Ovid's stage, to play her part in the destruction of the last daughter of Cadmus: madness to avenge madness.

Notes

1. There is a separate edition of this book on a small scale for the use of schools by Henderson, A. A. R., *Ovid: Metamorphoses III*, Bristol, 1979; Bömer's first volume of commentary ends with Book 3. The Valla/Mondadori commentaries on the poem include Barchiesi and Rosati on Books 3-4 (Milan, 2007).

2. On Cadmus see Gaertner, Hans, "Der Drachenkampf des Cadmus: Zu Ovid, *Met.* 3, 50-98," in *Anregung* 35 (1989), pp. 299-313, and the important article of Hardie, Philip, "Ovid's Theban History: The First *Anti-Aeneid*?," in *Classical Quarterly* 49 (1990), pp. 224-235; note also Feldherr, Andrew, "Metamorphosis and Sacrifice in Ovid's Theban Narrative," in *MD* 38 (1997), pp. 25-55.

3. At *Fasti* 1.490, Cadmus is cited as a stereotypical example of an exile.

4. Foundational to the bibliography on the Cadmus legend is Vian, F., *Les origines de Thebès: Cadmos et les Spartes*, Paris: Klincksieck, 1963 (with plates).

5. The question of the order of stories in Ovid's poem is a vexed one, filled with uncertainties; see further the important article of Cole, Thomas, "Ovid, Varro, and Castor of Rhodes: The Chronological Architecture of the *Metamorphoses*," in *Harvard Studies in Classical Philology* 102 (2004), pp. 355-422, which explores the matter of whether a lost comprehensive mythology handbook lurks behind the order of stories.

6. Still fundamental is the work of Constans, L., *La légende d'Oedipe étudié dans l'antiquité, au moyen âge, et dans les temps modernes*, Paris, 1881.

7. In Pseudo-Apollodorus 3.22 ff. the spring is Ares'. Hyginus (*Fabulae* 178) also identifies the serpent as Martian; so also Apollonius Rhodius, *Argonautica* 3. 1179 ff.. The theme of men born from dragon's teeth will recur in Ovid's telling of Argonaut lore; Jason performed a similar sowing. Ovid's anachronistic treatment of Cadmus' story, signaled by the simile of the Roman stage curtain (3.111-113), makes the Greek lore symbolic of the birth of the Romans.

8. Seneca, *Oedipus* 582 ff. has a marvelous scene of necromancy, where the prophet Teiresias summons the ghosts of the "Spartoi" (the ones "sown" from dragon's teeth); cf. Statius, *Thebaid* 4.564 ff.

9. *Histories* 1.32.

10. On Actaeon see further Nagy, Gregory, "On the Death of Actaeon," in *Harvard Studies in Classical Philology* 77 (1973), pp. 179-180 (on Stesichorus 236 P), Cancik, H., "Die Jungfrauenquelle: Ein religionswissenschaftlicher Versuch zu Ovid, *Met.* 3,138-255," in *AU* 25.6 (1982), pp. 52-75, Schlam, C. C., "Diana and Actaeon: Metamorphosis of a Myth," in *Classical Antiquity* 3 (1984). pp. 82-110, Lamar, Ronald Lacy, "Aktaion and a Lost 'Bath of Artemis,'" in *The Journal of Hellenic Studies* 110 (1990), pp. 26-42, Heath, John, *Actaeon: The Unmannerly Intruder: The Myth and Its Meaning in Classical Literature*, New York: Peter Lang, 1992 (published version of the 1982 Stanford thesis), and Schmitzer, Ulrich, "Transformierte Transformation: eine Fallstudie zu Erzähltechnik und Rezeption der *Metamorphosen* Ovids anhand der Actaeon-Sage," in *Gymnasium* 115.1 (2008), pp. 23-46 (with illustrations). For accounts in the mythographers, see Pseudo-Apollodorus 3.30 and Hyginus, *Fabulae* 180-181 and 191. The myth was exceedingly popular in the Middle Ages and Renaissance (Ronsard's *Amours* 1.120 is especially noteworthy, together with accounts in Petrarch's *Rime* and Maurice Scève's *Delie*, a work named after one of Diana's cult titles in imitation of Tibullus' first book of elegies). Notably, women writers of the French Renaissance responded to the lure of the story (Pernette Deu Guillet's *Rymes, Elégie II*, and Louise Labé, *Sonnet XIX*). For this vast

Nachleben see, e.g., Murphy, Stephen, "The Death of Actaeon as Petrarchist Topos," in *Comparative Literature Studies* 28.2 (1991), pp. 137-155, and Read, Kirk D., "Poolside Transformations: Diana and Actaeon Revisited by French Renaissance Women Lyricists," in Larsen, Anne, R., and Winn, Colette H., *Renaissance Women Writers: French Texts/American Contexts*, Detroit: Wayne State University Press, pp. 38-54. In the *Roman de Troie*, Achilles compares his love for Polyxena to Narcissus' predicament (on this and other medieval French passages see further Gilbert, Jane, "'I Am Not He': Narcissus and Ironic Performativity in Medieval French Literature," in *The Modern Language Review* 100.4, 2005, pp. 940-953). Besides frequent depictions in the visual arts, the story appealed to composers, e.g., Charpentier's *Actéon*.

11. The presence of Actaeon in the Hesiodic *Catalogue* is disputed. See Janko, R., "P. Oxy. 2509: Hesiod's *Catalogue* on the Death of Actaeon," in *Phoenix* 38.4 (1984), pp. 299-307, following on Casanova, A., "Il mito di Atteone nel Catalago Esiodea," in *RFIC* 97 (1969), pp. 31-46, both in favor of inclusion (so also Hirschberger's 2004 commentary and Most's 2007 Loeb, *contra* Merkelbach-West). Elsewhere in Ovid, Actaeon is mentioned at *Heroides* 20.103-104 (Acontius to Cydippe).

12. So also Diodorus Siculus 4.81.3. In Nonnus' lengthy account in *Dionysiaca* 5, the hunter eagerly takes in the site of the naked goddess, until a Naiad interrupts his lustful voyeurism by revealing his location. In Nonnus, the parents of the dead hunter come upon a deer's mutilated body and pass it by; Actaeon is forced to visit them as a ghost to tell them what happened so they may find and bury his cervine remains. The story is sometimes mentioned in passing in other accounts of Theban lore; so Euripides, *Bacchae* 240 and 340, and Seneca, *Oedipus* 751. Rembrandt understood that the Ovidian stories of Diana and Actaeon and Callisto's rape should be considered a unit; in a famous 1634 painting he essayed to present both scenes on one canvas, thus taking two of the most popular themes from the visual arts and joining them in an original unitary depiction. Diana and Actaeon, and the death of Actaeon, were the subjects of two of Titian's paintings for Philip II of Spain.

13. Anderson ad loc. is misleading; Ovid may have been the first to localize the myth there, but the name is not original to him.

14. Anderson strangely sees eroticism in the appearance of Diana towering above her companions, and in the beautiful imagery of the sun striking clouds and the purple dawn. But the images are baleful for those who recall the contexts of the Virgilian models. On the end of the story, Anderson comments that Diana is now bearing a quiver, whereas earlier she was hardly exhibiting any sort of epic grandeur or dignity, which rather misses the point.

15. For general commentary on the popular topos of animal transformations in Ovid, see Riddehough, G. B., "Man-into-Beast Changes in Ovid," in *Phoenix* 13.4 (1959), pp. 201-209 (a sensible, well-written article that remains valuable).

16. At Pseudo-Apollodorus 3.31, Actaeon is killed for his trying to woo Semele; Acusilaus is credited as the source.

17. See further Seaford, Richard, "Tragedy and Dionysos," in Bushnell, Rebecca W., ed., *A Companion to Tragedy*, Malden, Massachusetts: Blackwell Publishing, 2005, pp. 25-28, for the hypothesis that Dionysus was a character in Aeschylus' *Toxotides*. As Seaford notes, *Toxotides* was allegedly one of the plays in which Aeschylus was accused of having profaned the Mysteries, which may have been either those of Demeter and Persephone or Dionysus. Seaford makes the brilliant observation that Actaeon often is depicted as having seen himself in a body of water (cf. *Metamorphoses* 2.200), which may allude to the mirror used in Dionysiac mystery worship.

18. For a comparison of Diana's satiated anger and Juno's forthcoming rage against her rival Semele, see Feeney, D., *The Gods in Epic: Poets and Critics of the Classical Tradition*, Oxford, 1991, p. 201.

19. For Dante's reworking of Ovid's Semele, see Brownlee, Kevin, "Ovid's Semele and Dante's Metamorphosis: *Paradiso* XXI-XXII," in *MLN* 101.1 (1986), pp. 147-156.

20. Zeus' love for Semele was of course a very old story (as befitting the mother of even the latest of the Olympians); cf. Homer, *Iliad* 14.323, Hesiod, *Theogony* 940, besides the *Homeric Hymns to Dionysos*. She was the daughter of Cadmus and Harmonia (so Pausanias 9.5.2, *inter al.*). Nonnus, *Dionysiaca* 5.88 describes her exquisite beauty, which he compares to the Graces. Antonio de Literes (1673-1747) produced a *Júpiter y Semele*, one of the greatest of the Baroque *zarazuelas*; it ends with a vision of Semele enthroned in heaven, to the delight of Cadmus.

21. For a study of some possible Virgilian echoes in Ovid's portrayal of Juno and Semele, note Prauscello, Lucia, "Juno's Wrath Again: Some Virgilian Echoes in Ovid, *Met.* 3.253-315," in *The Classical Quarterly* N. S. 58.2 (2008), pp. 565-570.

22. On Beroe see Pappa, Panagiota, "Erat Beroe (Ov. *Met.* III 278): βιργιλιανές επιδράσεις," in *Dodone(philol)* 31(2002), pp. 263-278.

23. So Pseudo-Apollodorus 3.6.7, where Teiresias' mother Chariclo, who was beloved of the goddess, begs her to help her blind son. Athena grants him the knowledge of the songs of birds and a cornel wood staff to enable walking.

24. Besides the commentaries, note Morrison, A. D., "Sexual Ambiguity and the Identity of the Narrator in Callimachus' *Hymn to Athena*," in *BICS* 48 (2005), pp. 27-46.

25. See further Krappe, A.H., "Teiresias and the Snakes," in *The American Journal of Philology* (1928), pp. 267-276, and Coleman, Kathleen, "Tiresias the Judge: Ovid, *Metamorphoses* 3.322-338," in *The Classical Quarterly* N. S. 40.2 (1990), pp. 571-577. Most of the Teiresias bibliography considers his appearances in Sophocles' *Oedipus Rex*; Frazer's notes to the Loeb Apollodorus ad 3.6.7 are especially useful.

26. The most convenient summaries are Hyginus, *Fabulae* 75, Antoninus Liberalis 17, and the First Vatican Mythographer 16. Interestingly, many of the extant sources for the story locate it on Cyllene in Arcadia, which was sacred to Mercury; others place it on Cithaeron in Boeotia (the more logical location for a Theban tale). But why, then, the *difficilior traditio* of Cyllene? Did Hermes play a part in some version of the story? In any case, Ovid neatly balances two stories that apparently enjoyed two quite different traditions: Actaeon and Teiresias. In both cases, the poet chooses the details and version that suits his larger concerns.

27. On Narcissus note especially Vinge, Louise, *The Narcissus Theme in Western European Literature up to the Early 19th Century*, Lund, 1967; also Galinsky, *op. cit*, pp. 52 ff., Skinner, V., "Ovid's Narcissus: An Analysis," in *CB* 41 (1965), pp. 59-61, Meijers, J.J.M., "Narcissus," in *Hermeneus* 40 (1969), pp. 357-360, Manuwald, Bernd, "Narcissus bei Konon und Ovid (Zu Ovid *met.* 3,339-510)," in *Hermes* 103 (1975), pp. 349-372, Due, O. S., "Filolgiske selvbetragtninger og Ovids Echo og Narcissus," in *MT* 30-31 (1977), pp. 56-80 (Due also produced a 1977 Danish translation of the episode with commentary and consideration of the *Nachleben*), Gorissen, P., "Omtrent Narcissus en het Narcissusverhaal in Ovidius' *Metamorfosen*," in *Kleio* 10 (1980), pp. 49-82, Rudd, Niall, "Echo and Narcissus: Notes on a Seminar on Ovid, *Met.* 3.339-510," in *EMC* 30 (1986), pp. 43-48, Hunink, Vincent Jan Christian, "Ovidius als verteller: (*Met.* 3.339-510)," in *Lampas* 30.1 (1997), pp. 47-49, Gildenhard, Ingo, and Zissos, Andrew, "Ovid's Narcissus (*Met.* 3.339-510: Echoes of Oedipus," in *The American Journal of Philology* 121.1 (2000), pp. 129-147, and Egan, Rory B., "Narcissus Transformed: Rationalized

Myth in Plato's *Phaedrus*," in Zimmerman, Maaike, and van der Paardt, Rudi, *Metamorphic Reflections: Essays Presented to Ben Hijmans at his 75th Birthday*, Leuven: Peeters, 2004, pp. 143-159. Narcissus has of course held special fascination for some who enjoy the word "gaze" in article and book titles; so also, inexplicably, for Dutch classicists. For an interesting study of Ovid's myth and a form of magical divination by trance-like staring, see Nelson, Max, "Narcissus: Myth and Magic," in *The Classical Journal* 95.4 (1999-2000), pp. 363-389. Philip Hardie has studied the episode as a case of Ovid's blending Lucretian imagery with conventional elegy ("Lucretius and the Delusions of Narcissus," in *MD* 20-21 (1988), pp. 71-89. The story held immense interest for later literature and the visual arts, perhaps the finest example of which is the Old French *Narcisse*, a poem of some thousand lines that develops the character of Narcissus' spurned suitor into a fully fleshed out dramatic figure (besides coyly changing the gender and giving the "new" girl a name, Dané). For a comparison of Ovid's Narcissus and the *lai Guigemar*, see Gertz, SunHee Kim, "Echoes and Reflections of Enigmatic Beauty in Ovid and Marie de France," in *Speculum* 73.2 (1998), pp. 372-396. The great twelfth century troubadour Bernart de Ventadorn uses Narcissus as a symbol of the madness of love in his famous *Can vei la lauzeta mover*; the story figures at length near the beginning of the *Roman de la Rose*. The Narcissus story was of great significance to Milton (in his depiction of Eve), to name just one of the many anglophones inspired by Ovid; for a good paper on an over-studied problem, see James, Heather, "Milton's Eve, the Romance Genre, and Ovid," in *Comparative Literature* 45.2 (1993), pp. 121-145; note also Kilgour, Maggie, "'Thy Perfect Image Viewing': Poetic Creation and Ovid's Narcissus in *Paradise Lost*," in *Studies in Philology* 102.3 (2005), pp. 307-339. As we might expect, the Narcissus story has also provided ample fodder for the fanciful musings of the psychoanalysts.

28. Narcissus' story is not well attested in extant literature, and Ovid, as so often, has become the canonical account by dint of the power of his narrative. The main evidence includes Pausanias 9.31.7-9. He knows the tale of Narcissus falling in love with his own image, which he dismisses as nonsense. He prefers another version, in which Narcissus fell in love with his twin sister and gazed at his image as a way to recall her memory after she died. Conon (*Narrationes* 24) has a version in which a youth commits suicide after Narcissus spurns him, only to invoke Nemesis to wreak vengeance (cf. the similar Ovidian version). Lengthy descriptions of artwork by Philostratus the Elder (*Imagines* 1.23) and Callistratus (*Descriptiones* 5) do not much help in elucidating the myth. Ovid briefly mentions the story elsewhere at *Fasti* 5.223-226.

29. We may safely conclude that Ovid invented the connection between Narcissus and Echo. Elsewhere, the nymph makes sporadic appearances in surviving literature as early as the *Homeric Hymns*; she is often associated with Pan.

30. For a more scientific account of the phenomenon from a Latin poet, note Koenen, Mieke, "*Loca Loquuntur*: Lucretius' Explanation of the Echo and Other Acoustic Phenomena in *DRN* 4.563-614," in *Mnemosyne* 57.6 (2004), pp. 698-724.

31. For a good study of the wit and humor in this middle section of Ovid's Narcissus story, see Wilkinson, L.P., *Ovid Recalled*, Cambridge, 1955, pp. 165 ff.

32. See further Skinner, Marilyn B., "Rhamnusia Virgo," in *Classical Antiquity* 3.1 (1984), pp. 134-141. At Catullus c. 64.395 I read Baehrens' *Amarunsia* (i.e., Diana) with Mynors, Thomson, *et al.*, *contra* 'Rhamnusia.' Note also c. 66.71, and cf. c. 50.21 *vemens dea* probably = Rhamnusia.

33. So I interpret *ludere* here (vid. Lewis and Short II.G), rather than the usual idea of "mockery" or "making sport of" (the latter action can be unintentional; less so the

first). There is no hint in Ovid that Narcissus takes pleasure in enticing would-be lovers, despite his admittedly "hard pride" (354 *dura superbia*).

34. For possible comic influence on Ovid's Narcissus' lament, see Davis, G., "Ovid's *Metamorphoses* 3.442 ff. and the Prologue to Menander's *Misoumenos*," in *Phoenix* 32 (1978), pp. 339-342.

35. The madness theme also appears at 3.479 *misero praebere alimenta furoris*.

36. At 10.654 *posse putes* (cf. 3.453 *posse putes*), Ovid draws a subtle link between Hippomenes and Atalanta in the race with the golden apples and Narcissus' observation that "you would think that [he and his mirror image] were able" to touch; in the race narrative, the poet observes that you might think the runners able to speed over water dry shod, or standing ears of corn without touching the crops. Cf. also the mention of fruit in the Narcissus story at 3.483-484. The association is slight, but the point seems to be that neither couple will be successful in the end—and cf. Atalanta's aforementioned ambiguous features. Narcissus' name (cf. "narcotic") is from the Greek for "to become numb." Not only Narcissus' self-infatuation caused numbness, but also his adolescent pattern of flight into the forest world.

37. The fruit not yet ripe has an appropriately purple color to signal the impending death of another tragic youth (485 *purpureum . . . colorem*).

38. Anderson observes that the narcissus is not particularly attractive, "merely pretty." This may indeed be the point of the epic's first flower metamorphosis, since otherwise it seems difficult to understand why Narcissus needed to become a flower. In his perpetual self-gaze he will presage the heliotrope Clytie, who will at least turn her look outside herself.

39. For brief analysis (= lecture summary) of the rest of the book, note Little, D., "The Pentheus Episode. Ovid, *Met.* III, 511-733," in Adams, M., ed., *Aulla: Proceedings of the Ninth Congress of the Australasian Universities' Languages and Literatures Association, Melbourne 19-26 August 1964*, Melbourne, 1965, p. 30. In Nonnus' version of the Pentheus story, it is Teiresias who warns the blasphemer about the dangers from the new god.

40. The story is best known from Euripides' *Bacchae*. Aeschylus also treated the subject (cf. *Eumenides* 24), where Bacchus is said to have fashioned for Pentheus a death as for a hunted rabbit; for other accounts, note Pseudo-Apollodorus 2.36-37 and 3.5.2, Hyginus, *Fabulae* 184, Pausanias 2.2.6-7 and 9.5.4, and the long summary at Oppian, *Cynegetica* 4.230 ff. The Latin tragedian Pacuvius, as we shall see, may also lurk in Ovid's Pentheus narrative, which, in rivalry with Euripides, sets forth to provide a Roman tragic drama. Propertius mentions the death of Pentheus at c. 3.17.24.

41. Like Apollo, Bacchus was traditionally an inspiration for verse, and thus of peculiar concern to the Augustan poets. On this vast subject see especially Batinski, Emily E., "Horace's Rehabilitation of Bacchus," in *The Classical World* 84.5 (1991), pp. 361-378, as well as Nisbet and Hubbard ad Horace, c. 2.19, and Nisbet and Rudd ad c. 3.25. Bacchus knows no rehabilitation in Ovid's vision, where, as we have seen, Apollo is the preeminent god for poetry and all things positive in the Augustan world.

42. For the Pentheus tradition before Euripides, most convenient is Dodds' introduction to the same, especially pp. xxv-xxxvi (with consideration of both the literary and the visual evidence).

43. For a very different reading of Ovid's Pentheus from that found in these pages, see the fine article of Janan, Micaela, "The Snake Sheds Its Skin: Pentheus (Re)imagines Thebes," in *Classical Philology* 99.2 (2004), pp. 130-146.

44. See Bailey ad loc. The cult was introduced in Rome in 202 B.C., though Roman citizens were not allowed to participate in conducting the rites.

45. Note Cosi, D.M., "L'ingresso di Cibele ad Atene e a Roma," in *CRDAC* 11 (1980-1981), pp. 81-91, and Bremmer, Jan, "The Legend of Cybele's Arrival in Rome," in Vermaseren, M. J., ed., *Studies in Hellenistic Religions*, Leiden: Brill, 1979, pp. 9-22. Overly imaginative is Wilhelm, Robert McKay, "Cybele: The Great Mother of Augustan Order," in *Vergilius* 34 (1988), pp. 77-101. Better is Wiseman, T.P., "Cybele, Virgil, and Augustus," in Woodman, T., and West, D., eds., *Poetry and Politics in the Age of Augustus*, Cambridge, 1984, pp. 117-128. Something of the Roman hesitation to accept Cybele whole cloth can be see in Ovid's account at *Fasti* 4.250 ff., where the goddess notes that she had not come with Aeneas at the very beginning of the Roman adventure, but had waited five centuries: 253-254 *sed nondum fatis Latio sua numina posci / senserat, adsuetis substiteratque locis*. Rome was not yet ready for her, in other words. A good overview can be found at Vermaseren, M. J., *Cybele and Attis: The Myth and the Cult*, London, 1977.

46. Where see Fantham ad loc., and Boyd, Barbara Weiden, "*Itala nam tellus Graeca maior erat*: 'Poetic Syncretism' and the Divinities of Ovid, *Fasti* 4," in *Mouseion* 3.1 (2003), pp. 13-35.

47. For a study of Pentheus' attempt to fight Bacchus with an evocation of the dangerous symbol of the snake that had slain Cadmus' men, see James, Paula, "Pentheus Anguigena: Sins of the *Father*," in *BICS* 38 (1991-1993), pp. 81-93.

48. The whole passage is discussed at length by Otis, *op. cit.*, pp. 139 ff. Otis considers the possible sources of the Pentheus-Aconteus story, as well as Ovid's reasons for including the lengthy interpolation of the story from the *Homeric Hymn*.

49. Ovid may have borrowed the name of Acoetes from the *Pentheus* of the second century B.C. tragedian Pacuvius. No fragments of the play survive, but only a summary preserved at Servius *auctus* on *Aeneid* 4.449. There, we read that Acoetes was found instead of the god when Pentheus sent out a search party to detain Bacchus. We are, regrettably, unable to determine what Ovid found in the lost play, but Virgil's use of the name for Pallas' companion would also have figured in Ovid's composition. See further Otis, *op. cit.*, pp. 371-372, for rational analysis of the problem of Ovid's sources for his *Pentheus*. For a different view on the question of Pacuvius' play and whether we can accept Servius' evidence of its existence, see Haffter, H., "Zum Pentheus des Pacuvius," in *WS* 79 (1966), pp. 290-293. Haffter focuses on the curious introduction of a new character and the absence of the madness motif from Pentheus' description. If Pacuvius does not lurk behind Ovid, then Virgil becomes the sole known source for the Ovidian Acoetes.

50. More precisely, the pirates merely ply their trade on the Tyrrhenian Sea. But the point should not be pressed too pedantically.

51. The attempted rape of the handsome young god is implicit in Ovid's version and explicit in Hyginus, *Fabulae* 1.34 and Servius ad *Aeneid* 1.67. Note also Hyginus' *Astronomica* 2.17, which cites the *Naxica* of Aglaosthenes (c. 7th century B.C.), where the sailors were supposed to deliver Bacchus as a child to nymph guardians on Naxos, only to try to turn off course in the pursuit of ransom.

52. For a study of the extant versions of the story (the *Homeric Hymn*, Ovid, and Nonnus), see James, A. W., "Dionysus and the Tyrrhenian Pirates," in *Antichthon* 9 (1975), pp. 17-34.

53. See further Sharrock, Alison, "Gender and Sexuality," in Hardie, Philip, ed., *The Cambridge Companion to Ovid*, Cambridge, 2002, pp. 95-107.

54. It is arguable that Bacchus showed pity for Pentheus in allowing him the chance to repent of his ways by sending either Acoetes or by his own use of Acoetes' guise to tell a cautionary story. But none of this subtracts from the vicious violence that closes this book.

55. In the tale of the sailors there is a ring with Lycaon; both parties had sought to do violence to a god in mortal guise.

56. For the gender conflict inherent in the story of Pentheus' murder at the hands of his female relatives, see Segal, C. P., "The Menace of Dionysos: Sex Roles and Reversals in Euripides' *Bacchae*," in *Arethusa* 11 (1978), pp. 185-202. Gender ambiguity, as we have noted, is a key factor in Ovid's version of the attempted abduction of the god by the Tyrrhenian pirates, and was foreshadowed by Narcissus' own ambiguous sexuality.

57. Virgil enjoys playing with the names of disparate characters whose names share the same first and last letters (Arruns/Aeneas, Acca/Anna, Camilla/Cleopatra, etc.); it is possible Ovid thought of Palinurus' appearance after Virgil's autumn simile when he decided to describe Pentheus' murder with the same image. In a nice touch, Ovid roughly follows the outline of Virgil's fifth *Aeneid*: there the fake Beroe encourages the Trojan women to burn the ships, followed by the eventual loss of Palinurus; in Ovid the fake Beroe leads Semele to her fiery doom, followed by the loss of Pentheus. Further, Virgil's violent women are terribly transformed into the mad women of Ovid's vision of Pentheus' murder.

58. For a fine study of the shades of Bacchus in Aeneas at Dido's court, see Weber, Clifford, "The Dionysus in Aeneas," in *Classical Philology* 97.4 (2002), pp. 322-343; Mark Antony lurks in that scene, of course, and Bacchus is once again depicted in a dangerous light.

59. For a convenient, brief consideration of the complicated issue of Ovidian book divisions, note Hopkinson, Neil, *Ovid Metamorphoses Book XIII*, 2000, pp. vi-ix.

Chapter IV

But Not the Daughter of Minyas

If the fourth book of the *Metamorphoses* opens with any sense of anticipation, it is rooted in the uncertainty Ovid has created over what will follow the apparent triumph of Bacchus.[1] For the first time, there is no clear indication as we turn from one book to the next of what we shall encounter. The first word of the new book, the conjunction *at*, signals a new conflict: Bacchus still engenders protest and lack of acceptance. Alcithoe, the daughter of Minyas in Orchomenos, will not worship the new god. We might well expect a doublet of the story of Pentheus, and indeed Alcithoe and her sisters in crime will be punished for their impiety in denying the divine paternity of Bacchus (again, a reasonable charge given Jupiter's philandering). But for the space of half the book, Ovid will entertain us with the stories of the daughters of Minyas, all of them centered on the erotic theme that has recurred and sometimes dominated the first movements of the epic.[2] Soon thereafter we shall return in a great ring to the beginning of the whole Theban saga, as we witness Juno's destruction of more of Cadmus' line and, at last, the serpentine fate of Agenor's son. Ovid's *Thebaid* had begun with Jupiter's abduction of a Sidonian girl; it will end with the offspring of yet another of his affairs, which will allow the poet yet another exploration of the theme of questioned paternity and, rather in the manner of his Phaethon saga, yet another miniature epic, though this time a very different epyllion indeed. The present book will move us from the failed world of a Theban *Aeneid* to an Argive saga that will also evoke *Aeneid* lore, and with greater success.

But we are still seemingly very far in all of this from the contemporary world of Augustan Rome. In the stories of the Minyades, Ovid lures the audience yet again into a web of enchanting tales.[3] But the mammoth structure he is building brooks no haphazard construction; in ever widening rings, the poet continues to return to where he began. Jupiter had investigated the wickedness of mortals in his visit to Lycaon; since the destruction of humanity and mortal rebirth after the flood, it has been man that has suffered at the hands of certain seemingly capricious, violent gods (Jupiter and Bacchus). Some hint of (Augustan) order has been seen from Apollo and Mercury. But Ovid has effectively crafted a tense world that seems to lack permanence; he has devoted hundreds of lines to Cadmus' Thebes, but we have not been permitted to admire any Theban glory, rather, we have seen the slow decline of the city state, with occasionally dramatic bursts of divine retribution against certain of its people. The poet is laying the groundwork in these early books for the coming of Rome and the birth of the Augustan regime. For the present, we remain lost in a world seemingly without firm foundation, though, as with Pentheus, faint echoes of the future Rome can already be heard.

The priest summons all women, servant and mistress, to worship the new god of the vine (4.4-17). In language that echoes Virgil's description of Juno's wrath, the priest makes clear that if there is any disobeying of the command to worship, the god's divinity will be offended: 8 *saevam laesi numinis iram*. As in the Pentheus story, so now there is a clear announcement: the pleasing rites of the god, full of wild abandon and surrender to wine, conceal a violent underside that threatens destruction and dismemberment. The book opens with a long, cultic hymn to the god that mentions both Pentheus and the Thracian king Lycurgus (22-23).[4] There is Augustan imagery in the evocation of an Orient conquered by the god, India in thrall to Bacchus as far as the Ganges (20-21). Silenus is in Bacchus' train (26-27), unable to walk in his drunkenness as he uses a staff and an ass to balance his steps; we may be reminded of Virgil's Silenus and his song (which has influenced Ovid's early stories).[5]

The Minyades refuse to join the general throng of Theban women who cultivate the god. They remain at home as if dutiful Roman women, busy with spinning and the arts of Minerva (4.31-35). In another context, their behavior would be praiseworthy; here it is inappropriate in its timing (33 *intempestiva . . . Minerva*). The Minyades believe that Pallas is the "better god" (38 *melior dea*); a Roman would agree with the sentiment that the Minervan works of the loom are more useful than Bacchic revels (39). The Minyades are impious, though in a very different way from Pentheus; they seek no converts to their cause, except perhaps their servants whom they compel to join them in the labor of the loom. As they work, they decide to pass the time with stories.[6]

Interestingly, despite the eminently Roman interest the Minyades have in spinning, the first storyteller seems to know only tales from the exotic East.[7] She decides to pass over the story of Dercetis of Babylon, the Syrian goddess Atargatis, and that of her daughter (i.e., Queen Semiramis) with their respective fish metamorphoses (Hyginus, *Fabulae* 275 mentions Semiramis, daughter of Dercetis, as founder of Babylon). She settles on the etiological story of why the mulberry tree has dark fruit, a story "not commonly known" (4.53 *quoniam vulgaris fabula non est*) for the Minyades (and Ovid's audience?), but of wide renown for moderns entirely due to Ovid's treatment: the tragedy of Pyramus and Thisbe.[8] The tale is another example in the poem of an entirely human love, a story largely devoid of any divine machinery.[9] It is an appropriate tale for the first of the Minyades to tell, since the context of their story-hour is the impious decision of the women to prefer the works of Minerva to the worship of Bacchus (however admirable the preference of the one god for the other might be). The story is tragic in that it ends in the bloody, premature deaths of the two lovers, though they do find a certain sort of union in their mutual destruction, which contrasts greatly with the fate of the discarded divine amours we have seen thus far. Indeed, despite the admittedly pathetic nature of some aspects of the story, there is a real nobility to be found here, especially in Thisbe's suicide.[10] Eastern stories are appropriate enough in a Bacchic context; the Minyad does not realize that despite her Roman spinning, she is weaving an Eastern (Bacchic?) yarn.

The lovers are separated; there is no reason given for the parents' disapproval (4.55-62). A plan is quickly formed: Pyramus and Thisbe will seek union outside the walls of the city, at the tomb of Ninus, Semiramis' husband (83-92, an ominous assocation given Semiramis' murder of her spouse).[11] Thisbe arrives first at the tomb; love has made her bold (96 *audacem faciebat amor*). A lioness scares her off; having recently slain cattle, its maw is bloody and Thisbe's lost cloak soon bears gruesome clues of the slaughter, thus setting the stage for Pyramus' assumption that his beloved has been devoured. Upon finding the misleading evidence, Pyramus kills himself; his blood shoots high in the air and spatters the berries of a nearby mulberry tree:

> ut iacuit resupinus humo, cruor emicat alte,
> non aliter quam cum vitiato fistula plumbo
> scinditur et tenui stridente foramine longas
> eiaculatur aquas atque ictibus aera rumpit. (4.121-124)

> *As he was lying prone on the ground, his gore shot high in the air,*
> *not otherwise than when a pipe with weakened lead*
> *is broken and, through a small hissing opening,*
> *shoots forth long streams of water and breaks the air with the blows.*

Some scholars, under the mistaken impression that *eiaculatio* is good Latin for sexual climax, have taken this famous simile as evidence of an Ovidian attempt to mingle sex and death in a grisly spectacle.[12] Ovid is, instead, more interested in the prosaic world of Roman plumbing than any *eros/thanatos* connection.[13] We might well question the appropriateness of this urban image of pipe failure in an isolated foreign setting. We wonder how a Boeotian girl knew about the particulars of Roman waterworks. This is precisely Ovid's point; the Minyad is a Roman girl, marvelously anachronistic and, quite fittingly, seeing the world through Roman eyes as she serves Minerva like a praiseworthy Roman matron.

Pyramus' blood stains the mulberries with the purple color we have come to associate with the premature death of the young (127).[14] The union of these sad lovers in death represents a partial failure of their dreams; they do not know the joy of union as consummation of their mutual longing. Instead, they have the "devotion" that is expressed by suicide and mingled ashes. Their end will contrast with that of Salmacis and Hermaphroditus later in the Minyad story cycle, where the lover and her unwilling beloved are literally fused into one being, albeit again without consummation of their union in the strict sense.

Thisbe returns to the scene, worried that her lover might think she has forsaken him. She finds the body, and predictably, commits suicide; she begs that their parents might let them be buried together, though there is, presumably, no one at hand to hear the entreaty. Nevertheless, the Minyad notes, her prayers touched both gods and parents (4.164 *vota tamen tetigere deos, tetigere parentes*), and the request was granted: the gods see to it that the mulberry remains forever stained as a mark of the love that endured until and beyond death, and the parents allow a joint burial. This is the first appearance of the "gods" in an all-too mortal story; they approve of the lover's plea. The first Minyad story is eminently Roman: noble suicide, honorable burial, permanent memorial, even a nod to urban planning.

The next sister begins her story: Leuconoe. The names of the Minyades are disputed. Antoninus Liberalis (*Metamorphoses* 10) has Leucippe, Arsippe, and Alcathoe. Aelian (*Varia Historia* 3.42) has Leucippe, Arsippe, and Alcithoe. Ovid names only Alcithoe and Leuconoe; the teller of the story of Pyramus and Thisbe is left unnamed. Why the significant change? The name Leuconoe was perhaps borrowed from Horace c. 1.11, the celebrated *carpe diem* ode; it may mean "she who bears the mind of Apollo," which fits the Horatian context, where Leuconoe is warned not to worry about the future, and not to test Babylonian numbers (i.e., Chaldaean astronomy).[15] The name, and especially its Babylonian association, points to an evocation of Horace's ode, as does the possible connection between the Apollonian Leuconoe and the story she is about to tell of the sun and his loves. If correct, the suggested etymology of her name would link Horace's Leuconoe with Apollo *Leucatas*, the patron deity of Octavian's victory over the Eastern forces of Antony and Cleopatra at Actium. Ovid has magnificently defied expectations and reintroduced the world of Augustan Rome in the quiet room where these defiant women honor Minerva and shun the Eastern Bacchus with his oriental retinue. Leuconoe, she who bears the mind of Apollo, will tell her sisters of Apollo's loves.[16]

Her first story is not really in accord with her declared subject matter: the sun is not in love, but is rather the witness of the love of Mars and Venus (progenitors of so much of ancient Rome). The celebrated adultery had been told by Homer in the song of Demodocus at the banquet in Phaeaecia (*Odyssey* 8.267 ff.). The sun is not only the witness of the infidelity, but also the reporter; he reveals the whole matter to Vulcan, who promptly fashions his famous chains to trap the lovers and reveal their behavior to all Olympus (4.173-189). Just as Pyramus and Thisbe share an urn, and Salmacis and Hermaphroditus a new body, so Mars and Venus are entwined in Vulcan's invisible net, thus maintaining the theme in the Minyad cycle of trapped lovers (willing or not), in contrast to the poem's previous examples of separated amours.

Venus punishes the sun god (4.190 ff.).[17] In the first book, Apollo had been struck by Cupid's shafts; now Sol is subjected to amatory torture by Venus: she infuses the god with love of one Leucothoe, the "white goddess."[18] The commentators have noted the similarity of her name to the narrator's. Goddess indeed she would seem to be, as she surpasses Phaethon's mother Clymene in the god's affections (204), as well as Rhodos and Perse (the latter Circe's mother).[19] These other loves of the sun are associated with ancient mythological lore, while Leuconoe gives Leucothoe a quite historical setting: she is the daughter of Orchamus, an Achaemenid Persian monarch and descendant of Belus (209-213). Significantly, Belus is also the name of Dido's father. This Persian princess also surpasses Clytie in the god's affections; this lover, like Leucothoe, is otherwise unknown in extant literature: Ovid may have juxtaposed two old and established amours with two women of his own invention. The mention of Clytie, as we shall see, anticipates the heart of the story Leuconoe is unveiling.

Sol disguises himself at night as Eurynome, the maiden's mother. He enters her chamber, where the princess is spinning with her handmaidens. The scene is a replica of the Minyades' devotion to Minerva; this is another eminently Roman setting.[20] Once the witnesses are dismissed, the god reveals his identity:

> in veram rediit speciem solitumque nitorem:
> at virgo quamvis inopino territa visu
> victa nitore dei posita vim passa querella est. (231-233)

> *He returned into his true form and his accustomed gleam;*
> *but the virgin, as if terrified by the unexpected sight*
> *was conquered by the god's gleam, and, complaint put aside, endured the rape.*

Venus' revenge has led to another divine rape. The violence is somewhat mitigated by the girl's lack of protest, which contrasts with similar previous scenes; Ovid observes that she was conquered by the god's splendor. But the girl was unwilling, as she herself pleadingly declares to her father once he learns of the liaison (4.238 *vim tulit invitae*). The story is spread abroad by the jealous Clytie, whose gossip evokes the stories that followed the tale of Sol's ill-fated son Phaethon. The god had reported a divine adultery; now the tattletale suffers an ironic end. Interestingly, Clytie spreads the story of Leucothoe's "adultery" (236 *adulterium*), a word that hearkens back to the sun's complaint about Venus and Mars (171 *adulterium*), though of course the word was appropriate: Venus was Vulcan's husband, while there is no indication that Leucothoe is married. The whole story of Sol's entry into the girl's chamber and discovery of the women spinning reminds us of the assault on Lucretia in early Roman lore; the outcome of the two stories is very different. Orchamus buries his daughter alive (239-240).[21] The sun tries in vain to save his beloved; his attempts fail and the girl is lost. The only recompense for the whole episode of rape and murder is the sun's decision to turn the body into a fragrant incense plant. (254-255 *virga . . . turea*). Clytie, his *quondam* lover, is at once abandoned. Leucothoe is also, conveniently, a Persian princess with an ancestor whose name reminds us of

Dido. Ovid thus distances himself from her plight, Roman setting notwithstanding.

Especially if we connect the sun and Apollo, we can see in the story of this mysterious Persian girl, Leucothoe, a definite decline in the god's behavior. His actions can only be called rape, notwithstanding the girl's admiration for his divine splendor. His *post mortem* commemoration of his lover seems insufficient compensation for her suffering. Venus, of course, can be blamed for the whole episode, and Ovid can claim that it is not Apollo, but merely the son of Hyperion, who shares in guilt for the girl's abuse and death. Clytie, for her part, wastes away into a heliotropic sunflower (4.259-270). As we have noted, the story may well be an Ovidian invention; certainly the sisters of Leuconoe do not know for sure what to think of it:

> dixerat, et factum mirabile ceperat auris;
> pars fieri potuisse negant, pars omnia veros
> posse deos memorant; sed non est Bacchus in illis. (4.271-273)

> *Thus she spoke, and a marvelous deed had captured their ears;*
> *some of them deny that such a thing was possible, while others recall*
> *that true gods can do all things; but Bacchus is not among them.*

It is almost as if some of the sisters are obstinately ruining the otherwise pious sentiment that true gods can do all things by inserting a denial of Bacchus' divinity; or, possibly, the poet means literally that the god Bacchus was not present: the sisters deny his existence, and they have shunned his company. If the story of Clytie were invented by the poet (in addition to Leucothoe's story), then the comment of the sisters takes on a special note of irony.

Leucothoe's name, however, is most significant for understanding Ovid's purpose in relating her story. She prefigures another Leucothoe we shall meet later in the book, when we come to the destruction of yet more of Cadmus' house. That Leucothoe will become the Roman *Mater Matuta*, a dawn goddess, thus offering a parallel to this solar amour. This "white goddess" represents a failure in divine intentions; Venus had instigated her destruction by her attack on Sol, and it will be Venus, as we shall see, who saves another Leucothoe and helps to ensure her divinity. It is as if Leuconoe's obscure (invented?) story is an aborted prelude to the later tale. Interestingly, of the three sisters' stories we might reasonably judge that the accounts of Pyramus and Thisbe and Salmacis and Hermaphroditus are the most successful; the loves of the sun are less unified, the narrative almost consciously less polished and memorable.

Alcithoe is the most scholarly of the Minyades, or at least she is the most ostentatiously interested in showing off her mythological learning to her sisters in competition. She will ultimately tell the story of Salmacis and Hermaphroditus, another tale of love gone awry that may well be an Ovidian invention.[22] Alcithoe will not tell of Daphnis, the shepherd who was turned into a stone by a jealous, spurned nymph (4.277-278); the *praeteritio* evokes the world of Virgil's fifth eclogue and its lament for Daphnis, though in Virgil there is no mention of the nymph and petrifaction. Sithon was once a man and now a woman; this story, also mysteriously unknown outside Ovid, will also be passed over. The other ignored stories include two additional flower metamorphoses (Crocas and Smilax), and the transformation of Jupiter's once faithful infant guardian Celmis into adamant.[23]

The story she does tell forms a ring with that of Mars and Venus. The love goddess had a son with another divine partner, Mercury; the infant, Hermaphroditus, was raised (like Jupiter) in Crete (4.288-291). Ovid will delay revealing the name of the boy until the story's end, when the etiology of hermaphroditism is made clear. Alcithoe signals that the story will be of ill repute by announcing that it provides the etiology for why Salmacis' fountain makes men weak. Like the story of Mars and Venus, this tale offers another embarrassing account of the results of divine affairs. The fifteen year-old Hermaphroditus travels to Lycian Caria in Asia Minor; there he finds a marvelous pool of pure water (297-301), what seems to be a true *locus amoenus*. Here, we meet one of Ovid's most memorable creations, a Diana-like nymph who defies all the conventions of that familiar type. The nymph Salmacis does not enjoy hunting; she is not interested in running or archery. She is, in fact, unique: the only Naiad who is not in Diana's retinue (304). No other extant poet portrayed this sort of anti-Diana nymph; as we shall see, virginity is not a virtue she guards zealously. She enjoys bathing in her pool and beautifying herself by the water's edge; contrary to the view of some, we need not necessarily see in these actions the desire of the nymph to attract some man; Salmacis is a narcissist, with qualities that recall another youth near a pool (312 *et, quid se deceat, spectatas consulit undas*). Narcissus was of ambiguous sexuality, and so too Hermaphroditus, who looks like both his divine parents and who is close to Narcissus in age (fifteen against sixteen).[24] Ovid has thus far defined the ages of only these two youths, both of whom have appearances that confirm the liminality of both male and female traits. When Salmacis sees this handsome boy-girl, so much like both his divine parents, she falls at once in love with no need for heavenly intervention to set the attraction in motion (315-316). In a nice touch that also evokes Narcissus (besides Crocas and Clytie), Salmacis was gathering flowers when first she caught sight of the youth.

If we compare the story now commencing with its predecessor, Pyramus and Thisbe, we see a marked decline in the honorable qualities we might seek in the lore. The first story had a heroic element of bravery, with a tragedy that was at least commemorated in the eternal love of a shared burial and etiological commemoration. The present story will also lead to a perpetual union, though of a couple that does not share a bond of mutual love and affection. The nymph and the son of two major divinities will create a scenario of infamy; any man who bathes in Salmacis' waters is destined to be enervated. Venus is the mother of

Hermaphroditus, but she engenders neither the love of Salmacis nor the affair between Pyramus and Thisbe (at least not explicitly). Her direct action comes between the two stories, in the affairs of the sun, where we see the love goddess caught in the very un-Roman act of adultery (especially for the Augustan regime). Discovery of the adultery leads the enraged goddess to attack the sun (Apollo?), who is then smitten with love for Leucothoe, a Persian princess who evokes Dido (cf. the mention of Belus, and perhaps even the matter of her alleged "adultery," so strange and inexplicable a charge to level against her given the loaded nature of the word to a Roman audience—are we to think of Dido's failure to remain an *univira* to Sychaeus' memory?). After the tragic results of Venus' attempt to avenge her embarrassment on the sun, we read the twisted tale of her offspring's strange dalliance with a nymph whose neglect of the deeds of Diana reminds us of Venus' playacting the huntress in Virgil's *Aeneid*. Salmacis, in her beautification and lazy relaxation at poolside, evokes the spirit of the capricious goddess of love. Alcithoe's story is something of an embarrassment in itself for Venus, in much the same way as Leuconoe's story targeted the goddess. In contrast, the admittedly tragic love of Pyramus and Thisbe shows forth something of the indomitable spirit of humanity freed from divine influence (except in the assent the gods give to Thisbe's dying prayers, itself a testimony to immortal admiration for the heroism and mutual devotion displayed by the two young lovers). In Homer Aphrodite and Hephaestus are essentially divorced after the discovery of her affair with Ares; Ovid does not bother to describe how or when she commenced an affair with Mercury.

If Salmacis had not sought to beautify herself for a man before, now Ovid makes clear that she tends to her appearance before approaching Hermaphroditus (4.317-318).[25] We have noted that Venus committed adultery with Mars, and that Leucothoe was accused of the same crime by her father. The adultery motif continues in a subtle way with Salmacis' address to Hermaphroditus. She showers the youth with praises of his appearance, wondering if this is Cupid in disguise (320-321). If he has siblings, she muses, they are blessed; more importantly, blessed in Salmacis' eyes is the woman who is married to this man. If Hermaphroditus is already married, so much the better for his spouse; if not, blessed will be his future bride. If a marriage already exists, Salmacis shockingly suggests, let there be a secret affair: 327 *haec tibi sive aliqua est, mea sit furtive voluptas.* Salmacis is suggesting to Hermaphroditus nothing that his mother would not herself consider doing. Her overtures embarrass the young man; he blushes in shame:

hic color aprica pendentibus arbore pomis
aut ebori tincto est aut sub candore rubenti,
cum frustra resonant aera auxiliaria, lunae. (4.331-333)

Here his color is like that of apples hanging on a sunny tree
or that of ivory that has been tinted or when bronze

calls for aid for the moon that is red under gleaming white.

Brilliantly, Ovid evokes the simile of Lavinia's blush at *Aeneid* 12.61 ff. (itself borrowed from Homer's image of blood on Menelaus' wounded thigh (*Iliad* 4.141-147).[26] In the Virgilian passage, Lavinia's mother Amata begged Turnus to cease combat, since he was the security of her old age; she announced that she would not tolerate Aeneas as a son-in-law. Lavinia blushes, aware that she is the cause of so much suffering; Turnus, for his part, urges Amata not to create such ill omens before he proceeds to single combat.

Hermaphroditus, that young man who could be mistaken for a girl, is shocked at the mention of love—let alone adultery. He is implicitly compared to the virginal Lavinia, the object of Aeneas' erotic conquest.[27] The moon in eclipse evokes the image of Diana, whom Salmacis has never honored; in the lunar eclipse we see a comment on Salmacis' rejection of Diana's lifestyle. That rejection has led to the inappropriate pursuit of the huntress for this young man. The ruddy apples ripen on the tree and cannot be reached at Sappho fr. 105a Lobel-Page; we might be reminded of Ovid's previous evocation of Catullus' cut flower imagery and the desirability and attractiveness of the unplucked flower. The blushing is also significant of the suitability of a youth for marriage; Hermaphroditus should be ready to consider love, though, as in the case of Narcissus with Echo, clearly the nymph Salmacis does not hold particular attraction for him. Lavinia blushes for complex reasons centered on her wish to retreat and not be the cause of war in Latium; in her, too, we may perceive a hesitation over marriage.

Hermaphroditus, despite his age and especially his divine parentage, is not only ignorant of adultery but also of love itself (4.330 *nescit enim quid amor*); his reaction to Salmacis' overtures is childish in its lack of sophistication, as he imagines that he can merely walk away and escape without further attempts from the lustful nymph. We do well to consider that it is strange for a son of Venus and Mercury to be so skittish about love at fifteen. Salmacis hides, watching as Hermaphroditus walks off; soon enough he enters the pool, stripping off his clothes to the delight of the maddened girl (340 ff.). The scene is reminiscent of Diana's bath and the invasion of Actaeon into her private world; this time, the nymph who should be hunting with the virgin goddess will invade the tranquil waters of her own sacred haunt.[28] We see how the *intermezzo* of the sun's involvement with Venus and its ill effects have paved the way for the move from the love of Pyramus and Thisbe to that of Salmacis for Hermaphroditus. The ultimate victory of Salmacis in the forthcoming narrative of her attempted rape of the scion of Venus and Mercury is something of an act of revenge on Venus. The goddess' son will be the unwilling victim of his pursuer's unwanted advances for all time.

Salmacis does not much favor running, but Hermaphroditus is swift as he enters the water (4.352 *velox*) and presents a beautiful image of a handsome swimmer:

desilit in latices alternaque bracchia ducens
in liquidis translucet aquis, ut eburnea si quis
signa tegat claro vel candida lilia vitro. (4.353-355)

He leapt into the waters, leading his arms in turn,
And he is translucent in the liquid waters, just as if someone
concealed ivory statues or white lilies in clear glass.

His skin, now blush-free, gleams like ivory.[29] The lily image reminds us of his feminine characteristics and evokes Narcissus' mother, the nymph Liriope ("Lily-Face"). Salmacis strips off her own clothes and jumps in the water; she now shows energy and zeal as she entwines her body with that of her object of passion (356-360). Echo, when repulsed by Narcissus, had discreetly receded away. Salmacis, for her part, is at last aggressive in the chase and pursuit of quarry; the girl who took no interest in the hunting of wild animals now dives after sexual congress with the hapless youth.

A strange set of similes describes Salmacis' action as she madly pursues union with Hermaphroditus:

inplicat ut serpens, quam regia sustinet ales
sublimemque rapit: pendens caput illa pedesque
adligat et cauda spatiantes inplicat alas;
utve solent hederae longos intexere truncos,
utque sub aequoribus deprensum polypus hostem
continet ex omni dimissis parte flagellis. (4.362-367)

She entwines him like a snake, which the royal bird lifts
and snatches aloft: hanging there, she wraps around his
head and feet and entwines her tail around his spreading wings;
or as ivy is accustomed to weave around long trunks,
and as under the waters the octopus holds a captured foe
with its whips sent out from every part.

The first simile defies initial expectation; we do not think the serpent will be the victim of rapture at the claws of the eagle. The serpent returns us to the theme of Cadmus and the dragon; the eagle is the bird of Jupiter. The simile is the first indication that Salmacis will win; she seemed to be defeated by Hermaphroditus' repulse, but she will conquer him and achieve union with her beloved. The contrast between the gentle action of ivy and the more violent attack of an octopus shows the alternation of moments of successful joining with Hermaphroditus' fitful escape attempts.[30] Salmacis tires of the youth's struggles; she calls him "wicked" (4.370 *inprobe*) for his resistance and prays that the gods may grant them an eternal, inextricable bond. Some deity or deities answer the prayer (373 *vota suos habuere deos*); the two bodies grow together into one, as if someone had grafted a branch on a tree (375-379). The result is a seemingly monstrous creature, neither female nor male, with characteristics of both in one body, so that *femina* and *puer* are no longer suitable words to describe the whole (379-380). The octopus is here to remind us of Salmacis' water victory.

The tale recalls Teiresias' experience of both sexes, as well as the ambiguities of gender inherent in the Echo and Narcissus story. More generally, we can note the violent amatory behavior of gods such as Jupiter and the effects of that violence: love on earth has been corrupted, just as it is corrupt on Olympus, where Venus is unfaithful to Vulcan and the supreme god has a near broken marriage. But the creation of this new being is not the end of Ovid's story. Hermaphroditus sees that he has changed; there is a seeming inconsistency here, since there is supposed to be one creature now and not two. Apparently the mind of each remains, though there is but one face (4.374-375 *facies . . . una*). Hermaphroditus prays that any man who enters this particular spring as he did might exit a *semivir*, a "half man"—the same word Latin would use for a eunuch (there is no proper noun in Latin for a hermaphrodite *per se* other than the character's name). Venus and Mars grant their son's prayer:

> motus uterque parens nati rata verba biformis
> fecit et incesto fontem medicamine tinxit. (4.387-388)
>
> *Either parent was moved, and they ratified the words of their*
> *biform son, and they tinged the spring with a perverse medicine.*

Incesto has strong textual support, though *incerto* is also well attested. The question is which adjective was corrupted into the other. The problem for modern critics is to decide whether or not Ovid is imputing moral turpitude to the hermaphrodite. It is interesting that the emphasis in Ovid is on the enervation of the male; there is no comment on the implicitly equal effect of the male on the female. There is no discussion of how Salmacis is now more masculine; she was already aggressive, to be sure, as she fulfilled a rôle we have come to associate with male gods. But her lavish attention to appearance confirms her gender; she is no mannish woman. Hermaphroditism, in Ovid's view, is about the creation of a *semivir*, not a *virago*. The first description of the metamorphosis presents a monster that is not identifiable as either gender. Hermaphroditus' prayer (Salmacis is seemingly nowhere) is the entreaty of an emasculated half-man. He bore the image of both his parents already before his transformation (290-291); there is a deplorable element, too, in his psyche: he prays that others may suffer his (clearly unwelcome) fate. The taunts of Iarbas and Numanus Remulus echo in the implicit criticism of the effeminate hermaphrodite; there is no place for this creature in Roman society except as an object of mockery. Again, we can see the decline from the (heterosexual) love of Pyramus and Thisbe, thus far arguably the most successful romantic couple in the epic, past the bad behavior of the unfaithful Venus, and lastly the bizarre birth of the hermaphrodite, a new creation whose continued propagation (however controlled) is approved by Venus and Mercury's contamination of Salmacis' pool.

Alcithoe had decided not to sing of Crocas' floral transformation; now crocuses and myrrh suddenly appear, together with the sound of loud Bacchic instruments (4.391 ff.). The stories are over, and, as with Pentheus, we might expect that the Minyades will be punished for their ignoring the rites of the new god. Vines appear everywhere with clusters of grapes; the color purple in the girls' tapestry (398) becomes a symbol yet again of imminent doom. Terrible images of savage wild animals once again appear to frighten the impious; the scene is one of real horror as the shadows of night begin to descend, the day far spent with spinning and stories. The Minyades are transformed into bats (407-415), while the voices that had spoken so long in weaving yarns are now reduced to pitiful squeaks as the Minyades begin to take flight on their new (though still mammalian) wings. The etiology of the bat's Latin name *vespertilio* is explained by the time of Bacchus' transformation of the blasphemous sisters: evening has come.[31]

The destruction of the Minyades follows at once on the story of the origin of the hermaphrodite. Parallels can be drawn between the aggression of a Salmacis and the violence of Bacchus' female worshippers, and especially between the *semivir* Hermaphroditus and Bacchus, who himself exhibited both male and female traits. The sisters are punished for their stories as much as for their refusal to worship the new god. At this juncture, with two extended accounts of the destruction of those who would deny Bacchus' divinity, the poet returns to Juno, the eminently Roman goddess who will now attack one of the last of Cadmus' line, Bacchus' aunt Ino.[32] The attack is of course really aimed at her enemy, her *hostis* (4.428)—the god Bacchus.

We have already met Ino, who was one of the women who helped to rip apart her relative Pentheus. Ino is now a veritable spokeswoman for the god as she tells of his great strength (4.417 *magnas vires*) that has, of course, been used principally to destroy those who would reject him. Juno is filled with rage. She considers Bacchus to be little more than the son of a whore (422 *de paelice natus*), and she recounts his destruction of the Etruscan pirates, Pentheus, and the Minyades. In Juno's view, the actions of Bacchus have illustrated well just what madness can accomplish: 429 *quidque furor valeat*. Therefore, Juno decides that Ino should be infected with madness (431 *furoribus*) and suffer the same pain other members of her family have already experienced.

Ovid now attempts to copy what Virgil did with Juno near the beginning of the seventh *Aeneid*. There, the goddess had decided that it was time to invoke hell in her assault on Aeneas and his Trojans. Bacchus and his family present the same sort of target for the goddess; she will summon infernal powers now to attack the god's aunt Ino. The Ovidian context is less serious than the Virgilian, though the ultimate target is greater; it is clear that Juno has little use for the new

god except, perversely, as an example of how to use madness to achieve an end
(readers of the *Aeneid* would recall that there the goddess needed no such help to
discover the benefits of fury). Ovid will here seemingly begin a version of the
Iliadic *Aeneid* as he recalls Juno's summoning of Allecto; later in the book, we
shall see the master poet create an *Aeneid* within an *Aeneid*.

For now, with a vengeance, we are thrust into a world we know well from
Virgil: Juno's rage and the horrors of the infernal regions where she will
summon aid, as once the Fury Allecto engendered a war in Italy and would
gladly have set the world ablaze, had not the great goddess checked her
madness.[33] Ovid's underworld offers numerous parallels and points of
comparison to Virgil's; the poet is conflating Juno's approach to Allecto with
the great underworld drama of *Aeneid* 6. Ovid's vision is of course syncopated;
he takes some thirty lines where Virgil had several hundred.[34] Ovid's hell is
thoroughly urbanized, which again injects the anachronistic Roman theme into
the epic: Ovid's city of Dis is a sepulchral *simulacrum* of Rome, complete with
a forum (4.444). There is no sort of clear division in Ovid's underworld between
Tartarus and Elysium, and, appropriately, Ovid spends most of his time
describing the usual inhabitants of the worst regions of hell: Tityos, Ixion, the
Danaids, and Sisyphus are all in their usual places of torment. Juno does not
spend any longer than she needs to in this place of criminal horror; she orders
Tisiphone and her fury sisters to assist in the overthrow of the house of Cadmus
and the mad destruction of Athamas, Ino's husband.[35] Ino will be ruined by the
madness of her husband; this punishment will be the fitting recompense for how
they have spurned Juno (468-469 *qui me cum coniuge semper / sprevit*): the
Theban couple has spent time on the worship of the new god Bacchus, and,
besides, Bacchic revelry is incompatible with Junonian reverence, given the
goddess' rage over her rival Semele and the divine offspring she conceived.[36]
Ironically, Athamas is the son of Aeolus (and brother of Sisyphus); Juno had
sought the help of the wind god in *Aeneid* 1, and now she seeks to destroy the
son of the god as part of her plot to ruin Ino.

Ovid also describes elements of the Ino story at *Fasti* 6.473 ff. (on which
see the extensive notes of Littlewood).[37] There, Ovid follows the
aforementioned account of how Ino and Athamas attracted Juno's fury for their
part in the safeguarding of the infant Bacchus; as we examine Ovid's account in
the *Metamorphoses*, we shall make comparison to his other (essentially
simultaneously composed?) version from his calendar poem. There was also a
version of the story in which Athamas came upon his wife in Bacchic revel on
Parnassus after having giving her up for dead (Hyginus, *Fabulae* 4); Ovid uses
two different accounts in his two renditions of the lore.[38]

Tisiphone drives Athamas and Ino mad (4.481-511).[39] The description of
her execution of her task is slow and deliberate, with the poet lavishing his skill
on a scene where he clearly feels no rush to advance his story. Part of the effect
Ovid creates here is a true evocation of the key events of *Aeneid* 7; Tisiphone's

epic assault on the Theban couple has been viewed by some as a veritable mockery or parody of Virgil's narrative, since Athamas and Ino are not anywhere near as important to the *Metamorphoses* as Amata, Turnus, and the rest are to Virgil's work. But this seemingly inappropriate contrast is precisely Ovid's point; there is no mockery here of his predecessor's epic, but rather deadly seriousness: the East, more specifically Phoenicia—the land of Dido's Carthage—has brought forth a blight on the world. There is great irony here, of course, since in Virgil Juno is the patroness of the Carthaginians. But she is also a lover of Italy, and the *Aeneid* is in part the epic of how she becomes the special patroness of the Romans. So by the "time" of Ovid's epic, Juno is firmly on the side of Rome, and the nascent settlement in Thebes—a child of Phoenicia—is hateful to her not only in light of future Roman history, but also, more immediately, because of the Jovian paramours involved in its foundation (Europa, Semele). The new god Bacchus is loathsome to Juno both for his origins as an illegitimate child of Jupiter and for his rather un-Roman association with the East and less than sober religious rites. Rather nicely, when Juno sees the Danaids in the underworld (463) they are called the *Belides*, the daughters of Belus, which reminds us of Dido. Ovid has followed in Virgil's steps by presenting a Juno who—in contrast to her Virgilian predecessor—is hostile to the children of Phoenicia precisely because she is already patroness of the Rome that (in Ovid's world) is yet to be founded, though its spirit already infuses the entire drama.

The extended Tisiphone passage is *hommage* to Virgil and response to the Allecto narrative; in both poets the focus is on the study of *furor* or madness. Madness personified (4.485 *Insania*) accompanies the Fury in the execution of her tasks (cf. 528 *insania*). The snakes that are an avatar of the Fury and instrument of her spreading of insanity prefigure the snakes of Medusa, and reflect the serpentine nature of the poet's Theban cycle: the children of the snake are here driven mad by infernal serpents.

Athamas is now insane thanks to the Fury's work; he sees Ino holding their little boy Learchus, whom he seizes and whirls around as if he were a sling. The boy ends up dashed against some rocks (4.516-519); Athamas thinks he is a hunter in pursuit of quarry, and that Ino is a wild animal. The hunting imagery of the Actaeon and Pentheus stories thus returns; Ino, for her part, is no less crazed than her husband. She invokes Bacchus in her madness, Ovid's point being that Juno has simply followed the example of the new god. Ino grabs her other son Melicertes and flees Athamas; Ovid notes that it was not clear whether she fled out of sorrow for the loss of Learchus or because she was insane anyway from the Fury's action (519 ff.). Ino prepares to throw herself and Melicertes off a nearby cliff into the ocean. At this point, Venus intervenes in the narrative, ready to set in motion the transformation of the mother and child into gods.[40]

In the *Fasti*, after being driven mad for taking care of the baby Dionysus, Athamas murders Learchus and Ino flees with Melicertes. As in the *Metamorphoses*, the Theban woman throws herself over the edge with the child, but here the story changes direction dramatically. Ino is conveyed by nymphs all the way to the Tiber, where she encounters maenads who are stirred on by Juno to abduct Melicertes. In desperate need for help, Ino calls on the aid of Hercules, who just happens to be wandering by on his way back from Spain. Hercules frightens off the maenads, and Ino is received by Evander's mother, the prophetic nymph Carmentis, who announces the transformation of Ino and her son into marine deities. Ino is now known to the Romans as *Mater Matuta*, a dawn goddess. In striking contrast to the practice of Bacchic cult, serving women are barred from participation in her rites. The etiology for their exclusion is that a servant girl became Athamas' mistress and told lies about Ino.[41] Women pray to Ino for the children of others and not their own, since the goddess was a better aunt than mother. As Littlewood notes ad 6.525-526, in the Ino of the *Fasti* there is the calm and reverential demeanor of someone who is about to be transformed into a Roman goddess.[42]

A very different version is presented in the *Metamorphoses*. First, it is Venus who intervenes to save Ino and Melicertes. Here again Virgil lurks, and powerfully. Juno and Venus have opposing goals in the *Aeneid*, and here Venus acts to check the power of her enemy; the goddess' intervention is original to Ovid and fits his Virgilian theme. As she had done to save Aeneas from any further trouble on the sea voyage from Sicily to Italy, so now she invokes her uncle Neptune. Ino is her granddaughter, and, in the goddess' eyes at least, undeserving of her fate (4.531 *inmeritae neptis miserata labores*). Venus is specific in her request: she wishes mother and son to be changed into sea gods. Neptune agrees, and Leucothoe and Palaemon are added to the album of marine divinities. Venus' instruction to Neptune contrasts greatly with her similar invocation of Neptune in *Aeneid* 5 to protect the Trojan fleet, which led to the sacrifice of the helmsman Palinurus.

Venus' salvation of Ino and Melicertes also provides compensation for the story of the sun's infatuation with a woman of the same name as the new sea goddess, Leucothoe. Venus had punished the sun for his spreading abroad the story of her illicit involvement with Mars; an innocent girl had been killed in the process, much to the general shame of the immortals and their reputation. Now, in saving Cadmus' daughter from drowning, Venus makes the name "Leucothoe" known for the Greek sea goddess rather than the Persian princess.

Juno has been challenged; she retaliates against Ino's female Theban companions, who are ignorant of the fortunate fate of their friend and assume she has been lost at sea (4.543 ff.). Their grief reaches dangerous levels when they declare that Juno was unjust in her persecution of Ino; Juno rather predictably decides to turn them into monuments of her wrath (547 *saevae*, 550 *saevitiae*). The story of the transformations is probably not original to Ovid (see further Bömer ad loc.), though we have no narrative other than his. One of the women is exceptional in her *pietas* (551 *quae praecipue fuerat pia*); she is about to hurl herself into the water after Ino when Juno effects her petrification—we see a brief nod here to Juno's persecution of the *pius* Aeneas. Three more women are similarly turned into statues (554-559). Still others are turned into birds that skim the waters where Ino and Melicertes fell, probably some sort of gulls.

Juno's vengeance may seem insignificant in comparison to the new gods who grace the Greek (and Roman) pantheons, but the great Theban cycle now advances to its close with the fate of Cadmus, its progenitor (4.563 ff.). Under the heading "the Cadmeian victory," the monumental *Suda* records that Cadmus spent eight years laboring for Ares after his defeat of the god's dragon. In Ovid, the hero and his wife are now described as world-weary and tired on account of the long series of tragedies their house has known; interestingly, there is no hint of pride or rejoicing in the fact that a new god originated from their line. The old couple flees into self-imposed exile, where at last Cadmus reflects on his now seemingly ancient combat with the serpent. Rather oddly, he wonders if the snake had been sacred to a god (571 *num sacer ille*); it is as if he has forgotten the prophecy of his own serpentine transformation. He prays that if the trouble that has assailed his line relentlessly is due to his actions then, that he himself might atone for the offense now by being changed into a serpent. His "request" is at once granted, and Ovid indulges in a somewhat pathetic scene as Cadmus bids his wife to say farewell to the nascent serpent. She begs the immortals to allow her to share her husband's form; her wish finds fulfillment. The two new snakes slither off together, and, mindful of their original form, they do not harm mortals (602-603). We might think of the mysterious snake that appeared on the grave of Anchises when Aeneas visited Sicily for the memorial games the year after his father's death (*Aeneid* 5.84-93); that snake likely portended no ill but rather the powerful presence of the shade of the hero's father. For a Trojan audience, the snake at Anchises' tomb compensates for the baleful image of the serpents that had devoured Laocoon and his sons. Further, the presence of the snaky head of the Gorgon on Minerva's aegis shield allies the serpentine image with the Roman war goddess.

The end of Cadmus and Harmonia has some reminiscence of the theme we have seen with Pyramus and Thisbe and (though very differently) Salmacis and Hermaphroditus: eternal togetherness. No explanation is given for why the Theban progenitor should have experienced this metamorphosis, which is not described in particularly dark or chilling language. Ares had once harbored a Boeotian serpent that brought death; now, on the very borders of Illyria (4.568), Cadmus and his wife present the spectacle of friendly snakes. The transformation is not entirely welcome, though, in the sense that the new snakes are described as finding solace for their changed form (604 *versae solacia formae*) in the fate of their grandson Bacchus, whom suddenly they seem to remember. India has been thoroughly conquered (605-606 *debellata . . . India*) and worships the god; Greece is filled with his temples. The commentators have done well to note here that temples to Bacchus/Liber/Dionysus in Greece and Rome were in reality rather rare; Ovid imagines a Greece thronged with such structures. The mention of India, as we have seen before, carries an echo of the Augustan propaganda dream of a world under Roman sway (even if the actual foreign policies of the regime were rather more restrained and intelligent). The real cult of Bacchus, especially in Rome, was of a rather more controlled nature than Ovid might have us think; the point seems to be to underscore the god's triumph—he is an accepted part of the Olympian pantheon—and to defy expectation by remaining fixed on the topic of the disputes that continue to hound the god as his cult advances. A distant cousin of Cadmus, one Acrisius, denies Bacchus' Jovian divinity and keeps his worship out of Argos. Besides this blasphemy, Acrisius also denies that his daughter Danae conceived Perseus in union with Jupiter.[43] Thus begins the next movement of the book, and its last: the drama of Perseus. This epic story will continue into *Metamorphoses 5*, ostensibly as part of the continuing saga of the denial of Bacchus' divinity.[44]

The Perseus saga is part of the legendary history of Argos. With Bacchus, we have moved beyond the borders of Thebes and into a new tradition, though one firmly linked to the Theban cycle by the theme of denial of divinity. The story opens *in medias res*, a signal to the audience that this is another of the poem's miniature epics; like the Phaethon narrative, it will straddle two books. Perseus has already slain Medusa and is in flight over Libya, where drops of the Gorgon's blood fall and engender all manner of serpents (4.617-620). The passage links to the serpentine nature of Cadmus' transformation, but also looks forward to the baleful history of a north Africa that will be associated with Carthage (and even, in Ovid's future, the snake-infested Libya of Lucan's terrible vision). Besides Ovid's extended treatment, the Perseus and Andromeda story will figure in the *Astronomica* of Manilius (5.538-630).[45]

In Virgil, the wrath of Juno and fury of Allecto had inaugurated war in Italy. In Ovid, Juno's wrath has had mixed consequences for the house of Cadmus and, just as Aeneas was ultimately immune from Juno's assaults, so Bacchus now reigns without effective opposition. In Ovid's vision, Cadmus and Acrisius are related; both are descendants of Agenor (more or less), since Acrisius can trace his lineage back to Agenor's brother Belus. Arguably, the Perseus story is thus part of the Theban cycle for Ovid, though the poet has rather artificially pushed the family connection a bit far for his purpose. Besides the fact that a veritable universal history of myth would have had to include Perseus lore, Ovid wants to present another son of Jupiter to contrast with Bacchus. There will be much to admire in the heroic and romantic exploits of this young man, and also a conclusion to the Virgilian story that Ovid inaugurated with the wrath of Juno and summoning of the Fury Tisiphone: Perseus will evoke Aeneas in his erotic rivalry with Turnus, so that the conclusion of the Perseus narrative in *Metamorphoses* 5 will also be the end of an extended Ovidian treatment of Virgil's Iliadic *Aeneid*. This conclusion will allow the poet to forge a new beginning for an epic that might seem in danger of becoming unwieldy in its arguably ramshackle construction.

Thus far in the *Metamorphoses*, human love has positively contrasted with divine peccadilloes in the story of Pyramus and Thisbe, the only purely mortal story we have seen thus far, and a romantic tragedy that celebrates the heroic devotion of lovers. The Perseus story is the first that combines romance and the erotic theme with heroic endeavor. Cadmus had been a city founder and slayer of a monstrous serpent; he was not depicted, however, as a romantic hero. His (very) distant relative Perseus will be the epic's first "complete" hero, and as such he echoes certain aspects of Virgil's Aeneas, the putative prototype for a hero in the Roman epic tradition. And, indeed, when first we meet Ovid's Perseus, the hero is being tossed about hither and thither by discordant winds in a clear evocation of the beginning of the *Aeneid* (with its own *in medias res* opening). Perseus is alone as he alights far in the west, indeed at the very edges of the known world. Were he Aeneas, he would have gone too far in his quest for Hesperia; the Hesperia Perseus finds is the region of Atlas in the far west (4.628 *constitit Hesperio, regnis Atlantis, in orbe*). It is not at all clear in Ovid's narrative why the hero is this far west; if the Gorgon is envisaged as living beyond the River Ocean, then Atlas would logically be encountered on the way out to meet her; Perseus has been buffeted by the winds, and so Ovid creates a geographical disorientation for the hero and us.

The story of Perseus' petrifaction of Atlas is not well attested outside Ovid.[46] Ovid's version has affinities with the poet's narrative of Cadmus' early story; a dragon guards an orchard where Atlas has a tree of golden leaves and golden fruit (the motifs are clearly borrowed from lore about the golden apples of the Hesperides, and we may be meant to imagine that the famous apples are exactly what Atlas is zealously guarding here). Atlas had been warned that a son of Jupiter would deprive him of his gold, and so he tries to ward off the flying hero, noting (in line with a now familiar theme) that Perseus is a liar: Perseus' deeds are not glorious and (implicitly) Jupiter could not be his father (649-650 *gloria rerum. / quam mentiris*). Perseus had boasted of his Jovian birth and his great deeds, though he had not enunciated the latter in any detail. Ovid emphasizes the rather obscure account of Atlas' petrifaction (the first story in his *Perseid*) to highlight the hero's part in affirming the Jovian order.

Perseus is calm and reasonable; he tries to persuade Atlas with calm words (4.652 *cunctantem et placidis miscentem fortia dictis*). The adjective *cunctantem*, "hesitating," is of great significance in the *Aeneid*; here, it well reflects what Anderson considers the eminently Roman behavior of a Perseus replete with *gravitas*. Atlas is converted into a mountain of immense size once Perseus is finally forced to resort to Medusa's head to ensure victory over the Titan. In a significant detail, the petrifaction had been decreed by the gods (661 *sic, di, statuistis*). The heavens now rest not on the shoulders of some possibly rebellious giant who might seek to renew the terrible days of the titanomachy, but on the firm foundation of quite solid (and expansive) rock. Perseus is a Jovian hero in the tradition of those who bring order and restore peace. There are parallels, to be sure, to the attempt of Bacchus to reason with Pentheus through the story of Acoetes. But Perseus did not attempt to bring some new religion to the remote west; he merely requested rest and hospitality. Ovid emphasizes the rude and inconsiderate reception afforded the weary hero by Atlas from one who was merely seeking the due of any wayfarer, especially one of noble lineage and deeds (639 *hospes*, 642 *hospitium*). There are shades of Odysseus here, too, which will continue to appear in the Perseus narrative as it unfolds. The contrast with Bacchus is greater than any structural or superficial similarity.

Significantly, once the victory is won Aeolus' winds subside (663); the hero is free to continue on his journey (which we may perhaps localize in Africa, at the site of the modern Atlas mountains; Perseus will now travel east against the sun to the land of Ethiopia).[47] If Cadmus was an imperfect and unacceptable evocation of the Aeneas image, Perseus is a vast improvement. Indeed, we can see in Perseus a positive effect of the Junonian intervention that thrust us into a restaging of the erotic world of the second half of the *Aeneid*; far from a fallacious *post hoc* argument, such a reading fits Ovid's elaborate attempts to link Perseus' story with the fall of the Theban house: this hero represents an improvement over the past. With Juno's destruction of Athamas and Ino— notwithstanding the Venusian apotheosis of the latter and her son—an *Argive* hero (from Juno's beloved Argos) now captures our attention in a way no minor sea deity can. And, significantly, no Venus or Cupid is necessary to initiate the forthcoming tale of love.

The hero finds Andromeda awaiting the unjust penalty of sacrifice because of her mother's crime.[48] Manilius describes a bit more of the background of the circumstances (*Astronomica* 5.538 ff.).[49] Neptune sent a flood to destroy the land of Cepheus and Cassiopeia because of the queen's sin; at Aratus, *Phaenomena* 657 ff. we find her boasting that she was more beautiful than the Nereids (the version Ovid will follow), while Hyginus (*Fabulae* 64) has her boasting of her daughter's beauty. Perseus sees Andromeda chained to a rock, left to await slaughter at the hands of a sea monster. At first he thinks she is a statue, though soon enough he sees the breezes play with her hair and the tears on her frightened face (4.672 ff.). He is smitten with love, and, in striking contrast to the actions of Cupid and Venus with Dido in *Aeneid* 1 or any of several similar scenes in the present poem, there is no divine cause for his love: this is another purely mortal affection. Perseus is "snatched by the image of her beauty" (676 *correptus imagine formae*). The same phrase was used at 3.416 to describe Narcissus' infatuation with his mirror image. The outcomes of the two stories are very different, and comparisons are difficult; it is possible (though I think unlikely) that Ovid did not mean to recall the former story. Part of the point may be the apparent unattainability of both loves; Narcissus cannot win his mirror image from outside the waters, and Perseus is in love with a condemned victim of divine wrath, chained to a rocky crag to await her devouring. This time, however, heroism will win the day; Perseus suffers a moment not dissimilar to Narcissus' plight as he freezes in midair and nearly forgets to beat his wings (677).

The rehabilitation of questionable happenings from past stories now continues. Venus and Mars had been caught in the chains her husband Vulcan forged as proof of infidelity; now Perseus prays that he and Andromeda might be joined in chains (implicitly, nuptial ones). Perseus asks Andromeda who she is and why she is in her present predicament; with a modesty befitting some Roman *virgo*, the girl is described as ready to hide her face if she could but move her hands (4.681-683). Her eventual confession comes only so she might not appear to be guilty of some crime. Here we have nobility that in its heroism surpasses even the respectful love of Pyramus and Thisbe; this son of Jupiter has learned something of manners. The modest girl is not even compelled to speak for long; soon enough the monster appears.[50]

Perseus is described as a *hospes* (4.695) as he addresses Cepheus and Cassiopeia. The emphasis is once again on his status as a guest-friend; once again, he has affinities with Aeneas. Here again he seeks reception and recompense for labor; the story is well known. Perseus is brief (the monster, after all, is looming large and close): he should be preferred to all because of his past achievements and his present promise to save the girl from certain death; rather piously, he makes his promises with a note of *dis volentibus* (702 *faveant modo numina*).

We are immersed, then, in a miniature *Aeneid* within an *Aeneid*. In Virgil's world, now that the hero has been promised the maiden, the time would come for civil strife and rivalry and the injection of furious madness from Juno's hellish consultations. That episode has already come; here, the maiden is—unlike Virgil's Lavinia—in immediate danger. No other suitor has made himself known to challenge Perseus (excluding the terrible perversion of courtship embodied in the sea monster). And so, at once, the epic combat begins.

A magnificent simile describes Perseus' attack on the beast:

utque Iovis praepes, vacuo cum vidit in arvo
praebentem Phoebo liventia terga draconem,
occupat aversum, neu saeva retorqueat ora,
squamigeris avidos figit cervicibus ungues,
sic celeri missus praeceps per inane volatu
terga ferae pressit dextroque frementis in armo
Inachides[51] ferrum curvo tenus abdidit hamo. (4.714-720)

And as the bird of Jove, when in an empty field it spies

a serpent offering its mottled back to Phoebus,
attacks from behind, lest the beast twist back its savage mouth,
and it fixes its greedy talons in the scale-bearing neck,
so, sent headlong through the void in swift flight
the son of Inachus pressed down on the back of the beast and
buried his sword up to the curved hook in the right shoulder of the seething
   beast.

The eagle is the bird of Jupiter; Perseus is like an eagle in that he is presently a winged son of the god. The simile recalls the image of the eagle and the serpent that marked the watery combat of Salmacis and Hermaphroditus; yet another image from the less glorious part of the book has been reintroduced into a new and more honorable context.[52] Similarly, the dying sea monster is compared to a wild boar surrounded by hunting hounds (4.722-723); the Theban women who slaughtered their son and nephew Pentheus imagined him to be a wild boar: once again, Ovid rehabilitates a dark image from his recent narrative. That slaughter had been impious and indeed beyond all conventions of morality; this slaughter will save a princess who had been unjustly condemned from death at the hands of a beast that engenders no sympathy whatsoever from the audience. Perseus is a skilled warrior; as he combats the beast at close quarters, the bloody water and sea foam begin to weigh down his winged sandals, and so he seeks refuge on a convenient nearby rock to finish off his slaughter of the beast (730-734). In his defeat of the sea monster Perseus also presents a new image of heroism: Jovian-born and thus an exemplar of the Olympian order against primeval chaos (cf. his defeat of the defiant Atlas, whose custody of the globe on his shoulders represented an ever present threat to the world's stability). But Perseus is no inheritor of his father's propensity to violent infidelity; he seeks monogamous, marital union with Andromeda.

The shout of congratulations that rises up from the shore reaches the homes of the gods; in Perseus we see a figure not unlike Apollo in his triumph over the Python, a victory that had been described but briefly and without embellishment. We have seen nothing of the sort of heroism Perseus' actions reveal; he has traveled like Odysseus and sought a maiden's hand in marriage like Aeneas. In contrast with both of those heroes, he has succeeded in single combat with a portentous beast. In the imminent union of Perseus and Andromeda the audience witnesses the first seemingly unmitigated success in mortal amours; it is as if the pattern of decline we had noticed has been arrested by the Junonian intervention. Or, we might note that while divine amours have illustrated the dark side of love, the stories of Pyramus and Thisbe and now Perseus and Andromeda have shown the finest aspects of erotic love. And, significantly, the gods have largely been absent from both amatory adventures. Juno, a traditional patroness of marriage besides devoted lover of Argos, lurks in the background.[53]

In order to wash his hands more easily, Perseus puts down the Gorgon head. He takes special care with it to avoid damage; the head will play its part in the unfolding of the rest of the narrative of this Argive hero and his new bride. In the meantime, nymphs are entertained by how the head turns twigs into stone; the etiology is thus provided for the existence of Mediterranean coral (4.741-752). The scene is playful and deliberately comical; the twigs seem to acquire their own petrifaction properties and spread the stone in harmless fun from branch to branch under the carefree direction of the nymphs; it is as if they are celebrating the wedding with harmless magic entertainment that does serve to remind us of Perseus' deadly weapon that has already neutralized a Titan.

Juno is absent from the triple altars the hero erects to commemorate his victory (4.753 ff.). Mercury and Minerva are especially honored because in the tradition they had assisted Perseus with such vital accoutrements as his winged sandals; Minerva of course has a special association with the Gorgon head. Jupiter must be included as Perseus' father; it is noteworthy that Juno does not harass this Argive son of her husband. Perseus had been promised the kingdom in addition to the girl; the hero accepts her now without further dowry (758 *indotata*); he is seemingly without fault. And there has been, as yet, no hint in Ovid's narrative of any challenge to Perseus' claim over Andromeda; nothing like the drama of the seventh *Aeneid* has asserted itself to announce a coming struggle over the maiden's hand.

We can anticipate that now, with a marriage banquet and celebration in full vigor, the poet will finally describe the previous adventures of the hero in first person narrative, in imitation of the great banquet at Dido's palace in *Aeneid* 2-3. The rest of the book, only some forty lines, will proceed to the story of Perseus' slaying of the Gorgon—less time than was spent on the combat with the sea monster. Ovid's point in this syncopation of what was arguably the most famous story associated with Perseus is to hasten on to the main theme of his miniature *Aeneid*, the forthcoming rivalry between Perseus and Phineus for the hand of Andromeda. The audience has not been made to expect such a shift in action; for now, in the richly appointed palace of Cepheus, we anticipate nothing more or less than a magnificent epyllion on the death of Medusa. Perseus, however, will seem strangely reticent about his conquests.[54] The death of Medusa will be described with (for Ovid) uncharacteristic brevity.

The story begins with the daughters of Phorcys, the great sea god who was father of both the Gorgons and the Graiae, the grey-eyed sisters with whom Perseus begins his story.[55] The Graiae share a single eye between them, which Perseus proceeds to steal.[56] The Perseus narrative had opened *in medias res*, and now, just as with Aeneas' story to Dido's banquet assembly, the background to the saving of Andromeda is also described *in medias res*. The eye is apparently necessary for Perseus to find the sisters of the Graiae, the fearsome Gorgons. There is no hint in Perseus' exceedingly abbreviated speech as to why he in pursuit of Medusa's head.[57] There is, in fact, no mention in the hero's speech of his origins beyond the briefest of nods to Jupiter and Danae; the hospitality

theme Ovid weaves in through his *Perseid* demands that Perseus seem to be a
hero in search of a home and family.

In Hesiod (*Theogony* 270 ff.), the Gorgons are three in number: the
immortal Sthenno and Euryale, and the all too mortal Medusa. Hesiod knows the
story of Perseus' decapitation of Medusa; in his account the three Gorgons are
apparently all beautiful. Chrysaor and the famous steed Pegasus are born from
Medusa's blood.[58] Hesiod's passage also records the tradition that Poseidon
slept with Medusa. The tradition of the birth of Chrysaor and Pegasus is briefly
mentioned by Perseus (the former offspring left unnamed) at 4.785-786. Indeed,
the whole story is so brief that when Perseus rather unexpectedly seems to be
finished, one of the dinner companions asks for more, specifically, why Medusa
was the only Gorgon who had serpentine locks. Now Perseus tells the tale of her
transformation from beautiful young woman to petrifying monstrosity.
Neptune's rape of Medusa was not in some flower field (as in Hesiod), but in a
temple of the virgin warrior Minerva. The goddess avenged the defilement of
her shrine by punishing Medusa with the destruction of her fetching looks.[59]

When Minerva had seen the sexual union of Neptune and Medusa in her
temple, she averted her eyes and hid them behind her aegis. The fourth book
closes with an authorial comment that Minerva now bears the head of the
Gorgon on the same aegis shield.[60] The tradition that Medusa may have dared to
compare her looks with the goddess' provides an ironic twist to the final
mounting of the Gorgon head on the aegis; the goddess' fearsome battle avatar
will now be the transformed head of the woman who had dared to challenge the
goddess' precedence in loveliness. The more widely disseminated story of the
violation of Minerva's temple by sexual congress also underscores the goddess'
perpetual virginity and devotion to the same zealous defense of sexual purity
that has been familiar to us from the Diana myths of Callisto and Actaeon;
unlike that isolated goddess, Minerva is a very public goddess of war and
patroness of Athens; the mention of the aegis at the end of Book 4 is preface to
the goddess' important part in the drama soon to unfold, as Ovid advances his
transformational history of the world.

Book 4 thus ends with another briefly told element of the Medusa story; we
have moved backwards through the history of her doom and Perseus' victory.
The last word of this book is *angues*, the "snake," precisely to recall the start of
the whole Theban cycle and the appearance of the dragon snake that had slain
Cadmus' men and become the symbol of the new people of Thebes (especially
the *Spartoi*). Perseus' defeat of the Gorgon (with her snake tresses) is the final
defeat of the threatening image that had marred so much recent history; it
hearkens back to Apollo's defeat of the Python at the beginning of another new
world in the wake of the deluge. Minerva's twin serpents slew Laocoon and his
sons in the second *Aeneid*; this new hero will defeat the serpent, as it were, and
give over its head to Minerva as a trophy of his victory. The serpentine Salmacis
had subdued Hermaphroditus (who could but aspire to be a mere *simulacrum* of

a true bird of Jupiter); the eagle Perseus, the god's own son, has defeated the real serpent, Medusa. In the heroic exploits of Perseus there is ultimately a rehabilitation (at least partial) of Jupiter.

As with the previous book, we are left with a sense of closure and no clear idea of what will follow. Ovid will now surprise us with a return to the theme of the *Aeneid* (not to mention the homecoming of Odysseus to Ithaca), as Perseus is forced to do battle in a dining hall for the hand of Andromeda. Perseus will continue to prove himself the greatest mortal hero the world has yet seen, as he fights an epic battle to secure his bride. From the embarrassing and often deplorable behavior of the immortals, a new heroic world would seem to have taken shape, an age of heroes that distantly presages Rome. It is as if the world has been reborn in a new and better age. Soon, though, the goddess of the Medusan aegis will take rest with the Muses on Helicon and, with those nine daughters of Memory, she will take stock, as it were, of the new world. Since this is Ovid, that period of reflection will consist of more stories. Through them we shall travel yet again to hell, as we see another world unravel.

Notes

1. The standard commentary on this book and the next is Bömer, *P. Ovidius Naso Metamorphosen: Kommentar, Buch. IV-V*, Heidelberg, 1976. These two books are also well served by the comprehensive commentaries on the entire poem in other series.

2. Virgil had said that the second half of his epic was the greater work, and it was dedicated to Erato with an implicitly erotic theme; Ovid has picked up where his predecessor left off.

3. On the daughters of Minyas see Janan, Micaela, *"There Beneath the Roman Ruin Where the Purple Flowers Grow*: Ovid's Minyades and the Feminine Imagination," in *The American Journal of Philology* 115 (1994), pp. 427-448.

4. Lycurgus' story is very old; at Homer, *Iliad* 6.129 ff., the Thracian attacks Dionysus' band of nurses and is struck blind by Zeus. Aeschylus staged the story; at Pseudo-Apollodorus 3.34-35 we read that in a fit of madness Lycurgus chopped up his son and was eventually killed by his own horses after his people had bound him on Mount Pangaion in obedience to an oracle of Apollo. Diodorus Siculus 5.50.1-6 has a lengthy account of the impiety of Lycurgus and his Boread brother Boutes; in this version Lycurgus is struck mad after trying to rape the Bacchant Coronis, and throws himself into a well. Hyginus (*Fabulae* 132) has the terrible account of a mad Lycurgus seeking to rape his mother before killing his wife and son and throwing himself to a panther. Virgil once mentions the fierce Thracian king (*Aeneid* 3.13, with no hint of the Bacchic stories).

5. Bacchus' aunt Ino will engage in her own celebration of the god's achievements later in the poem, though to her ultimate doom at the hands of Juno; see further Leigh, Matthew, "Two Notes on Ovid," in *The Classical Quarterly* N. S. 50.1 (2000), pp. 311-313.

6. Ovid did not invent his general account of these dutiful spinners, though as usual he has manipulated his material. Antoninus Liberalis 10 reports that Nicander and Corinna told the story of how Bacchus tried to convince the Minyades to worship him; the god appeared as a maiden and failed in the attempt. Bacchus drove the women mad by changing into a bull, a lion, and a leopard; one of the women killed her son, tearing him to pieces with her sisters' help. Eventually the women went abroad as crazed Bacchants, until Hermes changed them into (respectively) a bat (cf. Ovid's story), an owl, and an eagle owl. Aelian, *Varia Historia* 3.42 tells a similar story, which was also known to Plutarch (*Quaestiones Graecae* 38). Aeschylus almost certainly treated it as well.

7. On these Babylonian stories note Perdrizet, P., "Légendes babyloniennes dans les Métamorphoses d'Ovide," in *RHR* 105 (1932), pp. 193-228.

8. The afterlife of this extraordinarily enduring story is an amazing example of the power of Ovid's verse; its ample *Nachleben* makes up in a sense for our complete ignorance of its *Vorleben*. Shakespeare was deeply struck by it; the story was retold in an Old French poem of over nine hundred lines that the author of the *Ovide moralisé* simply took over whole cloth for his "translation" of Ovid. The bibliography is predictably lengthy; note especially Duke, T. T., "Ovid's Pyramus and Thisbe," in *The Classical Journal* 66.4 (1971), pp. 320-327, Schmitt-von Mühlenfels, F., *Pyramus und Thisbe: Rezeptionstypen eines ovidischen Stoffes in Literatur, Kunst, und Musik*, Heidelberg, 1972 (with illustrations), Dooren, F. van, "De logische vertelstructur van Ovidius' Pyramus en Thisbe (*Met.* 4, 55-166), in *Lampas* 19 (1977), pp. 143-150, Perraud, Louis

A., "Amatores Exclusi: Apostrophe and Separation in the Pyramus and Thisbe Episode," in *The Classical Journal* 79.2 (1983-1984), pp. 135-139, Glendinning, Robert, "'Pyramus and Thisbe' in the Medieval Classroom," in *Speculum* 61.1 (1986), pp. 51-78, Holzberg, Niklas, "Ovids *Babyloniaka* (*Met* 4, 55-166) in *WS* 101 (1988), pp. 265-277, Knox, Peter E., "Pyramus and Thisbe in Cyprus," in *Harvard Studies in Classical Philology* 92 (1989), pp. 315-328, Gaillard, Jacques, "Le sang de Pyrame," in *CEA* 33 (1997), pp. 109-118, Keith, A. M., "Etymological Wordplay in Ovid's 'Pyramus and Thisbe' (*Met.* 4.55-166)," in *The Classical Quarterly* N.S. 51.1 (2001), pp. 309-312, and Shorrock, Robert, "Ovidian Plumbing in *Metamorphoses* 4," in *The Classical Quarterly* N. S. 53.2 (2003), pp. 624-627. The story of Pyramus and Thisbe was enormously influential on Chrétien de Troyes, who used many of its motifs to great effect in his story of Yvain and the lion in the *Chevalier au lion*.

9. We can be sure that Ovid did not invent the story of these young Babylonian lovers, but his sources are shrouded in obscurity. Later Latin authors did not much intrude on a story Ovid had told so well; note Hyginus, *Fabulae* 242, and otherwise very paltry evidence indeed. Echo was a nymph; Pyramus and Thisbe are all too human.

10. For the view that Ovid deliberately exaggerates the "lachrymose aspects" of the Pyramus and Thisbe story so as to avoid empathizing with his characters, see Galinsky, *op. cit.*, p. 128. The matter is one of subjective impressions and cannot be settled definitively.

11. Hyginus, *Fabulae* 240; at f. 223, Hyginus speaks of the same wall around Semiramis' Babylon that Ovid notes (4.57-58), while at f. 243 he mentions the suicide of both Thisbe and Semiramis, who threw herself onto a pyre when her horse was lost.

12. See Newlands, C. E., "The Simile of the Fractured Pipe in Ovid's *Metamorphoses* 4," in *Ramus* 15 (1986), pp. 143-153.

13. For a consideration of this simile as an example of the "aestheticization" of violent, gory death see Hardie, Philip, "Ovid and Early Imperial Literature," in Hardie, P., ed., *The Cambridge Companion to Ovid*, Cambridge, 2002, pp. 41-42. The Augustan poets usually make more of the aestheticism of gruesome female deaths; cf. Virgil's Camilla.

14. For good analysis of Ovid's brilliant play with *mora*, the "mulberry," and the Latin for "delay" and indeed "Rome," see Keith, *op. cit.*, p. 310 n. 11 (with good bibliography on Ovidian etymological wordplay).

15. On the name see further Carrubba, Robert W., and Fratantuono, Lee M., "Apollo and Leuconoe in Horace c. 1.11," in *Quaderni Urbinati di Cultura Classica* 74.2 (2003), pp. 133-136.

16. As we have noted, strictly speaking we are dealing with Helios/Sol, not Apollo (cf. 4.192 *Hyperione nate*), though the associations of Apollo with the sun, and the god's overall importance to the Augustan regime, compel us to think of the divine twin when we read solar lore. The deflection, however, from Apollo to Sol does allow the poet to disclaim Apollonian responsibility for the god's actions should it suit him.

17. For a good survey of the actions of the love deities in the epic, note Stephens, Wade C., "Cupid and Venus in Ovid's *Metamorphoses*," in *Transactions of the American Philological Association* 89 (1958), pp. 286-300.

18. As with Pyramus and Thisbe, Leucothoe's union with the sun is not well attested; she may be an Ovidian invention. Hyginus (*Fabulae* 14) names Thersanon as their offspring. On this vexed passage note Mantero, T., "Una crux nella narrativa

iginiana e l'ignoto figlio di Leucothoe," in *La struttura della fabulzione antica*, Sassari: Gallizi, 1979, pp. 129-198.

19. Rhodos and Perse are well attested as solar loves from a very early date (Hesiod, Homer, Pindar).

20. The scene of the lover finding his mistress spinning is a familiar topos; see further Maltby ad Tibullus c. 1.3.83-89, who notes that both matrons and virgins were idealized as devoted pliers of the weaving trade. The image ultimately goes back to Homer's Penelope.

21. For a clever solution of a possible textual crux here, which allows us to see a terrible parallel between the violent action of Orchamus and the traditional practice of sprinkling earth for the sake of minimal burial, see Harrison, S. J., "A Conjecture on Ovid, *Metamorphoses* 4.243," in *The Classical Quarterly* N. S. 47.2 (1997), pp. 608-609.

22. On this tale note Otis, *op. cit.*, pp. 156-159, Robinson, M., "Salmacis and Hermaphroditus: When Two Become One: Ovid, *Met.* 4.285-388," in *The Classical Quarterly* N. S. 49.1 (1999), pp. 212-223, Landolfi, Luciano, "*Forma duplex*: Ov. *Met.* 4, 378," in *BStudLat* 23.3 (2002), pp. 406-423, and Romano, Allen J., "The Invention of Marriage: Hermaphroditus and Salmacis at Halicarnassus and in Ovid," in *The Classical Quarterly* N. S. 59.2 (2009), pp. 543-561. For the *Nachleben*, note Silberman, Lauren, "Mythographic Transformations of Ovid's Hermaphrodite," in *The Sixteenth Century Journal* 19.4 (1988), pp. 643-652. Stirrup, B. E., "Ovid's Narrative Technique: A Study in Duality," in *Latomus* 35 (1976), pp. 97-107, considers this story along with Echo and Narcissus. For a close study of the rape of Hermaphroditus, note Murgatroyd, Paul, "Plotting in Ovidian Rape Narratives," in *Eranos* 98.1-2 (2000), pp. 75-92. Ovid probably signals the originality of the Salmacis story by the key word 284 *novitate*. In the emphasis on originality in these stories from Orchomenos, Ovid associates himself to some extent with the Minyades, who become his (implicitly Roman) spokesmen.

23. The story of Celmis the "smelter" (and discoverer of iron on Cyprus) is very poorly attested, but was not original to Ovid. For the metamorphoses of Narcissus and Crocas, note *Fasti* 5.225-227.

24. For an interesting attempt (*inter al.*) to connect Hermaphroditus with Odysseus, see Keith, Alison M., "Versions of Epic Masculinity in Ovid's *Metamorphoses*," in *Ovidian Transformations*, pp. 214-239.

25. Anderson ad loc. conveniently examines the (probable) Ovidian evocation of Homer's Odysseus with Nausicaa, with the gender shift appropriate, I would note, given the theme of the story.

26. On Ovid's blush and its Renaissance imitation in Beaumont's 1602 *Salmacis and Hermaphroditus*, see Krier, Theresa M., "Sappho's Apples: The Allusiveness of Blushes in Ovid and Beaumont," in *Comparative Literary Studies* 25.1 (1988), pp. 1-22.

27. Ovid's evocation of the Virgilian simile equates Salmacis with Amata; the point (especially for so brief an echo) need not be pushed too far.

28. For a study of Salmacis' desire (for that which is part of herself, in the author's view), see Paula, James, "Crises of Identity in Ovid's *Metamorphoses*," in *BICS* 33 (1986), pp. 17-25.

29. The passage is prelude to Pygmalion's ivory statue in Book 10. On the idealized image ivory presents, see Salzman-Mitchell, Patricia, "A Whole Out of Pieces: Pygmalion's Ivory Statue in Ovid's *Metamorphoses*," in *Arethusa* 41.2 (2008), pp. 291-311. The monégasque sculptor Bosio would make Salmacis the subject of a celebrated 1826 statue now in the Louvre; the piece decorates a high value Monaco airmail

semipostal stamp of 1948. Ironically, the same sculpture has become the "Golden Nymph" award used to honor victors at the Monaco television festival. "The Fountain of Salmacis" appears as a song on the 1971 *Genesis* musical album *Nursery Cryme*.

30. The octopus is mentioned very rarely in surviving Latin, though the word is old. Salmacis' arms and legs move so quickly that they appear to be multiplied.

31. Note Grant, Mary A., "Time Settings in the *Metamorphoses*," in *The Classical Weekly* 36.21 (1943), pp. 242-243.

32. Ino lore is well known to the mythographers (Pseudo-Apollodorus 3.26-29, Hyginus, *Fabulae* 2-4 and 224), though poorly attested elsewhere. Note also Fontenrose, Joseph, "The Sorrows of Ino and of Procne," in *Transactions and Proceedings of the American Philological Association* 79 (1948), pp. 125-167.

33. The first sign of restraint Juno shows in the *Aeneid*.

34. On Ovid's Tisiphone note Jouteur, Isabelle, "Tisiphone ovidienne (*Met.* IV, 451-511," in *Euphrosyne* N. S. 36 (2008), pp. 87-104.

35. At Pseudo-Apollodorus 1.84 and 3.28, Athamas and Ino are driven mad by Hera because they assisted in the nursing of the baby Dionysus. At 3.33 (and cf. Plato, *Leges* 672b), Hera is even guilty of infecting Dionysus with madness, which Plato cites as the explanation for some of how the Bacchic rites were inaugurated: madness as a result of madness. Athamas' madness was the subject of a lost play of Aeschylus; cf. Callistratus, *Descriptiones* 14 and Pausanias 1.44; Nonnus relates the story in *Dionysiaca* 10.

36. The subject appealed to republican tragedy; note Anto, V. d', "L'Athamas di Ennio e di Accio," in *BStudLat* 1 (1971), pp. 371-378. For the paltry Ennian remains, see Jocelyn ad loc., with full commentary.

37. See further Parker, Hugh C., "The Romanization of Ino: *Fasti* 6, 475-550," in *Latomus* 58.2 (1999), pp. 336-347.

38. In the version preserved in Hyginus (*Fabulae* 1-5), Athamas' new wife Themisto resolves to kill the children of Ino and orders her servant to signal the identities of the children with black clothes (as opposed to white for Themisto's own); the slave is actually Ino in disguise, who reverses the clothes and causes Themisto to become an unwitting matricide.

39. For consideration of some of the (broadly conceived) personified horrors of Ovid's epic (Invidia, the Fury Tisiphone), note Tissol, *op. cit.*, pp. 61 ff. Tissol considers the figures of Envy and Hunger rather "audacious" for epic; I am not sure that Ovid's personifications are "more extreme" than Virgil's Allecto.

40. The story is as old as Homer (*Odyssey* 5.333 ff., where Leucothoe rescues Odysseus); cf. Pindar, *Olympians* 2.22 ff., and *Pythians* 11.1 ff. The Elder Philostratus (*Imagines* 2.16) describes the scene.

41. Plutarch (*Quaestiones Romanae* 13) says that Ino killed her son after being rendered mad with jealousy of a slave; for this reason, female slaves were not permitted at the rites of *Mater Matuta*, with the exception of one who entered to have her ears boxed by the matrons. But the whole matter is shrouded in obscurity.

42. Littlewood ad *Fasti* 6.563 raises the speculation that Ino as dawn goddess may have been considered a war deity, with the power to sway engagements that commenced at dawn.

43. The celebrated story of Perseus, despite its enduring popularity (the subject of two modern films, a far greater cinematic presence than, *inter alia*, Virgil's *Aeneid* enjoys), is not well attested in our extant sources; Aeschylus composed a trilogy on the story. The mythographers are helpful here; Pseudo-Apollodorus 2.26 and 34 has the

familiar story of the golden shower Zeus employed to impregnate Danae (a story known also to Sophocles, *Antigone* 947). Homer knows of the Argive hero Perseus (*Iliad* 14.310), as does the pseudo-Hesiodic *Shield* (229). But apart from Ovid, we have no continuous narrative of his heroic exploits involving the Gorgon Medusa, Andromeda and the sea monster, and the eventual defeat of his domestic enemies. See further Phinney, E., "Perseus' Battle with the Gorgon," in *Transactions of the American Philological Association* 102 (1971), pp. 445-463, and Neschke, A. B., "Vom Mythos zum Emblem: Die Perseuserzählung in Ovids Metamorphosen (IV 607-V 249," in *AU* 25.6 (1982), pp. 76-87. Ariosto imitated Ovid's Perseus and Andromeda in his episode of Ruggiero and Angelica in the *Orlando Furioso*; see further Javitch, D., "Rescuing Ovid from the Allegorizers," in *Comparative Literature* 30 (1978), pp. 97-107. The subject of Perseus and the Gorgon is highly prevalent in vase painting; note the important article of Topper, Kathryn, "Perseus, the Maiden Medusa, and the Imagery of Abduction," in *Hesperia* 76.1 (2007), pp. 73-105. Topper provides a study of the scene on classical red figure vases that considers the shift from a monstrous to a beautiful depiction of Medusa. Jocelyn provides commentary on the surviving evidence of Ennius' *Andromeda*, which may already have been lost in Ovid's day. Euripides produced his own *Andromeda* in 412 B.C., on which note the edition of von Bubel (Stuttgart: Steiner, 1991), with commentary and translation, the outstanding Aris & Phillips edition of Collard, Cropp, and Gilbert (second volume, 2004), and Gilbert, John Carrington, "Falling in Love with Euripides (*Andromeda*)," in *Illinois Classical Studies* 24-25 (1999-2000), pp. 75-91. T. B. L. Webster reconstructs the play from the evidence of Ennius and Hyginus in "The Andromeda of Euripides," in *BICS* 12 (1965), pp. 29-33. The image of Andromeda freed from the rock where she has been exposed to a sea monster figures at Propertius, c. 1.3.3-4 *qualis et accubuit primo Cepheia somno / libera iam duris cotibus Andromede* (on which see Noonan, J. D., "Propertius 1.3.3-4: Andromeda is Missing," in *The Classical Journal* 86.4 (1991), pp. 330-336. As Richardson notes ad loc., Propertius is the sole source for the slumber of Andromeda after her rescue. The most useful survey of much of the disparate surviving accounts and their modern counterparts is Vicente, Cristóbal, "Perseo y Andrómeda: versiones antiguas y modernas," in *CFC* 23 (1989), pp. 51-96, which considers Euripides, Ovid, Manilius, as well as Lucian, together with the extensive use of the lore in Spanish literature from the Middle Ages through the seventeenth century. Haydn's opera is the most famous musical version of the story of Perseus and Andromeda; best is perhaps Lully's *Persée* (1682). With characteristic obscurity and learned allusiveness, Lycophron covers the main parts of the story at *Alexandra* 838 ff. Ogden's recent Routledge survey (*Perseus*, 2008) is very helpful.

44. In the mythographic tradition, we find that Acrisius is warned that a son of Danae will kill him; rather understandably, the aged monarch seeks to prevent the pregnancy and eventually casts out mother and daughter in a chest on the sea, where they land at Seriphos. The eventual death of Acrisius at Perseus' hands is not punishment for some slight against Bacchus, but of an accidental nature, though certainly there is a probable element of Jovian anger at what he thinks is the mistreatment of his lover and her hero son.

45. See further Voss, Bernd Reiner, "Die Andromeda-Episode des Manilius," in *Hermes* 100.3 (1972), pp. 413-434, and Coleman, K. M., "Manilius' Monster," in *Hermes* 111.2 (1983), pp. 226-232.

46. Note Philostratus the Elder's *Imagines* 1.29, and Polyidus, fragment 837, which cites a commentary on Lycophron for the story that Perseus was forced to turn Atlas into stone after the Titan would not allow Perseus safe passage.

47. Ovid thus provides the etiology for the Atlas mountain chain that figures in Virgil's *Aeneid*; we are still in the distant past of mythological chronology.

48. Ovid mentions Andromeda at *Ars Amatoria* 3.429-430 *quid minus Andromedae fuerat sperare revinctae / quam lacrimas ulli posse placere suas?*, as an example of the surprise appearance of love in the unlikeliest of places; at 3.191-192 *alba decent fuscas: albis, Cephei, placebas; / sic tibi vestitae pressa Seriphos erat* Andromeda is imagined as a dark-skinned girl clothed in flattering white as she returns with Perseus to his adoptive home of Seriphos. See further Gibson ad loc., who notes that the usual tradition was for Andromeda to be pale despite her Ethiopian locus (so Euripides and Heliodorus). The *Metamorphoses* is silent on her color (though Ovid's comparison of her to a marble statue at 4.675 may point to her paleness). Manilius is likewise silent.

49. The date of the *Astronomica* is problematic; it appears to have straddled the reigns of Augustus and Tiberius. The first book speaks of the disaster of Varus in the Teutoberg forest (A.D. 9) as recent history; we can assume the poet knew his Ovid, but beyond that speculation is difficult. As Goold has noted, were it not for the survival of the poem's archetype, we would have no reason to know of the existence of either the work or the author. The Perseus and Andromeda story is easy enough to justify for inclusion in an astronomical epic, but in Manilius' vision it achieves great importance from its placement as the climax to the poem's final book. For commentary on Book 5 see now Hübner's DeGruyter edition with text and translation.

50. Ovid's insistence on Andromeda's modesty may have influenced Manilius, who also underscores the same theme: 5.553 *servatur tamen in poena vultusque pudorque*; Manilius also emphasizes the girl's virginity (at 552, in a striking image that is without parallel, she hangs on a virgin cross: *et cruce virginea moritura puella pependit*). Manilius further makes clear that the girl's sacrifice is a terrible parody of nuptial rites (545 *hic hymenaeus erat*). Manilius' Perseus can barely hang on to Medusa's head as he sees the girl in midflight (a clear attempt to respond to Ovid). Manilius indulges rather more than Ovid in detail of Andromeda's lovely appearance before his Perseus goes off to meet the monster.

51. The Inachus is a river of Argos, and so appropriate to provide an epic patronymic for the hero; the reader mostly thinks of Io, however, the river's daughter and new Egyptian goddess. Perseus has replaced the image of the Eastern goddess (with her shades of Cleopatra): no careless or merely ornamental use of the circumlocution, then, but rather a subtle note of continued Perseid rehabilitation of previous stories from the epic. In general, Ovid's use of such periphrases in referring to his characters needs to be studied more comprehensively.

52. In Manilius the battle takes on more of the characteristics of a duel, with the prize (Andromeda) watching from her position as a captive audience and fearful for her heroic would-be savior. In both Ovid and Manilius the hero takes special care to bathe his hands after his slaughter of the kraken: the virgin must be touched with pure hands; I am not sure we can see comedy in the act of washing (so Anderson *et al.*).

53. Seneca (*Hercules Furens* 4 ff.) has Juno complain that Perseus and other products of her husband's affairs have been set among the stars.

54. Ovid wants to hurry to his main theme of suitors' rivalry, but in the process he also presents a Perseus who in his reticence is strikingly humble about his

accomplishments, a hero who needs to be prodded to tell even the most elementary aspects of his story.

55. The Graiae are named as daughters of Phorcys and Ceto at Hesiod, *Theogony* 270 (where see West); there they are women with beautiful countenances, gray from birth and two in number: Pemphredo and Enyo. At 332 ff., Hesiod describes the birth of the Gorgons from the same couple. The association of the two sets of sisters is thus as old as Hesiod; Phorcys and Ceto further produced Echidna, a monstrous snake with the face of a beautiful nymph and the body of a serpent, as well as the youngest of the dragons that guard the golden apples of the Hesperides, thus linking that story to the Gorgons'. In Hesiod the Gorgons live at the farthest point of the western world, beyond the River Ocean. Not surprising, then, that Alcman could pray that no man ever marry a daughter of Phorcys (fr. 1). The Graiae formed the chorus for the *Phorcides*, the second play of Aeschylus' lost trilogy on Perseus.

56. The story is alluded to at Pseudo-Aeschylus, *Prometheus Vinctus* 793 ff., where there are three sisters of swan-like shape that share a single eye and a single tooth, near the home of their sisters the Gorgons. Nonnus (*Dionysiaca* 31.13 ff.) has Perseus stealing the eye of Phorcys' old, one-eyed daughter. The gray color (of hair, presumably) mentioned as early as Hesiod engendered the tradition that the Graiae were old (if not positively haggish), but Hesiod first mentions their beauty.

57. One might almost think from the brevity of Perseus' narrative that Ovid was consciously avoiding competition with some other poetic treatment of the lore. By moving quickly in reverse order through the narrative, Ovid creates uncertainty over the direction of his story, and allows us to be surprised by his main theme, the forthcoming battle with Phineus.

58. Pseudo-Apollodorus 2.4.2 credits Poseidon with the paternity of these two creatures; Ovid and the other extant sources are silent and allow for a parthenogenic conception. Pegasus is the origin of the Muses' spring at Hippocrene, which will provide a natural connection between the Medusa lore of this book and the next one's description of the Muses' songs; see further Hinds, *op. cit.*, pp. 15-16.

59. Pseudo-Apollodorus 2.46 cites a tradition that Medusa was made ugly because she had dared to praise her beauty above Athena's. Ovid elsewhere alludes to Neptune's love for Medusa at *Heroides* 10.129 ff. The scene of Perseus' attack on the Gorgons appears on the Pseudo-Hesiodic shield (220 ff.). Pseudo-Apollodorus (2.38-46) preserves a story of how the Graiae directed Perseus to nymphs who had the necessary accoutrements for his victory over Medusa, including a helmet of invisibility; Hermes provides the hero with an adamantine sickle. In the Apollodorus narrative the Gorgons are all ugly, with huge tusks and golden wings, and all of them possess the power of petrifaction. In Ovid (4.782-783) the hero safely gazes at Medusa's reflection in his shield. A rationalized version of the lore appears at Pausanias 2.21.5-6, where Medusa is transformed into some Libyan warrior maiden who is decapitated by Perseus; Pausanias has frequent references to artwork depicting the beheading. Diodorus Siculus 3.52.4 has a similar account, where the Gorgons are depicted as veritable Amazons.

60. 4.802-803 should not be considered part of Perseus' speech, since then we must imagine that Perseus is ignorant of the fact that he is presently in custody of the Medusa head, which does not yet adorn the goddess' aegis. It would not be mere "anachronism" (cf. Anderson ad loc.) to let Perseus utter these closing words, but plain silliness on the poet's part.

Chapter V

While the Danaean Hero . . .

The fifth book of the *Metamorphoses* is the shortest thus far in the epic, but one of the poem's most important.[1] Essentially this is a two-part book, which opens with the conclusion of the story of Perseus before shifting its scene to a lengthy interlude with Minerva and the Muses.[2] There the main attraction is the famous account of the rape of Persephone by the lord of the dead.[3] As we shall see, Ovid's epic can be divided into three parts; this book marks the close of the poem's first movement: in Book 10, Calliope will give way to Orpheus. (There will also be a division into two halves, though more subtly).[4] Book 5 offers a companion to the underworld lore of its predecessor; there Juno had visited hell to summon the Fury Tisiphone against Ino, while here we see the establishment of the underworld's royal family. As the epic's first third draws to a close, the audience is left with a traditional view of both underworld and afterlife, a view that will only be challenged much later in the epic. And, in a stunning conclusion to the recurring theme of rape that has plagued the first movement of the epic, Diana will see to it that her beloved nymph Arethusa is rescued from Alpheus' lustful pursuit in the closing scenes of the book.

As the action begins, the wedding banquet of Perseus and Andromeda is interrupted by the sudden intrusion of Phineus, who is now introduced as a *quondam* suitor of the Ethiopian princess.[5] At last, Ovid moves to the main theme of his *Perseid*: a retelling of the Aeneas-Lavinia-Turnus triangle, with shades of the homecoming of Odysseus to Ithaca.[6] The hero has defeated three significant opponents in Medusa, Atlas, and the sea monster; now he shall set his new home in order.[7] The slaughter at a wedding banquet that is about to commence is modeled after the traditional account of the Battle of the Lapiths and Centaurs at a nuptial feast; in Book 12 Ovid will tell of that struggle, and many of the names of the dead from the present story will reappear there.

The conflict between Aeneas and Turnus was resolved in the closing lines of the *Aeneid* with the decision taken by the Trojan hero to slay his defeated opponent in vengeance for the loss of Pallas. That sacrificial offering of Turnus to Pallas' ghost closed six books of more or less continuous conflict in Italy. In Ovid, the battle comes after the marriage (Virgil, unlike his medieval imitators, chose to suppress any victorious, celebratory scenes of the nuptials of Aeneas and Lavinia). Phineus rises up to attack his brother's new son-in-law (5.8 ff.).

123

As if he were Virgil's Latinus, Cepheus tries to quell his brother's anger, noting that the preference here is not for Perseus *per se*, but for life rather than death in the kraken's maw. Readers of the scene will have different views on whether Perseus or Phineus should attract more sympathy here; certainly Phineus had given up Andromeda for lost and had not performed any heroic feat to save her from the sea monster.

Close to the book's end we shall see Diana successfully rescue Arethusa; for the present, Phineus complains that Andromeda has been stolen from him, and his challenge to Perseus carries the implicit threat that he will take Andromeda by force. Like Alpheus' pursuit of Arethusa, Phineus' claim will be in vain, and he will end up a petrified monument in Cepheus' hall.

Phineus hurls his spear at Perseus; his poor aim succeeds only in striking a nearby couch (34-35). Virgil's Aeneas had surrendered to madness in his decision to slay Turnus; Perseus is both ferocious (35 *ferox*) and possessed of a personal hatred for Phineus (35-36 *inimica / pectora*) as he rises to meet the challenge. But Ovid also indicates that Phineus is a scoundrel and criminal; he is a *sceleratus* (37) as he hides behind an altar, in Ovid's view an unworthy (*indignum*) place of hiding for such a rogue. Perseus hurls back Phineus' spear (emphasizing he was unarmed when Phineus tried to kill him, and that it was Phineus who started this battle). Rhoetus is struck instead, full in the face, and dies amid the tables strewn with food and drink (38-40).[8] The name is that of a Centaur during the famous Lapith combat (12.271 ff.), which may serve here to dehumanize the first victim of Perseus' wrath against Phineus.[9] The first blood of the combat causes general mayhem in the hall; Phineus has his supporters. The hospitality theme is underscored yet again; Perseus' status as a guest-friend, and more, has been terribly violated. This theme of abused hospitality was at the center of the Lycaon-Jupiter narrative.

Cepheus, again in imitation of Virgil's Latinus, gives up and leaves the hall; his last gesture is to call on the gods as witnesses that he did not countenance this violence (5.43-45). As host of the wedding party, he would bear responsibility for the violence about to erupt.

Minerva, however, is present, and she defends Perseus with her aegis; that breastplate does not, as yet, bear the Gorgon, but the passage looks forward both to her custody of the Medusa head, and the central part the goddess will play in the second movement of this book. The second supporter of Phineus to rise up (and die) is the Indian Athis, who at once recalls the image of Cybele's famous devotee Attis (Catullus c. 63). Athis was born under glassy waters, which reminds us of Hermaphroditus and the beautiful image he presented under the waters of Salmacis' pool. He is lavishly dressed in the Eastern (i.e., non-Roman style): he has a Tyrian mantle (as if he were a Carthaginian). His hair is perfumed with myrrh, which recalls the anger of Iarbas or Numanus Remulus against Aeneas and his Trojans and their perfumed locks.

From a Centaur's name, we have advanced to some half-man who evokes not only Catullus' Attis, but also Virgil's Chloreus and the Trojan customs that will be implicitly suppressed in the future Rome (as Virgil's Jupiter made clear

to Juno). Athis is skilled with missile weapons, especially the bow; Perseus does
not give him time to prove his skill—the boy's handsome face is smashed to
pieces under the blow of a firebrand from the nearby altar (where Phineus was
lurking?).[10] Perseus, the new Aeneas, is able to kill warriors the first Aeneas
could not plausibly kill because of his Trojan background.

As if Ovid were channeling the spirits of Nisus and Euryalus, the next
victim of Perseus is the Assyrian Lycambas, who was Athis' homosexual lover.
Lycambas mourns the bitter wound that has felled his close friend; 5.62 *acerbo*
points to the premature death of the *eromenos* Athis, who is sixteen. Perseus has
managed to find his own weapon in all the commotion; Lycambas' arrow shot is
ineffectual, but Perseus is able to drive his hooked sword into the would-be
avenging lover's chest. As was the case with Virgil's Nisus and Euryalus,
Lycambas is able to enjoy the solace of a shared death with his beloved (71-73).

Nisus and Euryalus were first introduced during Virgil's narrative of the
foot race in Sicily; there, Nisus had slipped in some sacrificial blood and had
tripped a competitor so his lover Euryalus could race ahead. Perhaps influenced
by this scene, after the death of *his* Nisus and Euryalus Ovid describes how two
other would-be assailants of Perseus slipped in the now gory floor of the hall, a
good example of how an echo of one passage can provide inspiration for a
seemingly insignificant, conventional detail in another (5.74-78). Like Rhoetus,
Phorbas is another Centaur's name (12.322); Amphimedon is borrowed from
Homer's Odyssean suitors.[11] Rhoetus is also a victim of the night raid of Nisus
and Euryalus (*Aeneid* 9.342 ff., describing Euryalus' exploits).

Erytus is killed with a heavy serving bowl that was embossed with rich (and
unspecified) ornamentation (5.79-84); the name is reminiscent of another of the
centauric monikers we shall encounter again in Book 12, in a passage clearly
imitative of this gruesome scene—Eurytion/Eurytus was the leader of the
centaurs who fought the Lapiths.[12] A great number of new victims now follows
rapidly; among them we find Caucasian Abaris (86), who shares a name with
one of Euryalus' victims (*Aeneid* 9.344). In Perseus' victory over Phineus'
supporters, we find victims who evoke Nisus and Euryalus, as well as casualties
that share names with the Latin victims of that ill-fated Virgilian pair; this hero's
exploits are comprehensive, though the slaughter is becoming excessive. But
part of the poet's trick is to create a situation where Perseus has no choice; he
did not start the combat, and the supporters of Phineus continue their assault
relentlessly.

Polydegmon is Babylonian; the ornate adjective *Semiramian* (5.85
Semiramio) reminds us of the Near Eastern stories of the Minyades and
continues the extraordinary emphasis on the very un-Roman enemies of
Perseus.[13] Phlegyas is another name associated with the Centaurs; he was king
of the Lapiths, and so again—as with Rhoetus and Abaris—again, Perseus is
shown to kill victims on both sides of legendary ancient battles.[14] Phineus, for
his part, is too scared to advance against Perseus; he hurls a javelin that
accidentally strikes Idas, who had been neutral in the refectory brawl (89-96).
Idas is the name of a Trojan slain by Turnus (*Aeneid* 9.575); the association with

Mount Ida makes it a name of unimpeachably (though not exclusively) Trojan associations.[15] Hodites (another Centaur name) falls by the sword of Clymenus; Phineus' friend Clymenus reminds us of Phaethon's mother Clymene, herself the wife of the Ethiopian king Merops: the combat of Perseus at Cepheus' palace rings back to the Ethiopian story from Book 2.

The aged Emathion watches the slaughter (like Idas), not choosing sides but shaking his head in horror at the slaughter that has marred the nuptials. Ovid now presents one of his grisliest scenes, for some readers a fine example of his black humor:

> . . . fuit et grandaevus in illis
> Emathion, aequi cultor timidusque deorum,
> qui, quoniam prohibent anni bellare, loquendo
> pugnat et incessit scelerataque devovet arma;
> huic Chromis amplexo tremulis altaria palmis
> decutit ense caput, quod protinus incidit arae
> atque ibi semianimi verba exsecrantia lingua
> edidit et medios animam exspiravit in ignes. (5.99-106)

> *. . . there was also among them aged*
> *Emathion, a lover of justice and timid with respect to the gods,*
> *who, since his years prevented him from fighting, by speaking*
> *did fight, and he strode forth and cursed the criminal arms;*
> *as he was gripping the altar with trembling hands,*
> *Chromis cut off his head with a sword, which straightway fell on the altar*
> *and there uttered the cursing words with tongue half-alive*
> *and at last breathed out its last amid the flames.*

"Emathion" is poetic metonymy for Macedonian or Thessalian; later in this book, near its close (669 *Emathides*), Ovid will use this appellation for the ill-fated Pierides, the daughters of Pierus of Macedon.[16] Emathion denounces the combat he sees before him; he himself has abstained from the fighting because of his advanced age. Ovid does not make clear who kills him; since Chromis is another name associated with the Centaurs (like so many of Perseus' victims thus far), we may draw some conclusions. The scene is ghastly and arguably overdone in its gruesome effects, though there are passages of both Homer and Virgil that are of similar if not equally gory effectiveness. Regardless of whether Perseus' partisans are responsible or not for the aged man's grisly end, his slaughter attests to the impious lengths this eruption of madness has reached.

Ovid had evoked the foot race in Sicily; now he nods also to the boxing match by mentioning two pugilists, the twin brothers Broteas and Ammon, who both fall by Phineus' hand (5.107-108). The death of Ceres' priest Ampycus looks forward to that goddess' part in the drama about to unfold in the battle of the Muses; the priest's death at the hands of the impious Phineus adds to the sacrilege of Emathion's grisly death at an altar. We might note that it was Aeneas and not Turnus who killed a priest at *A.* 10. 537 ff.

The unacceptable violence continues in the death of the bard Lampetides (5.111 ff.). Phineus started the violence, and it has taken on excessive proportions; Lampetides was presumably present at the banquet to celebrate the marriage of Perseus and Andromeda with song. Pedasus' slaughter of the innocent bystander carries echoes of Pyrrhus' vicious taunts of Priam in Aeneas' account of the fall of Troy:

> Pedasus inridens 'Stygiis cane cetera' dixit
> 'manibus,' et laevo mucronem tempore fixit. (5.115-116)

> *Pedasus, laughing at him, said, "Sing the rest to the Stygian*
> *shades," and he fixed the blade in his left temple.*

As the poet falls, he sings a *miserabile carmen* (118) that is nothing less than the bloodbath he sees around him. Pedasus is in turn killed by Lycormas; Ovid compares his death to that of a slaughtered bull to draw attention to the violation of altars and other basic conventions of warfare that we have seen thus far (121-122). Lycormas' weapon of choice is a doorpost; this creative use of available battle props spurs Pelates to try to rip away another post. Pelates shares his name with another Centaur; he is a North African (124 *Cinyphius*), as is Corythus (from Marmarica near Carthage), whose spear pins Pelates' hand to the door. The battle in Cepheus' hall has become both confused and civil in its nature; Perseus may not have started it (any more than Aeneas started the conflict in Latium), but the violence has indeed mushroomed out of control.

Dorylas is slain, one of Perseus' new friends (5.129 ff.); he had been rich in lands and the owner of the territory that produced the greatest amount of incense in the world (131 *turis acervos*), incense that would burn on the altars of the gods. Halcyoneus fells him with a terrible groin wound, adding the taunt that the rich Dorylas will now possess only the small plot of land where he falls.[17] Perseus avenges the wealthy wedding guest by ripping out the spear and returning it; Halcyoneus is stabbed through the nose, the spear exiting via his neck. In Virgil, the ostensible loser Turnus was a victor in that the new Rome would be Italian, not Trojan; at *Aeneid* 10.284, in a powerful (and probably deliberate) hemistich, he had observed that Fortune favors the brave (*audentis Fortuna iuvat*). Now, Ovid notes that Fortune aided Perseus' hand (140 *dumque manum Fortuna iuvat*), as more victims fall, beginning with another that bears a Centaur's name, one Clanis, who is slain together with his brother Clytius.

The battle had started with Phineus' ashen spear, and now an ashen spear is driven through Clytius' thighs.[18] Other Perseid victims are of questionable background; so Astreus, who is born from a Syrian mother to an unknown father (hinting, as the commentators note, at prostitution—possibly ritual), Aethion, a seer who was apparently not very good at predicting his own future as a partisan of Phineus, and Agyrtes, who killed his own father. Celadon (144) will reappear as a Lapith name; as we have noted, the slaughter has taken lives associated with both sides of that epic struggle. Thoactes is named as the king's arms-bearer; he was apparently Cepheus' servant.

Ovid summarizes what has been a dizzying and complex battle scene. Cepheus is apparently back in the hall; he is "pious in vain" (5.152 *frustra pius*) and allied with wife and daughter in favor of Perseus. Unlike Virgil's Amata and Lavinia, Ovid's Cassiopeia and Andromeda are firmly on the side of their new relative by marriage. Bellona, the Italian war goddess, holds sway, however, as the slaughter in the hall rages around Perseus. For those who would question the hyperbole of how Perseus is fighting alone against so many, we might compare Turnus, trapped in the Trojan camp and fighting single-handedly in the face of an onslaught. Certainly the passage is filled with hyperbole; a thousand men fight with Phineus (but Virgil, too, had Turnus claim a thousand victims at *A.* 11.397, in describing that day in the Trojan camp—the number is poetic exaggeration in both poets). Bellona has contaminated the Penates (155) precisely because the marriage of Perseus and Andromeda prefigures the union of Aeneas and Lavinia; Ovid has, in fact, described a battle at a wedding such as the narrative of the *Aeneid* would not permit. Ovid presented the completion of the victory over what we might have imagined was the last obstacle facing Perseus would face (the kraken), only to spoil what we might have expected as Virgil's climactic scene of celebration (the happy wedding) with a brutal battle that violates *pietas* as well as hospitality: the theme of Atlas and the *hospes* Perseus is central to this bloody melee.

Perseus is one man, then, against a huge multitude; the two leaders who face him are Molpeus and Echemmon, the former Chaonian, the latter Nabataean (i.e., Arabian), though bearing the name of a son of Priam (*Iliad* 5.160). Ovid compares Perseus to a tigress driven by hunger that is tempted by two herds. In the identical situation in the *Aeneid*, Turnus was compared to a lion frightened by hunters (*A.* 9.793 *territus*), which does not flee in terror, however, because of anger (*ira*) and manly courage (*virtus*).

Deftly, Ovid has turned Perseus from Aeneas into Turnus during the course of the battle. The Turnus image is not necessarily bad (in light of the final disposition of cultural affairs in Italy), but the hungry tigress is not Virgil's hunted lion. Perseus strikes Molpeus and wounds him in the leg; Echemmon is coming fast to attack, and so Perseus is willing to let Molpeus go—he is "content with flight" (i.e., Molpeus'): 5.169 *contentusque fuga*. The phrase is extraordinary in light of its origin. At *Aeneid* 11.815, it describes Arruns, fresh from his victory over Camilla, content now in flight as he flees the scene of his (perhaps treacherous) killing of the Volscian huntress. Arruns was content with his own flight; Perseus with the flight of another. The passage deserves more attention than it has received:

> Molpea traiecti submovit vulnere cruris
> contentusque fuga est; neque enim dat tempus Echemmon,
> sed furit et cupiens alto dare vulnera collo
> non circumspectis exactum viribus ensem

fregit in extrema percussae parte columnae (5.168-172)

He removed Molpeus with a wound to his transfixed leg
and was content with flight; for Echemmon did not give him time,
but he raged and, desiring to give a wound deep in the neck,
with his strength not carefully measured he broke his sword
on the very edge of the smitten column

The column is where Perseus stands to defend his rear; Molpeus leads Phineus' forces on the left and Echemmon on the right. The question is why Molpeus was let go with a leg wound. Echemmon seems to be the fiercer opponent; the conjunction *enim* usually corroborates a preceding assertion. In this case, Perseus' decision as to which side to strike first is made for him by Echemmon, who tries to attack with his sword but succeeds only in striking the column. The Virgilian passage compels us to consider whether it was Perseus who was content with his own flight, not that of Molpeus (one wonders how easily Molpeus could have fled anyway, given the nature of his wound). Perseus could not make up his mind, and Echemmon was not willing to grant him the *tempus* to decide.

Perseus ducks away from Echemmon's sword, and the overeager, indeed furious warrior strikes the column too hard. The blade breaks and impales itself in his throat; the horrible wound is not fatal, however. Echemmon is killed as he begs for mercy, just as Mago had pleaded with Aeneas to spare his life (cf. *A.* 10.536 *orantis*). Perseus has become just as bad as Aeneas after the death of Pallas, and, arguably, with less reason. What is certain—however we take *contentusque fuga*—is that Ovid is recalling the (striking) Virgilian passage, which forces us to consider Perseus as Arruns (a not very complementary association), and that Perseus does not achieve a glorious victory over these two leaders of his opposition: Molpeus is left subdued with a leg wound, while Echemmon is killed both because of his own action in striking the column, and Perseus' refusal to grant him mercy.[19] The denial of pity presages Phineus' own fate below; we might wonder where he has been lurking in fear during the great slaughter, and why his supporters have apparently not cared that their leader has been proven a coward.

Significantly, it is at this point that Perseus' *virtus*—the very quality that had sustained Turnus the lion—now begins to yield to the throng: 5.177 *Verum ubi virtutem turbae succumbere vidit.* Perseus will now imitate Juno; she had said that it was fitting to be taught by an enemy—Bacchus—and now Perseus will seek aid from his former opponent—the Gorgon Medusa. An argument can be made that the bloody war—how much time has elapsed?—has corrupted Perseus; certainly this extended sequence has made the hero more ambiguous than he seemed to be in Ovid's rapid flight through his previous exploits. The war in the dining hall has been civil (Phineus was Cepheus' brother), and its evocation of the deadly rivalry of the Iliadic *Aeneid* confirms the baleful associations of the combat that has been forced on Perseus (just as the struggle in the *Aeneid* was forced on Aeneas). And, further, this time the violent struggle follows the marriage; the wedding of Perseus and Andromeda was not the celebration of relief from trouble, but rather the locus for a terrible eruption of savagery.

Ovid admits that the first victims of Perseus' terrible unleashing of the power of the Gorgon deserved their fate. One of them, Nileus, is a liar who boasts that he was born of Nile (5.187 ff.); in a Roman context he is a fitting opponent for the hero Perseus. Eryx tries to rouse the throng to rush at Perseus and overpower him with numbers; he is of course petrified on the very verge of his attack, and we might think of the famous Sicilian boxer whose gloves Entellus owns, the gloves with which Eryx fought Hercules (*A.* 5.400 ff.). The mighty boxer, for Ovid's day the icon of a legendary age of past heroes who fought with demigods, is a fitting image to recall as this brave warrior is turned into a statue to decorate Cepheus' hall. One victim is a partisan of Perseus; the Argive hero had warned his supporters to shield their eyes (179-180), but in the confusion Aconteus did not pay heed. Two hundred are said to have survived, while the same number are petrified; again, a "thousand" enemies was poetic exaggeration, since that number seems to have shrunk significantly by this point in the combat.

Phineus realizes he has been fighting a divinely aided hero, and that his attack had been unjust (5.210 *iniusti . . . belli*). The scene is not reminiscent of Virgil, where Turnus had an arguably defensible cause; Ovid has portrayed Phineus with not a speck of sympathy for his claim to Andromeda (whom he was apparently willing to see sacrificed without a fight). Phineus now appeals to Perseus for mercy; we can anticipate the request will be refused. Phineus harms his own case by announcing that he did not attack Perseus out of *odium* or any desire for the kingdom, but rather because of the girl; again, the image of Andromeda chained to the rock calls into question Phineus' feelings (or at least bravery). Phineus does not make the appeal of Turnus to be returned alive to his aged father; he begs merely for his life.

We have observed that Perseus has become corrupted during the course of the battle in the hall. The corruption advances now to a deeper level. What he can grant, the hero says, he will: Phineus will not die by the sword (5.224-226). The other fate both the audience and the frightened wretch can guess. Phineus will be granted a sort of perverse immortality:

> quin etiam mansura dabo monimenta per aevum,
> inque domo soceri semper spectabere nostri,
> ut mea se sponsi soletur imagine coniunx. (5.227-229)

> *No, I shall grant that you remain as a monument through the age,*
> *and in the home of our father-in-law always you will be gazed upon,*
> *so that by her spouse' image there may be consolation for my wife.*

The word order of the last sentence is effective in revealing the horror of what Perseus has become; he imagines Andromeda taking comfort in the image of her petrified spouse. It is possible to imagine that Andromeda will, rather sadistically, enjoy the sight of the man who unjustly sought to kill her savior, and certainly there are passages in Homer's *Odyssey* that might make us question the decisions of Odysseus in his battle with the suitors and their supporters. Ovid does not allow any question: Phineus was wrong in what he did, and he is presented as a despicable coward and thoroughly unappealing, unsavory figure. But Perseus has done what Aeneas did before him (refuse mercy to a suppliant), and the last lines the hero utters to the cowering Phineus betray a certain blackening of his soul. The suppliant (234 *supplex*) is frozen forever in his pleading position, his hands raised up in prayer (235 *submissaeque manus*).

Perseus, of course, could not remain the idealized hero; that would spoil the hopes of the Roman future. And his actions are not conclusively wicked; unlike Virgil's Lavinia, we might also observe, Perseus' Andromeda actively champions his cause (5.152-153). And, significantly, his first deed after his victory is to avenge his grandfather Acrisius, an act of *pietas* indeed, even if, as Ovid reminds us, the king was undeserving (237 *inmeriti*), both because of his denial of Bacchus and his attack on his own grandson. Acrisius, we learn, had been driven out of power by his own brother Proetus.[20] Perseus petrifies his granduncle in vengeance for the exile of his grandfather; the story may well be original to Ovid.

Proteus is but the first of a new set of victims of the Gorgon head; Polydectes is next.[21] The king of Seriphos is mentioned allusively by Ovid, who expects his audience to know the basic tradition at least, namely that the king was enamored of Perseus' mother Danae and more or less prevented from satisfying his lust by the presence of the beautiful woman's son. Now having returned from his series of heroic adventures, Ovid's Polydectes doubts the veracity of Perseus' claim to have slain Medusa; his petrifaction silences the criticism. The theme is a familiar one; the doubter is punished for his impudence, though Ovid has refrained from punishing Acrisius for his doubt of Bacchus' divinity (or Perseus' birth from Jupiter—on the contrary, he has made Perseus a dutiful avenger of wrongs done to his grandfather). The main reason for the suppression of this theme in the case of Acrisius is the tradition of Perseus' own part in excluding Bacchic worship from his realms.

Minerva was traditionally associated with her stepbrother Perseus; she has not been a significant part of the narrative thus far (though the imitation of Homer's Odysseus further serves to highlight her place as patroness of Perseus' work). Now the narrative shifts, as we learn that Minerva leaves Perseus behind and makes her way to Thebes and Mount Helicon, the traditional haunt of the Muses (5.250 ff.). The return to Thebes is a ring of sorts with the great Theban cycle, of which Perseus' story is a pendant. Pegasus had already been to Thebes, it seems, and had given birth to the famous spring Hippocrene by a strike of his hoof.[22] Minerva visits Helicon to see the wondrous new spring, the symbol of

the poetic arts in this peaceful abode of the nine daughters of Memory.[23] Perseus
and Andromeda have disappeared from the epic, never to return; the glorious
deeds of the Argive hero are put aside: room will have to be made in due course
for other heroes.

We have observed that Perseus' seemingly perfect image of heroism is
somewhat tarnished by the long episode in Cepheus' dining hall, though he
remains the greatest mortal hero we have thus far encountered in the poem.
Divine action has thus far left us less than impressed; Jupiter in particular has
seemed prone to questionable activities with mortal women. In a sense, the
meeting of Minerva and the Muses is one of the purest of scenes Ovid has
created; ten virgins gather by a spring created by a horse's hoof in a *locus
amoenus* defined both by flowers (5.266) and, more importantly, the majestic
power of song. We are in the very workshop of poetry, at the waters every poet
hopes to quaff. We learn soon enough that attempted rape has entered the
discourse even in this sacred precinct, with the Muses' story of Pyreneus.[24] The
character is otherwise unknown; his name perhaps evokes thoughts of Achilles'
son Pyrrhus, fire, and the violation of holy places.

Ovid's Pyreneus could not be more of a bullying brute. He is Thracian, he is
ferox, and the domains he has conquered are ruled by injustice (5.277 *iniustaque
regna*, with transferred epithet). The story is reminiscent of Lycaon and the
"beginning," as it were, of the world in its wickedness: Pyreneus invites the
Muses to take refuge in his dwelling from a rainstorm. Ovid invites us to
conclude that Pyreneus is insane (291 *vecors*).[25] Not only does he try to rape the
Muses, but also, after they escape in winged flight, he climbs up to the roof of a
citadel and tries to fly after them, only to crash to the earth and dash his brains
out.

The brief story of Pyreneus is nothing less than a hearkening back to the
recurring theme of outrageous behavior (both human and divine) that had
characterized the world both before and after the deluge. After the (often
exemplary) heroism of Perseus (and his perceptible decline), it is as if we have
begun again, though with the hero Perseus and his implied opposition to
Bacchus and the (anti-Roman) excesses of the East as backdrop (much of
Perseus' victory is a very Augustan sort of attack against the forces associated
with Antony and Cleopatra). Just as Jupiter had told the assembled immortals of
the wickedness of Lycaon, so the nine sisters have told Minerva of a similar
experience of mortal mischief. The second half of this book will open with an
attempted rape of virgin goddesses; it will end with another attempted rape.
Neither will be successful, though they will frame the all too victorious
abduction of Persephone by her uncle.

Humanity might well complain that the immortals have had their fair share
of despicable and wretched moments, and so Ovid introduces the Pierides, the
nine mortal sisters of Macedonian Pierus, who have been transformed into
magpies (5.294 ff.).[26] Fundamentally, the contest of the Muses and the Pierides
will be a commentary on the relative merits of men and gods after more than

four books of evidence have been amassed and an apparently cyclical world seems once again poised for decline.

We know the result of this competition even before it begins; the magpies are the transformed losers, still talkative in their defeat. The Pierides had suggested the nymphs as judges of the contest (314), appropriate enough given how often the nymphs have been victims of immortal rape. The stakes of the contest are high: if the Muses lose, they must surrender Helicon and Aganippe to the Pierides; conversely, the Pierides will surrender the Emathian plains as far as snowy Paeonia in Macedonia. Given the poetic importance of Helicon, of course, the loss would be far greater to the Muses than their mortal challengers.

The first of the Pierides starts with a gigantomachy (5.319 ff.). Her story is unduly flattering to the opponents of Olympus; she is interested in attacking the coming of the Jovian regime. She presents the Olympians in flight, running in terror from Typhoeus to Egypt and the Nile's seven mouths; the shame (especially for an Augustan audience) would be profound. Even in Egypt, the gods are not safe; Typhoeus pursues them there and forces them to assume theriomorphic shapes that implicitly mock how Jupiter had disguised himself as a bull to rape Europa: now he is a ram hiding from the earth-born monster, and no wonder the north Africans show Ammon (i.e., Jupiter) with horns. But the Pierides are excessive; they do not restrict their comparison to Jupiter (which would have been impious enough), but continue with Apollo (a raven, in mockery of the story of Coronis and her death because of his unrestrained anger), Bacchus (a goat),[27] Diana (a cat), Juno (a cow, in mockery of her rival Io),[28] Venus (a fish, probably because of her traditional marine origins), and Mercury (an ibis bird).[29]

The Muses are not sure Minerva has time to listen to their reply; the goddess (and Ovid's audience) make time for the story.[30] The Muse Calliope, the muse of epic verse, now proceeds to tell the great story of Pluto's rape of Ceres' daughter Persephone.[31] The song is one of plaintive lament (5.338-339 *surgit et inmissos hedera collecta capillos / Calliope* **querulas** *praetemptat pollice* **chordas**), because it is a narrative of loss.

Ovid has two extended narratives of the famous story; besides the Muse's song, there is *Fasti* 4.417-618, the longest elegiac narrative in his calendar poem.[32] In the *Metamorphoses*, Calliope opens with a powerful threefold anaphora of Ceres as *prima*: she was the first to engage in farming, she was the first to yield up the fruits of the earth, and she was the first to give laws to men. Rather lavishly, Calliope praises Ceres as the giver of every boon (5.343 *Cereris sunt omnia munus*). There is learned irony here, of course; the Pierides sang of how the gods had disguised themselves in fear to escape Typhoeus, though we have seen such anthropomorphism only in the context of Jovian rape. The story Calliope is about to relate is essentially another divine rape, this time with a more significant victim than Europa.[33] Even the daughters of major Olympians are not immune from the threat of rape; Ceres' daughter Persephone will be stolen by her own uncle.[34] We should note that there has been labor and farming in Ovid's world before this story; Ceres, however, can still rightly be credited as the first giver of the gifts of cultivation. Only at the end of Calliope's story will there be any reference to the familiar myth of how Triptolemus spread the gifts of agriculture at the direction of the goddess. Ovid is moving through history more or less chronologically, but temporal precision need not be one of the poet's virtues.

Much has been made of the so-called programmatic nature of the story of Persephone's abduction, and about the different genres Ovid uses to tell essentially the same story in the *Fasti* and the *Metamorphoses*. [35] I suggest that the matter has been overdone, and that the story Calliope now sings is not especially programmatic, and that it plays more of a part in the poet's ultimate concerns about the afterlife and human fate (concerns philosophic rather than poetic), rather than any recurring (I am tempted to say tiresome) discussions of epic *versus* elegy. The Pierides have indeed sung the wrong sort of song, not because it was a gigantomachy *per se*, but because the wrong side was glorified; their song is prelude to the forthcoming poem of Arachne that will infuriate Minerva at the beginning of the next book. [36]

In one sense, what Hinds well labels "the endless deferral here of final generic classification" is a red herring of the poet. The *Fasti* is epic elegiac, the *Metamorphoses* is elegiac epic. The skilled poet could have reversed the two works. But the *Metamorphoses*, if only because of its meter, is an epic, first and foremost, whatever its characteristics. Calliope's song is an epic within an epic. For those who wish to find them, it will yield flaws (though I am not convinced that Ovid is consciously weaker in his narrative skills so as to offer a deliberate contrast between Calliope's style and his own). But her song will succeed in offering a rehabilitation of the divine actions of the first third of the poem. It will not be persuasive in every regard, but, as we shall see, for the first time in the poem a virgin goddess will save a potential rape victim, in a stunning change to established mythological tradition. [37] A certain order will be imposed on the world as this book concludes, an order whose standards of behavior will extend into the next book, as we examine more examples of divine retribution for mortal misbehavior.

The ostensible reason for Calliope's story in the wake of the Pierides' gigantomachy, though, is the locus of Sicily as the grave of Typhoeus: the gods did defeat the monster, after all, and he rests forever under Etna (the *Fasti* passage also opens with Sicily, though with no mention of its darker associations). Typhoeus is immortal, of course, and therefore still a threat; Pluto is compelled to inspect the foundations of his kingdom to ensure the safety of his underworld realm (again, there is none of this in the *Fasti*, where Pluto simply appears on the scene).

Pluto's presence is too irresistible a target for Venus Erycina and her son Cupid; she orders him to strike his uncle and spread their power to the underworld. The Venusian instigation of the rape is doubtless an Ovidian invention; in the *Homeric Hymn to Demeter* the earth conspires with Zeus to help Hades in his infatuation with Persephone by creating an especially desirable flower to tempt the maiden. [38] Hesiod knows the basic story (*Theogony*

912 ff.). In Ovid's version, Venus is distressed at none other than Minerva and Diana:

Pallada nonne vides iaculatricemque Dianam
abscessise mihi? (5.375-376)

*Do you not see how Pallas and javelin-throwing Diana
have departed from me?*

The virgin goddesses have displeased Venus; she fears lest Persephone soon augment their number (interestingly, according to Ovid Persephone is already planning a celibate life). Cupid obeys his mother and strikes his uncle with a particularly sharp amatory shaft; the stage is now set for the abduction of the maiden in a beautiful grove at Henna (in the very middle of the island).[39] Venus has struck another blow in the age-old struggle she maintains against Diana and the virgin denizens of the sort of *locus amoenus* we are about to enter. Cupid had struck Apollo of his own volition; Venus instigates this assault, and the plan is specifically for Pluto to fall in love with his niece Persephone (who conveniently happens to be picking flowers near where her uncle is inspecting the physical security of his realm). The whole scene of Cupid's attack is modeled, appropriately enough, on Cupid's assault on the poet at *Amores* 1.1.21-24 (where see McKeown). This *amor*, however, will end in a Jovian-sanctioned legal marriage: some sort of order is about to be effected after five books filled with lustful escapades. Cupid is once again firing his shafts, but this time the ultimate consequences might surprise both him and his mother.

It is perpetual spring in the lovely locale that will be the scene of intrusive violence (5.391 *perpetuum ver est*); the season will be less than eternal once Ceres is finished with avenging her daughter's loss.[40] The abduction is accomplished with breathtaking speed (395 *paene simul visa est dilectaque raptaque Diti*); in both his accounts Ovid notes that Persephone tore her robe (probably in the struggle). The horse-drawn chariot of Pluto will be mirrored in the dragon chariot of Ceres with which the book will close, as the goddess takes the Athenian Triptolemus across the world to spread the wonders of agriculture far and wide. The abduction of the maiden by an amorous god is a familiar motif, though here taken to epic lengths hitherto unseen in the poem.[41] Unlike his brother Jupiter, Pluto is silent as he abducts Persephone; he also wastes no time and brooks no delay with disguises or any dissimulation.

It is worthwhile here to note that the rape of Persephone presents an extended myth that offers an etiology for the traditional underworld pairing of Hades and his queen (as we shall see below, despite the resolution of the story and division of the year between Ceres and Hades, elsewhere in myth we always see Persephone in her underworld capacity, never again the carefree girl of spring). With regard to the ultimate questions of life and death that vex poets and philosophers alike, the end of *Metamorphoses* 5 presents a "traditional" underworld vision, just as we saw when Juno visited Tisiphone to attack Ino.

This is the underworld Ovid and his contemporaries inherited from Homer, the underworld that was rejected by Lucretius and so altered by Virgil. Ovid here introduces his underworld royal family for the first time; we have seen the traditional hell of Tartarus, and now we see the violent establishment of hell's ruling class. Ovid will return to this theme later in the poem, where he will respond to the views of both Virgil and Lucretius before him.[42]

There is a witness to the abduction: the nymph Cyane.[43] She is no virgin goddess herself, but the wife of the river god Anapis; her spouse had practiced courtship and not rape. Cyane's protests are ignored and her watery home becomes the transit point for Pluto's departure with his prize; the disconsolate nymph is lost in her grief and eventually melts away into water (5.425-437).[44] The metamorphosis of Cyane is paralleled by the similar transformation of Arethusa at the book's end; both nymphs are turned into water in connection with the intrusion of an amorous male deity.[45] Cyane's transformation is easy; it is no difficult feat to change a water nymph into water.[46]

Ceres begins her search for her lost daughter. In both Ovidian accounts the goddess lights two pine torches to guide her way (5.441-443 and *Fasti* 4.493-494).[47] In the *Metamorphoses*, Ceres arrives at the humble cottage of an old woman and a mysterious little boy (5.446 ff.); the goddess is tired and extremely thirsty. The old woman offers her a sweet drink that has toasted barley sprinkled on top (450 *dulce dedit, tosta quod texerat ante polenta*). Ceres is mocked by the boy for her greedy quaffing of the drink; the goddess immediately throws the unfinished portion at him and turns him into a speckled newt (451-461).

The story is unknown to the *Homeric Hymn* and is not mentioned in the *Fasti*. The drinking of a mixture of barley meal and water is, however, prominent in the hymn (206-209) and featured in the rituals at Eleusis.[48] The tale is not original to Ovid; it figured in Nicander (fr. 56 of the *Heteroeumena* and Antoninus Liberalis (*Metamorphoses* 24). The boy is utterly unsympathetic; we shed no tears for his transformation into a gecko (Latin *stellio*). Ovid does not make clear what if any relationship there is between the boy and the old woman (who is too old to be his mother); it is possible he is to be identified with the demonic figure that will tattle on the hungry Persephone in the underworld. Like Jupiter with Lycaon (although in a far less deadly context), Ceres has reacted to inappropriate behavior that threatens the laws of hospitality; in a sense this theme (cf. the Perseus saga) lies behind the whole narrative of Persephone's abduction: Pluto abused the same principles when he stole his niece. And so Cyane warned Pluto: 5.415-416 *non potes invitae Cereris gener esse: roganda, / non rapienda fuit.*

Upon return to Sicily, with no word of her daughter, Ceres comes to Cyane where, as we might have expected from the initial digression about the fountain, Ceres is enraged to learn that her daughter has been abducted (she could not have drowned, after all); in anger the grain goddess turns her wrath against the fruits of the earth, which now either lay barren or are destroyed.[49] Soon enough, the truth is revealed, though not by Hecate and Helios (as in the *Hymn*),[50] but by a second water nymph, Arethusa.[51]

Extremum hunc, Arethusa, concede laborem.[52] Arethusa was invoked as Theocritus' muse of Sicilian pastoral; she is the patroness of the great fresh water spring near Ortygia. The setting has been idyllic; the content of the story has become anything but pastoral. Arethusa now intervenes to save the world, essentially: in the story of Ceres' veritable decision to destroy the earth by ending her protection of agriculture, we see a third threat to the world: the deluge, the fire, and now Ceres' anger and the risk of global famine. The rivers of the world had suffered grievously in the destruction wrought by Phaethon's mismanagement of the sun's horses, and now Arethusa will plead for herself and, by extension, the rest of the world's waters (Ovid envisions the rivers as patrons of their native lands, since arguably Ceres' action would not be nearly as fatal to them as Phaethon's).

Arethusa has her own story to tell, after the immediate emergency has passed; she owes an explanation for why she has found herself in Sicily (5.493 ff.). Arethusa did not see the abduction (cf. the sun in the *Fasti*, and the witnesses in the *Hymn*); only Cyane saw any part of the actual capture, and she was liquefied in grief at her ineffective testimony. Arethusa was traversing from Pisa to Sicily when she saw Persephone in the underworld, unhappy and still frightened (*tristis neque adhuc interrita*), though enthroned as queen of the dead. Unlike Cyane, this water nymph is able to report her findings to Ceres and solve the mystery of Persephone's disappearance.

Calliope, it seems, has chosen a story that puts a twist on the divine rapes of the first movements of the epic; Pluto abducted Persephone, but for the sake of what to a Roman audience would be an honorable, indeed royal and desirable marriage. Jupiter seeks to persuade Ceres to accept that her daughter has a dignified lot; the goddess will have none of it.[53] The supreme god is willing to let Persephone be returned to her mother, on the condition (established by the Fates) that she fasted in the underworld.

In the *Fasti*, Mercury is sent to fetch the ravished girl; he reports back quickly that she broke her fast with three pomegranate seeds. In the *Metamorphoses* she was wandering in a garden and had seven seeds from the same fruit. The story is derived ultimately from the *Homeric Hymn*, where Hades secretly gives the girl a single seed once Hermes appears to escort her back to her mother. In the *Fasti* Ovid offers no real explanation for how or why Persephone ate, while in the *Metamorphoses* he presents a picture of a simple child (5.535 *simplex*) wandering in the garden (where she is overcome by hunger). But that simple child is destined to become the queen of the underworld and mistress of the dead.

Calliope's story puts less blame for the whole incident on Pluto; in her version, the rapist did not actively conspire to ensure Persephone's continued presence in the underworld by giving her food. In the *Hymn* Persephone experiences rebirth as she returns to her mother, only to face the prospect of a second "death" once she answers truthfully the question about her infernal diet. Pluto is presented as more innocent in Ovid's version because of the poet's wish to put the blame on Venus and Cupid for the whole affair; given the success

Diana will have at the end of the book in rescuing Arethusa from rape, we can see in Book 5 yet another manifestation of the frequent conflict between the virgin goddess of the hunt and her immortal opposite.

Persephone's consumption of the seeds was witnessed by Ascalaphus, the son of the nymph Orphne and Acheron; he reports the ill-fated "meal" and ruins Persephone's happy reunion with Ceres (5.538-542). The name is suspiciously similar to Ascalabus, the Greek for "lizard," the moniker of the boy-newt in Nicander and Antoninus Liberalis.[54] Persephone, though, is already truly the queen of the dead; in anger at Ascalaphus' revelation, she throws water from the river of fire, Phlegethon, at his head. Whatever the demonic status of the son of Acheron, he is susceptible to bird metamorphosis; he is at once transformed into an owl (Latin *bubo*), a bird of ill omen (543-550). Thus both mother and daughter are afforded the chance to punish wretched characters that sadistically cause them pain.[55]

Persephone undergoes her own metamorphosis from simple (and hungry) to vengeful queen of the dead in the time between eating the pomegranate seeds and smiting Ascalaphus for his loquacity. Distantly, the talkativeness of this son of the Acheron presages the noteworthy garrulousness of the Pierides. The Muses sing inspired hymns; in the Pierides and the tattletale Ascalaphus we see a chattiness that is offensive to the goddesses (cf. the silently eloquent nymph Cyane). Ovid will return to this theme in the next book, with his grisly account of the similarly silent Philomela and her dumb eloquence.[56]

Calliope now asks why the companions of Persephone have been changed into birds that retain the features of young women (5.551-563). Here, the audience is seduced by a story that deserves more attention than it has received. The etiology of the Sirens is explained in a dozen verses that relate how the maidens sought after their missing companion, and, having had no luck on land, how they finally prayed that they might travel in search for her over the waters:

> quae postquam toto frustra quaesistis in orbe,
> protinus, et vestram sentirent aequora curam,
> posse super fluctus alarum insistere remis
> optastis . . . (5.556-559)

> *Who, after you had searched in vain throughout the whole world,*
> *straightway, so that the sea also might know your care,*
> *you chose to stand over the waves on the oarage of*
> *wings . . .*

The gods granted their prayer and they were transformed into bird-women, women who continue to have "so great a dowry of voice" (562 *tantaque dos oris*)—strange, since there are plenty of birds with the gift of melodious voice. The Sirens want to continue their quest at sea; in *curam* there is a hint of how the Sirens will themselves become a source of anxiety for future navigators.

The connection of the Sirens to Persephone is not original to Ovid.[57] In his narrative, there is no hint of the baleful associations we know from Homer (*Odyssey* 12.39-54 and 165-200) and the end of *Aeneid* 5, where after the loss of Palinurus Aeneas' ships safely pass the rock where they once threatened sailors. In the tradition linking the Sirens with Ceres' daughter, we see an emphasis on the idea that Persephone's abduction represents a kind of death (and an eternal one at that). The Sirens will presumably abandon their search in mid-ocean and haunt their accursed rock (until the tradition of their own inevitable end). The story of their search for Persephone explains their extensive repository of knowledge; they have presumably seen so much of the world in their exhaustive quest for the abducted girl. The Apollonian detail that Aphrodite (from her shrine at Eryx) saved the Argonaut Butes from their seductive song (he would have been their sole casualty from Jason's Argo) may point to the same sort of tradition we saw in Ovid's Venus and her lament that Persephone would remain virginal in the manner of Minerva and Diana; certainly the Sirens are a part of the same celibate universe that shuns marriage and the affairs of Venus.[58]

The Sirens are unambiguously dangerous; they are a hazard for navigators until the tradition of their suicide (because of Odysseus' eluding their snares).[59] We may speculate that the loss of their companion has caused their apparent anger; certainly Persephone (who is abducted while plucking flowers, itself a destructive image) is emblematic of the grave in her capacity as the queen over hell. Her companions are therefore, not surprisingly, associated with death.[60] If they were ever made aware of the details of the abduction of Persephone (or is this the one thing they do not ever learn?), they would perhaps be especially hateful of men. Since Persephone herself becomes the mistress of the dead, it occasions no wonder that her companions are also connected to the underworld.[61] Persephone was abducted without them, but they, too, have become underworld spirits, faithful to their mistress to the last. The song of the Sirens, with its allure of arcane knowledge, carries with it shades of mystery religions (i.e., Eleusis) and exploration of the afterlife and its secrets.

Jupiter divides Persephone's year between Ceres and Pluto (5.564-571). There is no explanation in any of our sources for how there can be a solemn decree of fate that those who eat of underworld food may not leave hell, while now Persephone is permitted back for six months.[62] The story as told in our surviving witnesses is merely a lavish etiology for the passage of the seasons, which, we might bemusedly note, have apparently not existed for the past several books of Ovid's poems (though there is no mention in Ovid of Ceres' refusing to perform her labors during winter *per se*; she merely stops her labor while she is busy searching for her daughter). In the *Fasti*, Ovid had told a lengthy account of the birth of agriculture (4.503-562, of the goddess' visit to Eleusis); in the *Metamorphoses*, agriculture is already a given in a pre-abduction world of farming labor. Persephone will be a lawful wife (5.567 *coniuge*).

Ceres does not forget Arethusa; she now asks the river to tell her story (5.572 ff.), which thus forms a pendant to the main Persephone narrative (the basic outline is an old story, known to Pindar).[63] She was no Salmacis, but rather a nymph well practiced in the arts of the chase; she was also beautiful, and that beauty would serve as a curse. She is hot on account of the summer sun and her labors; she proceeds to dive into an inviting pool that seems amazingly clear and calm. The scene is reminiscent of Diana's fateful bath, where Actaeon would unwittingly intrude to his doom; there is also an echo of Hermaphroditus' watery wrestling with Salmacis. We know the nymph will be pursued; soon enough the river god Alpheus appears and asks why she is hastening away. The nymph is naked; she flees away, thus inciting the lustful god even more. Her nakedness was an innocent reaction to the heat; the erotic imagery is linked to a girl who is unaware of the force of her charms. As Alpheus pursues her, she is like a dove before the hawk:

> ut fugere accipitrem penna trepidante columbae,
> ut solet accipiter trepidas urguere columbas (5.605-606)

> *just as the doves flee the accipiter on trembling wing,*
> *and just as the accipiter presses on the trembling doves.*

The simile is an echo of Camilla's pursuit of the Ligurian (*A.* 11.721-724), an image borrowed in turn from Homer's description of Achilles chasing Hector (*Il.* 22.139-142).[64] In Virgil, the powerful virgin huntress Camilla is equated with the Homeric Achilles (and female raptors are larger than male ones, so that the Virgilian comparison is arguably more apt than the Homeric). In Ovid, the bird of prey is Alpheus; the hapless dove the nymph Arethusa. Some prefer to imagine that the point of Ovid's use of such similes is to take dramatic moments from solemn epics and insert them into the (lower register) of amatory verse, especially a scene such as this Apollo and Daphne-like escapade. But in the context of Calliope's song, the song of the muse of epic verse, we have nothing less than a retelling of the *Iliad* and the *Aeneid*, or at least a passing allusion to the two greatest poems the muse had produced, the epics of Troy and Rome. We should expect that Calliope would cite a simile that had appeared in both of those earlier epics.

Alpheus is essentially a doublet of Pluto; it was appropriate that Arethusa should reveal the truth of Persephone's abduction to Ceres, since she herself had suffered a similar ill fate as the object of lust for a male god. Like the *simplex* Persephone, Arethusa is somewhat rustic and unsophisticated (5.583 *rustica dote*). And Arethusa is one of Diana's band, her arms bearer, in fact (619); she prays to the divine huntress for salvation.

The goddess answers the prayer of her favorite; she encloses Arethusa in a thick mist. Arethusa herself speaks in similes; is she not like a lamb hiding from the wolves, or like a rabbit seeking to escape the pursuit of hunting hounds. These similes serve (as before) to remind us that the muse of epic is telling the story. Small wonder, then, that this rustic girl knows how to use them. The mist is indeed quite humid; Arethusa tries to slink away and escape her pursuer, but as she attempts to depart she is rapidly changed into water (perhaps the goddess intended for her to stay fixed).[65]

The transition is somewhat odd; she is a cloud, after all, and a certain amount of condensation can be expected, but are we to imagine Diana effected this transformation? In any case, in an exact replica of Pluto's action at Cyane's pool, the archer goddess strikes the ground to provide her favorite with an escape route (5.639). Arethusa emerges near Ortygia in Sicily; the fact that the same name once graced Diana's Delos makes it especially pleasing to her nymph. Unlike Persephone, Ovid's Arethusa makes a successful escape with Diana's help.[66] The story thus neatly rehabilitates the huntress for whatever questionable behavior we might have attributed to her in the Callisto and Actaeon narratives. It is significant that in Ovid's narrative, there is no successful pursuit for Alpheus; he does not follow Diana's escape channel to mingle his waters with his love's.[67] Ovid does not assert that Alpheus did not follow her; he does not explicitly contradict all of his predecessors. But someone without knowledge of the myth might well conclude from Ovid that Arethusa escaped without her would-be lover. Apollo had not succeeded in winning Daphne; his twin sister Diana will triumph in securing the escape of her beloved rustic nymph.[68] Diana's actions with Arethusa bear close comparison with her response to Callisto in particular; the goddess had not been invoked by that nymph, while here Diana shows herself ready to help when called.

As Arethusa finishes her story (or, more accurately, Calliope finishes), the goddess Ceres yokes her dragon chariot (5.642 *geminos . . . angues*) and restrains the mouths of her serpentine steeds with a bit (643 *frenis coercuit ora*). Here we see a victory over the Theban avatar; a subtle conclusion, of a sort, to that long saga as the first third of the epic draws near to its close. And Ceres does not approach Thebes now, or even Perseus' Argos, but rather Pallas' city: Athens. There she will teach Triptolemus the arts of agriculture. Ovid's universal history is advancing apace, with the dramatic introduction of Pallas' sacred city.

The story of Ceres' Athenian/Eleusinian sojourn is Homeric, and it appears in the *Fasti*, too, though—as in the *Hymn*—as part of the narrative of Ceres' quest in search of her daughter. In the *Fasti* Ovid tells a tender tale of the aged Celeus and his invitation for the sorrowful mother to come to his house, where she finds a sick infant for whom she prepares a sleeping potion. Ceres finds some poppy before entering Celeus' house and mindlessly breaks the fast she had inaugurated as she searched for her daughter; the detail is a foreshadowing of Persephone's own behavior in the underworld. Late that night, Ceres endeavored to make Triptolemus immortal; the boy's mother interrupts the scene and disturbs the ritual, but Ceres announces the child's future as the bringer of agriculture before departing on her dragon chariot.

In the *Metamorphoses*, there is no hint of the hymnic lore Ovid had incorporated into the *Fasti*; Triptolemus is instead some civilizer who travels over Europe and Asia (5.648 *Europen . . . Asida*) before arriving in the wilds of Scythia, where we might expect a less than welcome reception for the Athenian teacher of agriculture. Lyncus is king; his name already announces the lynx into which he will be transformed (650 ff.).[69] Triptolemus, we now learn explicitly, had traveled through the *aether* (654) to reach the distant east—he is like to a god since Ceres is conveying him aloft. Lyncus, apparently ignorant of the story of Lycaon, tried to kill the Athenian as he slept; Ceres at once changed him into a lynx and ordered Triptolemus to make his way onward—it would seem Scythia would remain uncivilized for a while longer.

The end of this first third of the epic recalls the beginning of the last book of Lucretius' *De Rerum Natura*, where Athens first grants both crops and life to mortal men: Epicurus is the Athenian credited with bringing solace to the world (6.3-4 *et recreaverunt vitam legesque rogarunt, / et primae dederunt solacia dulcia vitae*, of Athens). In Lucretius' vision, the glories of the opening of Book 6 soon give way to the devastating conclusion of his work, where the plague brings death and destruction to the noble city (a metaphor for the inevitable end of life, which readers of the poet's Epicurean gospel are supposed to be able to face with serenity). And just as it did for Virgil, so also for Ovid does the ghost of Lucretius continue to haunt the poet's pen.

Not coincidentally, the end of the first third of the epic—with its long story of Persephone and Arethusa—softly echoes the close of the first third of the *Aeneid*, where *Proserpina* had not yet taken a golden lock from the dying Dido's hair to commit her to Stygian Orcus (*A*. 4.698-699). In Virgil's vision, Proserpina is already the fully developed underworld queen, to whom Aeneas must offer the Golden Bough to gain access to Elysium.

And, as we approach the book's close, Calliope—the muse of epic—ends her long story on a note that exactly matches the beginning of history: the outrageous behavior of Lycaon of Arcadia. He had been transformed into a wolf; now the lynx Lyncus joins him in theriomorphic punishment, though, we might note, far off in remote Scythia, not anywhere in Greece (even the wilds of Arcadia). Triptolemus might have been some Alexander, sent to civilize the wild people of the world's edges; the blessings of Greek society are spreading far as part of the progress of Ovid's universal history.

Thus ends Calliope's story, with a return to where we had begun before the destruction of the world. Her song is learned:

Finierat doctos e nobis maxima cantus (5.662)[70]

Our oldest sister had finished her learned songs

The Muses are gifted with the power to know that which memory has taught; they know the history of the world.[71] In Calliope's song there has been more than mere cyclical roundabout, however; water, fire, and starvation had failed to ruin the globe, all thanks to the mercy of the gods. We have been treated in the fifth book to the heroic Perseus, purveyor of both great deeds and violence, and the civilizing Triptolemus, as the progression from Thebes to Argos to Athens brings us to the very cusp of what we might dare to consider a modern world (at least from the classical perspective). Between Perseus and Triptolemus, there seems more hope than not for humanity, and in the careful epic cycle Calliope has offered, the gods have been presented most favorably, climaxing with a stunning victory for virginity for Diana on behalf of her beloved Arethusa. The Lyncus pendant reminds us that the world still harbors wretches, but Lyncus is comfortably Scythian, an Eastern enemy not unlike those slain by Perseus in his father-in-law's dining hall. And, conveniently, Bacchus seems to have been forgotten and has made no appearance in the Muses' song.[72] The first story of Book 6 will take us to Asia Minor, to Maeonia; the "foreign" element in these stories of divine retribution will continue.

We know that the Pierides are already magpies; we are not surprised that these Macedonians are not moved by Calliope's song. The nymphs, of course, award the victory to the Muses:

> at nymphae vicisse deas Helicona colentes
> concordi dixere sono . . . (5.663-664)

> *But the nymphs said with one voice that the*
> *goddesses dwelling on Helicon had conquered . . .*

Some scholars have claimed the game was rigged, given that the semi-divine nymphs would favor the Pierides, but nobody told the Pierides what to sing or, more importantly, how to react in the aftermath of their loss. The Pierides had suggested the terms that they would now surrender their favored haunts to the Muses (and the Muses had not disputed those terms). The Pierides seem not to have considered that there was no good reason the Muses would ever want to exchange Helicon for Macedonian haunts.

But now the nine daughters of Pierus begin to revile the Muses (5.664-665 *convicia victae / cum iacerent*). Stunningly, even after the Muses announce that now they will suffer punishment, the Pierides laugh and spurn the goddesses' words (669 *rident Emathides spernuntque minacia verba*). The sisters had hurled reproaches at the Muses (*convicia*), and reproaches of the forest they become, as the Muses effect a transformation of the nine wretches into magpies, birds that to this day have a boundless love for talking (677-678 *nunc quoque in alitibus facundia prisca remansit / raucaque garrulitas studiumque immane loquendi*).[73] Even as the sisters are transformed, they continue to try to mock the Muses with obscene gestures (670-671 *magno clamore protervas / intentare manus*): their impudence knows no end. The Pierides will, in a sense, continue to speak in the behavior of the mortals we shall soon meet; Arachne, for one, will be a spokesman for their cause.

We do well to remember that it is Minerva's story that provides the foundation of the lengthy narrative of the Musomachia that we have just witnessed. The nymphs are the arbiters of that contest, but Minerva, too, stands as judge. She is the goddess not only of the domestic arts of weaving but also of battle; together with the Muses there is almost a self-sufficient Rome on

Helicon.[74] The second half of Book 5 has also presented something of a feminine epic, where the major characters are women (the Muses, Minerva, Venus, Diana, Ceres and Persephone, Cyane and Arethusa, the wretched Pierides). Women have been the victims of Jovian rapes; Jupiter is discreetly retiring in this book, careful not to offend either Ceres or Pluto (and he is in fact willing to compel Persephone's return, provided she fasted). A successful divine rape is framed by two accounts of the successful eluding of would-be rapists.

The fifth book of the *Metamorphoses* ends with the victory of the Muses and the punishment of their thoroughly dislikable mortal rivals. Like Lyncus, they now bear the marks of their true nature in their animal transformations. Once again, the poet has ended a book with no clear sense to the audience of what might follow next. Love of talking (5.678 *studiumque immane loquendi*) has, of course, characterized what has filled five books and what will fill another ten. But with that wink and nod, Ovid prepares to advance to the next third of his epic, a collection of books that offers the second great movement of his tripartite poem.

Ovid's first order of business will be to address a problem that the actions of Lyncus and the Pierides have illustrated all too well: the flaws inherent in men, in particular those that lead to outrageous (or at least offensive) behavior. Ovid will now fill a book with narratives of divine punishments for mortal missteps. Lurking behind the apparent quest of the gods to root out wickedness from the world will be the search for another hero, who will, soon enough, appear suddenly and indeed without warning. He will emerge, not surprisingly, from the narrative of yet another divine rape: from the outrageousness of the immortals comes the birth of mortal heroes.[75] But first, Ovid will follow the gods as wickedness is rooted out over the world. He will surprise us with how he ends his accounts of divine vengeance, but not until we have had our fill of the more or less just deserts of immortal retribution. Along the way we shall learn more about the nature of both the victor and the vanquished, as a parade of gods judges humanity in the dock.

Notes

1. Besides the usual commentaries, special mention must be made of the monograph of Stephen Hinds, *The Metamorphosis of Persephone: Ovid and the Self-Conscious Muse*, Cambridge, 1987, a book that offers a detailed, sophisticated account of the Persephone narrative and a call for Ovidian critics to read the poet carefully, line by line, word for word, since "nowhere are the [critics] more guilty of underreading than in the *Metamorphoses*." (p. xi). On Hinds note the important review of Richard Thomas (*Classical Philology* 85.1 (1990), pp. 77-80. The second book of Hill's commentary (Aris & Phillips, 1992) covers Books 5-8, rather briskly. There is also now the monograph of Patricia J. Johnson, *Ovid Before Exile: Art and Punishment in the Metamorphoses* (Wisconsin Studies in the Classics), Madison: The University of Wisconsin Press, 2008, which examines the contest between the daughters of Pierus and the Muses. Johnson sees Augustus in Minerva (*fortasse recte*). The new Italian commentaries (under the general editorship of Alessandro Barchiesi) cannot be praised sufficiently. The third volume, edited by Gianpiero Rosati, covers Books 5-6 with the same skill evinced by the first two.

2. On Ovid's battle of the Muses note Johnson, Patricia, and Malamud, Martha, "Ovid's "Musomachia," in *Pacific Coast Philology* 23.1-2 (1988), pp. 30-38.

3. For Ovid's version of Persephone's rape note Hinds, Stephen, "An Allusion in the Literary Tradition of the Proserpina Myth," in *The Classical Quarterly* N. S. 32.2 (1982), pp. 476-478, and Zissos, Andrew, "The Rape of Proserpina in Ovid, *Met.* 5.341-661: Internal Audience and Narrative Distortion," in *Phoenix* 53.1-2 (1999), pp. 97-113; note also Otis, *op. cit.* pp. 152 ff. In the afterlife of the myth, especially noteworthy is Stravinsky's *Perséphone* (with libretto by Gide), which was first performed in Paris in the spring of 1934. The bibliography on Demeter and Persephone is vast. I note the very helpful Penglase, C., *Greek Myths and Mesopotamia: Parallels and Influence in the Homeric Hymns and Hesiod*, London-New York, 1997, and, with caution, Suter, A., *The Narcissus and the Pomegranate: An Archaeology of the Homeric* Hymn *to Demeter*, Ann Arbor: The University of Michigan Press, 2004 (with Andrew Faulkner's important response in *The Classical Review* 54.2 (2004), pp. 286-288). For the evidence of a worship of Persephone distinct from Demeter, and the possible existence of a Sicilian great goddess, note the first part of the influential work of Zuntz, G., *Persephone: Three Essays on Religion and Thought in Magna Graecia*, Oxford, 1971.

4. Various attempts have been made by scholars to divide the epic into more or less neatly defined sections. Otis' work in this regard is rather *sui generis* and not as influential as its meticulous character might otherwise merit; Ludwig (*Struktur und Einheit*, de Bruyter, 1965) offers an even more complicated schema than Otis. I cannot imagine that either scholar's plan reflects the poet's intentions for his audience. For an epic in fifteen books, I think a division into thirds is most likely what the poet envisaged, along with a division into halves that raises the question of why the poem has an odd number of books. As we shall see, the division into halves offers problematic, yet interesting, results.

5. Pseudo-Apollodorus 2.43-44 briefly mentions the rivalry of Cepheus' brother Phineus and his petrifaction; Hyginus (*Fabulae* 64) names Agenor as the suitor. The episode is not well attested outside Ovid.

6. Hill ad loc. is not convinced of the connection between the two romantic triangles, but does not offer a challenge to the evidence the commentators and others have gathered.

7. Relatively little work has been done on the battle in the banquet hall; the second half of this book has eclipsed the first in scholarly popularity. See Hendry, Michael, "On Not Looking at a Gorgon: Ovid, *Metamorphoses* 5.217," in *Mnemosyne* 49.2 (1996), pp. 118-191. "Here Ovid is at his worst and his worst is very bad indeed." (Otis, *op. cit.*, p. 164). I shall not try to praise this section, though I think it has been unjustly ignored and reviled; I do not agree with those who feel that Ovid is a deliberate practitioner of bad verse for this or that reason. He is, however, interested in showing the decline of his hero under the dehumanizing experience of slaughter; it is significant that Perseus disappears from the action after this sequence, with no valediction. The sequence shows, too, that Ovid understood the point of the second half of the *Aeneid*.

8. For Ovid's manipulation of battle scenes from Virgil, see Keith, Alison M., "Ovid on Vergilian War Narrative," in *Vergilius* 48 (2002), pp. 105-122. Keith sees imitation in the Perseus-Phineus combat of both *Aeneid* 7 and, as prolegomenon to both, the historical reality of civil war in the late Republic. Regrettably, Ovid is not considered in the exemplary article of Weber, Clifford, "The Diction for Death in Latin Epic," in *Agon: Journal of Classical Studies* (1969), pp. 45-68.

9. Rhoetus is probably the Rhoecus who was associated with Hylaeus as a casualty of Atalanta (Callimachus, *In Dianam* 220 ff., Aelian, *Varia Historia* 13.1, and cf. Propertius c. 1.13).

10. Archery carries with it mixed connotations for an Augustan audience. Apollo is the preeminent archer, and in *Aeneid* 5 the archery contest brought with it Acestes' fateful portent—but it was also the weapon of Pandarus' truce-breaking in the *Iliad* and could carry negative associations of cowardice and unwillingness to face one's opponents at close quarters. We might also compare Ascanius' use of the bow (under Apollo's watchful eye) to slay Numanus Remulus in *A.* 9. On the Homeric view of the bow see further Farron, Steven, "Attitudes to Military Archery in the *Iliad*," in Basson, A.F., and Dominik, W. J., eds., *Studies on Classical Antiquity and Tradition in Honour of W. J. Henderson*, Bern-Frankfurt-am-Main: Peter Lang, 2003, pp. 169-184, and Sutherland, Caroline, "Archery in the Homeric Epics," in *Classics Ireland* 8 (2001), pp. 111-120.

11. Phorbas is a name with a rich history in the Greek and Latin epic traditions. At *Iliad* 14.490-491 we learn that the Trojan Phorbas was loved by Hermes beyond all his fellow Trojans; he is gorily murdered by Peneleos (note the identical first and last letters to Perseus). At *Iliad* 9.665, Phorbas is the father of Diomede, a mistress of Achilles with whom he sleeps during the embassy sequence. Phorbas is sometimes the father of the Argonauts' helmsman Tiphys, and, at the end of *Aeneid* 5 (in a related sense) the Trojan in whose guise Sleep menaces Aeneas' helmsman Palinurus.

12. And Erytus is an Argonaut at Apollonius Rhodius, *Argonautica* 1.52.

13. And Minerva will move us from Boeotia to the Near East for her attack on Arachne at the beginning of Book 6, which follows on Ceres' vengeance against Lyncus for his would-be attack on the Athenian Triptolemus, as the civilizing force of the Greek world moves east.

14. The minor victim Clytus appears at Hyginus, *Fabulae* 170 as a son of Aegyptus; Clytius below at 5.140 is a more common name, shared by several figures in the *Aeneid* (9.774, 10.129, 10.325).

15. Also the name of a Thracian at *Aeneid* 10.351, who sent three of his sons to fight in Italy (victims of Aeneas and the Trojans' onrush); at 14.694 below Idas is one of Diomedes' companions.

16. Liger slays Emathion at *Aeneid* 9.571; at 10.576 ff. Liger is a foolish warrior who insults Aeneas, which definitively clarifies the question of his allegiance in the earlier passage.

17. At 12.380 we meet another Dorylas, a Centaur. The confusion of the slaughter, where victims do not fall according to neat and easily characterized divisions, serves to remind the audience of the confused hazards of war—a theme of both Virgil and Ovid.

18. Ash is conventional enough for spears, but the wood here signals the beginning of the final stages of the long combat.

19. Many parallels can be drawn between Arruns and Aeneas.

20. Like much in Ovid, the story is obscure: Pseudo-Apollodorus knows it (2.2.1, 2.4.1), as does Pausanias (2.16.2, 2.25.7); the latter speaks of a division of empire between Perseus and Proetus, as well as an inconclusive battle that ended in a truce. Hyginus (*Fabulae* 244) says that Perseus killed Proetus, only to be slain in turn by his son Megapenthes. A scholiast on Euripides, *Phoenissae* 1109 records that Proetus went into exile in Thebes. Pausanias records that Perseus was a successful opponent of the introduction of Bacchic cults (2.20.3 and 2.22.1).

21. Better known than Proetus; Polydectes' story is known to Pindar (*Pythians* 12.9-16), who mentions Perseus' blinding of the Graiae, his avenging of the mistreatment of Danae, the shower of gold, and the patronage of Athena the hero enjoyed. Cf. Pseudo-Apollodorus 2.4.3. On Pindar's Perseus note the useful article of Koehnken, A., "Perseus' Kampf und Athenes Erfindung," in *Hermes* 104 (1976), pp. 257-265.

22. The main source is Aratus, *Phaenomena* 216 ff. (where see Kidd); Antonius Liberalis 9 says that Helicon began to swell because of the singing of the Muses (in their contest with the Pierides, on which see below) until Pegasus stopped its expansion by a strike of his hoof. At *Fasti* 3.449 ff., Ovid says that Pegasus created the spring after he objected to Bellerophon's ultimately successful attempts to bridle him (Ovid does not include any Bellerophon lore in his epic).

23. Hinds begins his monograph on this book with a highly detailed account of the striking of Pegasus' hoof and its literary implications for students of Aratus, Ovid, Germanicus, *et al.*

24. We have no evidence for this story other than Ovid, and he may well have invented the tale, which aptly fits his purposes at this juncture in the epic.

25. Anderson ad loc. oddly calls the Muse Urania "puritanical" for describing the would-be rapist thus.

26. Pausanias 9.39.3 says that Pierus had nine daughters who were named after the nine Muses, and that their sons were called the children of the Muses. It is entirely unclear where the story of the contest between the Muses and the Pierides arose. The fact that Antoninus Liberalis records the story (*Metamorphoses* 9) does point to a Nicandrian original, but beyond that we can say no more.

27. Because of his connection to goat sacrifice and tragedy.

28. She is also, of course, ox-eyed Hera.

29. Ovid is also playing with the anthropomorphic gods of Egypt; cf. the terrible animal head deities that face Octavian on the shield of Aeneas. Thoth had an ibis head. Many of these mocking metamorphoses were borrowed from Nicander.

30. For the important question of internal narrators and the omnipresent Ovid, see further Barchiesi, Alessandro, "Voices and Narrative 'Instances,'" in Knox, Peter E.,

Oxford Readings in Ovid, Oxford, 2006, pp. 284 ff. (translation of "Voci e istanze narrative nelle Metamorfosi di Ovidio," from *MD* 23, 1989, pp. 55-97). Calliope is the muse of epic, and, as we shall see, she makes a clever allusion to both Homer and Virgil before the end of her Persephone narrative to highlight her past achievements. Note also the important article of Cahoon, Leslie, "Calliope's Song: Shifting Narrators in Ovid, *Metamorphoses* 5," in *Helios* 23.1 (1996), pp. 43-66.

31. I usually refer to the goddess as "Persephone" and not "Proserpina" for convenience sake; Ovid uses both names in the *Metamorphoses* (and only the former in the *Fasti*) for metrical convenience (forms of "Persephone," e.g., are required for the first position in the hexameter).

32. See further Fantham ad loc. (who notes that the story of Persephone's abduction is the "longest secondary narrative in the *Metamorphoses*"; the longest primary narrative is that of Phaethon). The *Fasti* account is part of Ovid's commemoration of the Cerialia, an April festival in the goddess' honor that may have marked the (spring) recovery of Persephone, who was venerated as *Libera*, the free girl. The cult dated to 493 B.C. at Rome, and Augustus was responsible for restoring the temple that had burned down in 31 B.C. (it was rededicated in A.D. 17). There were two festivals that are attested at Rome (see further Fantham ad loc.), which Ovid conflates into one: the spring *Cerialia* and a high summer (Greek) ritual that was handled by priestesses from Magna Graecia; the narrative of Persephone's freedom was properly part of that celebration. But there is no good reason to imagine that the April Cerialia did not include due honor to the freed daughter, honor that was fitting throughout the warmer months of the year (though not as fitting, arguably, after the solstice).

33. Cicero also has a brief digression on the myth at *Verrines* 2.4.106-107, though apart from clear verbal echoes there is little of import that Ovid has adopted.

34. Venus and Cupid have moved to loftier targets than Apollo; Pluto is a difficult quarry for the amatory gods, and the appearance of the lord of the dead outside his realm is irresistible. But his pursuit of Persephone represents a worsening of the violence of rape; one of Ovid's themes is that the symbiotic relationship between gods and men means that the two classes of beings feed off of each other in imitative behavior. But the story of Persephone's abduction—which ends as an eminently Roman sort of marriage— is framed by the tales of two successful escapes from rape, something we have not seen before except in the case of Daphne, whose own fate was of questionable success.

35. Note, e.g., Hinds, *op. cit.*, pp. 131 ff.

36. Otis (*op. cit.*, p. 153) argues that the "story of Proserpina is far more akin to the impious stories of the Pieriae than the somewhat unsophisticated Muses can readily understand." In this Otis compares the abduction of Persephone to his "*maiestas-amor*" theme of the first movement of the epic; too many of the gods are rapists who abduct young women. But the story of this girl's abduction is very different from those previous stories, with nuances that lead to a legitimate marriage and, in a brilliant *dénouement*, Diana's successful rescue of Arethusa from rape.

37. The Pierides are an unworthy audience for the song. There is no question at the end of this book that the nymphs are correct in awarding the victory to the Muses. But this victory does not alter the fact that the Muses have left many questions unanswered, many potential counterarguments without response. Ovid will do the Pierides' work for them in the next sequence of books.

38. On the *Hymn* see Richardson, who argues (in my view rightly) that we can be sure Ovid knew the archaic text and imitated it. On the whole matter see further Hinds, *op. cit.*, pp. 52 ff. There are echoes of Callimachus' hymn to Demeter in Ovid, but

Callimachus does not deal with the abduction myth (see further Hopkinson's Cambridge commentary). Ovid in turn was a major influence on Claudian's *De Raptu Proserpinae* (where see Gruzelier, and Hall).

39. For the possible attacks on Augustan moral legislation and imperial ideology implicit in the poet's depiction of Venus here, see Johnson, Patricia J., "Constructions of Venus in Ovid's *Metamorphoses* V," in *Arethusa* 29.1 (1996), pp. 125-149.

40. Persephone's abduction is a traditional etiology for the seasons, though in Ovid agriculture has existed in some form for a while now. Ovid is not presenting a carefully arranged history of the world, and so at the end of his narrative Triptolemus is the bringer of the arts of cultivation far and wide; in this civilizing act there is a miniature Golden Age, as it were, which starts from his native Athens. In some sense this book of the epic marks the dawn of that city's influence (as we move from Thebes to Argos to Attica).

41. Scholars have widely accepted the argument that in the *Metamorphoses* Ovid presents an epic view of the abduction, whereas in the *Fasti* he proposes an elegiac reading (Hinds, *op. cit.*, p. 127; Myers, *Ovid's Causes*, pp. 163-164). This approach strikes me as rather much fuss over the obvious; the meter of the two poems reveals the two genres, and in the *Fasti* we have an elegiac epic, etc. Scholars have also noted that the Pierides perform exactly the sort of song Ovid rejected (against his will, we might note) at the beginning of the *Amores*, where Cupid prevented a gigantomachy (just as here Cupid will prevent Pluto's harmless return to his underworld lair and will initiate an "amatory" epic). We do well to note that Ovid had greater freedom in the placement of his episodes in the *Metamorphoses* than he did in the *Fasti*, where he was constrained by calendar exigencies. The Pierides sing the song that Ovid had been obstructed from completing in his youth; their gigantomachy is, however, not the most important reason why the Pierides are doomed (their bad behavior at the end of Calliope's song seals whatever doom they had already incurred merely by challenging the Muses). Cupid instigated Ovid's change of theme in the *Amores*, and he carries out his mother's orders in the *Metamorphoses*, thus instigating the Pluto-Persephone epyllion.

42. Virgil, too, presents a "traditional" underworld that would (more or less) be familiar to Homer, only to alter its course (and geography) when he introduces the concept of purification and rebirth of souls (e.g., the world of Pythagoras, Neoplatonism, and Stoic philosophy). I have argued elsewhere that at the end of *Aeneid* 6, Virgil has Aeneas exit the underworld by the ivory gate of false dreams to signify that in his view, neither Homer nor the Neoplatonists were correct in their conception of the afterlife, but rather that Lucretius was the teacher of truth: there is no life after the grave. See further my "A Brief Reflection on the Gates of Sleep," in *Latomus* 66.3 (2007), pp. 628-635, and my entry "Eschatology" in the forthcoming Wiley-Blackwell *Virgil Encyclopedia* (Thomas, R., and Ziolkowski, J., eds.). At this relatively early stage in his worldview, Ovid does not yet trouble his audience with opposing philosophical schools, but is content to remain in the world of traditional myth.

43. Her existence is exceedingly shadowy outside this scene, though Diodorus Siculus (5.4.1-2) does record that Hades created the spring at Cyane when he returned to the underworld with his captive bride. In Ovid's narrative (5.420-424) Pluto responds to Cyane's objections by striking the deepest part of her pool with his scepter, thus opening a presumably unwelcome entrance to his realm.

44. Pluto strikes the ground at the bottom of Cyane's pool; the earth opens a way for his chariot. In the description of the god's action (5.423-424 *icta viam tellus in Tartara fecit / et pronos currus medio cratere recipit*), there may be an echo of the *crater* from

which dreams drink truth and falsehood at Plutarch, *Moralia, De Sera* 566b, along with Orphic parallels—even if the metaphor is quite conventional.

45. See further Murgatroyd, Paul, "Ceres' Informants in Ovid," in *Eranos* 101.2 (2003), pp. 129-132.

46. On Ovid's "easy" transformations note Solodow, *op. cit.*, p. 183-184.

47. In the *Fasti* Ovid associates this with the ritual carrying of torches in the Eleusinian Mysteries; see further Fantham ad loc.

48. See Montanari, F., "L'Episodio eleusino delle peregrinazioni di Demetra (A proposito delle fonti di Ovidio *Fas.* 4.502-62 e *Metam.* 5.446-661)," in *Annali della Scuola Normale Superiore di Pisa* 4.1.3 (1974), pp. 109-137.

49. The story is known to the *Hymn* (cf. 305-309), but Ovid is very much an independent reader of his sources.

50. Ceres prays in the *Fasti* to the Parrhasian stars (4.577 ff.), i.e., the Greater Bear Callisto and the Lesser, Helice, to help in her hunt for Persephone. Callisto had been raped by Jupiter; she is an apt constellation for Ceres to invoke (even if the "scientific" reason is that the Bears never set and thus see all; cf. 4.576-577). But Helice does not reveal anything; she urges Ceres to consult the sun, since the "night is innocent of the crime" (581 *crimine nox vacua est*), a strange expression (see further Fantham, and Bömer): indeed Night had not witnessed the abduction, and apparently the stars can only see that which happens when they are shining (i.e., nocturnally).

51. In the *Fasti*, Arethusa is mentioned briefly (4.423) as the river that entranced the mothers of the gods as they frolicked near its waters. Cf. Virgil, *Aeneid* 3.694 ff. (with Horsfall), where we find the basic outline of Alpheus' union with her waters.

52. Virgil, *Eclogues* 10.1.

53. Ovid's two versions here have many correspondences; in both we find *praedone marito* at line end to describe Pluto (*F.* 4.591, *M.* 5.521). In the *Fasti* Ceres asks if her lot would have been better if the giants had defeated the Olympians and she were now a captive; given the Pierides' gigantomachy, the passage occasions interest for the question of composition of the two poems. Interestingly, Jupiter says that Pluto owns the "empty chasm" as his lot (4.600 *possidet alter aquas, alter inane chaos*), which (*pace* Fantham) brings up inevitable thought of the beginning of the *Metamorphoses*, even if the word does not refer to the primordial state of the universe. The point may be, yet again, Ovid's cyclical view: the ultimate fate of the dead is not dissimilar to that of the world before the coming of order.

54. This underworld demon is otherwise known only to Pseudo-Apollodorus 1.33, where his mother is Gorgyra and not Orphne. There may be a lost original source for the tale, but the presence of the two similarly named characters, both of whom hamper the reunion of mother and daughter, is significant.

55. For a very different view, see Anderson ad loc.; he considers Persephone the sadistic one as she takes pleasure in the transformation of Ascalaphus. Anderson strangely considers the forthcoming metamorphosis of Persephone's maiden companions into the Sirens to be equally evidentiary of the two goddesses' faults. But the Ovidian Sirens chose their own fate.

56. On Ascalaphus' owl and the boy-newt (another victim of Ceres' wrath), see Myers, K. Sara, "The Lizard and the Owl: An Etymological Pair in Ovid, *Metamorphoses* 5," in *The American Journal of Philology* 113.1 (1992), pp. 63-68. Note also Ronnick, Michele Valerie, "Stellio non lacerta et bubo non strix: Ovid *Metamorphoses* 5.446-61 and 534-50," in *The American Journal of Philology* 114.3 (1993), pp. 419-420 (a reply to Myers' article). Ronnick makes the important point that Ovid's Ascalaphus is

transformed not into a "screech" owl (as is often carelessly thought), but rather a "sluggish owl," an *ignavus bubo* (who is, nonetheless, a herald of ill omen [549-550] *venturi nuntia luctus, / . . . dirum mortalibus omen*). Somehow both a *stellio* and a *bubo* are less impressive than a *lacerta* or a *strix*; these transformations are as disgraceful as one could imagine.

57. Euripides, *Helena* 167 ff. may point to the tradition, which is conclusively evidenced at Apollonius Rhodius, *Argonautica* 4.892 ff. Hyginus (*Fabulae* 141) has them punished for not having helped Persephone.

58. In Apollonius (*Argonautica* 4.892) the Sirens are located on Anthemoessa, a "flowery" island off the western coast of southern Italy; they dwell in a locale not dissimilar, then, to where Persephone was abducted. See further Nelis, Damien, *Virgil's Aeneid and the Argonautica of Apollonius Rhodius*, Leeds: Francis Cairns, 2001, pp. 205-209. The Sirens were variously located; there was disagreement, too, as to names and number.

59. Lycophron, *Alexandra* 712 ff.; Hyginus, *Fabulae* 141.

60. At Plato, *Cratylus* 403d, the Sirens are used as an example of just how powerful death is; even they cannot escape the grave—where they are, of course, united at last with their mistress.

61. The attribution of song to the Sirens, as to the Muses, has engendered a great amount of scholarship on the question of female authority in poetic discourse. But the place of the Muses in the epic tradition makes it obvious to credit women with song; cf. Carmentis, the prophetic nymph, and *carmen*, etc. Tissol (*Face of Nature*, pp. 207 ff.) makes the point (as do others) that Ovid seems to question whether the Sirens deserved their fate. But Ovid makes it reasonably clear that the bird-women chose their transformation. Tissol *et al.* wonder about the well-known destructive powers of the Sirens, with the implication that they did not deserve that aspect of their transformation. We could argue that what is not in Ovid is outside the realm of consideration; Ovid wants us to focus on the story he has told and the details he has accumulated. We might also reflect that the ultimate destiny of the Sirens may not be the consequence of divine transformation, but the result of their own actions in the face of their seemingly endless quest: they asked for the wings, which the gods granted while also ensuring that their capacity for beautiful song remained. Some songs, though, are better left unheard. For Persephone as messenger of death, see Kenney ad *Heroides* 21.46.

62. At 5.568 ff., we read that the goddess' face and mind and mouth were all changed; she became as happy as the sun when it shines forth from the clouds. I take it this refers to Persephone, not Ceres (*contra* Anderson *et al.*), though perhaps the ambiguity emphasizes the common bond and mind between mother and daughter. In any case, it is notable that never again in myth do we encounter Persephone on earth or in heaven, and she is a regular feature of the underworld whenever heroes venture there; despite the pacification of Ceres, she becomes associated exclusively with the lower regions.

63. *Nemeans* 1.1-2.

64. In Quintus Smyrnaeus, Penthesilea is a dove before Achilles the hawk (*Posthomerica* 1.529-572).

65. The interaction of Alpheus with Arethusa is discussed at length by Stirrup, B. E., "Techniques of Rape: Varieties of Wit in Ovid's *Metamorphoses*," in *Greece & Rome* 24 (1977), pp. 170-184.

66. For a reading of Arethusa's escape as an artifact of Bronze Age sailing between the Peloponnesus and Sicily, see Bilic, Tomoslav, "The Myth of Alpheus and Arethusa

and Open-Sea Voyages on the Mediterranean: Stellar Navigation in Antiquity," in *IJNA* 38.1 (2009), pp. 116-132 (with maps).

67. Cf. Virgil's version at *A*. 3.694 ff.

68. At *Amores* 3.29-30, Ovid briefly mentions the traditional story: *quid? non Alpheon diversis currere terris / virginis Arcadiae certus adegit amor?*, where Alpheus is in pursuit of an Arcadian Arethusa, where the nymph's descriptor (somewhat odd) may point to the stereotypical woodland haunts and groves of that region (cf. Callisto).

69. The story is unknown until after Ovid; it may be an invention of the poet, though, as ever, we must be slow to ascribe originality too easily.

70. In the Vatican manuscript (11th century), Book 6 begins here: the punishment of the Pierides is thus closely linked with the punishment narratives that follow.

71. We should also remember that the Muses were not invoked in the proem to Ovid's epic. As Heyworth has noted ad Propertius c. 1.1, the old view that the Muses were the "chaste girls" (*castas paellas*) Amor taught Propertius to hate may well be worth considering. Ovid, the poet of amours, does not commence his transformational epic with mention of the Muses. Only at the close of the first third of his epic does he introduce them to his narrative, not as the inspiration of his song, but rather as the singers of their own poems in competition with would-be mortal rivals. Calliope's song, however, puts a seal on the drama of the first third of the epic: the poet is to be tamed, along with the rest of humanity.

72. On the contrary, the Pierides remembered him, though only for his goat-disguised flight from Typhoeus (where, arguably, chronologically he should never have appeared).

73. On the failure of the Pierides and other such defeated artists in the epic, note Leach, Eleanor W., "Ekphrasis and the Theme of Artistic Failure in Ovid's *Metamorphoses*," in *Ramus* 3 (1974), pp. 102-142.

74. And a female one at that, with idealized virginity in both the goddess and the daughters of Memory.

75. Throughout his epic, Ovid is deeply concerned with the symbiotic relationship between man and god. Each depends on the other, and the behavior of the one influences the other in kind. It will not surprise us that Boreas rapes Orithyia at the end of Book 6 right after the terrible story of Tereus, Procne, and Philomela.

Chapter VI

Tritonia Had Listened

The sixth book of Ovid's epic is highly episodic.[1] It devotes significant attention to accounts of divine retribution against mortal behavior. At the close of Book 5 and the first third of the epic, Ovid presented a worldview that had now been crowned with the colloquy of Minerva and the Muses on Helicon. The virginal goddesses had presented an Olympian order that began to offer rehabilitation for the tarnished reputations of amorous gods; the underworld was now Pluto's with Persephone, and the blessings of civilization had begun to flow out even to the barbarous East under the patronage of Minerva's own city, Athens. In some sense Book 6 begins with an air of finishing the process of global improvement and the establishment of a peaceful Jovian rule over the world (cf. Minerva's olive-wreathed tapestry below); the last vestiges of ruthless arrogance will be rooted out by avenging gods. The book will end very differently, as Ovid relates the most horrific tale thus far in the epic, and thereby sets the stage for a lengthy exploration of the nature of the hero.

The first target of immortal wrath is the Lydian girl Arachne.[2] Ovid shifts the scene quickly and deftly; Minerva approves what the Muses did to the Pierides, and sets off at once to settle the matter of Arachne, who has been rumored to boast that her skills in weaving surpass the goddess'. Minerva heads east, to Lydia; Arachne is not famous or noble by birth, but she is gifted in her arts (something the goddess does not deny). Arachne's father supports her work, while her mother is already dead as Ovid's story opens (6.10 *occiderat mater*).[3] The first real indication that Arachne's art is sublime is the admiration it engenders among the nymphs, who abandon their vineyards to inspect it (15-16 *deseruere sui nymphae vineta Tmoli, / deseruere suas nymphae Pactolides undas*; the locale looks forward to the story of Midas and his golden touch). The nymphs not only want to see the finished product, but also Arachne's creative process, so marvelous is the site of watching the lowborn girl work at her loom. "You would know," Ovid says, "that she had been taught by the goddess herself":

. . . scires a Pallade doctam. (6.23)

The apostrophe comes as something of a surprise. Thus far, in the span of less than two dozen lines, Ovid has crafted a delicate psychological portrait of a girl who suffers from what moderns might call an inferiority complex; her background is poor on both sides of her family, but she has a skill that surpasses that of any rival. Even the semi-divine nymphs want to come and see her artistry at work. Some degree of sympathy is already being inculcated in the audience; Arachne does not remind us of the magpie Pierides who insulted the Muses both with words and obscene gestures. But the end of the description announces directly to the audience that *Pallas* had been her teacher. This was no skill acquired absent divine favor; Minerva, the goddess of domestic crafts, had taught Arachne. The image of a woman spinning and weaving at home had profound resonance for Ovid's Roman audience, and this Lydian girl, foreign and yet thus far admirably Roman in her pursuits, had been educated in her craft by the master weaver herself.

Sympathy for the girl diminishes when we hear that Arachne disavowed any Minervan responsibility for her training:

quod tamen ipsa negat tantaque offensa magistra
'certet' ait 'mecum: nihil est, quod victa recusem!' (6.24-25)

Nevertheless, she denies this fact and, offended by having such a great teacher, she said, "Let her but contend with me; having been conquered, there is nothing that I would refuse!"

The Latin brings out the irony of Arachne's boast; the perfect passive participle *victa* looks forward to what the audience knows will be Arachne's ultimate fate, and the absence of the present subjunctive of the verb "to be" serves to underscore the *factual* rather than the *contrafactual* nature of Arachne's prayer. She means, after all, "If I were to be conquered, then I would not refuse . . . " But her defeat is already sealed by her arrogant attitude.

Those who would fault Pallas for injustice with Arachne must confront what the goddess actually says to this girl. Pallas disguises herself as an old woman, and announces to the young Arachne that the old have some qualities that are to be admired, wisdom in particular. Pallas urges the girl to seek fame as the greatest of mortal weavers (6.31 *inter mortales faciendae maxima lanae*), but to yield to the goddess. She promises pardon if Arachne would but make a prayer for forgiveness.

Arachne's response is excessive to the situation. She drops her work (6.34) and can scarcely restrain from hitting the old woman (35 *vixque manum retinens*). Ovid continues his masterful portrait; the girl is full of rage. She observes that the old woman has lived too long, and that she should restrict her advice to a daughter or daughter-in-law. And, to crown her blasphemies, Arachne wonders why the goddess herself does not come to contend with her in weaving. Her wonder does not last long.

In an important detail, once Pallas throws off her disguise and reveals herself to the Lydian upstart, Arachne blushes, however involuntarily:

... erubuit, subitusque invita notavit
ora rubor rursusque evanuit, ut solet aer
purpureus fieri, cum primum Aurora movetur,
et breve post tempus candescere solis ab ortu. (6.46-49)

... she blushed, and a sudden redness marked her unwilling
face and again vanished, just as the air is accustomed to
become purple, when first Aurora is moved,
and after a brief time it begins to whiten from the rising of the sun.

Anderson is not alone in thinking that similes such as this "have only a pictorial value." Such is the reputation Ovid has suffered for so long; he is no Virgil with similes and poetic descriptions that conceal great truths or profound reflections. He is merely an entertainer, a writer who, as it were, never composed a line he was not willing to retain, a writer who without much effort could draft a simile that serves no purpose other than to adorn and decorate a narrative. And, of course, Ovid can be read in such a lighthearted, relaxing way; his stories can charm and do little more.

Here, the purple once again signals the imminent destruction of a young life. It also links to the purple shellfish Arachne's father Idmon used to dye her wool (6.8-9). It also recalls Ovid's celebrated description of the dawn's blush at *Amores* 1.13. That elegy reproached Aurora for her insistence on forcing humanity to rise early; among the "victims" of the dawn's petulance are the spinning women who might otherwise delay their labor: *tu, cum feminei possint cessare labores, / lanificam revocas ad sua pensa manum* (23-24).[4] The dawn, of course, blushed at the end of Ovid's attack; the poet took it that she had heard his complaint (47 *iurgia finieram. scires audisse: rubebat*). Here, Arachne may be unafraid of Minerva (6.45 *sola est non territa virgo*), but she has heard the reproach.[5] Ovid does not tell us what time it was when Minerva had arrived at Arachne's, though the simile seems to point to the hour just before dawn, so that with the rising of the sun Arachne is like the dawn, whose purple light vanishes before the coming of full daylight. And, by recalling his image from the *Amores*, Ovid rather aligns himself with Minerva here, as Arachne is compelled to accept the justice of the goddess' complaint, even if by her very nature she is incapable of change.

The weaving contest begins in earnest. The process is described in great detail (6.53-62); this is a *locus classicus* in Latin literature for the practice of weaving (which would have occasioned no surprise for Ovid's audience, even if most modern readers might have to consult commentaries to follow the specific details). The canvases the two women are creating are full of color, especially purple and gold; Ovid again resorts to a magnificent simile to describe the effect:

qualis ab imbre solent percussis solibus arcus
inficere ingenti longum curvamine caelum;

in quo diversa niteant cum mille colores,
transitus ipse tamen spectantia lumina fallit:
usque adeo, quod tangit, idem est; tamen ultima distant. (6.63-67)

Just as after storms rainbows are accustomed to stain
the wide heaven with a huge curve after the sun's rays after struck through;
in which, though a thousand colors shine differently,
nevertheless the very passage deceives the eyes that gaze on it:
so far is each the same as that which it touches; nevertheless the extremes are
*   so different.*

Purple and gold are the principal colors Ovid emphasizes (61 *purpura*, 68 *aurum*); these royal colors are associated in Virgil with both Dido and Camilla, and here, as in the *Aeneid*, the colors have ominous associations. The rainbow itself is of mixed associations; rainbows are omens of bad weather (cf. Virgil, *Georgics* 1.380-381). Rainbows are often used in baleful contexts in the *Aeneid*.[6] So here, too, the seemingly beautiful image has dark associations for those who know their Virgil.

We now learn the stories that each woman has decided to present. In the previous book, the stories were recited as songs at a poetic contest; now the two competitors are silent as they decorate their respective canvases with wondrously woven songs. We learn first of the goddess' subjects (6.70 ff.). Near the close of Book 5, we had seen the introduction of Athens as a civilizing influence on the world, as Ceres had taken Triptolemus eastward in her dragon chariot. Minerva had heard that story, and she was, of course, the city's patroness. Not surprisingly, her first "song" now is the contest with Neptune by which she achieved her patronage over the city.[7] There is a famous "error" in the opening of her description:

Cecropia Pallas scopulum Mavortis in arce
pingit et antiquam de terrae nomine litem. (6.70-71)

Pallas painted the crag on the Cecropian citadel of Mars
and the ancient dispute over the name of the land.

The problem is that the *scopulum Martis* or Areopagus is quite different from the *Cecropia arx* or Acropolis. I do not think we are supposed to imagine that Pallas did not know the geography of her own city, but rather that Ovid is emphasizing the speed with which the goddess worked. She is in a hurry to defeat Arachne and punish her insolence; Ovid is also demonstrating the sometimes overpowering effect of the visual arts, where the eye is overwhelmed and confused by the images that confront it, and where initial appearances do not suffice to separate out the component parts of the picture.

The goddess shows Jupiter and the other gods sitting in judgment of the competitors; the subject of Pallas' canvas is a contest within a contest, and her victory over Neptune is another ill omen for Arachne. Pallas has her aegis (6.79); again, the chronology is not exact, but we are definitely moving past the events of Book 5 to the classical Athens the goddess protects. The victory Pallas wins over her uncle ought to be warning enough, but to clarify Arachne's fate the goddess decorates the corners of her canvas with four odd stories of divine retribution.

The first considers the mountains Thracian Rhodope and Haemus, which were once human beings (6.87-89). The apparent romantic couple (Rhodope = feminine, Haemus masculine) called each other Jupiter and Juno (89 *nomina summorum sibi qui tribuere deorum*), and for this blasphemy they were transformed into mountains. The story is otherwise unknown. It has a shade of the gigantomachy theme.[8] The giant theme seems to be a deliberate contrast with the second story, that of a Pygmy woman who is transformed into a crane after having been defeated in some obscure contest with Juno (90-92).[9] Both of these stories seem to be set in the remote past; the third concerns Antigone, the daughter of Laomedon of Troy, and must be imagined as an episode from more recent history. Antigone is changed into a stork for having dared to contend with Juno; again, the details elude us. The last story is the most unfamiliar; Cinyras has lost his daughters, who have somehow been transformed into the marble steps of a temple (a rather imaginative fate for someone who challenged a deity).

The border of the whole work is wreathed in olives, the tree of peace (6.101 *oleis pacalibus*): the scene represents the way the world should function, with the haughty duly punished and Olympian order in the ascendancy: no giants, no Troy, but Athens as the heart of a civilized world. It is the crowning summation of the picture the Muses painted in the preceding book.

The Pierides had begun to complain as soon as the nymphs awarded victory to the Muses; they squandered any chance they had to make reasoned arguments against the perhaps revisionist history the nine sisters had sung. Arachne has read the first third of the *Metamorphoses*. The first story on her canvas is that of Europa, the beginning of the long Theban cycle (6.103-107). Arachne emphasizes the moment of Europa's cry to her companions; she weaves together the story of Europa and that of Persephone, thus fashioning a ring between the two Olympian abductions. The rape of Asterie (108) is also Jovian; in the guise of an eagle Jupiter abducted the starry maiden. Leda (109) was ravished by Jupiter in the form of a swan; we can assume that Asterie's story was better known to Ovid's audience than to us, but the immense fame of Leda makes it probable that Arachne is showing how she knows all the stories of Jupiter's amours, major and minor alike.[10] The catalogue of his affairs continues; Danae has already been mentioned (113), while the reminiscence of Jupiter fathering the Muses after he disguised himself as a shepherd to seduce Mnemosyne links to the stories we have just heard in Book 5. The crowning moment comes when Arachne illustrates Jupiter's dalliance with his own niece, Persephone:

. . . varius Deoida serpens (6.114)

> *. . . and, as a spotted snake, Deo's daughter* [did he take]

There had been no hint of this incestuous union in the long narrative of Ceres and her daughter; here the rape comes as the climactic revelation in a sordid catalogue of divine misbehavior.[11] Arachne knows more than the poet has thus far revealed; Ovid has her allude both to stories he has told and tales he has not mentioned even in passing.

Arachne does not stop with Jupiter; there is more than enough immortal crime to provide material for her canvas. Neptune is next: in the form of a bull he seduced Canace, the daughter of Aeolus (6.115-116).[12] Neptune's amours begin as his brother Jupiter's did, with a bull disguise. Arachne proceeds to describe how Neptune disguised himself as Enipeus and became the father of the Aloidae (that is, the giants Otus and Ephialtes). As the commentators have noted, Arachne seems to be confused here; study of *Odyssey* 11 (235-254, 305-308) reveals two stories that Arachne seems to have conflated. Enipeus was the husband of Tyro; disguised as this mortal the god begat Pelias and Neleus. Iphimedeia, a separate conquest, was mother of the Aloidae. It is probable that here we have the same "mistake" we saw with Pallas, who could have been expected to know the layout of her beloved Athens. Working with speed, Arachne has confused two stories that appear within a short span of lines in Homer. We cannot fault Arachne for the error any more than we can blame Pallas for a similar slip. Medusa has already been mentioned as a Neptunian conquest; the story would have particularly aroused Minerva's ire. And, just as Jupiter impregnated his own niece Persephone, so Neptune had a dalliance with Ceres (118-119 *et te flava comas frugum mitissima mater / sensit equum*), where the epic circumlocution for the goddess underscores the inappropriateness of the rape: the most gentle giver of crops and mother of agriculture experienced Neptune in equine form.[13]

Apollo is Arachne's next target. Her knowledge of mythology is vast, though we must be careful not to assume that stories are obscure based only on the relatively paltry evidence that has survived. We know nothing about when Apollo disguised himself as a hawk or a lion (6.123-124) to seduce hapless maidens. Isse, the daughter of Macareus, is no more than a note in a grammarian. Bacchus mysteriously seduced Erigone with false grapes; again, the story is utterly unknown to us.[14] Saturn, lastly, bore the Centaur Chiron; the god's half-horse progeny has already appeared in the epic, but here Arachne alludes to how Saturn's wife interrupted him during his union with Philyra, whereupon the god rushed out in the form of a stallion—an escape trick that resulted in the equine form of Philyra's offspring.[15]

Arachne's picture is difficult to envision; the scenes are not described in any particular order, but the whole is wreathed with ivy, in contrast to Minerva's olive. Ivy is a clingy plant, and has been used already by the poet to describe inextricable bonds (cf. the Salmacis and Hermaphroditus story); Arachne's point may be that no amount of solemnity or divine *gravitas* can extricate the immortals from the embarrassing behavior contained within the ivy tendrils that frame this canvas.

Neither Pallas nor Livor (a close relative of Invidia, we might imagine) was able to find anything to carp at (6.129 *carpere*) in the tapestry.[16] The workmanship was apparently flawless. As for the subject matter, certainly the virgin goddess Pallas, the recent victor over Neptune for custody of Athens, would not attempt any justification of the images Arachne has depicted. Indeed, the divine actions of, e.g., Diana in the last book showed something of an attempt to move past the rampant immortal rapes of the past ages of history. The issue seems to be not the truth of the images but the author; the Lydian Arachne has no business pointing out the foibles of the gods, especially given her own ample faults. Pallas responds emotionally; she breaks the picture. She strikes Arachne four times in the head. Interestingly, the girl now goes and commits suicide.[17] Pallas does not kill her; the goddess does not punish her at once with some sort of transformation. Arachne is described as *infelix* and *animosa* (6.134); the point is that she cannot stand not having won.

Pallas pities her. She allows her to live on (thus in effect resurrecting her, though to an arguably terrible end), choosing to transform her into a spider (a creature that will go on spinning, though without making any more offensive pictures). The metamorphosis is clearly a punishment; Pallas wishes the curse to last through the generations, lest Arachne be secure in her future (6.137 *ne sis secura futuri*). She will hang (as was her choice), but for all time.

The story of Arachne serves as a warning, but her fellow Lydian Niobe does not learn anything from the cautionary tale.[18] Niobe was Lydian, and had known Arachne as a girl, but she married Amphion of Thebes, and so the story is set in that locale, where once those who would not worship Bacchus were punished. Here the question is the veneration of Latona, the mother of the divine twins whose cult was so central to the Augustan regime. Niobe is Lydian by birth and Theban by marriage; in the judgment of Augustan religion, she is damnable for her blasphemies against Apollo and Diana and their mother. Niobe is a proud woman in Phrygian gold (6.166 ff.); the reference increases our distaste for this most un-Italian, un-Roman woman who hails from the environs of old Troy. And Niobe's story offers a complement to Arachne's in that another virgin goddess will be involved in the destruction of offensive mortals; Minerva and Diana had been significant in the attempted rehabilitation of the gods in Book 5, and now they move to the forefront in the extirpation of outstanding examples of mortal arrogance that still exist in a world that has otherwise seemed to improve.

Niobe considers herself a goddess (6.172 *numen . . . meum*); her claim must be subjected to rigorous scrutiny. Tantalus is her father; the boast as to her paternity already makes her judgment suspect. Atlas is her grandfather; we might again raise an eyebrow at her pedigree. Jupiter was indeed the father of Tantalus and of Amphion, but such an ancestry does not guarantee Niobe's divinity. Her claim to possess divine power, her assertion of a *numen*, is inappropriate and exaggerated.[19] The Trojans and the Thebans are said to fear Niobe (177-178); again, the reverence is not impressive. Her husband Amphion was the brother of Zethus and son of Antiope; the less than glorious story of Niobe's husband's origins had been told on Arachne's tapestry (which of course Niobe never saw). Amphion is credited with having built the walls of Thebes by the music of his lyre; Niobe takes special pride in this accomplishment, which is presented as if it were to her credit.[20] Her fourteen children are mentioned last, because this greatest of her claims to supremacy and power will be the principal weapon by which her haughty arrogance will be destroyed. As with Arachne, this Lydian woman seals her own fate with no help from the immortals.

Niobe orders an end to the worship of Latona and her children; she demands that her Theban subjects take off the laurel from their heads (6.201 ff.).[21] The people obey, though silently (and wisely) they still worship the divine triad. The aftermath of the blasphemy is well known: Latona summons her twin children to avenge her. Latona's speech has interesting facets. She calls herself *animosa* (206), the same word used to describe Arachne; the goddess is spirited on account of her two children. Latona has just cause for pride, but she is humble: she yields the supreme place to Juno (207). She is, after all, another in the catalogue of Jovian amours, but she has the greatest pride in Apollo and Diana, and good sense to know the balance between said pride and arrogance. The goddess need not tarry on her complaints; the twin archers tell her to be silent and allow them to avenge the insult to them and their mother. We are back in the world of Pentheus and Thebes, though Niobe is a Lydian by birth and there is no question (as there was with the denial of Bacchus) of the arrogant wrongdoing of this foolish woman (and Ovid has done nothing to make her remotely sympathetic in our eyes; she is the image of excess that the immortals are now busy eradicating).

Niobe's sons are engaged in equestrian pursuits on an open plain; the horses are Tyrian, reminding us of their eastern, indeed Carthaginian origin, and they are covered in red cloth; we are reminded of Arachne's father dyeing her wool, and again the color (red = purple here) signals the impending death of the young. Apollo, the patron of the sudden death of males, begins his violent retribution for the slight to his mother. Ismenus falls, followed by Sipylus; the latter casualty reintroduces the image of the runaway chariot, as he falls and is mangled (not unlike Hippolytus) in the horse's gallop. Phaedimus and Tantalus are killed with one arrow as they wrestle in the *palaestra*; Alphenor is struck as he rushes to aid his brothers: his *pietas* (6.250 *pio . . . officio*) does not save him, and he suffers a grisly end as a piece of his lung is ripped out when he tries to remove the divine shaft. One arrow had slain two brothers, and so the "lost" arrow is made up in the case of Damasicthon, who is struck in the knee and then felled by a shot to the throat. The blood spurts high as the arrow is expelled (259 *expulit hanc sanguis seque eiaculatus in altum*), where the language recalls the bloody death of Pyramus. We are beginning to question the morality of Apollo's gruesome slaughter (if "morality" is a word we can use in this context), but when the last brother, Ilioneus, makes his plea, the god is moved to pity. The arrow had already been fired, but Apollo makes sure the wound is slight (however fatal). This is the sort of passage for which Ovid is famous, where critics have seen a touch of black humor; the point, however, is that the god of the inherited myth (Ovid did not invent the story after all) shows restraint. His anger and wrath have limits, and he can be moved by prayers. Not all divine action in the poem evinces the same pity.[22]

Niobe is angry that the gods have dared to strike her children; she is angry that they have such power (here there are shades of the theme of her pretension to divinity). Amphion commits suicide.[23] Niobe's insanity knows no limits; after a short indulgence of her grief, she asserts that Latona is still not as blessed as the mother of seven daughters (6.284-285). Like Arachne before her, Niobe is not afraid as Diana's bow makes its twang, and this time, the fearlessness is not made red by any blush of shame. No daughter makes a prayer for herself; Diana's shafts actually do their work faster than her brother's, and soon all of Niobe's children are dead save one. The mother makes the prayer for this last life; in the midst of the plea, the child is slain. Diana is crueler here than Apollo; the poet gives no indication that the goddess pitied any of the children. The audience would have known the transformation all too well: Niobe is changed into a rock, which is transported from Thebes to Lydia. Ovid thus provides the etiology for the crag on Mount Sipylus in Phrygia (cf. the name of Niobe's son who had tried to flee Phoebus' arrow as if he were a ship's captain fleeting a storm), where a trickle of water emanates that could be considered Niobe's perpetual tears.

As the story of Latona's wrath spreads, stories are told. Ovid does not make clear where exactly people began to talk of other divine acts of retribution; the very ambiguity of the geography makes clear that we are dealing with a fear that has spread far and wide. An anonymous figure tells of the Lycian farmers.[24] Ovid's narrator has eyewitness authority; he had been sent abroad to find select cattle, and had a native guide. He found an altar in the midst of a lake that was surrounded by trembling reeds (6.325-326). The altar is sacred to Latona, and commemorates the difficulty of her pregnancy and delivery of twins (despite Juno's wrath); Latona is imagined as giving birth near an olive tree (335), thus connecting her story with that of Minerva's wrath. The lake and its altar recall Latona's flight and her need for water in the fiery land of Lycia, the home of the chimaera.[25]

The Lycian farmers refuse to allow the tired mother to take water from the pool. Here Ovid provides a pendant to the destruction of Niobe; if we felt any sympathy for the fourteen slaughtered children, now we are forced to pity the weary mother and her newborns. Latona can scarcely make out her words as she begs for water, so great is her thirst. The hospitality theme returns to the fore; the Lycians should not hesitate to give a drink to the goddess.[26] Ovid has a moment of genuine humor when Latona points out to the farmers that if they are not moved by her plight, they should at least pity her infants, who, she says, are stretching out their hands from her breasts—and it happened that just then, Ovid says, they were doing just that (6.358-359 *'hi quoque vos moveant, qui nostro bracchia tendunt / parva sinu,'* et casu tendebant bracchia nati*). The whole effect is to make the Lycians utterly reprehensible as they deny the water; these wretches deserve whatever fate Latona imposes. The *convicia* (362) the farmers hurl at the goddess are an echo of the reproaches of the Pierides to the Muses. Just as the Pierides had made obscene gestures to accompany their impious words, so the Lycians deliberately stir up the water and make it muddy (in Antoninus Liberalis the farmers want their cows to drink and would presumably not want to disturb the water—in Ovid they are simply wicked bullies).

The goddess transforms the lot of them into frogs (6.370 ff.). Like Arachne, they are mostly belly now; they continue to make their raucous uproar known, whether they are above or below the surface of the water.[27] The story thus concludes with a fitting act of justice; Ovid allows no sympathy for the Lycians as they become amphibians. But one of the members of the audience remembers another story from roughly the same locale: the horrific fate of the satyr Marsyas.[28]

Ovid briefly tells the general outline of the story at *Fasti* 6.703-708. The story is also short in the *Metamorphoses*, but it is much more than a perplexing close to a series of divine acts of retribution. Rather, the Marsyas episode is of enormous importance to the Augustan political program. The satyr was a traditional boon companion of Bacchus and a symbol of the civic liberty of cities; he was the mythological progenitor of the *gens Marcia* and associated with plebeian accession to the college of augurs (the satyr was considered the father of augury).[29] But for the Augustan regime, Marsyas (especially the image of the bound satyr) was a symbol of Apollo's victories and the coming of order. And so the crowning of these tales of divine retribution is the story of Apollo's victory over the rebellious satyr. The scene Ovid paints in the *Metamorphoses* is gruesomely detailed; there is no description of the contest that preceded the flaying. Traditionally, the punishment came after a musical contest; according to the version preserved in, e.g., Pseudo-Apollodorus, Apollo played his lyre upside down and ordered Marsyas to do the same with his instrument; the satyr was unable to play and thus lost the contest.

Some salient points can be noted here. Marsyas was associated with Bacchus; the pendant passage of his torture here is a surprise after the punishments inflicted on the more than deserving Lycian farmers, Niobe, and even Arachne. Marsyas stands out as the pitiable one; Ovid does not describe why he is being punished, and there is no metamorphosis *per se*, but rather a terrible anti-metamorphosis: Marsyas' own innards are exposed. We have seen already how the worship of Bacchus was somewhat problematic for the Augustan regime; the death of the god's companion here, slaughtered by Apollo, is a stunning reminder of the problems Bacchic revelry posed for the Augustan order (and we should remember that a depiction of Marsyas, bound and awaiting Apollo's knife, decorated the *Aedes Concordiae Augustae*).[30] Minerva had invented the instrument of Marsyas' doom; she had thrown away the flute after she disliked how it disfigured her face (cf. Ceres' drinking and the mockery of the soon-to-be newt). And so Minerva is associated in Marsyas' doom; the point is that what the dignified virgin goddess had discarded might have been better left unplayed. Marysas is mourned as if he were some figure from pastoral:

> illum ruricolae, silvarum numina, fauni
> et satyri fratres et tunc quoque carus Olympus
> et nymphae flerunt, et quisque in montibus illis
> lanigerosque greges armentaque bucera pavit. (6.392-395)

> *That one did the country-dwelling fauns, the divinities of the woods,*
> *mourn, and the satyrs, his brothers, and Olympus, who was then also dear to*
> *   him,*
> *and the nymphs, and whoever in those mountains*
> *pastured wool-bearing flocks and horned kine.*

In an interesting touch, Olympus is viewed as Marsyas' *eromenos*; elsewhere he is a student or even the father of the satyr.[31] The detail may be original to Ovid, and it may be another attack on the figure whose conquest was a symbol of the coming of the Augustan order. Now one may wonder if Ovid saw irony in how the flaying of Marsyas was a symbol of Augustan concord, but the fact that the satyr's punishment comes at this juncture is no surprise in what is, we shall see, a profoundly Augustan poem. And given that Apollo's victim is a satyr, the punishment of this would-be flautist also allows for detachment; the other victims of the book have been all too human.[32] Bacchus is the ultimate target behind Apollo's actions; divine retribution has weighty targets in this veritable purification of the rebellious East.

The mourners of Marsyas cry so much that the earth receives their tears and changes them into water that she sends forth as an extraordinarily clear stream; the new river takes its name from the slaughtered satyr (6.396-400).[33] As the storytellers return to the present, all agree that Niobe was to blame for the destruction of her home; the only individual who mourns her is Tantalus' son, Niobe's brother Pelops (403-405). He reveals his ivory shoulder, a brilliantly allusive gesture that looks both forwards and backwards in the epic's narrative. According to the usual version of the tale, Tantalus had offered his own son as a banquet to the gods; this was the principal reason for his eternal torment in the underworld. Ceres, at the time, was distracted by her daughter's abduction; not thinking, she consumed part of Pelops in the stew. The gods resurrected the boy, but his shoulder was missing thanks to the goddess' careless repast. An ivory prosthesis atoned for the loss.

The story thus looks back to Ceres' loss, and forward to the terrible story Ovid is about to tell: the drama of Tereus, Procne, and Philomela.[34] Before Ovid, the story had already been briefly treated by Virgil, where the lore forms part of the song of Silenus that, as we have already noted, Ovid has mined for material for his epic.[35]

Whatever the origins of the slaughter of Marsyas in Augustan propaganda, the cruel method of the god's punishment of the arguably unfairly defeated satyr was unspeakably violent. We have noted that in Ovid's vision, there is always a palpable sense of the symbiotic relationship between gods and men. The actions of the immortals influence mortals, and *vice versa*. It is no accident that the story of Marsyas precedes one of the most horrific tales in the epic, a story that illustrates all too well the failure of any divine attempt to root out wicked behavior. In comparison to Tereus' acts, the behavior of Arachne and Niobe seems trivial.

The Theban royal family has been wiped out, and in some sense Niobe's story provides another note of finality for the ill-fated city: ambassadors come from throughout the Greek world to offer solace on the devastating loss of sixteen royals in one massive symphony of slaughter. Amphion's union with the Lydian Niobe has brought him ruin.

Argos is first; that city had replaced Thebes in ascendancy when Ovid commenced his Perseus narrative (6.414). Calydon gets a special mention (415 *et nondum torvae Calydon invisa Dianae*), which both looks ahead to Book 8 and the Calydonian boar hunt, and reminds us of the poem's current emphasis on divine retribution. Corinth, already wealthy (416 *nobilis aere*), sends an emissary; strong Messene is present.[36] Pylos is under the control of Neleus, Nestor's father; Troezen is not yet under Pittheus' rule. Mycenae is Peloponnesian because Niobe's brother Pelops was the father of Atreus; once again, Ovid subtly notes the chronological progression in his world history. All the cities of Greece come to lament Thebes' loss, with the sole exception of Athens. The glorious city, whose civilizing influence had been part of the climax of Book 5, is already suffering and, in Ovid's vision, is already in decline, or at least serious discomfiture: *solae cessastis, Athenae* (421).

Athens is at war. In Pseudo-Apollodorus, Athens was fighting the Theban king Labdacus; Ovid's version has barbarous hordes coming from overseas (6.422 *subvectaque ponto / barbara . . . agmina*). The mythographic version may preserve some trace of ancient rivalry between the two cities; in Ovid's account, Thebes has been "defeated," as it were, by Niobe's actions and Athens is under foreign assault. Athens is saved by a Thracian mercenary, Tereus. Tereus is married to Pandion's daughter Procne. Ovid does not bother to identify the reasonably well-known Athenian monarch; as for Tereus, traditionally he was a son of Ares (appropriate for a warlike Thracian), and in Ovid he traces his lineage to Mars under his ancient name, Gradivus.[37]

Juno was not the matron who oversaw the marriage, however, and Hymenaeus and the Graces were absent. Rather, the Furies were in attendance, and the sluggish owl makes a reappearance (a nice link to the Ceres story). The commentators compare the ill-omened "marriage" of Aeneas and Dido at the fateful hunt in Carthage, as well as Roman political unions and the anachronistic nature of Ovid's description of Juno as *pronuba*. But we might note that this is Ovid's first wedding (after a fashion) since the union of Pluto and Persephone. Pluto had abducted his niece to serve as hell's queen; that union, occasioned by

rape, has served as the prototype for Tereus' union with Procne. A violent marauder from Thrace has come to the heart of civilized Athens to save it from
foreign invasion; Procne is in some sense the price for Athens' salvation.

Five autumns go by without noteworthy event. The use of autumn as the
season to describe the passage of years is ominous; it reminds us of Ovid's imitation of Virgil's simile about the leaves in the first chill of autumn: this is the
beginning of the downfall of a nuclear family. Ovid's narrative builds suspense
effectively; Procne asks that she might have a chance to visit with her sister. She
asks Tereus either to let her return to Athens, or to summon Philomela to
Thrace. The story here may bear an Ovidian twist. In the mythographers, Tereus
either lied to Philomela that Procne was dead, thus seducing her by deception, or
he lied to Pandion that the one daughter had died, so as to gain the other. Ovid
emphasizes the hospitality theme yet again; Tereus enters the Piraeus and exchanges greetings with Athens' king, his father-in-law and ally. Ovid allows no
hint that this Thracian monarch will abuse his situation.

Philomela appears (6.451 ff.). Her beauty is such that she could be compared to the naiads and dryads, if only they had her adornment and rich finery.
We might think of Propertius' advice to his beloved not to worry about lavish
attention to appearance; Philomela could be some stunning woodland nymph,
but she is dressed in royal robes. Tereus burns for Philomela just as fire burns
ripe grain, leaves, or hay (455-457). The simile is reminiscent of Apollo's lust
for Daphne, which Cupid had inspired with his all too effective shafts. Tereus
needs no divine help to lust after Pandion's other daughter; Ovid recalls
Apollo's lust for Daphne here, to be sure, but absent the important factor of divine instigation. There is a hint in the simile of the Thracian's propensity for
destruction. Ovid is explicit about the blame in this instance:

> digna quidem facies; sed et hunc innata libido
> exstimulat, pronusque genus regionibus illis
> in Venerem est: flagrat vitio gentisque suoque. (6.458-460)

> *Indeed, her appearance was worthy; but his innate libido also*
> *drove him on, and the race in those regions is prone to*
> *Venus: he burned with a vice both of his race and himself.*

Tereus is not civilized; he has thus far maintained appearances, but his true
character is about to be revealed. Athens' situation must have been dire indeed
for Pandion to marry his daughter to this monarch, though the comment here is
Ovid's authorial remark as an Augustan Roman. Tereus is not completely lost
yet; he wonders about approaching Philomela's handlers the way a character in
amatory elegy might try to gain access to his love interest. His marriage to
Procne seems a distant memory now, however. He wonders if he should simply
seize this girl and defend his conquest by force.

There is a hint that this Thracian is not particularly bright (certainly he is besotted on account of his lust). He realizes that all he must do is fulfill Procne's order, and he might have both Philomela and the title *pius* (6.474) for fulfilling his wife's wishes. Philomela effectively joins her would-be rapist in pleading with Pandion to let her go; in an interesting detail, Ovid notes that Tereus lusted for her as he watched father and daughter embrace:

> . . . et quotiens amplectitur illa parentem,
> esse parens vellet: neque enim minus impius esset. (6.481-482)

> . . . *and however many times she embraced her parent,*
> *he wished he were her parent: indeed, he would not then be less impious.*

Tereus has learned from the example of Jupiter or Pluto; incest would not be beyond the scope of his crimes, were he only to have Philomela.

The day is far spent when Pandion hosts a royal banquet for his son-in-law; Bacchus, as we might expect, is present in the ample wine that soon puts almost everyone to sleep, sated with food and drink (6.488-489 *regales epulae mensis et Bacchus in auro / ponitur; hinc placido dant turgida corpora somno*). The association between the god and the forthcoming drama is deliberate. Tereus is awake; he spends the night anticipating his crime, but, significantly, he does not dare attempt anything while still in Pandion's palace—he is not yet devoid of all reason.

When morning comes, the farewells are exchanged; Ovid lingers over this departure scene, in which Pandion first feels the stirrings of trouble (6.510 *timuitque suae praesagia mentis*), though his fear does not prevent his agreement to send off Philomela. The barbarian Tereus (515 *barbarus*; cf. 533 *barbare*) has won his prize, and he is like an eagle that has captured a hare:

> non aliter quam cum pedibus praedator obuncis
> deposuit nido leporem Iovis ales in alto;
> nulla fuga est capto, spectat sua praemia raptor. (6.516-518)

> *Not otherwise than when with curved talons the predator*
> *bird of Jove has deposited a hare in a lofty nest;*
> *and there is no flight for the captive, the raptor gazes on his reward.*

Tereus is like Jove, the rapist god who is symbolized by the eagle, his avian avatar; he might be Jupiter conveying Europa over the sea. The situation is quite different, however; as soon as Tereus reaches Thrace he surrenders to his basest passions and secludes Philomela, raping her as she calls on her father, her sister, and most of all the gods (524-526). This passage is, in fact, the most violent description Ovid has thus far used to describe a virgin's violation; previous rapes were passed over relatively quickly. Even with the minute detail of how Tereus was descended from Gradivus, Ovid in this sequence recalls the passage from the opening of *Aeneid* 3 where the Trojan exiles learn of the death of Priam's son Polydorus, murdered in Thrace for filthy lucre. Ovid exceeds the violation of hospitality in that terrible scene; Philomela becomes his most pitiable victim thus far; she is like a frightened lamb or a dove that has somehow escaped the clutches of a wolf or a raptor (527-530). The commentators note the irony of how the dove marvels at the blood that marks its wet plumes, a foreshadowing of Philomela's own future as murderess; most striking, though, is the fact that lambs and doves do not often escape wolves and hawks. In Ovid's vision, the barbarous Tereus will presumably plan further visits to Philomela's forest prison.

The gods, of course, have been nowhere in the story. The book had opened with a series of tales of divine retribution; now the mood has changed, and the efforts of the gods to extirpate offensive behavior seem feeble and ineffectual in the face of Tereus' shockingly violent actions. We had moved at the end of Book 5 from Athens to the East; slowly we have moved back to Greece (starting with Niobe, the Lydian wife of a Theban monarch), and now Athens, the glorious center of civilization, has become the victim of a violent Thracian rapist who now holds two of her princesses in his grasp. Philomela's prayer resonates with Ovid's audience: if the gods have any divine power, Tereus will be punished (6.542-543 *si tamen haec superi cernunt, si numina divum / sunt aliquid*, and cf. 548 *audiet haec aether et si deus ullus in illo est*).

The horror increases as a result of Philomela's brave threats to tell the world of Tereus' crimes: he cuts out her tongue (6.549 ff.). Much has been made of Ovid's gruesome description of how the root still quivers and the freshly severed tongue not only twitches on the ground but seeks its mistress' feet as it dies. The tongue's flickering is even given a brief simile, where it is compared to the severed tail of a snake—a significant shift, we might note, from a lamb or a dove. The snake has lost its tail, but a snake it remains, a harbinger of how the shattered Philomela will soon enough take her revenge.[38]

Some have argued that Ovid's focus on outrageous detail here, especially the unrealistic scene of the crawling tongue, serves to distance the audience from the horror his characters suffer. On the contrary, we see here a forced stare at the visceral aspects of that horror; the crown of the terrible narrative comes when Ovid makes explicit what we might have hoped would be left implicit and unsaid: Tereus returns again and again to rape his mutilated victim (6.561-562). At the very least, Ovid has successfully moved the audience from any complaints about the behavior of the gods; even Apollo's flaying of Marsyas seems trivial in comparison to the ongoing violation of Philomela. But the terrible torture of the satyr, an image, to be sure, of the triumph of the Augustan order, has preceded the vicious torture Tereus imposes on Philomela. The symbiotic world of gods and men has been consumed by violence, and as the Thracian king returns time and again to the forest (Diana's haunt, we might add) to rape the Athenian girl, the violence is magnified and calls to heaven for vengeance.

Tereus lies to Procne that her sister has died (6.563 ff.). Ovid here reverses the tradition that Tereus had won the second sister by lying about the death of the first. Philomela endures her captivity for a year; she is bereft of all help (and the gods are noteworthy for their silence). Finally, Pandion's daughter decides to borrow a trick from Arachne and weave a tapestry that will allow the mute to speak. Purple threads on a white background will color the story of her abduction, rapes, and mutilation (purple again signals the imminent death of the young). Arachne had infuriated Minerva by highlighting divine rapes on her Lydian canvas; the Athenian princess will now close another poetic ring with her story of an all too mortal act of violence against women. The web is barbaric (6.576 *barbarica*) because the Thracian canvas will bear the evidence that reveals Thracian barbarity. Minerva had been present to smash Arachne's canvas; the story Philomela weaves is far worse than anything Arachne could have depicted, and this time there is no god to intervene.

The canvas is sent to Procne, and renders her mute as well (6.584 ff.). She is entirely bent on punishment. Ovid now introduces a magnificent scene that underscores the point he has been trying to make:

> tempus erat, quo sacra solent trieterica Bacchi
> Sithoniae celebrant nurus: nox conscia sacris,
> nocte sonat Rhodope tinnitibus aeris acuti. (6.587-589)

> *It was night, when the Sithonian daughters-in-law are*
> *accustomed to celebrate the biennial sacred rites of Bacchus:*
> *the night was aware of the rites, at night Rhodope sounded with the clashes*
> *of the shrill bronze.*

Ovid seems to have invented the scene; the other extant accounts make no mention of Bacchic rites (indeed, in Hyginus Tereus sends Philomela to another Thracian king, who returns her to Procne—apparently he was less savage than his countryman). Ovid contextualizes the dramatic scene of the sisters' revenge at the biennial nocturnal rites in honor of the god Liber. Once again we are thrust into a scene of Eastern horror of a sort we had thought finished. We are reminded of Pentheus' death at the hands of his mother and aunt, and Ovid's audience—well aware of the general outline of the story—knows that Procne and Philomela are about to initiate the slaughter of a male relative of their own, the boy Itys. Bacchus had been mentioned by metonymy at the banquet before Tereus abducted Philomela from Athens; now Bacchus is once again in power, having reemerged to preside over the vicious *dénouement* of the story. Silenus, his satyr, had told it in Virgil's pastoral vision; now, after the torturous end of another satyr, Bacchus' rites will witness the lengths human savagery can reach.

Procne is dressed in a costume that represents a blend of Bacchic revelry and a perversion of Diana's rites: she has a vine in her hair and a deerskin cloak (6.592-593). The scene of the rites is Mount Rhodope, the mountain Minerva had depicted on her tapestry during her contest with Arachne. In the obscure myth Minerva had depicted, Rhodope and Haemus had apparently been mortals (giants?); the couple had affected to be gods by addressing each other with divine names (Jupiter and Juno, presumably). Now Rhodope, the *female* half of that equation, is the scene for the violent revels in honor of the god whose divinity so many have questioned and rebelled against. In a stunning apostrophe, Ovid makes clear whom Procne is simulating:

> concita per silvas turba comitante suarum
> terribilis Procne furiisque agitata doloris,
> Bacchae, tuas simulat . . . (6.594-596)

> *Set in motion through the forest with a crowd of her own accompanying her,*
> *Procne is driven on by the madness of her terrible sorrow,*
> *and it is your madness, O Bacchus, that she simulates . . .*

Procne "rescues" Philomela, dressing her sister up in the costume of a crazed Bacchant (596-600). Ovid's scene is reminiscent of *Aeneid* 7, 385-399, where Amata abducted Lavinia and took her into the forest after Allecto had infused her with madness. Amata is crazed at the idea that Lavinia might be forced to marry Aeneas, and she takes her daughter out to the woods, where she is soon followed by a crowd of Latin mothers who join in the terrible Bacchic rites Allecto's madness has inspired.[39] There, Amata was possessed with the "simulated divine power of Bacchus" (*A.* 7.385 *simulato numine Bacchi*), where we might have expected to read *stimulato*. The Virgilian point is that Amata is not really possessed by Bacchus, but rather by Allecto's Junonian fury; in Ovid, Procne is playing Bacchus. Bacchus instigated the frenzy that led to Pentheus' murder; he is not, strictly speaking, present now in the forest groves of Rhodope as Procne carries out her terrible Bacchic liturgy, though his power is expressed in every crazed imitation of his own madness. The first part of the book had emphasized the need for mortals not to claim to surpass the gods; imitation, however, was apparently not forbidden.[40]

Once Procne has brought Philomela back to Tereus' palace, she removes her Bacchic accoutrements and faces her sister, who is overcome with shame and thinks she has wronged Procne in some way (6.605-609). Virgil's Amata had taken Lavinia into the forest with some terrible act of madness in mind; Virgil had not explained what Amata was thinking of doing, though the implication seems to be that she preferred the death of her daughter to marriage with Aeneas. Now, though she has removed her Bacchic clothing, Procne admits to Philomela that she has prepared some great deed to punish Tereus, though she is seemingly unsure what it is:

> . . . magnum quodcumque paravi:
> quid sit, adhuc dubito. (6.618-619)

> *I have prepared some great thing:*

what it is, still I hesitate . . .

Procne knows that whatever fate she settles on for Tereus, it will be great. Ovid is careful in his depiction of Procne and his allusion to Virgil's Amata. The key is *simulation*. We are not in Book 3, where Bacchus himself saw to the destruction of Pentheus, who had personally offended him. Procne is simulating the god; by removing the clothes that signify his worship, she reveals that her madness is quite her own. It is akin to the madness of Bacchus; the god has shown her the way.[41] Her son Itys shows her the details of how to execute her madness, as he enters the room, looking ever so much like his father (620-623).

Itys trusts his mother implicitly and runs to her embrace; the experience of the boy's affection causes Procne to hesitate, and Ovid's description offers interesting details into his character's psyche and the poet's plan:

> sed simul ex nimia mentem pietate labare
> sensit, ab hoc iterum est ad vultus versa sororis
> inque vicem spectans ambos, 'cur admovet' inquit
> 'alter blanditias,[42] rapta silet altera lingua?' (6.629-632)

> *But as soon as she felt that her intention was beginning to falter*
> *from excessive piety, from this one again she turned to the face of her sister*
> *and was gazing at both in turn, and said, "Why does the one move me*
> *with blandishments, while the other is silent with tongue ripped out?"*

Itys has not suffered, while Philomela has been unbelievably mutilated. Itys is the image of his father. Where Tereus is concerned, Procne goes on to argue, *pietas* is a crime (635 *scelus est pietas in coniuge Tereo*). What is most interesting is Ovid's description of how Itys' caresses turned Procne away from "excessive piety." The phrase in context should mean that Procne's devotion to her sister was excessive (in that it sanctioned the slaughter of her innocent son), but the Latin would more normally express the idea that Procne was slipping from her *mens* or intention out of an excess of *maternal* piety. The passage is vexed, as evidenced by the fact that *mentem* is but one attested reading; *mortem* is also found, which is next to impossible to construe intelligibly. Heinsius emended the text to *matrem*, which has found numerous supporters. But what the critics do not explore is why Ovid would consider Procne to be slipping away from her intention to kill Itys out of some excessive maternal piety.

I would suggest that Ovid means exactly what he says, and that the hesitation to slay Itys is, in context, actually a display of *nimia pietas*.[43] Look at who your husband is, Procne says to herself (6.634 *cui sis nupta, vide, Pandione nata, marito*). She accuses herself of being a degenerate, that is, of disgracing her lineage (635 *degeneras*). Allowing the son of the Thracian monster to live would be a disgrace to her noble Athenian blood. And, further, there is something of Diana here too: the sisterly bond must be the strongest. The gods did not intervene to save Philomela, and so Procne must take matters into her own hands. The story of Pelops also lies in the background, of course; Tantalus had conceived of serving his own son as a feast to the gods. That tale had been alluded to just before the present parallel narrative had commenced. Tantalus had less reason to slaughter Pelops than Procne Itys, some might argue; further, Procne will serve the child to his monstrous father and not to the gods. None of this is to say that the gods countenance what Procne is doing (though no one intervenes to save the boy), but in the end the narrative demands that all the members of this household be destroyed. The rapist's son will not survive his monster of a father.[44] Of course the brutality of Tereus has plunged the whole family into madness; the Athenian princesses will resort to an act of violence worthy of any Thracian madman in their plot to seek vengeance. In a perverse way, in order to achieve victory over Tereus, the sisters might conspire to outdo him in savagery. Arachne's canvas had inspired the Athenian goddess Minerva to surrender to rage and the destruction of the offensive artwork; the canvas of the Athenian princess Philomela will drive her sister Procne to madness.

The boy cries out as his mother approaches (6.636 ff.).[45] Procne is like a tigress now, a wild animal that has trapped a baby deer in a dense forest near the Ganges (636-637 *veluti Gangetica cervae / lactentem fetum per silvas tigris opacas*). Ovid brilliantly emphasizes two points here. First, metaphorically Procne is back in the forest now, not in the "civilized" realm of the palace (we should note that Tereus' unspeakable crimes were committed in the woods, not in the house where the "civilized" Athenian princesses will commit murder). Second, Procne is compared to a lion of the Ganges, which locates us in Bacchus' Indian haunts: we are back to the world of the wine god and his Eastern madness, and Procne is a savage, roaring beast from some Bacchic hell. Philomela will be loyal to her sister; she will cut Itys' throat even though her sister's wound to his side is sufficient for death. The sisters prepare to cook the body; Ovid ensures that we know the boy was still alive as the process started (644-645 *vivaque adhuc animaeque aliquid retinentia membra / dilaniant*). There is something here of Apollo's torture of Marsyas; again, mortals have imitated immortals. And, in contrast to Pelops' fate, this time there will be no divinely wrought resurrection of the innocent boy. Procne has removed her deerskin and, metaphorically, taken on the pelt of a tigress.[46]

Procne lies to Tereus and argues that only a husband may partake of certain meals that are sacred according to the rites of her fatherland (6.648 *patrii moris sacrum*), i.e., Athens. There is no such tradition that we are aware of, but Tereus of course is ignorant of Athenian custom. Ovid's point is that the Athenian princess is aware of her country as she prepares to destroy her Thracian husband. The theme of the whole sequence has been the *night*; Ovid lamented at the very outset of his story that mortals are oppressed with the cares of the dark night (472-473 *pro superi, quantum mortalia pectora caecae / noctis habent*), and now Tereus has such a "night of the mind" (652 *tantaque nox animi*) that he does not realize he has consumed his own son, and he summons the boy to his presence, thus inviting Procne to utter one of the finest retorts in the epic:

intus habes, quem poscis (6.655)

You have inside you the one whom you seek

The line underscores Procne's belief that the son is just as guilty as the father; the son looks like the father, he is as Thracian as the father, and there is a hint of a terrible logic in Procne's faulty reasoning: the son will grow up to be as awful as the father, and so death is an act of mercy.

As if she were some Bacchant with Pentheus' head about to grace a stake, Philomela now appears, her hair matted with blood in terrible fulfillment of the dove simile that had presaged her bathing in Itys' gore. She hurls the boy's head at his father's face (658-659). The night, of course, is the time for Bacchus' crazed rites, which have now been carried out inside the Thracian royal palace.[47] The "hospitality" of the dinner has been ruined in the most terrible of ways; Procne had simulated the god Bacchus, and now she has simulated an Athenian rite to underscore how she, a princess of civilized Athens, is avenging the violation of her sister by a savage Thracian.

Tereus calls on the Furies to avenge the death of his son as he rises to pursue the two women, but the Furies are nowhere at hand (6.662), since, of course, the two sisters have fulfilled their function already. In an interesting detail that has escaped much notice, Ovid notes that now Tereus was keen to bring forth his son's innards from his body (663-664 *et modo, si posset, reserato pectore diras / egerere inde dapes inmersaque*[48] *viscera gestit*), and now to mourn and call himself the tomb of his own son (665 *flet modo seque vocat bustum miserabile nati*). Of course were he sufficiently mad, he could have opened his own body with the sword he soon unsheathes to pursue the two sisters; *si posset* implies that he was not able to do this: apparently his reason is not entirely lost, and, besides, he is more interested in killing Procne and Philomela than himself. Interestingly, throughout the story, despite the vicious violence of Tereus, the Thracian remains capable of keeping up rational appearances (calm mendacity, etc.), in contrast to the wilder savagery of Procne. Of course, Ovid's point is that the two sisters have greater cause to be driven insane.

Soon enough the hunter and the hunted are transformed into birds; the whole thing happens astonishingly fast. Tereus is transformed into a hoopoe; Ovid is vague about the fate of the two sisters, saying that one escaped into the forest and the other to the roof of the palace, with the marks of the slaughter of Itys still staining both their breasts.[49] The Greeks were fairly sure that Procne became a nightingale and Philomela a swallow. Hyginus reverses the metamorphoses. Ovid, of course, is not clear which sister is which bird; the most the commentators can guarantee is that the swallow is likelier to be the bird that would seek the roof. At *Fasti* 2.853-856, Procne is the swallow, the harbinger of spring; sometimes the bird comes too quickly, and Tereus, Ovid notes, takes pleasure at the cold his former wife feels. In the aforementioned passage of the

Ars, Procne is also a swallow, though in the *Tristia* Ovid seems more confused as to the identity (cf. 2.3.90, 3.12.9-10, and 5.1.60). The two sisters were joined in the blood of Itys, but they are not together in their avian metamorphoses. The theme of separation was a major part of the story; in what we may construe as a punishment, the sisters are now deprived of each other's company for all time. The separation also underscores Tereus' problem; he is frustrated and does not know which sister-bird to pursue first, and as he chases one, the other escapes easily in a different direction.

Pandion dies early because of the loss to his house; we cannot be surprised. His power is weakened, however, in the manner of the Theban royal house; he has a son, Erectheus, whose extraordinary qualities make him more than suitable for rule (6.678 *iustitia dubium validisne potentior armis*). He has eight children, four sons and four daughters; two of the daughters are especially beautiful. The one, Procris, marries Cephalus; Ovid will return to her later, in his next book. The other daughter, Orithyia, is pursued by Boreas, the north wind, but his Thracian locale makes him an unsuitable suitor given the terrible story of Tereus—the Athenians have learned not to marry their daughters to Thracian husbands.[50] Erectheus is in a difficult position; Boreas is immortal and will not be dispensed with easily.

Boreas is in some sense a divine parallel to his mortal Thracian counterpart Tereus, though far less vicious.[51] The briefly told story of his rape of another Athenian girl serves to introduce his sons, who will participate in the voyage of Jason in quest of the Golden Fleece. The tale is a hearkening back to the old days of divine rape, the sort of story with which Arachne had decorated her canvas and that Minerva had found so offensive. The first part of this book was concerned with the theme of divine retribution; the gods (except for Bacchus) were absent from the lengthy story we have just finished. In a sense, Tereus was not punished terribly effectively because his victims, Procne and Philomela, had taken matters into their own hands; by the end of the tale, all three had committed such heinous acts that the avian transformation they share seems the only solution to the moral conundrums the story poses.[52] But if the gods were intent on a better world, not to mention a world where Athens, the city of Minerva, could be the bringer of civilization to barbarians, then the example of Triptolemus and Lyncus has been taken to a terrible new level of horror. There, Ceres punished the insolent Scythian king and safely took Triptolemus away from death; here, Minerva is absent as her city's princesses are abused and, now, Boreas prepares to rape another of Athens' daughters. It is possible to argue that the level of depravity displayed in the Tereus story is the lowest Ovid has yet revealed; whatever comfort we might have taken in the calm atmosphere of the Muses and Minerva on Helicon has long since disappeared. And Ovid does not bother to comment directly on the matter of whether Tereus or the sisters were more savage; he allows his readers to ponder the unanswerable for themselves.

Boreas is tired of waiting for Orithyia to succumb to his entreaties; he is tired of waiting for Erectheus to forget what a Thracian did to his sisters. The god recalls his mighty powers in a long soliloquy (6.687 ff.); he will take what he wants by force. Boreas comes rather close in this passage to the attitude of the giants, those beasts that had tried to scale Olympus; he asserts that he holds power in the air, over the sea, and on land, and, in an interesting passage, he observes that on occasion he enters the hollow parts of the earth and terrifies even the ghosts in the underworld with his blasts (697-699 *idem ego, cum subii convexa foramina terrae / supposuique ferox imis mea terga cavernis, / sollicito manes totumque tremoribus orbem*). The lines are reminiscent of the fears Pluto had for what might happen to his kingdom in the wake of the volcanic and other geological phenomena in Sicily, and they underscore the wind god's arrogant boasting about the extent of his power. And Boreas is, after all, abducting a daughter of Minerva's city—and the Athenian patroness will do nothing.[53] Orithyia will be taken to one of the wildest regions of Thrace and not be heard from again in Ovid's poem.

The commentators note that Ovid uses language that is reminiscent of Lucretius' descriptions of wind and other natural phenomena, but in a mythological context where the naturalistic philosophy of the Epicurean might seem out of place. But Ovid is not concerned here with mere wit or amused mingling of mythology and rational thought. Instead, he is once again reminding us of a poetic voice in the Latin tradition that will grow louder as the epic unfolds.

Orithyia is abducted and taken to the Ciconian realm of Thrace, an especially wild area where Virgil located the death of Orpheus (*Georgics* 4.520).[54] Orithyia gives birth to twin sons, winged like their father (but otherwise taking after their mother in appearance). The boys Calais and Zetes are born with red hair and without visible wings; as they grow up the wings appear and they become blonder (Ovid was aware of what happens to red hair as one ages).[55]

The tradition of the north wind's rape of Orithyia has no violence once the initial assault is past; unlike the tragic mess that resulted from Tereus' ferocity, we hear nothing more of this story except that these two winged sons of the wind god were companions of the Minyans, that is, the Argonauts, as they sailed in quest of the famous fleece:

> ergo ubi concessit tempus puerile iuventae,
> vellera cum Minyis nitido radiantia villo
> per mare non notum prima petiere carina. (6.719-721)

> *Therefore, when the boyish time of youth had given way,*
> *with the Minyans did they seek the radiant fleece with its shining hair*
> *through a sea not known, on the first ship.*

The tradition was that the Argo had been the first vessel ever to sail the deep; Tereus, of course, had used a boat to transport his prize back to Thrace, and the point cannot be pushed too far. But Perseus, the first hero of Ovid's epic, had used the oarage of winged sandals; Jason is the first hero who will use a ship to navigate toward his heroic quest.

The sixth book ends quietly, though with the clear expectation that Ovid will begin a version of the *Argonautica*. From Perseus, the Gorgon Medusa, and Andromeda, Ovid has advanced to the next great hero in the rough chronological order of his universal history. And, arguably, the world needs another hero after the breakdown in order represented by the horrific story of Tereus and his Thracian barbarity. Jason will, in a sense, do battle with the East, though in a manner that causes more problems than not. And, as we have seen is his wont, Ovid will not dwell equally on all aspects of the lore, and he will race over parts of the story we might consider quite important (and not always because some previous poet seems to have handled the material already).

The heroic theme that Ovid's *Perseid* inaugurated did not last long. Ovid will not spend much time on Jason either (less, in fact, than on his heroic predecessor). But Jason will commence a series of heroic narratives that will occupy the next several books. These stories of valor and daring, of tragedy and disaster, will take place in the world that Minerva, the Muses, and even Diana seemed to set in order in the second half of Book 5: a Jovian world, to be sure, a world of Olympian order, but one in which the worst excesses of the past would be excised. That order has been threatened, though (especially from a Roman, Augustan perspective) more locally and domestically than not; the violence of Tereus impacted the Athenian house of Pandion, but even that family showed its resilience in the successful reign of Erectheus. His daughter was raped by the wind, but that divine violation (and by a relatively minor god) resulted in the positive development of the birth of two heroes, though Ovid will dispense with them quickly and, if we can believe the surviving traditions, they will accomplish very little of note in their relatively brief lives.

The second third of the epic, then, will largely explore the nature of heroism, a necessary prolegomenon before any sort of examination can be undertaken of the great heroes of the Trojan cycle and, of greater concern to Ovid's contemporary audience, the hero Aeneas and the Roman founding. If the first third of the poem set the stage in the world's history for the coming of heroism, the second third will study that phenomenon closely, all as prelude for the Trojan and Roman cycles of the last third. At a time when humanity's fortunes seemed to be in decline, Perseus had appeared as a romantic hero whose bravery and deeds of valor could entrance a world that was in desperate need for figures to admire and emulate. Now, after horror such as the world had never seen, Ovid devotes several books to the problem of the hero. The gods were absent from the tragedy in Tereus' home; someone must take their place. Perseus had succeeded with ample divine assistance in his quest to slay Medusa; his own decline had come after the savage violence in his new father-in-law's dining hall. After that tarnishing of his heroic image, the immortals had returned to Ovid's main stage, only to be absent (and ineffectual) in the last movements of the book. Bacchus, of course, was the exception, though even he was technically absent: Procne, like Virgil's Amata, had *simulated* the god in wreaking her vengeance. We have observed that one of Ovid's concerns in this book has been the relationship between what the gods do and the influence their actions have on mortals (cf. the Roman concern with *exempla*). The hero is a natural part of that poetic meditation and discussion, since by their very nature heroes both emulate the gods (in practice, both for good and ill), and seek to surpass them.

Something else lurks in the background, too, a theme that, soon enough, we shall come to identify as Ovid's greatest concern. The ultimate quest for any hero is the conquest of death and the journey to the underworld; so Aeneas had visited the infernal regions and seen a vision in Elysium that portended the great future of Rome. Ovid, too, will unveil his own reading of Virgil's underworld philosophy, though slowly and at his own pace. As we move from Calliope to Orpheus to Pythagoras, we shall see that the poet who had envisioned the world in eminently Stoic terms at its creation has been haunted all the while by the same poet who left Virgil spellbound: the Epicurean Lucretius. And we shall come to realize that, in an important sense, Ovid's main purpose in his epic is to respond to the eschatological vision Virgil offered in the sixth *Aeneid*.

But for now, we ride with the winged sons of the wind on the world's first ship. With them we shall voyage into another book, where we shall meet a new hero and his greatest challenge, the beautiful sorceress who, in Seneca's terrifying vision, would soon announce to her husband and the world that there are no gods.[56]

Notes

1. The older (1972) volume of Anderson's commentary covers Books 6-10; best now (together with Bömer's encyclopedic coverage) is Rosati in the Fondazione Lorenzo Valla series.

2. The story is another canonical Ovidian tale; a brief reference to the lore can be found at Virgil, *Georgics* 4.246-247, *aut dirum tiniae genus, aut invisa Minervae / laxos in foribus suspendit aranea cassis* (where see Thomas). Servius ad loc. either did not know about the weaver girl (he complains about the use of the feminine *aranea*), or he did and let pedantry win out over mythological allusion. But Virgil's slight nod does not allow us to imagine how much Ovid invented. On Arachne note von Albrecht, M., "L'épisode d'Arachné dans les Métamorphoses d'Ovide," in *REL* 57 (1979), pp. 266-77, Lausberg, M., in *Boreas* 5 (1982), pp. 112-123, Tupet, A. M., "La magie dans les métamorphoses d'Arachnè" (Ovide, *Mét.* 6, 135-145), in Frécaut, J. M., and Porte, D., eds., *Journées ovidiennes de Parménie: Actes du Colloque sur Ovide (24-26 juin 1983)*, Bruxelles: Editions Latomus, 1983, pp. 215-227, Harries, Byron, "The Spinner and the Poet: Arachne in Ovid's *Metamorphoses*," in *PCPhS* 36 (1990), pp. 64-82 (where Arachne is an image of the exiled poet; see also Lausberg above), Hardy, Clara Shaw, "Ecphrasis and the Male Narrator in Ovid's Arachne," in *Helios* 22 (1995), pp. 140-148, and especially Oliensis, Ellen, "The Power of Image-Makers: Representation and Revenge in Ovid *Metamorphoses* 6 and *Tristia* 4," in *Classical Antiquity* 23.2 (2004), pp. 285-321.

3. It might be a promising line of investigation to study cases in Augustan poetry of ill-fated women whose mothers die early (e.g., Virgil's Camilla).

4. As McKeown notes ad loc., wool working was a symbol of chastity (since the nocturnal toil kept the women from extracurricular dalliances).

5. The nymphs are frightened by the goddess' presence, and their assembly in Arachne's dwelling creates a parallel situation to how the Heliconian nymphs judged between the Muses and the Pierides.

6. At 4.700-702, Iris descends to Dido to release her from torment; at 5.609-610 and 657-658, Iris descends to Sicily to instigate the burning of the Trojan fleet; cf. 9.14-15, where Iris is sent to stir Turnus up so he will attack the Trojan camp in Aeneas' absence. The mottled snake that appears on Anchises' tomb is compared to a rainbow (5.88-89), in language that is almost repeated from the end of Book 4 (Dido's recent death is very much on the mind of Aeneas in Sicily, and Anchises' memorial games are, in a sense, funeral games for Dido). Anchises' snake may also portend Palinurus' eventual end.

7. Herodotus 8.55 is the most famous surviving description of the contest.

8. In the *Homeric Hymn to Demeter* (422) "Rhodope" is one of the companions of Persephone, and the name may have been on Ovid's mind after the stories of Book 5, but there seems to be no connection between mountain and maiden.

9. Cf. Antoninus Liberalis 16, which seems to tell the same story (with not much more than Ovid in the way of details); why cranes were associated with giving warnings about war is unknown (though perhaps their distinctive sound seemed a suitable harbinger of martial ills).

10. Asterie is an obscure figure for moderns; Pseudo-Apollodorus (1.4.1) has a story that she disguised herself as a quail to escape Zeus' advances (presumably she was a nymph or some semi-divine creature to have the power of metamorphosis, since there is no mention of any prayer to a deity for help). But every other story Arachne relates was of a successful Jovian rape. As for the daughter of Nycteus, Antiope (6.111), the story

was a favorite of Propertius (c. 1.4.5, 2.28.51, and especially 3.15.12, 19, 22, 39). Over two hundred lines of Euripides' *Antiope* survive; the play was probably an influence on Ovid.

11. The story was not original to Ovid; cf. Callimachus' *Aetia*, fr. 43.117 Pfeiffer, for a scanty reference to the union and the birth of a chthonic Dionysus.

12. Pseudo-Apollodorus 1.7.3-4.

13. See Pausanias 8.25.4-10, 42.1-6. As with the story of Jupiter's affair with his daughter Persephone, so here the Lydian girl provides details Calliope had omitted from her rendition of the story of Ceres' daughter's abduction. While searching for her daughter Persephone, Ceres had been pursued by Neptune; she disguised herself as a mare, but the god followed suit as a stallion and overpowered her. Arachne is doing the work of the Pierides in responding to the Muses' song.

14. The possibility does exist that Arachne has blended well-known stories (e.g., Leda and Danae) with lies. She may well have embellished certain details or even invented some affairs out of whole cloth. I consider this possibility unlikely, but it is odd to have such a collocation of so many obscure stories in so brief a span of lines. Again, Arachne apparently knows her mythology very well.

15. Cf. Apollonius Rhodius, *Argonautica* 2.1231-1241.

16. Bömer and others have wondered if *Livor* here should be considered a "personification" like Invidia. More interestingly problematic is how Pallas is referred to as a *virago* (130), a warrior. I suspect Ovid's point is that Pallas is not only skilled in weaving, but also in battle and so much else; Arachne has but one skill (however great). Further, we should not forget that Arachne was trained by Pallas: the goddess taught her weaving and, we might add, contempt for the misbehavior of male gods (Arachne is envisioned as a virgin like the goddess). There was no mention of fault in Pallas' tapestry; both canvasses were probably perfect (or at least impossible to critique), and so no victor was possible. And both contestants, so similar, were unable to accept this reality.

17. And by hanging, a particularly ignominious end for the ancients.

18. Niobe was among the most well known of mythological figures. The *locus classicus* for her fate (and that of her children) is Homer, *Iliad* 24.601-617 (where see MacLeod in particular); the mythographers, of course, remember her, and there were tragedies by Aeschylus and Sophocles. But Ovid's is, yet again, the "canonical" account, the only complete surviving version. See further Otis, *op. cit.*, pp. 147 ff., Brown, A. D. Filton, "Niobe," in *The Classical Quarterly* N. S. 4.3-4 (1954), pp. 175-180, Voit, L., "Die Niobe des Ovid," in *Gymnasium* 64 (1957), pp. 135-149, Holtsmark, Erling B., "Unhappy Niobe: Ovid, *M.* 6.284-5," in *Eranos* 86 (1988), pp. 71-73, and Feldherr, Andrew, "Reconciling Niobe," in *Hermathena* 177-178 (2004-2005), pp. 125-146. Propertius c. 2.20.7-8 mentions Niobe's pride and the death of twelve children; at *Amores* 3.12.31 Ovid observes that it was "we poets" who made Niobe into flint, or Callisto in a bear. See further the helpful article of Hollis, A. S., "A New Fragment on Niobe and the Text of Propertius 2.20.8," in *The Classical Quarterly* N. S. 47.2 (1997), pp. 578-582. On the significance of the Homeric Niobe, note Ahern, Charles F., "Two Images of 'Womanly Grief' in Homer," in Tylawsky, Elizabeth, and Weiss, Charles Gray, eds., *Essays in Honor of Gordon Williams: Twenty-Five Years at Yale*, New Haven: Henry R. Schwab, 2001, pp. 11-24.

19. At 6.313 and 315, as all who hear of the fate of Niobe's family venerate the true *numina* of Latona and her twins. And cf. 331 *numen* below; Ovid's point in this whole section is the power of divinity.

20. Apollonius Rhodius, *Argonautica* 1.736-741 has a summary of Amphion's musical feat.

21. Though the sense is quite clear, 6.201 is significantly corrupt; Anderson's *statis* may be correct (though Ovid's normal metrical practice argues otherwise, and Tarrant does not cite the conjecture). This section is plagued by an unusually high number of textual problems, and is perhaps indicative of lack of final authorial revision of this narrative.

22. The god could presumably have spared the boy, though we might be reminded of Coronis and the regret Apollo felt after killing his *quondam* lover.

23. This may be Ovid's own version; the suicide theme relates back to Arachne. There was no reason for Ovid to use the story that Apollo slew the father with the sons (so Hyginus), which would have made the god seem more bloodthirsty than he already is.

24. This tale, which appears at Antoninus Liberalis 35, is attributed to Nicander. See further Clauss, James J., "The Episode of the Lycian Farmers in Ovid's *Metamorphoses*," in *Harvard Studies in Classical Philology* 92 (1989), pp. 297-314.

25. 6.339-340 *Chimaeriferae . . . Lyciae*, i.e., the Lycian home of the monster Bellerophon slew. Ovid does not tell the story, though he alludes to it more than once; the chimaera was Turnus' avatar in the *Aeneid*, which may provide a clue to why Ovid omits the story in his epic.

26. In Antoninus Liberalis, Latona wants to bathe the divine infants; Ovid increases the pathos by having the goddess insist that she does not want the pool for bathwater, but rather for a life-sustaining drink. Further, in Antoninus the point of the story is why the country is called Lycia, from the Greek for wolf: wolves led the goddess and her infant twins to the pool. In this detail we also see something of the origin of the connection between wild animals and Diana.

27. Some scholars have made much of the fact that Latona seems patient with the farmers, in contrast to her treatment of Niobe. But Latona is weak and overcome with thirst and, further, Niobe had spent quite some time living in wanton arrogance.

28. The story is told at Pseudo-Apollodorus 1.4.2 and Hyginus, *Fabulae* 165.

29. See further Littlewood ad *Fasti* 693-710.

30. Littlewood has the bibliographical reference to Kellum, Barbara, "The City Adorned: Programmatic Display at the *Aedes Concordiae Augustae*," in Raaflaub, K., and Toher, M., eds., *Between Republic and Empire: Representations of Augustus and his Principate*, Berkeley: The University of California Press, 1990, pp. 276-308.

31. Hyginus, *Fabulae* 161, 273.

32. For a rather different reading, see Galinsky, *op. cit.*, pp. 134-135.

33. See further Livy, *Ab Urbe Condita* 38.13.6, with Briscoe's commentary. H. J. Rose has a brief note that wonders if Ovid borrowed the detail about the river of tears from some Near Eastern folktale at "The Rivers of Tears," in *The Classical Review* 42.5 (1928), p. 171; note also his "The River of Tears Again," in *CR* 43.2 (1929), p. 61. Normally Marysas' blood formed the river.

34. The story is well attested outside Ovid. The usual mythographic treatment can be found at Pseudo-Apollodorus 3.14.8 and Hyginus, *Fabulae* 45; Antoninus Liberalis 11 tells essentially the same story, though with the names changed. The story is very old; Hesiod alludes to it ad *Opera et Dies* 568-569 (where see West, and Zaganiaris, N. J., "Le mythe de Térée dans la littérature grecque et latine," in *Platon* 25 (1973), pp. 208-232). Sophocles had a *Tereus*, which was undoubtedly a source of Accius' treatment of the same; several fragments are preserved of what Cicero attests was a quite popular play. The barest traces remain of Livius Andronicus' treatment. See further Monella, Paolo,

Procne e Filomela: dal mito al simbolo litterario, Bologna: Pàtron, 2005; also Jacobsen, G. A., "Apollo and Tereus: Parallel Motifs in Ovid's *Metamorphoses*," in *The Classical Journal* 80 (1984), pp. 45-52, Pavlock, Barbara, "The Tyrant and Boundary Violations in Ovid's Tereus Episode," in *Helios* 18 (1991), pp. 34-48, Kaufhold, Shelley D., "Ovid's Tereus: Fire, Birds, and the Reification of Figurative Language," in *Classical Philology* 92.1 (1997), pp. 57-71, Segal, Charles, "Philomela's Web and the Pleasures of the Text: Ovid's Myth of Tereus in the *Metamorphoses*," in Wilhelm, Robert M., and Jones, Howard, eds., *The Two Worlds of the Poet: New Perspectives on Vergil*, Detroit: Wayne State University Press, 1992, pp. 281-295, Ciappi, Maurizio, "La metamorfosi di Procne e Filomela in Ovidio, *Met.* 6.667-670," in *Prometheus* 24.2 (1998), pp. 141-148, Peek, Philip Sheffield, "Procne, Philomela, Tereus in Ovid's *Metamorphoses*: A Narratological Approach," in *Antichthon* 37 (2003), pp. 32-51, and Feldherr, Andrew, "*Intus habes quem poscis*: Theatricality and the Borders of the Self in Ovid's *Tereus* Narrative," in Arweiler, Alexander, and Möller, Melanie, eds., *Vom Selbst-Verständnis in Antike und Neuzeit/Notions of the Self in Antiquity and Beyond*, Berlin: Walter de Gruyter, 2008, pp. 33-47. The story of Procne and Philomela is the subject of one of the surviving Virgilian centos, *Progne et Philomela*, on which see McGill, Scott, *Virgil Recomposed: The Mythological and Secular Centos in Antiquity*, Oxford, 2005. In the prologue to the *Cligés*, Chrétien claims to have composed a treatment of the subject; in the *Ovide moralisé* one Chrestiiens li Gois is credited with the nearly 1500 lines of such a treatment.

35. See further Clausen, and Coleman, ad loc., Hudson-Williams, A., "Some Passages in Virgil's *Eclogues*," in *The Classical Quarterly*, N. S. 30.1 (1980), pp. 124-132, Boneschanscher, E. J., "Procne's Absence Again," in *The Classical Quarterly*, N. S. 32.1 (1982), pp. 148-151, and Peirano, Irene, "*Mutati artus*: Scylla, Philomela, and the End of Silenus' Song in Virgil *Eclogue* 6," in *The Classical Quarterly* N. S. 59.1 (2009), pp. 187-195. It is noteworthy that Ovid borrows this terrible tale from Silenus's song right after the slaughter of *another* satyr, Marsyas. For an argument that Ovid's version of the myth is a late transformation of an original story that focused on fertility rivalry, see Suter, Ann, "The Myth of Prokne and Philomela," in *The New England Classical Journal* 31.4 (2004), pp. 377-386.

36. 6.417 *Messeneque ferox*, "strong Messene." Nonius 425,23 notes that *ferox* is a synonym of *fortis*, while *ferus* = *saevus*. The distinction is not always maintained, but is good to remember.

37. Servius ad Virgil, *Aeneid* 1.292 says Gradivus was Mars' proper title when he raged (*saevit*). Not "archaic, or arcane, but perhaps a little bookish" says Horsfall ad *A.* 3.35 (though the title's occurrences in Livy's first pentad and Ovid's *Fasti*—Horsfall does not mention this passage—do not exclude an archaic flair for the moniker). All of this is verbiage though to excuse the fact that we are ignorant of the origins of the title or its precise signification.

38. Much ink has been spilled over the mutilation of Philomela, usually as part of gendered readings of the poem (see further, e.g., Spentzou, Efrossini, "Theorizing Ovid," in the *Brill Companion*, pp. 384 ff.).

39. On the Virgilian passage see my "*Laviniaque venit litora*: Blushes, Bees, and Virgil's Lavinia," in *Maia* 60.1 (2008), pp. 40-50.

40. Virgil had also compared Dido to a Bacchant (*A.* 4.300-303), but the more apposite passage here is Amata with her daughter Lavinia.

41. Ovid here raises the spectacle of Procne as Medea, the subject of a famous lost tragedy that was part of the early work of the poet. Not surprisingly, Ovid's next major movement in the epic will be to explore Jason and Medea lore. Ovid's point in the evoca-

tion of Medea here, however, is to highlight how shocking it is for the Athenian Procne to become like her barbarous Eastern counterpart. See also Larmour, David H., "Tragic *Contaminatio* in Ovid's *Metamorphoses*: Procne and Medea, Philomela and Iphigenia (6.424-674); Scylla and Phaedra (8.19-151)," in *Illinois Classical Studies* 15 (1990), pp. 131-141. Procne is mentioned immediately after Medea at *Ars Amatoria* 2.383-384 *altera dira parens haec est, quam cernis, hirundo: / aspice, signatum sanguine pectus habet.*

42. *Blanditiae* recur in the narrative as an important theme. At 6.496, Philomela was *blanda* as she begged Pandion to let her go with Tereus to see Procne, just as Procne had been blandishing (440 *blandita*) when she sent Tereus to Athens. Here Procne imagines that Itys is using blandishments to tempt her away from her terrible resolve, while the Thracian north wind Boreas will use the same device (685 *blanditiis*) to woo Orithyia, to no avail (thus leading to his divine rape). Procne is suspicious of her son's charms precisely because of the ill use of the same trick by Tereus and, it would seem, other Thracian men, including the divine wind.

43. It is possible to take *ex nimia mentem pietate labare* of Procne's own thoughts, though this seems less likely.

44. For an interesting study of the transformation of women from wild to civilized in the poem, see Vesley, Marc Eric, "Women and Civilization in Ovid's *Metamorphoses*," in *SyllClass* 16 (2005), pp. 61-83.

45. On the tragic influence behind this passage, note Curley, Daniel, "Ovid, *Met.* 6.640: A Dialogue Between Mother and Son," in *The Classical Quarterly* N. S. 47 (1997), pp. 320-322.

46. In Virgil, Dido memorably insulted Aeneas by saying no mother bore him, but rather Hyrcanian tigresses (*A.* 4.367); the adolescent Camilla wears a tiger skin (11.577), probably a gift of Diana's, since there were no tigers in ancient Volscia. Ink has been spilled over when tigers were first exhibited in Rome, and when Augustus first saw one, but Ovid's point here is that Procne has been transformed into a Bacchic monster.

47. Itys was slaughtered and cooked in a secret area of the house (6.638 *utque domus altae partem tenuere remotam*) so as to conceal the crime until dinner, but *inside* the house nonetheless. The civilized Athenians have brought Bacchus into the home.

48. Of the attested variants, *emersaque* is clearly the wrong reading here, though it might carry a hint that he was beginning to vomit and wanted to be able to regurgitate all he had eaten as quickly as possible (i.e., *reserato pectore*). *Semesaque* is appealing for its vividness, though it is difficult to take it as "half-digested."

49. On the metamorphosis note Solodow, *op. cit.*, pp. 178-179.

50. For the story of Boreas' rape of Orithyia, note Apollonius Rhodius, *Argonautica* 1.212-223.

51. Cf. even the subtle correspondence of 6.473 *molimine*, of Tereus' lies to win Philomela, and 694, of the struggles of Boreas in the sky.

52. We might note that in Hyginus the transformation of the women is explicitly due to the mercy of the gods; the original story, however, probably lacked this detail (for a truly merciful divine intervention might have changed only the women, rather than condemning them to an eternity of being pursued by the hoopoe). In Ovid's vision, all three are rather equally punished. The hoopoe remains militaristic after the manner of its Thracian origin; the swallow and nightingale are forever stained with the red color that commemorates Itys' bloody end. Ovid commented on what "public opinion" thought of, e.g., Diana's treatment of Actaeon; the narrative of Tereus and his involvement with two Athenian princesses offers no such opportunity to debate moral culpability. But the avian

metamorphosis of the three players in the tragic drama does make the point that the punishment they suffer is eternal.

53. At *Amores* 1.6.53-54, Ovid invokes Boreas to assist him in breaking down his beloved's door: *si satis es raptae, Borea, memor Orithyiae, / huc ades et surdas flamine tunde foris*. As McKeown notes ad loc., normally in a paraclausithyron the komast complains about the north wind that buffets him on the threshold; Ovid invokes Boreas as a potential ally. At Propertius c. 2.26.51, Orithyia is pictured as denying that Boreas was cruel, though at c. 3.7.13, Boreas is an object of fear (*timor*) for the ravished girl.

54. See further Thomas ad loc. Orpheus is imagined as another Pentheus, torn apart by raving Bacchants. The parallel to the Tereus story and the actions of the Athenian sisters there is clear; Boreas, of course, is no mortal but rather a demigod. Boreas is also not credited with anything remotely approaching the savagery of his mortal counterpart; Tereus' violence (and the reaction it elicited from the daughters of Pandion) has marked the zenith of madness thus far in the epic.

55. Ovid will but briefly return to these two sons of the wind. In Apollonius, they are killed by Heracles after they press the Argonauts to give up the pursuit of the lost Hylas. In Propertius (c. 1.20), they are pictured (uniquely) as amorous pursuers of the young man, chasing after him on their wings as he drives them off successfully. See also Pseudo-Apollodorus 3.15.2, and Richardson ad Propertius c. 1.20.25-31 (and Heyworth's *Cynthia* for the textual difficulties in the passage).

56. Seneca, *Medea* 1026-2027 *per alta vade spatia sublime aetheris, / testare nullos esse, qua veheris, deos*.

Chapter VII

And Now the Minyans

The seventh book of the epic is devoted largely to the deeds of heroes, specifically Jason and Theseus, though Ovid takes his narrative in directions we might not expect were we looking for a mere summary in epic verse of the heroes' *curricula vitae*.[1] At the close of Book 6 we were prepared for Ovid's *Argonautica*, and the sons of the north wind open this book with a brief mention of how the Argonauts had encountered the blind and aged Phineus, who was tormented by the Harpies.[2] The story begins—as did Ovid's *Perseid*—in *medias res*; Ovid blithely passes over everything that happened to the Argonauts before they reached Colchian Phasis. Before ten lines of the book have passed, the poet reveals his main interest: the love of the king's daughter Medea for the hero.[3] There will be no extended dramatic depiction of the heroic exploits of either Jason or Theseus; the latter hero's deeds will be but briefly enumerated in a hymnic catalogue.

Rather than an epic in the style even of Ovid's *Perseid*, Book 7, then, is instead a return to the overtly erotic theme that had dominated the early movements of the poem.[4] Ovid's lengthy examination of heroism will include a detailed study of love, a resumption of a theme he had never really abandoned; the fact that Virgil had invoked Erato at the beginning of the second half of the *Aeneid* is never far from the poet's mind. Ovid's *Metamorphoses* has been called an epic of love; while the amatory interest will ultimately prove subordinate to other concerns, the threat of passionate love to the hero is of major interest to both Virgil and Ovid (cf., as we have noted, Lucretius' attack on passion in *De Rerum Natura* 4). Medea is consumed with fury (7.10 *furorem*) as the present book opens, a madness that cannot be quelled by reason (*ratione*). This granddaughter of the sun is on fire with passion for the stranger who has arrived in her father's land.

Ovid's Medea resurrects the same image for his audience that Virgil's Dido did for his: the specter of Cleopatra with Antony. Medea is like a student learning what we have already mastered from Ovid's earlier books: "some god" (7.12 *nescio quis deus*) is behind her love, she realizes (we know about Cupid); she thinks that what she is experiencing must be "love" (13 *quod amare vocatur*).[5] Perseus had represented an earlier sort of hero, a man oppressed by a less complicated situation: no tradition of his story revealed any domestic trouble with

Andromeda *per se* (rather, his love for her was the cause of strife with others, just as Odysseus' loyalty to Penelope ultimately caused the destruction of his fellow Ithacans on his return). In Medea, *Jason* will find his destruction (as will his children and his prospective new wife and father-in-law). For from the beginning, Ovid's Medea knows that her mad passion for Jason is wrong:

> excute virgineo conceptas pectore flammas,
> si potes, infelix! si possem, sanior essem!
> sed trahit invitam nova vis, aliudque cupido,
> mens aliud suadet: video meliora proboque,
> deteriora sequor. (7.17-21)[6]

> *Drive out from your virgin breast these flames you have conceived,*
> *if you are able, unhappy one! If I were able, I would be healthier!*
> *But a new force drags me, though unwilling; I see the better things and I approve them:*
> *I follow the worse.*

Ultimately, *deteriora* will encompass child murder.

Medea's circumstances are both similar to and different from Dido's. Medea is a virgin; she has no ghost of a husband demanding loyalty. But as with Dido, the hospitality theme is at the fore of the conflict (cf. 21 *hospite*); Jason is a guest, a status that does not demand the princess' passionate love, but Medea is perhaps correct that her father's tasks for the hero are unduly harsh (14-15). Here the poet is preparing for the parallel story of Theseus that will succeed Jason's; both heroes were assisted to a great extent by foreign princesses, women who would eventually be abandoned (though under very different circumstances). In the present book, Ovid will suppress any mention of Ariadne; Medea will take center stage as the image of a scorned woman, and throughout this book the reader is haunted by the memory of *Aeneid* 4. There, Carthage's queen had only been able to utter threats that portended doom for the future, as Rome would face the avenger of Dido's blood in Hannibal. Ovid shows the sorceress in all her glory, and as we see Medea encourage daughters to hack at their father so he may be submerged in boiling water, we see a terrible realization (on a far more savage scale) of the sadistic wish of Dido to have Aeneas lost at sea, calling in vain for her help.

Medea summarizes briefly the tasks Jason has been asked to perform: he must yoke fire-breathing bulls to plough a field, then face the armed offspring of sown dragon teeth, and lastly the serpent that guards the Golden Fleece (7.29-31). Interestingly, Medea observes that without her help, Jason will be "savage prey" (*fera praeda*) for the serpent: the epithet is transferred from serpent to victim, but also looks forward to the rhetorical attacks on Jason, Aeneas, etc., from spurned women: only a wild animal would behave thus and abandon a beloved.[7] Indeed, Medea observes that if she does not help Jason, one would think her the offspring of a tigress (32), an echo of Dido's insult of Aeneas. As we might expect, Ovid's Medea anticipates what the audience knows will be the result of this passion; Medea expresses fear that if she helps Jason, he might leave without her or, worse yet, prefer another to her. Were he to do this, she would wish him dead (43 *occidat ingratus*). But, for now, Medea is sure that he would never abandon her, partly because of his nobility (44 *nobilitas*), but mostly because he is handsome (43-44 *vultus in illo / ea gratia formae*): hardly reliable proof, but exactly the first thing Dido raved over in Carthage.

But Medea is not completely lost; she will demand a pledge from Jason, and she will call on the gods as witness.[8] Medea is sure she will be secure in Jason's honor, and she will be celebrated through the cities of Greece as the hero's savior (7.49-50). She refers to the Greek cities as *Pelasgian*, i.e., one of the oldest names for the Greeks: here we see a hint of the ambitious Medea who craves domination over ancient Greece.[9] Medea also gives voice to sentiments some in Ovid's audience might appreciate; she wants to go with Jason to Greece in order to appreciate culture. She recognizes that Colchis is a barbarous land (53 *barbara tellus*). Fame, however, is never far from her mind; she even imagines the same sort of glory Horace had predicted for himself:

> . . . quo coniuge felix
> et dis cara ferar et vertice sidera tangam. (7.60-61)

> . . . *happy with my husband*
> *I shall be considered dear to the gods, and I shall touch the stars with my head.*

At the close of his first ode, Horace observed that if he were to be inserted among the lyric bards, he would scrape the heavens with his lofty head (35-36 *quod si me lyricis vatibus insereres, / sublimi feriam sidera vertice*). Medea's words, of course, are Ovid's, and so there is a bit of learned humor on the poet's part, perhaps even an echo of the lyric tradition of Euripidean tragedy that helped make Medea so memorably famous. But the echo of Horace mainly serves to underscore Medea's madness; she has conflated the poet's art with the madness of passion and desire for a wealthy, famous spouse. There may also be the slightest hint that Ovid's Medea hopes to rival Dido in the poetic tradition.[10]

Medea's *furor* is not all consuming, however. Significantly, in Ovid's vision the sorceress restrains her emotions and returns to reason; *pietas* and *pudor* defeat Cupid (7.72-73). In Ovid's depiction of divine amours, there is never any such reasoned debate over the appropriateness or suitability of a prospective dalliance; the god simply takes what he wants. Medea is more reasoned and nuanced; her very intelligence adds to the terror she engenders. After spending most of her speech giving in to her passion for Jason, the Colchian princess remembers the loyalty she owes her family (*pietas*) and, presumably, the sense of decorum that (especially from a Roman perspective) would demand a less aggressive, less forward approach to a potential amour (*pudor*—again, unlike Dido, Medea is a virgin and no widow).

At this point, Ovid's narrative takes an interesting turn. Medea goes off to an altar of Hecate that is deep in a dense forest (74-75). There is no reason given for the visit; her passion cools and she seems in control of her reason. But then, without warning, she sees Jason, and the dead flame rekindles (77 *exstinctaque flamma reluxit*).

Why did Medea go to the altar of Hecate, and why was Jason there? In Virgil, such consorting with infernal powers was part of the last movements of Dido's story, not the very beginning. In Apollonius, Jason is urged to seek Hecate's help (3.478 ff.). Ovid creates a montage that leaves his reader somewhat dazed and off-balance; he does not care to tell us why Medea went to the forest (where passion should indeed be extinguished), or why Jason was there; Medea is Hecate's favorite, and if Jason were urged to seek the help of the goddess, an encounter would be understandable. What *is* clear in Ovid's narrative is that while Medea is struck by Jason's appearance, it is Jason who first approaches Medea and asks for help. It is over very quickly; the hero both asks for help and promises marriage (7.90-91 *hospes et auxilium submissa voce rogavit / promisitque torum*,[11] with shades of the hospitality theme again).[12] Once again, the narrative moves very quickly: Jason receives the magic herbs by which he might quell the power of the fire-breathing bulls. There is no romantic interlude, but rather a quick return by the hero to his dwelling.[13]

The scene shifts to the trials Jason must endure; Ovid here is the master painter, depicting his scenes with dizzying speed to reflect the magical spells associated with the Black Sea witch. King Aeetes is dressed in royal purple and bears an ivory scepter; the colors are baleful. Jason meets the fire-breathing bulls without fear, all thanks to Medea's assistance. Ovid compares the bulls' sounds to loud furnaces or to lime kilns, the latter another of his very precise, anachronistic similes that has caused critical commentary: what is the poet's purpose in evoking such features of the modern world? The usual explanation is that the poet is being irreverent with the tradition by inserting what sometimes strike the reader as ridiculous comparisons (cf. Pyramus' spurting blood and the broken water pipe) into his epic narrative. Similes from the manmade world are not, I would argue, necessarily evidence of irreverence; from the pen of a Roman poet, they evoke the importance, indeed the solemnity, of the urban world. They join the time-honored images of nature in providing poetic comparisons (and are not without epic precedent in Homer).[14] For ultimately, as with Virgil's Aeneas and Dido, Jason will forsake passionate love for the urban love of Glauce, the Corinthian princess; it matters not whether he intended to leave Medea completely—the point is that his quest for "civilized" power would bring him to the bed of Corinth's heiress. This civilizing influence is what rebels against Medea's powers, which here are seen defeating the bulls whose sounds are akin to those we might hear in the factory district of some ancient town.

Jason yokes the deadly bulls and ploughs the virgin field; he soon sows the dragon's teeth whence armed warriors will arise (7.115 ff.). The situation now is parallel to what Cadmus faced in Thebes; the earth gives birth to soldiers in arms, just as an infant is fashioned in its mother's womb. The comparison is inexact; these are fully grown warriors with weaponry, not small babies awaiting full maturation. The point may in part be that these warriors appear suddenly and at once; Cadmus' warriors had appeared slowly (Ovid described them with the simile of the stage curtain slowly rising). Jason's warriors intend to fight their maker, not themselves. The hero throws a rock amid the newborn soldiers and engenders civil war (139-142). The passage does not make clear why the warriors turn on each other; elsewhere in the tradition throwing the rock had been Medea's idea. Here, the sorceress mutters a secret incantation to help her lover (137-138). Cadmus had merely witnessed civil war; Jason causes it, and, implicitly for those who know the tradition, with Medea's help (cf. Cleopatra's Antony). In contrast to the situation with Cadmus' dragon-sown warriors, here there would be no internecine conflict were it not engendered by Jason, who is now already bewitched by Medea's spells.

Jason still needs to slay the dragon that guards the Golden Fleece; Ovid moves rapidly now through his narrative, covering epic ground even more swiftly than he had done thus far in his miniature *Argonautica*. There is a palpable rush here not only to move to elements of the story the poet wishes to emphasize, but also to advance his main themes; there is a constant tension in the *Metamorphoses* between the slowly unfolding main point of the epic (which will be simple and unified), and the many and varied stories that make up his universal history. Not everything can be told in great detail, but nearly everything must be at least mentioned. The fleece, in any case, is unimportant; the real prize is Medea, and with her Jason returns to Thessaly (7.156-158 *heros Aesonius potitur spolioque superbus / muneris auctorem secum, spolia altera, portans / victor Iolciacos tetigit cum coniuge portus*). And she is, we should note, a *coniunx*, even if Jason might not think so when the time comes to enter into a nuptial alliance with Corinth. She would not merit this title in Roman eyes, but, in contrast to the reception of Virgil's Aeneas, Ovid's Augustan audience demands no such legal niceties from this Argonautic hero. He has made his error, just as Aeneas did with Dido (but Venus and Cupid could be blamed for some of that), and, more importantly, just as Antony had with Cleopatra (where no one believed a god responsible).

Perseus had ample divine help in securing his victory over the Gorgon (and, by extension, the sea monster that threatened his beloved Andromeda). His *objet d'amour* played no part whatsoever in his heroic victories over either monsters or rival suitors in Cephalus' palace. Jason, in contrast, has relied on the aid of a foreign sorceress. His achievements in Colchis have been great, but he has secured them not through the aid of the immortals *per se*, but through the assistance of a passionate Eastern princess. Jason's flawed approach (and we must remember that in Ovid's narrative it is Jason who initiates the request for Medea's help) leads to a perversion of what would normally be admirable behavior. So when Thessaly comes forth to celebrate Jason's victories, only his father Aeson is absent, overcome by old age and feebleness (7.162-163). Jason approaches Medea and asks her to help the elderly king, and, in what we might consider a supreme example of *pietas*, he asks that she take some of Jason's years and add them to his father's span of life.

The intentions are noble and laudable; the problem is Jason's invocation of a foreign witch. Medea is not a caricature of evil; she is moved by her husband's piety, even as Ovid notes that the thought of her abandoned father occurred to her mind (7.170 *dissimilemque animum subiit Aeeta relictus*). Medea was no practitioner of *pietas*, but she can recognize it in another, just as she understood all too well the very Roman concept of *pudor*. Asclepius had incurred divine wrath by raising the dead, and Medea does not agree that she can transfer years from anyone to another, but she does declare that if Hecate helps her, she can restore Aeson's youth.[15] Perseus had ample divine help; Jason invokes Medea. Later in this book, when we meet Theseus we shall note that in Ovid's brief description of his early glories, neither gods nor men are mentioned as aids; that will change with Ariadne, but Theseus overall will mark an improvement over Jason.[16]

Hecate was involved in Dido's rites before her suicide; the three-formed goddess makes regular appearances in passages replete with magic.[17] Hecate's connection to Medea is familial; Medea's father Aeetes was the brother of Perses, Hecate's father.[18] The connection of Hecate to Diana is reinforced by the tradition that Hecate's mother, the Titan Asteria, was Latona's sister.[19] Hecate was, like her cousin Artemis, traditionally a virgin goddess. A Titan, she allied with the Olympians and thus was on the winning side in Zeus' rise to power.[20] In the *Homeric Hymn to Demeter*, it was Hecate who reported the fate of Persephone to her mother; the goddess eventually became Persephone's close companion. Artemis had been a companion of Persephone in the *Hymn*, and the two goddesses were frequently conflated.[21] In Roman verse, the goddess became associated with a divine triad: the three-form goddess that manifested as Artemis on earth, Selene in heaven, and Hecate in the underworld. Her patronage over magic rites and necromancy was thus assured.

Medea's invocation of Hecate is thus a family affair. The sorceress goes off under the light of a full moon, ready to invoke the goddess Night, Hecate, Tellus, the stars and the moon (7.192 ff.).[22] The passage is the first full account of what the audience already knows; Medea is a powerful witch of proven ability. Phaethon could not control his father's solar chariot; Medea is able to make her grandfather's car go pale along with Aurora's dawn. Medea reviews her threefold accomplishments on behalf of Jason: she would have us think that she surpasses in her power all the great mortal figures we have already met. Certainly the impression the audience has thus far is that the Colchian princess is far stronger than Jason, who seemingly could do nothing without her aid.

Nothing, of course, is particularly loathsome or even especially troublesome in the catalogue of Medea's accomplishments. Now, she prays that the vigor of youth may return to her husband's aged father, and that she may be admired for her devotion and positive efforts to help her spouse. Her prayers are answered;

the dragon chariot that is her divine means of transportation appears from the heavenly ether (7.219 ff.). Medea begins her ride to collect the herbs she needs for her rejuvenating rites. The sorceress surveys the mountains and rivers of Thessaly in a passage that recalls previous Ovidian catalogues, including the damage another descendant of the sun did in a chariot ride through the sky. This time, the virtual goddess is in supreme control as she is driven by serpents on a magical quest.

Having returned to her adopted home, Medea begins her magic rites. She constructs two altars, one to Hecate and one to Youth (7.234 ff.). She sacrifices a black sheep. She prays that the lord of the underworld and his abducted wife Persephone might not hasten to take away Aeson's life. Aeson's nearly lifeless body is brought outside to the altars for the climax of the ritual; Jason and other witnesses are sent away so they may not witness the secret liturgical acts, which are akin to the all-female nocturnal revels of Bacchic madness (257-258 *passis Medea capillis / bacchantum ritu flagrantis circuit aras*). The efficacy of the magic is not in question; the practice is. We are reminded of Dido's rites before her suicide, and the solemn curse by which she condemned Aeneas' Romans to the horrors of the Punic Wars. She is a barbarian (277 *barbara*), and we might wonder at how she uses a branch of the gentle olive (278 *ramo . . . mitis olivae*) to stir the terrible concoction she prepares in her cauldron—though, after all, this terrible liturgy will result in new life for Aeson. The whole mess is prepared as Medea, with rather shocking speed, cuts the throat of the aged king. She fills the wound and his veins with the foul mixture, and all the revulsion such magic rites might engender is perhaps forgotten: the old man is restored to his appearance of forty years before. Medea has successfully made Aeson young again; *pietas* has been served as the king becomes a vital prince.

Interestingly, at this juncture Ovid inserts the brief but important note that Bacchus was impressed by the magic, and by the knowledge that he could borrow the same trick to restore youth to the faithful nurses of his infancy (7.294-296).[23]

Procne and Philomela had evoked the specter of Bacchus in their madness after what they had suffered at the hands of Tereus. Medea goes beyond this image, in that for once a god comes to a lesser being and seeks assistance: Medea can apparently do more in this regard than the wine god, and her benefit (7.296 *munus*) will return Bacchus' wet nurses to youthful vigor. If Bacchus is terrifying, Medea is made all the more ominous by her tutelage of the god. Jason has fallen under the spell of a sorceress who is able to instruct the most dangerous of the immortals.

At this crucial juncture, with the seemingly pious presence of the god signaling an ominous turn in the story, Ovid introduces Pelias, who has thus far been absent from his version of the *Argonautica*.

According to the mythographers, it had been Jason who contrived to use Medea to slay Pelias.[24] In Pseudo-Apollodorus, Aeson faces death at Pelias' hands, but is allowed to commit suicide (so also Jason's mother). Who was this enemy of the Argonaut leader? The usual story was that Pelias had been warned that he ought to beware a man who came to him with a single sandal; Jason of course lost a shoe in a river and was thus revealed to be the threat to Pelias' crown (Ps.-Apoll. 1.9.16). The quest for the fleece was instigated as a way to eliminate the peril to Pelias. So there is, in a sense, a good reason why Medea would turn against the Thessalian king; her method, however, will be ghastly and involve treachery:

neve doli cessent . . . (7.297)

Lest trickery be absent . . .

Medea will convince the daughters of the aged Pelias that she can rejuvenate their father. Again, the story is not original to Ovid, though it is significant that in his narrative it was Jason who first requested help from Medea in Colchis, and the Colchian sorceress who here embarks on the trip to Pelias, seemingly of her own accord. Again, as elsewhere, Ovid does not deny the tradition that Jason inaugurated Pelias' death, but his silence—in contrast to his detail of Jason's earlier active solicitation—is important. Jason has now been suppressed from the narrative, and it is Medea—the Black Sea Cleopatra—who reigns supreme on Ovid's stage. The death of Pelias is not a subject for mourning (arguably he needed to die to safeguard Jason, though the image of the aged king is something less than frightening), but by Medea's abuse of the laudable *pietas* of Pelias' daughters (the savage means by which she achieves the king's demise), and the admiration of Bacchus for the potency of the witch's magic, the audience begins to appreciate how dangerous Jason's union with this woman is.

Medea toys with the innocent daughters of Pelias; Ovid reveals a sadistic streak in this witch. She pretends to have to think about the request that Pelias be restored to youth; after feigned deliberation she offers—of her own accord—a demonstration: an aged ram will be transformed into a lamb (7.309-311). As the commentators have noted, Medea alters her method here: at once she slits the ram's throat and throws the carcass in a cauldron together with her magic herbs and potion. A lamb, of course, emerges safe.

Medea had wanted trust from Jason (7.46 *fidem*); now her promises to the Peliades obtain faith from the rejuvenation of the ram (322-323 *promissaque postquam / exhibuere fidem*). The trust the elegiac lover had hoped for is now broken in the terrible magical rites that will pervert the pious relationship of loyal daughters to their father. Tereus had destroyed Pandion's daughters; now Medea will make Pelias' daughters the killers of their father. Jason had promised Medea a bed (91 *torum*), and now the daughters of the king stand around his bed (334 *torum*)—the repetition of the word reveals that Jason did not necessarily mean "marriage" by his use of the noun. Medea makes clear what is at stake in her orders to the women: if they have any *pietas*, they will kill their father. The scene is vintage Ovid, another *tableau* that would make a modern horror film director proud: the aged king awakens to find his daughters hacking at his body as they avert their eyes from the seemingly (and really) impious act the Colchian has imposed on them. Pelias begins to plead with his pitiable daughters; Medea finishes him by slitting his throat and throwing him in the cauldron.[25]

Ovid here echoes the horror of the Tereus, Procne, and Philomela sequence; there the sisters slew a child and cooked him so his father could consume his own son's flesh. Here desperate daughters hack at their father so he may be submerged in boiling water. The difference is that the instigator of this madness is the "wife" of the newest hero to grace the world, the woman who was most responsible for the hero's successful feats.

Medea's status as a semi-divine creature (?) is ambiguous; she is capable of being punished, and so despite her great powers, she flees away (7.350 ff.) to escape retribution for her murder of the king. The sorceress begins a reverse flight; she had traveled to find the necessary ingredients to rejuvenate Aeson, and now she will flee punishment for her slaughter of Pelias. Interestingly, she passes over a locale made famous by the fate of one Cerambus, who is said to have escaped Deucalion's flood by the aid of nymphs who lent him wings.[26] The flood has thus far been the greatest natural disaster to afflict the earth, and Cerambus escaped it—just as arguably Medea has now made a name for herself as one of the most despicable characters in the poem, if not the most criminal— the audience, after all, knows that she slew her children, and more, to punish her husband.[27]

Cerambus is a type of Medea; now the witch travels over lands made famous by various metamorphoses that have not received much critical attention. The first is a seemingly obscure petrifaction of a snake (7.357-358). The snake in question had tried to eat the head of the dead Orpheus; Apollo intervened to spare the poet the mutilation. Medea also flies over where Paris received a pitiful partial burial. Between the two examples of the horror of lack of burial, Ovid locates a mysterious (otherwise unknown) metamorphosis where a bullock was changed into a deer by Bacchus to cover up the fact his son (of unknown identity) had stolen it. Next is Maera (also otherwise unknown), who was changed into a dog that now terrifies the locals with its barking (362). Then come the women of Cos, who were changed into cows at the time Hercules' band left their island (again, an unknown story, though it is known that Hercules had gone to Troy and then returned to Greece via Cos). Next are the Telchines of Rhodes, whom Jupiter plunged into the sea to drown; Ovid mysteriously says they "blighted all things by their very eyes" (366 *quorum oculos ipso vitiantes omnia visu*) and thus were punished.[28] Medea passes over Cea, where Alcidamas, Ovid says, would one day marvel that his daughter had become a dove.[29] At this point, Ovid embarks on the longest single metamorphosis story in Medea's travelogue: the swan Cycnus.

We can pause, then, and examine the first half of Medea's voyage. The first story, that of Cerambus, echoes Medea's own ride: he escaped the deluge. Then two eerie stories of implied corpse mutilation surround the seemingly pious Bacchus, who covers up his son's theft (and we might note that Bacchus had borrowed Medea's example to restore youth to his nurses). Women who were apparently punished for some transgressions are next: Medea will escape all punishment. The Telchines are sorcerers like Medea herself; given the evidence of the first fragment of Callimachus' *Aetia*, Ovid may have enjoyed a smile in composing the scene of their punishment. Finally, Alcidamas' daughter suffered avian transformation because her father broke faith; she died in childbirth.

The stories Medea's journey evokes do not merely reflect some effort of the poet to display his knowledge of obscure mythological changes. While they do serve to load Ovid's universal history with yet more tales, however briefly told, most of them can in some ways be linked to Medea's own story (cf. the tradition of her own brother and how she saw to his being chopped up and thrown overboard to slow Aeetes' ship, thereby just raising the specter of the horror of unburied body parts littering the waters).

The middle of the catalogue of changes concerns the story of Cycnus, which can be found in a somewhat different version at Antoninus Liberalis 12. Cycnus was loved by Phyllius, who was charged to perform a series of tasks to win his beloved's favor: the taming of wild birds, of a lion, and finally of a bull. Here the three amatory challenges echo the three parts of Medea's aid to Jason, which began with the fire-breathing bulls. Cycnus rejected the accomplishment of the would-be lover, who in anger refused to turn over the promised bull. Cycnus then threw himself off a rock and might have been thought dead, but instead the would-be suicide was transformed into a swan. His mother Hyrie, in grief at the supposed loss of her son, was so overcome by her mourning that she turned into a pool of water (7.371-382).

We might have expected Phyllius to be the one to throw himself off a rock; Cycnus is apparently quite angry that he was denied the bull. It is unclear why he tells Phyllius that he would one day wish that he *had* surrendered the animal (377 *cupies dare*); the swan is among the most magnificent of creatures and a bird of exceeding beauty, and perhaps the point is that Cycnus was going to be willing to surrender to Phyllius, but only in his own good time; by refusing to turn over the animal, the would-be lover has lost a magnificent prize in Cycnus. The connection of the story to Jason and Medea comes from the evocation of the labors Medea performed (ultimately in vain) for her lover; of course it is Medea who is able to escape Jason on wings. The story thus foreshadows how Jason would reject Medea, despite her assistance in such matters as the taming of the fire-breathing bulls, and that Jason will rue the day he forsook Medea—who will escape in the air, just as Cycnus did.

Combe is next; her obscure and otherwise unknown story also relates to Medea: she escaped her children by transformation into a bird. The Latin is ambiguous: 7.382-383 . . . *in qua trepidantibus alis / Ophias effugit natorum vulnera Combe* could mean either that Combe had been threatened with death from her children, or that she had assaulted them (the latter interpretation is, I think, the likelier in context). In any case, the story relates to the fate of Pelias as well as that of the children of Medea and Jason.

The sorceress next passes the island of Calaurea, sacred to Latona (7.384-385). Here a king and queen were transformed into birds; the myth is otherwise unknown and we cannot speculate on what is signified. Mercury's Mount Cyllene is next, though in Medea's travel adventure it is a locale famous for the future incest of one Menephron with his mother (386-387).[30] The River Cephisus follows, whose tutelary divinity mourns that Apollo had changed his son into a fat seal. Medea also sees the house of Eumelus, who was mourning that his son now lived in the air.[31] The seal story is utterly unknown, but Eumelus killed his own child for what he thought at the time was a just reason (or at least he surrendered to a temporary rage), and so there might be a foreshadowing of Medea's forthcoming murder of her children.

Medea at last arrives in Corinth (7.391 ff.). Here, Ovid concludes his long list of transformations with the tale that it was at the site of this ancient city that men were once sprung from mushrooms (392-393 . . . *hic aevo veteres mortalia primo / corpora vulgarunt pluvialibus edita fungis*). The story is, again, utterly unknown outside this passage, the last in an extraordinary chain of stories where most of the metamorphoses are not otherwise extant. Many of the tales, however, do fit with details of the Medea story, both the events Ovid has already described and the story's imminent conclusion. It is possible (though I would argue unlikely) that the unknown stories were invented by the poet and reflect in part the great knowledge of the demi-goddess, who, like her grandfather, can see all things. Certainly the stories were in part chosen from the more obscure and recondite tales of change available to the poet.

I suspect that part of Ovid's point here comes in his description of what happened after Medea reached Corinth. The poet is at his laconic best:

sed postquam Colchis arsit nova nupta venenis
flagrantemque domum regis mare vidit utrumque,
sanguine natorum perfunditur inpius ensis,
ultaque se male mater Iasonis effugit arma. (7.394-397)

*But after the new bride had burned up from Colchian poison
and either sea saw the burning house of the king,
the impious sword was bathed in the blood of the sons,
and, having avenged herself wickedly, the mother fled Jason's weapons.*

Ovid does not bother to tell how and why Jason arrived in Corinth; the story was well known. Jason is already married to a new princess in the rapid temporal compass between Medea's departure to slay Pelias and her return. We are almost in something of a dream world; presumably Medea left to kill Pelias (at Jason's behest?) and then returned, having surveyed so much of the Greek world, exactly to the city where now Jason was married to a new royal princess, the Corinthian Glauce. Events have been syncopated; the catalogue of metamor-

phoses has, in a sense, told the intervening tale with a transformational eloquence mere linear narrative could not have surpassed. The dramatic events of
Medea's vengeance against Jason at Corinth, the stuff of so many Euripidean
trimeters and lyric choruses, are here abridged into four lines that are part of
Medea's travelogue—where Athens is the next destination.

Medea enters the citadel of Pallas in the goddess'own city (7.398 ff.), to
which Ovid now returns after a long absence. The witch has now entered the
"last" Greek city, the Minervan haunt that had so recently promised to be the
bringer of civilization via the gift of agriculture. Some last briefly told metamorphoses are occasioned by her arrival. Periphas and Phene were apparently a
royal couple of ancient Athens.[32] Periphas was so wise and just a monarch that
his people began to ascribe to him the honors due only to the gods; Zeus wanted
to destroy him, but Apollo intervened and secured the supreme god's agreement
that Periphas would be transformed into an eagle and Phene a vulture (the former Zeus' own bird, the latter of indeterminate significance). Alcyone has also
recently been at Athens; she was the granddaughter of Polypemon, and had recently been transformed into a halcyon bird.[33]

The stories are odd, but they may both point to divine intervention to save
victims of "questionable" guilt via the device of avian metamorphosis. There
may be a connection to Medea's escape from punishment—twice, and hence
two stories—via flight.

There is something jarring about seeing Medea sheltered in Athens, the city
of Pallas; Jason is forgotten (and easily, given Ovid's consistent focus on his
amour). Aegeus, the new Athenian monarch, receives Medea with *hospitium*
(7.403—the return of that important theme), but in his own way he exceeds the
expectations of hospitality: he marries the girl, and this time there is no question
of the legality of the union (*thalami quoque foedere iungit*). Medea, after all, is
the lynchpin that joins the stories of two great heroes: Jason and Theseus. And
there is a warning, here, too, for Medea: her powers have been supernatural, and
despite the double reminder that she must flee from punishment, she has seemed
unstoppable in her magic. She has now arrived in a second Greek city, not unlike Cleopatra in her union with not one but two prominent Romans; there is
more than a shade here of Medea as whore, symbolized by Halcyone's transformation story.[34] And, now, another Greek hero will be impacted by this Eastern sorceress, as Theseus returns to his father's home after a long absence.

Iamque aderat Theseus (7.404); Ovid announces the second of the heroes in
his new sequence.[35] He is rather like Perseus in that some heroic accomplishments already lie in his past; Ovid will return to those later (405 *bimarem
pacaverat Isthmon*).[36] The situation is much the same as with Pelias; Medea will
soon be ready to prepare another potion.[37] Theseus is to be poisoned with
wolfsbane as is he were some public enemy (420 *hosti*); Ovid does not bother
with the background to why Aegeus would agree to enlist Medea's aid in mur-
dering this heroic visitor. The story was well known; Aegeus had had a long lost
son, and Medea was the first to recognize that Theseus was the rightful heir to

the Athenian throne. She thus contrived his death, and enlisted the unwitting support of the father to slay the son (once again, this monster has violated all dictates of *pietas*).

Aegeus recognizes the Athenian or even family marks that adorn Theseus' sword as he prepares to drink the potion Medea had mixed to his ruin (7.423-424). Thus we have Medea's third escape from punishment; again, she is able to flee through magic arts (*nebulis per carmina motis*), though once again we are reminded that she would presumably be susceptible to penalty had she not fled.[38] She is an image of victory, though, over both mortals and immortals: she suffers no ill effect for her many crimes, she is never transformed or otherwise penalized by a deity for her sins. She is master over serpents, as evidenced by her dragon car. We may see in Ovid's conception of this sorceress an image of Cleopatra, who succeeded in eluding Octavian's grasp by her suicide.[39] But Theseus, like Octavian, survives any designs the sorceress might have had on his life. He also succeeds in escaping from any passionate encounter with an Eastern temptress.

Athens has had much to mourn in the days since Ceres took the city's native son Triptolemus over the lands on a divine chariot to spread the gifts of agriculture. Now, just as Argos could rejoice in Perseus, so Athens can bask in the glories of a new hero. And, unlike Jason (who represented a decline in heroism in comparison to Perseus—not surprising after the preceding narratives that detailed such horrors as the story of Tereus)—Theseus will be celebrated for great victories that were achieved by his own valor. The Athenians sing of his glory in defeating the Cretan bull at Marathon (7.434).[40] The whole scene is a marvelous respite from troubled circumstances; Ovid allows Athens and his audience to celebrate (and even the mention of Bacchus by metonymy for wine does not concern us). There had been a tradition that the Cretan bull was actually the means Jupiter used to convey Europa (cf. Ps.-Apoll. 2.5.7); if Ovid had that tradition in mind, than the slaying of the bull represents a return to the pursuit of order and "rehabilitation" of the gods that we observed earlier. Theseus safeguards Ceres' sacred Eleusis by eliminating the wrestler Cercyon, who was a bane of travelers (439); protection of the innocent wayfarer from perils on the road is, in fact, a major theme of Theseus' exploits: Procrustes with his fatal bed (438), Sinis with his trick of tying people to trees to rip them apart (440-442), Sciron with his habit of hurling people (including his daughter) off a cliff (443-447). And in Ovid's narrative, the hero performs these exploits almost as if he were a civil servant, charged with cleansing the countryside of the wicked: he is, in fact, not dissimilar to the gods at the start of Book 6, who swept over the world and punished the especially guilty. The terrible crimes of Tereus (and his victims) had polluted Athens; now Theseus removes the blight from Attica and beyond. For a moment, we are allowed peace in a spirit of reflective pride.

Ovid now ruins the glorious celebration by stating an important part of his overall philosophy (however commonplace and clichéd); Aegeus had a problem, since no pleasure is without trouble:

... usque adeo nulla est sincera voluptas,
sollicitumque aliquid laetis intervenit. (7.453-454)

... so indeed it is that there is no pure pleasure,
and something troublesome intervenes amid happy things.

The Cretan king Minos is preparing war against Aegeus' Athens; he was avenging the loss of his son Androgeos.[41] A brief catalogue follows of the islands that were convinced (either by bribe or otherwise) to ally with Minos. Here we have a distant foreshadowing of the Trojan War as Minos prepares to wage war on Athens and summons a contingent of allies to help in his attack, and Minerva's city faces yet another threat to its stability.[42] We are also reminded of the doors of Apollo's temple at the opening of *Aeneid* 6, with their depiction of Cretan lore. Ovid will, in time, complete the images Virgil left unfinished.

The catalogue that now commences is prolegomena to Ovid's main narrative here, namely the visit of Minos to Aeacus' island of Aegina. The story does not appear outside Ovid; some would judge this tale another authorial invention (perhaps rightly). The poet will now link Aeacus' Aegina and its rejection of Minos' request for military alliance with the story of Cephalus.[43] The visit of Minos to Aegina is also a perversion of Aeneas' visit to Evander's Pallanteum to seek allies against Turnus. Cephalus' visit to Aegina will provide the correct parallel: he will follow on the heels of Minos and secure Aegina'a assistance in the Athenian struggle against Crete.

For Ovid's Aeacus refused to ally with Minos because of his country's ancient ties to Athens; the Cretan king goes off with a threat, though he is unwilling to expend his forces on an attack against the island. As soon as his ships depart, an Athenian vessel appears in port; the ship carries Cephalus and his sons Clytos and Butes. Athens, not unexpectedly, is seeking Aegina's aid in repelling Minos' threatened invasion. Aeacus grants the request; he has plenty of men in the full bloom of youth, though Cephalus notes that many men seem absent from his previous visit to the island, thus inviting Aeacus to tell his tale of prior woe.

Aegina had been a love of Jupiter; Juno hated her rival and punished the island that bore her name by sending a plague to devastate Aeacus' realm.[44] Thus commences Ovid's contribution to the great literary tradition that began, we might conjecture, with the beginning of Homer's *Iliad* and the plague Apollo sent on the Greeks in response to Chryses' prayer. We are free to think that Ovid decided to insert a plague into his epic merely because Lucretius and Virgil before him had done the same, and it had become an expectation of hexameter verse that such a topos would appear somewhere. Athens had suffered a famous historical plague, and so Ovid was simply following Lucretius' example by his insertion of such a narrative; since Ovid's mythological chronology would not really permit a retelling of the great fifth century epidemic, he would need some earlier, perhaps invented lore, and Athens' ally Aegina was as good a target for his plague as any.

Lucretius' plague comes as the poet's final expectation for his reader: if you have mastered everything the Epicurean has taught, you will accept the horrors of such a disaster with serenity (Lucretius, *De Rerum Natura* 6.1138-end).[45] In Virgil, the plague is a reminder that it matters not how much *labor* you exert on the care of your cattle; sometimes, as once at Noricum, plague strikes your animals and they die (*Georgics* 3.478-566). In Ovid, the narrative of the Aeginetan plague, like the whole sequence of Minos' threat to Athens, comes right after the glorious catalogue of Theseus' exploits: no pleasure without anxiety. Ovid's plague is not the result of natural disaster; it comes as the direct result of Juno's anger over Jupiter's perpetual illicit amours. In the chronological narrative of Ovid's universal history, the plague serves first as a reminder of the continuing impediments to human progress; Theseus can kill local marauders and mythological monsters, but no one can prevent plagues. Juno's wrath remains alive; we have not heard of a Jovian affair for some time, but his dalliance with Aegina has destroyed a population.[46] Lucretius had focused on men and Virgil on animals; Ovid will combine the emphases of his two predecessors and destroy both men and beasts under the scourge of this Junonian plague.[47]

The gods can play no part in an Epicurean didactic poem; nor would Virgil's *Georgics* permit divine responsibility for the blight at Noricum. Ovid blames Juno for the Aegina disaster (and Jupiter, indirectly). One almost imagines that the outburst of divine wrath over the island is a reaction to the unpunished actions of Medea (chronology notwithstanding). In Ovid's vision, the plague will lead to the repopulation of the island by ants changed into men: the famous Myrmidons. The story of the transformation is very old (Hesiod, fr. 205 Merkelbach-West). Ovid seems responsible for linking it to a plague; the usual story was that Aeacus had come to Aegina and prayed to Zeus that his loneliness might be relieved by companions. In Ovid's vision, Jupiter will counteract his wife's arguably unjust attack on the island by repopulating it with a race that would one day become famous for its exceptional martial heroism. Again, chronology aside (and Ovid's chronology in this section is very loose indeed, since, for instance, Procris—soon to be introduced as Cephalus' wife—was sometimes a sister of Cecrops, the grandfather of Aegeus), Ovid is giving us another example of divine cleansing in this section: the plague eliminates one population and gives rise to a better one. It is a reversal of the myth of the decline of the ages; in Ovid's cyclical view of history, despite setbacks that engender legitimate anxiety, we are moving (however slowly) towards a better future—an Augustan dawn.

It is a commonplace of plague descriptions that the author notes the ineffectuality of the medical arts. Apollo was a patron of medicine, and since he was the progenitor of the first great literary plague, it is a testimony to their power that his arts cannot provide relief. In *Aeneid* 12, Aeneas suffers a mysterious arrow wound that is serious enough to remove the Trojan hero from battle; the doctor Iapyx tries to heal the wound, only to confess that it is beyond his skill. Venus is compelled to descend to earth and cure a wound we might think would otherwise have been fatal (of course the author of the wound is not definitively identified; it may well have been Turnus' divine sister, the nymph Juturna). Ovid's plague also defies all medical arts; Juno's power is too great. Aeacus notes that there was a great temple of Jupiter (whose affair had caused the plague); the prayers offered there were in vain. The horror that unfolds is Lucretian; the Aeginetans fight over the flames, just as had happened at Athens in the terrible closing lines of the *De Rerum Natura* (7.610 *deque rogis pugnant alienisque ignibus ardent*).

After the great description of woes, we expect at 7.614-615 to read that it is Jupiter who is moved by pity, though it is in fact Aeacus, who prays to the god for relief: *Attonitus tanto miserarum turbine rerum, / 'Iuppiter o!' dixi . . . .* Aeacus prays either that his people might be returned to him, or that he too might die. Jupiter agrees to hear him; there is no explanation for why the god was previously deaf to entreaties—clearly nearly everyone was supposed to die first. There is a sacred oak, Jupiter's tree; Aeacus prays that the many ants he sees on it might be transformed into his new population. That night, Aeacus dreams that his wish was granted; in the morning, he discovers he has a new people, born from the ants. We see here a return of the Ovidian theme of rebirth after disaster; the scale is not global, but the effect is the same. An old population has died, and a new people has arisen from nature. The workmanly nature of the ant can be expected to reside in the newborn Aeginetans (655-657). And Ovid can expect that his audience will know that these are the future companions of Achilles, who led the Myrmidons to Troy.

Otis and others have argued that Ovid does not do much to emphasize the divine nature of the plague.[48] On the contrary, the very salvation of the ant-men from the plague is a testimony to its divinely inspired nature; Jupiter resolves the punishment his wife had inflicted. That punishment had effected a cleansing that would result in the birth of the same warriors whose proud name would one day be associated with Achilles.

The Myrmidons are a ready army to accompany Cephalus back to Athens; for now the night soon comes and sleep overtakes all (7.661 ff.). In the morning, Cephalus and his sons meet in the palace of Aeacus, and discussion soon centers on the javelin Cephalus is carrying, which seems to be of unknown wood and tipped with a golden point (672-673 *ignota ex arbore factum / ferre manu iaculum, cuius fuit aurea cuspis*). Thus begins one of Ovid's most memorable and beloved stories, the ill-fated love of Cephalus and Procris.[49]

Ovid had already told this story, at *Ars Amatoria* 3.687-746 (where see Gibson). There, the tale was a cautionary one about the need for lovers to have trust. The story was quite popular, it would seem, though few versions survive.[50] In Ovid, the setting of the story of Procris' death is the forest, a true *locus amoenus* after the horrors of the Aeginetan plague. Significantly, the tale of Cephalus and Procris and the danger of mistrust comes soon after Medea's ill-fated affair with

Jason (and Ovid's audience would also recall the similar case of Theseus' Ariadne, who had also betrayed her father and would, however excusably on Theseus' part, be abandoned as was Medea). It has been some time since we have had a positive example of mortal (or immortal) love; Ovid will balance and contrast this tale of tragedy with the unremittingly happy affair between Baucis and Philemon in his next book.

Phocus asks about the beautiful javelin Cephalus is carrying. The aged Athenian announces that his wife had been the sister of the ravished Orithyia; Ovid thus returns us in a ring to the narrative that had ended right before the sailing of the Argo and the adventure of Jason with Medea (and Theseus, etc.). Orithyia had been raped by the north wind; Cephalus becomes the first victim in the poem of female divine rape (7.703-705 *lutea mane videt pulsis Aurora tenebris / invitumque rapit*). He had been hunting; the scene is usually one of either Diana's virgin coterie in blissful retreat or the invasion of said peace by a male intruder. Here, the male hunter is raped by the dawn goddess, though, he protests to his audience, he could only think of Procris. In other versions, Cephalus was guilty of an affair; Ovid may be inviting the audience to wonder how truthful the repeated protestations of this aged widower about his loyalty to Procris might be.

Cephalus chooses to return to Procris, and rejects the goddess; males, of course, have this power, it would seem, in contrast to female victims of divine rapine. The spurned Aurora curses her would-be lover; as Cephalus returns home, he begins to wonder if *Procris* has been unfaithful (and, again, in some versions she had been). Aurora is clearly the instigator of the doubts; she allows Cephalus to change his appearance to try to test Procris' fidelity. But Cephalus finds his wife as faithful an exemplar of the Roman ideal of the *univira* as he could have wished (7.734-736). The chastity of Ovid's Procris, however, has its limits:

> . . . non sum contentus et in mea pugno
> vulnera, dum census dare me pro nocte loquendo
> muneraque augendo tandem dubitare coegi. (7.738-740)
>
> . . . *I am not content, and I fight toward my own*
> *wounds, until by saying that I would give a sum for a night*
> *and by augmenting my promises, at last I compelled her to hesitate.*

As the commentators have noted, Ovid's Procris is less culpable than her mythographic homonyms, but she does hesitate, and Ovid allows us to indulge in the commonplace that the paranoid are, sometimes, right to be paranoid: Procris is susceptible to corruption.

Ovid's Procris now becomes something akin to Virgil's Dido, who was oddly compared to Diana in a simile whose inappropriateness to Carthage's widowed queen highlighted the conflicted state of Dido's mind. Cephalus is triumphant that he has "caught" his wife; furious and ashamed at his trickery, Procris flees the house and city and becomes a Diana-like woman in the forest (7.745-746 *offensaque mei genus omne perosa virorum / montibus errabat, studiis operata Dianae*). She is no virgin huntress, of course, but she becomes one now in hatred of men. Diana gives Procris two presents: a swift dog and the magical javelin that occasioned Cephalus' story. The implication in Ovid's version is that the non-virginal Procris had been accepted into Diana's coterie; she succumbs, however, to Cephalus' entreaties and returns to her husband, to whom she gives the dog and the weapon. One imagines Diana was not pleased.

Soon enough, Thebes was ravaged by a monstrous fox (7.759 ff.). Ovid does not identify the animal specifically, but refers allusively to a beast known from the tradition.[51] Strange, though, is the poet's assertion that this came after Oedipus' defeat of the Sphinx; the text here is troubled by an apparent interpolation (762) that seems to indicate that Themis was avenging the loss of that horror by sending another bane to the city. Help is sought far and wide; Ovid is here foreshadowing the great drama of Book 8, the Calydonian boar hunt. Cephalus comes with his exceedingly swift dog Laelaps (whose Greek name = a violent storm). The dog and the fox are ultimately changed into marble statues as Cephalus watches from a height; there is no indication of why or how the metamorphosis occurred; Cephalus opines that some god wanted them both to remain unconquered, forever frozen in memory.

Cephalus' story serves to deflect the main point of his long narrative, namely how the javelin figured in the ruin of him and his wife. But the first part of the story is not mere poetic distraction or digression. The description of the animals' chase owes much to the famous simile in which Aeneas chased down Turnus (*A.* 12.753-755), where the Trojan was compared to an Umbrian hound that seems to have caught its prey, though it has not (cf. *Met.* 7.785). Why would Ovid echo that epic combat, which ended in the death of Turnus and not some divinely inspired petrifaction that would = a tie? I do not think the evocation of a dramatic moment from the *Aeneid* is accidental; nor do I think Ovid indulged in the somewhat eerie story of the lonely chase of the hound and the fox for mere narrative leisure. The Virgilian combat had ended with Aeneas' slaying of Turnus, an act that questioned whether the Trojan had absorbed his father Anchises' underworld admonition to the *Roman* Aeneas to spare those who are subjected to you; the Trojan hero does not advance to the Roman future that we know from Jupiter's dialogue with Juno would not be Trojan but Italian. Here, the combat is frozen: there will be no capture, no death, no successful use of Diana's hunting hound to destroy the marauding fox (which had apparently been sent by some other angry deity). Cephalus will find that his wife's gift is useful in that the fox is no longer a threat to Thebes, but the gift will be lost in the marble memorial of the strange chase on the plain. In contrast, the other gift, the javelin, will finds its mark and kill its prey.

Gaudia principium nostri sunt, Phoce, doloris (7.796). Why were Cephalus' joys the beginning of his sorrow? Did he rejoice in the successful vanquishing of the fox? Does *gaudia* refer to his happiness in having won back his once disaffected spouse? After the narrative of the animal hunt, we might almost forget the beginning of the marriage, since Ovid's resumption of the story of Cephalus and Procris seems to treat the newlywed stage of the union as if there had been no serious problem. Procris had revealed that she could be seduced; Cephalus, for his part, engenders suspicion for those who know that in some versions of the story, he was a willing paramour of Aurora. He goes to hunt in the early morning, exactly when Aurora would just have finished her duties (804 *sole fere radiis feriente cacumina primis*). He prays rather suspiciously for the "aura" or "breeze" to come to him (811-813 *aura . . . auram . . . aura*). Cephalus notes that his language was ambiguous and might well have fooled someone into thinking he was having an affair with the goddess; he blames the fates (816 *sic me mea fata trahebant*), and, after all, Aurora had cursed him for his earlier rejection of her advances.

We are reminded of the stories of the raven and the crow as Ovid reports that someone heard Cephalus praying for his breeze, and swiftly reported to Procris that Cephalus must be having an affair with a nymph named Aura. Procris waits until the next morning and goes to the forest to see what Cephalus is doing.[52] Cephalus calls for the breeze, thus causing his wife to groan; she makes a sound by crunching some fallen leaves with her foot, and the hunter Cephalus hurls the javelin his own wife had given him, the former gift of Diana to her new huntress.[53] We know the result: Procris will be slain by the irrevocable and unfailing weapon. Interestingly, one of the Athenians (not Cephalus) had said that the spear always hit its target *and* always returned to its author (7.683-684 *fortunaque missum / non regit, et revolat nullo referente cruentum*). Here, the story seems false: the weapon does not return to its master of its own accord, but Cephalus rushes to his wife and draws out the shaft himself. The story ends romantically (if perversely); Procris dies happy once she learns that there was no "Aura," and that her husband has remained faithful to her (at least in this version of the myth).[54] Unlike Laelaps, Cephalus captured his quarry.[55] The book ends quietly, as Cephalus is dissolved in tears and receives the Aeginetan allies for Athens' fight against Crete.

Ovid refers to Cephalus as a *heros*, a hero, as the book ends (7.863). Indeed, as we have observed, he is like Aeneas, off to Arcadian Evander to seek allies against Turnus. Like Aeneas, Cephalus has succeeded in his mission; he has his soldiers to help fight Minos. But the loss of his wife hangs heavily in the air— there is a reminiscence here of how the trip to Evander to seek allies would result in the death of Pallas (and of course Aeneas had lost his wife Creusa, not to mention his ill-fated affair with Dido, long before he arrived at Pallanteum). As the book ends, we might well expect that Ovid will begin the next with the results of the expedition back to Athens, in which case we shall be disappointed.

Book 7 of the *Metamorphoses* is part of a long sequence of narratives concerning heroes, though, as is Ovid's fashion, he ranges far and wide in his history. This book ends as it began, with a story of love and the violation of trust.

The Cephalus of the *Metamorphoses* is innocent of an affair with Aurora; he is a victim of the goddess, cursed because he rejected her advances. Previous versions of the tale color Ovid's narrative, however: as in the Ovidian rendering in the *Ars*, the problem is one of trust. Still, we can blame Aurora for the mess, and critical attention to Ovid's story should not neglect this important element of the narrative.

Not much has been made of Aurora's responsibility for the tragedy of Cephalus and Procris, and even less has been made of Diana's part in the drama. When last we saw the goddess, she had saved her beloved Arethusa from rape; together with Minerva, she had been part of the world's improvement. Her part in this story has been subtle, but highly significant: Cephalus is an avid hunter (exceedingly avid, we might say). Procris ran off to the forest and became a devotee of the goddess after she was found guilty of succumbing to the temptations of infidelity for riches and presents: a willing prostitute, we might well conclude, now moving to the opposite extreme and playacting Diana. Her hunter-husband's pleas lead her to *reject* Diana and resume her married life, and to surrender two of the virgin goddess' special presents to her husband—an element of the story that has also not received much attention. Was the fox sent to the city of Thebes by Diana (a true foreshadowing of the Calydonian boar)? Was the petrifaction of the goddess' hound Laelaps also Diana's doing, a means both to take back from Cephalus that which he should never have owned, and to memorialize it forever? Certainly the javelin becomes the instrument of punishment for any offenses Procris has created, and a memorial in its own way of Cephalus' crime and his lifelong loss. Aurora punished Cephalus because he rejected her advances; she had tried to violate the sanctity of Diana's forests by raping the loyal husband. But Procris offended Diana, and she falls victim, in a sense, to both goddesses—the one a jealous and spurned rival, the other not pleased with Procris' rejection of her. Both members of this unhappy couple reject goddesses; both are destroyed. There is much of Dido in Procris.

In the case of Jason and Medea, no god was responsible for either's actions. Medea felt violated by Jason, and, as the powerful granddaughter of the sun, she was able to do something about the wrongs she had suffered. Her vengeance carried no consequences. Cephalus and Procris are all too mortal, and thus easy prey for the gods; in the aged Cephalus who comes to Aegina, there is a hint of Aurora's Tithonus, who lived too long. Cephalus is still being cursed for his rejection of the goddess, as he spends every day in lament over his wife. He lost the hound Diana had given Procris; he retains the javelin that was the instrument of his wife's death. In the next book, the larger story of Aegeus' suffering from Minos' threatened invasion will be delayed once more by the long story of another ill-fated love, that of Scylla and Minos. Among many other themes, there, too, a passionate love will end badly. Ovid continues to warn against the dangers of such passion (and of disregarding the gods); in a sense, the story of Cephalus and Procris resumes the themes of the beginning of Book 6, with the sometimes questionable behavior of deities who seek to punish mortals. Again, Ovid maintains the theme of the symbiotic relationship of gods and men in a world in serious need of healing. For now, both Theseus and the Myrmidons offer some hope to that beleaguered world.

Cephalus and Procris fatally mingled the worlds of love and the hunt. The question is not primarily one of blame or fault, any more than it was Callisto's fault that Jupiter raped her in the guise of Diana. What matters to the divine huntress is that her pure sanctuary has been invaded, in this case by Aurora's rape of Cephalus, the abandonment of the goddess' service by Procris (who succumbed to her husband's charms), and Procris' inappropriate bestowal of the goddess' sacred gifts on her husband. To leave Diana's service *and* give her presents to a man is more than the goddess can countenance, and her one-time devotee will die by the goddess' own weapon, hurled by the man she preferred to Jupiter's virgin daughter.

Ovid's Cephalus was the victim of Aurora's rape and her curse, which can be blamed for his subsequent treatment of Procris. In Ovid's narrative, Procris comes off the worse: she was willing to be seduced by bribes to commit infidelity, and she forsook Diana. What lesson, if any, does the poet offer here? What should Cephalus have done differently? Should he have preferred Aurora to Procris? (We might compare Odysseus' situation with Calypso and Penelope). He is punished for devotion to his wife. Is the point that he was devoted enough to forsake a goddess, while the object of his devotion was willing to succumb to mortal bribes? Was Cephalus' passion for Procris misplaced, his admirable behavior wasted on an unworthy object of devotion? In this reading, Cephalus balances Jason: the former lavished fidelity on a woman who did not merit it, while the latter forsook a woman who, arguably, deserved better treatment. Theseus, the unifying hero (who is introduced between the two stories), shows a more successful way: he will utilize the services of his foreign princess, Ariadne— and, conveniently, he will not have to worry about the future, because Bacchus will demand the girl as bride. Theseus, of course will abandon his lover to the god, just as Aeneas abandoned Dido after Mercury related Jupiter's orders. No god, alas, awaited Dido's embrace.[56] Interestingly, Cephalus' punishment for his transgressions against Aurora will not end; he is a living memorial of his inadvertent murder of his wife, just as Laelaps and the fox were frozen in stone. Procris—not unlike Virgil's Dido—finds some release in death, as she breathes her last with the assurance that her husband had not broken his faith to her.[57]

We have argued that in Book 5 there was, as it were, an attempted rehabilitation of the world after the divine rapes of the early movements of the epic. The world set in place by the actions of Diana and Minerva was in the process of being cleansed anew in the first half of Book 6. But the cruel fate of Marsyas showed that the gods could be excessive in their lust to extirpate offense from the world; the savage example of the satyr's flaying was followed at once by the terrible drama of Tereus and the daughters of Pandion: the world was once again in turmoil, and the gods seemed absent—save Boreas, who resumed the pattern of divine rape as the book ended. In a world without divine recourse, we should

not be surprised to see the rise of heroes—Jason was as needed in his time as
Perseus had been in his—but either should we be amazed to see a Medea, a
semi-divine creature whose evil seems to operate uncontrolled. For in the absence of divine oversight, sorceresses like Medea can run rampant indeed.
Medea's savagery ruined one hero (Jason), and threatened to plunge Athens into
renewed sorrow by the destruction of a second (Theseus).

Perseus achieved his victories with ample divine help; Jason relied just as
heavily—and more—on Medea. The early victories of Theseus that Ovid related
so briefly in the present book were recounted absent divine or feminine intervention. Theseus seems to represent an improvement over the two heroic types previously introduced. In the midst of the glorious recounting of his victories, trouble intervenes, which takes the form of Minos' threat to Athens, the recounting
of the plague at Aegina, and the personal tragedy of Cephalus. Ovid has moved
from the macro- to the micro- level of tragic drama, each time increasing the
pathos by dwelling longer and longer on the suffering: from the great civilizing
city of Minerva, we have moved to the tiny allied island to the personal plight of
a husband who had accidentally killed his wife. In the midst of this catalogue of
woe, the first real inkling of the future hero Achilles has been voiced: Aegina's
new population is comprised of the fearsome Achillean soldiers, the Myrmidons.
From the tiny island will spring some of the greatest soldiers of the Trojan cycle,
a theme the poet will resume in Book 11.

For now, Ovid will continue his *Theseid* in his customary oblique and digressive fashion.[58] Theseus has been blameless in his deeds, though we might
question why there is so much danger from Minos if Athens had in Theseus a
truly awe-inspiring hero who might win the day against Crete (why was there a
need to send the aged and weary Cephalus to Aegina to beg allies?). One man,
of course, cannot defeat many armies; Theseus is no Perseus with the aid of a
Gorgon's head to do his heroic work for him. And, in time, the Athenian hero
will win his own victories over the Cretan monarch.

Theseus has been identified as a cleanser of the countryside from pests both
human and animal; in this the hero was a type of the avenging gods as they
brought destruction to such undesirables as Arachne, Niobe, and Marsyas. In the
next book, after his traditional adventures with the Minotaur and Ariadne are
related in due course (and with characteristic brevity for such major and well
known stories), Ovid will present Theseus once again as a potential cleanser of
his native Greek locales from harm, as Calydon calls for help with Diana's wild
boar. That story—like the plague at Aegina and its resultant Myrmidons—will
also presage the *Iliad*, as Ovid recounts the lore surrounding Meleager, the ill-
fated hero who had been used as a cautionary story during the great embassy to
Achilles in the *Iliad*. Theseus, the greatest hero so far in the epic, will have a
fittingly great longevity in Ovid's narrative that will match his valor (even if he
is usually in the background and not a direct participant in the events Ovid unfolds).

We are thus moving ever closer to Achilles, and, in turn, Aeneas, Rome, and Augustus. Much history remains to be recounted, though soon enough Ovid will reach the midpoint of his epic, the middle of his eighth book. There are questions about interpolated lines, lines here and there that ought to be excised from our text.[59] But it is haunting that the midpoint of the next book, deep in the drama of the boar hunt at Calydon, will come with a line about avenging one's brother while fearing the same fate as one's brother (8.442 *ulcisci fratrem fraternaque fata timentem*), a line that would have deep resonance indeed for a Rome so often riven by civil strife. The midpoint of Book 8 and the poem will come amid a tale that links Homer, Virgil, and Ovid in a magnificent triad centered (for the Roman poets) on the alluring image of a Diana-like girl.

Meleager had been a cautionary tale of Phoenix to Achilles about the matter of returning to battle. Phoenix's story offers a different tale of Meleager's exploits from what we have in Ovid. In Homer, Meleager's Calydon is under assault when the hero withdraws from battle because he is angry with his mother. He refuses to succumb to the offer of presents to return, and only reenters the fray when his wife Cleopatra reminds him of how much a captured city suffers (*Iliad* 9.528-600). As Benardete has brilliantly observed, in withdrawing from combat Achilles became, in effect, like a Trojan. Achilles became an active enemy of his fellow Greeks. *His* Cleopatra will be Patroclus, silent in death. He must not be a Trojan; he must return to the war as a Greek, and the instrument of his return will be his lover, the ill-fated Patroclus.[60]

But Ovid had read not only Homer, but also Virgil. In the *Aeneid*, Turnus surrenders his best chance to win the war against Aeneas because the savage will of Jupiter demanded it. The instrument of that savage wrath was the heroine Camilla, whose death was instigated by two immortals, Jupiter and Apollo. That death caused Turnus to give in to rage and abandon his ambush for Aeneas, the plan by which he might have destroyed his Trojan enemy at one stroke. In her dying words, Camilla—Turnus' Patroclus—sent her companion Acca to advise Turnus not to give up that ambush, but to maintain his position and plan. Her death, in other words, would not mean defeat for the Latins, were Turnus but to keep his nerve and pounce on Aeneas according to plan. Meleager's Cleopatra had urged him to return to battle to save Calydon; Turnus's Camilla similarly urged him to stay in battle to save Latium by defeating the Trojan invader.[61] Homer's Meleager and Achilles ultimately listened; Virgil's Turnus would not, since the will of Jupiter demanded that he give in to anger and let his rage over Camilla's death ruin his sense (a victim of passionate love, the poet implies) and thus cost him his victory.[62] In Homer's vision, the death of the *eromenos* precipitated the heeding of the lessons of Meleager; in Virgil, the death of the *eromenos* precipitates the scuttling of those same lessons.

Ovid had read his Virgil. In the next book, the hero who was Homer's cautionary *exemplum* to Aeneas will reappear, and so, in every sense, will Virgil's Camilla. One of the contestants at the forthcoming Calydonian boar hunt will be the Arcadian Atalanta, whose characterization in Books 8 and 10 will be modeled step by step after that of Virgil's Camilla. Like Turnus, Ovid's Meleager will give in to his passion for a beautiful huntress, to his doom. Homer's Achilles did not heed the story of Meleager, and by his delay arguably cost the life of his friend and lover Patroclus (whose name is the mirror image of Cleopatra). Virgil's Turnus and Ovid's Meleager gave in to passion (just as Homer's Achilles had given in to his rage), and both perished; Turnus' passionate anger came after Camilla's death (just as Achilles' did after the death of Patroclus).[63] The passion of Ovid's Meleager will cause his own end, while Atalanta will survive her lover. Ovid's Meleager is very distant from Homer's, thanks mostly to the intervening examples of Homer's Achilles and Virgil's Turnus. Phoenix had essentially argued that by staying out of battle, Achilles was becoming a Trojan; by giving up his ambush, Turnus becomes a Trojan by helping Aeneas to win: Achilles was supposed to reenter battle, while Turnus is supposed to stay in it.[64] Both Turnus and Camilla do not realize how Roman they are, of course—more Roman, indeed, than Aeneas given the ethnic disposition of the future city— they are protomartyrs for Rome because their actions help pave the way for Aeneas' victory and the eventual founding of an *Italian* Rome.

Turnus, Aeneas' rival, thus became his inadvertent helper (with Jupiter's aggressive prodding). Rome's civil strife was already presaged in the conflict in Latium, as future brother slays future brother; civil strife will lie at the heart of the Meleager story Ovid will now unfold (it is an underlying theme in Homer's account). Erotic passion (and the danger it engenders) is also central to the story, as it is to many of the other tales Ovid is about to relate. Antony, after all, had surrendered himself to Cleopatra.[65] The middle of the *Metamorphoses* is an *hommage* to the main themes of the *Aeneid*, and thus serves as prolegomena to Ovid's own account of Troy lore and the coming of Rome . . . and, most importantly, the setting of the stage for Augustus.

Ovid will now continue his *Theseid*, though, as we have observed, Theseus himself will recede far into the background. The poet will unfold his continuing history through one of his longest books, as a diverse group of new stories marches us ever closer to the poet's as yet unknown and dimly glimpsed goals. As the poet reaches the zenith of his drama and the midpoint of his epic, he will focus on a huntress, another Diana-like figure who will destroy the men she encounters. Virgil's heroine Camilla will soon reappear in Ovidian dress, as we travel with Atalanta to Calydon.

Notes

1. E. J. Kenney is the author for the forthcoming commentary on Books 7-9 for the Fondazione Lorenzo Valla *Metamorphoses*.

2. The classic extant account is the *Argonautica* of Apollonius Rhodius; Euripides' *Medea* is a major influence here. Ennius most likely adapted Euripides' play and composed another of his own on the same theme (see further Jocelyn ad loc.). Pacuvius and Accius also treated aspects of the lore. Pseudo-Apollodorus 1.9.16-28, and Hyginus 12-23, offer mythographic summaries of Jason's quest. Virgil's Dido was largely modeled after Apollonius' Medea. In post-Ovidian times Valerius Flaccus composed an *Argonautica*, and Seneca a *Medea*; of Ovid's *Medea* the barest traces remain. The story of the Colchian sorceress has made its mark on literature and the arts through the centuries; of special (and very different) note are Charpentier's *Médée* and Pasolini's Medea. Ovid has a verse epistle of Hypsipyle to Jason (6), as well as Medea to Jason (12), thus making the Argonaut the recipient of two of the *Heroides*; given his tragedy and the evidence of the *Heroides* and the *Metamorphoses*, the story was clearly of intense interest for the poet. On *H.* 12 note the important article of Hinds, Stephen, "Medea in Ovid: Scenes from the Life of an Intertextual Heroine," in *MD* 39 (1993), pp. 9-47. For an argument that Ovid did not write *H.* 12, but rather a later poet under the influence of the "other" Ovidian Medeas (tragic and epic), see Knox, Peter E., "Ovid's Medea and the Authenticity of *Heroides* 12," in *Harvard Studies in Classical Philology* 90 (1986), pp. 207-223. Hosidius Geta produced a *Medea* cento. For the *Nachleben*, Morse, Ruth, *The Medieval Medea*, Woodbrige, Suffolk, and Rochester: Boydell and Brewer, 1996, is useful.

3. On Ovid's Medea note Rosner-Siegel, J. A., "Amor, Metamorphosis, and Magic: Ovid's Medea (*Met.* 7.1-424)," in *The Classical Journal* 77 (1982), pp. 231-243, Wise, V., "Ovid's Medea and the Magic of Language." in *Ramus* 11 (1982), pp. 16-25, Wilhelm, Michelle P., "The Medeas of Euripides, Apollonius, and Ovid," in *The Augustan Age* 10 (1990-1992), pp. 43-57, and Newlands, Carole E., "The Metamorphosis of Ovid's Medea," in Clauss, James J., and Johnston, Sarah Iles, *Medea: Essays on Medea in Myth, Literature, Philosophy, and Art*, Princeton, 1997, pp. 178-208.

4. I say "overtly" because, as we have seen, Ovid's *Perseid* is dominated by the specter of Perseus' fateful love for Andromeda, which is the precipitate cause of the battle in Cepheus' banquet hall, over which the poet lavishes what some would call excessive narrative attention. But there is no study whatsoever of Perseus' or Andromeda's romantic feelings, much as Virgil suppresses any erotic theme for the relationship between Aeneas and Lavinia (which he reserves instead for his depiction of Aeneas-Pallas and Turnus-Camilla). Again, we see that passionate love is fraught with peril; Perseus succeeds with Andromeda, and Aeneas with Lavinia, in part because of the absence of passion.

5. But soon enough she decides that the "greatest god" is dwelling in her (7.55 *maximus intra me deus est*).

6. On these famous lines note Schmizter, Ulrich, "*Video meliora proboque, deteriora sequor*: Ovid und seine Medea," in Kussl, R., ed., *Spurensuche*, München: Bayerischer Schulbuch Verlag, 2003, pp. 21-47.

7. For a different view (read *mera praeda*, "merely prey"), see Kenney, E.J., "Textual Notes on Ovid, *Metamorphoses* 7-9," in *The Classical Quarterly* N. S. 51.2 (2001), pp. 545-550.

8. 7.46-47 *cogamque in foedera testes / esse deos.* These are the lines that Seneca imitated in the devastating verses that close his *Medea* (where see Costa).

9. At *Fasti* 2.627, Medea appears with Ino, Procne and Philomela, Tereus and the Tantalids (Atreus and Thyestes) in a catalogue of the wicked who are banned from the February festival of the Caristia.

10. Creatively, Ovid lets his character do the talking for him, just as his Medea will identify her lust for Jason as a fault and not a marriage (in contrast to Virgil, who makes an authorial comment on Dido's actions).

11. *Torus* need not connote marriage (cf. 332 below, of Pelias' sickbed); certainly to a Roman audience, there is no legally binding marriage here, any more than there was between Dido and Aeneas.

12. Ovid here has none of the moral ambiguities we find in Virgil's Aeneas and Dido: Jason knows he is wrong, and so he asks for help with subdued voice (he need fear no eavesdroppers in the forest, and the tone of voice reflects the inherent shame). He knows he is asking a daughter to betray her father and country. Medea is susceptible to a handsome face, but Jason takes the initiative here in seducing the princess, as he grasps her right hand in making his nuptial pledge (7.89).

13. 7.99 *tecta,* "dwellings," has occasioned question: where was Jason staying? Ovid is playing with the same matter Virgil raises in the *Aeneid*, where the poet frequently uses language appropriate to city-building to describe the temporary shelter of Aeneas and his Trojans. Jason leaves the wild world of the forest and returns to civilization, as it were.

14. Hill has a good note here, comparing Homer's description of Polyphemus' blinding and the simile of the blacksmith.

15. Aeneas' father Anchises lurks in the background as well; he was (mercifully for him, we might think) already dead by the time Aeneas met Dido, and so he played no part in his son's dalliance with Carthage's queen.

16. And also over Perseus, who, in Ovid's vision, is corrupted by the battle in Cephalus' dining hall, in imitation of Virgil's conception of a corrupted Aeneas (where passion for Pallas destroys his humanity via the slaughter of Turnus). Perseus is not passionately in love with Andromeda (Odysseus certainly was with Penelope), but the end result is the same: the archaic hero Perseus, whom we spend so much time with and yet never fully come to know, falls victim to the passions that excite violent slaughter in an inappropriate setting. Therefore he cannot be graduated to the highest levels of heroism.

17. For magic in Ovidian love narratives, note Segal, Charles, "Black and White Magic in Ovid's *Metamorphoses*," in *Arion* 3rd Ser. 9.3 (2001-2002), pp. 1-34.

18. Diodorus Siculus 4.45.1.

19. Cf. Cicero, *De Natura Deorum* 3.18. Elsewhere Hecate is a daughter of Demeter or Nyx.

20. See Hesiod, *Theogony* 404 ff., and Boedeker, Deborah, "Hecate: A Transfunctional Goddess in the *Theogony*?," in *Transactions of the American Philological Association* 113 (1983), pp. 79-93.

21. Cf. Aristophanes, *Ranae* 1358 (with Dover's notes).

22. Ovid has Medea invoke the triple Hecate here, and the moon, which some have found inconsistent. The passage is a good reminder of how poetry cannot abide strict mythological exactitude.

23. Oddly, Anderson ad loc. judges that "the story is not terribly important here."

24. Cf. Pseudo-Apollodorus 1.9.24, Hyginus, *Fabulae* 24.

25. Cicero, *De Senectute* 83 seems to preserve a version of the story in which, bizarrely, Pelias is rejuvenated; the text however is not sound and the passage does not

make it entirely clear what is happening to Pelias (see further Powell ad loc.). Plautus, *Pseudolus* 868 ff. does have a mention of Pelias being made young again, but it is not clear there that the speaker is to be trusted with his mythological details.

26. Antoninus Liberalis 22 has a slightly different version, where Cerambus (the "beetle") is changed into an insect after not believing the nymphs and Pan that a storm would drown his flocks.

27. At *Heroides* 12, Ovid spends half the poem having Medea recite all she did for Jason in Colchis; she blames Jason for the instigation of the murder of Pelias at the hands of his own daughters. In his verse epistle Ovid does not describe the death of the children, though the end of the poem has ample foreshadowing of some ominous event.

28. Ovid is almost certainly referring to the mysterious Telchines of Callimachus, *Aetia* fr. 1 Pfeiffer, who are said to have complained that the aged Callimachus had not yet composed a long epic on a continuous theme. They were held to be a race of Rhodian sorcerors. See further Hopkinson ad loc.

29. Cf. Antoninus Liberalis 1, where the father went back on his promise to marry his daughter to a certain Athenian, who complained to the gods. They helped the young man seduce the girl, who then died in childbirth and was changed into a dove.

30. Hyginus, *Fabulae* 253, also refers to this story, but he may be borrowing solely from Ovid. The tale of maternal incest may distantly foreshadow the matter of Hippolytus and his stepmother Phaedra, which would cause such woe to Medea's forthcoming target Theseus.

31. Antoninus Liberalis 18 helps here: Eumelus was duly reverent to Apollo, so reverent that he killed his own son when he was offended at the boy's perceived mistreatment of a sacrificial lamb. Eumelus at once regretted his anger (cf. Apollo and Coronis), and the god took pity and transformed the boy into a bird.

32. Antoninus Liberalis 6 has the story, which is of quite unknown origin.

33. The story would be unknown save the evidence of Probus ad *Georgics* 1.399. Apparently this girl was thrown off a cliff by her (grand?)father for violating her chastity. She was transformed into a halcyon bird (which may imply, as with the preceding story, that some divinity pitied her—perhaps her lover?). Her father was Sciron, who would be defeated by Theseus (7.443-447 below), so that Ovid here foreshadows the coming *Theseid*.

34. And we might note that in striking contrast to Virgil's Dido, there is barely any hint of sympathy on Ovid's part for Medea; there is nothing in this eminently Augustan epic of the pathos we feel for the Colchian princess in Euripides or Apollonius.

35. Among the various artistic creations of Theseus' *Nachleben*, special mention may be made of Lully's *Thésée*, which focuses on the Medea theme in the Theseus story throughout its five acts.

36. Pseudo-Apollodorus has the story of Theseus' upbringing (vid., e.g., 3.15.6-7, 16.1). Plutarch's *Theseus* offers a detailed account of much of the lore; note also the extant remains of Callimachus' *Hecale* (where see Hollis).

37. I thank my colleague Bridget Buchholz for pointing out to me that Ovid's Ceres (the benefactor of Athens) distantly presaged the Medea cycle in her consumption of the old woman's brew (5.449 ff.), which the goddess then uses as the instrument of her punishing transformation of the newt-boy.

38. Medea's method of escape here is not entirely clear; she may have conjured a mist to conceal her departure, or, more probably, she once again employed her dragon chariot.

39. The question of Cleopatra's suicide has been of perennial interest to students of the classics. Adrian Goldsworthy has produced a 2010 Yale joint biography of Antony and his Egyptian queen that reevaluates the old evidence. Horace, c. 1.37 offers a classic account of the noble queen, victorious in some sense through the suicide by which she escaped the humiliation of a triumph. I suspect that Octavian was happy to allow Cleopatra to kill herself; her "victory" only redounded to his greater glory, by making her appear to be a far more dangerous foe than the reality warranted. Ovid's Medea is not unlike Egypt's queen in her "escape" from punishment, and serpents may have played a part in both women's dramatic exits.

40. In Pseudo-Apollodorus' *Epitome* (1.4-6), Theseus was sent to defeat the bull as part of Aegeus' attempt to eliminate him; when the hero succeeded in slaying the monster, Medea offered the poison brew. This version is similar to the instigation of Jason's quest for the fleece; Ovid's account does not necessarily exclude the same reading. What is important is that Ovid's Theseus does not require help, in contrast to his Jason.

41. Ovid offers no background here; Pseudo-Apollodorus 3.15.7 says the Cretan youth was a competitor in the Panathenaic Games and was sent by Aegeus against the Marathonian bull, which killed him. But there is no clear sense from the evidence as to whether or not Minos had just cause to blame Athens for his son's death.

42. Among the islands Minos "captures," special note should be made of "Siphnos" at 7.466 (if Heinsius' conjecture for the unmetrical received text is correct); Ovid says the island was betrayed by Arne, who in punishment was transformed into a jackdaw (a notoriously rapacious bird). The story is otherwise unknown, though the commentators cf. Tarpeia; most likely is that Ovid is recalling Medea's betrayal of her father, and the tradition that Ariadne did the same to help Theseus: another linkage between the heroes Jason and Theseus.

43. On Ovid's framing device for his main Theseus narrative, note "Ovid's Framing Technique: The Aeacus and Cephalus Epyllion (*Met.* 7.490-8.5)," in *The Classical Journal* 86 (1990-1991), pp. 35-44. On Cephalus here note Brenk, Frederick O., "*Tumulo solacia* or *foedera lecti*: The Myth of Cephalus and Prokris in Ovid's *Metamorphoses*," in *The Augustan Age* 2 (1982-1983), pp. 9-22.

44. This Aeginetan plague is otherwise unknown. For the tradition of Jupiter's lust for Aegina and his taking her away to the island to save her from her father's wrath, note Pseudo-Apollodorus 3.12.6, Hyginus, *Fabulae* 52, and Pausanias 2.29.2.

45. And, of course, cf. Thucydides 2.46-55.

46. Hyginus 52 agrees with Ovid with respect to Juno's anger over Aegina; Hyginus has one snake poison the island's water, not Ovid's many thousands (7.534).

47. Tarrant finds evidence of several interpolated lines in Ovid's plague narrative.

48. *Op. cit.*, pp. 175 ff.

49. See further Segal, Charles P., "Ovid's Cephalus and Procris: Myth and Tragedy," in *GB* 7 (1978), pp. 175-205, "The Innocence of Procris: Ovid *A.A.* 3.687-746," in *The Classical Journal* 75 (1979), pp. 15-24, and Sabot, A., "Heur et malheur d'un amour conjugal: Céphale et Procris (Ovide, *Métamorphoses*, VII,661-862," in Frécaut, J. M., and Porte, D., eds., *Journées ovidiennes de Parménie*, Bruxelles: Editions Latomus, 1984, pp. 199-214, Viarre, Simone, "Doublets mythologiques chez Ovide: de l'*Art d'Aimer* aux *Métamorphoses*," in Porte, D., and Néraudeau, J.-P., eds., *Hommages à Henri Le Bonniec*, Bruxelles: Editions Latomus, 1988, pp. 441-448, and Ahl, F., "Homer, Virgil, and Complex Narrative Structures in Latin Epic: An Essay," in *Illinois Classical Studies* 14 (1989), pp. 17-21.

50. Pseudo-Apollodorus 3.15.1, Hyginus, *Fabulae* 189, 241, Antoninus Liberalis 41 are the main sources besides Ovid.

51. Pseudo-Apollodorus 2.4.6-7, where Zeus is responsible.

52. Anderson argues that Procris does not go at once, but waits—thus showing a greater sense of reason. But Cephalus always went out to hunt just after dawn. In the *Ars* Ovid does highlight her maddened state; she is like a Bacchant as she races off to the woods (3.710 *evolat, ut thyrso concita Baccha, vias*); her *mens* returns once her husband explains what had happened (730), though by then it is too late and her husband fires his fatal shot.

53. Ovid brilliantly evokes the passage in the *Ars* where he described Procris' reaction to the news that Cephalus was having an affair, where at 3.704 the poet compared Procris to leaves growing pale in late autumn or early winter (one of his favorite images for death): *pallescunt frondes, quas nova laesit hiems*.

54. The end of the Cephalus and Procris narrative is not dissimilar to the Pyramus and Thisbe story; the differences only highlight the parallel. The hound and the fox were frozen forever in a marble pose that commemorated their chase; Cephalus will carry the weapon of his wife's death for the rest of his life.

55. The metamorphosis of the hound and the fox can be taken as a warning to Cephalus to abandon the hunt. Just as the combat between Aeneas and Turnus ended in the ruined redemption of the former (who slew his enemy in wrath, in contrast to Homer's Achilles, who returned Hector's body and found his salvation in the final book of the *Iliad*). Cephalus' continued pursuit of hunting (especially at dawn, a rather stupid time given his offense to the goddess) will lead to the death of his wife and his own undoing. We see something of Dido's playacting of Diana in Ovid's Procris.

56. For a different view of the Cephalus and Procris epyllion, note Galinsky, *op. cit.*, pp. 150 ff.

57. I think it no accident that Ovid's Cephalus and Procris epyllion comes so soon before his Meleager and Atalanta. In Virgil, the same line is used to introduce the fateful hunt where Aeneas and Dido consummate their union, and the opening of Book 11, the climax of which is the *Camilliad* (4.129 = 11.1 *Oceanum interea surgens Aurora reliquit*). Aurora is the central actor in the Cephalus and Procris tragedy. Her actions are petty and spiteful, and motivated purely by revenge for Cephalus' slight to her ego; but the hero can do nothing in the face of the goddess, he has no recourse (the plague at Aegina also symbolizes this helplessness). The point, ultimately, is an evocation of the helplessness of Virgil's Turnus in the face of the dictates of fate and Jupiter's savage will: he has no chance, any more than Ovid's Cephalus can escape Aurora's wrath. Ovid will return to some of the themes of his Cephalus and Procris narrative in Book 11's Ceyx and Alcyone epyllion. The Virgilian Camilla narrative was introduced, in a sense, by the dawn formula that opens Camilla's book; not accidentally, Ovid introduces his version of the Camilla and Turnus story with the Dawn of the Cephalus and Procris tale. Procris and Camilla have some affinities (especially in their manner of unforeseen death from the air, and their estrangements from Diana, however different).

58. Ovid's method, as we have seen, allows him to tell as many myths as possible in his epic, even at the expense of always maintaining a focused narrative continuity.

59. There are 11,995 lines in Tarrant's Oxford text, which means that even with allowances for interpolations and excisions (and the fact that no poet could expect someone to pay attention to the exact midpoint of such a massive epic), the "exact" middle of the *Metamorphoses* comes within the story of the Calydonian boar hunt, with ample room on either side of the "midpoint" for error. Ovid could expect that his audience would note

that the "middle" of the epic must come in the middle of Book 8, and I would argue that it is no accident the boar hunt and story of Meleager and Atalanta is the middle of both book and epic.

60. See further Benardete, Seth, *Achilles and Hector: The Homeric Hero*, South Bend, Indiana: St. Augustine's Press, 2005, pp. 100-101 (reprint of the original 1985 publication of the St. John's Review, itself a corrected version of his 1955 Chicago thesis).

61. Virgil loves to play with the parallelism afforded by the identical first and last letters of the names of different but related characters.

62. Though, it is important to note, the "indignant" spirit of both Camilla and Turnus (who share the same death line), would be vindicated by the divine agreement that the future Rome would be Italian and not Trojan.

63. The "wrath" of Homer's Achilles is twofold. On the one hand, there is his anger over Briseis that causes him to withdraw from the war; this is the anger that the story of Meleager is supposed to quell. The second wrath is his reaction to the death of Patroclus and rage against Hector; that anger will be quelled in the haunting scene in Priam's tent, where the two men learn what Virgil would call the *lacrimae rerum*.

64. Elsewhere I have noted how the possibly lycanthropic Camilla becomes, in a sense, an image of the she-wolf that nurtured Rome, in that she inadvertently nursed Aeneas by the part she played in his escape from Turnus' ambush; see especially my "Chiastic Doom in the *Aeneid*," in *Latomus* 69 (2009), pp. 393-401. Achilles does not listen to Phoenix, and Turnus ignores Camilla; the latter hero had, regrettably, not read the *Iliad*, though Virgil makes it clear that Jupiter demanded the Rutulian's actions and instigated the whole scenario at the end of *Aeneid* 11.

65. In Homer, Meleager's wife is Cleopatra; Virgil also plays with the Cleopatra image in his depiction of Camilla, though in *Aeneid* 11 Virgil crafts an allegory of Actium that is brilliantly turned on its head as Camilla, the possible image of Cleopatra, is rehabilitated and becomes a symbol of Italian patriotism and heroism.

Chapter VIII

Now the East Wind Fell

The eighth book of the *Metamorphoses* brings us to the halfway mark in Ovid's epic.[1] As we have already observed, that significant halfway point will come in the midst of Ovid's tale of the Calydonian boar hunt and the ill-fated love for Meleager for the Arcadian huntress Atalanta. The midpoint of the *Metamorphoses* will look back to the great themes of Homer's *Iliad* (the embassy to Achilles and Phoenix's cautionary tale of Meleager), and those of Virgil's *Aeneid* (the crucial decision of Turnus to abandon his best chance to win the Italian war by surrendering to rage over the death of Camilla). Nestled in Ovid's version of the boar hunt and the doomed relationship between Meleager and Atalanta will be yet more reflections on the nature of Rome's great bogey, civil war (especially within the same family).

Book 8, like its predecessor, is part of a larger consideration of the deeds of heroes. In Book 7, Jason and Theseus were introduced; the former more as a foil for his benefactor and lover Medea than for any heroic achievements. Theseus came next, and he remains the ostensible background subject of the increasingly dense story Ovid is unfolding. Theseus' father Aegeus is in dire straits because of a planned attack on Athens by Minos of Crete; forces are being marshaled on both sides for an impending war (the first, we might note, in the epic, and a presage of the Trojan War). Book 7 had opened with emphasis on Medea and how Jason had discarded her; Book 8 will open somewhat similarly, with another sea voyage and another strange story of love: the tale of Nisus and Scylla.[2]

The story of Scylla's betrayal of her father and city to Minos is a familiar one; to a Roman audience, it most evokes the treachery of Tarpeia.[3] The betrayal of the Capitol to the Sabines during their war against Romulus was the Roman example of a familiar motif: the native girl falls in love with the enemy commander and is willing to violate all bounds of *pietas* in betraying her father and/or country to the invader.[4] Minos is attacking Athens; in Ovid's universal history, Athens represents thus far the height of world civilization; Megara is Athens' ally, and Minos is seeking to besiege it as book and story open.[5] In a sense, then, Roman history is dimly forecast and even beginning as the heroic *Theseid* continues (without Theseus). Ovid, in fact, never speaks of the war against Athens *per se*; in his narrative Minos returns to Crete after this episode, never to leave.

Ovid included the Scylla story in part because, once again, he wished to echo the cosmogonic song of Silenus, the sixth eclogue.[6] There, as in the *Ars Amatoria*, Scylla the daughter of Nisus of Megara is confused with the monstrous canine horror associated with Charybdis.[7] The *Metamorphoses* keeps the two women distinct; we shall meet the "other" Scylla in Book 13.

Scylla's father Nisus had a purple lock on which his kingdom depended.[8] He also had a daughter, who of course would prove his undoing. As Ovid's story opens, Scylla is watching the siege from the royal tower where the stones were said to have retained the power of music ever since Apollo had left his lyre there (he had helped to build the walls).

Apollo, then, is something of a patron of Megara; Scylla is able to play with pebbles that make the stone resound because the god had once labored there and bestowed the gift of eternal music. Like Helen showing Greek warriors to Priam, Scylla watches the war and learns the names and habits of the foreign combatants—but she is alone. Most of all, she notices the "face of the European leader" (8.23 *faciem ducis Europaei*): Minos, the son of Jupiter and Europa.

Here we see something of the great heroic cycle that began when Jupiter crossed the Hellespont with Europa on his taurine back: Minos is the son of that ultimately Phoenician princess. Here, he is besieging an Athenian ally that is marked by Apollo's gift. Megara is a prefigurement of Rome, and Scylla of Tarpeia. The enemy might as well be Carthaginian. Apollo's gift is right in front of the girl, but she thinks Apollo stands forth in the archer Minos (8.30-31 *inposito calamo patulos sinuaverat arcus: / sic Phoebum sumptis iurabat stare sagittis*).

Scylla's soliloquy reminds us of Medea's somewhat similar debate with herself. Scylla knows that she is contemplating a terrible deed in considering the possibility of betraying her city to Minos (8.54 *tantum ne posceret arces*), but, as we might expect, she quickly rationalizes the unthinkable. Seneca's Medea would exclaim to Jason that he should now testify to the world that there are no gods; certainly Ovid's Medea gave the impression that some powers are nearly unstoppable, as the Colchian witch spread malice from city to city without divine intervention. Scylla is impious not only to country and father (she voices the wish that she might not have a sire), but also to the gods: 72-73 *sibi quisque profecto / est deus*, for her, everyone is a god for himself. Nisus has a purple lock, and that baleful color will not make Scylla blessed, as she wrongly imagines, but rather cursed for all time (79-80 *illa mihi est auro pretiosior, illa beatam / purpura me votique factura potentem*).

As he did with Medea, so with Scylla Ovid moves astonishingly quickly; the young princess manages to elude all the guards she had mentioned and make her way both to cut off her father's lock and to bring it to Minos; the whole journey takes less than eight lines, and one of those may well be interpolated (8.81-89; 87 is suspect).[9] Minos has thus far in the narrative been a largely unsketched figure, but a vile one if only because of his threat to strike Athens, which has been presented in the most favorable terms as the bringer of civilization via the gift of Ceres' agriculture and as the sacred city of Minerva, a veritable prototype of Rome. But Minos is the son of Jupiter, a future lord of the dead, and here he will have nothing to do with Scylla. He cannot imagine that Crete, which he identifies as Jupiter's childhood home, would ever contain such a monster as Scylla (97-100). Aegeus the *Athenian* had welcomed Medea and exceeded the bounds of hospitality by making her his wife; Pandion, too, had invited trouble to his house by marrying his daughter to a Thracian. Minos will not allow Scylla to sully his home.

Ovid continues his virtual redefining of Minos by noting (with his typical oblique speed) that Megara was, of course, defeated, and that Minos imposed unspecified terms on the conquered: but he was "most just" (8.101-102 *captis iustissimus auctor / hostibus inposuit*).[10] Minos abandons Scylla, who becomes like Catullus' Ariadne or, most especially, Virgil's Dido: she has been abandoned by a would-be lover who had accomplished much from her affections. She is right: Minos has won because of her deed. She is Medea, wondering how Jason could forsake her after she betrayed her father and country to help him. Minos, the Jovian son of the Phoenician Europa, has too much honor to accept her crime, however.[11]

The commentators have noted that the Athenian war disappears from Ovid's narrative: Minos returns to Crete, and we hear nothing more of any planned attack on Minerva's city. This is a deliberate omission of the poet, but to what end? Was Minos so horrified at Scylla's betrayal of her father that he retreated home and abandoned his planned attack to avenge his son's death? Why would the "most just" of monarchs not fulfill what he would consider the demands of *pietas* owed to his son by attacking Aegeus' city? We might note, too, that unlike the Sabines' treatment of Tarpeia, Minos is just indeed to Scylla—he does not kill her. Perhaps, in light of Tarpeia's fate, we should conclude that Ovid's Minos is *too* just where this traitor is concerned: he should have killed her, as the Sabines rightly punished Tarpeia. Megara is allied with Athens; the great city has now suffered from the Tereus story, Medea's involvement with Aegeus, and the betrayal of her ally by the king's own daughter.[12]

Athens, too, does not escape some manner of defeat in Ovid's version; there may be no attack narrative or invasion, but Athens will pay to Crete the famous tribute of young victims for the Minotaur (8.169 ff.). Athens has allies from Aegina, but has lost Megara; Ovid expects us to conclude that Aegeus' city is weak enough to be compelled to sacrifice its elite youths to Minos' bull—which calls into question the king's justice.

Scylla mentions Minos' own embarrassment in her attack on the king she considers perfidious. Minos' wife conceived a wild passion for a bull; Daedalus helped Pasiphae sate her lust by crafting a wooden contrivance, by which she was able to conceive the Minotaur. This story had formed part of the artwork that Daedalus crafted for the doors of Apollo's temple at Cumae. The climax of that artistic endeavor had been the loss of his own son, which he was unable to complete because of grief for the dead Icarus. Virgil completed the scene for him in the loss of Marcellus, whose ghost haunts the procession of future Roman historical worthies at the end of *Aeneid* 6, which is thus ringed by Icarus and Marcellus.[13] Minos may be destined for underworld glory, but on earth he has a family life that bespeaks his ruin: a dead son Androgeos, a wife Daedalus helped to mate with a bull, and a taurine stepson. Jupiter had abducted Minos' mother in the guise of a bull, and the bull (so central to Cretan lore) continues to haunt Europa's progeny.

In Minos, then, we can see the frankly vile result of Jupiter's infidelity. The god who absconded with a Tyrian girl in the costume of a bull has sired a son whose wife is passionate for real bulls, a son who feeds his wife's monstrous progeny with Athenian men and women—the stories of Tereus and Medea lurk in the background, and once again Athens is the victim of savagery. In Ovid's vision, part of Minos' justice is his refusal to accept Scylla's betrayal: even the monster has limits. The specific limit is one a Roman audience would appreciate: Minos will not accept the violation of paternal *pietas* by which Scylla made her would-be love victorious over Megara.

As Minos leaves Megara, Scylla follows—somewhat fantastically. Her father is now a bird (8.145 ff.). In the *Ciris*, Jupiter pitied Nisus and returned him to earth from the dead, allowing him to live in avian transformation as a *haliaeetos ales*, a "sea-eagle" that is usually taken to be an osprey.[14] Nisus attacks his daughter, who lets go of Minos' ship; she is herself transformed into a bird, the *ciris*, so named from her propensity for cutting.[15]

There is no explanation in Ovid for why father or daughter becomes a bird. Ovid once again employs his typical narrative rapidity; he does not tarry over the story, even at the expense of what we might consider necessary details. The osprey will pursue the ciris for all time, as a memorial of the lesser bird's crime.[16] No god is credited with either transformation, though (*pace* some critics) Scylla is clearly punished with eternal harassment.[17] The whole situation is presented by Ovid as parallel to the ultimate fates of Tereus, Procne, and Philomela. Birds, of course, are somewhat removed from the earth, and so the blight of the unspeakable crime, while always readily remembered, is, in a sense, taken away by the avian transformation.

Minos, however, has the problem of the Minotaur, for which Daedalus crafts the famous labyrinth (8.159 ff.). The labyrinth is crafted like the Phrygian Meander (162-168), a simile that reminds us of the ultimately Phrygian origin of Minos' line: Ovid does not allow us to forget the implicitly Carthaginian associations of Jupiter's conquest of Europa and the cycle her rape inaugurated.[18] The labyrinth's architect, Daedalus, was said to have been exiled from Athens for murder; one Athenian would solve Minos' problem and another, in a sense, would end it (Theseus' defeat of the monster).

Ovid moves with rapidity through reasonably well-known stories: Theseus comes to Crete to solve Athens' tribute problem.[19] Ariadne helps him solve the mystery of the labyrinth, and the hero leaves with his lover. In Ovid's quickly moving narrative, Theseus abandons Ariadne on Naxos, and is cruel to do so (8.175 *crudelis*); it is Liber who comes and brings aid to the rejected girl, taking her to heaven and perpetuating her honor by transforming her crown into a constellation (177-182).

Ariadne lore is extremely complex. She first appears in Homer (*Odyssey* 11.321-325), where she is killed on the island of Dia (= Naxos) by Artemis for the crime of having left Dionysus for Theseus. But in Hesiod (*Theogony* 947-959), she is Dionysus' wife, seemingly for all time. What is perhaps most significant in Ovid is that Theseus leaves her for no clear purpose; Ovid does not say that the god ordered it, though of course his narrative is so briefly sketched that one could take his account to mean Bacchus told Theseus to leave her—or not:

vela dedit comitemque suam crudelis in illo
litore destituit; desertae et multa querenti
amplexus et opem Liber tulit . . . (8.176-178)

He set sail and, cruel one, deserted his companion
on that shore; to the girl who was deserted and complaining of much
Liber brought embraces and help . . .

Ovid keeps Theseus in the story, though barely; Daedalus is soon to be the poet's main concern in his *Theseid*, just as Daedalus' artwork opened the sixth *Aeneid*.[20] The story of Daedalus and Icarus will balance Scylla and Minos; both involve failed flights. Scylla attempted to pursue her illicit love over the seas and was transformed into a bird that is forever attacked on account of its crimes. Daedalus will escape Crete on his own wings (the master craftsman, as it were, needs no gods to transform him into a bird). He will attain his desired goal of freedom, but at the cost of the loss of his son: the murderer will atone for his crime by the blood of Icarus.

If Augustus could not find a successor and had, in a sense, lost his son (Marcellus), then we can find a parallel to the *princeps*, who, like Daedalus, made his own metamorphosis, as he transformed the Roman state.[21] Ovid makes the astounding claim that Daedalus made nature new: 8.189 *naturamque novat*.[22] His action, of course, resulted in the death of his son. The parallels are not exact, but the outcome is the same for both the Athenian craftsman and the Roman emperor. That the story of Daedalus' flight was a favorite of Ovid is illustrated by his longer version at *Ars Amatoria* 2.19-98, where the tale illustrates the impossibility of constraining winged beings (i.e., Cupid); the stories are quite similar, and there, too, Daedalus announces that he must reinvent the laws of nature: 42 *sunt mihi naturae iura novanda meae*. But just as no inventor, however fabulous, could constrain a winged being, so no *princeps*, no matter his talent or ability, could constrain a successor—indeed, finding a suitable heir was a herculean task. Ovid boldly announced in the *Ars* that he was preparing to detain winged love (98 *ipse deum volucrem detinuisse paro*)—Medea, Ovid says, could not keep Jason for all her magic arts—she had not read his poem, after all.

Phaethon, too, lurks behind Ovid's Icarus; in Book 2, the boy traveled alone, and against his father's will. Now the boy travels under the careful tutelage of his father, and still perishes. Ovid foreshadows Icarus' doom by noting how the boy played with his father's work (8.197-200); he impedes Daedalus' work by his childish antics (*impediebat opus*). The flight, in a sense, came too early in the boy's life; he was not yet ready to advance with his father. Scylla had run in vain to catch Minos, and her father soon joined the pursuit, though chasing his daughter, not his conqueror. Daedalus will lead his son away from Minos, in a reverse of the previous situation, where the daughter had led the father. Scylla was a murderess; so is Daedalus (as Ovid will soon make clear). Scylla and Nisus were mysteriously transformed into birds; Daedalus transformed himself and his son into birds.

The famous flight begins; like Sol with Phaethon, Daedalus cautions his son against watching the potentially dangerous stars and chasing after them (Icarus' eyes must stay fixed on his father, and the boy must follow where the man leads). Those who would change nature are akin to the gods, for they have the power of metamorphosis; so the earthly observers of the two flyers think that they are gods, and watch as they ply their way through the ether that is properly the abode of the immortals (8.219-220 *quique aethera carpere possent, / credidit esse deos*). Herein is part of the doom; usually such behavior occasions divine retribution (in the *Ars*, Daedalus makes it clear that he is not seeking to usurp divine prerogatives). The story was well known to Ovid's audience both from literature (we can assume) and from vase paintings; Icarus does not listen to his father. The boy is drowned after he flies too close to the sun (shades again of Phaethon) and falls to the water; no god, however, was necessary to cause this death. The boy's own recklessness leads to his doom; Daedalus finds the body and buries it on the island that now bears his son's name.

At this point in the narrative, on the lonely island of Icaria, Ovid notes that a partridge clapped in celebration on account of Daedalus' misfortune (8.236 ff.). Ovid has not explained why Daedalus was trapped in Crete; he has made it clear the great craftsman was in exile, but he has not alluded directly to the story of Daedalus' act of murder. Daedalus' sister had entrusted her son to his uncle for the sake of his education; the boy was exceedingly bright and had already created the saw and the compass without any tutelage.[23] Daedalus was jealous of the boy's abilities and hurled him off the Acropolis, pretending that he had fallen (250 ff.).

Minerva makes her return at last to the epic: she favors the intelligent (8.252 *favet ingeniis*), and she saves Perdix by transforming him into the talkative partridge. The bird is not necessarily especially intelligent (though its garrulous nature speaks to some ability); its vigor of mind went into its wings and feet (254-255 *vigor ingenii quondam velocis in alas / inque pedes abiit*).

Daedalus had prayed that he might escape Crete and return to his native Athens, whence he had been exiled for his killing of Perdix (apparently no one believed his story of the fall). Ovid says Daedalus was now received in Sicily, by the kind King Cocalus (8.260-262); we must assume that Daedalus could not return to Athens, and that the allusion to the story of Perdix is a reminder that the aged inventor is still barred from his home. Minos will be but briefly mentioned once again (9.437), and there in a comment from his father Jupiter that the great king is now old and dishonored. But that mention is both exceedingly brief and far distant after this passage. The usual tradition was that Minos pursued Daedalus to Sicily and was killed there.[24] According to one account, the Cretan monarch was actually scalded to death by Cocalus' daughters (cf. Medea's instigation of the death of Pelias).[25] No mention in Ovid, then, of the local tradition that Daedalus had made a landing at Cumae (whence Virgil's *Aeneid* 6).

Ovid now returns in a ring to the theme with which he had begun his *Theseid*: Athens is in rejoicing because the hero has freed Pallas' city from its dire tribute to Crete, and all is well (8.262). Athens has indeed been *lamentabile*; from Tereus, Procne and Philomela through the hazards of Aegeus' dalliance with Medea and the Cretan problem, there has been ample room for tears in the goddess' city. Once again, Ovid offers a brief respite, and the goddess is there, honored along with her father Jupiter and the other gods. No wonder Daedalus is barred from the city; the murderer's presence, especially given Minerva's favor for the brilliant Perdix, would be unacceptable.

But what of Minos? No agreement in Ovid that the Cretan king eventually died in Sicily; again, however brief the mention, 9.437 proves he is still alive at some future point. He, too, is now discarded from the narrative without any sort of satisfactory coda; both Daedalus and Minos, Ovid seems to be indicating, deserve to leave the scene without any real farewell. If Virgil's "later" account can be appended to Ovid's narrative, we are left with an image of the inventor that is much the same as the scene on Icaria—Daedalus in mourning for his son. Daedalus is, admittedly, given something of a comfortable "end" in Ovid: Cocalus is willing to fight for his guest, and the Sicilian monarch was considered *mitis* (8.262), "gentle"—he was, after all, defending an exiled killer. Minos, the savage feeder of beautiful girls and handsome youths to a man-bull, is left implicitly defeated and ignored. Europa's son receives nothing of the comfort the Athenian Daedalus—killer or not—is afforded.

At last we come to the middle of the book and the epic: the great drama of the Calydonian boar hunt. This is the zenith of the *Metamorphoses* and the high point of the epic: it is the central panel in the multifarious decorations of transformations with which Ovid has adorned his canvas. The story of Ceres and Triptolemus presaged the present narrative; Ceres had been willing to grant immortality to the Athenian infant, and here, Meleager could well have been immortal from the visit of the Fates to his infant home.

The story was of immense popularity in antiquity, far more than its modern appeal might make clear.[26] The basic story is that Calydon's King Oeneus incurred Artemis' wrath by failing to honor her with the other immortals (out of innocent forgetfulness rather than deliberate slight); the angry goddess sent a giant boar that ravaged the countryside. Meleager was the local hero who managed the fight; the story seems to have an early kernel of competition over the spoils of the boar, where in an ensuing fight between the Calydonians and the Curetes. Meleager kills one of his uncles, which arouses his mother's ire; she sides with uncle over son and prays for Meleager's death. Meleager withdraws from the battle, to the discomfiture of his side; finally he returns after the heartfelt pleading of his wife Cleopatra. Meleager's fate is unspecified in the account we hear from Phoenix during the embassy to Achilles in *Iliad* 9. In Hesiod's *Catalogue* (fr. 25.12-13 Merkelbach-West), Apollo slays Meleager in battle soon after his return to combat (cf. Achilles' death at the hands of the archer Paris). The story was of intense interest to the tragedians, notably Euripides; Accius composed a *Meleager*.[27]

Ovid's story commences in the usual way: Calydon has offended the goddess, whose anger (8.279 *ira*) must be satiated. Diana's rage is so great that her boar threatens both the fruits of Ceres (291-292) and Minerva's olive (295). The boar threatens even the bulls that have been a symbol so often in the epic of tremendous, savage power (297). To combat this beast, Meleager and others assemble in pursuit of heroic glory.[28] The catalogue of heroes begins in earnest (301 ff.), in imitation of, *inter al.*, Virgil's catalogue of Italian heroes at the close of *Aeneid* 7. First after Meleager are the divine twins, Castor the horseman and Pollux the boxer. Jason is here, noted almost blithely as the builder of the world's first ship, with no mention of the tragedy he has so recently suffered. Theseus is next, together with his friend Pirithous; again, Athens' hero is but briefly noted, though from the beginning of the story and the framing narrative of Ovid's *Theseid* we might have expected a more significant part for the son of Aegeus. The two sons of Thestius are important as the brothers of Meleager's mother Althaea; Ovid expects that his audience will know who they are.[29] Caeneus is here, no longer a woman (305); Virgil notes *her* presence in the underworld (*A.* 6.448-449).[30] Phoenix is present, an obvious nod to Homer's embassy scene to Achilles and a representation of the generation of heroes from before the expedition to Troy; Achilles' father Peleus is also a combatant (309)—we are moving ever closer to Troy and Rome (in a nice touch, at 365-368, Pylian Nestor will use his spear to pole vault into a nearby tree and thus save himself from the boar).[31] Amphiaraus is among the fighters, not yet destroyed by his wife Eriphyle, Ovid tells us (316-317).[32]

Last in the catalogue is the Arcadian huntress Atalanta,[33] just as Camilla is the last figure in Virgil's listing of the Italian heroes:[34]

> ... nemorisque decus Tegeaea Lycaei:
> rasilis huic summam mordebat fibula vestem,
> crinis erat simplex, nodum collectus in unum,
> ex umero pendens resonabat eburnea laevo
> telorum custos, arcum quoque laeva tenebat;
> talis erat cultu, facies, quam dicere vere
> virgineam in puero, puerilem in virgine possis. (8.317-323)

> ... and the Tegeaean glory of the Lycaean grove:
> for her a polished buckle bit the highest part of her robe,
> her hair was simple, collected into one knot.
> and from her left shoulder there was hanging an ivory
> case for her weapons, and her left hand was also holding a bow;
> such was she in her dress, and her face was such that truly you could say
> that it was a virgin's in a boy, and a boy's in a virgin.

Both Camilla and Atalanta are the glories of their native lands; Turnus addresses Camilla as the *decus Italiae* (*A.* 11.508), while Atalanta is the glory of the Lycaean grove. The adjective is a reminder of Lycaeus, the wolf king whose lupine transformation had opened the mortal catalogue of triumphs and woes in the *Metamorphoses.* We have encountered the sexually ambiguous look before; the young Achilles was said to have such an androgynous appearance.[35] The point is that the young woman is at an age not yet ready for a man; Meleager may be ready for her, but she is not a suitable partner for him. Camilla, too, is a virgin who spent her girlhood and adolescence in the service of Diana; despite leaving the goddess' forest haunts to participate in the war in Latium, she remains a virgin and is thus not ready for any sexual designs Turnus may have on her; Atalanta's looks are more an indication of precocious age than any sexual ambiguity *per se.*

Atalanta lore is very old; she makes her first appearance in extant literature in the Hesiodic *Catalogue* (fr. 73 Merkelbach-West). There, Atalanta is the daughter of Schoeneus and exceedingly beautiful as well as swift, though she shuns marriage. The fragments that follow tell of the famous race (on which more later); Hesiod says that she ran as swiftly as a Harpy.[36] Atalanta is praised for her hunting skills at Callimachus *In Dianam* 215-224, where she is the daughter of Iasius and famous for her killing of wild boars, as well as victories over Centaurs (cf. her appearance in Propertius c. 1.1).[37] Aelian begins Book 13 of the *Varia Historia* with Atalanta lore, saying she was the Arcadian daughter of Iasion and had been abandoned in the forest, where she grew up suckled by a she-bear. As in the *Theognidea*, once again Atalanta is a blond; she slays Centaurs who invade her sylvan haunt.

Two Atalantas, then, can be identified in the mythological tradition, though if we want to count the names of fathers, we might find three or even four. Three stories tend to emerge: the participation in the Calydonian boar hunt and adolescent killing of Centaurs, as well as the famous foot race with the golden apples.[38] Indeed, Gow called the Atalanta question an "inextricable problem." I would argue that the confusion became part of the tradition, and that both Virgil and Ovid took advantage of the confused lore and used it as a metaphor for the conflicted state of both Camilla and Atalanta in their respective epics. Both women will make two appearances, Camilla in *Aeneid* 7 and 11, Atalanta in *Metamorphoses* 8 and 10. Numerous parallels will emerge between both women. Two other poets, Catullus and Propertius, essentially open their poetry collections with references to Atalanta lore (Catullus, interestingly, to "one" Atalanta, and Propertius to the "other").

Meleager loves this girl, though a god forbids it (8.325 *renuente deo*). Already, there is trouble: perhaps here we have an allusion to the tradition that either an oracle or the girl herself had rejected marriage. Atalanta is identified as a problematic *objet d'amour*; she causes destruction for those who would be infatuated with her (as does Camilla with Turnus). In a nice touch, Ovid says that Meleager kept his silence regarding the girl, since the *greater work* (328 *maius opus*) demanded his attention—a neat reference to the seventh *Aeneid* and the "greater work" of Virgil's *Iliad*. No Lavinia for Aeneas until combat with Turnus, and no Atalanta for Meleager until after the hunt. And indeed, the following description of the actual boar hunt is, as the commentators have noted, the most "epic" description in the poem. This is a miniature *Iliad*, as befits an allusion to the embassy to Achilles and the ramifications of the choices of Homer's Achilles, Virgil's Achilles (for Aeneas was told that "another Achilles," that is, Turnus, would be found in Italy), and Ovid's Meleager. As we shall soon see, the mention of the *maius opus* signals the coming of the epic's second half, as it did in Virgil's *Aeneid*.

The boar soon appears, and the combat begins (8.338 ff.). Jason distinguishes himself only by overshooting the boar; he employs excessive force and consequently misses the mark. Soon enough, he will disgrace himself in a failed attempt to correct the mistake he makes here. Mopsus, the son of Ampycus and a seer, prays to Apollo that he might strike the boar; we might compare Apollo's devotee Arruns and his similar prayer to strike Camilla. Apollo, Ovid says, granted what he could; the missile struck the beast, but without a wound—Diana, Apollo's sister, removed the iron point. In the *Aeneid*, Arruns had prayed that he might both kill Camilla *and* return home, however inglorious; Apollo heard the first part of the prayer, but the breezes scattered the second. Here, Diana does not allow the weapon to strike the boar—she does not thereby render the beast immortal, since later it will be fatally struck—but for now, she blocks Mopsus' shot, since another is destined to slay this animal (and note that at 372-377 the Tyndaridae, Castor and Pollux, would have been able to strike the boar had it not gone into the woods).

Apollo's action only serves to irritate the boar even more, and casualties begin to accrue; the boar lunges at the crowd of hunters like a shot from a catapult (8.357-360), another magnificent, anachronistic simile.[39] Soon thereafter, it is Atalanta who draws first blood from the beast. She is the "Tegaean one" (380); Ovid never names her in this long description of the hunt, which serves to increase her mystery and allure.[40] Meleager has obviously been watching Atalanta more than the boar; he is the first to notice that she has struck the beast and drawn blood, and at once he announces it to his companions. He had earlier kept silent about his interest in the girl; now, in the heat of combat against the beast, he cannot resist praising her and announcing already that she will win the prize as the first to have wounded the animal. The ensuing scene is not dissimilar to the situation in the equestrian battle before the walls of the Latin capital, where Camilla's actions shamed her enemies and roused Jupiter to stir up Tarchon to ask his Etruscans why they were allowing a woman to vanquish them. There, Tarchon upbraids his soldiers for being more interested in the pursuit of love and wine than of battle (using the metonymy of Venus and Bacchus).[41] Like Camilla in the *Aeneid*, Atalanta shames the contestants in the Calydonian boar hunt by drawing first blood from Diana's beast—the master huntress shows her eminent skill, just as the Volscian huntress shows that she can easily transfer the skills of sylvan pursuit of wild game to the equestrian battlefield.

The Arcadian Ancaeus (a countryman of Atalanta) is the spokesman here, the Tarchon of the scene; he is working under no divine inspiration, however, and is blasphemous as he announces that he will show how far superior men's weapons are to women's: he will destroy the boar, even if Diana herself should forbid it. Of course Diana has her revenge at its sweetest: the chauvinist is destroyed by a gory wound to the groin, the most visceral description of an injury in the entire passage, and the one wound Ovid wanted us to remember from this epic engagement, as Ancaeus' entrails all rush out of the gaping wound to the upper part of his groin.

Pirithous is next; he hopes to succeed where the others have failed, but Theseus warns him to be careful (8.404 ff.); there is almost a hint here of how Apollo advised Ascanius to stay out of the Italian war after the death of Remulus. Pirithous is not destined to strike the boar; his shaft was wonderfully aimed, but an oak branch blocked it (410)—a probable nod to Jovian divine intervention.[42] Jason appears in sequence after Theseus (the two great heroes nearly side by side again, as they were in Book 7); here the Argonaut leader hurls a spear that misses the boar again, but this time strikes a hapless hunting hound, pinning the canine to the ground (411-413). If Jason's fortunes were bad at the end of the Medea episode, they have not improved here.

Meleager finally takes his turn, having only appeared thus far to celebrate the success of his infatuation. He strikes at the boar with two spears, and his second hits the mark; he is able to advance to close quarters and dispatch the beast (8.418-419). The other competitors slowly advance, struck by the size of the boar and still in fear of it as they approach; they dip their weapons as if in a ritualistic "washing of the spears."[43]

Meleager killed the boar, and he merits the prize of the spoils. No one could have questioned that economy. But the victor had already promised that Atalanta would take the prize for having drawn first blood, and now he announces that she will have the spoils. She is silent in Ovid's narrative and makes no audible comment that Ovid reports:

> illi laetitiae est cum munere muneris auctor;
> invidere alii, totoque erat agmine murmur. (8.430-431)

> *For her it was a source of joy, both the gift and the author of the gift;*
> *the others looked askance at this, and in the whole assembly there was a mur-*
> *mur.*

In the crowd's action *invidere*, there is of course also a hint of jealousy: they wanted the pelt of the beast, and if they could not have it, certainly a woman should not win it, especially if she had not slain the boar. Significantly, Ovid notes that Atalanta was pleased not only with the gift, but also with its author; she is possessed of a capacity to appreciate the obvious affections of a man. Ovid seems to be depicting a change that has come over the girl; the girl with the boyish face has become aware of the first stirrings of romantic interest.

The sons of Thestius, Meleager's uncles, protest (8.432 ff.). They also threaten Atalanta, and perhaps also Meleager, telling her that she should beware lest her lover be far off from her (435 *ne sit longe tibi*). The threat is vague but definite; the two men take away the prize and, Ovid says, the right of giving the prize. Meleager strikes with sudden anger; Plexippus is soon stabbed in the heart. Ovid notes that the uncle was not expecting the blow; Meleager's rage is hot and fast. Ovid pauses over the fate of the other uncle, as we reach the exact midpoint of the book (and, at least in Ovid's intention, also the poem):[44]

> Toxea, quid faciat, dubium pariterque volentem
> ulcisci fratrem fraternaque fata timentem
> haud patitur dubitare diu calidumque priori
> caede recalfecit consorti sanguine telum. (8.441-444)

> *As Toxeus was in doubt as to what he should do, equally wishing*
> *to avenge his brother and fearing his brother's fates,*
> *scarcely did Meleager allow him to to be in doubt, and he reheated*
> *the weapon that was hot with the first brother's gore with his kin's blood.*

The passage is an extraordinary one. Toxeus wishes to avenge his brother, but he fears his brother's fate; he is torn between running away and attacking Meleager. The moment of hesitation is quite brief: Meleager slays him. Althaea, Meleager's mother and the sister of the slain man, soon sees the corpses of her relatives as she was already piously offering thanks to the gods for her son's victory. The family unit has been thrown into disarray by Meleager's love for Atalanta (lust and infatuation, more accurately); there is civil strife in Calydon because of the hero's emotional attachment to this girl.

Meleager, we might note, has slain Diana's boar (thus possibly offending the goddess), and he has managed to attract a girl who had previously been devoted to the works of Diana.[45] Soon enough, his mother is afflicted with her own *amor* (8.450): love for punishment. She no longer mourns for her brothers, once she learns the author of the deed. She is hot only to avenge the loss, even at the cost of her son's life. Her means of revenge is now described: the firebrand that the Fates had marked as responsible for the length of Meleager's life (451 ff.). The scene is dramatic; we can understand why Dryden appreciated it so much, even if we might disagree with his praise of Althaea before Virgil's Dido. Four times does Althaea try to burn the wood; four times she hesitates before condemning her son to death. The scene is a doublet of Scylla trying to decide between father and would-be lover; it is a doublet of Procne as she decides (in a sense) between father and son. It evokes too the choice of Medea between punishing Jason by the slaughter of their children or not. Althaea is like a ship lashed by the power of both wind and tide (470-474). But she is the daughter of Thestias (473), and the audience knows what her final choice will be.

It is a terrifying scene as Althaea invokes the Furies to oversee her dread deed (8.480 ff.). Althaea realizes the political implications of the loss of her son; the royal family will be ruined, and Calydon will be plunged into grief and loss. Althaea herself plans to commit suicide after the death of her son. She hurls the brand into the fire; the very flames, Ovid notes, were unwilling to receive what is in effect her son's life (514 *stipes, ut invitis correptus ab ignibus arsit*). Meleager has behaved questionably in the episode thus far; his infatuation with Atalanta has clouded his judgment, and his killing of his uncles displayed a surrender to rage that does not, of course, negate his heroic status. It is not that surprising that Ovid says that Meleager overcame the agony of the invisible flames with great fortitude as the fire began to cook his viscera. He complains that he is not dying a heroic death, since he cannot see his killer; he laments that Ancaeus had suffered a better end in the grisly fate granted him by Diana's boar. He calls on his relatives, including his *wife* (521 *sociamque tori*): he was married, after all, as we know from Homer (to Cleopatra), though this is the first explicit mention in Ovid's poem that he was married when he met Atalanta. The Arcadian girl, for her part, is long gone from Calydon; she will reappear in a very different context, two books hence; for now, the cause of Meleager's death (which he does not realize) has departed away, and he has seemingly forgotten her. In a sense, Atalanta has been abandoned, like other women we have encountered in Ovid's heroic cycle. Turnus, too, considered himself betrothed to Lavinia when he met Camilla.

Meleager dies quietly, as the fire burns out with his life (8.522-525). As Althaea foresaw, Calydon is plunged into mourning; once again Ovid returns to the theme of sorrow after joy. The lament of Meleager's sisters has occasioned comment, because of the seemingly excessive language with which Ovid describes it:

> non mihi si centum deus ora sonantia linguis
> ingeniumque capax totumque Helicona dedisset,
> tristia persequerer miserarum fata sororum. (8.533-535)

> *Not if to me a hundred mouths sounding with their tongues*
> *and a capacious genius and all Helicon had the god given me,*
> *could I follow through the sad fates of the miserable sisters.*

Here, Ovid enters much storied poetic ground, from Homer to Virgil, by way of Ennius and others.[46] As often, the question is one of propriety; is Ovid having fun with the epic tradition and merely indulging in comedy for his own amusement, and perhaps that of his learned audience? Or are we to take the poet seriously, in the sense that this scene is one of his most important? If we begin with the idea that the very midpoint of the epic is a crucial part of the unveiling of Ovid's plan, than a major evocation like this passage should not surprise us. It was not haphazardly inserted here, as well in this locus as any other; it is a reminder of the significance of the evocation of Meleager lore both from Homer and from the Turnus-Camilla episode that is so central to the resolution of the *Aeneid.*[47]

The sisters of Meleager remind us of the sisters of Phaethon, who, we now realize, distantly presaged this terrible day. The Meleagrides cannot stop crying for their brother, and it is Diana, not surprisingly, who decides that Calydon has suffered enough: she turns the girls into guinea fowls (8.542-546).[48] The passage deserves more attention than it has received. Diana was responsible for the boar, but her presence in the coda to the scene lets her assume blame for the entire tragedy. Meleager (and Atalanta) killed her boar; the hero's death atones for that. His "conflict" with the goddess is symbolized in part by his dalliance with the virgin Atalanta, who is not his wife—he already has one. He abandons Atalanta on his deathbed, however praiseworthy his devotion to the "ally of his bed"—where was she during the hunt, as he flirted with the Arcadian? Atalanta, a Diana-like figure, rejoiced in not only the pelt of the boar, but also the giver—unlike Virgil's Camilla, who never displays a single hint of departure from her Diana-sworn virginity, Ovid's Atalanta does begin to shift.[49] Diana pities Meleager's sisters—she is always partial to sororial coteries—and, like others in the present extended cycle, they experience avian transformation. This time, it is clearly meant as an act of mercy.

Not if the gods had given me all of Helicon, Ovid announced: for in the central panel of his epic, he has annotated and challenged both Homer and Virgil. Phoenix had seen the boar hunt; in Ovid's vision, he had seen Meleager and Atalanta. In Homer, Meleager was urged to return to battle for Calydon against the Curetes; his wife Cleopatra successfully secured his reentrance and Calydon's victory (even if Meleager always ends up dead in the various traditions, like Achilles). Achilles ignored Phoenix's cautionary story and stayed out of battle. He returned only after the death of Patroclus, which spurred him on to a new sort of rage, a madness that would only find redemption in the closing movements of Homer's epic. Turnus needed no aged hero to urge him back to battle against Aeneas. In the drama of Book 11, Turnus crafted a battle plan in response to Aeneas' reported movements against the Latin capital. His plan would have worked, as the dying Camilla knew; like Homer's Cleopatra, she urged Turnus not to abandon his plan, notwithstanding her death (and, as Virgil crafted his scene, did he smile at the fact that *another* Cleopatra had fled Actium?). Turnus ignored Camilla—his Patroclus—and in ignoring her, he handed Aeneas the victory in Latium. So did Jupiter demand, with his savage will.

Ovid's Meleager, of course, had no chance to read Virgil's *Aeneid* and learn the lesson of the hazards of emotional attachments to Diana-like women and their tempting allure. By devoting the very midpoint of his epic to this lore, Ovid firmly places himself in the epic tradition of *Iliad* and *Aeneid*—not surprisingly, given that by the very fact of his universal history, Ovid's poem should encompass all his predecessors in all their array. This is an epic poem, with epic grandeur . . . and moving ever closer to Augustus and the end of history.[50] Ovid's Meleager dies as a hero in every respect, with Roman devotion to family and Stoic fortitude in the face of agony. Homer's Achilles found redemption from his wrath, and won his desired wish of eternal fame (despite a rather ignominious end in the tradition that was not, we might note, dissimilar to the end Virgil's Camilla suffers). Virgil's Turnus and Camilla were both indignant at the perceived injustice they had suffered (Turnus realized it was Jovian in origin; Camilla not), but both found *post mortem* redemption in the final disposition of Rome.[51]

Ovid now returns to his *Theseid*. The hero has participated in the boar hunt, and now he returns to Athens. Along the way, he is sidetracked by the swollen river Achelous (8.547 ff.). As the commentators delight in noting, the river is west of Calydon, the wrong way to Athens. Did Ovid not know his Greek geography, or did he not care? More likely with our learned poet who deserves to be taken seriously (in his forays into comedy), the error is deliberate. The rest of Book 8 will be devoted to four stories, essentially, two of punishment and two of reward (more or less). All involve mortal interaction with the gods. The gods had seemingly been absent from much of the early part of Ovid's heroic cycle and before: where were they when Tereus, Procne, and Philolmela attended to their ghastly deeds? Where were they when Medea slaughtered children with impunity and drove off in her dragon chariot? In a world teetering on the verge of disorder and a virtual return to chaos from the fury of the likes of a Medea, in the boar of Calydon Diana has restored order (just as she did with Minerva before the recent eruption of madness).[52] Now, in quiet reflection of that restoration of order, the hero Theseus will hear stories that attest to that renewal. It is true that the tales are set in the "past" of Theseus' sojourn with Achelous—but we have not heard them yet, and that is what matters to the master poet. Theseus takes the wrong way home—the world has changed, and the hero learns of its metamorphosis, in the company of a river god, and in the respite afforded by the god's hospitality. The very presence of the error serves to highlight the ensuing set of stories, just as the great evocation of Helicon announced the zenith of the poet's epic.[53] Now, Ovid introduces his version of the *maius opus*, the epic's second half (cf. 328 above). Meleager delayed his expression of love for Atalanta because the "greater work" of the boar hunt called him (and so there was no love expressed between Aeneas and Lavinia in the *Aeneid*).

The river is in flood, and Theseus will wait for the waters to subside (8.562 ff.). The hospitality theme returns; the river is most glad in having such an honored guest (*hospite tanto*). Theseus is accompanied by both Pirithous and Lelex of Troezen, who will tell the story of Baucis and Philemon. A feast is held; wine is drunk. Theseus sees a land mass in the mighty river that seems to be one island, and yet perhaps more; the distance makes precision difficult. Achelous notes that there are five islands, once naiad nymphs; these women had once forgotten him in their sacrifices to the local gods. Like Diana (579), Achelous was offended and punished the unintentionally blasphemous nymphs. The naiads are swept out to sea and form the Echinades, sometimes conflated with the Strophades, whence the Harpies fled after the Argonauts drove them from Phineus.[54] The river god is less powerful than Diana; his range is not as extensive, but these women are perpetual memorials to his attack on their impiety.

Perimele is a contrasting example; her island is a memorial to kindness (8.590 ff.). The story is clear enough (and only extant in this Ovidian version); we have seen the motif before. A girl is raped by a god; her father punishes her for "unchastity," and she is "saved" from drowning when the god prays for her safety. Perimele is changed into an island by Neptune's granting of Achelous' wish.[55] The girl is like so many other raped nymphs in the epic, and, like Callisto, she is granted some sort of solace for her misfortune in eternal memory.

Pirithous—whose own doomed future is known to Ovid's audience—causes shock now by stating openly that the gods cannot effect metamorphoses. He presents the atheistic view Seneca's Medea would appreciate; there are no gods. Lelex will tell a story that attests to divine power: the enduring tale of Baucis and Philemon, one of Ovid's most popular stories.[56]

In the context of the early movements of Ovid's *maius opus*, the story most echoes Aeneas' reception by Evander. In imitation of Virgil, Ovid will soon begin his great Hercules cycle, in reminiscence of how the epyllion of Hercules and Cacus formed an important part of the Evander episode in *Aeneid* 8. The Phrygian locale of the story is crucial, and not just as a launching pad for scholars to ponder whether the tale has Near Eastern origins. Baucis and Philemon will be presented as nothing other than simple Italian peasants, the old stock of Italy, the sort Juvenal would laud.[57] They are living in Phrygia, where the story may well have originated. They represent exactly what Jupiter had announced to

Juno: the suppression of all things Trojan in the future establishment of Rome. Here, at the very beginning of his *maius opus* that rivals the second half of Virgil's *Aeneid*, Ovid presents the image that will be announced at the end of *Aeneid* 12, in the climactic discussion between Jupiter and Juno that reconciles the goddess' wrath and represents the quelling of madness in Virgil's *Iliad*, the reinvention of the madness of Achilles that has been transferred to Turnus (the *alter Achilles* in Latium), and his patroness Juno. Baucis and Philemon are Romans living in Phrygia, and they are Italian.

Jupiter had visited Lycaon in Arcadia to investigate rumors of despicable behavior; in Phrygia, no doors open to him and his son Mercury as they seek hospitality (the continuing theme now for so long).[58] They find the home of the aged and poor Baucis and Philemon, who live as the hardy stock of primitive Italy, where slaves and masters are unknown, and where poverty is considered a light thing and not of any consequence (8.629 ff.). The mention of their *penates* (637) has special meaning here (Ovid likes this sort of anachronistic detail about household gods); they are Romans in every sense that matters, just as Evander's small dwelling carries such resonance for a Roman audience aware of the tradition of the *casa Romuli*. A modest meal will be prepared; cabbage was considered a veritable symbol of humble menus for the Romans, and meat was something of a luxury for the poorer classes, and so the little portion of pork Philemon prepares for his guests is a sign of the honor with which the old couple welcome their guests.[59] We should remember that poor Romans were not vegetarians (any more than the Roman legionaries were).[60] The whole scene, of course, is a delicious mockery of the tastes of wealthy Romans, who would shun a meal of this sort with snobbish derision, all the while celebrating the virtues of the scene as the idealization of the life of the early Italians. For poets like Ovid, satirists and philosophers, this scene provided the exact image of what the wealthy and educated did not necessarily practice, but what they lauded as the image of praiseworthy poverty. The scene is happy; Jupiter and Mercury enjoy the meal, refreshingly different (and thus novel) from their usual fare.

Jupiter and Mercury may be enjoying the novel experience, but the poverty of Baucis and Philemon's meager wine supply is too much, of course, for the gods to accept; they magically refill the drinking bowl (8.679 ff.). Their hosts soon realize the miracle; they are filled with reverential fear. We have seen no humans in the epic as perfect as this old couple; every step they take is full of admirable quality and blameless demeanor. The goose that they prepare to slay is probably a nod to the sacred geese that saved the Capitol; certainly the goose had significance for early Roman history, which may explain why the couple would never think to use it for a more sumptuous meal before now; it is a cherished pet of sorts.[61] The goose is not stupid; it flees to the gods as the old couple chase it. The scene is comic as the goose wears down the aged pair, but also touching; their piety is heartwarming and heartbreaking at the same time. On such as these is the strength of Roman character built.

The gods prepare for the *dénouement*: Baucis and Philemon will seek the high ground with the gods, while flood waters envelop all their neighbors (8.689 ff.). The passage has obvious affinities with the deluge that originally swept over the world after the murderous inhospitality of Lycaon; there is also an echo of the punishment of Achelous for the naiads that had neglected his worship. Baucis and Philemon mourn the loss of their neighbors; they know compassion, and they pity the victims of the divine retribution for the disregard of hospitality the other locals have shown. Ovid does not mean for us to worry about the propriety or lack thereof of the gods' action; what matters is that the virtue of hospitality has been affirmed, that Baucis and Philemon are shown to be humble and pious, and to know how to sympathize with the miserable, and that once again, the power of the gods to punish transgressions has been affirmed.

The humble dwelling is now a richly adorned temple; it had been the home of such wonderful, praiseworthy old Romans, and it had held the gods: it is like the little hut of Romulus, like Evander's cottage that had held both Hercules and Aeneas. Jupiter is *Saturnius* (8.703) because Ovid wishes to evoke the spirit of the Golden Age; he asks the aged couple what they wish. Significantly, Philemon speaks to his wife before answering; he may be the *paterfamilias* of this small unit (why no children?), but he consults with his consort of so many years. They pray to be temple guardians and to die together; after many years they are transformed into trees that grow side-by-side, as close as possible. Lelex is the perfect storyteller, for he claims eyewitness status: he saw the trees, and he hung wreaths there and venerated the custodians of the gods.

Theseus is the most affected by the story (8.726 *Thesea praecipue*); unlike Pirithous (whose reaction Ovid does not record), Aegeus' son is moved by the tale and wants to hear more stories. Ovid has not focused closely on the Athenian hero, but what he has revealed is mostly positive; the only criticism we could level is how *crudelis* Theseus had abandoned Ariadne on Naxos, but even there, Ovid did not disavow the usual story that Bacchus had demanded that the girl be left behind. Theseus contrasts with his close friend; he respects the gods, he venerates their power, and he wants to hear more of their marvelous deeds (*facta mira*). Achelous will oblige him, as we move to the great story of Erysichthon, one of the great blasphemers of the epic, one of the contemptuous villains whose punishment is so memorable. He will be Ovid's Cacus.

The story was of intense popularity in Hellenistic times, and serves as the main focus for Callimachus' hymn to Demeter.[62] The tale was Hesiodic, as proven by recovered fragments of the *Catalogue of Women* (especially fr. 43a Merkelbach-West; note also Philodemus' testimony at fr. 43c). The mythographer Palaephatus knows the story (*De Incredibilibus* 23), as does the scholiast on Lycophron, *Alexandra* 1393.

Achelous begins his response to Theseus by noting that while there are some for whom metamorphosis is a solitary event, a one-time circumstance that spells a perpetual change in status, for others there are repeat transformations, among whom the sea god Proteus is most notable (we must expect a river god to be most familiar with marine phenomena). The introduction is misleading; we expect, perhaps, to hear something connected to the famous shape-shifter. Instead, we are privileged with a very different tale indeed, as Achelous uses the sea god to shift to his real focus, the wife of Autolycus, the daughter of Erysichthon (whose name, Mestra, is never mentioned by the poet—cf. his similar refusal to name Atalanta during the boar hunt).

Mestra's father is like Pirithous; he has no respect for the gods, and he even violated a grove that was sacred to Ceres. Diana and Minerva had reentered Ovid's narrative, and now Ceres makes her reappearance, as the divine punishments of Books 5-6 are recalled. Lelex had hung wreaths in honor of Baucis and Philemon at the time he visited their virtual shrine in Phrygia; in the case of Erysichthon's impiety, there was a huge oak tree (sacred to Jove), itself a grove in its immense size, and the cult site where many votive offerings had already been made (8.743 ff.). Lucan would adapt this passage to great effect in his *Pharsalia*, where Caesar would desecrate a grove that was sacred to the Druids.

Erysichthon is Thessalian; he is the Dryopeian one (8.751 *Dryopeius*), an adjective that will link his tale to the very different tree violation story of Dryope that Ovid will soon relate.[63] Erysichthon could not be more overtly impious; he does not care if the tree is sacred to Ceres; even if the goddess herself were the tree (755-756 *sed et ipsa licebit / sit dea*), still he would order his companions to begin to chop it down. The blood starts to flow, of course, just as Polydorus' grove began to bleed at the beginning of the third *Aeneid*, when his ghost was inadvertently disturbed. Ovid compares the blood to that which flows from a sacrificed bull; Erysichthon, of course, like Virgil's Laocoon, will become the sacrifice to appease the wrath of the offended goddess.

Erysichthon, a modern reader might think, is mentally ill; when a companion of this seemingly crazed lumberjack tries to stop him from desecrating the now bleeding tree, he turns his axe against the man and decapitates him on the spot (8.767 ff.). A nymph, of course, dies in the tree; the dryad prophesies that the solace for her cruel slaughter will be the death of Erysichthon. Astonishingly, Erysichthon still continues his work, and the huge tree is felled. As scholars have observed here, Erysichthon is akin to the impious giants that threatened the Olympian order; he has no redeeming qualities whatsoever, and Ovid's depiction brooks no sympathy for his fate. He is a *contemptor divum*, rather after the fashion of Virgil's Cacus, though, more than Mezentius (who, despite his cruelty, is presented with restraint and heroic pathos by Virgil in the tenth *Aeneid*). Cacus had hung the heads of his victims as trophies; Erysichthon decapitates the one man who dared to try to intervene to stop the sacrilege. Ovid will soon enough begin his *Herculeid* as part of his larger heroic cycle (and in a nod to the order of events in the second half of Virgil's *Aeneid*), but here he most evokes the story Aeneas (= Theseus?) heard of the brigand Cacus and his savage ways. The story of Cacus, of course, would have special relevance to Theseus, who himself had started his career by clearing the Athenian countryside of similar outlaws. Ovid's Erysichthon is presented as a man of not only contemptuous attitudes toward the immortals, but no respect for human life or law; he is as dangerous as a Procrustes or a Sinis.

When Ceres had searched and mourned for her lost daughter, agriculture had suffered from the goddess' neglect; now, when she hears what this woodsman has done to the tree sacred to her, she shakes all of the world's crops with a nod of her head: 8.781 *concussit gravidis oneratos messibus agros.* There is a faint hint here of the danger Ceres' anger poses to global agriculture; she is enraged here, much as she had been with the boy she changed to a newt. This offense has been arguably greater than the mocking lad's had been; it requires a novel and creative act of revenge. Ceres will borrow a page from the punishment handbook of Minerva, the other goddess Ovid has associated with the retribution due to especially offensive mortals: she will visit the "goddess" Fames, the mistress of hunger.

Ceres hopes to make Erysichthon pitiable, were the lumberjack to be pitiable to anyone in light of his savage actions (8.782-783). The antithesis is vintage Ovid; no one cares about Erysichthon, and we—like the gods—will take a voyeuristic, indeed possibly sadistic pleasure in seeing what the goddess has in store for this wretch. The punishment is fitting not so much to the crime as to the goddess; the corn deity will make sure that her enemy is punished with perpetual hunger. If the penalty is appropriate to the crime or criminal, it would be due to the insatiable nature of Erysichthon's offense: his rage knew no quelling, his madness no relief, and so he will be tormented by a hunger that is without end. It is tempting to see a deliberate pair of panels in Ovid's narrative, where the archaic *Homeric Hymn* is echoed first, followed by the Alexandrian one by Callimachus, with its very different emphases.

Minerva had been able to approach Invidia; Ceres is not allowed to visit Fames, who is literally her opposite (the same relationship did not obtain for Minerva with the instrument of her revenge). An oread is chosen as the messenger for the great goddess; like Minerva with Invidia, she will not dare to draw too close to the disgusting Fames (8.809-810). When Ceres had taken the Athenian youth Triptolemus on his global mission to spread the powers of civilization to distant, eastern lands, Scythia had been the locale for the offensive mistreatment of guests exhibited by Lyncus. Scythia is also Ovid's locus for the goddess Ceres will now employ on her quest to destroy Erysichthon; the poet thus effects a parallel between the two stories of Ceres' punishments (and, in a nice touch, the goddess will not return to the place she had fled in disgust with Triptolemus). The oread will be allowed, in fact, to use exactly the dragon chariot that the goddess had used for her previous trip with Athens' young hero (794). Ovid may also be nodding to the tradition of Prometheus' punishment in the Caucasus mountains; he was tormented with the opposite of eternal hunger, as a bird of prey daily fed on his liver. The Titan was a type of the impious giant who challenged Jupiter's new order; Erysichthon is like the giants of yore. To underscore the connection, Ovid says that the home of Fames in Scythia was located on the mountain top men call Caucasus: 797-798 *rigidique cacumine montis / (Caucason appellant)*. Hercules, of course, had freed Prometheus from his torment; his appearance will, not coincidentally, follow Erysichthon's story, but there will be no heroic rescue for this sinner.

There is a nice contrast between the pitiful blades of grass that Famine gnaws at (8.799-800) and the humble but satisfying meal of Baucis and Philemon (admittedly with the presence of gods who always refill the wine cups). As we might expect, Ovid lavishes attention on the revolting picture of the personified Hunger, whose stomach is nonexistent, whose breasts hang free and seem attached to the frame of her spine (805-806). Hunger will enter the *thalamus* of Erysichthon (817), and there she will embrace him as he sleeps, as if she were his wife. The revolting image, worthy again of some horror film, is among Ovid's most memorable. Hunger, of course, has a home to return to that is not unlike the poor hovel of Baucis and Philemon; both dwellings knew want, though with very different outcomes.

Dreams—and bruxism—now plague Erysichthon; sleep also torments the contemptuous blasphemer with images of food. Ovid personifies Somnus here as well; the winged being will play his part in the destruction of Ceres' enemy. Erysichthon was probably already mad, but when he wakes from sleep, he rages with a mad desire for food (8.828 *furit ardor edendi*) that surpasses the hunger of the ocean for water or fire for further sustenance (8.835-841). Callimachus spends more time describing the efforts to feed the hungry man, but Ovid does not always give in to what some would call excess.

Erysichthon's story eventually becomes one of simple economy; he cannot afford to continue to buy food without respite. His daughter is soon the only "possession' left that can be used to alleviate his perpetual pangs. It is interesting to note that Callimachus' Erysichthon is too young to have a daughter, and that in the old tradition (from Hesiod), Mestra is not sold into slavery or quasi-prostitution, but rather given as a bride with an expected price. Ovid's Erysichthon is presented in the worst possible light. The story that Achelous had told of the Echinades islands had included a note that Perimele, one of the islands, had been a victim of the river god's rapine; when her father tried to kill her, Achelous had prayed to Neptune that the great god of the waters might save the girl from death. Neptune had acceded to the request and transformed Perimele into an island. Now, Mestra makes her prayer; we learn (if we had not already known from the tradition), that the girl had been raped by Neptune (8.850-851). Thus Ovid rings together the story of Achelous and Perimele with the tale of Neptune and Mestra. The Neptunian rape is Hesiodic; in Ovid, the sea god grants the prayer of his *quondam* lover and transforms her into a fisherman, even as her father pursues her (852-854). The scene is wonderfully comic, in a way that makes us feel amusement at Erysichthon's fate; his daughter hates him now too, and rejoices that she is asked about her own whereabouts (862-863 *et a se / se quaeri gaudens*). Her rejoicing will not last too long, as Erysichthon soon discovers her trick.

Pirithous had doubted that the gods could cause metamorphoses; Lelex had told the story of how Baucis and Philemon were transformed into trees (together with the whole drama of how their locale was ravaged by floods and their home turned into a richly appointed temple). Achelous had followed that story with an observation that sometimes the gods wrought multiple transformations, the ostensible reason for telling the story of Erysichthon, whose daughter is turned into a fisherman, and then back again into a girl after she successfully deceives her father. Caenis had prepared the way for this story; she requested sex transformation from Neptune after rape, and had been turned into Caeneus; in Virgil's underworld, of course, Ovid would have read how she was once again a woman in the circle of those afflicted by *durus amor*.

Multiple transformations show forth even greater power than simple ones; the shifting transformations also become a metaphor for the poet's epic, as he immerses himself in the diverse works of his epic and elegiac (and other) predecessors, both Greek and Latin. The reality of multiple transformations also attests to the possibility of *return*: metamorphosis can be final, but it can also, sometimes, be temporary, as with Mestra. There is a lesson here, too, for those who would effect political change.

Ovid does not make clear exactly how Erysichthon came to realize that his daughter now had the power of shape shifting; the woodsman had seen how his daughter's footprints ended right where the fisherman was angling, and while initially deluded, the fakery does not deceive the hungry man for too long. Presumably, Neptune has made Mestra into a female, mortal version of Proteus, since the text indicates that she now has the power to change her form (at will?). The reason for this gift is to avoid her father, but it somehow does not quite work, since Erysichthon is able to sell her to master after master, each one of whom she escapes by a transformation. The economic process must be imagined as rather dizzying; just as Mestra resumes her normal form, she is sold again, and must evade a new master by some metamorphosis. Apparently she never strays too far from home, for her father is always able to catch her and use his daughter to augment the budget for his never-ending meals. In describing Erysichthon's realization that his daughter could change forms at will, Ovid uses a remarkable word:

ast ubi habere suam transformia corpora sensit (8.871)

But when he sensed that his own daughter had bodies that transformed

The adjective *transformia* occurs only here in the *Metamorphoses*, and once in the *Fasti* (1.373 *ille sua faciem transformis adulterat arte*), of Proteus, the subject of Achelous' introduction to the story of Mestra and Erysichthon.[64] The word is, of course, central to the main theme of the epic. But why the mention of

Proteus at the beginning of the story? In the *Fasti*, Ovid introduces Proteus in the same context as Virgil at the end of the fourth georgic: he is the savior of Aristaeus, the ill-fated beekeeper. In the *Georgics*, the seer Proteus announces that Aristaeus' apiary losses will be made right once Orpheus' shade is appeased; the epyllion of Orpheus and Eurydice follows. Ovid here signals movement toward his own Orpheus lore, which will bring the second third of his epic to its conclusion. That second third will thus conclude with more underworld allusions, as Ovid once again evokes the lessons of the sixth *Aeneid*, and as we move ever close to the poet's complete unveiling of his epic's plan.

The end of the story of Erysichthon is suitably grisly; he cannot keep up with the power of his hunger, and it is as if his daughter cannot be sold fast enough to maintain his diet. The delay in waiting for every new, craved morsel is too great; Erysichthon eventually consumes that which is most readily at hand: himself. Ovid restrains himself: he does not describe the process of autophagy in anything approaching the gory extremes we know he is capable of depicting. His silence makes the whole matter all the more horrifying.

Achelous abruptly ends his story (8.879); he is a consummate storyteller, who knows exactly how to leave his audience breathless as he omits the terrible climax of Erysichthon's punishment (*quid moror externis?*). Pirithous, again, is silent in the aftermath of the tale. Ovid now moves toward his next transition: Achelous himself, it turns out, has the power of changing his shape. He seems weaker in this regard than Mestra; he has the power, but it is limited in scope. Sometimes he appears as he is in front of Theseus and his band; at other times he is a serpent, and at still others, a bull (881-882). The god has three forms, then, though apparently there is always evidence of the bull in the horns he wears (river gods, of course, were usually depicted as horned). One of Achelous' horns is broken off, and the god groans in lament as the book ends. Ovid thus effects an effective transition to the *Herculeid* that will commence in the next book, though since Achelous does not say he will reveal the cause of the loss of his horn, the direction the poet will now take is unclear, and suspense is thereby effectively crafted as we move forward.

The eighth book ends quietly, with a river god's groan. Thus opens a new section in Ovid's heroic cycle, though we do not as yet know the direction it will take; Hercules, the hero of *Aeneid* 8, will now appear as the cause of Achelous' pain. By his learned nod to Proteus, Ovid has also begun, in a sense, the song of Orpheus that will soon enough come to full measure.

The middle of the epic has been reached, and we have entered Ovid's *maius opus*. The first third of the poem had ended after the great account of the rape of Persephone and the establishment of the royal family of a traditional underworld; following on that account, Diana had saved Arethusa from rape and select immortals had begun a veritable process of global cleansing of ill. The cruel slaughter of the satyr Marsyas by Apollo had signaled the coming of a resurgence of violence, savage and seemingly without end or divine recourse, violence that engulfed even Minerva's own city of Athens. Those unremitting horrors had been quelled by a new series of acts of divine retribution for mortal violence, most notably the great boar that ravaged Calydon. Since the satisfaction of the archer goddess' wrath, the world has returned to the peace it knew in the days when Minerva could calmly engage in immortal discussion on the slopes of Helicon with the Muses.

As we advance through this second third of the epic, in a world once again reborn (as symbolized by the floodwaters that destroyed Baucis and Philemon's Phrygian home, where the Italian couple survives as all their Phrygian neighbors are drowned),[65] Ovid moves us closer to Orpheus, a figure whose presence signals an underworld that Homer would not recognize, but that is very familiar to readers of the stunning vision with which the sixth *Aeneid* ends: the world where souls are reborn into new forms, the ultimate metamorphosis for those willing (like Bacchus) to be born twice. Achelous has signaled the entrance of Orpheus into Ovid's epic by his allusion to Proteus in the introduction to his Mestra and Erysichthon story, which Ovid neatly confirmed by his careful use of the rare adjective *transformis* only twice in his extant poetry, once of Proteus, and once of the girl whose story the example of Proteus presaged.

At the midpoint of the *Metamorphoses*, Ovid evoked the whole tradition of the *Iliad* and the *Aeneid* in the carefully fashioned story of Meleager, Atalanta, and the Calydonian boar hunt; in the midst of Meleager's lust for Atalanta, Ovid (in imitation of his poetic predecessor) announced the beginning of his *maius opus* with an appropriately erotic theme that might as well have been dedicated to Erato, the muse of amatory verse. Ovid has also pursued the themes of the early movements of the second *Aeneid*: the reception of a great visitor into a humble dwelling, the vanquishing of an impious giant who embodies rebellion against the Olympian order, and the introduction of Hercules as the great hero of a bygone age. Lastly, in brilliantly realized allusion to the end of the fourth georgic, Ovid has also announced the coming of Orpheus, as the new poet moves both forwards and backwards in the pages of his much admired and beloved predecessor. Admiration and love, of course, do not preclude the seeking of increased poetic glory: Ovid is, after all, most fundamentally the poet of the universal history, the author who does aspire to receive all of Helicon as his inheritance from the Muses.

There is humor in the *Metamorphoses*, and moments of comedy that both amuse and enchant. But Ovid's epic is a serious one before all else. He is concerned with the weightiest of philosophical and theological problems, and he offers serious commentary on the most haunting of questions. His work, we have come to realize, is an intensely engaged dialogue with Homer and Virgil (especially the latter, given the shared language and close proximity in time).

As we turn the page to another book, we can expect the coming of Hercules, whose appearance has been so amply signaled. Theseus has not yet left the stage, though now another hero will come into focus, a figure imbued with so much solemnity by the Augustan regime as a symbol of the coming of Olympian (i.e., Augustan) order. If the examples of Jason and Theseus have taught us any-thing, it is that we cannot expect Ovid to provide any extended, glorious epic rendering of the deeds of the hero. His *Herculeid* will follow the pattern of his other epyllia in its selective brevity.

Soon enough, though, Ovid will remind us once again of Caenis/Caeneus, as we enter a world where love in its myriad forms is seen as sometimes quite unnatural, even unholy: the polar opposite of the love displayed between the pious Baucis and Philemon. The shift may seem unusual and without reason, but the poet has his reasons, as the victims of love gone awry in Virgil's underworld are recalled, and as we move ever closer to the arrival of a philosopher bard whose songs could move rocks, and whose presence signals the coming of both deeply felt tragedy and a new, perhaps more hopeful conception of the fates of the dead. Looming even more distantly in the future is the lesson of another poet, who would shatter such fantasies and brook no fondly held illusions.

Notes

1. Besides the usual commentaries (most important Bömer's fourth volume of 1977, containing Books 8-9), excellent notes are available in Hollis, A.S., *Ovid Metamorphoses VIII*, Oxford, 1970. There is an expurgated school text by Gould and Whiteley. Note also the lengthy article of Boyd, Barbara Weiden, "Two Rivers and the Reader in Ovid, *Metamorphoses 8*," in *Transactions of the American Philological Association* 136.1 (2006), pp. 171-206.

2. In Latin poetry, besides Ovid the main surviving evidence is the pseudo-Virgilian epyllion, the *Ciris* (where see Lyne's 1978 Cambridge edition). The *Ciris* almost certainly postdates the *Metamorphoses*. The first extant appearance of the story is at Aeschylus, *Choephoroi* 612 ff. (where see Garvie). Pseudo-Apollodorus 3.15.8.2 has the basic outline of the story, without the metamorphosis (his Scylla is executed by being tied to Minos' prow and left to drown; note also Hyginus, *Fabulae* 198). Virgil knows the story (*Georgics* 1.404-409); Callimachus seems to have treated it in his *Aetia*, and Parthenius as well.

3. The subject of Propertius c. 4.4, where see Hutchinson.

4. In Ovid, Scylla has no special motivation for her infatuation with Minos. In the *Ciris*, Juno punished Scylla because of some desecration of the goddess' temple and act of perjury. See further Knox, Peter E., "Cinna, the *Ciris*, and Ovid," in *Classical Philology* 78.4 (1983), pp. 309-311. In the *Ciris*, Cupid is (rather remarkably) Juno's aid in punishing Scylla, which Knox takes as a borrowing from Cinna's *Zmyrna*, where Cupid assists Venus in acts of retribution. Ovid's girl needs no divine instigation, which increases her guilt in the audience's eyes.

5. In the sweep of Ovid's narrative there is no indication of why Minos decided to besiege Megara and not Aegina; Ovid says he did not want to expend his forces on the latter. As Book 8 opens, he is willing to launch a difficult attack on Megara.

6. 6.74-77 *quid loquar, aut Scyllam Nisi, quam fama secuta est / candida succinctam latrantibus inguina monstris / Dulichias vexasse rates et gurgite in alto / a! timidos nautas canibus lacerasse marinis*, where see Coleman, and Clausen.

7. *Ars Amatoria* 1.331-332 *filia purpureos Niso furata capillos / pube premit rabidos inguinibusque canes*, where see Hollis. Some scribes attempted to interpolate lines to separate the two women. Note also *Tristia* 2.393-394 (with Owen), and *Ibis* 362, as well as Tibullus, c. 1.4.63 (with Murgatroyd, and Maltby).

8. *Purpureus* in the *Ars*; *ostrum* in the *Metamorphoses*; Hollis ad 8.8 wonders if "scarlet" is better here than "purple," but note 80 *purpura*, 93 *purpureum*, where I doubt scarlet is the best translation. Ovidian colors remain largely understudied; note the brief start offered by Edgeworth, Robert Joseph, *The Colors of the Aeneid*, New York-Frankfurt: Peter Lang, 1992, pp. 14-17.

9. 8.87 *fert secum spolium celeris progressaque porta*, while offering no essential new information and being both repetitive and limp, is also difficult to explain as a scribal interpolation.

10. See further Hollis ad 101-102. Minos was not consistently portrayed as a just lawgiver, but often as a wild and savage individual (and there is nothing in Ovid before this scene to make us think he is anything but a violent warmonger).

11. In a nice touch, besides the usual attack that the man who runs away was born of a tigress, Scylla also claims that Minos must have been born from Charybdis (8.120-121),

a nod to the lore that her namesake was the whirlpool's neighbor. She, not Minos, is the monster.

12. And Minerva has been nowhere for any of it.

13. In the Virgilian appropriation of Daedalus lore, there is also a hint that the master craftsman, who was able to contrive a way for Pasiphae to mate with a bull, for Theseus to navigate the labyrinth, and for himself and his son to escape Minos' prison, is not able to sketch his lost son, and, in a sense, cannot help with the all-encompassing problem of the Augustan succession: Daedalus cannot solve the intractable problem of who will replace the savior Augustus. Marcellus might well have, but, like Icarus, he died; Daedalus cannot depict Icarus, while Virgil can draw Marcellus. Neither can make a living successor for the *princeps* out of the tragedy of lost youth.

14. See further Hollis ad 145-146.

15. From the Greek verb.

16. The ciris' identity is notoriously vexed; Hollis follows Thompson's conclusion that the bird most probably belongs to mythology and not ornithology. Of course the fantasy element also explains how Scylla is able to pursue Minos' ship and hang on in lustful pursuit of the king.

17. I share Hollis' lack of understanding of Otis' conclusion that Scylla's transformation is the logical result of her situation (*op. cit.*, p. 65).

18. In the comparison of Minos' labyrinth to the Phrygian Meander there is also a hint of the Roman stereotype of Punic perfidy.

19. Later in the book (8.262 ff.) Athens will duly rejoice in Theseus' victory, thus closing the ring that opened with the celebration of the hero's deeds before he met Aegeus and Medea. Ovid does not bother to tell us why Theseus, the hero who had helped to rid so much Greek territory of beasts and brigands, waits for two cycles of Athenian youths to be sacrificed to the Minotaur before intervening, or how Athens needed to pay tribute at all when such a great hero resided in her walls. In Pseudo-Apollodorus (3.15.8), the war drags on and Minos despairs of victory; he prays to his father for help. Athens is then struck by a pestilence (cf. Aegina), and eventually the Athenians are told they must give Minos whatever he asked. Minos then demanded the tribute of the youths for the Minotaur, and of course Theseus is among the elite children to be sent as human sacrifices. We cannot be certain which sources and traditions Ovid had in mind, and his poem must ultimately be studied for its own text: what he omits is just as important as what he includes. Thus far in the *Theseid*, the title character has been barely present, as Ovid focuses on other concerns and uses the general progression of heroic history as canvas for rather different, less than heroic images.

20. The story (in both of Ovid's versions) has occasioned a considerable bibliography. Note especially Ahern, Charles F., "Daedalus and Icarus in the *Ars Amatoria*," in *Harvard Studies in Classical Philology* 92 (1989), pp. 273-296, Schubert, Werner, "Explizite und implizite Mythendeutung : (Ovids Daedalus-Ikarus-Erzählung, *Met.* 8, 183-235)," in *Eirene* 28 (1992), pp. 25-31, Davisson, Mary H. T., "The Observers of Daedalus and Icarus in Ovid," in *The Classical World* 90.4 (1996-1997), pp. 263-278, Pavlock, Barbara, "Daedalus in Ovid's *Metamorphoses*," in *The Classical World* 92.2 (1998-1999), pp. 141-157, and Gärtner, Thomas, "Zur Bedeutung der mythologischen Erzählung über Daedalus und Icarus am Amfang des zweiten Buchs von Ovid's *Ars Amatoria*," in *Latomus* 64.2 (2005), pp. 649-660. The tale offers Ovid at his very best; Silius Italicus (*Punica* 12.89-103) cannot compare. Hyginus, *Fabulae* 40 offers the basic story in the usual mythographic treatment.

21. I consider the parallels between Daedalus and Augustus more likely than those raised by some between Daedalus and Ovid.

22. Some commentators make a distinction between making nature new and making one's own nature new. But the essence is the same.

23. Note Pseudo-Apollodorus 3.15.8 and Hyginus, *Fabulae* 39.

24. Cf. Herodotus 7.169.

25. So the Apollodoran *Epitome*, 1.15.

26. *Iliad* 9.529 ff. offers the most extensive surviving archaic evidence; the mythographers cover the story somewhat dully (Pseudo-Apollodorus 1.8.1 ff., Hyginus, *Fabulae* 171-174; note also Antoninus Liberalis 2).

27. Some two dozen fragments remains thanks to the lexicographical interest of some words; the Atalanta theme was clearly central to the action. For the afterlife, note Swinburne's 1865 *Atalanta in Calydon*.

28. See further O'Connor, Joseph F., "Ovid's Meleager," in *The Augustan Age* 10 (1990-1992), pp. 34-42, and Segal, Charles, "Ovid's Meleager and the Greeks: Trials of Gender and Genre," in *Harvard Studies in Classical Philology* 99 (1999), pp. 301-340.

29. Plexippus and Toxeus.

30. Ovid will return to his/her story later, at 12.189 ff. and 459 ff., during the battle between the Lapiths and the Centaurs (Caenis was a daughter of the Lapith king who requested a sex change after Poseidon raped her). The legend was very old (Hesiod); see further West, Grace Starry, "Caeneus and Dido," in *Transactions of the American Philological Association* 110 (1980), pp. 315-324.

31. A cautionary note here on this catalogue is warranted. Many of the names are important in classical literature and the epic tradition; others seem mere names in a catalogue. It is a testimony to the learning of Ovid's audience and the attention the poet demanded of his readers that we find 313 Hippasus and 371 Eurytides, i.e., the son of Eurytion = *Hippasus*. *Pace* some of the commentators, I think Ovid expects you to know the patronymic and to remember.

32. Both Caenis and Eriphyle are in Virgil's underworld, and the evocation of the two women in this passage is perhaps coincidental, but more likely a reminiscence of Virgil's catalogue of the victims of *durus amor* in *Aeneid* 6.

33. Ovid also mentions her in the context of the boar hunt at *Heroides* 4. 99-100 (Phaedra to Hippolytus): *arsit et Oenides in Maenalia Atalanta; / illa ferae spolium pignus amoris habet.*

34. On the parallel, see further my "*Posse putes*: Virgil's Camilla, Ovid's Atalanta," in Deroux, C., ed., *Studies in Latin Literature and Roman History XII*, Bruxelles: Editions Latomus, 2005, pp. 185-193. Atalanta is also last in the catalogue at Hyginus, *Fabulae* 173, where Arcadia is the last locale that sent aid to Oeneus in Calydon.

35. With the image of the boy Achilles at Scyros cf. Horace's description of the boy Gyges at c. 2.5.21-24 (with Nisbet and Hubbard), where Horace observes that you could insert Gyges into a choir of girls.

36. See further my "*Velocem potuit domuisse puellam*: Propertius, Catullus, and Atalanta's Race," in *Latomus* (2008), pp. 342-352. I have argued there that the comparison to the Harpy may point to a connection between Atalanta and the snatcher she-wolf Harpalyce, along with the origins of Virgil's Camilla in native Italian myth and folklore. Schoeneus is, after all, the father of Harpalyce at Hyginus, *Fabulae* 206.

37. Atalanta is also the daughter of Iasius at "Theognis" 1283-1294 West, where the blond girl tries to run home to escape marriage, though in the end she yields to Aphrodite in unspecified ways and to unknown consequences.

38. Pseudo-Apollodorus 1.8.2 mentions Atalanta at Calydon, and, at 1.9.16, her presence on the Argo; in both occasions he names *Schoeneus* (usually associated with the race) as her father; at 3.9.2, the mythographer is aware of confusion over her father's name. Apollonius Rhodius, *Argonautica* 1.769 has the more plausible story that Jason refused her passage on the Argonaut, afraid that a single beautiful woman might cause more trouble than she was worth.

39. The simile may be meant to recall the death of Aconteus at *Aeneid* 11.616, where the hero fulfills the meaning of his name (Greek "javelin"); there may be a connection between the Mopsus prayer and its reminiscence of Virgil's Arruns and the probable link between Camilla-Arruns and Cydippe-Aconteus, on which see the forthcoming article of McOsker, M., and Fratantuono, L., "Camilla and Cydippe: A Note on Virgil, *Aeneid* 581-582," in *Quaderni Urbinati di Cultura Classica* (2010), pp. 111-116.

40. There may also be an indication of her confused origins in Ovid's refusal to use her name.

41. A rather ironic point given the help that Venus bestowed on the Trojans, the Etruscans' allies.

42. The text is vexed here, but *aesculea* is almost certainly the correct reading.

43. *Pace* Anderson, who notes (unfairly) the rather empty courage of those who did nothing in the hunt and now bloody their spear shafts.

44. As we noted in the previous chapter, line 442 marks the probable midpoint of this book (questions of interpolation aside); the midpoint of the entire poem is less easy to pinpoint precisely, though it certainly occurs during this episode.

45. The huntress can hunt any game; Diana's devotees, it would seem, can go after even Diana's boars. But, we might note, Atalanta herself will soon enough be doomed, though for complex reasons that go beyond Diana; like Virgil's Camilla, she has left Diana's world and the goddess' protection.

46. *Iliad* 2.488-490; *Georgics* 2.43-44; *Aeneid* 6.625-626. See further Hollis ad loc.

47. Hollis ad loc. concludes that the passage is comic, hypothesizing that Callimachus may have been the source of the humor, if not Nicander. That begs the question of why Ovid should insert comedy here.

48. And, we might note, the Greek name for this bird, the "meleagris," is an attested, real bird—unlike, it seems, the ciris.

49. It is true that Ovid, unlike Virgil with Camilla, does not make explicit that Atalanta had any particular devotion to Diana. But the character is presented as a Diana-like figure, a quiver-carrying virgin (unlike the non-virginal Venus, Dido, and Procris pretenders, or the strange case of Salmacis).

50. "Six books of falsehood," as Benardete labeled the Iliadic *Aeneid*: a reading of Virgil that is prolegomena, I would argue, to understanding anything written in the shadow of those six books. For in the failure of the Augustan succession, we see proof that the *princeps* represents, in an important sense, the end of history.

51. Though, in light of the evidence of Homer's Achilles in the underworld of the *Odyssey*, we are tempted to wonder what their response might be.

52. In a sense, the same Diana who saved Arethusa also saved Atalanta (and notice the similar names): Meleager's death meant no consummation of a relationship with the Arcadian huntress.

53. I wonder, too, if the wrong way trip of Theseus is an allusion to the ivory gate by which Aeneas entered, as it were, the second half of the *Aeneid*.

54. Pseudo-Apollodorus 1.9.21.7.

55. The passage is vexed by an unusually extensive series of doublets in the manuscript tradition. Essentially there are two versions, one longer and one shorter, of the girl's metamorphosis into an island. Hollis defends most of the possibly interpolated lines, arguing persuasively that if someone inserted them, he was perhaps the most consummate interpolator of classical Latin poetry who ever lived. I suspect the lines were cut in part because of the erotic description of how the lustful river god fondled Perimele's breasts as she was being hardened into an island. (Gould and Whiteley ad loc. discreetly omit any mention of the matter, and refer in their introduction to their expurgation of the text).

56. The story is utterly unknown before Ovid, though much speculation has been offered as to its origins (Near Eastern flood myths, lost Greek lore). Callimachus' *Hecale* would be an appropriate influence, given the story's place in Ovid's larger *Theseid*; Ovid, *Fasti* 5.493 ff., of the divine visitation of Hyrieus, is something of a doublet, though the point cannot be pressed too far. Hollis has extensive commentary here on the motif of the gods visiting humble abodes; Bömer is especially thorough. See further Gamel, M.-K., "Baucis and Philemon: Paradigm or Paradox?," in *Helios* 11 (1984), pp. 117-131.

57. Cf. s. 11.79-79, 82, with Courtney, and Ferguson.

58. Otis (*op. cit.*, pp. 201) offers speculation on why the theodicies of Baucis and Philemon and Erysichthon are placed between Meleager and Hercules, but his first conclusion, that Ovid needed to prevent repetition and monotony, is unpersuasive.

59. On the diet of the Roman poor see further Littlewood ad Ovid, *Fasti* 6.169-170, and, more generally, Emily Gowers' *The Loaded Table* (Oxford, 1993). 8.651 ff. is vexed by another problem of doublets and possible interpolations, an interested coincidence (?) after the same problem in the Perimele narrative. 8.693 ff. is also textually problematic; there is no definitive answer for the question of the presence of so many textual variants in so short a scope poses.

60. As Adrian Goldsworthy does well to remind us, in view of the persistent view that Roman soldiers did not eat meat.

61. A goose was Molorchus' planned offering at *Aetia* 3, but a Callimachean mention of a goose does not exclude the associations with early Roman history.

62. On which see Hopkinson's Cambridge edition, with full commentary, Bulloch, A. W., "Callimachus' Erysichthon, Homer, and Apollonius Rhodius," in *The American Journal of Philology* 98.2 (1977), pp. 97-123, and Robertson, Noel, "The Ritual Background of the Erysichthon Story," in *The American Journal of Philology* 105.4 (1984), pp. 369-408. Note also McKay, K. J., *Erysichthon: A Callimachean Comedy* (Mnemosyne Supplement 7), Leiden: Brill, 1962. For the Ovidian story, note also Griffin, Alan H. F., "Erysichthon—Ovid's Giant?," in *Greece & Rome*, Second Series 33.1 (1986), pp. 55-63, and the important article of Thomas, Richard F., "Tree Violation and Ambivalence in Virgil," in *Transactions of the American Philological Association* 118 (1988), pp. 261-273; note also Henrichs, A., "Thou Shalt Not Kill a Tree: Greek, Manichaean, and Indian Tales," in *BASP* 16 (1979), pp. 85-108. For the fascinating story of the possible survival of the lore in oral tradition on the island of Cos, see Hollis ad loc. (and his "Appendix III"). For the similarities between this tale and Arachen's fate, note Horowski, J., "De Call. Hymn. VI, 24-115 et Ovid Met. VI, 5-146," in *Meander* 16 (1961), pp. 141-148.

63. This reading must be preferred to *Triopeius*, which has enjoyed inexplicable editorial favor; see further Hollis ad loc. (*recte*), and cf. the same confusion at 8.872 below.

64. No other extant Latin writer uses the adjective.

65. A truly marvelous Ovidian reading of the end of the *Aeneid*.

Chapter IX
The Neptunian Hero . . .

The ninth book of the epic continues Ovid's heroic cycle and his *Theseid*, which now also becomes a *Herculeid*.[1] By book's end, it will not be entirely clear whether or not we are still immersed in either epyllion. Theseus has remained largely in the background (a good place to be if one wishes to avoid suffering any tarnishing of one's heroic armor). Once again, Ovid resorts to "another" narrator, this time the river god Achelous, to introduce the definitive hero of the ancient pre-historical world (educated Greeks and Romans considered "history" proper to start with the Trojan War).[2] Theseus inquires as to Achelous' broken horn; Ovid names the son of Aegeus the *Neptunian hero* (9.1), for which we may consult Pseudo-Apollodorus.[3] Some considered Theseus the true son of the god; the mythographer records that Aegeus was drunk on his way back from Delphi and stayed at Troezen with Pelops' son Pittheus, who had his guest sleep with his daughter Aethra. Poseidon apparently also slept with Aethra on the very same night, and so the paternity question proved difficult indeed.

Ovid is playing here with the somewhat similar situation of Jupiter's son Hercules, whose mother Alcmena had a quite mortal spouse, Amphitryon; the question of Hercules' paternity will soon be raised as part of the fight between Achelous and the great hero. Achelous will explain the cause of his mutilated forehead; he begins with Meleager's sister Deianira. The story begins, then, in a parallel to Meleager's own tale: a woman was the source of Achelous' pain. Deianira will have two suitors, Achelous and Hercules; the contest is an old motif, and we might well think of Aeneas and Turnus. All other suitors for the girl retire in the presence of the two great challengers (9.13). Like Aeneas, Hercules has been harried by Juno, who was angry at the offspring of yet another Jovian dalliance; like Aeneas, Hercules had been driven through a gauntlet of harrowing experiences because of the anger of heaven's queen.

The issue of divine paternity that Ovid raises at the beginning of this book is also linked to the major divine discussion that will mark its midpoint (cf. 9.400 ff. below). Ovid is still immersed in his "second *Aeneid*," his *maius opus*, and in this book he will revisit the major themes of the great council of the gods that inaugurated that book. The issue is a simple one, of profound implications: can the gods intervene to help their favorites? The time is right for the matter to be discussed: not only are we lost in Ovid's evocation of the second half of the *Aeneid*, but we are also in his *Herculeid*. It was Hercules who would be troubled by the impending fate of Pallas (cf. *A.* 10.466 *tum genitor natum* and ff.). Pallas had wanted to be a new Hercules, as if Turnus were another Cacus infesting Latium. Pallas does not understand the ultimate disposition of Rome, and he misreads the situation, especially as it applies to him personally.[4] As Ovid moves ever close to the appearance of Orpheus in his epic universal history, the philosophical concerns that are at the heart of Virgil's vision now begin to appear with increasing frequency and greater intensity.

Achelous, of course, is a true god, however minor; he is almost pathetically akin to Virgil's Aeolus. Hercules is all too mortal, despite his enormous strength and valor, though, and the god will not yield without a fight. Achelous raises exactly the argument Turnus makes to Latinus: Hercules is a foreigner, while he is a native:

> nec gener externis hospes tibi missus ab oris,
> sed popularis ero et rerum pars una tuarum. (9.19-20)

> *Nor have I been sent as a son-in-law from foreign shores,*
> *but I am one of your people, and one part of your affairs.*

Latinus had been told to seek a foreign son-in-law (which, technically, Turnus the Rutulian was); Achelous pleads the strength of shared locale. Juno might be happy at Achelous' attacks on Hercules; either the hero is a liar and no son of a god (a recurring theme since the Phaethon story), or he was born from adultery (9.25 *adulterio*: the charge is particularly pointed for an Augustan audience).

The two heroes clash in a wrestling contest (9.31 ff.); Achelous describes the fight as being similar to the competition of two bulls for the prize of the most beautiful heifer in the flock (46-49). The simile most echoes Virgil's account of the clash between Aeneas and Turnus (*A.* 12.715-722). In both passages the herd is frozen in silence as the heifer watches and wonders which hero will conquer and win her hand. The competition between Aeneas and Turnus for Lavinia is, of course, the main erotic theme for the second half of the *Aeneid*; this is Ovid's reason for evoking this image at the beginning of his *Herculeid*. The victorious Hercules prefigures Aeneas, who will win Lavinia's hand. And, further, the outcome of both contests is predetermined; we know from the very outset (even if we were ignorant of the tradition) that Achelous lost his bout with Hercules. His story, after all, opened with his lament over the broken horn—a favorite Ovidian device for opening new stories: beginning with the end result. This, too, is a commentary on the nature of fate and predetermined outcomes.

The commentators have also compared our present Ovidian passage, and its Virgilian predecessor, to Ennius' description in the first book of the *Annales* of the contest of Romulus and Remus over what the name of the future city would be.[5] The conflict of the twins is another type of the same situation that obtains between Aeneas and Turnus, and serves to highlight the internecine strife that stands at the very heart of Roman history. The wrestling bout, as we already knew, swiftly favors Hercules; he gains the upper hand and compels Achelous to resort to transformations. Achelous changes his form into that of a snake, which allows Hercules to allude to his infancy battle with Juno's serpents, and the conquest of the Lernaean hydra.[6] Neither as snake nor as bull can Achelous withstand Hercules, and soon enough the contest is over and, to add insult to injury, Achelous loses one of his horns, which naiads dedicate to the goddess Copia, "Abundance"—the formation of the cornucopia, a nice "Roman" touch to the combat—something good for Rome out of the defeat of the river god.[7]

The etiology of the cornucopia leads to the entrance of a nymph who serves the harvest of autumn from the horn, with a rich fruit course for dessert. The party has gone on for some time; the guests perhaps welcome the dawn (9.93 *lux subit*); they leave as the sun rises.[8] Interestingly, Theseus and his two companions do not wait for the river to subside. They had stopped at the behest of Achelous to allow the waters to recede; now they leave with the morning, though the waters are still in flood. Ovid had had Theseus take the "wrong way" back to Athens; now the guests leave even though the floodwaters are still deep. And so, with another somewhat mysterious "error," Ovid ends the cycle of stories that were told in Achelous' watery haunts. We leave Theseus again, and the poet himself digresses with more of his *Herculeid*. We have barely met the great hero; the defeat of the river god was hardly among his most glorious deeds, and besides the wrestling match there has only been brief mention of the defeat of serpents in infancy and the second canonical labor, the Hydra of Lerna.

Now, in contrast to Achelous (who escaped relatively unscathed from his combat with Hercules), we meet the centaur Nessus.[9] The situation of the hero and his new wife is identical to Theseus; the river Euenus is swollen, and, interestingly, while Hercules would have no trouble crossing himself, apparently he is willing to allow the centaur to help his wife make the transit (one wonders why he could not help her himself); Ovid makes clear that Deianira feared the river and the centaur alike (9.111). The audience knows the story, which Ovid relates with brevity: Nessus attempts to abduct the terrified girl, Hercules warns him, the centaur ignores the threat and is felled by an arrow in the back that protrudes through his chest. As he dies—as much from the shot as from the Hydra's blood that coats the hero's shafts—he gives his blood-soaked tunic to Deianira and advises her that it will be a charm against the possibility of lost love.[10]

Ovid spends no time here on Hercules' great deeds. Even in the narrative of the early *Theseid*, the poet had allowed for a brief mention of the hero's exploits as part of the celebrations in his honor in Athens. All we learn of Hercules is that his fame fills the world and satisfies the hate of his stepmother Juno (9.135 *odiumque novercae*). It is true that the stories were exceedingly well known, but so are plenty of others that Ovid details. Ovid spends the most time in his *Herculeid* detailing the death of the hero.[11] He had already addressed some of the issues inherent to this lore at *Heroides* 9, where Deianira makes her appeal to

Hercules; in the *Fasti* he tells the story of Hercules and Cacus succinctly.[12] Ovid's treatment of Hercules in the *Metamorphoses* owes much to his earlier presentation of the hero in the *Heroides*, where Achelous and Nessus are also linked (139-142).[13] In her lament, Deianira mentions far more Hercules lore than Ovid includes in the *Metamorphoses*. We might think that Ovid was more interested in the hero's end than in his traditional catalogue of exploits. We are reminded of Ovid's focus on Jason and Medea rather than the Argonaut voyage. The defeat of Cacus in the *Aeneid* would seem to have been replaced by the far less serious (perhaps even semi-comic) wrestling match with Achelous. For Ovid, the destruction of Erysichthon corresponded to the defeat of Virgil's Cacus. Ovid will focus on a different Hercules in his epic, and Hercules' catalogue of deeds will be part of a setting very distinct from the celebrations that honored Theseus' exploits. For Ovid, Hercules will be preeminently the Stoic hero, the example of valor in the face of unbearable torment. Ovid's Hercules is not so much a rethinking of Virgil's as a companion piece; in Virgil, the hero had been an Augustan symbol of the conquest of evil and the spreading of the Olympian order; in Ovid, the hero—his work done, if you will, in quelling monsters old and new—will take his deserved rest.

Hercules has completed the conquest of Oechalia; he is piously paying his vows to Jupiter (9.136 ff.). But word has reached Deianira that Hercules has fallen in love with a princess of the Oechalian royal family, Iole. In the Sophoclean tradition, it was the herald Lichas who announced this dalliance to Deianira; in Ovid's version, no doubt under the influence of Virgil's Aeneas and Dido story, it is Rumor who brings the word (though it will be Lichas who brings the fatal garment to Hercules, since Rumor cannot carry Deianira's laundry to Hercules). The situation is parallel again to that of Jason and Medea. Ovid has emphasized the relationship of the hero to a woman, Deianira; he details the story of the hero's preference of another, royal woman to his love. The woman resorts to a type of magic; Deianira is no Medea in this regard, but the centaur-blood aphrodisiac scheme (with poisonous effect) is reminiscent of the magic of the Colchian sorceress. Deianira remembers that she is the sister of Meleager, who lost his life because he surrendered to excessive passion for Atalanta:

quid si me, Meleagre, tuam memor esse sororem
forte paro facinus, quantumque iniuria posit
femineusque dolor, iugulata paelice testor? (9.149-151)

What if, Meleager, mindful that I am your sister
I prepare a great crime, and give testimony of how much
a woman's grief is able to accomplish, with the slut having been slaughtered?

Hercules will die much in the same way as Meleager, set on fire with torturous pain; where the life of the Calydonian hero ended in agony as the firebrand was extinguished, the (earthly) life of the future god will be destroyed in the flames of a suicidal funeral pyre that offers relief from pain and an image of Stoic purgation and rebirth. Both heroes die because of passion, and both die ignorant of the real causes behind their sudden and premature demises. Of course Deianira does not realize that she is not so much invoking the tradition of what her stepbrother did to Plexippus and Toxeus, as she is echoing Althaea's rage at Meleager. In any case, Deianira should know that the tragedies she is evoking all spell doom.

Hercules' very piety only serves to hasten his end; the flames at the altar where he is burning incense to Jupiter cause the poison to work faster (9.161).[14] Achelous had groaned even at the mere memory of losing his horn to Hercules; the great Stoic represses all cries as long as he is able (163 *solita gemitum virtute repressit*). Of course the Stoic repression is only temporary; the agony is so great that the hero's cries befit someone of his size and strength. He is a giant, and so his blood hisses as when hot metal is plunged into chilled water (170-171); the image is reminiscent of Homer's description of the gory hissing of Polyphemus' eye when Odysseus plunged his stake into it. Hercules, of course, assumes that Juno is the cause of the torment, and he prays to her for death. What would kill a lesser man can only cause endless agony for a Hercules. Now Ovid will indulge in a catalogue of what the hero did; it is, of course, remarkable that the agonized Hercules can recite so carefully all his deeds.

Busiris and Antaeus are stories well known in the tradition.[15] Both are reminiscent of the sort of victories Theseus won in Attica. Geryon and Cerberus are among the canonical labors, as is the slaughter of the Cretan bull (9.183-186). Hercules also mentions the labors of the Augean stables and the Stymphalian birds, as well as the capture of Diana's Cerynthian hind. Next are the girdle of the Amazon Hippolyta and the golden apples of the Hesperides, followed by a minor centauromachy and the labor of the Erymanthian boar. Hercules had already mentioned the Hydra; he repeats it here, along with the flesheating mares of Diomedes. Lastly, he mentions the first of the traditional labors, the slaughter of the Nemean lion; when he had crossed the Euenus he had his lion pelt. All of these stories were common mythological knowledge; Ovid dispenses with them rapidly (even if, again, we may observe that for a man in torment, Hercules does very well with his catalogue of feats). The Nemean lion was traditionally the first of Hercules' labors; the hero ends with the beginning of his exceptional deeds of valor. The labors become part of the death agony.

Jason had suffered at the hands of Medea, and it seemed that there were no gods, as the sorceress acted with impunity. The Stoic Seneca may well have been influenced by Ovid's dying Hercules when he composed the end of his *Medea*,[16] as the hero observes ruefully:

. . . et sunt, qui credere possint
esse deos? (9.203-204)

. . . and there are those who are able to believe

that the gods exist?

Hercules is like a wounded bull as he climbs Mount Oeta (9.205-206); Ovid once again uses taurine imagery to describe the hero, who is like his father (who had abducted Europa in the guise of a bull).

Ovid devotes some space to the fate of Lichas, who was not the bearer of ill tidings to Deianira, but who had brought the deadly garment to Hercules (9.211 ff.). As the hero ascends Mount Oeta, he sees Lichas hiding under a hollow rock; he grabs him and hurls him into the sea in the manner of a catapult, only stronger than any such siege engine (218). Ovid does not develop the nascent simile, but instead defies audience expectation and describes how Lichas began to harden in midair, just as rain freezes and changes to snow and then to hail. Lichas eventually becomes an outcropping of land in the sea, a place where sailors fear to land because they see its human appearance (227-229). The meteorological simile, seemingly ridiculous in context, was inspired by Lucretius (*De Rerum Natura* 6.495 ff., especially 527-529).

The simile has not attracted much attention, especially anything beyond the usual observation of some that Ovid is having fun with the tradition, inserting ridiculous passages to amuse a learned audience. Here, two points can be raised. Once again, Ovid has "made a mistake," as it were. As the commentators note, a missile speeding through the air will become hot, not cold. Lichas should be catching on fire before he freezes and congeals. Again, the "error" is a signal of the poet for the audience to stop and ponder. In the midst of this Stoic funeral, Ovid now inserts a Lucretian allusion that seeks to explore the scientific causes behind natural phenomena. Lichas does not deserve his fate; so, arguably, will be the case with Dryope below. Hercules murders his onetime friend, and becomes a god; Apollo will rape Dryope, who will succumb to what most would consider an undeserved end. Small wonder that soon enough Ovid will consider the important question of the limits of divine power, especially in a world that may be predetermined.

Hercules prepares to mount his suicidal pyre (9.229 ff.). The surrender of his bow to Philoctetes is another presage of the coming Trojan War; Philoctetes, the honored squire, contrasts with the hapless Lichas, the last victim of Hercules' notoriously violent temper. The Stoic hero prepares for death as if he were enjoying some banquet in calm serenity (237-238). The gods take pity on Hercules' torment, and Jupiter bids them not to worry: he intends to make Hercules a god, since, after all, part of the hero is immortal and cannot be subdued by flames. The part that Alcmena gave her son will be consumed by the flames; the remaining part will reign on Olympus and, we soon learn, will be joined to a goddess—so much for Deianira, and Iole.

The passage owes something to the end of *Aeneid* 12 and the reconciliation of Juno. Jupiter observes that if any immortal should be displeased with his decision regarding Hercules, such a god would then indeed be unwilling to grant the reward, but they will recognize that it is deserved, and they will be unable to prevent it (9.256-258 *si quis tamen Hercule, si quis / forte deo doliturus erit, data praemia nolet, / sed meruisse dari sciet, invitusque probabit*). Juno recognizes that the comment is primarily directed at her, and she sorrows (261 *indoluisse*) over it, but she cannot change anything. Indeed, Jupiter carefully (and rather Stoically) presents the whole affair as being predetermined; Hercules cannot be entirely killed, since he is the son of a god (other such children, of course, die rather often in classical epic—we need but think of Zeus' own words in the *Iliad* regarding Sarpedon). Indeed, this theme will be reintroduced soon enough by Ovid later in the book, as the poet continues to explore the notion of fate, the freedom or free will a predetermined world does or does not have, the alliance of Jupiter with the dictates of fate, and the relationship between these issues and notions of transformation and metamorphosis.

Hercules had begun his career by killing Juno's serpents, and now he is compared to a serpent that has sloughed off its old skin and become as new (9.266-270). The commentators have noted the ambiguous nature of the simile; the snake has both positive and negative associations, as we have seen in both Ovid and his predecessor Virgil. The snake was, however, the beginning and end of Cadmus' Theban career, and Hercules is, after all, another Theban (cf. the significant 9.112 *Aonius*, i.e., "Theban"—only Ovid uses this Latin epithet for the hero).[17] In one sense, Hercules but shares the fate of his Theban progenitor, quasi-immortality or not. The snake-killer has become a snake; this has no basis in the mythological tradition, of course, but the poet can make his own mythology using the creative power of a simile.

I would suggest that if Hercules represents Augustus, and if we are to find some undercutting of the *princeps* in Ovid's description of the hero, then it is at least as valid to wonder if the undercutting is not necessarily of the *princeps*, but of the tenets of Stoic philosophy. Stoic predetermination, after all, is at the root of Jupiter's address to the gods about Hercules' impending apotheosis: the hero is assured of divinity according to some predetermined outcome, rather than any new decision or edict of the supreme god.[18] In the death of Hercules—or, more precisely, the death of his mortal flesh—there is a fulfillment of the Stoic belief in the virtual purgatory that purified the human soul before it could rejoin the ethereal fire whence it originated. Hercules' torments appealed to Stoic sensibilities because they seemed to represent (especially in the painfully fiery torment engendered by Nessus' blood poison) exactly the sort of purgative process Stoic philosophy preached. The Lucretian simile, and, I would argue, the ambiguous image of the serpent underscore Ovid's questioning of the veracity of Stoic doctrine. More than Augustan carping, the poet has philosophical targets here (so also Virgil in *Aeneid* 6); Ovid's concerns are now more with eschatology than politics. Criticism of Augustus, after all, would require criticism of Hercules himself, and we are hard pressed to find that in this passage. But we do find subtle hints of criticism of the Stoic program. All of this contributes further to Ovid's interest in responding to Virgil's own ultimate story of metamorphosis, namely the rebirth of purified souls in the sixth *Aeneid*.

And, after all, Hercules has weight (9.273 *pondus*) as he ascends to the heavens; he is no light spark. Atlas feels the burden. The notion that the gods are heavier than human beings is a commonplace, but it does not accord well with Stoic ideas of fiery purgation. The mention of Atlas allows for a bit of appropriate humor, too, given the audience knows the story of how Hercules had an encounter with Atlas during the quest for the golden apples at the western limits of the world; when last we met the Titan, he had been petrified by Perseus into the Atlas mountain chain; now those mountains can be imagined as feeling extra weight pushing down on their summits.

Ovid briefly describes the aftermath of the hero's "death," in a section that owes something to Euripides' *Heraclidae*.[19] Eurystheus persecuted Hercules' family, and in Ovid's next scene, Alcmena is lamenting to the pregnant Iole (who has been taken by Hercules' eldest son Hyllus) that she hopes the girl's pregnancy will be easier than her own had been (suffering as she was under the burden of Junonian persecution). Hercules' Stoic endurance owes something to his mother, we now realize; like her son, she raises her hands to heaven as she is tormented by birth pangs in her labor to deliver the mighty son of Jupiter (cf. 9.209-210 and 293).[20] Juno did not only resort to snakes in the infant's crib, but to pressuring Lucina, the goddess of childbirth, into delaying Alcmena's delivery of the destined mighty hero. Again, the emphasis is on how the Stoic hero's mother had suffered so greatly at the very outset of her son's life. Alcmena's words would have moved hard rocks (9.303-304); Ovid exactly echoes the language he used to describe the "hard" Lichas as he petrified after Hercules threw him into the sea (cf. 225 and 304).

Galanthis, the "weasel" (and so Ovid announces her transformation in advance), is one of Alcmena's attendants; she tricks Lucina so her mistress may give birth. In Ovid—and no other surviving source—the girl laughs at her successful trick, thus sealing her doom (9.316). Juno[21] effects the metamorphosis of the lying girl into the rodent, complete with the punishment that weasels would ever bear their young through the mouth. We have seen this sort of pendant passage before; Juno, one of the preeminent of Roman goddesses, the goddess who would be reconciled to the Roman founding and subsequently venerated as one of Rome's greatest goddesses, is given a small victory as the "final word" in the story. Ovid appends the story of Galanthis to allow a Junonian victory as the coda to his Herculean apotheosis. There was a Hellenistic tradition that Alcmena's serving girl became a dutiful minister to Hecate in the underworld, and that Hercules built a Theban shrine to the girl who was responsible for facilitating his birth—Ovid omits all mention of this, of course, since his goal here is to allow Juno to triumph "in the end," even if she lost in her wish to have Hercules destroyed. In another Junonian "victory," Ovid devotes very little time to Hercules in his heroic cycle. And while we lament Alcmena and her suffering at Juno's hands, we also feel no sympathy at all for Ovid's weasel-like handmaiden—a story that Ovid has somewhat altered here to suit his purposes, and a quiet introduction to other tales, that of Dryope in particular, where the poet will make significant changes to the lore he inherited.

The story of the weasel Galanthis and Juno's revenge stirs Iole as she listens to her former's husband's mother. She, too, has understood the power of transformations, since her own stepsister was changed. Ovid returns now to the central theme of the stories told in Achelous' cave: the gods have the power to effect metamorphoses, and Iole's story of Dryope is yet another illustration of the theme, as was Alcmena's Galanthis.[22] After the birth of the new hero and his brief appearance on Ovid's stage, the poet returns to his previous theme.

Ostensibly, Iole's story of Dryope is meant to balance Alcmena's tale of Galanthis, though the girl's tale is longer and more developed than the mother's. Dryope is reminiscent of Daphne; we learn that she was raped by Apollo, though later happily married to a mortal:

> . . . quam virginitate carentem
> vimque dei passam Delphos Delonque tenentis
> excipit Andraemon, et habetur coniuge felix. (9.331-333)

> . . . the one whom, though lacking her virginity
> and having suffered the violence of the god who holds Delphi and Delos,
> Andraemon took up, and he was considered blessed in his wife.

The passage is interesting. Ovid may have invented the detail that Iole and Dryope were sisters. The commentators have taken Ovid's description of Dryope's premarital sexual history as a case of *hysteron proteron*, though it possibly Ovid means what he literally says: Dryope was not a virgin, and she was subsequently raped by Apollo and then (thirdly), she was married to Andraemon, and the union was considered blessed. This is Apollo's first explicit rape in the epic; the god plays no other part in the story. This is a blight on Apollo's image in the epic, however briefly mentioned. What is intriguing is that the only known possible source for Ovid's story, Nicander, apparently told a very different tale indeed.[23] In his version, it seems that Dryope did nothing wrong; she was innocent of any wrongdoing whatsoever. She gives birth to a son, the local nymphs decide she is wonderful enough to make her one of their number, and they take her away, leaving a poplar tree in her place. Her son, Amphissos, establishes games in his mother's honor.

The argument from silence is a perilous one, but it is odd that the one extant tradition we have besides Ovid paints such a different story. Ovid's Dryope is a nursing mother; the baby is not yet one year in age (9.338). The mother has gone to a lake to pick garlands for the local nymphs, which Iole takes as evidence of her piety and reason to be indignant at her fate. She spies a lotus flower, purple in color, imitating *Tyrian* purple, to be precise—a baleful allusion. Iole is with her as Dryope picks some blossoms to offer as an object of pleasure for her baby (innocent enough, of course, though originally she was there to pick flowers for the nymphs). Iole is about to join her in picking flowers (an image of destruction, we might recall from our discussion of Persephone and her friends in Sicily). Suddenly, the sisters see the flowers bleed (344-345), and the realization comes quickly that this is a sacred place, a holy haunt the young mother has violated. The commentators duly note that Ovid here echoes the scene of the inadvertent desecration of Polydorus' grave at the beginning of *Aeneid* 3.[24] The nymph Lotis, Iole says, had assumed the shape of the flower when she was hiding from the advances of the god Priapus. Ovid was interested in the story; he discusses it also at *Fasti* 1.415 ff. There, Priapus pursues Lotis very carefully at night, trying to sneak into her nymph dwelling to rape her, exercising exceedingly cautious behavior so as not to wake up the slumbering girl. An ass begins to bray; Lotis wakes up and is able to escape, while the tumescent Priapus is left as an object of mockery (and the donkey a slain sacrifice). In the present passage, Lotis transforms herself—apparently permanently—into a water flower that Dryope has desecrated (however unintentionally). The story is reminiscent of Erysichthon, though of course so very different. Iole describes the Lotis lore in interesting terms:

> scilicet, ut referunt tardi denique agrestes,
> Lotis in hanc nymphe . . . (9.347-348)

> *Evidently, as the slow rustics still tell,*
> *the nymph Lotis was in that [flower] . . .*

Did Iole learn the story after her stepsister's transformation? Did Iole know it, but not Dryope? Would not a close friend of the local nymphs know about the famous nymph and her lotus flower?[25] What exactly is meant by *tardi*? Are the local rustics a slow and shambling lot, or are they also dull-witted? Or does the adjective mean "too late," and the passage indicate that the locals learned all too late of who was in the flower (just as Aeneas and the Trojans learned of Polydorus' fate?).[26] In any case, there is no warning, the transformation soon begins (and is an obvious punishment of the nymph). Dryope knew that something terrible had been done when she saw the blood, and she began to venerate the nymphs (9.350 *adoratis . . . nymphis*). This might well be a conventional gesture for a friend of the local goddesses who realizes that she has committed a sacrilege; in any case, the appeal is futile as the arboreal metamorphosis commences.

The transformation is among Ovid's most pathetic. The nursing infant feels his mother's milk begin to harden; soon there is nothing left of the young mother but her face (which takes a rather suspiciously long time to disappear). Enough time, in fact, is given to the Dryope-tree so that her husband and father may arrive; Iole is allowed to lament that she cannot share her sister's fate. Here I do not see a remembrance of Dido's Anna or Sophocles' Ismene, but rather a reaction to how close Iole came to sharing Dryope's fate.

But there is a reason for Dryope's pitiful and extended end. Ovid's source material apparently contained not only an innocent Dryope who had not played with any flowers, but also a celebrated figure, a woman who was honored by her son with games after she became a part of the woodland revels. In the original story, we might remark at the unique (?) nature of the honor Dryope enjoyed: how many mothers are taken into the company of the nymphs, a member of a coterie of sisters we usually associate with Diana and other virgins, would-be victims (like Lotis) of amorous gods? Apollo's first love, Daphne, had eluded him in one sense, though, in a perhaps more important way, she became his forever by virtue of the ever-youthful laurel that would be his sacred emblem. Dryope—and the association of names is deliberate—makes a powerful declaration of her innocence in Ovid, almost as if she knew the tradition Ovid had altered and had resolved to use her dying words in eloquent protest of the poet's injustice:

'si qua fides miseris, hoc me per numina iuro
non meruisse nefas. patior sine crimine poenam.
viximus innocuae.' (9.371-373)

'If there is any faith in the miserable, I swear by the divine powers
that I did not merit this unspeakable thing. I suffer penalty without crime.
I have lived innocent.'

Dryope could not make a more solemn appeal to her relatives; she uses an extraordinary two future imperatives (9.377 *facitote*, 378 *facitote*) to order that her son remember to drink milk and greet his mother under the tree; she also gives the timely warning about plucking flowers, and enjoins them to remember to think that all of them conceal the bodies of nymphs (380-381). This passage is the poem's most poignant and explicit declaration of noble protest against the seemingly unjust, even cruel actions of the gods. For the pathetic aspects of the metamorphosis do not erase the savagery that lies behind the victim's rape and her death because of flower mutilation. Part of the strength of Dryope's oath of innocence comes from her definition of her fate as *nefas*, truly an unspeakable wrong. The use of the plural is not terribly unusual, though here it may have special meaning in the case of the young mother of a suckling. In the perfect *viximus* we see both an aorist: "I lived innocently," and a true perfect: "I have lived innocently." Dryope's verb tense encompasses the present "transgression" and her past life. Is there something of Dido and Anna in Dryope and Iole?

I would suggest that there is a probable connection between Dryope's fate as a victim of Apollo's rape and her unjust end as a victim of Lotis' anger.[27] Like Daphne, this Apollonian amour will remain a tree, though one that in Ovid's vision—and, apparently, *not* that of his predecessors—will remain nothing save a memorial of one woman's ill fate. No laurels will be gathered here, and no son establishes memorial games to honor his ill-fated mother. Apollo's crime is effaced in the arguably greater injustice of the hapless mother's arboreal metamorphosis. In any case, Dryope is a victim of what the audience might judge to be unfair treatment, and, as we saw with the *Apollonian* fate of Marsyas, Dryope's story will soon be followed by new tales of perversion, though this time with diverse endings. The stories of Byblis and Iphis will provide similar and yet quite different "responses" to the injustice of Dryope's fate. Ovid's emphasis on that injustice is underscored by his transformation of the young man of the existing tradition into an infant.

Ovid makes clear that this transformation is a death; his language is unusually explicit: 9.392 *desierant simul ora loqui, simul esse*: "and, at the same time her mouth ceased to speak, and she ceased to exist." This is a true transformation, in the most terrible of senses; for a while the tree retains the warmth of the once living human body (392-393), but Dryope is no more, and the warmth does not linger forever. Ovid also does not make Dryope's tree anything special or memorable: the place may be sacred (but that, too, is left unnamed), but the tree is anonymous. In Nicander, Dryope had been honored with a poplar (not transformed into one); in Ovid, she *becomes* a tree and does not even merit a new species to serve as a memorial. How far distant from Daphne's honored end is the fate of this woman (and, it would seem, once again part of the point of comparison is that Dryope is not a virgin—the first detail Ovid used to describe her). This tree retains no feature of the original being, only the transient warmth—a last, silent and futile protest from the trapped and enclosed victim who is no more. As for the baby boy, he is forgotten as Ovid moves to other concerns; Ovid does not, of course, reveal the fate of Dryope's tree, which she prayed might be dried or burned if she were lying about her innocent life.

Nor does Ovid allow Iole and Alcmena much time to weep over the fate of Dryope. Suddenly, without warning, Iolaus appears at the door (9.397 ff.). He was Hercules' half-brother, the son of Iphicles, and had been a participant in the Calydonian boar hunt. Now, he is young again, having seemingly undergone a transformation that has restored his lost youth. Hebe, the goddess of youth (and ironically, a daughter of Juno) had acceded to her new husband Hercules' prayers and granted the stepbrother his lost years. Iole could not save her stepsister; her *quondam* lover Hercules is able to give life back to his half-sibling. Ovid's first point here is that Hebe is now Hercules' wife; Iole has been forgotten, just as Deianira had been before her. The presence of Iolaus at the door is a powerful indicator of Hercules' new domestic situation—and 400 *Iunonia*, of Hebe, is deliberate—Juno has been reconciled to the new god in her midst. Iole can see her fate all too clearly. And now, at this juncture, Ovid will begin one of the more extraordinary passages in the poem, a sequence that owes much to the divine machinery of the *Aeneid* and the Virgilian consideration of the powers of the gods, the mechanisms of fate and the presence of free will in a predetermined world, the Stoic questions raised by the *Herculeid* (of which Iole's story is a pendant), and the coming stories of perversion and chaos in a world that once again seems on the brink of chaos.

For Dryope, in the final analysis, would seem to have suffered because such was her fate, though she was of course unaware of her destiny (9.336 *fatorum nescia*). Iole, the one-time wife of the Stoic saint, told of the transformation of her sister that was her predetermined fate. But what if the poet had changed her fate for his own purposes? Does poetry become in itself an image of the idea that there are no predetermined outcomes—or, perhaps, that while some things cannot be changed, other things can—which is, after all, an important part of the message of the reconciliation of Juno at the end of the *Aeneid*. And just as Ovid appears to have changed the lore surrounding Dryope, so, we might note, does he alter the tradition of Hercules' stepbrother Iolaus.[28] For elsewhere, Iolaus is granted youth for but a day, so that he might be able to exact retribution on King Eurystheus. It would seem to be no coincidence that we find two altered stories in immediate succession. The poet has powers beyond fate, and here Ovid exploits them well to suit his own purpose and, ironically, underscore this book's commentary on the philosophical problems Virgil raised in the tenth *Aeneid*.

When Hebe decided to grant Iolaus extra years of life, she began to swear that this would never happen again, that her gift would not be bestowed on another (9.401 ff.). As she started to utter her oath, Themis checked her and uttered a prophecy about the future of Thebes, the city of Cadmus whose early history had dominated so much of the opening movements of Ovid's epic. The saga of Thebes, as we have seen, was among the most enduringly popular; the drama of the seven against Thebes was the premiere battle of "prehistorical," mythological antiquity before Troy. Hebe is about to make an extraordinary promise in light of what we know about subsequent mythological history: the goddess of youth envisages a world where the gods do not interfere in human affairs. Since Hercules was a Theban (and since Ovid has not yet described later Theban history), Themis predicts the future in highly allusive, oracular style: she knows it is destined that gods will interfere in the affairs of Thebes. Themis' prophecy encompasses more than just the matter of making mortals young again (which is, of course, what Medea herself did); Themis realizes that Hebe's prophecy raises important theological issues about the place of the gods in human affairs. So she starts with the notorious blasphemer Capaneus, who was slain by Jupiter's lightning bolt (404-405).[29] The famous Eteocles and Polynices are mentioned but briefly. They are allusively introduced not only to name two famous Theban figures, but also to commence Ovid's main point here, the mess of a story that is the rejuvenation of the sons of Callirhoe.[30]

Amphiaraus did not want to go to Thebes as one of the seven with Polynices who would seek to overthrow Eteocles; Amphiaraus' wife Eriphyle received a necklace from Polynices to bribe him.[31] Amphiaraus "died," as did all the seven except Adrastus (and so Eriphyle is among the women we meet in Virgil's underworld near Dido).[32] But he enjoined his sons to seek vengeance on their mother, and ten years after the original expedition, the "Epigoni" went off to avenge their fathers. Eriphyle was at her old tricks; Polynices' son had given her a robe to bribe her son Alcmaeon to join the expedition. Alcmaeon killed his mother and was pursued by the Furies. He was eventually purified, and married Arsinoe, the daughter of Phegeus, to whom he gave the fatal presents of the necklace and the robe. But he was driven mad again and left Arsinoe, eventually remarrying Callirhoe. Callirhoe wanted the two bribes and declared that she would not stay with Alcmaeon unless he produced them; not surprisingly, when the ill-fated lover returned to Phegeus, the king had his sons ready to ambush and kill his former son-in-law. Callirhoe—herself now loved also by Jupiter— begged that the supreme god grant years to her sons so that they could go and avenge Alcmaeon. Jupiter granted the request, and Hebe was expected to do her work again (9.416-417). Once again, Ovid fulfills the demands of a truly universal epic by making the briefest of allusions to as many stories as possible.

The complicated lore that Themis predicts (a wonderful test for the learned audience) serves only to point out that at some future date, the goddess of youth would exercise her powers on behalf of someone other than Iolaus. But the larger implications of the story are not lost on the immortals. There was no compelling reason why Iolaus should have been made young again; it was clearly nothing other than a favor for Hercules. And Callirhoe, too, was in the tradition another of Jupiter's amours; small wonder that she should be allowed to benefit from Hebe's skills. Aurora is the classic example of an immortal afflicted with longing for the rejuvenation of a lover, the decrepit Tithonus; Ovid notes that even Venus was worried about Anchises, a future concern (9.424-425 *Venerem quoque cura futuri / tangit, et Anchisae renovare paciscitur annos*)— the first mention in the epic of anything having to do with Aeneas lore. Civil war soon erupts in heaven, since every god has a favorite:

cui studeat, deus omnis habet; crescitque favore
turbida seditio (9.426-427)

One whom he favors, each god has; and there grows with partisanship
a noisy sedition

The scene is parallel to the debate between Juno and Venus at the council of the gods at the opening of *Aeneid* 10.[33] That council opened in the aftermath of Turnus' stunning achievements in the Trojan camp, while Aeneas was off with Evander raising allies. Jupiter had resolved the argument between his sister/wife and daughter by declaring what some would call "neutrality" or immortal nonintervention in whatever the "fates" or "destiny" of an individual hero might be, divine favorite or not. Jupiter himself would seemingly violate his own decree in the very next book of Virgil's epic, where he would ensure that Camilla was destroyed before she could destroy the Trojans, and Virgil makes explicit near the end of the eleventh *Aeneid* that Jupiter's savage will demanded that Turnus abandon his ambush and thus secure Aeneas' salvation.[34]

Here, in Ovid's miniature divine council, Jupiter asserts his time-honored position: no one can withstand the decrees of fate, and he prefers to align his positions with those of fate. In the Jovian theology that is unfolded here, the point would be that Callirhoe was *fated* to have her sons become young again. Aurora's Tithonus is not so fated, and so she will not be able to call on Hebe to restore his years. Of course, such a system only appeals to the recipient of the boon; but Jupiter can make the argument that there are numerous examples that can be adduced of favorites he was not able to help. The specific cases Jupiter raises are of the traditional three judges of the underworld, Aeacus, Rhadamanthus, and Minos. This is the first mention of the Cretan king for some time now; he is aged and despised (9.437-438), no longer the fearsome would-be invade of Athens or beloved of Scylla. The three underworld judges are all still alive, it would seem, and so the mention of the famous triad is interesting in that all three would eventually receive an honored place (though Jupiter would argue that such was their fate). Rhadamanthus and Minos were brothers, both sons of Europa; the generations have duly passed since the close of Book 2 and the Phoenician girl's taurine abduction. The gods in Ovid do not put up much of a fight; they cannot deny that the three cited cases are all weary with years.

Minos had been a major character for some time in the epic, and Ovid cannot dismiss him so briefly now. A brief tale is related, a story that raises similar questions to some of the preceding episodes we have just seen: Ovid seems to have changed the "vulgate" tradition. The case in point is Miletus (9.443 ff.). Minos, Ovid says, was once powerful and fearsome, but was now so weak that he feared for his own kingdom of Crete. Miletus was a young son of Phoebus Apollo and an otherwise unknown woman, Deione. Minos was afraid of Miletus and the young man's possible designs on his kingdom, but he was unwilling to expel him for fear of causing even more trouble with the youth. But in Ovid's brief rendition of the "facts," Miletus flees of his own accord and founds the famous city in Asia Minor that bears his name; no reason is given for why the youth was apparently afraid of the aged monarch (or at least very eager to flee Crete). Miletus was handsome and desirable; the daughter of the River Meander (which Ovid had used as a symbol for the Cretan labyrinth) joins with Miletus and gives birth to twins, the girl Byblis and the boy Caunus, thus introducing Ovid's next lengthy tale.[35] It is important to note that Ovid does not make clear whether Miletus or the nymph Cyanee instigated the relationship.[36]

The story of Miletus is obscure. Antoninus Liberalis 30 preserves something of Nicander's version, also by way of introduction to Byblis lore. But there, Milteus fled Crete because Minos had sexual designs on the youth. Pseudo-Apollodorus (3.1.2) has a similar tale, where Minos and Sarpedon both desire the handsome Miletus, and Miletus favors Sarpedon, thus driving Minos to anger and war. Minos is on the verge of conquering his enemies when Miletus decides to flee.

Ovid either changed the story or suppressed the salient detail: Miletus was Minos' desired *eromenos*, and the young man fled in consequence of his rejection of the king's overtures. Homosexuality was always considered suspect in ancient Rome;[37] as for Minos, thanks to the story of Pasiphae's obsession with a bull, the family acquired a reputation for sexual perversion. Here, Minos' pursuit of Miletus—and his old and feeble age is probably meant to increase the revulsion—is something Ovid expects his learned audience to know from other sources. Miletus flees to Asia Minor, to Phrygia—itself a place of questionable background for a Roman audience. There, a story of perverted love will unfold, the amour of Byblis for her brother.

Byblis was well known to Ovid's audience, no doubt better known than her father. Parthenius was probably the conduit by which the story reached the Augustan elegists; Nicander also told the tale (Antoninus Liberalis 30).[38] Ovid had already alluded to Byblis' story, however briefly (*Ars Amatoria* 1.283-284).[39] Ovid introduces the story with a rare explanation for *why* exactly he is telling it: Byblis is an example for girls to illustrate the point that they should love what is allowed:

> Byblis in exemplo est, ut ament concessa puellae

> *Byblis serves as an example, that girls should love what is conceded* (9.454)

Ovid is clear here: Byblis has no business loving her brother Caunus, who is described as an "Apollonian brother" (9.455 *Apollonei . . . fratris*); we are supposed to think of the chaste relationship between the divine huntress and her immortal brother. This is not a Roman story; the foreign name of the girl and the Asian locale make this story another Ovidian example of perversion in a far-off place. We have observed that Ovid introduces this tale soon after the arguably unjust fate Dryope suffered. Dryope's story fits with Jupiter's recently enunciated views on fate; all we must say in response to a tragedy like Dryope's is that it was her "fate" to die as she did. Here, Ovid presents Miletus as the innocent victim of Minos' advances, and the undeserving father of the perverse Byblis (soon enough, an even worse figure will emerge in Myrrha, who loves her own father). The fact that Miletus is a son of Apollo makes the situation even more relevant to Jupiter's recent discussion with the immortals: being the son of a god does not free you from trouble. Further, the unspecified cause of Miletus' flight from Minos paves the way for how Byblis' brother Caunus will follow his father's example in trying to escape his obsessive, amorous sister.

Byblis might as well be one of Virgil's women in the underworld's Fields of Mourning. At first, she loves her brother without realizing her affection has inappropriate dimensions; "she is deceived by the lying shade of piety" (9.460 *mendacique diu pietatis fallitur umbra*). Ovid subtly introduces the subtext that the gods themselves have brought about this improper love; they have engendered Byblis' madness by the fact that on Olympus brothers marry sisters: Jupiter has no room to critique this relationship. The excesses of the gods, most recently typified by Dryope's unjust fate and the inadequate resolution of the debate about the nature of fate and the limits of divine favor for the gods' individual cares, are now displayed in even greater relief, as we meet a woman who yearns for exactly the same sort of relationship the supreme god enjoys. Byblis is even as jealous as Juno; if she approaches her brother and there is some more beautiful woman in his company, she is envious (463 *siqua est illic formosior, invidet illi*). Byblis realizes that there is a crucial distinction between siblings and lovers (something the Olympians do not seem ever to consider); she laments when Caunus calls her "sister," and prefers her given name (466-467). She prefers to call her brother her "master" (466 *dominus*), a word that is harmless enough as a salutation, though it spells doom for her future in its evocation of her future wish that Caunus might be her erotic *dominus*.[40] Byblis is in fact very concerned with names and labels; soon enough she wishes that her name might be changed, as if that would suffice to allow for her incest (487 *si liceat mutato nomine iungi*).

Byblis knows that what she is feeling is wrong (as does Ovid, who refers to the girl's longing as an "obscene expectation" at 9.468 *spes . . . obscenas*; cf. 509 *obscenae procul hinc discedite flammae*); she blushes in her sleep when she dreams of sexual union with Caunus. She wakes from her dreams and wishes they would not come true (474 *quam nolim rata sit*); she takes comfort in the idea that she can enjoy her forbidden longing in the privacy and quiet of night, in her world of dreams (479-481). Like Ovid reproaching the dawn in his *Amores*, Byblis laments that the night is too short for the extreme pleasures she experiences as she imagines lustful congress with Caunus; she invokes Venus and Cupid, though this mad obsession has been credited to no immortal. Later, in her letter to her brother, she will attest that she did everything she could to flee the "violent arms of Cupid" (543-544 *pugnavique diu violenta Cupidinis arma / effugere infelix*).[41] Her calling of heaven to witness (542 *sunt mihi di testes*) is reminiscent of Dryope's call for the gods to be witnesses of her innocence.[42]

Interestingly, Byblis wishes that she and her brother might have different grandparents (9.490-491); the point is that then they would different parents and thus not be siblings, but the reference to the older generation does point to Apollo: he had no manner of inappropriate relationship with his sister; had he, Byblis would certainly have used it as an example from family history. But Byblis does invoke the case of Saturn and Ops, of Ocean and Tethys, and, the climax of her ascending tricolon of divine incest, Jupiter and Juno (497-499). Byblis focuses on her dream life; she realizes that she is "forbidden" to have Caunus, and so she wonders what her sexual dreams of union with her brother can mean:

quid mihi significant ergo mea visa? quod autem
somnia pondus habent? an habent et somnia pondus? (9.495-496)

*What therefore do my dreams signify for me? Moreover, what
weight do dreams have? Or do dreams even have weight?*

Most recently, the matter of *pondus* was raised in the case of Hercules, upon whose accession to heavenly honors Atlas felt the sky grow heavier on his back. As we imagine Byblis' suitability for Virgil's *lugentes campi*, we might also think of the underworld Gates of Sleep and the dreams that are sent to men.

Byblis has an answer to her evocation of heaven's example, though we might not find it satisfactory: the gods can marry siblings because they have their own laws (9.500-501). This does not necessarily mean that the gods are not as "moral" as men (whatever that concept might mean if translated for an Augustan audience), but it does indicate the same sort of hard lesson the recent debate on fate revealed: some things cannot be changed, others can. The gods can do as they wish in this arena (not in all areas, it would seem). There is no rationale other than that they operate under different laws than mortal men. Byblis thus has no answer; she cannot reason her way to justify incest, and so she prays that the passion either dissipate, or that she die so her brother may kiss her corpse (503-504): if we had any doubts of her intentions, her pathetic wish dispels them. The reference to her death is an allusion to the "other" version of the story, the one Ovid alludes to in the *Ars*: Byblis committed suicide to preserve her honor. Again, Ovid has worked in this book with the recurring theme of changed stories and altered details as part of his reflection on the nature of fate and predetermined destiny and the poet's ability to transform traditions.

Byblis resumes citing other examples in her continuing quest to defend her obscene thoughts: the children of Aeolus married each other. Aeolus was a wind god, so his children are semi-divine, though obviously much closer to the situation at hand than the lofty Olympians. Ovid had already covered that sibling lust in *Heroides* 11, where Canace wrote to her brother Macareus.[43] Line 508 is among the most wonderfully self-referential in the epic, as Byblis asks how she even knows about the loves of the children of Aeolus: *unde sed hos novi? cur haec exempla paravi?* Byblis has apparently spent some time reading Ovid's prior works.

Dryope had spoken of the *nefas*, the true injustice, of what had been befallen her; Byblis knows that she is also contemplating a *nefas*, and she prays that she may love her brother only insofar as it is right (9.510 *nisi qua fas est*). She knows that she is embarking on a mad quest (512 *furori*; cf. 541 *quamvis intus erat furor igneus*). Byblis decides that if Caunus were to pursue her, she would not reject him, and so she will pursue him. If love (515 *amor*, perhaps best if capitalized) compels her, she will speak; otherwise, she will write a letter—a marvelous self-reference to the poet's own *Heroides*.

Ovid essentially writes a miniature version of one of his letters of heroines; Byblis had not been one of the women of that previous collection, her "place" having been filled by Canace. Ovid lingers at length over the debate Byblis has with herself; she is uncertain what to write, and she continues to draft and redraft her words to her brother. (9.522 ff.). Soon enough, Byblis has no sense of what is *fas* and *nefas*; she invites old men (551 *senes*) to worry about such questions of moral theology, and she essentially invites Caunus to abjure traditional morality and be joined with his sister (implicitly, after the example of the immortals—there is something in this tale of Byblis as inappropriate imitator of divine practice, a twist on the idea of mortal women as rivals of divine goddesses for the affections of their brother-husband gods):

> quid liceat, nescimus adhuc, et cuncta licere
> credimus, et sequimur magnorum exempla deorum. (9.555-556)
>
> *What is permitted, we still do not know, and we believe that*
> *all things are allowed, and we follow the examples of the great gods.*

Ovid's heavenly debate had been brief; Byblis' verse epistle as the newest of the *heroides* further explores and refines issues first raised in Jupiter's council with his fellow divinities. Byblis' words are usually taken to mean that because of their youth, she and her brother have a justification for not knowing what is permitted; it is as if they have not yet reached the age of reason. She has of course proven this view wrong by her previous thoughts and the varied expressions of her tortured mind thus far, but the lines have more universal resonance than simply the judgment of a single mad girl: certainly if mortals follow the example of the gods (starting with the practice of sibling incest), than it would seem that all things are indeed permitted—except, Jupiter would have us believe, that which is contrary to fate. Again, after the outrageous fate of Dryope, which would seem to call into question fundamental assumptions about justice and the expectations of the gods for mortal behavior, Ovid presents us with Byblis, who makes the perhaps legitimate argument that her outrageous request of her brother is, after all, merely following divine precedent.

Deianira had heard about Hercules' affair with Iole from Rumor; Lichas, however, had transported the fatal shirt to the hero. Now, a nameless go-between brings the letter of the sister to her brother (9.568 ff.). Ovid closes a ring now with that previous story. Hercules had killed Lichas because he blamed the herald for having brought the clothing that spelled the hero's doom; now Caunus threatens to kill the messenger who brought the fateful letter from Byblis (576-579). Caunus, it would seem, has not lost his sense of right; he cannot even bring himself to read the entire letter. Further, when Hercules had thrown Lichas into the sea, Ovid had described the fall of the herald through the air to the freezing and congealing of water into snow and hail. Now, when Byblis' messenger returns with the news of Caunus' anger, Byblis is filled with icy chill (582 *et pavet obsessum glaciali frigore corpus*).

It would seem a foregone conclusion that it is Byblis' fate not to be in happy union with Caunus; mortal siblings are not supposed to mate. An omen had warned Byblis: when she passed the writing tablet to her messenger, she dropped it (9.571-572). She remembers the omen now, and imagines that perhaps the day was poorly chosen. The conventions of Roman religious practice would have appreciated this sentiment; the issue is not necessarily what you

contemplate, but when you envisage carrying out your plan (598-600).[44] Byblis
credits the god with having warned her (599 *deus ipse monebat*); she has been
following the gods' examples, though ignoring the warnings of omen. For the
third time, Byblis mentions the word "madness" (602 *furores*); despite the divine exempla that seem to rationalize her pursuit of Caunus, she knows what she
is doing: her problem is a conventional one (she cannot help herself). Byblis
knows, even at this very late stage, that it was best not to have started the whole
process in the first place:

> nam primum, si facta mihi revocare liceret,
> non coepisse fuit. (9.618-619)
>
> *For the first thing, if it were permitted for me to call back my deeds,*
> *would have been not to have started.*

Unlike Dryope, Byblis recognized that even if she were to do nothing more, she
could never be considered innocent in her brother's eyes (9.628); she also now
blames Cupid as the god who pressed her on (624-625 *vel certe non hoc, qui
plurimus urget et urit / pectora nostra deo, sed victa libidine credar*).[45] The verb
urget was used at 8.328 by Ovid to describe how Meleager deferred his lust for
Atalanta because the *maius opus* of the Calydonian boar hunt was pressing him.
Meleager did give in to his lust, however, both in surrendering the boar's pelt to
the Arcadian girl and in killing his brothers after they insulted him.[46] Byblis
needed no god to press her on to pursue her lust; while we may consider such
deities as Cupid to be mere metaphors for human emotions, we must then decide
why sometimes the poet depicts divine interference, while at other times, as in
the Byblis story, the gods are seemingly absent.[47]

Caunus finally follows the example of his father Miletus, who had fled
Crete because of Minos' unnatural lust for him: he decides to escape himself, to
flee from his persistent sister (9.633-634).[48] Now, Byblis embodies multiple
images of madness. She is like Medea or Ariadne, abandoned by her "lover."
She is like Scylla pursuing Minos, in that she decides to head off in pursuit of
Caunus. Ovid describes Byblis' flight in terrifying terms: the women of the surrounding locale see her run off in howling pursuit, as if she were a raving Bacchant (641-644). The passage marks the return of a mad Bacchic revel; when
last we met the god he was settling into something of domestic order in his relationship with Ariadne, whose crown adorns the heavens; now the familiar old
picture returns: Byblis is as mad as those women who slaughtered Pentheus, or
the terrible story of Tereus, Procne, and Philomela (and the image also presages
the coming death of Orpheus).

Byblis covers much ground on her way to Caunus; as the commentators
note, the distance between his old and new cities is only about a hundred miles,
but the direct route involves inhospitable terrain, and the actual journey reveals
how far he wanted to escape from his sister. Appropriately, she travels through

Lycia, which Ovid identifies as the home of the Chimaera (9.647-648), the fire-breathing monstrosity whose image is a veritable symbol of Byblis' raging. At last, Byblis falls, her face biting not the dust of heroic epic, but fallen leaves, the autumnal image of death (650-651).

Byblis is a granddaughter of Apollo, the god of healing, and it is appropriate that the local nymphs who see the fallen girl take it upon themselves to try to conjure a cure.[49] Byblis cannot stop crying, and she wets the ground with her constant tears. The local nymphs give her a perpetual fountain of tears for her lachrymose lament; Ovid asks what greater gift they could have given (9.658 *quid enim dare maius habebant?*), which need not be sarcastic: Byblis will become a fountain, a water nymph of sorts, usually an object of veneration. The process of her aquatic transformation is described with three brief similes: just as drops of pitch fall from a slashed tree, just as bitumen drips from the heavy earth, and just as snow melts in the sun, so Byblis—now identified not as Miletus' daughter, but as Apollo's descendant (663 *Phoebeia Byblis*) undergoes metamorphosis into a fountain. The image of the melting snow nicely reverses the chill she had earlier experienced; the nymphs succeed in applying Apollo's medical arts to this hapless girl. Once again, as with Lichas' fatal fall, Ovid employs naturalistic images to describe fantastic events.

Not much has been made of the significance of Byblis' end. She is a rebel against the immortals, though an unintentional one; her lust for her brother is unnatural and obscene, but her points about the gods are unassailable in their validity.[50] The gods have indeed shown the way for all manner of mortal sin. In the context of Ovid's *maius opus*[51] the transformed Byblis is modeled after Virgil's Juturna, Turnus' sister.[52] After the briefest of mentions in *A*. 10, Virgil introduces the sororial water nymph as a significant character in Book 12. The parallels are of course not exact; Juturna has no sexual designs on her brother, and Turnus does not exactly flee his sister. But Juturna, a victim of Jovian rape, becomes a living image of protest and complaint against the gods as she strives again and again to help her brother and to save him from his fated end. She goes so far in these attempts that it is possible she is the author of the mysterious arrow shot that wounds Aeneas and confounds his medical doctors; Venus herself is forced to intervene and save her son from a potentially fatal wound (12.321 ff.). Aeneas would tell his son to learn of fortune from others, and true virtue from his father's example (rather ironic given the hero's divine healing); Juno tells Juturna to "learn her sorrow" (12.146 *disce tuum, ne me incuses, Iuturna, dolorem*). Once Juturna is forced to give up her help of her brother and to abandon him to his Jovian fate (just as she had suffered at the hands of the supreme god), she returns to her watery haunt, to her shedding of tears (12.886 *multa gemens*)—an appropriate activity for a water nymph.[53]

Ovid's Byblis is, arguably, not only left unpunished, but also rewarded; fountains were sacred in Roman religion, and there is no explicit mention (cf. Salmacis' pool) that the new fountain is particularly ill-omened, though the black ilex tree under which it flows is possibly baleful (9.665 *nigraque sub ilice manat*), but, more importantly, the ilex is an evergreen, and it features at the site of Horace's Bandusia.[54] Byblis has been transformed by the poet from a crazed lover of her brother, a girl who was in no control of her mad emotions, into a quiet fountain, a peaceful element of a true *locus amoenus*, who offers silent testimony by her tears not so much to the fury of a girl and her unrequited love, as to a profound accusation of the gods, a true successor to Virgil's Juturna.

Minos remains the point of reference: Miletus had fled the aged king's advances, and now word of his daughter's transformation might have been expected to arrive on the island of Crete, had not that island had its own story to tell (9.666 ff.): the tale of Iphis and Ianthe.[55] The tale is simple: Ligdus was a poor Cretan who lived a blameless life but had little money. When his wife Telethusa was about to give birth to their child, he prayed for a boy; because he was afraid of his family's impoverished condition, he ordered that if a girl should be born, the infant should be killed at once. Nothing Telethusa says or does is able to dissuade Ligdus from his awful sentence. At last, the night comes when the delivery seems imminent, and in a dream—perhaps—Telethusa sees a divine vision of Isis.[56]

We have met Isis before, in the metamorphosis of Jupiter's amour Io. Now she is in full array as a preeminent Egyptian goddess, and she is accompanied by a veritable pantheon of Egypt's anthropomorphic gods: Anubis, the barker, is there, along with Bubastis, who was conflated with Artemis,[57] Apis and Harpocrates,[58] and, of course, Isis' husband-brother Osiris (we might think of the Byblis problem once again, and the good example she gave of divine sibling love).

The whole scene, barking Anubis the jackal-headed one and all, is reminiscent of the shield of Aeneas in *A.* 8; this is the divine world that was ranged against Octavian at Actium. In Ovid's narrative, the scene is one of positive outcome for Telethusa; Isis tells her not to be afraid of disobeying her husband's orders and to raise the child (literally, that is—the Egyptian goddess gives a quite Roman instruction at 9.699 *tollere quicquid erit*). The passage rings back to the story of Galanthis; this time, Isis promises that there will be an easy delivery, that Lucina will perform her job well under Isis' helping hand (698 ff.).

Augustan propaganda aside, Isis and her cult had been popular at Rome for some time before Octavian ever arrived on the scene.[59] There would be nothing terribly unusual in a Roman girl having a devotion to Isis,[60] especially before childbirth (and Telethusa is not Roman after all), but the passage makes us wonder about the outcome of this birth. We might note that Roman husbands might object to the notion of women disregarding their orders, however savage; Isis' mystery religion is at the heart of her subversive injunction here for a wife to ignore her husband. And, we must note, in Nicander the goddess who assisted in the birth process was not Isis or any Egyptian deity, but the mother of the divine twins herself, Leto (no stranger to difficult pregnancies she).

The concept of the *pondus* or "weight" returns in Ovid's rather unsympathetic description of the child's birth: 9.704-705 *pondus in auras / expulit*. The phrase does not engender much happy feeling about the delivery. The baby was a girl of course, but the mother lies and claims it is a boy; fortunately Ligdus decides to name it after his father, Iphis, a name of common gender. The baby is raised with a lie, though a pious one (711 *inde incepta pia mendacia fraude latebant*), and, also fortunately, the child is handsome whether you thought it a girl or a boy. Here, Ovid recalls the virgin in a boy and boy in a virgin paradox of his Atalanta at Calydon:

> . . . facies, quam sive puellae,
> sive dares puero, fuerat formosus uterque. (9.712-713)

> . . . *a face, which, whether you were to attribute it to a girl,*
> *or to a boy, would have been handsome in either case.*

The scene is set: thirteen years pass, and Iphis is betrothed by her/his father to the girl Ianthe (714 ff.). The two had grown up together and, familiarity in this case bred love: 720 *hinc amor ambarum tetigit rude pectus.* Byblis had argued that she and Caunus were young, and we did not really believe it a reasonable excuse (Ovid had not divulged their ages). Here, both girls have the wound of love (720-721 *aequum / vulnus*), but, Ovid says, *fiducia erat dispar* (721): their trust or confidence was unequal.[61] Ianthe, Ovid says, thought that Iphis was a man and expected that she would have a man as her husband. Iphis, on the other hand, knows that she is a girl and despairs of being able to have the object of her passion.

We might say that Iphis is possessed of tendencies toward lesbianism, a concept that was known to the Romans, of course, though mythology is practically devoid of any lesbian relationships, and the whole matter makes only rare appearances in extant Latin literature.[62] Atalanta had a similarly gender ambiguous face, where one might wonder if there were a boy or a girl; she also participated in the manly world of the Calydonian boar hunt, where she did well. But there is nothing in *Metamorphoses* 8 to make us think that Atalanta was "mannish," what the Romans would term a *tribas*; rather, she was possessed of gender ambiguous facial features, notably a woman, but a woman who could perform ably at a man's activity.[63] Iphis, we might note, makes an argument from nature: there is no lesbianism in the animal world, and therefore there is none among humans (9.731-734). In consequence of her unattainable love, Iphis wishes that she did not exist (735 *vellem nulla forem*).[64]

Iphis utters a stunning commentary on homosexuality, since we can extrapolate from her speech that the same argument she makes about female-female unions could be made, *mutatis mutandis*, about male-male unions: even Pasiphae of Cretan shame was at least heterosexual in her orientation toward her beloved bull. Daedalus could therefore help her, but he cannot help Iphis (9.735 ff.). We can connect the presence of Isis and the Egyptian deities with this mess; they did not urge Telethusa to raise her daughter as if a boy, but they figured in the decision to deceive Ligdus, and the gender concealment was arguably the only way to save Iphis' life. The notion of what is *fas* returns: Iphis tells herself to seek what is right, what is sanctioned by nature (748 *et pete quod fas est, et ama quod femina debes*).

Byblis could visit Caunus without suspicion because of family connection; Iphis is able to marry Ianthe because they have been betrothed according to the cruel turn of fate, but nothing can come of the union, even if the gods were to lend aid (9.754 *ut dique hominesque laborent*), a reference to the origin of the problem. Iphis' successful birth seemed unlikely absent divine intervention, but the gods would seem unable to fix this problem.

The wedding day arrives: 9.760 *luxque iugalis est*; Iphis has no problem like Byblis in the sense that she must decide whether or not to approach the nuptial rites; everyone expects a wedding, and while Iphis desires Ianthe, soon enough the secret will be unavoidably revealed. Telethusa of course knows of the problem, and does what she can to delay the wedding. Ianthe, for her part, is praying for it to come: she loves Iphis, whom she imagines to be a boy.[65]

Telethusa makes her appeal to Isis. She correctly notes that Isis is the reason Iphis lives at all; she prays that Isis may heal the situation (9.775 *medere*; cf. 653 *medeantur*, of the action of the nymphs with Byblis—the healing metaphor returns). The goddess gives favorable omens; there will be help. And what exactly could the goddess do here? There is only one solution to the problem, and the audience either knows the story or can guess the ending: Isis must see to it that the girl becomes a boy. As the mother and daughter leave the temple, the girl is indeed transformed into a boy (785 ff.). A votive tablet of thanks is soon fashioned; the tablet, interestingly, says that Iphis, once a girl and now a boy, renders his gifts in gratitude for the vows he had made. We have not heard a word about this vow; we know Telethusa prayed, but Ovid did not indicate any such offering from Iphis. While it is certainly fine to imagine that the girl made prayers with her mother, it is odd that Ovid described the mother's vows at length and then has the tablet specify the girl-boy (admittedly, the recipient of the divine boon), especially after the girl had noted that nobody could change the laws of nature, that no Daedalus could solve her problem. Isis has proven her wrong of course (and the case of Teiresias, apparently unknown to her, has already illustrated the possibility of gender change in Ovid).

The details do not really concern Ovid; the old husband Ligdus is forgotten, and Ianthe—who always thought she would have a husband—gets her wish, though we must imagine she does not notice any real discernible change in her lover's appearance; at 9.786-790, Ovid describes those surface alterations, which are admittedly seemingly minor. The point he wishes to come to is the wedding, and it is an exclusively Roman affair: Juno is there, with Venus and Hymenaeus. In fact, this is one of the happiest endings of any book of Ovid's epic; certainly we have as yet never seen a book close on such a note of unremitting joy. There is no perversion here, no terrible change to crown some illicit passion; only a typical Roman wedding remains, with a shift from the gods of Egypt that made everything possible to the Roman immortals now in attendance on the nuptial liturgy.

Whatever we make of the presence of the Egyptian deities in this story, the first action they took led to a crisis that precipitated the second intervention, and the successful gender transformation concluded with an unmistakably Roman celebration of a happy marriage. We might note that the youths seem to be of the same age, which is not very Roman (but of course, Ovid might argue, we are in Crete, whether Juno is *pronuba* or not—an always convenient argument when anachronistic features that presage or evoke Roman custom cannot be pressed too far). In this case, the similarity in age helps to avoid an overtly anachronistic scene, and also allows for an emphasis on the mutual love the two youths had for each other as they were raised in close proximity and in shared tutelage. And, too, Ovid has offered an unmistakable critique of homosexuality: Iphis as girl and Ianthe as girl have no future together, since nature argues against it. And, if we situate the story in the context of the Jovian council, we could make the facile Olympian argument that it was Iphis' *fate* to be transformed into a boy, the panacea of an argument for any eventuality.[66] If the gods had not intervened, that, then, would have been Iphis' fate. The audience wants something more, and Ovid will not disappoint as we proceed through his remaining books. In the context of Ovid's virtual recreation of Virgil's *Aeneid*, it is possible that in the condemnation of homosexuality that lies at the heart of the Iphis and Ianthe story we are meant to recall the fates of Nisus and Euryalus. The second intervention of the Egyptian deities also represents something of a conquest of their earlier, perhaps inappropriate, designs.

We are lost now, perhaps still in a *Theseid*, perhaps in a *Herculeid* and its pendant episodes. There is no clue as this book ends as to the direction the poet will take, no indicator of what will follow on the blessed occasion of this Cretan marriage (where the infamy of Pasiphae's passion for a bull and Minos' lust for Miletus seems to have been erased in the happy union of the boy Iphis and the girl Ianthe).

As we turn the page and continue Ovid's unfolding universal history, his *carmen perpetuum*, Hymenaeus, the saffron-clad god who had just presided over the wedding of two blessed Cretan youths, will have darker tasks to perform, as he presides over the ill-fated nuptials of Orpheus and Eurydice. With that second wedding, Ovid will plunge his audience into the very heart of his philosophical and theological concerns regarding the afterlife, the place of the gods and men in the universe, and the dictates of fate. He will thereby offer his commentary on the haunting close of the fourth georgic, and the mystical drama of the sixth *Aeneid*. And, by way of a surprising climax, he will end the second third of his epic by finishing the drama he started at the beginning of its second half, as a beautiful huntress returns, this time to race for apples of gold.

Notes

1. Standard commentary = the fourth volume of Bömer; besides Anderson on 6-10, anglophone students often consult Hill on 9-12 (Warminster, 1999). Kenney's commentary on 7-9 for the Fondazione Lorenzo Valla is forthcoming.

2. On Ovid's Hercules see further Galinsky, G. K., "Hercules Ovidianus (*Metamorphoses* 9, 1-272)," in *WS* 6 (1972), pp. 93-116.

3. 3.15.6-7; 16.1.

4. On the passages from the tenth *Aeneid*, see further Harrison ad loc.+

5. Fr. 47 Skutsch (with detailed commentary, pp. 222-223); the Ennian passage is preserved by Cicero in *De Divinatione* 1.

6. 9.69 *Lernaeae . . . echidnae*, a nice touch given Achelous' recent story about the *Echinades*.

7. Not often mentioned in extant poetry; note Horace, *c. saeculare* 57-60, where Copia makes a return along with other personifications.

8. Ovid does not make explicit that the guests stayed up all night, but that seems likely since there is no mention of sleep (though the poet likes to hasten through these blander transitional passages).

9. No account of this story predates Sophocles' great tragedy, the *Trachiniae* (where see the very different commentaries of Easterling and Davies). Note also Pseudo-Apollodorus 2.7.6.4, etc.

10. Nessus apparently has plenty of time to remove his tunic and tell Deianira what magic the shirt will effect, all while Hercules apparently watches.

11. For the mythographic treatment see Pseudo-Apollodorus 2.7.7.5, and Hyginus, *Fabulae* 35-36.

12. For Hercules and Cacus in both Virgil and Ovid, note Schubert, Werner, "Zur Sage von Hercules und Cacus bei Vergil (*Aen.* 8, 184-279) und Ovid (*Fast.* 1, 543-586)," in *JAC* 6 (1991), pp. 37-60.

13. The appearance of both stories in the ninth unit of their respective works is probably a coincidence, though an interesting one.

14. Of course given the torture of the poison, the flames serve something of a good purpose for Hercules in hastening the process, though of course in the end it will take flames to cure the pain.

15. Pseudo-Apollodorus 2.5.11. And, with Busiris and Antaeus, the hero is recalled as the slayer of an Egyptian, besides the evocation of a gigantomachy.

16. Seneca's (?) *Hercules Oetaeus* is deeply indebted to Ovid's Hercules.

17. Some critics see a reference to Augustus in the image of Hercules becoming an object of reverence with august weight (9.270 *coepit et augusta fieri gravitate verendus*); such critics almost invariably also find some sort of Ovidian undercutting of the *princeps* in the comparison. Certainly Virgil's Hercules is a type of Augustus (though but one of several); there is no reason not to see a nod to Augustus here, faint or not, but I see no real criticism of Augustus in Ovid's brief coda detailing Hercules' apotheosis.

18. There is a hint, too, in Jupiter's speech of the debate at the divine council at the start of *Aeneid* 10, where Jupiter said that everyone would exercise their own fate.

19. Where see Wilkins' Oxford edition, with full introduction and commentary.

20. The story was Hellenistic (Nicander); cf. Antoninus Liberalis 29, though the tradition that Hercules' birth was difficult is very old (see further Bömer ad loc.).

21. Or possibly Lucina, since Ovid does not actually name the *dea saeva*, though it is reasonably clear he means the savage goddess *par excellence*.

22. Ovid's version has become the canonical one. Antoninus Liberalis 32 preserves a prose paraphrase of a story from Book 1 of Nicander's *Heteroeumena*. Relatively little has been written on the story; see further Simonetti, G., "Tecnica descrittiva delle *Metamorfosi* ovidane: l'episodio de Dafne e quello di Driope," in *RCCM* 19 (1975), pp. 95-105.

23. See Antoninus Liberalis 32.

24. Where see Horsfall, and Eve Adler's superlative discussion in *Vergil's Empire: Political Thought in the Aeneid.*

25. No mention of the lore survives outside the pages of the *Metamorphoses* and the *Fasti*. There may be a slight hint of connection between Ovid's note that the future weasel Galanthis laughed at her trickery of Lucina, and so was punished, and that in the *Fasti* Priapus is made a laughing stock for his tumescence after his failed rape of Lotis (where part of the humor is that the god is always erect).

26. So Hill, probably correctly.

27. In the boy's name Amphissos, did Ovid also see a cruel pun or similarity with Amphippos, i.e., a *desultor*, thus conjuring up images of Dryope as partner of multiple men—cf. again the odd placement of *virginitate carentem* before *vimque passam dei* already noted. Interestingly, Ovid notes that the boy's grandfather Eurytus had given him the name (9.355-356); we have seen the anger of fathers who have tried to kill daughters they considered unfaithful; are we to think that Eurytus was critical of his daughter's behavior?

28. Presuming Euripides' *Heraclidae* is reliable as representing the "vulgate" account.

29. For much of this Theban lore we must rely on Aeschylus in his *Septem contra Thebas*, where see Hutchinson.

30. A coherent account of this tangled tale can be found at Pseudo-Apollodorus 3.6.2-3.7.6.

31. In Pseudo-Apollodorus, Polynices learns about the necklace bribe from "Iphis," which may be part of why Ovid ends this book with the story of another "Iphis" and Ianthe. The whole Theban saga is redolent with the theme of civil war, of course, and so is appropriate for a Roman audience to ponder.

32. *A.* 6.441 ff., the *Lugentes Campi*. Euripides, *Supplices* 925-927 (*inter al.*; note also Pindar's ninth *Nemean*) has the version where the gods took Amphiaraus away alive, chariot and all, in a sort of rapture of a blessed soul; Ovid alludes to this version at 9.406-407.

33. Note especially Jupiter's "verdict" at *A.* 10.107-113.

34. *A.* 11.901-902.

35. The Byblis story has attracted a fair amount of scholarly attention, some of it fanciful. Note especially (with very different approaches Nagle, Betsy Ross, "Byblis and Myrrha: Two Incest Narratives in the *Metamorphoses*," in *The Classical Journal* 78 (1983), pp. 301-315, Janan, Micaela, "The Labyrinth and the Mirror: Incest and Influence in *Metamorphoses* 9," in *Arethusa* 24 (1991), pp. 239-256, Jenkins, Thomas E., "The Writing in (And of) Ovid's Byblis Episode," in *Harvard Studies in Classical Philology* 100 (2000), pp. 439-451, Shilpa, Raval, "A Lover's Discourse: Byblis in Metamorphoses 9," in Arethusa 34 (2001), pp. 285-311. and "Rhétorique élégiaque et ruse de la passion

dans la lettre de Byblis (Ovide, *Mét*. IX, 454-665)," in Laurence, P., and Guillaumont, F., eds., *Epistulae Antiquae IV: Actes du IVe Colloque international l'épistolaire antique et ses prolongements européens (Universitaire de Tours, 1er-3 déc. 2004)*, Louvain-Paris: Peeters, 2006, p. 125-145.

36. *Pace* Anderson ad loc., who makes Miletus the aggressor, either by rape or seduction.

37. The subject is fraught with controversy (and an overdose of Foucault). The most helpful overview is Williams, Craig, *Roman Homosexuality: Ideologies of Masculinity in Classical Antiquity*, New York: Oxford University Press, 1999 (second edition, 2010, with foreword by Martha Nussbaum), though the reviews here are especially important; note, e.g., N. Endres' appraisal at *AJPhil* 122.1 (2001), pp. 143-147. Essentially, the Romans cared about who penetrated whom, and about the citizenship of the penetrated. Adrian Goldsworthy is correct in his laconic view that despite arguments to the contrary, "dislike of homosexuality was fairly widespread in most social classes at Rome, and it was seen as something that weakened men" (*Caesar: Life of a Colossus*, New Heaven: Yale University Press, 2006, p. 67).

38. *Erotica pathemata* 11 (where see Lightfoot). Note also White, H., "Parthenius and the Story of Byblis," in *CL* 2 (1982), pp. 185-192, which examines the fragments of Nicaenetus cited by Parthenius ad loc.

39. Where see Hollis; note also Hyginus, *Fabulae* 243.

40. See further the short note of Knox, Peter E., "Ovid, *Metamorphoses* 9.466," in *The Classical Quarterly* N. S. 34.2 (1984), p. 489, on the meaning of Byblis' use of *dominus*.

41. And cf. 9.553 *conveniens Venus est annis temeraria nostris*, where Byblis observes that a reckless Venus is appropriate for her and her brother's youth.

42. Cf. 9.624-625, where Byblis observes that Caunus will not believe that she has been a victim of Cupid, but will instead think she is depraved by her own lust.

43. The verse epistle has attracted even more attention than the Byblis story; note Williams, Gareth, "Ovid's Canace: Dramatic Irony in *Heroides* 11," in *The Classical Quarterly* N. S. 42.1 (1992), pp. 201-209, Casali, Sergio, "Tragic Irony in Ovid, *Heroides* 9 and 11," in *The Classical Quarterly* N. S. 45.2 (1995), pp. 505-511, Phillippides, Katerina, "Canace Misunderstood: Ovid's *Heroides* XI," in *Mnemosyne* 49.4 (1996), pp. 426-439, and Casali, Sergio, "Ovid's Canace and Euripides' *Aeolus*: Two Notes on *Heroides* 11," in *Mnemosyne* 51.6 (1998), pp. 700-710; Reesen has a commentary on *Heroides* 11, 13, and 14 (Leiden: Brill, 2001).

44. The whole matter is of special interest to the poet of the *Fasti*.

45. I.e., Caunus will now think that she has been conquered by her own lust, not that she has been the victim of the god.

46. A topos that goes back to the tradition of Thersites mocking Achilles for his reverential pity for the dead Penthesilea.

47. It is appropriate that there be no divine characters in the first major tale after the heavenly debate about fate and its evocation of the Virgilian immortal council on non-intervention.

48. Ovid signals the imitation of Miletus' action at 9.635 *Miletida*, where he refers to Byblis as the "daughter of Miletus"—the patronymic has special force.

49. Cf. the medical metaphor in 9.653 *medeantur*, most likely the correct reading of this vexed passage.

50. In a nice touch, the lovelorn girl who called her brother *dominus* is herself now a *domina* (9.665).

51. And the aforementioned reappearance of the verb *urget* reinforces Ovid's reminders of what he is doing in these passages since the Calydonian boar hunt.

52. On Juturna see my forthcoming "*Decus fluviorum*: Juturna in the *Aeneid*," in *Athenaeum* (2011), and, from the bibliography there, note West, Grace Starry, *Giuturna*, in *Enciclopedia Virgiliana* II, pp. 764-767, *Eadem*, "Women in Vergil's *Aeneid*," Dissertation California-Los Angeles 1975, pp. 276-283, *Eadem*, "Vergil's 'Helpful' Sisters: Anna and Juturna in the *Aeneid*," in *Vergilius* (1979), pp. 10-19, Traina, A., "*Soror alma* (Verg. Aen. X.439)," in *Maia* (1991), pp. 3-7, and Perkell, Christine, "The Lament of Juturna: Pathos and Interpretation in the *Aeneid*," in *Transactions of the American Philological Association* (1997), pp. 257-286. Ovid mentions Juturna at *Fasti* 1.463-464 (where see Green) and 2.585 ff. (where see Robinson's notes).

53. In Ovid's *Fasti*, Juturna resists Jupiter and hides in hazel and water to escape his amorous pursuit; in Ovid, there is no clear indication that Jupiter ever managed to complete his conquest of Juturna, while in Virgil the supreme god grants her divine status as recompense for the rape.

54. c. 3.13.14, where see Nisbet and Rudd.

55. We have no idea where Ovid obtained this story; Antoninus Liberalis 17 has a version that he claims was part of Book 2 of Nicander's *Heteuromena*, but the account is changed even to the details of the character names, and in ways that make no clear sense in light of Ovid's extended retelling of the story. Hill and others speculate that there may have been an intermediate version; in any case, Antoninus Liberalis does not offer much in the way of help here. See further Wheeler, Stephen M., "Changing Names: The Miracle of Iphis in Ovid, *Metamorphoses* 9," in *Phoenix* 51.2 (1997), pp. 190-222, Pintabone, Diane T., "Ovid's Iphis and Ianthe: When Girls Won't Be Girls," in Rabinowita, Nancy S., and Auanger, Lisa A., ed., *Among Women: From the Homosocial to the Homoerotic in the Ancient World*, Austin: The University of Texas Press, 2002, pp. 256-285, and the superlative article of Lindheim, Sara H., "The Mapping Impulse in *Metamorphoses* 14 (and 9)," in *Transactions of the American Philological Association* 140.1 (2010), pp. 163-194.

56. 9.688 *aut stetit aut visa est*, a nice way for Ovid to offer the possibility that it was, after all, just a dream.

57. Cf. Herodotus 2.137.

58. I.e., the child of Horus, the subject of Catullus c. 74.4 and 102.4.

59. The most useful reference is Witt, R. E., *Isis in the Graeco-Roman World*, London: Thames and Hudson, 1971.

60. Though it would still be worthy of sarcastic and critical comment.

61. The English translation "expectation" or "hope" is not good for Latin *fiducia* here.

62. Latin *tribas* is really not a "lesbian" in the modern sense, but rather a woman of overtly masculine tendencies (who may well be a lesbian, of course, though that is not the case in Ovid's Iphis and Ianthe story). Cf. Martial, *ep.* 7.67, the oft-cited passage on this rarely attested (and thus easily controversial, not to say politicized) subject.

63. Cf. Virgil's depiction of Camilla, where the Volscian huntress is explicitly (if stereotypically) identified as a woman possessed of feminine tendencies—at least in the matter of appreciating and being drawn to beautiful objects of clothing.

64. Anderson is right ad loc. that this can mean both "I would wish that I were not in existence" and "I would wish I were not a female" (*pace* Bömer, and Hill). The feminine singular adjective is all the more poignant given Iphis' situation, which is all about a gender problem.

65. And again, we think of Atalanta: Ianthe loves a girl she thinks a boy, while Meleager loves a girl who has boyish features.

66. The second half of the *Aeneid* also addresses homosexuality, in the epyllion of Nisus and Euryalus, where the love of the young Trojans is situated within the context of the abolition of that which is associated with old Troy. But Virgil praises Nisus and Euryalus with a great authorial intervention that calls them blessed (*A.* 9.446-449): they are, paradoxically, the only successful couple in the *Aeneid*, as they share death and are remembered with the poet's special praise. See further my "*Pius amor*: Nisus, Euryalus, and the Foot Race of *Aeneid* 5," in *Latomus* 69.1 (2010), pp. 43-55. It is not an accident that Virgil includes the story of Nisus and Euryalus in the same book of his epic that contains the taunts of Numanus Remulus against the stereotypically effeminate Trojans. As Ellen Oliensis has correctly observed on Virgil's depiction of "homosexuality" in the *Aeneid*, the subject remains ultimately outside the poem's main concerns, since Dido and Lavinia represent alternate futures, while Nisus and Euryalus represent no future. Iphis' argument about the demands of nature is also felt in Virgil's vision of the birth of a new city. In any case, any possible inappropriateness engendered by Egypt's immortals is nicely overshadowed by the Roman deities' attendance at a most traditional wedding as the book closes.

Chapter X

And Then, Veiled in Saffron . . .

With the tenth book of the poem, Ovid concludes the second third of his epic.[1] Ostensibly, we are still in a cycle of heroes, though as Book 9 ended, we were left with no clear sense of what direction the poet would pursue in his universal history. Hymenaeus, we quickly learn, is the bridge between books; the god of nuptial celebration wings his way from Crete to the wild regions of the Thracians, specifically the Ciconian inhabitants of Thrace, where once Boreas had taken Orithyia after his abduction of the Athenian girl (6.710). Hymenaeus has been summoned by Orpheus, and in the context of weddings, the audience is at once attuned to the story of the ill-fated union between Orpheus and Eurydice.[2] Ovid will ring this baleful union with the equally doomed union of Venus and Adonis at the end of the book.

"Orpheus" was the "author" of a voluminous quantity of celebrated literature in ancient Greece.[3] Part of the Orphic corpus was cosmogonic poetry, and, if we can believe the philosophers of late antiquity, in the Orphic vision of creation Zeus and Persephone had had an illicit relationship that resulted in the birth of Dionysus. Hera, as we might expect, was furious; she ordered the Titans to kill the child, and the infant Dionysus was cooked and devoured. A gigantomachy predictably followed; the Titans were defeated by Zeus' thunderbolts, and man arose from the ashes of the defeated rebels. As for Dionysus, his heart was saved (cf. the story of Pelops' shoulder), and a new Dionysus was born after Zeus somehow used both the organ and the mortal Semele to engender a reborn god.

In Virgil's underworld, after Aeneas arrives in Elysium on his quest to visit the shade of his father Anchises, Orpheus is the first figure he encounters: *A.* 6.645 *Threicius longa cum veste sacerdos*. In Virgil's conception of the afterlife, the appearance of Orpheus signals the beginning of his description of how souls are reborn to a new life (*A.* 6.679-683 and ff.). The idea that souls might be reborn into new bodies—a concept of obvious appeal to a poet of transformation and metamorphosis into new bodies—is unknown to Homer. Homer's afterlife admits the existence of Isles of the Blest, but his Elysium is a final resting place, not a stopover *en route* to some new beginning. The idea that souls could be reborn was attributed to the sixth century B.C. philosopher Pythagoras, a figure almost as shadowy as Orpheus. Virgil's Elysium was located under the Eridanus, the River Po (*A*. 6.659); we might recall Ovid's Phaethon and the location of his fiery end. Virgil's Orpheus does not speak, but he is accompanied by Musaeus, another figure associated with a lost body of writing. His works were connected to the rites of Demeter and Persephone; the whole evocation of such eschatological lore, philosophy that is utterly at variance with Homer's conception of the afterlife, is a useful device, of course, for Virgil to introduce his catalogue of the reborn souls that will be the future great worthies of Roman history.

Virgil's Orpheus is depicted with reverential glory at the start of the great vision in Elysium; Ovid's is a widower on the very day of his wedding (10.8 ff.). In the *Georgics*, Eurydice had been fleeing from Aristaeus when she was bitten by a serpent; in Ovid, the girl is like Persephone—accompanied by some female companions—when she is bitten in the ankle and dies. Orpheus makes his mortal laments, but since those complaints avail him nothing, he soon travels to the underworld to make his appeal to Pluto and Persephone.[4]

As Ovid's Orpheus begins his appeal to the infernal gods, he notes that all mortals are owed to the underworld: 10.18 *in quem reccidimus, quicquid mortale creamur*.[5] There is no escape from death. Interestingly, Orpheus then attests to his honesty, in language that deserves close examination:

> si licet et falsi positis ambagibus oris
> vera loqui sinitis . . . (10.19-20)

> *If it is permitted, and if you allow me to speak*
> *true things, with the wanderings of a false tongue having been put aside . . .*

Ambages: Ovid had used the same word of the wanderings of the Cretan labyrinth (8.161 *variarum ambage viarum*), in imitation of Virgil (*A*. 6.29 *dolos tecti ambagesque resolvit*). The labyrinth had stood forth as a veritable image of the underworld in Virgil's conception, an underworld that began conventionally, in geography and language that would not have aroused much protest from Homer. But in Virgil's Elysium, the arrival of Aeneas at the haunts of Orpheus and Musaeus had introduced a new vision of the underworld, an afterlife that would appeal not to Homer but to Pythagoras, to the Neoplationists, even to the Stoics: a world where souls are reborn in some process of purgation (which to the Stoics leads ultimately to union with the ethereal fire). Ovid's Orpheus asks the "traditional" underworld gods if it is permitted for him to speak the truth, to lay aside the labyrinth, as it were: to cast off the vain myths of the Homeric underworld. After all, his quest is to see Eurydice reborn; in the Homeric conception, there is no possibility of rebirth. But in the Orphic system, a second birth is no unreasonable expectation.

Orpheus here asks if it is permitted to speak the truth, thus implying that possibly it is not; he asks that lies may be put aside, thus implying that others have lied. On the surface, Orpheus is discussing the reason why he has visited the court of the infernal deities. Orpheus pledges that he has not come as a hero in pursuit of Cerberus—a reminder of the recent *Herculeid*. Rather, he has come for his wife, whose "growing years" (10.24 *crescentesque . . . annos*) were taken away from her, a reference to the recent immortal debate about the powers of the gods to give youth and rejuvenation. Eurydice was not even yet fully grown when she was snatched from her new husband. Indeed, the theme of mendacity is further underscored when Orpheus asks about the presence of *Amor* in the underworld; he says that he would have been able to endure the loss of Eurydice, had Amor not intervened to conquer him—and he wonders if Amor is known among the dead, though he imagines the god must be familiar even there, if the story of the abduction of Persephone is true.[6]

Another undertone to Orpheus' appeal to the gods is the question Ovid posed in Book 9: what of fate, and what of the powers of the gods to contravene an individual's fate? Orpheus asks that Eurydice's fate might be unwound (10.31 *properata retexite fata*), which would seem to violate the stern laws of fate (unless, of course, it happens to be Eurydice's "fate" to be restored to life); if it should not be the girl's fate to be restored (38 *quodsi fata negant veniam pro coniuge*), then Orpheus begs that he might also be allowed to die (which, again, would either be in accord or not with his "fate").

Orpheus had enormous power over song; his appeal to the gods stops all of the notorious sinners in their tortured actions: Sisyphus no longer rolls his rock, but sits on it to listen to the bard. The Danaids stop trying to fill their sieves with water. The commentators have pointed out that the song of Orpheus is not all that splendid; certainly it does not seem the sort of poetry that might move even Pluto and Persephone—though, it is good to note, we do not hear the *music* that is implied at 10.40-41 *nervosque ad verba moventem / exsangues flebant animae*. This scene is the first appearance of Pluto and Persephone since the abduction in Book 5. Ovid more or less closed the first third of his epic with the rape of Persephone; here, in the book that closes the epic's second third, he returns to the underworld divinities, the gods who now share power in infernal rule. What is more significant than the quality or lack thereof of Orpheus' song is the idea that the gods can grant the sort of request that Orpheus is making. We had just been told that such special favors could not be granted at the whim of a deity; now the idea is raised that Pluto and Persephone can make a decision about Eurydice and her "fate."[7]

The Rhodopeian hero is not supposed to turn around and look at his wife. The motif can be paralleled, but the point here is mostly that the gods have contravened the decrees of fate, and Orpheus is not to look on the contravention until he has reached the upper air. Ovid once again utilizes his flair for rapid narrative: there is no great debate in Orpheus' mind as to whether or not he should look back to see if Eurydice is following; Ovid does not say that Orpheus thought the underworld gods might have lied to him about Eurydice's salvation.[8] He looks back, and Eurydice is lost. The girl does not complain about her second death (technically, the resumption of her first, since she had not yet reached the upper air); she knows that the problem was that Orpheus loved her too much, that he could not wait to see her.

Orpheus is stunned by this "second death" of his wife (10.64 *gemina nece coniugis*). Ovid compares him to an unknown figure that was petrified by the sight of Cerberus in chains; the story must refer to the successful labor of Hercules in bringing the god to the upper world for a temporary visit to Eurystheus' court.[9] Ovid then compares Orpheus to the case of Olenos and Lethaea, a couple cursed because the wife was excessively proud about her beauty. When she offended some goddess sufficiently strongly, her husband—ever loyal—decided to try to share her penalty, and the gods decided to let them be transformed into two stones on Mount Ida.[10] The stories mimic what Orpheus himself had more or less alluded to: first, the poet had said that he had not come to abduct Cerberus, and, second, he had offered to share his wife's fate if she could not return to the upper world (in a sense, the hero's eventual death violent fulfills this wish). The second story involves divine retribution for excessive faith in one's abilities, with possibly interesting applications to the case of Orpheus.

For seven days, Orpheus waits to reenter the underworld; he is not permitted entrance (10.74 ff.). Eurydice had not blamed her husband for her second death, but Orpheus complains that the underworld gods are cruel. Orpheus is Thracian; he eventually returns to his mountain haunts on Rhodope and Haemus, and shuns the company of women. Ovid does not explain this decision; he says it was either because he had fared so badly with Eurydice, or, more positively, because he had made a vow to her and desired to maintain his loyalty to his first wife. It is the third spring (78-79, with the sun in Pisces in March), and Orpheus teaches the people of Thrace about homosexuality:

> ille etiam Thracum populis fuit auctor amorem
> in teneros transferre mares citraque iuventam
> aetatis breve ver et primos carpere flores. (10.83-85)

> *That one indeed was for the people of Thrace the author of*
> *transferring one's love to tender males and those on this side of youth,*[11]
> *and of taking the brief spring of age and the first flowers.*

We may compare Virgil, *Georgics* 4.516 ff., where Orpheus shuns all manner of love; there is no mention of ephebophilia or pedophilia in his account. Again, there can be no question that for Ovid, Orpheus' pederasty is a vice.[12] The great resident of Virgil's Elysium, the tragic figure of the close of the *Georgics*, had asked that he might speak the truth in the underworld, and what he asked for was something that contravened the usual order: he wanted Eurydice to have the chance to live again, to experience resurrection and rebirth. The gods were willing to grant the request, which the very appellant himself ruined by his disregard for instructions.[13] The gods were not supposed to grant such extraordinary favors, but the very one who made the claim that the boon of rebirth was possible is the agent of its failure. Now, in grief, the master of song becomes the teacher of the (implicitly savage) Thracians of the art of pederasty.

Orpheus is in a grove devoid of shade; he begins to sing (10.86 ff.). Soon, his song attracts an astonishing catalogue of trees, as many "characters" from the *Metamorphoses* make a reappearance for the bard's concert. The poplars are present, once the Heliades—Phaethon's mourning sisters. The linden recalls the story of Baucis and Philemon. The laurel is unmarried Daphne (92 *et innuba laurus*). The ash has been noted as a spear-wood before. The aquatic lotus had spelled doom for Dryope. Other trees can be paralleled from other stories; it is as if Orpheus is singing the *Metamorphoses*. One of the trees that arrives is the pine, which Ovid notes was sacred to Cybele, the great Trojan mother goddess, since, the poet says, it was . . .

grata deum matri, siquidem Cybeleius Attis
exuit hac hominem truncoque induruit illo. (10.104-105)

pleasing to the mother of the gods, since indeed Cylebeian Attis
cast off his manhood for this and was hardened in that trunk.

The story has deep resonance for the Orpheus story Ovid has thus far crafted, and for the Trojan origins of Rome. Nowhere else in the extant literature is there any record of Cybele's devotee Attis having been transformed into a tree of any sort, sacred pine or otherwise. Ovid was undoubtedly influenced by the great galliambic account of Attis's crazed revel and castration at Catullus c. 63.[14] Attis had discarded his manhood (Ovid's *exuit hac hominem* brilliantly alludes to this self-mutilation); here, he is also divested of his manhood, not by castration but by arboreal transformation into Cybele's pine. As we have seen, Cybele is a problematic deity for a Roman audience, despite her impeccable Trojan pedigree. The Attis-tree's presence here forms a ring with the transformation of Atalanta and Hippomenes into Cybele's lion near the end of Orpheus' song.

Besides the pine, the cypress is present, and here, too, a young man lurks: there was once a youth named Cyparissus, who was loved by Apollo (10.106-108).[15] Ovid now inaugurates a marvelous perversion of another major theme of the second *Aeneid*, the story of Sylvia and her stag.[16] Sylvia's poor animal was a household pet; the Fury Allecto had made sure that the death of the animal, slain by Ascanius as he hunted, would help to ensure the commencement of war in Italy between Trojans and Latins. Cyparissus' pet deer is quite different from Sylvia's. It is ridiculously adorned with gold, silver, and pearls; gems are mounted on its collar in a garish scene of excess.

Once again, Ovid has adopted a scene from Virgil's *maius opus*. From the early history of Italy and Sylvia's rustic deer in its sylvan haunts, so emblematic of the pure spirit of the old world Aeneas and his Trojans had invaded, we have the depiction of a deer that is fortunately huge (10.110 *ingens cervus erat*), given the amount of jewelry it is wearing. The sun had been in Pisces three times when Orpheus forsook women and began to pursue pederasty; now Cancer is the zodiac sign as the stag seeks relief from the summer heat (126 ff.). Sylvia's stag had been slain by Aeneas' son Ascanius; Cyparissus' pet deer is wounded by Cyparissus himself.[17]

Orpheus had wanted to die if Eurydice could not be saved; Cyparissus wants to be able to cry for all time (10.136 *ut tempore lugeat omni*). The death of Sylvia's stag had helped to precipitate the war in Latium; the death of Cyparissus' flashy deer will serve only to precipitate the metamorphosis of its pathetic owner. The point is not mere mockery of the epic tradition.[18] The point rather is that Orpheus' pederasty has signaled a perversion in nature, which was presaged by the story of Iphis and Ianthe. That story had ended with the "happy" ending of a marriage; Orpheus' ill-fated union with Eurydice has, in Ovid's version, produced a pederast. For a Roman audience (with critical reaction to the metamorphosis from devoted husband to boy-lover), the point in undercutting Orpheus is to call into question the philosophy he represents, a theological worldview familiar from his appearance in the sixth *Aeneid*. Lies indeed: Orpheus had preached the chance of renewal, he had claimed that he had not come to tell falsehoods, but truths. But his song has proven mendacious.

The passage also proves a perversion of Apollo and his devotion to trees. Apollo is horrified at the loss of his lover; he dedicates the cypress to his mourning and declares that the tree will always be mourned by the god, and always mourn for others. This is a replica of the Daphne passage from Book 1; there the laurel represented so much that was sacred for Rome; here the cypress is the memorial of the god's love for a boy. The cypress is the last tree that assembles for Orpheus' song; once it has arrived, the bard can begin his verses (10.143 ff.).

Calliope's song had been recalled in *Metamorphoses* 5, as we learned of Pluto and Persephone; Orpheus begins his song from Jupiter, and he invokes Calliope, his Muse-mother (10.148 ff.). Orpheus is no Ovid now: Ovid had complained at the beginning of the *Amores* that he had tried to sing a gigantomachy, but Cupid had insisted on snatching away feet so as to make epic verse into elegiac. Orpheus notes that he has often sung of Jupiter's power and the coming of order (subjects that would be laudable to an Augustan). In a reversal of the Ovidian poetic program, Orpheus declares openly that he will sing of songs in a lighter strain (152 *nunc opus est leviore lyra*): he will sing of boys loved by the gods. The audience can guess that after the mention of Jupiter, Ganymede will come; there is a nod here to Virgil's Juno, who complained about the honors accorded to the Trojan cupbearer by her pederast of a husband. Orpheus will move (rather irreverently) from the thunder-bearer of a gigantomachy to the lover of a Trojan boy. Ovid will also sing of girls who were set on fire by passions that were not natural: 153-154 *inconcessisque puellas / ignibus attonitas meruisse libidine poenam*). No penalty for the boys loved by gods (who are conceived of as passive); penalty for the active girls, women who are set on fire by lusts that are not conceded to them.

Orpheus is ultimately doomed (not just in Ovid, but in preexisting tradition) to be killed by crazed women; no accident, then, that Ovid has the singer choose the ominous theme of potentially dangerous women. We have come to a very different sort of song from what we heard on the slopes of Helicon, with the Muses and Minerva.

Significantly, Orpheus announces that this dual theme will be boys loved by gods, and women afflicted with irrational passions. By this juxtaposition, Orpheus elevates pederasty (his new pursuit) by linking it to the gods (hence the introduction of Apollo and Cyparissus).[19] Orpheus' song has affinities to the tales of the Pierides, who chose to focus on the peccadilloes of the immortals; the (heterosexual) pursuits of the deities are here forgotten.[20]

And so the song begins with Ganymede, the Trojan cupbearer.[21] This had been one of the causes of Juno's unrelenting anger at Aeneas' race; Ovid alludes briefly to Juno's fury (10.161 *invitaque Iovi nectar Iunone ministrat*). In a nice touch, Ovid has Orpheus note that Jupiter only condescended to change himself into an eagle, the bird that carried his bolts, to abduct the boy; the mention of the "lying wings" (159 *mendacibus . . . pennis*) nods to the mendacity theme from earlier in the book. The story is briefly told (there was not much to relate); Hyacinthus receives more attention.[22]

Apollo had another love; he would have taken him to Olympus if fate had granted more time (a recurrence of the theme of the immutability of destiny). The story will find a parallel at the end of the book, with Venus and Adonis: here, too, the immortal lover spends his time hunting with his *objet d'amour*.[23] Hunting is soon forgotten, however, as an erotic scene is crafted of the handsome young couple as they strip and prepare to throw the discus in the noonday heat (10.174 ff.). Apollo makes his throw, and the "Taenarian" youth runs to grab it (183 *Taenarides*). The adjective is baleful: Taenarus was an entrance to the underworld.[24] The discus bounces back from the hard earth and strikes Hyacinthus in the forehead, instantly killing him. Ovid notes the powerless of the medical god in the face of the accident; again, the passage will form a ring with the death of Adonis later in the book. Given the flower metamorphosis the audience expects, Ovid could not resist comparing the death of Hyacinthus to the droop of a dying flower.

In Virgil, the image of the dying flower first describes the death of the *eromenos* Euryalus (*A.* 9.433-437); it also describes Pallas' end (*A.* 11.66-68, of the dead would-be *eromenos* of Aeneas). Ultimately, these flower similes derive from Homer's description of the death of Gorgythion (*Iliad* 8.306 ff.), Priam's son, shot by Teucer.[25] In both Virgil and Ovid, it is used, then, to describe homoerotic death.[26] Once again, Apollo prays for death; the god notes that fate does not allow this. Apollo blames himself for the death, but he also asks what his fault actually is, unless having played with the boy and having loved him is a fault (10.200-201 *quae mea culpa tamen, nisi si lusisse vocari / culpa potest, nisi culpa potest et amasse vocari*).[27]

At 10.205-208, Apollo announces that he will always remember Hyacinthus in song, and that a new flower will be inscribed with Hyacinthus' marking, and

that one day a great hero will be linked to the same flower. The reference is to
Ajax and a story Ovid will relate at 13.396-398.[28] Merkel deleted these lines;
Tarrant brackets them as suspect, though there is no compelling reason to excise
them. Ovid proceeds to say that Hyacinthus' blood ceased to be blood, but began to be transformed into a purple flower; the color is in fact brighter, Ovid
says, than Tyrian purple. The color (and place) usually has baleful associations;
here there is no exception, since the death of a young man is memorialized in the
purple (and cf. Virgil's description of the death of Marcellus). The flower is
inscribed with the Greek exclamation αι αι in commemoration of Apollo's grief
(cf. Cyparissus' desire to lament for all time). Interestingly, besides the mention
of Ajax, Ovid also notes that the Spartans did not consider it an object of shame
(217 non genuisse pudet) to celebrate their native son's memory with the annual
festival of the Hyacinthia. It is almost as if Ovid thinks that his audience (with
its Roman prejudice) might smile at the association between the story of the
eromenos Hyacinthus on the one hand, and Ajax and the Spartans on the other.[29]

Orpheus now makes something of a sharp transition, even for Ovidian narrative. Orpheus suddenly asks if someone wonders whether Amathus (in southern Cyprus) is proud of the Cerastae and the Propoetides (10.220 ff.). There is
an altar before the gates of the Cerastae; the blood on it would seem to be of a
sacrificial animal, but Venus (the patroness of Cyprus) was shocked to learn that
the Cerastae had slaughtered strangers on the altar. The story is an allusion to
the tale of Lycaon and his lack of hospitality, the first, primeval crime of Ovid's
epic; it serves to transition us to the second of Orpheus' themes, the loves of
women who were possessed by irrational and illicit passions. Venus wants to
abandon Cyprus because of the pollution, but she decides instead to transform
the Cerastae into bulls (savage animals that match the savagery of the original
humans).[30]

Cyprus also held the Propoetides, who denied that Venus existed. These
women are said to have been the first prostitutes, and as their shame passes, they
are transformed into hard flint (10.238-242). The Latin name Cerastae probably
indicated a feminine proper name; now the Propoetides, women beyond question, are the first to engage in the selling of their bodies for profit. Women have
been introduced, then, as both the slayers of strangers and the sellers of their
bodies for money—besides being blasphemers who deny the goddess Venus'
existence (it does not seem to have occurred to Orpheus that his rejection of
women might also be offensive to the goddess). The disgraceful behavior of the
women of Cyprus offends Pygmalion, thus leading to Orpheus' next story.[31]

Ovid's Pygmalion has become the definitive version of the story, but the
tale had been told before the Augustan Age; according to Clement of Alexan-
dria, it had been the subject of a third-century B.C. treatment by Philostephanus.
Like Orpheus, Pygmalion decides to live as a bachelor because of his disgust at
the behavior of women. He is also a sculptor; his statue exceeds the beauty of
any woman (10.248-249 formamque dedit, qua femina nasci / nulla potest). The
statue is chaste (251); you would think it would want to be moved, if reverentia

did not stand in the way. The statue's ivory is emphasized (248, 255 x2, 274, 275, 283).[32] Pygmalion decorates his statue much the same way in which Cyparissus' deer was decked out; still, in language Propertius would approve, the statue was just as beautiful when it was unadorned. Pygmalion treats the statue as if it were his wife, calling it the partner of his bed (268 *tori sociam*, the phrase used earlier to describe Meleager's wife). The despicable behavior of women has driven Pygmalion to union with an ivory statue; he is a creator figure, and, in a sense, ultimately the creator of a new woman (with divine help, of course), though his new creation will be purely for his private pleasure. Scholars have rightly detected an onanistic subtext to the whole affair.

The Cerastae had sacrificed humans instead of animals; real animals, appropriately, are slaughtered to mark Venus' festal day (10.270 ff.). Pygmalion goes to the altar of the goddess to pray, and asks that he may have a wife similar to the ivory statue—the goddess knew, Ovid says, that he really wanted the statue. Pygmalion makes an irresistible prayer: if the gods can truly do anything, then they can grant this (274 *si di dare cuncta potestis*). Like wax melting in the sun, so the statue begins to warm as soon as Pygmalion returns home and begins to fondle it. A marriage is celebrated; Venus is present and blesses the new couple. After nine months, the baby girl Paphos is born, who would give her name to one of the goddess' favorite Cypriot haunts.

Falsehood and mendacity have been recurring themes in Book 10.[33] One of the biggest falsehoods, though, is the very nature of this story of Orpheus: it does not fit his announced subject of loves that are not conceded to women, of irrational passions. The ivory that is understandably mentioned several times may, I have suggested, help signal the falsehood theme: Virgil's ivory gate of false dreams may underlie Ovid's narrative. *Metamorphoses* 10 is a virtual commentary on the Virgilian Gates of Sleep.

Orpheus, the singer of the set of songs, has cast himself in the part of the gods—those who would pursue youths in the manner of Jupiter and Apollo. Now, after providing what might have been a plausible introduction to a series of tales about women and their irrational passions by way of the Cerastae and the Propoetides, he has told a story that by no means fits his declared intention. Certainly the Pygmalion story follows naturally on what has preceded; if women are so vile, why not create your own woman and indulge in an ultimately masturbatory fantasy? But Orpheus could just as easily have had his subject pursue a homosexual relationship, or declared that the behavior of women leads logically to homosexual unions.[34]

But Paphos, the child of this seemingly perfect union, has a son, Cinyras. Thus begins a story that most certainly does fit Orpheus' declared theme: the incestuous love of Myrrha for her father.[35] Just as Ovid led us from the happy story of Iphis and Ianthe, (which also involved a transformation that facilitated a wonderful nuptial union), to the tragedy of Orpheus and Eurydice and all its baleful consequences for the poet-philosopher, so now the story of Pygmalion and his statue (nameless in Ovid) will lead to the lust of Myrrha for her father

Cinyras.
The falsehood theme is underscored yet again as Orpheus begins his tale:

> . . . procul hinc natae, procul este parentes
> aut, mea si vestras mulcebant carmina mentes,
> desit in hac mihi parte fides, nec credite factum,
> vel, si credetis, facti quoque credite poenam. (10.300-303)

> . . . far from here be ye daughters, far from here ye parents
> or, if my songs were soothing your minds,
> let trust in me be absent for this part, and do not believe that it happened,
> or, if you will believe, also believe in the punishment of the deed.

The story of Myrrha was quite popular in antiquity. Pseudo-Apollodorus (3.14.4) states that it was the subject of an epic poem of Panyasis; Catullus' friend Cinna wrote a *Zmyrna*, which has survived only in fragments.[36] Significantly, it is only Ovid who draws a connection between Myrrha and Pygmalion, and it is reasonable to think that Ovid was the first to posit a connection.

Interestingly, Orpheus emphasizes how he rejoices in the fact that Thrace is so far removed from the rest of the world that it is suitably distant from the locus of such an infamy as Myrrha's incest. Thrace, of course, was the home of the savage Tereus; Orpheus, too, has been a defender of pederasty. In his view, as in the view of Pygmalion, women are the cause of the world's problems, and we might note that the singer is undergoing his own metamorphosis, from devoted lover of Eurydice to embittered misogynist.

Cupid, Ovid notes, did not engender this love of Myrrha for her father; it was one of the three Furies. In mythology those dread sisters usually avenge those who slay their parents; Orpheus acknowledges that it is a crime to hate a parent, but claims that Myrrha's crime was worse (10.314-315). Orpheus does not waste any time on the details of Myrrha's perversion; he launches right into his story with Myrrha as the desirable object of numerous suitors, a girl, however, who has eyes only for her father.[37] Once again, rapid narrative advances Ovid's purpose; Myrrha prays that her feelings might pass, but before her entreaties of the gods go too far, she wonders if her desire for her father really is a crime (323 *si tamen hoc scelus est*).

Myrrha soon advances to an argument from biology: in the animal kingdom, there is no apparent prohibition on sex with one's parents (10.323 ff.). We are reminded of the Thracian origins of Orpheus and how the bard had thanked the gods that his haunts were far removed from this land, where a girl is willing to follow the base practice of animals; Thrace has a well-deserved reputation for its own vile habits. Myrrha prays for a world without law; she complains that nature has no problem with what she is asking (we might compare the story of Iphis and Ianthe, where the problem was that nature did not allow two girls to unite in fruitful marriage).

We have observed that Ovid may be responsible for the connection between

Pygmalion and Myrrha, which would mean that Myrrha's story should be a Cypriot tale. But Ovid localizes the etiology of myrrh in Panchaean Arabia (10.307 ff.).[38] Pseudo-Apollodorus (3.14.3-4) relates that Cinyras came to Paphos and married one Metharme, Pygmalion's daughter.[39] From their union came Adonis (cf. Ovid's own account of Adonis lore at the end of this book). But Ps.-Apoll. also notes that in Panyasis, who apparently related the story of Myrrha in a fifth-century B.C. account, Cinyras was an Assyrian, and the father of Smyrna.[40] Smyrna (like the Propoetides) refused to honor Aphrodite, and so she was cursed by the goddess with a passion for her father. Ovid's Myrrha notes that in some locales, even among humans incest is permitted; she proceeds to speak in language that evokes the story of Byblis, as she observes that she would be allowed to indulge her love if she were not Cinyras' daughter (334-340). But, as we might expect in Ovid, Myrrha waffles back and forth with indecision about what her course of action should be.

Byblis' story had prepared the way for Myrrha's, though the circumstances and outcome are very different. Byblis had experienced sexually satisfying dreams of union with her brother Caunus; Myrrha chides herself that not only should she avoid physical corruption by sexual union with her father, but that she should also avoid any mental conception of such a passion. She understands that her feelings constitute madness (10.355 *furor*). She is aware that her lust is criminal (367 *sceleris sibi conscia virgo*).

In Orphic cosmogony, Dionysus was the son of Zeus and Persephone. That relationship has been barely alluded to in Ovid, but it was well established in Greek myth. Myrrha's story involves divine incest, though of a less often described sort than the far more common relationships between divine brothers and sisters that Byblis was able to adduce to defend her feelings for Caunus. Orpheus is telling a story with condemnatory language—in fact, he has used some of the poem's harshest descriptions for the unseemly nature of the tale—but he is, after all, only describing exactly what Zeus experienced with Persephone. Ovid is enjoying a joke with his learned audience; the pederast Orpheus has railed against the feelings of Myrrha, though he is the mythical singer of a quite incestuous origin for Dionysus. Further, we may note that in Orpheus' version of Myrrha's story, there is no place for Venus; Myrrha could easily have been another blasphemer who had spurned the goddess, thus meriting this punishment. But instead, Orpheus' version presents a girl who can be blamed for her own feelings. There is no immortal here to share the blame for the unspeakable crime.

Pygmalion had fallen in love with his creation; his granddaughter Myrrha has fallen in love with her creator. The one story has led directly into the other; the transition has had great significance indeed. Orpheus had warned girls not to listen to his story (10.300 *procul hinc natae*), together with parents (*procul este parentes*)—deliberate language, of course, given the nature of the story, but also odd if the tale is meant to be a warning against incest! If they must listen, though, Orpheus does not want people to believe his tale; if they must believe that it happened, then he wishes they would remember the penalty Myrrha suffered along with her sin.[41] Orpheus made no comment on the veracity of his Pygmalion story; he presented it as presumably worthy of believe. The repeated mention of "ivory" to an audience versed in Virgil's underworld and aware of the significance of the figure of Orpheus in that underworld (and in afterlife lore in general) might cause some doubts, however, about the truth of *that* tale as well—especially if Ovid really did graft Myrrha's tale on the other as no one else had ever done. Orpheus' point, in any case, is that "happy marriage" leads to doom; for did not Hymenaeus bring disaster when he sped from the happy nuptial union of Iphis and Ianthe to savage Thrace, where he brought not marital joy but disaster to Orpheus and Eurydice?[42]

Parallels also exist between Myrrha's story and the forthcoming tale of Atalanta; in both cases, a plethora of suitors awaits the girl and her father (10.356-360). In this case, Myrrha is somewhat truthful to her father: she wants a husband like him. Finally, and perhaps because of the increasing pressure from the suitors, Myrrha finds herself on the fateful night when she will decide what course to pursue. Ovid compares her to a mighty tree felled by ax blows (372 ff.); she finally decides suicide is her best option.[43] The time is night; bad things often happen under cover of darkness in classical poetry.[44] Myrrha's impromptu hanging is interrupted by her nurse, who is reminiscent of both Anna with Dido (the nurse encourages the girl's passion) and Phaedra's nurse in Euripides' *Hippolytus*.

Ovid devotes time to the discussion between the girl and her nurse; finally, the occasion for the incest arrives: the nine nights of the festival of Ceres. Ovid does not describe exactly what festival we are to envision; the ritual abstinence from sex he details as the proximate cause of Cinyras' willingness to sleep with an "anonymous" girl brought to his bed by the nurse could fit any number of (celibate) liturgical celebrations. Ovid mentions Ceres so we may remember how the story of the goddess and her daughter was at the heart of *Metamorphoses* 5; he wants us to recall that lore from the end of the poem's first third as he prepares to finish the second third of his epic.

It is midnight, and the stars hide themselves out of shame at what is about to happen, in particular Icarius and Erigone.[45] Icarius was murdered because he had learned how to make wine from Dionysus and had given the drink to some shepherds who became drunk and thought he had drugged them; they killed him. His daughter searched for her lost father, and when she learned of his death she committed suicide. The point is clear; Erigone was a pious daughter, and Myrrha should have proceeded with her suicide rather than what is about to happen. The *bubo* makes a return (its origin was also in the Ceres and Persephone myth): numerous omens warn Myrrha that her course of action is baleful. Myrrha holds on to her nurse with her left hand (10.455), another unlucky sign. Significantly, Myrrha does hesitate on the brink of the incest (462 *cunctantem*), but the nurse prompts her to pursue the wicked deed; in Orpheus' conception, Myrrha was crazed and possessed of a madness that is evidence of why women are to be shunned, but the nurse, too, is execrable: her actions also provide ample fodder for criticism of women. Here, old women and young conspire in crime. Ovid recalls the Tereus story; that wretched man had received his own innards into himself, and here, in striking language that recalls that prior story of cannibalism, Cinyras receives his own viscera on his bed, now made obscene by his daughter's presence there (465 *accipit obsceno genitor sua viscera lecto*).

Cinyras, of course, is complicit in the crime; he was willing to be unfaithful to his wife, and with a younger woman. Now, he refers to his bedmate as *filia*, as he tries to calm the fears of a woman he assumes is merely a skittish virgin. In Orpheus' conception, Cinyras—who is heterosexual—is contaminated by lust for women; his lust has led him to deflower his own daughter. The point of the festival to Ceres is that Cinyras could not even wait nine days for his wife to return to his bed; his lust for sex has led him to impregnate his own daughter, for Myrrha leaves his bed heavy with child (10.469 *plena patris*). The sex continues; Cinyras is enamored of his new paramour. When he finally realizes it is his daughter—it certainly takes him long enough to have light brought in to the room—he decides to kill her in a fit of angry passion at how she has befouled his bed. Myrrha flees (476 ff.).

The Ceres festival had been nine days; Myrrha flees for nine months, which conveniently fits her pregnancy. The child will never be born; Myrrha prays that she may be transformed in such a way that she will not be a disgrace either to the living by her continued existence among men, or to the dead by her demise.[46] The gods agree; they transform the mother and unborn child into a tree (10.479-502).

The passage is interesting for several points. It is Myrrha who prays for the metamorphosis; it does not come as a punishment *per se*. Indeed, there is honor in her tears (10.501 *est honor et lacrimis*); like the Byblis fountain, the Myrrha tree has its revered quality for the sap distilled from its bark. It will be remembered for all time (502 *nulloque tacebitur aevo*). The conclusion of this incest story is not, then, dissimilar to the previous account of a girl's love for her brother; then again, Myrrha makes a confession of her wrongdoing and is aware at the end that she has done wrong. Further, she has no desire to see her child be born; there is, in fact, not a word about Myrrha's thoughts regarding the infant, and every indication that what has brought Myrrha to the point where she prays for neither life nor death is the time for her delivery: nine months have passed, and, practically, she can no longer go on in her flight from her crime until, presumably, she delivers the child. Instead, the baby will be sealed in the bark for all time with its mother; Myrrha will not allow the evidence of her crime to see the light of day. It is, in a sense, a most effective abortion.

But the child has intentions of its own. The infant is still alive; it continues to grow as it approaches the time of its delivery, and the tree begins to swell as the fetus looks for a way out (10.503 ff.). Lucina takes pity on the tree's labor pains; soon enough the baby bursts out of the bark and falls on the soft grass, a newborn boy of exquisite beauty (510 ff.). The boy will be none other than

Adonis.[47]

Ovid notes that even Envy, *Livor*, would praise the child's appearance; the mention of personified Spite is ominous. He is compared to the naked Cupids of art, which foreshadows his story with Venus and her archer son. The passage is interesting:

> . . . sed, ne faciat discrimina cultus,
> aut huic adde leves, aut illis deme pharetras. (10.517-518)

> . . . *but, lest dress should create a distinction,*
> *either add a light quiver to the one, or take it away from the other.*

Adonis and Cupid look alike, and one should either take away Cupid's quiver (which would have prevented the story Orpheus is about to relate), or one should give one to Adonis. Since Cupid is not about to lose his trademark weapon, if we follow the suggestion here, Adonis would gain a quiver—a presage of his short-lived career in hunting.

Adonis is apparently a hunter, in fact, when Venus is accidentally wounded by her son Cupid's arrow. The goddess quickly falls in love with the exceedingly handsome young man, and, as Orpheus relates, the love would be vengeance for what had happened to Myrrha. In Orpheus' narration of Myrrha's tale, there had been no mention of the goddess' possible part in the obscene love of the girl for her father; it would be easy enough to blame Venus for any illicit love, however, and the point is that in the goddess' love for Adonis she will find her undoing.

The falsehood theme returns: Venus dresses like Diana, exactly as she did when she appeared to her son Aeneas in the first book of Virgil's epic: 10.536 *ritu succincta Dianae.* Venus forsakes even heaven as she spends all her time roaming through sylvan haunts with Adonis, careful, of course, only to hunt safe game, rabbits and does. Venus encourages her mortal lover to be a coward; she is worried that if he should hunt serious game (as Diana or, e.g., Virgil's Camilla might), he will expose himself to risk. Wolves are to be avoided; bears and boars too—and lions. The lion, Venus notes, is hateful to her: 552 *invisumque mihi genus est.* The comment elicits a story, of course, and Orpheus will proceed to tell a tale within a tale, as Atalanta races with Hippomenes and is captivated by golden apples.[48]

Myrrha was an example of a girl who had given in to an illicit, irrational passion; the product of her incestuous union with Cinyras was Adonis. In Ovid's conception, the death of Adonis will in some sense blot out the infamy of the incest; Venus, in the matter of Adonis, is depicted as also suffering from an irrational passion, the result of her son's arrow prick. The goddess will be driven to pretend that she is her divine opposite. And in the disguise of that immortal opposite, she will tell the story of Atalanta to Adonis as a cautionary tale for why he should avoid lions (or, more precisely, why she hates the animals she has just warned him to avoid).

This is the second appearance of Atalanta in the epic; it has not been long since the Calydonian boar hunt and the disastrous results of the passion of Meleager for the Arcadian huntress. Atalanta wandered off after that story, seemingly out of Ovid's epic consideration. Now she returns, and there is no mention of the previous story whatsoever; it is as if the girl of the Calydonian boar hunt had never existed.

Virgil's Camilla similarly makes a "reappearance" in the *Aeneid* after a significant absence. Camilla is introduced at the end of the catalogue of Italian war heroes in Book 7, and is then ignored for more than three books as the war in Latium rages. Finally, she reappears in Book 11, and Diana tells the nymph Opis a lengthy story, a veritable epyllion, of the background of the young woman who is about to reenter the war narrative. Diana relates the childhood and adolescence of Camilla before Virgil proceeds to the story of her exploits in battle, her *aristeia* and death. The parallel is exact: Ovid has modeled his Atalanta on Camilla, as he now reintroduces his Arcadian heroine to his epic through a divine story, in this case, a tale Venus (disguised as Diana) relates to Adonis.

We have already observed that there may well have been *two* Atalantas, the one associated with the boar hunt, the other with the famous race.[49] Ovid may well have been aware that there were two mythological women of the same name, women who shared numerous characteristics in addition to a name. But if there were indeed two Atalantas, Ovid does not seem to have been much bothered by the mythological confusion. Pseudo-Apollodorus 3.9.2 (where the Atalanta who runs the race is the daughter of Iasus, not, as in Ovid and elsewhere, Schoeneus) seems to have thought the two Atalantas were one woman. Ovid mentions Atalanta at *Amores* 3.2.29 and *Ars Amatoria* 2.185 and 3.775 as well as *Heroides* 4.99.[50]

We have noted that the story of Atalanta first appears at Hesiod, *Eoeae* fr. 73 Merkelbach-West.[51] There, Atalanta is the daughter of Schoeneus (as in Ovid); Schoeneus was the son of Athamas and Themisto.[52] The famous race with a would-be suitor is detailed; Hesiod compares Atalanta to a Harpy in her speed (and note that at Hyginus, *Fabulae* 206, Schoeneus is the father of *Harpalyce*).[53]

In Pseudo-Apollodorus, where Iasus is Atalanta's father, we have a story not dissimilar to Diana's Virgilian tale of Camilla's upbringing.[54] Iasus was a descendant of Arcas; his daughter was exposed to wild animals because her father wanted a son. She was suckled by a she-bear, and raised as a solitary huntress in the forest. Centaurs tried to rape her; she killed them. She eventually participated in the Calydonian boar hunt; she was finally reunited with her father, who wanted her to marry. She offered the idea of the race; Melanion won her with the gift of Aphrodite's apple stratagem. The two newlyweds had sex in a precinct of Zeus, who in anger turned them into lions.[55] The story that the lovers were changed into lions first appears in Palaephatus (late fourth-century B.C.?); the story seems to have been known to Hesiod.[56] Palaephatus has no explanation for the metamorphosis.

Jim McKeown wisely notes on *Amores* 1.7.13-14 that "since they are almost certainly local variants on the same legend, the two versions cannot be fully distinguished." What ultimately matters for Ovid is the celebration of the confusion in the lore that was undoubtedly felt even in his day. As Virgil did with his Camilla, so Ovid takes advantage of confused traditions to craft a metaphor for the conflicted world of the adolescent female.

As Ovid's story opens, an anonymous god warns Atalanta that she should not marry; certainly the Meleager story might have confirmed that warning. Atalanta does what many troubled women of mythology do: she runs off to the dense forest, where she shuns the world of men; the mention of her many suitors links the story to that of Myrrha, who was similarly pursued, presumably for her beauty. In Atalanta's case, the poet makes explicit mention of the girl's good looks (10.562-563). Atalanta scares off potential suitors by establishing the rules of the race: if the prospective husband can outrun her in a foot race, he may win her; otherwise, he will forfeit his life.

Hippomenes wonders why anyone would risk his life for a wife; soon he sees the naked Atalanta as she prepares to run, and he understand the willingness of many men to undergo such risks (10.575 ff.). Atalanta's racing is the Ovidian parallel to Virgil's Camilla and her *aristeia*; Ovid's Atalanta is the destroyer of men by her running, just as the exceedingly swift Camilla dispatched so many men in combat. In the context of Ovid's *maius opus*, of his evocation of the second half of the *Aeneid*, his depiction of Atalanta offers a response to Virgil's Camilla. But, in line with the poet's falsehood theme in this book, Venus is no Diana, and Atalanta is, ultimately, no Camilla.

By language and theme, Ovid also underscores that the participants in the race exhibit extreme bravery, in contrast to the cowardice to which Venus summons Adonis. The goddess cannot help but note that Atalanta was as beautiful as she was (such a claim can be made by the goddess, while for mortals such boasts would be fatal); she was as beautiful as Adonis, if he were a woman (579 *si femina fias*), a nice Ovidian nod to the recent lore about sex changes and a reminder of how Atalanta had the beauty of a virgin in a boy and a boy in a virgin.

Atalanta runs no more slowly than a Scythian arrow; Anderson ad loc. argues that Ovid may be evoking the Parthian bogeyman, which Virgil also quietly echoed for Camilla. Hippomenes watches the race; Atalanta's skimpy attire (she appears to be wearing some sort of footwear and knee ribbons of quite uncertain identification) flutters in the wind.[57] A flush comes over the girl, which Ovid describes by use of a splendid simile:[58]

inque puellari corpus candore ruborem
traxerat, haud aliter, quam cum super atria velum
candida purpureum simulatas inficit umbras. (10.594-596)

And her body took on a ruddy color on her gleaming girlish figure,

scarcely otherwise, than when over the gleaming atria
a purple awning stains the shadows with borrowed color.

Ovid employs another anachronistic simile, this one a domestic picture of sorts, quite out of place, we might think, for the race, though the contest is an attempt to domesticate this girl who had been reared by animals. The purple color is once again baleful; Atalanta is not exactly blushing, but rather she is turning reddish pink from the sun's heat and the exertion.

Atalanta speeds to her victory; the conquered runners are executed (10.599). In the mythographic versions, Atalanta chases after the suitors with a spear and stabs them as she catches them near the finish line; their heads decorate the racecourse as a warning to others. It is true that Ovid has no such detail; it is hasty, though, to conclude that Atalanta has no part in the terms or the punishment of the losers. She is, after all, *inmitis* (573 "cruel" or "pitiless"); there is no hint in Ovid that she feels sorry for these contestants, or that she loathes the whole business.[59] She is, in fact, responsible for the terms (cf. especially 572, with its solemn future imperative).

In the context of Orpheus' larger song and the bard's pederastic background, Atalanta presents an unappealing figure, a beautiful woman who lures hapless men to death for lust. Hippomenes is willing to succumb to her looks and seek to pursue her; he challenges Atalanta to contend with him, the great-grandson of the god Neptune. There is a shade here of the taunts used by some against Camilla, challenges that she should step down, for example, and contend on foot and not by horseback; the Ligurian son of Aunus (*A.* 11.700) had urged Camilla to stop trusting so much in her horse and to fight on foot—Camilla obliged him, to his doom.

Atalanta has a metamorphosis of sorts in reaction to Hippomenes' challenge. Ovid gives her an extraordinary, somewhat extended speech, where she asks which god was envious of beautiful young men (we might think of Adonis and his handsome looks), a god who could motivate such a handsome man to seek marriage—which presumably he could pursue very easily with another girl—at such a risk. Atalanta is not proud of her looks; she observes that in her opinion, the risk is not worth taking: 10.613 *non sum, me iudice, tanti.* Atalanta insists—as if to convince herself, we can be sure—that she is not moved by Hippomenes' looks, but rather by his young age.

Atalanta, who had fled marriage because of an oracle, has succumbed to Hippomenes, and without any divine intervention. Like Camilla, Atalanta had been more or less forced into her lifestyle; Camilla had no choice in her father Metabus' dedication of his infant daughter to Diana, and Atalanta had no recourse from the terrible prediction of the oracle that marriage would spell doom. Now, rather like Venus and Adonis, the young couple—we had been reminded they looked like the goddess and her paramour—are in a mutual trance of sorts. Atalanta is unmistakably struck by the young man's looks, his courage, even his descent from Neptune (10.617). Atalanta opines that Hippomenes is able to be desired by another woman, a wise girl (621-622 *tibi nubere nulla / nolet, et op-tari potes a sapiente puella*). The sentiment has not been much appreciated; Atalanta is almost implying that she is not necessarily a particularly wise girl, certainly not if she is beginning to waver in her determination not to fall victim to the oracular warning about her romantic life. In a nice touch, Ovid has his Atalanta note that Hippomenes looks rather the same way *she* did at the boar hunt:

at quam virgineus puerili vultus in ore est! (10.631)

But what a virginal visage is in that boyish face!

Hippomenes is a mirror image of Atalanta, just as Adonis is of Venus. Atalanta notes that if she were going to marry anyone, it would be Hippomenes, but, of course, the curse weighs heavily on her and so she vacillates—just as Byblis had over her brother, or Myrrha over her father.[60]

Atalanta is at a liminal stage of life, lost somewhere in adolescence; she does not know what love is, and she does not understand her feelings for Hippomenes. Indeed, for the virginal huntress, Hippomenes is her first love:

'unus eras, cum quo sociare cubilia vellem.'
dixerat, utque rudis primoque cupidine tacta,
quod facit,[61] ignorans amat et non sentit amorem. (10.635-637)

'You were the one, with whom I would be willing to join beds.'
Thus she spoke, and, as one inexperienced and touched by first desire,
what she does, she knows not; she loves, and she does not feel it is love.

The imperfect *eras* is a nice touch; Atalanta imagines that this suitor, too, will be vanquished and killed.

The assembled people, and Schoeneus, demand the race (10.638). If Atalanta were taking the time to deliver as long a speech as she just made, either spoken or silent, it is no wonder people would call for the contest to begin. In other renditions of the lore, Schoeneus was the one who devised the whole contest; Ovid has Atalanta assume responsibility. Venus now tells Adonis that Hippomenes invoked her; this prayer is a parallel to how Pygmalion similarly called on the goddess to help him with his infatuation with his statue (and note that Ovid gives the detail that Atalanta's upper back and her shoulders were *ivory*-like as her hair fluttered in the wind).[62] Venus is, of course, open to the request; she has no reason not to grant it—though again, we might note that perhaps the goddess should have noted the bravery of Hippomenes, in contrast to the pusillanimous behavior she enjoined on her lover Adonis.

Venus has a sacred grove at Tamasos in Cyprus; the grove has an apple tree that bears golden fruit (10.644 ff.). The goddess goes to the tree and fetches three golden fruits (*aurea poma*) that she secrely gives to Hippomenes, and she teaches him how to use the trick of the apples to snare Atalanta and win her hand.[63]

Here, Ovid echoes Virgil's depiction of the demise of Camilla. Just as Camilla was distracted by the gold and saffron adornment of Chloreus, so Atalanta will be distracted by Hippomenes' tossing of the golden apples.[64] In both cases, the distraction will lead to doom for the young woman. In case we had any doubt about the intended comparison to Camilla, Ovid inserts a verbal echo of Virgil's description of the Volscian huntress. The scene is the very start of the race; Atalanta and Hippomenes hear the signal and set out in breathless running:

posse putes illos sicco freta radere passu
et segetis canae stantes percurrere aristas. (10.654-655)

You would be able to think that they were skimming over the seas with dry foot and racing over the standing stalks of white grain.

The passage echoes Virgil, *Aeneid* 7.808-809, of the swift Camilla upon her entrance at the close of the catalogue of heroes in the Italian war:

illa vel intactae segetis per summa volaret
gramina nec teneras cursu laesisset aristas.

That one could fly over the tops of the untouched grain, nor would she have harmed the grass or the tender stalks in her course.

This is the closest demonstrable echo of Virgil's *Camilliad* in Ovid's Atalanta epyllion; the echo, however, is but a signal to the audience of the more pervasive correspondences between the two women and their conflicted situations.

The crowd favors Hippomenes in the race as it proceeds through its first stages; he is the underdog and the hero the assembly hopes will finally achieve victory after so many executed contestants. Atalanta herself may have been rejoicing just as much or more than Hippomenes in the favor of the crowd for the brave young man (10.659-660); she is filled with mixed emotions as she competes. Virgil, of course, while depicting Camilla's fatal distraction over Chloreus' raiment, never indicated that there was any sort of sexual awakening on the part of his Volscian huntress. Certainly Turnus was driven to extreme emotional distress by Camilla's death, and it is reasonable to posit that the Rutulian had feelings for the girl that may have extended to romantic or sexual attraction—but Camilla is a virgin to the end, and there is no wavering from her devotion to Diana's injunction of celibacy. Not so with Ovid's Atalanta, who, even as she runs—even before the apples are thrown—rejoices as the crowd favors her suitor Hippomenes.

Atalanta is the better runner, however, and so even though she tarries—again, before an apple has been thrown—nevertheless she always surpasses Hippomenes. It is almost as if she could not possibly be outrun by the youth; divine intervention was needed here to conquer her. The same is true for

Camilla, who is only defeated after the explicit intervention of both Apollo and Jupiter; the implication in Virgil is that absent such powerful immortal help, the Trojans and their allies would have been utterly routed by Camilla's Volscian cavalry.

Hippomenes is getting tired; his mouth is already dry from running so fast in the heat (10.663 ff.). He throws his first apple.

The tossing of the three apples is preserved in Hesiod; the papyrus fragment breaks off, however, where the suitor has won and is panting at the finish line. The apples appealed to the Hellenistic poets.[65] The first apple does little to check the maiden's course; neither does the second. The very speed of Ovid's narrative reflects how fast it all happened; nowhere do our sources indicate the length of the course, but the implication is that this race is a sprint.

Camilla was destroyed in part because of her distraction over the gold of Chloreus, but Jupiter and Apollo played their parts in her destruction, as also in Turnus' emotional reaction to her death and his abandonment of the ambush of Aeneas that would have spelled doom for the Trojan. In Ovid, too, Atalanta's distraction is not the sole cause of her loss; the implication of the narrative is that she would have defeated Hippomenes, even given the stratagem of the golden fruit. For after Hippomenes throws the third apple—and this time he throws it far off the course, something he might have considered doing with the other two—this time, Atalanta hesitates to think about whether she should try to retrieve it (she has two, after all). Venus makes clear to Adonis that she compelled the girl to fetch the fruit:

> an peteret, virgo visa est dubitare: coegi
> tollere et adieci sublato pondera malo
> inpediique oneris pariter gravitate moraque (10.676-678)
>
> *Whether she should seek it, the virgin was seen to question: I compelled*
> *her to pick it up, and I added weight to the apple she fetched*
> *and I impeded her equally with the heaviness of the burden and her delay*

The concept of weight, *pondus*, returns again; Venus underscores the fact that she caused Atalanta's loss, and with more than just the stratagem of the apples (which would seem to have been ineffectual minus this "extra" assistance, just as Jupiter's reversal of Camilla was followed by Apollo's aid in destroying the Volscian girl).[66]

The Calydonian boar hunt had been occasioned by Diana's anger over lack of honor; Venus now, too, is upset when Hippomenes forgets to honor her (Atalanta would not necessarily have known about the goddess' help unless her new husband had told her). Venus decides to make an example of the two of them, so that never again will she be spurned by any who seek her help.

Venus stirs up a sudden and uncontrollable lust in Hippomenes; as he and Atalanta are passing a temple dedicated to Cybele, he cannot help himself and engages in sexual intercourse in the sacred precinct (10.686 ff.). Here, too, we have a nod to Virgil's Camilla; Chloreus had been a devotee of Cybele. Of course in Virgil, after the distraction came sudden death; in Ovid, the destruction is engendered by the distraction, and comes after Venus instigates the violation of Cybele's temple precinct. It is significant—and not much noticed—that *Hippomenes* is overcome by lust; Ovid does not say that Venus afflicted Atalanta in the same way. The girl who had been warned not to marry now faces a lustful husband who cannot wait to have sex; they defile a temple with their forbidden union (689-690 *illic concubitus intempestiva cupido / occupat Hippomenen a numine concita nostro*). The temple near where the desecration occurred was founded by Echion; it is probably no accident (Ovid rewards those with long memories) that Echion was the father of *Pentheus* (3.513-514).

Cybele wonders whether to destroy the couple at once by drowning them in the Styx; instead she decides to turn them into lions.[67] The lions are not merely left to roam the wild and live together as beasts; they are tamed by Cybele's chariot, frightening to others, but completely subordinate to the Great Mother, who uses them as a mode of transportation.

No fate could be farther from Camilla's; where the Volscian huntress had been transformed into the veritable protomartyr of Italy, a heroine whose example spurs the women of Latium to risk their lives for the country, Ovid's Atalanta is transformed into a slave beast of burden—she has completed a transition from virgin huntress to animal servant, her punishment forever known as a mark of how she was the victim of Venus and Hippomenes' divinely inspired, inopportune lust. We might compare Pygmalion, too, with Hippomenes.

Venus hated Hippomenes and Atalanta for the lack of gratitude after she had shown so much favor; she now hates the lions they have become. The implication is that the lions hate her as well; Venus warns Adonis that he should only pursue animals that offer their backs in flight, never those that charge directly and face the hunter head-on (10.706-707). The lions are vicious to everyone except their master Cybele (703 *aliisque timendi*); the dumb animals would not necessarily know that Adonis is a favorite of their enemy Venus, but they will be just as dangerous in any case—and, by implication, Adonis is not any better a hunter than Venus herself.

The lions were part of Cybele's established iconography; Ovid seems to have been the first to link Atalanta and Hippomenes to the image. No doubt Virgil's Camilla and Chloreus influenced him; further, Cybele is the representative of the "old" Troy, the Troy Chloreus symbolizes in the *Aeneid*, the Troy that will be suppressed in an Italian Rome. We have moved from the ivory statue of Pygmalion to the ivory shoulders of Atalanta; both stories represent a certain falsehood: Pygmalion's onanistic love for a statue, and Atalanta's reinvention of Camilla as victim of Cybele, not triumphant heroine of Italy. The presence of the Attis tree in the audience, of course—itself a strange thing—signaled the Cybele tale that has ended the song.

Adonis learned something from the Atalanta story, and it was not fear of lions. He learned *virtus* (709), which was opposed, Orpheus sings, to Venus' warnings. Adonis learned, in short, the art of being a man; Venus had, in effect, emasculated him (just as Cybele emasculates her male devotees). In a nice ring with the Calydonian boar hunt, a boar appears (no lion), and, like the memorable victim of the earlier hunt, Adonis is gored in the groin—exactly where a lover of Venus should be fatally wounded (10.715-716). Earlier, Ovid had explored the question of fate and the limits of divine power; Venus declares that fate will not have everything according to its destined dictates (724-725 *at non tamen omnia vestri / iuris erunt*; she will have a memorial of her grief (apparently, we could argue, this boon was allowed by fate). After all, Venus observes, Persephone was once allowed to transform a girl into mint.[68] The story is a deliberate insertion of a reminder about the Ceres-Persephone lore that had been so important to the close of the epic's first third; here, as the second third draws to a close, Ovid mentions *Persephone*. The flower metamorphosis is accomplished; Ovid uses a strange simile to describe the transformation of Adonis' blood into a flower:

> intumuit sic, ut fulvo perlucida caeno
> surgere bulla solet . . . (10.733-734)
>
> *It swelled, just as a bubble is accustomed to rise, thoroughly transparent,*
> *from the yellow mud . . .*

Caelo is the reading of all the manuscripts, and has occasioned controversy; Merkel emended to *caeno*, which has had some defenders (however halfhearted) who prefer to imagine a bubble arising from mud. Anderson (who defends *caelo*) is right to underscore the originality of the simile. The comparison is unclear; Venus sprinkles the gore with nectar; the gore then somehow swells. There was a silver *bulla* on Cyparissus' deer (10.114).[69] With hesitation, I agree with Merkel (and Tarrant) in preferring *caeno* here.

More interestingly, I would argue, Ovid compares the color of the Adonis-flower (an anemone) to that of *pomegranates*, a clear evocation of the Persephone lore for those who missed the mint. Ovid thereby conclusively links the close of the epic's second third to the close of its first. Venus, rather like Apollo, cannot cure her love (Hyacinthus, Adonis). Both become flowers; both represent divine attempts to circumvent fate (cf. flower metamorphosis as rebellion against the dictates of destiny, and Persephone's condemnation to spending half a year in the underworld).

Orpheus had announced that he would sing of pederasty and of out of control girls; for the former, he told of Ganymede very briefly, and of Hyacinthus at greater length. If he were providing his arboreal audience with a balanced song, we might have had a short story, then a longer one, on the second theme. But Orpheus is less than in full control of his faculties (despite his fine stories), and after the pederasty theme, things rather fell apart, it would seem. There were two brief tales of women behaving inappropriately (the Cerastae and the Propoetides). The latter story led to the Pygmalion episode, since if women behave as terribly as Orpheus would have us believe, small wonder a man would shun them and prefer a statue. But the "offspring" of that tale (in which there was no inappropriate woman except the women who prompted the story in the first place) was the girl Paphos. She was the mother of Cinyras, the father of Myrrha, who did fit the description of Orpheus' announced second theme. And Myrrha was the mother of Adonis, which would provide a natural enough linkage to his tale. Further, Orpheus had not said he would sing *only* of the love of male gods for young men; technically his story of Venus and Adonis fits the first of his announced themes. But why should Venus tell Adonis the story of Atalanta, which would seem to have precious little to do with them, and which had no connection to Adonis lore in the tradition before Ovid?

Part of Ovid's plan is the modeling of Atalanta after Camilla, which the poet's narrative strategy accomplishes deftly and brilliantly. But it is difficult to arrange Orpheus' songs into some neat balance; if we try to align 1) Hyacinthus and 2) Adonis as the frame, then inside the frame we have 1) Pygmalion, 2) Myrrha, and 3) Atalanta, and of course Atalanta is really inside Adonis. And this does not include the minor tales. A homosexual and a heterosexual pair of god-loves = a frame for three tales of heterosexual love, of which the first ends successfully (notwithstanding its baleful descendants), and the other two more or less badly (Myrrha's tree is honored; Cybele's lions certainly less so). Ovid has given Orpheus' song no neat organizational principle. Of course Atalanta and Venus are both conceivably girls who loved that which was not conceded to them; Hippomenes and Adonis were never intended for them. And, arguably, Pygmalion was loved by the gods; Venus favored him with a tremendous boon because of his piety. But this is not very convincing. As we shall see, one of the problems with trying to organize Orpheus' song is that *it is unfinished.*

As we arrived at the end of the first third of the epic, a new world had, in a sense, been fashioned; the goddesses Minerva, Diana, and Ceres were advancing over the world, spreading both divine retribution for mortal transgressions and, in the case of Ceres, the blessings of agriculture and civilization. And, more significantly for Ovid's overall philosophical and theological concerns, a "traditional" underworld had been populated with its royal family of Pluto and Persephone.

Now, as the second third of the epic draws to its close, Orpheus, the poet philosopher of rebirth and renewal, of purgation and the hope of a better future, holds forth. He is now the master of song, not Calliope or the Muses on Helicon, but Calliope's child in the mountain wilds of a barely civilized Thrace. The solemn figure whose presence presaged the great vision of the souls of future Romans in Virgil's underworld has been replaced with a maddened pederast who fled from the tragedy of the second loss of his wife. In place of the Virgilian image of the huntress warrior Camilla, a model for Italian patriotism, we have the figure of Atalanta, dominated by Cybele and all the spirit of old Troy that must die before the coming of an Italian Rome. Ovid would seem to offer a pessimistic view of the *Aeneid*, though, of course, his own *Aeneid*—and its after-math—has not yet come.[70] But the deliberate emphasis on falsehood throughout the book calls into question many of its implications—most importantly, the truth of the philosophy Orpheus represents, with its promise of rebirth and renewal. The matter was of great concern to Virgil, who ended his fourth georgic with Orpheus and Eurydice; Ovid, at the close of the second third of his epic, returns to the underworld themes of Book 5 to present another view of the after-life—but one whose tenets he seems to reject.[71]

Orpheus had warned that his audience should not believe the story of Myr-rha, which calls into question the veracity of the story of her son Adonis as well (and, perhaps, the tale of Atalanta's race). Certainly the detail of Atalanta's sub-jugation to *Cybele* (as opposed to Jupiter) may be suspect; here Ovid is respond-ing to Virgil's *Camilliad* and his poetic predecessor's pervasive theme of the final ethnic disposition of Rome.[72] Orpheus wanted to sing of women who were given over to irrational passions; such women, soon enough, will destroy him. In *Metamorphoses* 10, Ovid presents a *lying* Orpheus, a figure who promises resur-rection but does not deliver, a singer who says he will tell of youths loved by the gods and of women given over to loves not granted them, only to tell of Pygma-lion and his ivory statue: Orpheus is a liar, as he himself admits before he sings of Myrrha.[73]

Orpheus had shunned the world of women and was in pursuit of the love of young men (or even boys); his decision will lead to his own doom, as Ovid opens the last third of his epic with the death of the philosopher bard, and as the present book ends the only certainty would seem to be that Ovid will soon relate the fate of Calliope's doomed son. The death of Orpheus will be part of an ex-plosion of Bacchic rage that seems to portend a new era of madness for the world. The death of the would-be singer of rebirth will also be part of the begin-ning of Ovid's Troy cycle, as the poet's universal *carmen perpetuum* prepares to arrive at the gates of Priam's celebrated city. But along the way, Ovid has sev-eral more tales to tell, stories that will bring us both rivers of gold and halcyon birds.

AND THEN, VEILED IN SAFFRON . . .

Notes

1. Bömer's magisterial commentary continues with his 1980 volume on Books 10-11; the Fondazione Lorenzo Valla *Metamorphoses* commentary has a projected fifth volume by J. D. Reed on Books 10-12.

2. Despite the abundant *Nachleben* of this enduringly popular tale, the earliest surviving version of Orphic failure is that found at the end of the fourth georgic, where Proteus relates the sad story of the loss and foiled recovery of Eurydice to the beekeeper Aristaeus (*G.* 4.453-527). In Virgil, Orpheus and the nymphs are angry at Aristaeus because his pursuit of Eurydice led to her demise. See further Bowra, C. M., "Orpheus and Eurydice," in *The Classical Quarterly* N. S. 2.3-4 (1952), pp. 113-126, Segal, Charles, "Orpheus and the Fourth Georgic: Vergil on Nature and Civilization," in *The American Journal of Philology* 87.3 (1966), pp. 307-325, Segal, Charles, "Ovid's Orpheus and Augustan Ideology," in *Transactions of the American Philological Association* 103 (1972), pp. 473-494, Johnston, Patricia J., "Eurydice and Proserpina in the *Georgics*," in *Transactions of the American Philological Association* 107 (1977), pp. 161-172, Jacobson, Howard, "Aristaeus, Orpheus, and the *Laudes Galli*," in *The American Journal of Philology* 105.3 (1984), pp. 271-300, Heath, John, "The Failure of Orpheus," in *Transactions of the American Philological Association* 124 (1994), pp. 163-196, and Gale, Monica R., "Poetry and the Backward Glance in Virgil's *Georgics* and *Aeneid*," in *Transactions of the American Philological Association* 133.2 (2003), pp. 323-352.

3. The scholarly literature is enormous, as is the impact of the lore on later literature and art. Students can do far worse than to start with W. K. C. Guthrie's classic *Orpheus and Greek Religion: A Study of the Orphic Movement*, London: Methuen, 1934 (second edition 1952; reprinted Princeton, 1993, with a new foreword by L. J. Alderink). For the *Nachleben*, nothing can compare to Cocteau's 1949 cinematic masterpiece, *Orphée*.

4. On the *Georgics* passage, which lies behind much of the language and style of the Ovidian, see further Thomas ad loc., and Mynors.

5. And cf. 10.32-33 *omnia debemur vobis, paulumque morati / serius aut citius sedem properamus ad unam*, and ff.

6. Throughout, the undertone is that such things as love do not exist in the underworld, since the stories about them are not true: Pluto never really abducted Persephone, and so there is no love among the dead.

7. Of course we could argue that it was Eurydice's "fate" that she might be reborn again, and her "fate" that her husband Orpheus would not follow the instructions he was given, and thus she would be lost again; but Ovid's language makes it clear that the gods have granted a request (10.46-47 *nec regia coniunx / sustinet oranti nec, qui regit ima, negare*). Pluto and Persephone are agents of fate, to be sure—but the clear implication of the story is that they have granted a boon to the worthy singer.

8. 10.56 *ne deficeret* has an uncertain subject: is Ovid saying that Orpheus was afraid that Eurydice was falling behind on the difficult journey, or is the poet saying that Orpheus was afraid that he was failing his wife by moving ahead too quickly. The point is not much different either way. More interesting is the close collocation of a form of *carpere* (10.53 *carpitur*, of the taking of the path up to earth) and *avidus* (56), of Orpheus in his eagerness to see Eurydice. Ovid seems to be recalling Virgil's description of the snatching of the Golden Bough; the Sibyl had told Aeneas to "pluck" the Bough (*carpe*

manu), but in his eagerness, the Trojan hero greedily broke it off (*avidusque refringit*). Aeneas did not do exactly what the Sibyl ordered, and so the Bough protested by its hesitation (*cunctantem*). Here, the hero's greed (*avidus*) will have deadlier consequences. The Bough was an offering for Persephone; significantly, Ovid notes first that Persephone acceded to Orpheus' request, before he mentions her husband (10.46-47). The Bough was the means for Aeneas to see his father's ghost, a feat Aeneas successfully accomplished; Orpheus fails in his mission. Of course if the afterlife is a falsehood, both men fail.

9. The tale is otherwise quite unknown.

10. The name "Lethaea" may connote the underworld stream of oblivion, though as with the previous story of petrifaction, it is unknown outside this brief account. For the name Olenos cf. Valerius Flaccus, *Argonautica* 3.204.

11. Anderson insists that *citraque iuventam* means "men," though the phrase is not really that clear; it could also be taken to mean those who are just on the verge of *iuventus*, which seems better than to imagine it means those who are just on the *other* side of youth.

12. Hill ad loc. here is very wise.

13. A disregard that Ovid characterizes in language that recalls the Trojan hero Aeneas' disregard for the letter of the Sibyl's instructions concerning the Golden Bough.

14. See further Fordyce ad loc., and Nauta, R. R., and Harder, A., eds., *Catullus' Poem on Attis: Texts and Contexts*, Leiden: Brill, 2005. The presence of the Attis-pine here may be another part of the falsehood theme that recurs throughout this book.

15. The story of Cyparissus is not paralleled in extant literature, though Bömer, and Anderson, offer some relevant speculations. It is likely Ovid had some etiological explanation for the tree in the lore available to him, though some of the details are undoubtedly his own.

16. Cf. *A.* 7.496 ff., where Ascanius shoots the helpless deer, thus inaugurating the war in Latium.

17. There is a parallel to Cephalus' slaying of Procris (note the favorite trick of first and last letters of names); there is something less than intelligent about Cyparissus' mistake, in contrast to Cephalus' situation with his spying wife.

18. A lamentably large amount of the literary criticism on Ovid always returns to this point, and rarely advances past it.

19. And, also, note that in the case of the pine, Ovid alludes to Attis because that young man sacrificed his manhood, thus becoming effeminate: another presage of the song Orpheus will now sing. Later, we shall learn that Orpheus also intends to sing of one boy loved by a goddess—Venus' Adonis—though for now, the implication is that he will sing of how male gods practice pederasty.

20. Cf. also Arachne's song from the beginning of *Metamorphoses* 6.

21. Homer knows the story (*Iliad* 20.230-237).

22. The story was old; note Euripides, *Helena* 1469 ff. (with Dale, and Allan); Nicander knew it (*Theriaca* 902 ff., with Gow and Schofield). But the only extended account that has survived is Ovid's, which, once again, has become the canonical version. Note also the fragmentary *Hyacinthus* of Euphorion.

23. Hunting is usually not a good shared pursuit for lovers; the virgin goddess' haunt is typically baleful for romance, as we saw with Cephalus and Procris. Anderson is incorrect to say that Apollo is regularly "too dainty" to hold nets, and so here we have a reversal of his usual practice; the point is that the god is willing to be the servant of the mortal and to abase himself before the object of his pursuit. There is nothing particularly unusual about having Apollo hunt; the point here is that he hunts with his potential lover.

24. Another significant Ovidian epic circumlocution.

25. The evocation of Virgil's Nisus and Euryalus is fitting in this second half of Ovid's epic.

26. Very different is the Catullan use of the cut flower imagery at c. 11.21-24, and cf. c. 62.39-47.

27. Apollo's rhetorical questions have interesting subtexts for an Augustan Roman audience.

28. Note Hopkinson ad 13.398 *nominis*.

29. The Spartan festival was a lament for how flowers die in the extreme heat of midsummer.

30. And appropriate, given that Ovid says these monsters originally had horns anyway, whence the name *Cerastae*.

31. See further Bauer, Douglas, "The Function of Pygmalion in the *Metamorphoses* of Ovid," in *Transactions of the American Philological Association* 93 (1962), pp. 1-21, Elsner, John, and Sharrock, Alison, "Re-viewing Pygmalion," in *Ramus* 20 (1991), pp. 149-153, and Elsner, John, "Visual Mimesis and the Myth of the Real: Ovid's Pygmalion as Viewer," in *Ramus* 20 (1991), pp. 154-168. The story has enjoyed an immensely popular afterlife; Rameau's *Pigmalion* is especially noteworthy.

32. We might think of Virgil's ivory gate of false dreams, even though Pygmalion's wish will ultimately be granted—Ovid may, however, be warning us that the story is false.

33. Cf., too, 10.291-292 *oraque tandem / ore suo non falsa premit*.

34. The story of Pygmalion would not then have been a suitable subject, given its preexistence and lack of any overt homosexual theme; Ovid may, however, be playing with the same idea he raised in the Narcissus story, where the title character falls in love with himself, which means that (questions of orientation aside), he is a man in love with another man, a mirror image of sorts. Pygmalion is not in love with himself, but with his creation and whatever of the artist is in the art.

35. On Ovid's Myrrha see further Clarke, W. M., "Myrrha's Nurse: The Marathon Runner in Ovid?," in *Classical Philology* 68.1 (1973), pp. 55-56, Lowrie, Michèle, "Myrrha's Second Taboo: Ovid, *Metamorphoses* 10.467-468," in *Classical Philology* 88.1 (1993), pp. 50-52, Dyson, Julia T., "Myrrha's Catabasis," in *The Classical Journal* 94.2 (1998-1999), pp. 163-167 (where Dyson well notes that Myrrha's visit to her father's bedroom evokes Aeneas' to Anchises in the underworld, which would thereby highlight another facet of Ovid's concern with Orphic lore and the Virgilian underworld), and O'Bryhim, Shawn, "Myrrha's 'Wedding,' (Ov. *Met.* 10.446-470)," in *The Classical Quarterly* N. S. 58.1 (2008), pp. 190-195.

36. See further Hollis, Adrian S., *Fragments of Roman Poetry, c. 60 B.C.-A.D. 20*, Oxford, 2007, for convenient text and commentary. Note also the mythographic versions at Hyginus, *Fabulae* 58, and Antoninus Liberalis 34. Anderson is rather blithe in saying we can ignore the influence of Cinna and concentrate instead on Ovid's poetic art; better would be to state that the subject was of clear interest to the neoterics as the ideal sort of subject for their art, and that given the length of his treatment, Ovid most probably crafted a significant challenge to Cinna's epyllion. Lyne thought that he had identified new fragments of Cinna in the Pseudo-Virgilian *Ciris*; see further Hollis, *FLP*, p. 33.

37. Anderson notes that Ovid never says that Myrrha is beautiful, so as not to provide any reason to "excuse" the incest. But the fact that the suitors have come to pursue her can be taken as sufficient evidence of her good looks.

38. Part of the point of the story from the Augustan Roman perspective is that these

sorts of things happen in the East. And, of course, Orpheus' pederasty is conveniently localized in Thrace, far too from Rome; Orpheus' comment about his celebration of the fact that Thrace is so far removed from the locus of Myrrha's incest has amusing relevance to a Roman reading about what has happened in *both* Thrace and Arabia.

39. And Pygmalion is a Cypriot king in his version.

40. Myrrha-Smyrna-Zmyrna are all the same woman.

41. 10.301 *mulcebant* is interesting; what could possibly "soften" the minds of those who hear the story of Myrrha? The point is partly that if you enjoyed the tale of Pygmalion and want to keep listening, then this story is one where you must believe not only the crime but also the punishment (so it has some "moral" after all); there is also a sly authorial comment on the nature of the audience that might take pleasure in hearing such lurid, sordid tales as that of the beautiful daughter and her lustful, incestuous cravings.

42. Cinyras would have been happy, after all, if he had not had offspring (10.298-299); the idea is a commonplace, but in the context of Orpheus' song it celebrates the idea of union without fruit.

43. The simile of the tree may be borrowed from Virgil, *A.* 2.626 ff., where it describes the fall of Troy, though the correspondences are not exact. Ovid was no doubt interested in comparing Myrrha to a tree given her ultimate fate.

44. Cf. 10.454 *et tenebrae minuunt noxque atra pudorem.*

45. Note Pseudo-Apollodorus 3.14.7, and Hyginus, *Fabulae* 130.

46. Probably a virtual translation of Nicander; see further Hollis, *FLP*, p. 32.

47. The story of Venus and Adonis has had an astonishing appeal in literature and the arts; given its popularity, it is perhaps noteworthy that there is no earlier extant version than Ovid's, save the late first/early second-century B.C. *Epitaph* of Bion, a poem of ninety-eight verses (where see Reed's Cambridge edition with full commentary; the poem is almost certainly Bion's, though some doubts persist). The work is an imitation of Theocritus' lament for Daphnis in his first idyll. Fr. Sappho 140A Lobel-Page preserves a ritual lament for Adonis. Adonis' birth from the myrrh tree is known from a fragment of Panyasis.

48. See further my *Posse putes* in Deroux, ed., 2005; note also Anderson, William S., "*Talaria* and Ovid, *Met.* 10.591," in *Transactions of the American Philological Association* 97 (1966), pp. 1-13.

49. Gantz, T., *Early Greek Myth: A Guide to the Literary and Artistic Sources*, Baltimore: The Johns Hopkins University Press, 1993, is a convenient resource for Atalanta and other stories.

50. Hill ad *M.* 10.560-707 makes the incorrect distinction that the *runner* is mentioned at *Ars* 3.775 *Milanion umeris Atalantes crura ferebat*, which alludes to the *huntress*. Hill omits mention of *Heroides* 16.265, of Hippomenes' victory over Schoeneus' daughter, *Her.* 21.123-124 (of Acontius and apples), as well as *Tristia* 2.399 and *Ibis* 369-370.

51. See here the good notes of G. Most to his Loeb edition (= fr. 47).

52. Athamas had another son, Leucon; Hesiod fr. 70 Merkelbach-West says that Leucon's daughters married the grandsons of Orchomenus, the son of Minyas. Orchomenus was a cult site for the worship of the Graces; Hesiod compares Atalanta to the Graces—commonplace enough, but perhaps indicating a connection between the grace-like Atalanta and the marriage of her cousins to descendants of Orchomenus. Note here West ad *Theogony* 907-908, and Janko on Homer, *Iliad* 14.267-270. Pausanias (8.35.10) speculates that Schoeneus may have emigrated from Boeotia to Arcadia, where he locates the *dromoi* of Atalanta near Schoenus.

53. See further Lightfoot's *Parthenius*, p. 448 n. 177. Virgil's Camilla seems to be an amalgam of Penthesilea and Harpalyce. Note that in Nonnus (*Dionysiaca* 12.71-75), "Harpalyce" kills her son after her father—Clymenus, (who is, amazingly, the son of *Schoeneus*)—rapes her. She undergoes bird metamorphosis. The Harpalyce story can be found at Parthenius 13 (where see Lightfoot); there Harpalyce kills not her son but her younger brother. Indeed, as with Atalanta, there were apparently two Harpalyces, one a huntress (cf. Virgil's mention of the girl in *A.* 1), the other a victim of incest. In all these tales of huntresses, the father is often a significant figure (Camilla, Atalanta, Harpalyce); see further my *Velocem potuit* (*Latomus*, 2008), and my commentary on *A.* 11.

54. But note that at Pseudo-Apollodorus 1.8.2, Atalanta, the daughter of *Schoeneus*, is a participant in the boat hunt.

55. For Atalanta's alleged over-sexuality after marriage (and, perhaps, even before), note Gibson ad Ovid, *AA* 3.775, with the heroine's legs in a sexual scene. Ovid was fixated on Atalanta's attractive legs almost as if he were Rohmer filming *Le genou de Claire* (cf. *Amores* 3.2.29-32). Suetonius, *Tiberius* 44.2 records that the emperor had a Parrhasius painting of Atalanta performing fellatio on Meleager—possibly a pornographic commentary on her childhood suckling by wild beasts. The painting may well have been a pornographic mockery of the virginal Atalanta (cf. the implications of Ovid's Venus— not to mention Virgil's—in the guise of the virginal Diana). Ovid's boar hunt narrative does not allow much time for any sexual congress between Atalanta and Meleager.

56. See further Merkelbach-West fr. 41, where Philodemus seems to attest to Hesiod's knowledge of the transformation.

57. 10.593 *genualia* is a *hapax*; see further Bömer, and Anderson. A Homeric scholium (fr. 74 Merkelbach-West) makes the claim that Hesiod is later than Homer because he shows Atalanta and her suitors naked; Merkelbach-West wonder where Hippomenes put the apples if he were naked, and note that our surviving fragments from the Hesiodic version of the race show Atalanta's chiton seductively fluttering in the wind, blown by the west wind around her breasts. Note further West, *The Hesiodic Catalogue of Women*, Oxford, 1983, p. 135. D'Alessio believes that Hesiod ended the books of the *Eoeae* with "truly exciting" narratives like the race (in Hunter, ed., *The Hesiodic Catalogue of Women: Constructions and Reconstructions*, Cambridge, 2005, pp. 213-216). Ovid may be imitating Hesiod in the sexually charged eroticism of the fluttering *talaria* and *genualia*. The *talaria* were associated with Mercury (almost a technical term for his winged sandals); Atalanta, like Camilla, plays a psychopomp rôle in leading men to their premature deaths.

58. On this simile note Dyson, Julia T., "Lilies and Violence: Lavinia's Blush in the Song of Orpheus," in *Classical Philology* 94.3 (1999), pp. 281-282. If Dyson is correct in her analysis, we have yet more influence of the pervasive presence of the second half of the *Aeneid* in this section of Ovid's epic.

59. Anderson rather seeks to excuse Atalanta from being directly responsible for the terrible terms the losers suffer.

60. Some scholars have imagined that Atalanta makes the whole speech to herself in silent soliloquy, which seems a most unnatural way to take the Latin.

61. Better than *quid facit* (despite the latter's great manuscript support) since the emphasis is on how she does not know the thing she was doing. See further Bömer, and Hill ad loc. But the difference is not terribly significant.

62. 10.592 *tergaque iactantur crines per eburnea*.

63. Pseudo-Apollodorus (3.9.2) makes the assertion that in Euripides, Atalanta ended up married to Hippomenes—but no fragment survives to confirm the claim. It is

unclear from the mythographer whether he means the marriage was quasi-permanent or not.

64. We might also note that Book 10 opens with the saffron-clad Hippomenes, the god of nuptial celebrations; the book more or less opens and closes with the ill-fated unions of two couples, Orpheus and Eurydice and Atalanta and Hippomenes. Neither couple is destined for nuptial bliss. The name "Hippomenes," while not invented by Ovid, may have appealed to the poet for its equine associations, given the central place of horsemanship in Camilla's *aristeia*.

65. Note Theocritus, *Idyll* 3.40-42, with Gow, and Hunter ad loc.; also Philetas, fr. 18 Powell, a quote from the scholiast on Theocritus 2.120. See further Littlewood, "The Apple in Greek and Latin Literature," in *Harvard Studies in Classical Philology* 72 (1968), pp. 147-181, especially pp. 152-153. Nonnus (*Dionysiaca* 12.87-89) also blames Aphrodite's apples for Atalanta's undoing.

66. Or, if one prefers, the intervention of Venus during the race can be joined with her forcing Hippomenes to have sex with Atalanta in Cybele's temple, thus introducing two gods into the narrative, much as two gods felled Camilla.

67. Gibson ad *Ars* 3.775 wonders if the tradition of leonine metamorphosis is a reference to "rear entry" intercourse; cf. Atalanta's apparently oversexed nature in some of the lore.

68. On the story see Strabo 8.3.14; the story is quite obscure. Apparently Menthe was a lover of Hades; Persephone trampled her and transformed her into mint. No one else preserves the tale.

69. A different sort of *bulla*, to be sure, though it is interesting that this relatively rare word occurs once at the beginning and once at the end of this book. Notably, the *bulla* was also an ornament worn by noble Roman youths, which was put aside upon maturity and consecrated to the Lares; vid. Cicero, *Verrines* 2.1.58, and cf. Persius, s. 5.30. *Dignus bulla* = "childish" at Juvenal, s. 13.33. The association is appropriate both for Cyparissus' deer and Adonis, and Ovid may have had this association in mind. Adonis give up the *bulla* in that he dies; he is associated with it forever, however, because he dies young. The birth of his *bulla* from mud may reflect the pederast Orpheus' mockery of the whole scene, but the passage has not been convincingly explicated.

70. See further Dyson, *op. cit.*, p. 288.

71. Euripides, *Alcestis* 357 seems to preserve a version where Orpheus, a true purveyor of resurrection, succeeded in bringing back Eurydice. I suspect that elaboration of the story of Eurydice's attempted recovery by Virgil and Ovid offers a different twist on an old story; Orpheus was, after all, successful in bringing Eurydice back to life even in our two Roman accounts, but the point of the poets is not so much his achievement as on his failure in following the precise instructions necessary to complete the resurrection. The fact remains that he was able to win a concession from the infernal gods. The operative theme in this book is falsehood, which covers a multitude of sins. The matter of precise execution of underworld commands is also central to the hesitation of the Golden Bough after Aeneas does not do exactly what the Sibyl commanded.

72. As we have noted, lions were an established part of Cybele's iconography; it was a small leap for Ovid to connect Atalanta's transformation with the Great Mother.

73. The Myrrha story was well known and difficult to call a lie; Orpheus' remark (which he limits to the Myrrha section—10.302 *in hac . . . parte*, despite the obvious link the tale has to Adonis), ostensibly just an expression of shock at the horror of incest, is a signal, however, in a book of falsehood about the mendacious nature of Orpheus' song. Further, Orpheus' song is to trees; one wonders why then he tells daughters and parents

to depart before Myrrha's song (10.300), not to mention the aforementioned implications of 301 *aut, mea si vestras mulcebant carmina mentes*—Orpheus as singer of beautiful lies.

Chapter XI

While with Such a Song . . .

Book 11 of Ovid's epic opens in the aftermath of Orpheus' song, which ended, we soon find, without natural conclusion.[1] Orpheus' song, unlike Ovid's, is not a *carmen perpetuum*. As Book 11 commences, Orpheus is in the process of singing to the trees, the wild animals, and the stones (no humans), when the peaceful sylvan glade is interrupted by sudden violence. The daughters-in-law of the Ciconians (11.3 *ecce nurus Ciconum*) appear, and they are clothed in animal skins; they are maddened (*lymphata . . . pectora*).

The eleventh book of Ovid's *Metamorphoses* is one of his most extraordinary, with echoes both loud and faint of Books 5 and 11 of Virgil's *Aeneid*, and, like Virgil's poem, a "surprise" ending that parallels the divine conversation between Jupiter and Juno that comes near the end of *Aeneid* 12. This "*Aeneid* in miniature" becomes a deliberate trick of the poet before he launches into his own examination of Homeric and Virgilian lore proper in Books 13-14 of his epic. Book 11 of the *Metamorphoses* is a stunning opening to the last third of Ovid's epic, a grand introduction to the great themes that will dominate the final major movement of the poet's perpetual song.[2]

Virgil had already said that Orpheus was killed by crazed maenads (*G.* 4.520-527), but the story was by no means definitive. Some believed Orpheus committed suicide after Eurydice's death; others that Zeus killed him with a thunderbolt for teaching things men were not meant to know.[3] But most seem to agree that Dionysus' crazed female worshippers slew him. Aeschylus has a version that makes easy sense: Orpheus revered Apollo, and Dionysus' followers killed him in consequence. The mythographer Conon says that Orpheus would not allow women to participate in the liturgical rites of his mystery religion.[4] Orpheus lore was, like much of Greek mythology, riddled with contradictory variants; Plato has a story that Orpheus was only given a phantom Eurydice, because the gods were upset that the hero did not have the courage to visit the underworld by dying.[5] Ovid also drew on the fourth-century B.C. elegiac poet Phanocles for some of the details surrounding Orpheus' demise.[6]

For Ovid's narrative, the salient point is that Orpheus dies, and violently. The first maenad declares that she has found the *contemptor* of women, the one who spurned their company; she throws a spear at the "Apollonian bard" (11.8 *vatis Apollinei*), a detail that may reflect the aforementioned tradition that Or-

307

pheus was killed because he proposed the worship of Apollo rather than or in preference to that of Dionysus. Orpheus has been contemptuous of women; he has preferred boys to women in his grief over the double loss of Eurydice. The song of Orpheus highlighted Apollo's infatuation with Hyacinthus. Apollo, of course, was a Greek deity and there was nothing the Augustan regime could do to deny the fact that he was associated with the love of boys as well as women.[7] In the case of Orpheus, as we shall soon see, the poet's pederasty does not prevent him from receiving *post mortem* favors from Apollo.

A second woman throws a stone at Orpheus; it falls harmlessly to the ground, conquered by the music (which has no effect on the women—Orpheus did tell daughters to be gone before the story of Myrrha, which may be a reference to the tradition of his exclusion of women from his rites). But soon the insane Fury reigns (11.14 *insanaque regnat Erinys*); madness rules all as the women hurl weapons at the poet. The Bacchants have their own musical instruments, and there are too many of them; soon Orpheus becomes red with the blood of the stones (15-19). We are reminded of the slaughter of Pentheus, and of other victories of Bacchus over his enemies. Ovid's Orpheus has not forsaken Dionysus or blasphemed like Pentheus or the daughters of Minyas, but he has rejected the overtures of women, especially the local women of his own native haunts—and Bacchus rules over them. The women slay the animals gathered to listen to the bard (one wonders what they thought of Myrrha's appeal to the incestuous practices of the animal kingdom). Ovid describes the vicious attack in a powerful double simile, the second part of which is another of his anachronistic comparisons:

et coeunt ut aves, si quando luce vagantem
noctis avem cernunt, structoque utrimque theatro
ceu matutina cervus periturus harena
praeda canum est, vatemque petunt . . . (11.24-27)

And they go around him like birds, when they see the bird
of night wandering in the light, or as when, with the theater built up on either
*   side,*
the deer is the prey of the hounds on the morning sand, and they attack the
*   bard . . .*

The deer image reminds us of Actaeon; the owl image is more obscure. The bird of night is out of place in the day; the deer is out of place in the arena. The *noctis avem* reminds us of the usually nocturnal character of Bacchic revel; Virgil highlighted this quality in his description of Orpheus' death: *G.* 4.521 *inter sacra deum nocturnique orgia Bacchi.* In Ovid, the women of the night are slaughtering by day, during the very workday of the farmer, in fact; Orpheus, the underworld bard, is imagined as the bird of night.

More significantly, there are farmers nearby, and when they see the maenad horde, they flee in terror. The crazed women seize the farming implements to use as weapons against Orpheus; they slaughter the oxen the farmers had left behind.[8] Orpheus is soon ripped apart by the violent action of the women of Bacchus. The women have abused the use of civilization: the very instruments that remind us of Ceres' providential blessings on agriculture, the works Triptolemus tried to spread even to remote Scythia, have here been turned against the poet philosopher.

Nature mourns for the dead Orpheus, as the Thracian river Hebrus brings his head down its course. In Virgil, the Orphic head cried of Eurydice as it floated downstream; in Ovid, there is a threefold repetition of the head and lyre's mournful lament (flebile), as the banks respond to tongue and instrument. But the subject of the song is unspecified; Ovid's Orpheus, after all, had turned pederast. The head ends up on Lesbos—where an interesting coda describes the fate of both the mortal and immortal remains of the singer. A vicious snake attacks the head (11.56-58); Apollo intervenes and transforms the serpent into a stone sculpture, with its head frozen in a gesture of attack. At 7.358, Ovid may well have mentioned this snake (which no earlier extant source records), though it is perhaps difficult to imagine Ovid that expected his readers to remember the previous mention of a petrified serpent. We can study Apollo's intervention here in light of the subsequent fate of Orpheus' shade (11.61-66), and the fate of those responsible for his dismemberment.

Orpheus has been to the underworld before; this time he enters Elysium (the arva piorum). There, he finds Eurydice (invenit Eurydicen), and they walk in three styles: side by side, with Orpheus following, and with Orpheus leading but safely looking back.

Eurydice makes no appearance in the sixth Aeneid. In Ovid's stunning conclusion to the long song and the whole Orphic drama that ended the second third of his epic, the poet has found release in death and a return to his heterosexual marriage; he has seemingly abandoned the pursuit of boys and young men, and he has resumed the marriage for which he had previously made a journey to the land of the dead. Ovid's depiction of the happy couple has affinities with Virgil's Dido and Sychaeus; after Dido's silence in the underworld with Aeneas, the poet depicted her in reunion with her dead husband.

Bacchus is not pleased that the maenads have killed his bard (11.67 ff.). The passage comes as something of a surprise; we had no reason to think he did not approve of the bard's death. Bacchus sees to it that the maenads are suddenly overtaken by roots in the ground; before long the women are transformed into trees, a fitting end for the invaders of the sylvan grove where Orpheus had performed for an arboreal audience.[9]

Apollo, then, and Bacchus both participate in the rehabilitation of Orpheus. The Orphic cosmogony had sung of the birth of Dionysus; it is eminently fitting that the wine god should be displeased that his bard had been ripped to pieces. This is the first time in the epic that we have seen any dissension in Bacchus' mad kingdom; indeed, after the maenad metamorphosis the bard decides to leave Thrace altogether (11.85 ff.) and move to Lydia. His anger over the loss of Orpheus is such that even the punishment of the crazed women is not sufficient (*non satis hoc Baccho est*).

In the Orphic tradition, the bard was associated with both Bacchus and Apollo; Ovid neatly reconciles a complicated myth history by having both gods on good terms with Orpheus in his *post mortem* rehabilitation and avenging. Orpheus has been honored; he resides in Elysium (as in Virgil), though with his wife returned to him. It is almost as if the events of the preceding book had never occurred; it is as if the madness that had descended on the bard has been cured. He wanted Eurydice back, after all, and now in death he has her. There is no other extant source for the punishment of the murderers of Orpheus; the obvious problem for mythographers was how to reconcile the wild action of the maenads with the fact that Orpheus was "one of them" in an important sense. Ovid solves the problem creatively and with originality: Bacchus never approved the rogue action of his servants. They acted without divine approval (again, apparently it was Orpheus' *fate* to die this way, despite Bacchus' lack of approbation), and so they are punished.[10] And, presumably, Orpheus and Eurydice will spend eternity in "wedded bliss" in Ovid's underworld. There is no mention of Orphic lore of rebirth and renewal; they are together, and the poet's head has been saved from desecration.[11] Virgil did not afford Orpheus this *post mortem* blessing at the close of the fourth georgic, though in the *Aeneid* he resides in Elysium in revered glory (even if *sine coniuge*). But in Virgil's underworld, Orpheus' presence signals the coming recitation of Rome's history in the future tense, as we learn of the rebirth of souls from Anchises. In Ovid, we might as well be back in Book 5 again now, in a traditional underworld of permanent endurance. There will be no renewal for Orpheus and Eurydice.

Bacchus may be in a new Lydian locale, but his usual assembly of satyrs accompanies him. Silenus is not there. In Ovid's vision, in an echo of the sixth eclogue, Silenus has been captured by Phrygian rustics; they lead him to King Midas.[12]

The story of Midas' golden touch is one of the most enduring of myths; Ovid's rendition is the reason. No earlier version exists. Herodotus (8.138) has a note that in the gardens of Midas, Silenus was caught; this is undoubtedly evidence that there was a pre-Ovidian connection between Silenus, Midas, and (probably) a reward for the return of the satyr to his divine master. But only Ovid has survived to tell the story.

Ovid uses interesting language to describe Bacchus' reward to Midas:

huic deus optandi gratum, sed inutile fecit
muneris arbitrium gaudens altore recepto. (11.100-101)

For this one, the god made the choice of choosing a
pleasing but useless gift, since he rejoiced in his foster-father's return.

The story marks a return to the discussion Ovid had started on Olympus about fate and free will; Midas is given the *arbitrium* of choosing something he wants, even if it is disadvantageous or without use. Midas used the gift badly, Ovid says (102 *ille male usurus donis*), though one could argue that it is difficult to use the free will of choosing a pleasing but disadvantageous gift badly! The point seems to be that Bacchus has given Midas free reign, and the king has used it carelessly—though again, some would argue everything was predetermined and merely followed Midas' fate, which was unknown to the king (though perhaps not the god). As most everyone knows, Midas asked for the golden touch.

Midas is the Berecynthian hero (11.106); he is king in the land of Cybele, the very birthplace of the coming Troy, and traditionally a son of Cybele. His first attempt at aurifaction is tested on a twig, which leads us to an evocation of Virgil's Golden Bough: 109 *ilice detraxit virgam: virga aurea facta est*; cf. *A.* 6.208-209 *talis erat species auri frondentis opaca / ilice.* In his application of the golden touch, Midas plucks the Golden Bough, as it were, in a prefiguring of what his Trojan countryman Aeneas will one day do. But Midas is but a shadow of a future reality; for him, the Golden Bough is harbinger of impending doom. Midas is a symbol of the unsuitability of the Phrygian element to assume the veritable symbol of the arrival at the vision of the future Rome and its historical greatness.[13] In Virgil, the Golden Bough preceded the underworld vision; it was the necessary key to gain admittance, the symbol of forthcoming knowledge. In Ovid, the Bough comes after Orpheus; it announces to the reader that there are secrets yet to be revealed, that Orpheus, who had just been consigned with Eurydice to a most traditional (indeed plausibly Homeric) conception of the afterlife, is not, in the end, the final word on the soul's fate. The Midas story announces a future theme on the ultimate disposition of the human soul; Midas' Golden Bough announces the beginning of the final third of the epic, where we move beyond Homeric tradition and Orphic mystery to a new vision of the last things.[14]

Midas is a creator god; he is the father of new beginnings, and all that he gives life to is gold. The waters he touches could cheat Danae (11.116-117); he is like Jupiter in a shower of gold. Soon, of course, the problem of Midas' gift becomes known; he has too much gold, and there is a hint here of the golden finery of a Chloreus or some other Phrygian. Excess is part of the stereotype of the Lydians and their splendid reputation for gold; the story of Midas is as much an etiology for the gold deposits of the River Pactolus as for the fabulous wealth of the local royals. Midas is now like Erysichthon; he is lost in a world where no amount of food or drink can sate him (and, as the commentators have noted, his table seems to be heaped rather high anyway, as a sign of excess).[15]

Midas prays for relief; Ovid notes that the divine power of the gods is gentle: 11.134 *mite deum numen*: Bacchus will allow Midas to wash off the golden touch in the waters of the Pactolus. The passage deserves more attention than it has received; as an authorial comment on divinity, it does not seem quite true in light of what we have read through two thirds of the epic (it can be read, though less easily, as merely a comment on the current situation).[16] Midas will be freed from his curse, in something of an exception to the usual pattern in the poem; there will be no consequences for his bad decision. Of course part of this easy escape is the tradition that Midas' stupidity would return to haunt him in other ways; but this does not fully explain Ovid's remark. Part of the point would seem to be that Ovid is being deliberately mendacious; Murphy does well to compare *Fasti* 2.45-46, where Ovid explicitly denies that any water can remove bloodguilt.[17] Ovid may have had the *Fasti* passage in mind when he wrote this section of the *Metamorphoses*; in any case, Midas washes in the river and is purified. The Pactolus becomes a symbol in some sense of the underworld's Lethe, the stream of oblivion.

Ovid is not finished with Midas. The tradition existed that he eventually acquired ass' ears.[18] The once wealthy king now goes to the other extreme; he despises wealth and decides to live in the forest wildernesses (a fitting home, we might note, for a Bacchic servant). He remains just as stupid as ever, Ovid notes (11.148-149). We cannot assume that Ovid invented the reasons for his acquisition of donkey ears; in any case, the story the poet relates reminds us of past musical competitions in the poem. The god Pan challenges Apollo; the goat god can expect an easier punishment if he were to lose than the hapless Marsyas. Midas happens to be present for the contest; given his Bacchic proclivities, he would no doubt favor Pan, and indeed the satyr's song charms the onetime king (162-163).

Apollo stands to sing. Ovid probably had a statue in mind: 11.169 *artificis status ipse fuit*. Interestingly, the god of music is dressed in Tyrian purple (perhaps indulging in the local fashions); his lyre has gems and "Indian teeth" (167 *dentibus Indis*), that is, ivory. We have never heard of such a lavish description for Apollo's instrument before; it certainly stands in contrast to Pan's humble, rustic pipes. Tmolus is quick in his verdict: Apollo wins, and there is implication that the mountain god was charmed as much by the god's imposing, handsome appearance as by the quality of the song.

It is not surprising that Midas favors Pan; it is also perhaps the case that Pan's song was better. There are numerous reasons why Midas is stupid here; he was not the judge, and should have remained silent. He invited Apollo's wrath, which was indeed gentle—Ovid's point about the *mite numen* has some force here. Pan, we might be tempted to think, may have sung a pastoral melody, and Apollo a Callimachean epyllion (note 169 *docto*).[19] In any case, Midas soon finds his ears turned into those of an ass. Apollo has treated him with unusual kindness; it is almost as if the two gods who had participated in Orpheus' rehabilitation are especially gentle with this dull-witted clown, who now bears exactly the emblem of his sluggish stupidity. Midas is understandably embarrassed by the transformation, and so he assumes a purple tiara (of Persian associations) to cover the evidence (11.180-181).

Midas could not be more Phrygian or barbarian; now he has ass' ears to complete the picture. He is the son of Cybele, the Great Mother whom we so recently met in connection with how she acquired her lions. The whole scene mocks the tradition that will be suppressed in the future Rome; further, the fact that Midas assumes the Golden Bough to lead us into the last third of the epic is a signal that we should beware of the revelations we learn as we move forward.

Bacchus and Apollo can be taken as divine symbols of the two clashing worlds, those of Troy and Rome. In Midas, both gods have been reasonably gentle. This makes sense for Bacchus, given the affinities of the Phrygian for the wine god and his deliverance of Silenus. For an explanation of Apollo's gentle demeanor—in such contrast to his behavior with Marsyas—we have Rome's restrained tolerance of Cybele and her cult. Rome could not disavow Troy, and Midas, the stupid ass, is not killed—he merely dresses the part. There is something of this tolerance of Troy, too, in the deliberately "local" dress of Apollo: the god was displaying favor toward the region's traditions, respect for the local culture, as it were. Midas in his idiocy failed to see the point.

There is real comedy in the *dénouement* of Midas' tale; his barber cannot keep the ludicrous secret. In the reeds that eventually betray the secret the barber "buried" in the earth, we see a fitting link to Pan's reed pipe and the instrument that Midas had foolishly preferred to Apollo's lyre.[20]

Fittingly, after Ovid's commentary on the clash between Troy and Rome, *Ovid begins his Troy theme.* Apollo leaves the scene of his victory over both Pan (and, by extension, Bacchus) and Midas. But he does not cross the Hellespont (11.194-195), staying instead on the Asian side of the strait. Apollo travels to an altar consecrated to Jupiter, an altar that is situated just between the famous promontories of Rhoeteum and Sigeum. We are, essentially, at the site of the future city of Troy. The altar is dedicated to the "Panomphaean Thunderer" (198 *Panomphaeo . . . Tonanti*), that is, the thunder god from whom comes all voices—Troy, that is, the future Rome, is the destined lord of the world, the mortal avatar, if you will, of Jovian power and the Olympian order. Laomedon is building the walls of Troy.[21]

In Ovid's version, which more or less accords with his predecessors, Apollo and Neptune agree to build the walls of Troy in exchange for gold (the recurring mention of gold is another reminder of Phrygian greed in Roman eyes). Laomedon is like a Carthaginian in his perfidy (and Phoenicia, of course, is not *that* far off from Troy)—the Trojan monarch not only denies the price, but lies and says he never promised it anyway. Interestingly—especially in light of the Homeric antecedents and the question of whether both gods helped to build the walls in the preexisting tradition—it is *Neptune* who destroys the walls of the city; the god of the Augustan regime, conveniently, is not implicated in the direct destruction of the city. Neptune is savage; he also demands that the king's daughter be sacrificed to him, as if she were Perseus' Andromeda (11.211-213).

Hesione is quickly freed by Hercules; Ovid is playing loosely with his chronology, of course, since his universal history is not telling us exactly what had happened at every place on earth at a given moment. Hercules had been promised horses; once again, the amazingly stupid Trojan (cf. Midas) refuses, and Hercules smashes the walls again.[22] Hercules is aided by the hero Telamon, and he (not Neptune) receives Hesione as his prize. Telamon's brother was none other than Peleus, who did not need Hesione or any other wife from conquest, since he had received a goddess, Thetis—as Ovid observes, there were many other grandchildren of Jupiter, but only Peleus out of all mortals had been granted a divine wife.

The scene is now set for the continuation of Ovid's Troy lore; at long last, so close to the beginning of the last third of the epic, we begin the great saga Homer had made immortal. Achilles is now allusively and obliquely introduced, as Ovid recalls Proteus' prediction to Thetis that any child she bore would surpass the deeds of his father—a dangerous oracle indeed for a Jovian world.[23] Peleus is the noble son of Aeacus, one of the underworld's three judges; Jupiter orders him to take Thetis as his wife (no doubt with no complaint whatsoever).

An elaborate ecphrasis describes the location for Peleus' union with Thetis (11.229 ff.). The myrtle wood near the quasi-harbor where the two will meet is appropriate; the myrtle was sacred to Venus. There is a grotto in a grove that is sacred because the goddess Thetis so often retires there; Ovid notes (to the delight of the commentators) that the place was more artificial than natural:

> est specus in medio, natura factus an arte,
> ambiguum, magis arte tamen . . . (11.235-236)
>
> *There was a cave in the middle, whether made by nature or by art,*
> *it is unclear, nevertheless, more by art . . .*

Some god—or poet—had a hand in this cave, this locus for the union of the couple whence Achilles. Peleus approaches Thetis as a true grandson of Jupiter; the goddess is asleep—clearly Peleus has received Jovian approval for his approach of the beautiful—and naked—immortal. Thetis is like Proteus, the marine god who had made the prophecy of her special offspring in the first place: she has the power to transform herself, and soon she is a bird, then a tree— Peleus is able to capture both. A tigress, however, makes the point—Peleus releases his grip on his prey (245-246).[24] Peleus is devout; he immediately makes prayers, rather polluting the sea with wine, sheep entrails, and incense.

Proteus gives advice to the son of Aeacus; we might observe that the advice is not very creative: the suitor is simply to bind Thetis while she sleeps, and then, no matter what form she takes, retain the bonds—until, of course, she resumes her true shape (it does not seem to have occurred to the originator of the story that the goddess could just as easily flee at that point). As the commentators have observed, Proteus' advice is both Homeric (*Odyssey* 4.414-424) and Virgilian; at *G.* 4.387-414, Cyrene gives her son Aristaeus, the forlorn beekeeper, exactly the same advice to capture Proteus so that he can learn how to reconstitute his hives. In typically rapid Ovidian narrative, Peleus is soon in possession of both a new divine wife and a baby destined to be famous:

... confessam amplectitur heros
et potitur votis ingentique inplet Achille. (11.264-265)

... and the hero embraced her after she confessed,
and he attained his prayers, and he filled her with great Achilles.

Peleus would seem to be among the most blessed of mortals; he has a magnificent goddess for a wife, and a son of assured fame and valorous report. Ovid mentions that there was one blight on his record, namely the death of his brother Phocus.[25] Ovid tells the story obliquely, and would have us think Peleus was guilty of the murder (there is no mention of Telamon, let alone the tradition that all Peleus did was help hide the body). Ovid was not original in blaming Peleus for the murder, but he may be the first to have crafted the story that Peleus sought safety with Ceyx after he was forced to leave Aegina.[26]

Peleus approaches Ceyx, where he seeks shelter and hospitality; he does not, however, reveal his crime. Ceyx is in a depressed mood; when asked about his obvious sorrow he proceeds to tell the story of his brother Daedalion (11.291 ff.). The story begins with its ending; Ceyx will reveal the etiology of the hawk, the bird that terrifies all others.[27] Ceyx outlines how both he and his brother were the children of Lucifer, the Morning Star, but with very different temperaments; Ceyx was always a man of peace and family life, while Daedalion was brutal and pursued war. He was exactly like what he is now, a hawk that terrifies doves (299-300).[28] Daedalion has a daughter of fourteen years of age, Chione; she has many suitors, but the only two who matter are Apollo and Mercury.

The story of Chione's attraction of these two gods is very old (Hesiod, fr. 64 Merkelbach-West). Apollo decides to wait until night, while Mercury seizes her at once, first putting her to sleep—Apollo comes at nightfall in the guise of an old woman. From Mercury, Chione conceives Autolycus, the prince of thieves;[29] from Apollo, she bears Philammon, a noted musician.

Rather bizarrely, Chione's reaction to what some would call an abundance of divine favor (and others two rapes) is to claim that she is more beautiful than Diana. Clearly Chione was pleased with herself for having borne the children of two gods; why she should claim to be lovelier than Apollo's virgin huntress sister is difficult to explain. The answer may lie in the goddess' reaction; she shoots the girl at once with an arrow and kills her. By her action, Diana effectively erases at least part of the evidence of her brother and half-brother's rapes; one imagines Diana was not pleased with any of the business and only to happy to eliminate Chione.

Daedalion is overcome with grief over the loss of his daughter; he does not listen to his brother Ceyx' words of consolation (11.328 ff.). Finally, at the very scene of her funeral, he runs off as if he were a bullock stung by bees (emphasizing the sudden, sharp pain of the father's grief). Daedalion runs to Mount Parnassus, where he is about to hurl himself down from a promontory in suicide. Apollo takes pity on his would-be father-in-law, and transforms him into a

316 CHAPTER XI

hawk, an accipiter that terrorizes other birds (339 ff.).

The passage is interesting if Ovid is indeed the originator of the idea that Daedalion was transformed into a hawk. Ovid gives no reason for why Apollo should consider it appropriate to change Daedalion into a bird that attacks other birds; there is nothing in the narrative to explain this part of the metamorphosis. I suggest that Ovid is indeed playing with Virgil's Camilla simile of the accipiter and the dove; as in the story of Camilla, so here we have a case of divine sibling rivalry in the conflict between Apollo and his sister, who are at rather cross purposes in their reaction to the Chione affair. The divine conflict between the Latonian twins is at the heart of much of the drama of *Aeneid* 11, where Apollo is faithful to his devotee Arruns, and Diana to her votary Camilla. Indeed, the theme is relevant to Ovid's earlier concern with the image of Apollo in Troy: how does one reconcile the god of the Augustan regime with the world of Cybele and all that must die about old Phrygia? Ovid's narrative precedes Virgil's in the chronology of mythology—Daedalion and Chione come long before the Trojan War and its Italian aftermath. Ovid's narrative succeeds Virgil's, of course, in the chronology of when the two poets actually wrote. Here, Apollo makes Daedalion a savage hunting bird, a bird that will later become none other than Camilla in Latium. Apollo will help to destroy that hawk, his own creation, as it were. And we might well note that female accipiters are larger than males—something Virgil seems to have known.

The next story fits brilliantly into Ovid's probable evocation of Virgil's *Camilliad*: the story of the wolf that attacked the cattle of Peleus (11.346-409). The tale is not Ovidian in origin. Lycophron mentions it briefly (*Alexandra* 91-92).[30] Ovid is generally credited with the linkage of the story to the larger Ceyx tale, though the reason for the link is usually unexplained. Onetor, the custodian of the flocks Ovid had noted that Peleus had left roaming around when he visited Ceyx for shelter, comes with a terrible tale of what has happened to the sheep. Ovid dwells on the herdsman's rendition of what transpired on the beach; as usual, Ovid's lengthy description has a point—the poet wants the audience to stop and pay attention to his story. There was a temple near the site where the sheep roamed, dedicated to marine gods, and also a marsh overcome with willows. From that swampy ground a huge wolf appeared (366 *belua vasta, lupus iuncisque palustribus exit*). The wolf destroys everything; all the flocks are slaughtered—the wolf is more rabid than hungry (369-370 *qui quamquam saevit pariter rabieque fameque, / acrior est rabie*). Some of the guardians of the flock die with their fleecy charges. Onetor wants Peleus to lead an attack on the wolf and save what might be left from the lupine marauder (376-378).

Servius' commentary on both the Virgilian Camilla and Harpalyce preserves lore about wolves and rapine. For Harpalyce, the story is told that the girl was killed because she raided flocks (cf. her name, the Snatcher She-Wolf); for Camilla, the story is told that her killer, Arruns, was one of the *Hirpi Sorani*, worshippers of Apollo Soranus (i.e., Apollo of Mount Soracte). Rites were being conducted on Soracte to Dis Pater when wolves suddenly appeared and snatched away the sacrificial offerings. Shepherds pursued the wolves until they came to a cave; a mysterious exhalation from the grotto killed the shepherds, along with causing a plague. An oracle revealed that the only way to solve the problem was to imitate wolves, to live, that is, off of plunder. Hence the locals were known as the *Hirpini*, from the Sabine word for wolf.[31] The story of the plunder of Peleus' cattle is another example of lupine raids on flocks.

Elsewhere, I have offered the speculation that Virgil's Camilla is lycanthropic (so also Harpalyce), and that Camilla is envisaged as another of these predatory wolves, launching raids on flocks, as it were, as she dazzles the equestrian battlefield in her *aristeia*.[32] I suspect that in the etiology of the hawk, and in the lupine slaughter of cattle, Ovid is recalling Virgil's Camilla. At a basic level of narrative structure, the evocation of the central figure from *Aeneid* 11, followed by an extended story that borrows heavily from *Aeneid* 5, capped by a reminiscence of the conclusion of the divine machinery of Virgil's epic from *Aeneid* 12, afford Ovid's Book 11 a tight unity of theme: a summary of the *Aeneid* before Ovid commences his own treatment of the same lore.

Peleus is not surprised by the raid; he knows why the wolf has attacked. The Nereid Psamathe (Ovid does not name her at first; cf. 11.398)[33] was the mother of Phocus; she is angry for the loss of her son. Ceyx is ready, however, to go off and face the wolf, when his wife Alcyone appears and begs him not to go. Peleus intervenes; he says that battle is not required, but rather propitiatory prayer. The assembly goes to a lofty tower to survey the lupine carnage. Peleus' prayer, however, does nothing to move Psamathe; fortunately, however, he has a divine spouse, Thetis. She decides to intercede for her beleaguered husband. The wolf is called back from the slaughter (presumably by the Nereid that had sent him), but the beast continues his attack (401-402 *sed enim revocatus ab acri / caede lupus perstat, dulcedine sanguinis asper*). Finally, the animal is transformed in mid-bite into a harmless marble statue.

Peleus, however, cannot stay in Ceyx's presence. His bloodguilt is obviously in need of serious purification, and so he departs, an exile once again. He goes to Magnesia in Thessaly, where Acastus absolves him of his guilt (11.407-409). We have observed that in Antoninus Liberalis, Acastus' kingdom is the locus for the lupine attack.[34] And, indeed, the whole mess that has befallen both his brother Daedalion and his recent guest Peleus will lead Ceyx to worry very much about what further trouble might befall his household and realm. His concern is well-founded, as Ovid prepares to tell the most extended story of this book, the celebrated epyllion of Ceyx and Alcyone, which, as we shall see, has continuing affinities with both Virgil's eleventh *Aeneid* and its sister book, *Aeneid* 5, as Ovid continues the early movements of his great Troy-Rome cycle.[35]

Peleus had thought that prayer was sufficient to repel the wolf the Nereid had sent against his flocks. He was wrong on this count; only his divine wife was able to intervene—and the divine intervention, we might observe, is parallel to the divine intervention that destroyed Camilla. It represents another example of the seemingly inappropriate actions of immortals to help their favorites; we have been told in both Virgil and Ovid that such things are not permitted (and by Jupiter, the supreme god). Yet exceptions seem to abound to this general edict of non-intervention. Thetis is able to "slay" the wolf, in effect, but she cannot cleanse her husband of his bloodguilt, apparently.

The transformation of the wolf into a marble statue is identical to the transformation of the fox into marble that we encountered in Book 7.759 ff., which preceded the story of Cephalus and Procris (something of a doublet of Ceyx and Alcyone).[36] That earlier story had shown Diana's anger over the misuse of two of her presents, a hunting dog and a javelin; the dog ended up marbleized along with the fox, while the javelin would prove Procris' undoing and the symbol of Cephalus' own bloodguilt, as it were.[37] Procris had playacted Diana in the forest, angry at the treatment she had received from her husband; she was no Diana, however, in that she was a non-virgin, besides being a married woman willing to succumb to bribes for infidelity. She was also willing to surrender the goddess' presents to her reconciled husband. Procris is more Dido than any sylvan denizen, divine or otherwise.

Diana reappeared in the Ceyx story, as the king related the account of his brother's daughter Chione and her comparison of herself to the goddess— Chione, too, like Procris, was no true Diana. Falsehood had been a theme throughout the Orpheus song; in the case of Diana and her devotees, it is a pervasive theme, from Virgil (recall Venus and Dido and their playacting) to Ovid (Procris, Venus with Adonis). It lies behind the oldest extant version of the Ceyx and Alcyone story, where the pitiable couple of Ovid's forthcoming epyllion were destroyed because of arrogant pride: they fancied themselves to be Zeus and Hera in their salutations to each other.[38] While there will be some faint echoes that show Ovid was aware of this tradition, in his version of the Ceyx and Alcyone story, there will no explicit divine retribution for any wrongdoing.

Peleus was in error about how to stop the wolf; Ceyx wanted to fight it. His wife stopped him. Camilla's killer was Arruns, who, with ample help from Apollo, slew the Volscian with his divinely guided shaft. Numerous parallels exist in Virgil between Arruns and the eerie figure of Sleep who appears in *Aeneid* 5, near the very end of the book, to eliminate Palinurus, Aeneas' helmsman. The overarching structure of the Ceyx and Alcyone epyllion Ovid will now detail is centered on an evocation of the end of *A.* 5, itself a parallel to the Camilla-Arruns episode in *A.* 11. Ovid began with reminiscences of *A.* 11, however subtle; he spends the second half of this book on an evocation of the end of *A.* 5 and Sleep's dispatch of Palinurus.

In part, the poet is playing with the numbers of his books; I suspect *A.* 11 was in his mind as he crafted his own *M.* 11, and the theme of Cybele and the death of old Troy has clear connection to Camilla and Chloreus; Camilla was also on the poet's mind after Atalanta. The conflict between Apollo and Bacchus in Ovid over the question of Troy parallels the divine conflict in Virgil between Apollo and Diana over Camilla. Reflections on *A.* 11 naturally lead to study of passages in *A. 5*, its sister book.

Parallels abound, then, some more obvious than others. But why? Why should Ovid turn *Metamorphoses* 11 into a pastiche of reminiscences of *Aeneid* 11 and 5, just before he commences his *Iliad* in *Metamorphoses* 12 and his *Aeneid* in *Metamorphoses* 13-14?[39] I suspect that Ovid considered that in the figure of Camilla, Virgil had invested the greatest prominence: she is the mortal reason Turnus loses the war in Italy, though both she and Turnus become, as it were, immortal symbols of the future Italy and Rome. Palinurus, is, like Camilla, another example of divine intervention in human affairs; he dies as a Trojan prefiguring of Camilla.[40] He also dies as the only major Trojan casualty whose death is "needless" in light of the future Rome (Nisus and Euryalus, for example, must die in part because of their homosexual union—and Pallas, the Patroclus of the *Aeneid*, is not Trojan but Arcadian). Palinurus is a true sacrifice to seemingly capricious gods. But his loss, unlike Camilla's, holds no great significance for the outcome of the war in Italy; it is prefigurement, not fulfillment. Further, the gods had ample reason to demand Camilla's death; the death of her precursor is without warrant. Rather nicely, then, on the very edge of commencing his *Iliad*, Ovid neatly recalls the entire *Aeneid* by evoking Books 11 and, at much greater length, 5.[41]

Apollo played a part in the death of Camilla, and he was also associated with the death of Palinurus: Aeneas complained in the underworld that Apollo had never foretold of the loss of the helmsman on the way to Italy. Ceyx, troubled over so much, decides to consult Apollo's oracle (11.410 ff.).

Ceyx is compelled to visit the Apollonian oracle at Claros, in Ionia at Colophon, because, Ovid says, Phorbas was making the journey to Delphi impossible (11.414 *invia cum Phlegyis faciebat Delphica Phorbas*). The story is once again obscure; what is significant for our poet, though, is the fact that "Phorbas" is the Trojan in whose guise Sleep appeared to Palinurus on the deck of Aeneas' flagship at the end of *Aeneid 5*. Ovid here signals his intention to recall the events of the penultimate book of the first half of Virgil's epic.[42] In Virgil, a sea journey was the locus for the appearance of Phorbas to Palinurus, while in Ovid, a sea journey is occasioned because of Phorbas. Phorbas and his Phlegyans, in fact, remind us of exactly the sort of violent predators Palinurus will reveal as his murderers in Virgil's underworld, when he describes what happened to him after he was lost overboard.[43]

Virgil's Palinurus has no wife; his model in cyclic epic, Protesilaus, did: Laodamia. And so, too, does Ovid's Ceyx; Alcyone has already been introduced as a nervous wife, anxious for her husband's safety. Protesilaus had to go to Troy alone, and Ceyx will have to travel to Claros by himself. With mention of Phorbas, Ovid has signaled his intention to recall Virgil's Palinurus, and with Palinurus, we think of Protesilaus and his wife, who in some ways parallel Ceyx and Alcyone.

Alcyone makes a lengthy appeal to Ceyx; she is terrified at the prospect of a sea voyage. The topos is among the most common in classical elegiac poetry and elsewhere; Alcyone is the daughter of the wind god Aeolus (11.431 *Hippotades*),[44] and so Ovid recalls all the machinery of storms from the first *Aeneid*; Palinurus was a leading figure in the troubles at sea in *A.* 3 and 5 (though not 1). The storm in *A.* 1 was instigated by Juno out of her hatred for the Trojans; there is no similar divine work behind the storm that will befall Ceyx, though Ovid may have had the tradition of Juno's anger at Ceyx in mind when he crafted his story.[45] Ovid will now enter the heart of one of his finest tales, a masterpiece of the epyllion art, practiced, appropriately enough for the poet of love, in an elegiac mode.

Alcyone wants to go with Ceyx (another commonplace of elegy); Ceyx cannot allow this, and in the end the one concession he makes is that he will return within two months (11.450 ff.). There is something of Dido and Aeneas as Ceyx prepares his departure; Alcyone is only momentarily calmed by her husband's promise of a relatively quick return, and when she sees the boat being prepared and outfitted, she loses her composure and has to be carried off by attendants; Ceyx tries to find every excuse for delay, but his men are already rowing his vessel out to sea. The departure scene, as the commentators have noted, owes something to *Heroides* 13, where Laodamia sees her newlywed husband Protesilaus go off to war. Ceyx and Alcyone are not newly married, and Ceyx is not going off to war. The comparison is still valid; Ovid's story is also reminiscent of Hero and Leander, with its similar theme of the lover lost at sea.[46]

The storm comes up suddenly and without warning; Ceyx and his men are halfway to their destination (11.478 ff.). Again, there is no stated cause for the storm (Ovid does not need one); no indication is given that the gods are behind the disaster. The unnamed helmsman of the boat says that he does not know how to navigate in this tempest (492-493); the language echoes that of Palinurus after the Trojans have left Crete (*A.* 3.201-202). Palinurus makes a few appearances in *A.* 3 that presage his scene at the end of *A.* 5, a book that opens with a storm; it ends with calm seas. Venus had visited Neptune and asked for a safe passage on the last leg of the Trojans' journey from Sicily to Italy. The sea god had granted the request, though at the demand of one life, a sacrificial offering the god did not identify (and Venus never asks whose life must be lost). Nor does Neptune give any reason for why someone must die so that the Trojans may complete their journey. What is clear in Virgil is that the Trojans no longer need a helmsman, once Neptune is in charge of piloting Aeneas' flagship to Italy.

The storm grows worse; Ovid uses another double simile to compare the sound the battered ship makes to the way the gates of a citadel groan when a battering ram or a ballista rams against them (11.508 ff.). Then, the poet says that the waves lashed at the ship and overwhelmed it, just as lions will charge with strength and bravery into the weapons of hunters. Here, it would seem the ship is imbued with power and might; it is like a group of hunters with weapons arrayed. Ovid thus compares the assault on the ship to attacks from the world of men and the world of nature; part of the point is the ancient commonplace that men are better off not sailing in a world before meteorological forecasting could help safeguard a ship's crew. A double simile is not sufficient for Ovid here; he proceeds to say that once the ship's hull was breached, the water came pouring in just as when a soldier, more daring than his companions, decided to try to leap over the walls of a besieged city. After many attempts, the soldier finally succeeds in his seemingly reckless mission and finds himself alone, one man among a thousand within the walls of the city. In the case of Ceyx's boat, the tenth wave overwhelms it at last.[47] The hero is finished; his boat destroyed and both captain and crew lost to the waves.

What is interesting in these similes is the comparison of Ceyx's lone boat to a city. In the first instance, the citadel of a city is being battered by ram and siege works; in the second, a lone enemy soldier leaps over the walls of the city—usually that would spell doom for the brave but foolish warrior, though here the image is one of success: the ship is overcome, and so we must imagine the citadel and city of the similes are likewise conquered. Virgil never plays with the idea that the ships conveying Aeneas and his men to Italy represent the destined city of the Trojan exiles; he does describe Aeneas' camp in Italy in language that evokes the first settlement of the future Rome (distantly foreshadowed and in roughly the right place geographically—close enough, at any rate, for epic poetry). Here, Ceyx's ship is like a city under siege, a city that is finally conquered. His ship presages the fall of Troy, whose end began, in some sense, with Protesilaus' brave leap—the soldier of the simile, after all, recalls Protesilaus. To underscore the point about urban penetration and the destruction of a city, Ovid adds what amounts to a third city simile, as he compares the nervousness of Ceyx's crew to the terror in a conquered city:

> . . . trepidant haud setius omnes,
> quam solet urbs aliis murum fodientibus extra
> atque aliis murum trepidare tenentibus intus. (11.534-536)

> . . . all are nervous, scarcely less than a city
> that is accustomed to be nervous when some are digging outside the walls
> and other are inside and in possession of the wall.

The death toll mounts from the waves and destruction; Ceyx, of course, is intent only on his beloved wife. One last wave overwhelms the ship for good and all; rather bombastically, Ovid compares its effect to what would happen if Athos and Pindos were suddenly ripped up and thrown into the water (in other words, how great a wave would result). A huge wave would be needed to overwhelm a city, of course; still, some critics have found this whole storm sequence overwrought, while others have emphasized that Ovid wanted one lavish storm scene in his epic.[48] Part of the poet's point, too, is to highlight the important significance of what this storm precedes; it comes right before the great narratives of Troy and Rome, two major cycles that are largely centered on the conquest of cities. The repeated insistence on comparing Ceyx's boat to a besieged city is part of this game; so, too, the decision to evoke both Protesilaus and Palinurus, as two similar figures from the two different cycles the Ceyx and Alcyone epyllion introduces.[49]

When Troy fell, Virgil noted that after the exiles had gathered in preparation for their westward flight, the Morning Star, Lucifer, arose over Mount Ida (*A*. 2.801-802)—a new day dawned, really for Rome, not Troy—the first sign of hope for the nascent city. In Ovid, Lucifer hides in obscure darkness from the storm (11.570-572); he could not help his beloved Ceyx, and by veiling himself in darkness, he reflects both his inadequacy and the fact that it was, after all, impossible to see the lights of heaven. Lucifer mourns, and Ceyx, for his part, consistently laments for his lost wife.[50]

We have noted that one tradition held that Ceyx and Alcyone were punished for ascribing divine honors for themselves. That tradition may lie behind Ovid's description of how Alcyone prayed especially to Juno for the return of her husband. In an interesting detail, Alcyone prays not only that Ceyx may return safely, but also that he may never prefer another woman to her (11.580-581), a definite echo of the main theme of the Cephalus and Procris narrative, which was concerned with the matter of marital fidelity and trust. In the case of Ceyx and Alcyone, Ovid notes that this alone of all the wife's prayers would be granted to her. Juno is of course the wife of the unfaithful Jupiter and a patroness of marriage; she is an appropriate deity for Alcyone's prayers, though the main point may well be an evocation of the tradition that Juno was the origin of the punishment of the arrogant couple, and the storm her doing. Thus Ovid calls Alcyone *Aeolis* (573) as she begins her invocation of the goddess, in evocation of Aeolus as the agent of Juno's bidding in sending the storm that bedeviled the Trojans in *A*. 1.

Juno cannot tolerate the constant appeals of a woman for her dead husband. She orders Iris to visit the god Sleep, so that he may send a dream to Alcyone in the form of Ceyx:

vise soporiferam Somni velociter aulam
exstinctique iube Ceycis imagine mittat
somnia ad Alcyonem veros narrantia casus. (11.586-588)

See swiftly the slumber-inducing court of Sleep,
and order that he send a dream in the likeness of Ceyx
to Alcyone, so that it may report the true events.

Iris could presumably have relayed the message herself, were the goddess disinterested or disinclined to do it herself. The main reason for Ovid's introduction of Somnus is to evoke the end of the fifth *Aeneid*, where Somnus appeared to Palinurus in the guise of the Trojan Phorbas. Somnus urged Palinurus to give in to rest and to abandon his maintenance of the flagship's rudder; Palinurus would have none of it, since he was aware of the dangers inherent in a seemingly tranquil sea. Somnus argued with Palinurus for only so long. Finally, the god of slumber sprinkled Palinurus with Lethaean dew and hurled him overboard; the helmsman was clinging so staunchly to the ship's rudder that it came off with him as he was thrown into the sea.

After Palinurus is thrown overboard by the god, the fleet proceeds on course.[51] Aeneas somehow senses that the fleet is sailing without a guide, and when he comes up on deck to investigate, he laments that Palinurus has trusted too much in a serene sky—perhaps he thinks that Palinurus fell asleep, assuming the seas were calm and did not need his direction at the rudder. Elsewhere I have argued that Neptune is responsible for the noisy surf that seems to surround the island of the Sirens as Aeneas' flagship draws close to their lair.[52] The god is in command, and Palinurus is a final sacrifice to the Sirens (much as the storm in A. 3 is followed by the encounter with the Harpies, so that Virgil rings the two storm scenes with encounters with bird women).

Sleep did not actually kill Palinurus, though readers of the fifth Aeneid might well think he did. For the "true" story of what actually happened, we must wait until Aeneas encounters Palinurus' ghost in the underworld. There, we learn that Palinurus became a human ship, a navigator of himself as he managed to swim to the Italian coast, where he was murdered by unknown brigands for unknown reasons. The ultimate fate of Palinurus is echoed in the original reason why Ceyx had to travel to Claros: Phorbas was besieging the way to Delphi, thus forcing Ceyx to make a dangerous sea voyage to another Apollonian oracle. In Virgil, Phorbas was the figure who stood at the beginning of Palinurus' final journey, the "man" responsible for hurling Palinurus off the ship and into the midst of an impromptu sea voyage where the helmsman would have to conduct his own body to his destination—only to die upon arrival at the hands of murderous miscreants. And, as we have noted, Aeneas will complain in the underworld that Apollo never warned him that such an event would befall his helmsman. Palinurus will beg Aeneas to ensure that his body is buried; the Sibyl will rebuke him, though with the prediction that the day will come when the sailor will give his name to the promontory near where he died (the etiology of Cape Palinurus).

In Ovid, Sleep will be the instrument of Juno's announcement to Alcyone that her husband Ceyx is dead (11.592 ff.). Virgil was brief in describing Sleep, who, after all, appeared in the guise of Phorbas. Ovid's description is among his most memorable creations, a poetic tour de force that serves two main purposes: first, it charms and delights the reader; second, and more seriously, it underscores the evocation of the fifth Aeneid.

The ecphrasis begins with a detail that Sleep's abode is located near the land of the Cimmerians. Here Ovid nods to Homer and the beginning of his underworld narrative (Odyssey 11.14-19), where the Cimmerians were mentioned as a geographical locus for where Odysseus made his own katabasis; Ovid is nodding to the underworld tradition in Virgil, where Palinurus would be encountered by the hero Aeneas. Sleep was the mythical brother of Death; while Sleep

324   CHAPTER XI

did not directly kill Palinurus in the *Aeneid*, the helmsman's death was the direct
consequence of the god's actions. Ovid's Sleep seems rather harmless, especially in comparison to Virgil's character; he can barely rouse himself from his
bed. This is not so much humorous mockery of Virgil as an instrument to maintain suspense: readers of the *Aeneid* are left wondering what Ovid's god will do
next.

Sleep's action in the *Aeneid* constitutes a rare example (for that epic) of a
god actively participating in the death of a mortal; Somnus' murderous deed
forms a ring with the nymph Opis and her fatal shooting of Camilla's killer Arruns.[53] In Ovid, Sleep will be charged with sending a dream to Alcyone that announces the truth of what happened to her husband; in Virgil, the "truth" would
be revealed in the underworld by the hero's own shade.

There is a reminiscence here, too, of the Virgilian Gates of Sleep (*A.* 6.893-
901). In the Homeric conception (*Iliad* 24.12), Dreams live at the edge of the
River Ocean, near the Gates of the Sun; the matter was by no means settled,
since in Hesiod (*Theogony* 211 ff.) they live in Tartarus. Hesiod' description of
the dwelling of Sleep and Death at *Theogony* 758-760 (where see West) is influential here, but the matter is a rather complicated mess. In Virgil, Sleep lives at
the entrance to the underworld proper (*A.* 6.273-284), where *somnia vana*,
"empty dreams," also make their residence—an elm is their place of dwelling.[54]
It is unknown what source (if any) Virgil used for this dream locus; it appears
nowhere else in extant lore. They are *vana* because they lack substance; the adjective does not *necessarily* indicate that dreams are mendacious, but it certainly
can carry that connotation.[55] Dreams, after all, ultimately cannot be trusted on
face value; the dreamer does not necessarily readily know if the dream vision is
true. In Ovid's conception, *somnia vana* (11.614) are all arrayed around the
slumbering god on his magnificent ebony bed. They are as numerous as the
sands of the sea, the leaves in a forest, or the ears of grain at harvest.[56] Obviously, some of them might be true and others false; all lack substance, and so
are, in a sense, *vana*; similarly, all can be easily (and wisely) distrusted.

There are so many dreams all flitting about that Iris has to move some with
her hands (11.616-617), a delightful touch; how different from Virgil's Somnus
is Ovid's, who can barely rouse himself from his couch to speak with the rainbow goddess. The scene has real charm and beauty, which contrasts with the
serious undertones; the very description of the god's dwelling is designed to lull
the reader (we think of Orpheus' description of his song's power to soften and
soothe, *mulcere*).[57] Such was exactly the reaction Virgil's Somnus was trying to
engender in Palinurus, to no effect. Iris, for her part, is Juno's regular assistant in
carrying out missions; we might note, however, that she is an appropriate go-
between here (Minerva went to Invidia by herself—though Ceres sent a nymph
to Fames). After all, Iris was the goddess who assisted Juno in her scheme to
have the Trojan women set fire to Aeneas' ships after the games in *A.* 5, so Iris'
appearance here recalls her destructive influence there.

Dreams are without substance, given how they imitate that which they are not. Iris' order to Somnus is to send a dream that will imitate the appearance of Ceyx. The message the dream will convey is real; but the dream vision, of course, is not really Ceyx. The return of the husband is an echo of what Protesilaus was allowed to do in the case of Laodamia; in the usual tradition of his "resurrection," Hermes had brought him back for a brief time so that he could speak to his wife.[58] In Ovid, there will be no return to life for however short a while. Rather, a dream will convey the news to Alcyone that her husband has drowned. In Virgil, Palinurus' shade was encountered by Aeneas in the underworld, so that the ghost could reveal its fate to its master.[59]

There were different accounts of the dwelling place of Sleep, and so Ovid could enjoy some latitude in his description. The fact that Ceyx is dead and that Sleep is being summoned to craft a dream of the drowned husband makes clear enough the connection between Sleep and his deadly brother; the Ceyx dream might as well have been summoned from the underworld. But Ovid next tells us that Sleep roused one of his thousand sons—apparently a dream—by the name of Morpheus. The word reminds us instantly of the Greek for "shape" or "form," as in the very title of the poet's work. Morpheus does not occur before this passage, and he does not appear after in extant classical Latin. But the invention— and I would argue that the character is an Ovidian creation—is of the utmost significance given the connection of the character's name to the central theme of the poem—change of form, meta-*morphosis*—and the central significance of the Gates of Sleep whence dreams true and false emanate at the end of the sixth *Aeneid*.[60] If Morpheus is an Ovidian invention, the poet's game is all the more apparent; Morpheus is a false vision, not because his story is a lie, but because he is not Ceyx. Similarly, at the end of *A.* 6 the problem is not the truth of the vision in the underworld that Anchises presented to Aeneas—we know, after all, in light of future Roman history that what Aeneas saw is all too true—but because in Virgil's conception, *there is no afterlife*. Virgil moves from a traditional underworld that Homer would have recognized to a strange world of Orphic and Pythagorean philosophies, where rebirth into a new life, a sort of reincarnation as part of a process of slow purgatory and renewal, serves as the mechanism to allow Anchises to unfold Rome's past (from the vantage point of Virgil's audience) in the future tense (from the vantage point of Virgil's hero Aeneas). But if there is no afterlife, if death is the end of all, then neither Homer nor the songs of those who would preach reincarnation are true. That "other" voice that haunts the pages of the sixth *Aeneid* is the voice of Lucretius. We shall hear more of that voice as we continue through the last third of Ovid's epic.

Morpheus, Ovid says, is the dream weaver who imitates men; another craftsman, known as Icelos to the gods and Phobetor to men, is responsible for imitating animals (11.635-641). Once again, Ovid appears to be inventing figures. "Icelos" does what his Greek name indicates—he is "like" something, but not what he seems. "Phobetor" is the one who brings fright, since, Ovid would seem to be saying, animals usually bring fear and terror in dreams. Another dream master, Phantasos, is responsible for all that lacks the breath of life (643 *anima*). Morpheus is the one who is needed for this job, of course; Ovid describes how Somnus went past all the others partly to offer a poetically charming description of the process, but also to emphasize how, in the end, all the dream weavers do exactly the same thing: they merely replicate reality, for they are but images of the substances they mimic.

Morpheus' visit is something of an act of mercy, to be sure, though a terrible one: he assumes the form of the drowned Ceyx (11.650 ff.). Morpheus is a liar, we might note; he says that he is the shade of Ceyx (660 *inveniesque tuo pro coniuge coniugis umbram*). Again, the story of Protesilaus has been changed: Ceyx is not allowed to return to his wife, he is, we must imagine, for now at least among the unburied dead (like Palinurus). Morpheus is imitating the shade's reality (for those who want to accept that the shade has any reality, of course). Morpheus himself plays with the idea of falsehood, that theme Ovid had explored so often in the Orpheus narrative: 662 *falso tibi me promittere noli*, "Do not falsely promise me to you." But the lies continue, and more plainly; Morpheus says that it is not some uncertain herald who brings the news of the death, but the husband himself:

> ipse ego fata tibi praesens mea naufragus edo. (11.668)

> *I myself, present to you, a shipwrecked man, announce my death.*

Morpheus' Ceyx is made to sound as if he were some shipwrecked epigrammatist, lost at sea or washed up on some beach and in need of burial (the real point of the ancient terror about death at sea). Morpheus imitates the gestures of Ceyx and his tears, and the wife is, of course, fooled. Ceyx had affinities with Palinurus; now it is Alcyone who has been visited by "Sleep," if we can equate Sleep's dream messenger with the god himself. Alcyone, unlike Palinurus, has been deceived, though of course under very different circumstances. Alcyone soon underscores her deception to her nurse, as attendants rush in after the devastated wife is roused from her dream-filled sleep:

> umbra fuit, sed ut umbra tamen manifesta virique
> vera mei. (11.688-689)

> *He was a shade, but, nevertheless, it was the manifest and true shade of my husband.*

The dream image was so real to Alcyone that she is fixated on where it appeared; she even proceeds to look to see if there are any tracks that leave evidence of its presence. Sleep's Junonian deception has worked.[61]

Alcyone had wanted to go with Ceyx on his sea voyage; in her mind, they would have been together come what may, and the one would not have to live with the death of the other. In a neat commentary on the nature of Morpheus' visit and his replication of Ceyx, Alcyone observes that in the death of Ceyx, she herself has been tossed by the waves and drowned at sea; she is so devoted to her husband that it is as if she were in bilocation, out there on the water, experiencing her own drowning. The natural outcome of this line of thought, of course, is that she will resolve to commit suicide and thereby make real what has been thus far but an image.[62]

The scene is now inspired by Ovid's own telling of the tragic story of Hero and Leander in the *Heroides* (18-19).[63] In this case, the appearance of Ceyx's body is unexpected; Alcyone assumed that her husband was forever lost at sea. So certain is she of this that at first she thinks the body she sees is that of another drowned shipwreck; she pathetically hopes that he has no wife (11.720-721).[64] There was a pier nearby; this will be the locus for Alcyone's decision to jump into the water after her husband.[65] The scene offers a subtle last reminiscence of the juxtaposition of the manmade and the world of nature; this clash was part of Ovid's point in emphasizing that Ceyx's boat was like a city under siege.

Alcyone's attempted suicide is arrested by an avian metamorphosis (11.731 ff.). Like Atalanta and Hippomenes, Alcyone can now skim over the surface of the water; she has been transformed into a bird that utters plaintive cries appropriate to its grief-stricken, overwrought emotional state. The bird heads to the drowned corpse to bestow kisses on the lifeless lips. There were apparently witnesses to the marvel; some claimed that they saw the body respond to the bird by lifting its head, while others said it was just the motion of the waves— another pathetic detail that balances emotionally charged fancy with rational thought. In general, though, it should be observed that throughout the lengthy narrative of his Ceyx and Alcyone epyllion, on the whole Ovid refrains from engaging in the sort of pathetic description that might easily elicit a smile from his audience. He wishes more or less to maintain a serious tone in this book, as befits its epic subject and themes.

At this point, Alcyone's husband is also transformed into a bird. Ovid gives no credit for the metamorphosis to any god; the point is that the couple remains together in their marital bond for all time (11.742-744 *fatis obnoxius isdem / tunc quoque mansit amor nec coniugiale solutum / foedus in alitibus*). Both husband and wife have been transformed into kingfishers, birds that will build their nests during the so-called "halcyon days" near the winter solstice in December. For the brief, peaceful time when they nest, Ovid notes that Aeolus finally acted on behalf of his grandchildren, and calmed the wind and wave (747-748).

The ending, then, is happy: very different indeed from the Cephalus and Procris story. Whatever the preexisting tradition, there is no trace of punishment in Ovid's account, unless we wonder at why Ceyx had to die in the first place. These birds have eternal love and perpetual fidelity; they have peace for the continuation of their species every winter. Part of Ovid's point is the glorification of marital fidelity; we had seen a hint of this in the very different story of Pyramus and Thisbe, the ill-fated young couple that found eternal union as the result of their tragic, violent ends.

We have shown how the Ceyx and Alcyone story echoes the eerie episode

of Sleep's attack on Palinurus and his subsequent loss at sea. In Virgil's conception, Palinurus' shade finally appeared to Aeneas in the underworld and explained what had happened to the lost helmsman, who did not drown as Aeneas
(and perhaps the audience) had assumed, but who was murdered by brigands
upon arrival in Italy—like his Greek model Protesilaus, the first casualty of the
war in a foreign land. Ceyx avoided his Phorbas, his brigands, by choosing to
travel by sea and not land. His resulting death (at sea and not on land) led to the
"attack" of Somnus on Alcyone. In Ovid's conception, the Phorbas figure and
the Sleep figure were separated; in Virgil, Phorbas/Sleep was responsible for
Palinurus' death (the nameless brigands in Italy were merely responsible for
striking the last blow in an assault Somnus had started on deck). In Ovid, Phorbas threatened Ceyx; the hero avoided him, but his wife Alcyone faced Sleep.
Alcyone was deceived with an image of Ceyx, a false image that was conjured
by the somnolent god. Ceyx himself—his shade—never speaks to Alcyone,
never appears to his wife in some nocturnal vision (cf. Virgil's Hector and Creusa). In the morning light of reality (as opposed to the night of vain dreams),
Alcyone saw the body of her drowned husband, the reality that Aeneas never
saw in the case of Palinurus. In Ovid's vision, a storm without any discernible
cause destroyed Ceyx, and an equally mysterious transformation has given the
sad story something of a "happy" ending.

The Ceyx and Alcyone story is the longest single narrative in the book, and
what follows it would seem to be anticlimactic. But Ovid has a surprise left, an
ending that rivals the surprise that comes near the end of Virgil's epic.

Some anonymous old man sees the kingfishers, and points to another bystander that the love the birds have preserved is praiseworthy. But he also notes
another bird, a diver of exceptionally long neck. Thus begins Ovid's brief account of the transformation of Priam's "other" son, Hector's half-brother Aesacus. The story is obscure; Pseudo-Apollodorus has an interesting version
(3.12.5), where Priam marries Arisbe after the capture of Troy by Heracles.
They have a son, Aesacus, who is transformed into a bird after his wife died and
he was consumed with grief. Priam then gave Arisbe to Hyrtacus and took a
second wife for himself, the famous Hecuba, and her first son with him was
Hector.[66]

In Ovid's account, Aesacus is the son of Priam and Alexirhoe. This attribution can be paralleled by Servius ad Virgil, A. 4.254, but that citation may be
influenced by Ovid. Ovid's Aesacus is a loner; he prefers not to be in Troy, but
enjoys the surrounding country (11.764-766 *oderat hic urbes nitidaque remotus
ab aula / secretos montes et inambitiosa colebat / rura nec Iliacos coetus nisi
rarus adibat*). He is the antithesis of an urban personality. He is no city-founder
or urban dweller; he is admirable, we might think, in that his actions almost
seem to mimic the venerable sylvan lifestyle of Diana. But he is a Trojan, not an
Italian, and he is certainly not a virgin huntress. In a brilliant touch that is another testimony to Ovid's tremendous poetic skill, Aesacus falls in love with a
very special girl:

non agreste tamen nec inexpugnabile amori
pectus habens silvas captatam saepe per omnes
aspicit Hesperien patria Cebrenida ripa
inectos umeris siccantem sole capillos. (11.767-770)

Nevertheless he did not have some boorish heart, or one that
was unconquerable by love, when he saw Hesperia, whom he often
tried to catch through all the woods,[67] *as she was drying her locks that were*
flowing over her shoulders, on the banks of father Cebren.[68]

Aesacus, the "first son," as it were, of Priam, is captivated by the love of *Hesperia*. The nymph is not otherwise known; there can be question, I would argue, that Ovid means for us to think of the only Hesperia that could have occurred to an Augustan audience: the western land of *Italy*. On the very cusp of his *Iliad* and *Aeneid*, Ovid has presented Troy's scion in pursuit of Italy.

The nymph will have nothing to do with him; she flees in terror. We are, after all, very far from the Italy predicted at the end of *Aeneid* 12, very far from the final reconciliation of Juno and the disposition of the ethnic status of the future Rome. Hesperia is like a deer before the "tawny wolf" (11.771-772 *fulvum . . . lupum*), a reference to the "tawny wolf" that will nurture Romulus and Remus according to the great prophecy Jupiter makes to his daughter Venus at the beginning of the *Aeneid*.[69] Like a duck, the nymph Hesperia flees the hawk, the accipiter; by the mention of the wolf and the hawk, Ovid neatly rings the end of the book to the beginning, with the lupine predation of Peleus' flocks and the etiology of the hawk.

Aesacus does not stop his pursuit.[70] Ovid's Hesperia now links back to an even earlier ring than the hawk and the dove, as she steps on a poisonous serpent in an evocation of Orpheus' loss of Eurydice (11.773-776). Hesperia falls dead from the bite, as Eurydice is reborn in Troy.[71]

The Trojan is horrified by the loss of his *objet d'amour*; now he repents of having pursued her and laments her death. Aesacus claims that he has destroyed two lives by his pursuit; he is ashamed to live on after Hesperia, and resolves to commit suicide—a neat recollection of the story of Ceyx and Alcyone. He throws himself from a lofty crag into the sea (783-784). Tethys takes pity on the scene and saves him; she changes him into a bird (again, echoes of Alcyone's story). Aesacus is not grateful for the avian metamorphosis; he wants nothing more than to commit suicide, and so he hurls his new form into the water in a second attempt. His light feathers do not allow him to find the death he so desperately seeks; he tries again and again to submerge himself into the water, failing each time. He wastes away with his constant attempts to kill himself; finally he becomes a *mergus*, a "diver," with long neck and long joints, his head far from his body (allegedly a sign of his emaciation—793 *fecit amor maciem*). He will waste away for all time out of longing to die; grief has overcome him, as well as desire for the girl he has lost by his own (premature) pursuit. Hesperia was not yet ready for Troy.

The ending of the eleventh book of the poem is a stunning close to Ovid's preparations for his confrontation with Homer and Virgil in Troy and Rome. In Ovid's vision, Hesperia—none other than Italy herself—is killed. She will not be taken by Priam's first son; Troy will not capture Rome. Aesacus, as it were, correctly realizes that the ultimate fate of Troy is linked with Rome; he knows that he has destroyed himself in pursuing her—tragically, too early—and his suicide reflects his awareness that without Rome, Troy has no final destiny. He finds that he cannot die; despite constant attempts, he lives on, however emaciated: Troy's memory will not die, the Trojan element haunts Rome, since even if Rome is to be Italian and not Trojan, the distinction only makes sense because of the memory of what old Troy was (and, implicitly, why from a Roman perspective it must be suppressed).

Ultimately, Troy will be reborn in Italy. That is the foundational theme of Virgil's *Aeneid* and, as we shall soon enough see, of Ovid's *Aeneid*. The final nature of that settlement in Italy, the result of the fusion of the Trojan and the Italian, is a more vexed question; indeed, it is the central problem of Virgil's epic. Virgil ends his poem with a surprise; we had no expectation of the stunning revelations Jupiter makes to Juno in the speech that bookends the speech he made to Venus in *A.* 1.[72] Ovid has replicated that surprise in the eleventh book of his epic, a marvelous nod to his poetic predecessors and a splendid mark of appreciation for Virgil's achievement.

And Hesperia is like Eurydice. Eurydice's death brought Orpheus to the underworld, where he could try to practice his art of renewal and rebirth. He was unable to save Eurydice; she died a "second death," as it were, and through the poet's own fault. Orpheus could not cure Eurydice's mortal ill; he could not save his wife, despite whatever the Orphic poems and Orphic philosophy said about resurrection and a second life. In the end, though, Orpheus' death brought him back to the underworld of Homer and his Eurydice; they are united forever, just as Ceyx and Alcyone are together for all time. Hesperia is no bird; she is most certainly *not* linked to Aesacus, who is alone and has wasted away in his longing for that which he can never obtain. He will not follow the example of Orpheus; Ovid's description of the ultimate fate of Orpheus and Eurydice in the underworld serves as contrast with the fate of *this* victim of snakebite and her suitor. The marriage of Orpheus and Eurydice ultimately ends in eternal union in the underworld; the would-be rape of Hesperia by Aesacus ends in failure for the Trojan and a punishment, in effect, of eternal wasting: he wants nothing more than to die, and death will elude him for all time. Ceyx and Alcyone also find peace in death, and a certain type of immortality; the yearly appearance of the halcyon birds is a testament to their undying love and fidelity, and they are remembered happily and with tranquility after so much turmoil. There is something here of the honor the Sibyl offered Palinurus, honor that brings little consolation, of course; Palinurus is not unlike Camilla, whose soul goes indignant to the underworld, though she, too, will know *post mortem* glory and an honored name.

The evocation of Orpheus and Eurydice from the beginning of Book 10 also offers Ovid another chance to provide his narrative with a tightly constructed ring, in this case centered on the fate of another girl—and a most important one—who falls victim to a serpent.

And so, on the very cusp of his *Iliad* and *Aeneid*, Ovid offers *Book 11* of his epic, his *carmen perpetuum*, in which he has echoed first Book 11 and then Book 5 of Virgil's *Aeneid*, before moving back to Book 11 and, with it, a pendant in which he offers commentary on the final resolution of Book 12. It is a virtual *Aeneid* in miniature, before he addresses in his epic narrative the "real" events of both *Aeneid* and *Iliad* (the latter the necessary prolegomena to the former).[73]

We do not know for sure how Ovid will proceed as we leave the saddened Aesacus in his constant, failed attempts to commit suicide, though we know the poet cannot long delay the Greek expedition to take Troy, which represents its next destruction after Laomedon's perfidy with Apollo, Neptune, and Hercules, as well as the symbolic death of Troy in its quest to find Hesperia. Soon enough, the poet who does not disappoint and who so favors rapid narrative (ever advancing toward his main goal) will show us the ships assembled at Aulis, as the *Iliad* is reborn in Alexandrian miniature.

Notes

1. The Anderson commentary on Books 6-10 (1972) and 1-5 (1996) is projected to be finished for Oklahoma by Garth Tissol; I am grateful to Professor Tissol for supplying me with a handy copy of his article "The House of Fame: Roman History and Augustan Politics in Ovid's *Metamorphoses* 11-15," from *Brill's Companion to Ovid*, when I was away from my library. On Book 11, there is a small Oxford commentary by G. M. H. Murphy (1972) that has vocabulary and is aimed at lower-level Latin students, though with useful notes for more advanced readers.

2. Much of this chapter deals with the vast question of intertextuality. For an introduction to the subject, best is Casali, Sergio, "Ovidian Intertextuality," in the *Blackwell Companion to Ovid*, pp. 341-354.

3. Cf., e.g., Pausanias 9.30; Diogenes Laertius 1.5.

4. Guthrie, *op. cit.*, pp. 31 ff., provides a helpful overview of the testimonia, both literary and visual.

5. *Symposium* 179d, where see Dover, and Bury.

6. Most conveniently available in Powell's *Collectanea Alexandrina*.

7. Suetonius, *Divus Augustus* 68, records that in early youth Octavian was accused of sexual vice; Sextus Pompey called him effeminate, while Antony accused him of sex with Caesar (and Lucius Antony accused him of sex with Aulus Hirtius in Spain, and that he would practice a primitive form of electrolysis on his legs). All of these accusers would have been hostile to him. But it was generally accepted that Augustus was a womanizer and adulterer with women.

8. 11.37-38 *cornuque minaces / divulsere boves* must mean they tore apart the oxen that threatened them with their horns; Hill argues that they tore the oxen from their horns, to use the horns as weapons. But this is an unnatural way to take the Latin, and, besides, the maenads have already been shown to be interested in slaughtering everything they encounter, animals as well as men. If we read *cornu minaci*, the construction becomes a bit easier, though the textual variants reveal early trouble with the passage.

9. For the textual problems of 11.71-72, which do not impact the meaning in any significant way, see especially Murphy ad loc.

10. As Ovid notes at 11.92-93, Orpheus had taught the conduct of the Bacchic rites to Midas of Phrygia and Eumolpus of Athens; he was a proselytizer for the Bacchic cause, and the god has reason to be displeased with his female devotees.

11. Oddly, though, there is no mention of burial for the decapitated head.

12. See further "Ovid's Midas: A Case of Poetic Schizophrenia," in *The Classical Journal* 64 (1968), pp. 70-73, and Roller, L. E., "The Legend of Minos," in *Classical Antiquity* 2 (1983), pp. 299-313.

13. 11.108 indicates that Midas sought a twig from a branch that was not too high up in the tree; Merkel condemned the line (see further Hill ad loc., and Tarrant's apparatus), but Ovid may have had the Golden Bough in mind, and while Virgil does not specify how high the Bough is, the implication is it is reachable—and why not Midas' as well.

14. There is just possibly another allusion to the Virgilian Bough in Bacchus' instruction to Midas at 11.139 *carpe viam*, which echoes the Sibyl's (ignored) direction to Aeneas to "pluck" the Bough (*carpe manu*); but, as we have seen, *carpere* is a very common verb and the echo cannot be pushed too far.

WHILE WITH SUCH A SONG . . .

15. 11.119-120 *mensas . . . exstructas*.
16. Less likely a reading, since only Bacchus is really involved in the current story.
17. A reference to the idea that the Achelous could purify Amphiaraus' son Alcmaeon from guilt for slaying his mother.
18. Aristophanes, *Plutus* 287; note also the *Greek Anthology* 5.56. But the story is not elaborated in either reference, and Ovid's version is, once again, the first surviving account.
19. Though sometimes overmuch is made of every appearance in Latin verse of this adjective. Also, Pan's song is in the Phrygian or Trojan manner (11.162 *barbarico*), which denotes rude and uncouth verse—hardly suitable for pastoral, or for the aesthetically pleasing Alexandrian style.
20. In a neat little ring, Midas' barber will mumble his master's secret into the ground, just as later in the book Ceyx will murmur his wife's name into the waves after his shipwreck.
21. The story of the perfidious Trojan founder is Homeric; Hill ad 194-220 conveniently gathers the relevant passages, and note also Bömer's exhaustive cataloguing.
22. For the mythographic version, note Pseudo-Apollodorus 2.5.9 and 2.6.4, where the horses are those that Zeus gave in compensation for the abduction of Ganymede.
23. As Hill notes ad 11.221-265, Frazer's notes in the Loeb Apollodorus are unusually rich for Achilles lore, and provide a good starting place for study.
24. The metamorphoses are not original to Ovid; cf. Pindar, *Nemeans* 4.62-65).
25. The story is not well recorded in the extant sources. According to Pseudo-Apollodorus 3.12.6-13.1, Peleus and Telamon conspired to kill their brother because he was better than they at athletic competitions. Telamon actually committed the murder, but Peleus helped to conceal the body. Both were expelled from Aeacus' Aegina and driven into exile—hence Peleus' presence in Phthia.
26. Ovid hereby begins his (long) introduction to what will become the single most extended story of the book, that of Ceyx and Alcyone. The tale has aroused significant commentary; note especially Fantham, Elaine, "Ovid's Ceyx and Alcyone: The Metamorphosis of a Myth," in *Phoenix* 33 (1979), pp. 330-345, and Rudd, Niall, "Ceyx and Alcyone: Ovid, *Metamorphoses* 11, 410-748," in *Greece & Rome* Ser. 2, 55.1 (2008), pp. 103-110. For convenient summary of the problems of sources, see Otis, *op. cit.*, pp. 392-394.
27. See further Bömer, and Murphy, for the possible influence of Boeo's *Ornithogonia* in this section of the epic. The story of the transformation of Daedalion into a hawk may be original to Ovid; it is found elsewhere only at Hyginus, *Fabulae* 200, but, again, the argument from silence is weak. But in extant literature only Ovid links Daedalion with Ceyx.
28. It is possible that Ovid has in mind the Virgilian description of Camilla (*A.* 11.721-724) as a raptor that eviscerates a dove, but the idea is a fairly common one.
29. The grandfather of Odysseus.
30. And note Antoninus Liberalis 38, where the story is credited to Book 1 of Nicander's *Heteroeumena*. In Antoninus, we find Peleus accidentally killing Iros, who had performed the hero's purification for his brother's death—the accident apparently occurred during the Calydonian boar hunt. Peleus fled; the wife of his new host lied that he had tried to seduce her. Eventually he bought flocks to pay back Iros' father for the death of his son. Iros refused the offering, upon which a wolf came and attacked the sheep; the gods pitied Peleus and turned the wolf into a stone. See further Bömer, and Hill, ad loc.
31. See further *Madness Unchained*, pp. 348 ff., and the relevant notes in my com-

mentary on *A.* 11.

32. I have emphasized in previous work that Camilla's lycanthropy is a speculation. As I have noted, absent new evidence, the idea remains speculative. I remain bemused that it seems to have aroused ire in some critics, who, I must conclude, do not approve of speculation.

33. Her name is saved for the prayer, to underscore that in supplicatory invocations the divine name is important.

34. And cf. *Fasti* 2.39-40, where it is made explicit that Peleus was the killer of Phocus (not merely a helper of his murderous brother Telamon).

35. There are numerous parallels between the next to the last books of Virgil's *Odyssey* and *Iliad*, on which see further my "The Penultimate Books of Virgil's *Aeneid*," in *Quaderni Urbinati di Cultura Classica* 80.2 (2005), pp. 147-150.

36. The wife died there, the husband here; this time, however, the couple are "joined," in a sense, while the earlier couple was separated.

37. I note that Ovid brilliantly links these two episodes together in Books 7 and 11 of his epic, where the audience might recall Camilla's presence in the same two books of Virgil's poem.

38. See further Hill ad 410-748 (introductory remarks). Note, too, that while there is plenty of bad behavior on the part of both Cephalus and Procris, there is no such blameworthiness in the present tale.

39. Which is, in a deliberate, brilliant nod to his great epic predecessors, the shortest book in the epic. Ovid also allots but one book to his *Iliad*, and his briefest, but two to his *Aeneid*, and among his longer (Books 12 and 13 contrast as the shortest and longest books in the *Metamorphoses*).

40. And of Pallas; on Palinurus see further my *"Princeps ante omnis*: Palinurus and the Eerie End of Virgil's Protesilaus," forthcoming in *Latomus.* I argue there that Palinurus is modeled on Protesilaus; Ovid seems to have agreed, where Ceyx and Alcyone echo Protesilaus and Laodamia.

41. He had already focused significant attention on 11 in the Atalanta epyllion from *M.* 10.

42. For the scanty remnants of the lore, see further Bömer, and Hill; Murphy rather misses the point when he dismisses the appearance of these bandits as "specious motivation" for the dangerous sea journey to Claros.

43. The brigands may also be a nod to the version of "Alcyone"'s story mentioned briefly by Ovid at *M.* 7.401 ff., where Alcyone is the daughter of an Athenian brigand; she is thrown off a cliff by her angry father and is transformed into a bird. Probus ad Virgil, *Georgics* 1.399 mentions this story as well as the more famous one, which Probus credits to Nicander. In the scholia to Aristophanes' *Aves*, we learn of a version where the punishment Ceyx and Alcyone suffered for calling each other gods was the storm that killed Ceyx, which Otis rightly thinks is the version that was most influential on Ovid.

44. Hippotas was the father of Aeolus.

45. See further Otis' appendix on Ovid's sources for his version of the lore.

46. Hero and Leander are the subject of *Heroides* 18-19; their story lends itself well to that verse epistle collection.

47. A strange notion, which Tarrant thinks was original to Ovid. Hill notes that on British beaches, the seventh wave is considered the greatest.

48. See further Bate, Marcus, "Tempestuous Poetry: Storms in Ovid's *Metamorphoses, Heroides*, and *Tristia*," in *Mnemosyne* 57.3 (2004), pp. 295-310.

49. The Cephalus and Procris epyllion, with its emphasis on Diana, similarly pre-

cedes the Calydonian boar hunt.

50. There is also something of the Orpheus and Eurydice story in the separation of Ceyx and Alcyone.

51. Interestingly, Virgil observes that the fleet is unafraid, *A.* 5.863 *interrita*, which Mackail and others have taken to mean the ships are not frightened by Neptune's promise, namely, that one life must be sacrificed; most have seen it as a confirmation of the god's direction of the fleet to Italy.

52. See further my forthcoming *Princeps ante omnis* article on Palinurus (*Latomus*, 2011).

53. Of course the master poet can work on many levels of correspondences simultaneously. And so while Virgil's Palinurus and Arruns have affinities, so too do Palinurus and Camilla.

54. See further Austin ad loc.

55. Cf. the adjective's appearances at *A.* 2.80 and 11.715; it is a rather understudied word that deserves closer examination; the Ivory Gate sends forth *falsa insomnia*.

56. Murphy notes well that Ovid likes triple similes.

57. Cf. 11.625 *mulces*, in Iris' description of Sleep's actions.

58. Hyginus has a "standard" account at *Fabulae* 103-104; see further my Palinurus article for the interesting account of the mythographer Conon, which helps explain why Virgil crafted *A.* 5 the way he did (ship-burning followed by Palinurus).

59. Palinurus has no wife, though in his prefigurement of the loss of Pallas, Aeneas' would-be lover were the *Aeneid* not necessarily skittish (given its Roman context) about replicating the Achilles-Patroclus bond, there is something of the "abandoned wife" motif in Aeneas' underworld encounter with his lost helmsman.

60. I have presented my views on a massive problem in the 2007 *Latomus* article "A Brief Reflection on the Gates of Sleep." Those conclusions are summarized at *Madness Unchained*, pp. 196-198. I argue that the Virgilian Gates represent a rejection of both a Homeric and an Orphic/Pythagorean vision of the afterlife in favor of a Lucretian theology.

61. In this scene Ovid also subtly recalls the phantom Aeneas that Juno substituted for the real one to help delay the inevitable death of her beloved Turnus (see further *A.* 10.611 ff.); both Virgil and Ovid are in debt to Lucretius' consideration of sense and perception in *DRN* 4.

62. Reading 11.701 with the emended (so Heinsius) *et sine me me pontus habet* instead of *et sine me te* or *et sine te me*; see further Tarrant's apparatus ad loc.

63. Convenient summary of what (relatively little) we know about the lore = Kenney, *Ovid: Heroides XVI-XXI*, Cambridge, 1996, pp. 9-15. The story is essentially known to us from Ovid, Virgil's *Georgics*, and the fifth-century A.D. poem on the subject by Musaeus; a fragment of a poem found in 1982 (see further Kenney) may be part of the hypothesized lost Hellenistic original.

64. See further especially Hill for commentary on the body's appearance at 11.714-725: "these lines [are] among the most memorable in the *Metamorphoses*." Rather lavish praise for lines that, while unobjectionable, are not particularly distinguished.

65. It is not entirely clear that we are supposed to imagine that Alcyone has attempted suicide. She certainly resolved at 11.704 ff. that she would "come to be companion" to her husband (705 *et tibi nunc saltem veniam comes*—this was the night before she unexpectedly found the body the next morning). She hurled herself into the water to go to her husband, which does not necessarily imply a suicide attempt, but given her state and what she said the night before, it seems the most reasonable interpretation.

66. I am tempted to posit a connection between this Hyrtacus and the father of Nisus in the *Aeneid*, and, for that matter, the eternal union of Ovid's Ceyx and Alcyone and Virgil's great authorial apostrophe to Nisus and Euryalus, who are, in death, in a sense the only "successful" couple to be found in Virgil's epic.

67. 11.768 *Silvas captatam saepe per omnes* is usually translated as I have rendered it, namely that Aesacus tried to catch her through the forests time and again, which rather does violence to the Latin. Better is to take it as meaning that he saw her again and again in the woods, with an eye to catching her.

68. The Cebren is not mentioned in Homer. Cf. Statius, *Silvae* 1.5.21. The Cebren is a foreshadowing of the Tiber.

69. *A.* 1.275 *lupae fulvo . . . tegmine.*

70. Ovid's appellation of *Troius heros* for Aesacus (11.773) emphasizes Ovid's evocation of the lore of Trojan attempts to invade Italy.

71. There is no sense in Ovid's narrative that we are to imagine Rome is somehow doomed to die or enfeebled in the death of Hesperia, shocking as her loss might be; rather, the point is that Rome will not be captured by Troy. Death is preferable to that, and Hesperia's death signals the impossibility of such a successful rapine. Further, the greater emphasis in Ovid's story is on the emaciation of the *mergus*, as it tries again and again to die, though without success. The epic's past stories of such attempted suicides have come to a conclusion in the refusal of old Troy to give up the ghost. There is also something in the emaciated diver of the image of the Troy that haunts Rome and will not die.

72. And, for the major question of fate and destiny and what can and what cannot be changed, Virgil offers the point that the rage of Juno, the wrath of the goddess that corresponds to the wrath of the Homeric Achilles, is ultimately quelled because her madness succeeds in winning a major confession. It was fated that Troy found Rome; it was not fated, perhaps, that Rome be Trojan. Jupiter does not lie to his daughter in *A.* 1, but, as we have noted elsewhere, one imagines she would be very unhappy indeed were she privy to the colloquy between husband and wife in *A.* 12. Venus is *laeta* in the first *Aeneid*; by the end of the epic, it is Juno who is *laeta*, though for very different reasons.

73. The presence of Morpheus and the evocation of the Gates of Sleep further cement the book's status as a miniature *Aeneid*. I have argued elsewhere that the penultimate book of Virgil's *Aeneid* summarizes for the audience many of the themes of that epic, appropriately enough on the very cusp of the final resolutions of mortal and immortal affairs in Book 12. Book 11 of Ovid's epic does much the same thing, on a scale of detail that leaves the audience dazzled.

Chapter XII

Priam, Unknowing . . .

The twelfth book of the *Metamorphoses* is the shortest in the epic, though its subject is one of the most important in the literature of classical antiquity: the Trojan War.[1] As the book opens, the audience has no clear expectation about the direction of the narrative. The principal source lying behind Ovid's work and the reader's anticipation would of course be Homer's *Iliad*; in Ovid's recent past, Virgil had retold the *Iliad*, in effect, in the second half of his *Aeneid*. Besides that, there was the vast repertoire of cyclic epic and allusions to Troy lore in both lyric poetry and the tragic corpus; the basic outlines of the story were well covered by a wide variety of sources at the poet's disposal. One of Ovid's most important tricks in this book will be to defy expectation. Book 12 will cover the entire war in chronological scope, in the sense that it begins with the Greeks at Aulis and ends with the death of Achilles, but no reader could expect to encounter what Ovid highlights in his narrative. Most of the book, in fact, is spent on one combat, that of Achilles and Cycnus, and the aftermath, where the Greeks gather for a banquet and the aged Nestor tells the story of the battle of the Lapiths and the Centaurs. By book's end, Ovid would seem to have avoided covering much of the ground we would expect from an *Iliad* (admittedly, some of the material will be reserved for the great debate over the arms of Achilles in Book 13), but, as we shall see, the poet's main point is to present the themes he wants the audience to have absorbed both from Homer and Virgil. One of the most important of those themes for Ovid is the concept of the unfair fight, the battle against a seemingly superhuman foe (or a seriously mismatched opponent); that image lies behind the combat between Hector and Patroclus, which of course leads to the reentrance of Achilles into the war. The image recurs again and again in both Homer and Virgil (e.g., Turnus and Aeneas); for Ovid, the theme is so important that he will devote the bulk of this book to the stories of both Cycnus and Caeneus as he explores the meaning of indestructibility, a theme that also relates to the main topic he had raised after the death and apotheosis of Hercules: what can the gods do for their favorites? What help can they give to their special devotees, and how does this help or lack thereof relate to the larger issues of fate and free will?

As the book commences, Ovid once again employs rapid narrative; throughout this section of the poem, Ovid will effect a contrast between the

337

length of Homer's *Iliad*, not to mention the *Odyssey* and the now lost cyclic epics, and his comparatively short account. Within ten lines, the Greeks are ready to advance against Priam's city to avenge Paris' absconding with Helen of Sparta. Ovid had preceded his account of Troy lore with numerous recollections of the Palinurus episode from *Aeneid* 5, and as Book 12 of his epic begins, he is able to tie together Virgil's *Aeneid* 5 with his Troy cycle yet again: at Aulis, as the Greek fleet prepares to sail, a serpent attacks a nest of birds.

The omen is Homeric; as the commentators note, Ovid is especially careful here to imitate his Homeric model almost exactly.[2] But with the audience still thinking of Palinurus from the lengthy Ceyx and Alcyone epyllion, the evocation of Homer's serpent at Aulis recalls the snake that appeared at Anchises' grave in Sicily at the beginning of *A.* 5, the presumably positive omen that represents either the *genius* of Aeneas' father or of the place.[3] Once again, the snake is of ambiguous signification; here, as in Homer, it portends both good and bad: Troy will fall, Calchas prophesies, but only in the tenth year (since the serpent devours eight nestlings and their mother). The transformation of the snake into stone (reminiscent of the previous petrifactions of fox and wolf in conjunction with the Cephalus/Procris and Ceyx stories) is also Homeric; obviously the metamorphosis nicely fits Ovid's main theme, but here the snake symbolizes the beginning of Troy's end, just as Laocoon's serpents in Virgil symbolize the coming end of Troy in even more terrible fashion.[4]

The sacrifice of Iphigenia so that the Greek fleet might leave Aulis is an old story, though, as so often in Greek mythology, there was a varied tradition. Some believed that Iphigenia was not really killed, but that some animal or other substitute saved her life at the last moment.[5] For Lucretius, the image of the beautiful virgin sacrificed by order of her own father Agamemnon so that ships might sail is the supreme example of the wicked power of religion, which dictates that a girl must be stabbed so an expedition may set out with favorable winds. For Lucretius, the sacrifice of Iphigenia is the single best example of why one should withhold belief in the efficacy of religious practice.

Ovid appreciates the tradition that Iphigenia was saved by a last minute substitution; the appearance of a deer for the sacrifice fits neatly into his epic's transformations, and also spares Diana the onus of being responsible for the slaughter of an innocent virgin. Given Diana's place in Augustan religion, it was useful to Ovid's program to suppress the Lucretian emphasis on sacrifice and mention the substitution, though the language Ovid uses casts doubts on the whole affair:

supposita fertur mutasse Mycenida cerva. (12.34)

It is said that she exchanged a doe for the Mycenaean girl.

Ovid's Diana is moved to pity for Iphigenia (12.32 *victa dea est*); it will not do to have Diana approving the slaughter of blameless girls. The fleet sails; soon enough it arrives at Troy.

Ovid had preceded his retelling of the vast Troy lore with a detailed ecphrasis of the house of Sleep. To balance that description of the quietest and most peaceful place imaginable, he now has a description of the house of Rumor (12.39 ff.),[6] the one personification that Virgil had himself employed, the great beast that had brought the news of Aeneas' landing in Carthage and dalliance with Dido to Iarbas. Ovid builds suspense; we have no idea at first what he is describing as he starts his ecphrasis of the house at the center of land, sea, and sky. The description of Rumor's house has echoes of Virgil's details about the underworld; here, the baleful influence of Rumor is as much about the coming destruction from war as any hint of falsehood.

The war begins, of course, with Protesilaus, whose lore had recently been evoked in the remembrance of Virgil's Palinurus. Protesilaus is killed by Hector; in Homer, his killer is unnamed, though the tradition predates Ovid that Troy's greatest champion slew the first Greek to land on enemy soil. The first blood in the war was Protesilaus', but Ovid quickly moves to both Hector and Achilles—the latter is introduced almost casually, with nothing in the way of introduction. His first exploit is the death of Cycnus.

Only Ovid reports that Cycnus underwent any sort of metamorphosis; this son of Neptune appeared in the cyclic *Cypria*, but little survives in the way of pre-Ovidian evidence for this character. This is not the Cycnus of 2.367 ff., who was transformed into a swan after the death of Phaethon.

Cycnus—an indestructible warrior, as Achilles soon finds out—is the son of Neptune; he is a parallel to Virgil's Messapus, another son of Neptune who was said to be impervious to fire and the sword (*A.* 7.692).[7] Troy was destined to withstand the Greeks for nine years, only to fall in the tenth; Achilles is defended by the tenth of the layers of his mighty shield from Cycnus' attack. The Neptunian hero is struck a second and a third time, all in vain (12.95 ff.). Achilles is like a bull that is taunted in the arena.[8] The simile is another anachronistic image, of course, but the point would have had great appeal to Ovid's audience: in Neptune's invulnerable son, we have the perfect image of the hero's seemingly fruitless quest against an unfair opponent. The bull in the arena is an object of fear, but also mockery—the *toreador* taunts the animal as it grows increasingly angry and frustrated. There is something in Ovid's description of this combat that is reminiscent of Virgil's depiction of the struggle between Aeneas and Turnus, where the Rutulian hero is all too aware that his opponent has divine protection—Turnus has no doubt he would triumph absent such immortal interference, and he is aware that Jupiter is his enemy.

Achilles cannot slay Cycnus, but he can recount his previous exploits, which of course serves Ovid well as he attempts to tell as many stories as he can in as short a compass as possible. Significantly, he first announces his capture of Lyrnesos (12.108 ff.). Lyrnesos was the home of Briseis, Achilles' war prize.[9] In the anger of Achilles over Briseis and her eventual loss, there is something of Turnus' anger over Lavinia. Tenedos and Thebes are next; the latter has particular resonance as the city of Eetion (110 *Eetioneas implevi sanguine Thebas*), Andromache's slaughtered father. Ovid also mentions the famous story of Telephus, the Mysian king who found himself "twice experienced" in Achilles' spear (112 *opusque meae bis sensit Telephus hastae*). The story is most conveniently found in Pseudo-Apollodorus (3.17-20); Telephus was wounded by Achilles during an abortive Greek assault on Mysia (they had mistaken it for Troy). Later, Apollo told Telephus that he would be cured by the man who had wounded him; Telephus found Achilles and promised to show the way to Troy in exchange for a cure, which was accomplished by the scraping off of rust from Achilles' spear.

Achilles decides to resume his attack, but—rather unexpectedly—he hurls his weapon not at Cycnus, but at Menoetes. The story does not appear anywhere outside Ovid, but the name is of rich Virgilian associations.

There are two characters in the *Aeneid* whose fates Ovid is recalling here. The first was the helmsman of the Trojan hero Gyas on the Chimaera during the boat race in Sicily (*A.* 5.160-182). Gyas' ship was winning the race when the overzealous captain ordered Menoetes to draw in closer to the rock that marked the turning point of the race; Menoetes wisely urged against such a plan, and in anger, Gyas hurled him overboard. The whole episode presages the loss of Palinurus at the hands of Sleep later in the book, and forms a ring between the two men who are thrown off their decks. Menoetes is mocked as he comes up from the sea, spitting up draughts of salt water; the passage is a comic presage of the deadly reality that Palinurus will face when he comes up from the sea onto Italian soil and is slain by unnamed assailants.[10]

In *Aeneid* 12 (517-520), there is brief mention of a second Virgilian Menoetes, an Arcadian ally of Aeneas who is slain by Turnus. Virgil notes that he was a poor fisherman, his father a tiller of rented land.[11] In Achilles' killing of the hapless Menoetes, seemingly a sort of throwaway character whose purpose seems to be to prove to Achilles and possibly the audience that the hero can still kill people, Ovid makes a direct comparison between his Achilles and Virgil's Turnus. By recalling Menoetes, Ovid also neatly links his recent evocation of Virgil's Palinurus episode to the opening movements of his description of the war at Troy. Most importantly, Ovid opens his *Iliad* with one of the major themes of the *Aeneid*: the concept of the unfair combat, the hero fighting against a seemingly impossible enemy.

Achilles is enraged: after killing Menoetes, he strikes again at Cycnus and thinks he has at last drawn blood—but the gore is only from Menoetes. Achilles descends from his chariot and moves to close combat with Cycnus. Achilles goes into a mad fit of anger and begins bashing Cycnus with shield and sword-hilt over and over, forcing his opponent to give ground and retreat. Cycnus stumbles backward into a huge boulder (12.134-137). Achilles looms over him and picks him up, whirling him around in the air before smashing him to the ground—again, Ovid effectively conveys the hero's rage. The theme of Achilles' anger is the center of Homer's *Iliad*; in that epic, Achilles was angry because of the loss of Briseis, while in Ovid's conception, the hero is overcome with rage because he is fighting a semi-divine figure that is apparently unstoppable. This theme is one of the central issues in the *Aeneid*; Turnus cannot effectively challenge Aeneas because Aeneas has divine power and fate or destiny on his side. Turnus rages against this unbalanced, unfair combat; he is a heroic figure partly in that he challenges fate even though he knows he will lose, and yet he does not surrender.[12]

Achilles proceeds to strangle Cycnus (12.140 ff.). He cannot destroy the swan-man with any blade, but he can choke the life out of him. But when he proceeds to strip the body of its arms as spoils of war, he finds the armor empty, the body gone—Cycnus has been transformed into a swan. The swan is not there, it would seem (that would have been ridiculous), but the mysterious son of Neptune has vanished. He has been defeated, and yet Achilles has been cheated of victory.

Ovid has adapted an episode from cyclic epic and utilized it as the first extended story in his *Iliad*; it is striking that given the relatively short length of the book, so much attention is devoted to this strange tale. Cycnus is defeated—Turnus would enjoy no such triumph over Aeneas in his single combat—but the vanquished foe escapes the clutches of his enemy by divine intervention. He is transformed into a bird, and a beautiful, admirable one at that; he disappears, though Ovid is not quite finished with the image or the lore, as we shall see before too long. And we see shades of the mermaid-rescue of Aeneas' fleet in *A. 9*.

There is another Cycnus in the *Metamorphoses*, whose story was briefly related while Medea was in her flight after the grisly slaughter of Pelias (7.371 ff.). He was the object of Phyllius' amorous pursuit; he put forth challenge after challenge to the would-be lover, culminating in the demand for the capture of a fierce bull (we recall Ovid's comparison of Achilles to a taunted bull in the arena). The bull was refused, and Cycnus threw himself off a cliff and was transformed into a swan. As we have noted, it is not at all clear why that Cycnus told Phyllius the day would come when he would regret not having granted the bull; most probably, the point is that Cycnus would have acceded to the pursuit, and the day would come when Phyllius would regret that he had refused that last demand of the now beautiful and noble bird. In the present sequence, *Achilles* is the bull, the taunted animal some anonymous bullfighter—Cycnus—is challenging. Try as he might, the bull cannot vanquish the challenger. Achilles slays Cycnus, and yet he loses him; like Phyllius' lover off the cliff, here the invulnerable son of Neptune escapes pursuit and is impervious to capture (though his arms remain as a sign of the defeat and the loss of the body).[13]

A "Cycnus" first appeared in Book 2, then, after Phaethon's death; then we waited five books for another, who appeared during Medea's flight; then we waited another five books, and here, in the most extended Cycnus narrative, Achilles' first detailed combat in Ovid's *Iliad* is his fight with a third swan. There is a nice balance in the introduction of the name in Book 2, which rings neatly with the reappearance of Cycnus at 11.580-619 below, and the two narratives of the *eromenos* of *Met.* 7 and the invulnerable warrior of the present combat.

As we shall soon see, Neptune is not pleased with the defeat of his son; he views the conquest of Cycnus as a loss for his offspring, despite the miraculous transformation that is probably the doing of the god. In Ovid's conception, the death of Cycnus is the direct cause of the death of Achilles. Neptune will seek Apollo's help in seeing to the destruction of Achilles. In this double divine intervention, where Apollo will be sought to oversee the death (by a missile shot) of the hero, there is a direct evocation of Virgil's depiction of Camilla's death at the hands of Arruns, with the divine assistance of both Jupiter and Apollo. Achilles was enraged that this semi-divine hero should escape his grasp; he triumphed over the son of Neptune, but at the cost of his life. Homer's *Iliad*, of course, offers no detailed rationalization for the death of Achilles, no explanation for why the hero must die. He is fated to die young if he goes off to battle, and his return to combat after the loss of his beloved Patroclus signals his impending doom. Ovid offers explanation: Achilles challenged the divine order by seeking what we might term a fair fight, one in which a hero is not completely invulnerable. When he could not vanquish Cycnus by a blade, he tried and succeeded with strangulation; he will pay for his "victory"—the first Cycnus had mourned for the dead Phaethon, who had affected divine pretensions; the last Cycnus will be the cause of Achilles' death, who dared to challenge a god by killing his son.[14]

The struggle between Achilles and Cycnus leads to a truce; the reason for the stalled combat is not given. Presumably the Trojans are discomfited by the loss of their quasi-divine fighter; it is less clear why the Greeks should be willing to have a halt in operations. Achilles has reason, for now, to rejoice; he has defeated a seemingly unconquerable foe. Not surprisingly, when the Greeks retire to enjoy a banquet and feasting, they tell stories from the war at Troy, and Achilles has no better story to tell than his recent defeat of the son of Neptune (12.157 ff.).

Nestor is the old man of sandy Pylos; he had seen better men than those assembled at Troy. He, too, has experience of warriors who seemed impervious to any weapon. He proceeds to tell the story of Caeneus.[15] Ovid had already introduced this figure, though briefly, as a contestant in the Calydonian boar hunt.[16] As we have noted, Caeneus was a victim of Neptunian rape; his/her story fits in well after the long episode of Neptune's son Cycnus. Caenis asked to be changed into a man (from Caenis to Caeneus) after her divine violation; as Caeneus, he fought against the Centaurs in their great battle with the Lapiths. In Virgil, Caeneus is once again Caenis (*A.* 6.448); Virgil is the only extant source that has the warrior revert to his original female form once in the underworld.

Nestor is urged to tell the story; Achilles is especially eager to hear it (the whole assembly had been dazzled by his tale of Cycnus, and so he is clearly in command of the choice of topics, and he presses for the aged hero to tell of Caeneus/Caenis). Nestor announces that he recalls no story better than that of the transformed hero/heroine; he declares that he has lived for over two hundred years and is now in his third century—an Ovidian trumping of the Homeric tradition that had him living into a third generation of men.[17]

Caenis was sought by many suitors on account of her great beauty; report of her even reached Achilles' own father Peleus, who, Nestor observes, would have tried to marry her if he had not already been married to (or at least promised to) Achilles' divine mother Thetis. Rumor, *Fama*, has been a hallmark of Ovid's *Iliad* since the first word reached the Trojans of the arrival of the Greeks on their soil; extraordinarily, Nestor twice announces that *fama* claims that Caenis was raped by Neptune, and that Neptune subsequently asked her what she wanted by way of a present (12.197 *ita fama ferebat*; 200 *eadem hoc quoque fama ferebat*). Nestor is signaling that the story may or may not be true; he claimed that he remembered the story of Caenis/Caeneus better than any from his youth, but of course the part about the Neptunian rape and the compensatory promise predates Nestor's experience of the hero. Caenis prays that she may never again have to fear the trauma of rape by virtue of a transformation into a man; Neptune grants the wish immediately, and adds the unasked boon that the new man be impervious to any weapon.

Caeneus/Caenis is a relatively minor figure in Virgil's *Aeneid*, merely one shade among many in the underworld's Fields of Mourning that offer some commentary on the far more significant character of Dido. Ovid adapts Virgil's lore for his own purposes, greatly expanding the character's place in his epic and, by way of his narrative of the battle at the wedding banquet, linking his character in certain important ways with Virgil's Camilla. Nobody, of course, put Caeneus/Caenis lore into the Troy cycle before Ovid: Camilla, too, is most probably a "new" figure for Virgil epic's vision, and, by Virgil's association of her with his retelling of the *Iliad* in Italy, she becomes part of the neo-Homeric narrative the poet is crafting.

The scene then shifts to where Nestor was an eyewitness: the marriage of Ixion's son Pirithous to Hippodamia, the famous wedding where the Centaurs were invited. Ovid will now relate the combat of the battle of the Lapiths and the Centaurs, one of the most enduringly popular themes of mythology, both literary and artistic. Homer's Nestor also speaks of his involvement in the great event; it is unclear where the tradition started that the battle was occasioned by the marriage of Pirithous and Hippodamia.[18] In Ovid, the whole scene is most directly influenced by the poet's previous description in *Metamorphoses* 5 of the battle between Perseus and Phineus in Cepheus' banquet hall.

The story of Achilles' combat with Cycnus rings Ovid's *Iliad*, and the point of the tale, we have argued, is to underscore the theme of the hero's fight against an unfair opponent, the divinely aided hero who, in some sense, cannot be vanquished. Cycnus dies, but his death results in the death of Achilles; in Homer, Achilles died because he slew Hector after Hector had slain Patroclus, but without any specified reason for why it should be necessary for Thetis' son to have made a choice between a long life without eternal glory, and a short one with undying fame. In Ovid, the hero—like Virgil's Turnus—is ultimately defeated after refusing to cease his struggle against another divinely aided hero.[19]

We have observed that Ovid's *Iliad* is ringed by the hero's combat with a rather superhuman foe, and the consequences of that struggle in the hero's death. Between the bookends of the Cycnus story, we soon find that Ovid—perhaps surprisingly—intends to fill the bulk of Book 12 with a detailed account of the bloody battle between the Lapiths and the Centaurs, which of course ends with the victory of the former, though the seemingly invulnerable warrior Caeneus is one of the casualties, slain by the concerted effort of countless Centaurs. We might be tempted to think that in the narrative of the combat at the wedding of Pirithous and Hippodamia, we are likely to find an *Iliad* in miniature.

Once the combat is over, we shall see that a listener has an objection—Nestor has eliminated almost any mention of the great Hercules and his part in the defeat of the Centaurs. Nestor is angry, though not with the questioner; he is bitter about Hercules, whom he blames for destruction in his own home of Pylos. And he proceeds to tell of how Hercules destroyed yet another Neptunian hero, Periclymenus, who had been given the power to assume any shape. That death, as we shall examine in turn, will also presage the end of Achilles. In a nice touch, it was Nestor who tried to forestall the strife between Achilles and Agamemnon in the first *Iliad*; here, Nestor has the floor for almost all of Ovid's *Iliad*, and he will tell the tale of how a marriage reception ended in a bloodbath.

The mention of Hercules, though, as pendant to the Lapith-Centaur combat is highly significant. For it was with Hercules that the whole debate had started on Olympus about what the gods could and could not do for their favorites. The death of Periclymenus is an example of the limits of immortal aid, as was the case with the death of Cycnus and the death of Caeneus. All three represented Neptunian efforts to shield the beneficiary from harm; in all three cases, the beneficiary dies. In the aftermath of the drama of *Metamorphoses* 11, which so recalled *Aeneid* 5 and the case of Palinurus, we are reminded of the fact that it was Neptune who announced to Venus that one life must be sacrificed as the price of the Trojan fleet's successful arrival in Italy. One life had to be given for all. In a sense, Achilles' death is the one life that ensures the fall of Troy, of course; his death is nowhere linked to the fated fall of that city to the Greeks, but his loss is certainly the greatest the Greeks suffer before the walls fall.

In the story of the battle at the wedding, Hippodamia, the "Horse Breaker," is abducted by the amorous Centaur Eurytus (12.219). There is an obvious play here on the Trojan abduction of Helen: Eurytus is akin to Paris, and, even, to Aeneas, who—at least in Turnus' eyes—stole Lavinia.[20] Significantly, Ovid compares the action of the Centaur and his fellow horse-men to the rapine that accompanies the fall of a city (225 *captaeque erat urbis imago*). The other Centaurs follow the example of Eurytus and begin to abduct Lapith women, which is of course the image Turnus (and especially Amata, etc.) try to present of Aeneas and his Trojans: just as Paris abducted Helen, so these new Trojan exiles will come to abduct the women of Latium. The entire scene that now commences, the goriest battle in all of the *Metamorphoses*, is centered on the underscoring of this erotic theme: the great battles of Homer and Virgil were all occasioned by the abduction of a woman.[21] The Trojans are the stereotypical abductors of women, and here they are effectively semi-dehumanized by the implicit comparison to Centaurs—who were notoriously bibulous as well as amorous. Erato was the muse who was invoked to preside over the second half of the *Aeneid*, and the erotic element overshadows the battle between the Lapiths and Centaurs—no wonder, then, that Ovid will highlight the erotic theme in the midst of combat, as a male Centaur is killed and his female lover chooses suicide out of grief.

In case there was any doubt that Ovid is replaying both Homer and Virgil, the Centaurs begin shouting *arma, arma* (12.241, with effective anaphora) as Theseus, the great son of Aegeus, draws first blood. *Arma, arma* will reappear at this book's close (621 *armis arma*), as Ovid transitions from the death of Achilles to the contest between Ajax and Odysseus for possession of his divine arms.

Amycus is the first Centaur to kill a Lapith; he is impious, of course—he snatches a large lamp from the very *penetralia* of the house (245) and smashes it in the face of Celadon, leaving the hero's face a confused mass of bone and gore.[22] The action is compared to that of the slaughter of a bull at sacrifice. The Centaur is quickly dispatched by a Lapith; the general slaughter has begun. The Lapith in this case is a Macedonian, from Pella; his name is Pelates, Greek for either "invader" or "neighbor," either of which might be an interesting descriptor for a Macedonian guest at this Thessalian wedding.

The Centaurs only become more impious; Amycus had stolen a weapon from the inner chamber of the dwelling (the very bridal chamber, in fact); next Gryneus decides to use the sacrificial altar to furnish weapons of flame (12.258 ff.). Gryneus hurls a firebrand at the Lapiths, and Broteas and Orion are struck. Orion's mother, Ovid notes, was a noted witch, Mycale; Bömer (and Hill) provide commentary on these names, some of which are simply borrowed from other accounts of the battle.[23] Ovid had already established that this battle would be the goriest in his epic thus far (just as the war at Troy exceeded the sanguinary savagery of any previous struggle); Gryneus has a grisly end, as the Lapith Exadius shoves antler horns in his face, thereby gouging out his eyes—one of which hangs on the antlers, while the other falls on his beard in a messy congealed mass of blood and ocular material.

The next Centaur who appears in a combat vignette is Rhoetus. The name, as the commentators celebrate, is of extraordinary complexity, simply because there are so many figures in extant literature who bear either the same name or the closely related Rhoecus.[24] One or the other name appears not only elsewhere in Ovid, but also in the *Aeneid* (9.344-345, of a victim of Euryalus' night raid, and 10.388, of Anchemolus, a victim of Pallas from the ancient line of Rhoetus—*Rhoeti de gente vetusta*).[25] Rhoetus is victorious over not one but two Lapiths (at least indirectly); he also snatches up a sacred firebrand, which he proceeds to use against Charaxus. That apparently giant Lapith tries to throw a huge stone at the Centaur, but only succeeds in killing his friend Cometes. The Centaur laughs as he finishes the job of smashing Charaxus with the torch, which he buries in the hapless Lapith's brain (12.285-288). Soon the mighty Centaur has also killed Corythus and Euagrus; Corythus, we are told, was especially young, with just the first down of manhood appearing on his face.

The name is borrowed from 5.125, though its origins are unknown. Here, in the premature death of the young hero, Ovid may be recalling the highly significant mention of the same name at Virgil, *Aeneid* 3.170, where "Corythus" (or Corythum?) is identified as a destined home for the Trojan exiles. Crete will not be their home, the Penates say; Corythus must be sought.[26] The place was in Etruria, but beyond that, as Horsfall has noted, we cannot know for sure. Still, in the evocation of the destined home of the Trojans through the death of this tragically young hero, we have a taste of the continuing impiety of the Centaurs, and how insofar as they represent the Trojans, they are fighting against their own future, as it were. Dryas, whose name means someone who dwells in the wood,[27] finally ends Rhoetus' fiery but brief *aristeia*.

The death of Rhoetus leads to the flight of many Centaurs (12.302 ff.), among them Pholus, who at Virgil, *A*. 8.294 is recalled as a victim of Hercules.[28] Dryas slaughters a large number of additional Centaurs; one of those who flees is Nessus, who, in a nice touch, is told by the augur Centaur Asbolus that he need not flee, since he would be preserved for the bow of Hercules—a good reminder that Ovid has moved back in Nestor's story to a time long before the death of Nessus in his attempted abduction of Deianira.[29]

At this point, Ovid returns to an earlier theme he had raised as part of his preparation for the war in Troy—the Palinurus story (12.316-326). Aphidas is a Centaur who, like his fellows, is given to drink and sluggish slumber; he has had too much wine to drink at the wedding, and has taken advantage of a bearskin from Ossa that is part of the hall's decoration. While he was sleeping, Phorbas saw him. The name has been used previously by Ovid to describe the brigand who was infesting the road to Delphi, the brigand whose presence forced Ceyx to abandon any thought of traveling safely by land to consult Apollo's oracle, and who compelled him to go instead to Claros by a dangerous sea voyage.[30] Now, Phorbas will aim his javelin at Aphidas, who sleeps an eternal sleep. The name, of course, is a deliberate evocation of the Phorbas in whose guise Sleep appeared to Palinurus on the deck of Aeneas' flagship, and once again provides a tight narrative cohesion by forcing the audience to remember the whole evocation of *Aeneid* 5 that Ovid had used as prolegomena for his Troy lore. Phorbas tells the sleeping Centaur that he will mix his wine with the Styx and drink it there, just so we do not miss the connection of the character to Sleep, the god who was directly responsible for the loss of Palinurus, who would eventually plead to be able to cross the River Styx.

The passage thus provides a magnificent example of how Ovid works carefully even in these usually unappreciated gory battle sequences to underscore and emphasize the themes he has raised elsewhere in his epic. If we had more surviving literature, undoubtedly we would find numerous other examples of the same practice. Not surprisingly, Phorbas now disappears from the narrative; there is no retribution for the killing of Aphidas, and the character somewhat mysteriously vanishes from the scene—appropriately enough, given the eerie figure he evokes.

We have noted that Rumor, *Fama*, hangs over all of Ovid's *Iliad* (and, by extension, his *Aeneid*).[31] Rumor's presence does not mean that the stories Ovid relates are false; nor does the presence of the winged demigod signify that we should hunt for insignificant changes in established traditions that might be Ovidian inventions (as opposed to the major alterations we have noted elsewhere in the epic, which are not specifically credited to the presence of Rumor). *Fama* is an ill-omened creature, to be sure, but in the *Aeneid Fama* only portended ill if the idea was that Aeneas should stay happily with Dido in Carthage. Virgil's *Fama* is disgusting, more so in fact than Ovid's (cf. *A.* 4.195 *foeda*, the same adjective Virgil uses to describe the revolting Harpies). But the disgusting nature of the goddess does not change the veracity of her story to Iarbas. And it is Iarbas' prayer that leads directly to Jupiter's decision that enough time has been lost in Carthage, and that Mercury must be dispatched to hasten the Trojan hero on his way to his Italian destiny. At *A.* 9.473 ff., it is Fama who brings the news of the death of Nisus and Euryalus to the latter's mother; again, the news is terrible and the message bitter to bear, but the story is quite true. We might note that in both these actions of the Virgilian Rumor, the Trojans suffer the consequences of the true tale the goddess speaks.

In Ovid, then, we might expect to see a similar application of Rumor to the spreading of bad news for the Trojans. The major Virgilian appearance of Fama was to herald Aeneas' inappropriate relationship with Dido; the second appearance was to announce the death of the *eromenos* Euryalus to his mother. Both appearances, then, have something to do with a questionable relationship that must be ended as part of the foundation of the future Rome: Aeneas cannot stay with a Carthaginian queen and widow, and there is no place in the nascent Rome for the erotic union of a Nisus and a Euryalus. Rumor will see to it (or at least give witness to the fact that) that all these unions, however desirable *in se*, must end.

In the context of *Metamorphoses* 12, with its application of the truly ancient Battle of the Lapiths and the Centaurs to the drama of the *Iliad*, Rumor first brought the news to the Trojans that the Greeks had landed—another baleful announcement from a Trojan point of view. This is more serious for the Trojans than the death of one young hero like Euryalus; this is the news that the beginning of the end of their city has come. Paris abducted a wife; so Eurytus tried to abduct Hippodamia, the "Horse Breaker," who by virtue of her abduction will lead to the destruction of the equine Centaurs.[32] The Centaurs are impious in their conduct of the battle; in the struggle between Perseus and the friends of Phineus in Cepheus' dining hall, we saw the corruption violence could bring to all, both the instigators and the victims. There, though, man fought against man;

here, man fights against animals. The fact that we cannot but associate the Centaurs with the Trojans is telling. Eurytus' decision to attempt the abduction of Hippodamia will lead directly to the slaughter of countless Centaurs; the battle was one of the great experiences of the hero Theseus, and of course Ovid could have told the story in his *Theseid* many books ago. He chose instead to use the Lapith-Centaur battle as a paradigm for the combat at Troy.[33]

But all of this Lapith-Centaur combat has been occasioned by Nestor's desire to speak of Caeneus/Caenis.[34] For this hero/ine, G.S. West has provided the best commentary.[35] Ovid is clearly borrowing on Virgil's brief but significant account of this man-woman, who, we would think from her underworld location, died because of a *durus amor*. The final reversion of gender, from man to woman in the underworld, may be Virgil's own invention, as West notes. But West notes that Virgil's conception of this character is nuanced by his attribution of a female shape but a masculine name (he calls "her" *Caeneus*, as if she were not fully man or woman). As West points out, part of the point in Virgil's depiction of the character as a facet of Dido (whose attendant in the underworld she virtually is) comes with the fact that Dido does in Virgil's underworld what the masculine Ajax does in Homer's: she ignores Aeneas, just as her Homeric predecessor had ignored Odysseus.[36] In Ovid's conception, the character will be explicitly described as having been once upon a time the greatest of men, but now, perhaps, a very feminine entity indeed—a female bird.

As we shall soon see, Ovid bases much of his Caeneus/Caenis story on Virgil's Camilla. In numerous significant details and evocations, Ovid will echo episodes from Virgil's narrative. The first and most significant connection is the cavalry battle; the contest at the wedding of Pirithous and Hippodamia is, after all, an equestrian battle since one of the opposing sides is composed of Centaurs. Camilla, for her part, straddles the world of both men and women, which finds parallel in the bi-gendered Caeneus/Caenis. But the connections go far beyond these general considerations (see further below).

So in structure, then, we have an "*Iliad*" that begins and ends with Achilles, the victor over a seemingly indestructible foe, who will die because of his successful defeat of the enemy he should not have been able to kill. The actual story of "battle" in Ovid's version of Homeric epic is a "cavalry" battle, as much a cavalry battle as there could be, since the warriors of Book 12 are real horses, not merely men on horseback. The set piece battle of *Aeneid* 11, with its equestrian combat and infantry battle that never actually takes place, represents the poem's themes in miniature: the Latins would have won, and dramatically so, were it not for direct divine intervention to help slay the seemingly unstoppable (cf. Caeneus/Caenis' invincibility)—the Volscian Camilla.

And, what is more, Ovid will not end his account of the *Iliad* without a comment on one of the most important questions from both that poem and its Virgilian imitation, a question he has already raised: what of fate, what of the favors the gods might do for some and not others? That question had been occasioned by the blessings Hercules had received, and, as pendant to his *Iliad*, Ovid will return to and, at last, resolve that difficult question.

Virgil's Turnus, we have observed, was the new Achilles. So the Sibyl announced in the underworld; the comparison was made explicit to Aeneas before he arrived in Italy. The comparison is not exact in the sense that Virgil models his account step by step after Homer's Achilles; sometimes Aeneas plays the part, while at other times it is clearly Turnus' rôle. Other than Achilles' victim, Cycnus, the main warrior of *Metamorphoses* 12 is Caeneus, who is the ostensible reason for Nestor's story. If Caeneus is meant to evoke Camilla, and Achilles Turnus, Ovid thereby fashions a fine commentary on his predecessor's epic and some of its main themes. However, Turnus and Camilla were joined in Virgil in a way more intimate than any sexual union (cf. Aeneas and Dido) could have provided: he gave them the same death line, the line with which he ended his epic.

And so it is not surprising that at the end of this book, we shall see Achilles die in much the same way as Virgil's Camilla. *That* will be the hero/heroine's final gender transformation. There is no underworld presence for Caeneus/Caenis in Ovid. There is an avian metamorphosis, but no gender change that is definitive; Ovid will end the Caeneus/Caenis story with the masculine name of the character (cf. Virgil's practice), but the Latin word for bird, *avis*, is conveniently feminine (and so the confusion is nicely maintained). If the character is supposed to evoke Camilla, then in having the male Caeneus killed in a way that that does not recall Camilla's death, followed by Achilles' death in way that *does* directly evoke Camilla's end, Ovid neatly plays with the gender ambiguity of both Caeneus/Caenis and Camilla. It also helps that in Virgil, direct comparison is made between Camilla and Achilles in the important simile of the hawk and the dove, which is modeled on Achilles' attack on Hector, where Achilles is the hawk and Hector the hapless dove.[37] Just as the Caeneus-bird is in some sense both masculine and feminine (it has the name "Caeneus," but the bird is apparently female), so the masculine Achilles will die in a way that recalls the feminine Camilla. Ovid makes clear that there is a distinction between the hero while alive—who was undoubtedly a male, despite his past and notwithstanding the taunts of his Centaur enemies—and the *post mortem* metamorphosis into a bird that is, in contrast, feminine—even if it still bears the original, masculine name.[38] No surprise that the principal point of comparison between Virgil's Camilla and Homer's Achilles—the bird image (hawk as predatory *accipiter*)—is the source of the end of the Caenis story, where the greatest of men becomes a feminized bird.

Ovid has found his own way to link his Turnus and Camilla. In a nice twist, we are also deceived in our expectations. In the Cycnus story, the subject and main point was the idea of the indestructible foe. That invulnerable opponent was Achilles' enemy, and I have argued that we are to see something of the lessons of Virgil's Aeneas—he cannot be effectively fought because of divine favor and intervention. Caeneus/Caenis is then introduced as *another* example of an indestructible figure. And, indeed, despite death, the character will achieve avian metamorphosis and some sort of eternal memory thereby (cf. Camilla's fate). But Caeneus is a *Lapith*, not a Centaur, and we are clearly supposed to associate the Centaurs with the Trojans. Caeneus was on the same side as Nestor in the fight at Pirithous' wedding. *This* seemingly indestructible hero/ine is on the same side, in a sense, as Achilles.

In another brilliant linkage, Ovid's Cycnus, the indestructible, also reminds us of Messapus' contingents in the catalogue of Turnus' allies at the end of *Aeneid* 7. Messapus was another virtually indestructible Neptunian hero, and Virgil compares his men to a flock of singing birds, specifically *swans* that sing beautifully as they return from their feeding (*A.* 7.698-702).[39]

The end result is, as throughout so much of this last third of the epic, a magnificent amalgam of the lessons of both Homer and Virgil, and a splendid reading of the poet's Augustan predecessor.[40]

The gory battle continues (12.327 ff.); Theseus' friend Pirithous sends several Centaurs to their deaths, one of whom falls off a precipice as he tries to flee the hero's assault—he ends up impaled on the broken branches of an ash tree. The majority of the Centaurs' names either appear in the *Perseid* and/or cannot be paralleled elsewhere, at least as Centaurs.

Ovid had more or less abandoned Theseus some time ago; here, in this story from the past, Theseus has a more dramatic *aristeia* than during the time when he was ostensibly the central character in the epic. He rushes in to defend Pirithous from attack (12.343 ff.). Theseus is soon attacked by Demoleon; when the Centaur is unable to rip up a huge pine, trunk and all, he breaks off part of it and throws it at the hero. Pallas, Ovid notes, warned Theseus to move out of the way in time—or, Ovid adds, that is what Theseus would have one believe (360 *credi sic ipse volebat*). The detail is a neat reminder of the falsehood theme and even the authority of Rumor over this part of the epic; the statement is a subtle comment on whether or not the gods have the power to intervene and save the lives of their favorites: Nestor is an old man, but he has his doubts about the goddess Minerva's aid here.

The tree does not strike Theseus, but it does inflict a gory wound on Crantor, whom Nestor identifies as Achilles' father Peleus' arms-bearer. Peleus immediately tries to avenge his squire; Demoleon is struck by a shaft, the point lodged in his lung (12.366 ff.). Ovid gives a brief vignette of Peleus' achievements since, after all, he is Achilles' father and was the hero whose marriage to Thetis opened the whole Troy cycle. Peleus' last victim was slain with Nestor's help. Nestor describes the gruesome scene—probably the grisliest in the entire epic—as he takes aim at the Centaur. After wounding him, Nestor lets Peleus finish the job, since he was standing closer to the hapless horse-man. Peleus moves in and stabs Dorylas in the stomach; his viscera fall out and he bursts open his intestines as he tramples on them, finally tripping in his own innards and falling dead, his belly empty from loss of organs (388 ff.).

At this moment of tremendous violence, Ovid—no doubt with some degree of black humor—juxtaposes a very different scene, a brief love interlude between Cyllaros and Hylonome.[41] On a thematic level, the episode serves to remind us of the erotic dimension of the whole Trojan saga, of which the present combat is a type. Cyllaros is described as being an exceedingly handsome Centaur; his hair and beard are of gold (12.395 *aureus, aurea*—a striking anaphora). His blond human body contrasts with a black equine form, though with a white tail and legs. Cyllaros is sought by many female Centaurs as a desirable mate; only Hylonome manages to enchant and capture him. She, too, is exceptionally beautiful, and her loveliness is enhanced by how much attention she pays to her appearance (Ovid's description implies that if Centaurs are to maintain a beautiful appearance, they need to put in extra work). Cyllaros is struck down by an unknown hand; his heart is barely scratched, but the wound is fatal. Hylonome had been fighting beside him; she rushes to her dying lover and hurls herself on the same weapon in suicide. Nestor notes that she uttered some words before her death, but the surrounding din of the battle did not permit him to hear them.

Bömer's commentary focuses here on the parallel between Cyllaros and Hipponome and other couples in the *Metamorphoses* that find union in death.[42] There is a nice reminiscence in the death of Cyllaros of the mysterious arrow shot that wounds Aeneas (*A.* 12.320), where Juturna probably struck Aeneas with a serious enough wound that his physician Iapyx (Palinurus' brother) could not heal him, thus requiring the intervention of Venus to save the Trojan. The scene is a highly significant one from Virgil's last book, and its reminiscence here, in the midst of Ovid's *Iliad*, is a good example of how a small detail can be used to recall the whole machinery of another epic. The effect is to give the seemingly lumbering narrative of Ovid's poem a real cohesion and a close connection to its epic predecessors.

Cyllaros and Hipponome are among the tragic "successful" couples of epic, like Virgil's Nisus and Euryalus and Ovid's Pyramus and Thisbe. They find eternal unity in death, and theirs is an erotic love, a love that might well have been foreign to the marital experience of many an Augustan Rome, living as they did in an age where the concept of marriage for fulfillment of romantic love was something rather foreign. Cyllaros and Hipponome die essentially together and joined forever in the eternal memory of their love, which, of course, the poet's art ensures.

The scene also recalls a battle sequence from *Aeneid* 10 where Cydon is described as almost being killed by Aeneas (*A.* 10.324), where Cydon is distracted by Clytius, his *eromenos*. Cydon would have been killed had not seven of his cohort attacked Aeneas, who is defended by his Vulcanian helmet and shield— the first mention of Aeneas' divine weapons in combat. Venus (332 *alma Venus*) deflects weapons from her son so he is only grazed. The scene is important as the first time that, strictly speaking, any gods intervene in battle and thereby arguably violate the virtual non-intervention edict that Jupiter had issued during the divine council with which *Aeneid* 10 opens. If Ovid were recalling both the Cydon and Clytius scene and the mysterious wounding of Aeneas, then the point would be to emphasize two instances in Virgil's epic where Aeneas was protected by his divine mother.[43]

So the story works on several levels; it charms and offers the sort of appealing vignette that the Alexandrians would have appreciated; it also allows for a subtle recollection of an important point from Ovid's immediate epic predecessor. Foundationally, the poet of love reminds the audience that love is the foundation of the entire martial saga he is now engaged in retelling.

The Centaur Phaeocomes provides the next brief scene from the chaotic slaughter (12.429 ff.). He hurls a huge log at the Lapith Tectaphos, striking him in the head. Five lines (434-438) describe the terrible aftermath, as the brain is squeezed out from every possible facial aperture, just as curds are strained in making cheese. The lines in question have no good manuscript support, and were apparently interpolated by some later hand—though two questions arise. First, this is already Ovid's shortest book, and strikingly so. Cutting another five lines is more significant than it would be in another book of the epic. Further, why these lines, with creatively gory simile, should be inserted into an already detailed description of the battle is difficult to explain. Why here—and only here?—would some would-be Ovid insert a brief passage? We cannot know the answers to these questions, but these stand forth as the likeliest example in the poem of extended "supplement" and interpolation by some unknown hand.

Nestor's *aristeia* continues; whatever Phaeocomes may have done to Tectaphos, Nestor avenged the Lapith death. Nestor was wounded in the ensuing melee, and has the scars to prove it; he notes that those were the days when he should have been sent to Troy—he would have either killed Hector, or at least significantly impeded the Trojan's progress (12.445 ff.). The passage reminds us of how Hector's ghost appeared to Aeneas to urge him to flee the destroyed city of Troy, noting that if Troy had been able to be saved, he, Hector, would have done it. This is the commonplace of a sentiment that is ultimately rooted in the Hesiodic myth of the ages; things were better once before, and all things are in perishable decline—a sentiment that is also at the heart of Lucretian philosophy (cf. the end of *DRN* 2).

Nestor quickly moves through other casualties in epic style, as the death toll mounts (12.449 ff.). Mopsus is the most notable of this next set of figures, as he pins Hodites' tongue to his chin and his chin to his throat; Mopsus is also a seer who was traditionally involved in the Centaur-Lapith battle.[44] He was also named as a participant in the Calydonian boar hunt. Caeneus, meanwhile, has killed five Centaurs (459 ff.). Ovid is now ready to return to the ostensible reason for the whole Nestorian digression: the strange fate of the man-woman Virgil had so briefly mentioned in his underworld.

At this point, the Centaur Latreus (the "Barker") appears; the figure does not appear elsewhere. He rides in a circle (cf. Camilla's victim Butes and the intricate, ballet-like dance of death Camilla seems to lead him on at *A.* 11.694 ff.). Latreus begins to mock Caeneus; he knows his/her history and begins to reproach the warrior for being a woman. In the *Camilliad*, Jupiter stirs up the Etruscan Tarchon and he upbraids his men for falling prey to a woman; compare, too, how Camilla told Ornytus that he was bringing great news to the shade of his father, namely that he had fallen by Camilla's weapon, and how the nymph Opis expresses resentment that one such as Arruns (Camilla's killer) will fall by Diana's weapon. In the pendant to the catalogue of Italian warriors at the end of *Aeneid* 7, Virgil had noted that Camilla had forsaken the works of the divine Minerva, the distaff and the spindle. Latreus tells Caeneus that *she* should be spinning and leave fighting to men. Caenis had been raped by Neptune; Latreus urges Caeneus not only to remember that he was born a woman, but that he was raped. Caeneus says nothing in response, but hurls his spear, which is swiftly buried in the Centaur's side, just where the man and the horse are joined.

As Nestor had already established, Caeneus is impervious to weapons; Latreus is wounded but still dangerous, and he tries in vain to attack the seemingly indestructible man-woman. Latreus tries to grab at Caeneus' *ilia* (12.486), a word that describes the lowest part of the abdomen, extending down to the groin; Catullus uses it at c. 63 in the singular to describe Attis' ill-fated male member. The word does not necessarily refer to the genitals, but, especially in light of Catullus' famous use, it certainly evokes the image; it has been the locus for several wounds in this combat, and here it carries special significance given Caeneus' sexual change. The sexually charged wounds of several of the casualties of the Lapith-Centaur combat look forward to the transgender issues that surround Caeneus' story.

Caeneus cannot be harmed, it would seem; he strikes back and drives his sword—and his hand—into the Centaur. Like Turnus, trapped in the Trojan camp, Caeneus is soon one man against an army: all the Centaurs turn to attack him. He is able to withstand their blades and shafts, but, as with Achilles in the combat with Cycnus, the Centaurs have tricks against the impervious.

The Centaur Monychus continues the same sort of taunts that are familiar from the *Camilliad*: Caeneus is scarcely a man, and one person should not be able to do so much damage to an entire army. Of course the Centaurs are terribly impious, and so Monychus notes that clearly, if a half-man can destroy all of them, then they must not be the children of Ixion, who was so great that he could conceive the expectation of capturing Juno herself.[45] The Centaurs represent the Trojans in this miniature epic; Ixion had tried to rape the goddess who is most associated with marriage and the Roman marriage bond; he is an appropriate progenitor of the quasi-Trojans who are fighting at this wedding reception.

Essentially, Monychus' suggested plan for slaying Caeneus is identical to what Achilles did with Cycnus: strangulation and the cutting off of air. Trees and rocks must be uprooted so the man-woman can be buried under an immense weight and thus destroyed (12.507 ff.). Caeneus is soon barely able to move, to lift his head up and gasp for air; he cannot move all the trees and rocks that are used to pin him to the ground. Some people, Nestor says, believed that Caeneus died and went down to Tartarus; this is a nice nod to Virgil. Mopsus, however, said that he saw a bird rise up from the site of the burial alive; Nestor as eyewitness says that he also saw it, though for the first and the last time on that very day. Mopsus sees the bird circling the Lapiths and making a sound; the seer greets the bird as an honored Lapith hero:

'o salve,' dixit, 'Lapithaeae gloria gentis,
maxime vir quondam, sed nunc avis unica, Caeneu.' (12.530-531)

'O hail,' he said, 'glory of the Lapith race,
once the greatest man, but now a unique bird, O Caeneus.'

Turnus called Camilla the virgin glory of Italy; after Arruns succeeded (with divine assistance) in slaying the Volscian huntress, Camilla's death roused the women of the Latin capital to greater valor and to risk their lives for their country (previously they had been hiding in a temple with Amata and Lavinia, offering sacrifices to Minerva to protect them).[46]

Caeneus was mocked by the Centaurs; they, of course, live as half man and half horse, and so it is questionable that they should be mocking anyone for being *semi-* anything. Caeneus, the man-woman, becomes an example to the Lapiths of renewed courage in the face of the marauding equine raiders, and soon the Centaurs are clearly defeated in the new Lapith onslaught. There is something here, too, of the situation in *Aeneid* 12 where the Rutulians are struck by how Turnus will be fighting alone against Aeneas.

Nestor's story is essentially over; Caeneus' example has spurred the Lapith men on to victory, just as Camilla's example spurred the Latin women to fight against the Trojans who were besieging their capital city. The recollection of the glorious victory of men over horse-men is interrupted by Tlepolemus, a son of Hercules.[47] Not surprisingly, he is displeased that his mighty father has essentially been forgotten in the narrative of what happened at the marriage of Pirithous and Hippodamia. In Homer, there is no question that Tlepolemus is an unpleasant sort; he is almost reminiscent of Thersites (note the identical first and last letters of the names, a trick to link related characters that Virgil employs very often in his epic, Ovid less so). In the cyclic tradition Thersites had questioned Achilles over the latter's attitude toward the Amazon Penthesilea (Virgil's Camilla is a rebirth of the Penthesilea image); here, Tlepolemus is upset that his father seems to have been passed over for glory.

Interestingly, after addressing Caeneus as being once upon a time the greatest of men (12.531 *maxime vir quondam*), Mopsus then calls him/her/it (?) a unique bird (*avis unica*), a feminine entity, which, as we have noted, is partly because the word for bird is (rather conveniently in this case) of feminine gender in Latin. The bird is also unique—it will have no identity as a species, and no descendants—it is unclear whether or not it is immortal. In this regard, there is something of the preservation of the virginity that Caenis was robbed of by Neptune's rape. In the underworld, as aforementioned, there seems to be ambiguity over the shade's gender; in Ovid's account, it seems clear that we are left with a feminine image, which also accords with the evocation of Virgil's Camilla.[48]

The Caeneus story also works well in an epic battle between humans and Centaurs: the latter creatures invite Ovid to explore the possibilities of combat with half-men horses (or half-horse men, depending on your point of view), while the Caeneus story does the same with gender issues.

Nestor admits that Hercules was a great man; he confesses that Hercules won immense glory over the globe. But he also calls Hercules a *hostis* (12.548), by noting that Hector and other Trojans are also great warriors, but we do not for that reason praise an enemy. Interesting, Nestor uses the word *hostis*, which in Latin denotes a public enemy, not a personal one—an *inimicus*. While it is true that Hercules destroyed Pylos and might thus reasonably be termed a *hostis* to Pylian Nestor, the tone of the story and its details make clear that Nestor harbors a very understandable, *personal* grudge against the hero who slew his brothers. I suspect that the point of the term is to evoke Virgil's Turnus, who famously announced that Jupiter was his *hostis* so soon before his death at Aeneas' hands. In both cases, the enmity is formal and public; it may have a private dimension, but it is also practically ratified by all the solemn conventions that can accompany war (cf. Juno's throwing open of the gates of Janus' temple in *Aeneid* 7, a deliberate anachronism to solemnize the coming war in Italy by a very Roman goddess). Hercules, the symbol of the Jovian order, is *hostis* to Nestor, just as Jupiter was to Turnus.

Nestor recalls that Tlepomelus' father Hercules had destroyed Elis as well as Pylos (12.549 ff.). The story that Hercules destroyed Pylos is not unique to Ovid.[49] But in Homer (*Iliad* 11.670-671), Elis was destroyed not by Hercules but by none other than *Nestor* himself. We have noted that Nestor is old and forgetful; this is also a part of the story that he had intended to omit (but he has personal grudges and thus a vested interest in the tale). We have also observed that Ovid has been interested in the theme of falsehood, and that Ovid has introduced the whole section of his Troy lore with Rumor, with whatever consequences we can take from that. Here, since Ovid and his audience knew Homer very well, we must assume that Nestor has either made a mistake (certainly possible for someone over three hundred years of age), or, more likely, that he is gilding the lily, as it were, regarding Hercules' destructive exploits. This is ancient history for the assembly listening to Nestor's story; there are no other eyewitnesses in the Greek camp to the events that Nestor is relating. He might be able to be caught in mendacious remarks, but his very *gravitas*, and especially his place as a direct observer of events, make his account gain weight with his audience—notwithstanding Tlepolemus' objection, since, after all, he remembered what Hercules used to say about the Centaurs (a much more exciting battle to relate than the capture of Elis or even Pylos).

Nestor was one of twelve sons of Neleus, and all twelve died at Hercules' hands, Nestor alone excepted. One brother, Periclymenus, is of special interest, Nestor says (12.555 ff.). Periclymenus had the power of transformation; he could assume any shape he wished. Neptune, his grandfather, had given him this power as a boon. Periclymenus tried many shapes in turn, and finally settled on the form of an eagle, the bird of Jupiter:

vertitur in faciem volucris, quae fulmina curvis
ferre solet pedibus divum gratissima regi (12.560-561)

He turned into the form of the bird that is accustomed to bear
in its curved feet the bolts that are most pleasing to the king of the gods.

Periclymenus proceeds to scratch at Hercules' face and attack him; the transformation is not meant to provide a means of escape from the mighty foe, but
rather to attack more effectively.

Hercules shoots at the bird with an arrow, which wounds Periclymenus
where his wings join his side. The wound is not great—the situation is like that
of Cyllarus, who was barely scratched, though in the heart and fatally—but the
bird-man plummets to the ground, now devoid of strength or ability to stay aloft.
When he hits the ground, the arrow that had been only lightly sticking near the
wing is driven hard into the breast and exits the left side of the throat (the unlucky side); Nestor's brother is dead.

Because of the very personal matter of the slaughter of his brothers, Nestor
will not sing the praises of Hercules; he does not deny that he was a great figure,
but he chooses to remain silent about him and thus avenge his brothers. Since
Nestor is one of the last men alive, we can assume, who remembers the early
deeds of Hercules as an eyewitness, his silence is powerful.

Why this pendant on the strange death of Periclymenus? Periclymenus is
presented in Ovid as a would-be challenger to the Jovian order; he assumes the
form of the bird of Jove, which Ovid takes the trouble to note is the carrier of
Jupiter's special weapon of choice, the lightning bolts. Hercules destroyed a
would-be challenger to his father, Jupiter; the fact that Periclymenus and his
brother Nestor are the descendants of Neptune may carry a hint of rivalry between the two Olympian brothers. Periclymenus, by assuming the avatar of the
eagle, is an implicit challenge to Jovian supremacy, and he is destroyed by the
Herculean bringer of Jupiter's vengeance. In this evocation of enmity to Jupiter,
we have an image of Turnus' own awareness that Jupiter, not Aeneas *per se*,
was his enemy. Periclymenus must die as a symbol of the coming of order and
the accession of Jupiter to supreme power, but Nestor will not sing of Hercules
and celebrate his achievements; of course there is a certain poignancy in the fact
that in order to explain why he has omitted mention of the great hero, he must
detail how Hercules killed his own brother.

Periclymenus' choice of transformation was probably not inspired by any
attempt to challenge Jovian authority, but it was a reckless and unfortunate self-
metamorphosis that spelled doom for the shape-shifter. Nestor is old; in his
brother's shape-shifting there is also something of a reminder of the great age of
old heroes, where such happenings were more common in a world where divine
favor was more readily granted.

Turnus was a victim of the savage will of Jupiter, as readers of the *Aeneid* learn at the end of the *Camilliad* in *A*. 11; here, at the end of Nestor's own rendition of an *Iliad*-like combat, we have not only the remembrance of Camilla in Caenis, but also the brief epilogue about the fate of those who would assume Jovian power (as anyone who challenges Jupiter's order and loyalty to "fate" is guilty of doing). Turnus fought on against Aeneas, though he knew he was fighting Jupiter, and Periclymenus dared to attack Hercules in the form of Jupiter's own bird—a scion of Neptune using Jupiter's eagle to attack Jupiter's son. The great poet of transformation has shown another definition of what is meant by *carmen perpetuum*: he has taken his source material, Homer and Virgil, and woven them into his own epic narrative, replete with stories not found in either of his predecessors, retelling the older epics of *Iliad* and *Aeneid* with his new material as subject matter—all in a tightly constructed tissue of homage to his epic predecessors. It is a breathtaking and dazzling achievement.

Hercules was an instrument, then, of Jovian retribution; small wonder that he should be favored in exemplary ways, as Ovid emphasized in his brief *Herculeid*. Hercules kills the Neptunian scion Pericylemenus, and without suffering any consequence; there is no punishment for this attack on Neptune's favorite, no revenge from the marine god. This narrative contrasts greatly with the closing sequence of this book, where Neptune seeks revenge on Achilles, who is not under the same special protection of Jupiter as Hercules. Indeed, one of the powerful underlying themes of this section of Ovid's epic is the idea that Achilles is not privy to any special favor to save him from his chosen fate, any special favor that results in some transformation or, as in the case of Hercules, deification. Ovid chooses to insert the Hercules lore between the death of Caeneus and that of Achilles to remind us that Achilles will not enjoy the fate of his Jovian heroic counterpart, who was saved from a pyre and allowed to become a god. Small wonder, then, that Ovid will make sure to detail how Achilles' body is burned—thus offering an instructive parallel to the pyre that was the locus for Hercules' self-immolation. That Stoic suicide ended in apotheosis; Achilles' will end in ashes that can barely fill an urn—though undying glory will follow him, and a martial spirit that will live on past his death. There may also be parallels between Ovid's Hercules and Virgil's Aeneas, and between Ovid's Achilles and Virgil's Turnus.

Hector had predicted that Apollo and Paris would be involved in the death of Achilles, and it is with the great hero's demise that the end of Ovid's *Iliad* is concerned. Ovid returns in a great ring to Neptune, who is angry over the death of Cycnus. Here there is a hint of the god who demanded Palinurus' sacrifice at the end of *Aeneid* 5; here there is an evocation of exactly the sort of divine intervention we saw again and again in the case of Virgil's Camilla, where two gods conspired to destroy the Volscian huntress. All of this stands in the shadow of the larger question of what the gods are allowed to do for their favorites, or to punish those they especially detest or at least wish to see eliminated in light of some larger goal.

The anger that Neptune feels for Achilles is, in Ovid's eyes, unjust:

mente dolet patria saevumque perosus Achillem
exercet memores plus quam civiliter iras. (12.582-583)

He sorrowed in his fatherly mind, and thoroughly hated raging Achilles,
and he exercised unforgetting anger in his mind, more than is civilized.

The passage may well have inspired the opening of Lucan's *Pharsalia*, with its mention of "wars more than civil," *bella . . . plus quam civilia*, where *bella* corresponds to the Homeric wrath and the Virgilian arms, and the Lucanian arms are more than civil because they involve two men who were related by marriage, Caesar and Pompey. Here, Achilles is *saevus*—interestingly, the same adjective was used in threefold repetition to describe Jupiter at the end of *Aeneid* 11, where the chief god works to ensure that his wishes will be carried out in conformity with "destiny." Neptune here is like Virgil's Juno; he cannot forget, he cannot give up his anger; Juno, of course, could not kill Aeneas, but Achilles has no special protection of the sort the Trojan hero enjoys. Neptune's anger goes beyond the bounds of civility, but there is also a hint of civil war here, especially for a Roman audience—Achilles' mother Thetis, after all, is a *marine* goddess, and so Neptune is engaging in something of a civil war to destroy Achilles, just as Apollo was guilty of the same, and worse, when he conspired to destroy Camilla, the devotee and favorite of his own sister Diana.

The relief of Juno's anger was the main theme of the *Aeneid*; in Virgil's conception, the terrible anger of Achilles that had marked Homer's *Iliad* had been transformed into the goddess' anger over the fate of the Trojan exiles who would one day found a city that would destroy her beloved Carthage. Here, Neptune's anger will instigate the death of Achilles, not that that death will, of course, have any effect whatsoever on the ultimate fate of Troy to be destroyed—we are reminded in this passage of how Neptune assured Venus at the close of *Aeneid* 5 that he would have done even more for Troy, had he been asked, and so he will certainly assist in making sure Aeneas' ships make it safely from Sicily to Italy, even if a life must be sacrificed so ships might sail (cf. Iphigenia at Aulis).

The war at Troy has been carried on for some ten years when Neptune approaches Apollo (12.584 ff.). He address his nephew as *Smintheus*, a deliberate evocation of the obscure title of the god that the priest Chryses used to address Apollo in the first book of the *Iliad*: Ovid wishes to recall, here at the end, the whole mechanism of Homeric epic that had started with the wrath of Achilles, occasioned, as it was, by the abduction of Briseis in response to the surrender of Chryseis, and all that.

Apollo is a patron of the Trojans in Homer (and so, not surprisingly, he is involved in helping in the killing of Camilla, and, more generally, he is a suitable god to preside over the Augustan regime as its patron—he is, after all, a patron of the original, home city of the Trojan exiles). Neptune address Apollo as his most favored nephew—this is nothing more than blandishment before a request. More interestingly, he asks Apollo if the archer god does not agree with him that it is lamentable to see the walls of Troy destroyed, given that the two of them had built the original city—even if only in vain. Neptune further laments the many who have died in defending Troy—especially Priam's son Hector. All of this is further attempt at flattery of Apollo, sympathetic as he is to the Trojan cause.

Neptune would be happy to destroy Achilles with his trident, were the hero to dare to fight him directly (there may be a nod here to Achilles' great combat with the river in the *Iliad*). Since Neptune and Achilles cannot fight each other in single combat, let an arrow, unforeseen and from afar, do the same task the god's trident would have accomplished. Jupiter, of course, did not strike down Camilla; he stirred up Tarchon and his Etruscans, but he did not intervene directly to kill the Volscian. We have noted that it is relatively rare in classical epic for an immortal to kill a mortal directly and unambiguously. In the *Aeneid*, for example, there is the brief allusion to Minerva's use of the Jovian lightning bolt to kill Ajax, the son of Oileus; perhaps most tellingly, there is Diana's nymph Opis and her shooting of Arruns to avenge Camilla—but there, too, Diana herself does not do the killing, but rather she entrusts it to another—a variety of the same sort of divine intervention by which Apollo aids Arruns or, as here, Paris.

The commentators make much of the fact that in Homer, Poseidon and Apollo are not exactly on the same side, at least in the matter of Hector and the preservation of his body. Apollo initiates a debate among the gods about the matter, while Poseidon explicitly refuses to do anything to stop Achilles from dragging Hector's body around Patroclus' tomb. Ovid's Neptune is deliberately loose with his rendition of sympathy for his nephew; he argues in language that is designed to let his nephew hear exactly what he wants. Apollo needs no encouragement to go after Achilles, given his Trojan favoritism. In all of this, one wonders where Jupiter is, especially given the question of the preservation of favorites and extraordinary divine actions. But it is probable that there is a fair amount of subtle deception on Neptune's part in his remarks to Apollo, deception that, no doubt, Apollo would not have minded: the sea god's point is to secure the help of his nephew, though little effort, as we see, is required.

Apollo descends to the Trojan battlefield to see to the destruction of Achilles; Ovid makes it clear that the god agreed with his uncle, that the intentions of the two immortals were the same. Apollo had appeared to Ascanius to oversee the shooting of the braggart Numanus Remulus; there he had been disguised (and to Arruns, invisible); here he openly identifies himself to Paris, who is memorably depicted by Ovid as doing exactly what we might expect of the less than magnificent warrior—he is taking shots at the crowd in battle, but the arrows come rarely, and the targets are not significant. Apollo almost mocks him for spending his time aiming at plebeian foes:

... quid spicula perdis
sanguine plebis? (12.601-602)

... why do you waste your shafts
on the blood of commoners?

Apollo directs Paris' shot at Achilles (12.604-606). There is no question that this
is an ignominious end; Paris is no great warrior, but, as Ovid reminds Achilles in
an authorial apostrophe, a mere kidnapper of Greek women. Ovid makes a
splendid observation to the dead hero:

at si femineo fuerat tibi Marte cadendum,
Thermodontiaca malles cecidisse bipennem. (12.610-611)

But if it had to befall you to be slain by a woman's Mars,
you would prefer to have fallen by the Thermodontiacan axe.

The reference is to the icy river Thermodon, the home of the Amazons, the
home of Penthesilea, who arrived to help the Trojans immediately after the
events of Homer's *Iliad*.[50] If Achilles had to fall by a woman's hand, he would
have preferred to have been the casualty of the beautiful Amazon.

The passage reminds us of Camilla, of course, who is the Penthesilea of the
Aeneid; Penthesilea, however, had fallen by the hand of Achilles, and was given
honor in death by the identity of her killer. Achilles was slain by the cowardly,
womanly Paris; Camilla, for her part, was killed by someone far inferior to her,
the fanatic Apollonian priest Arruns. Camilla's soul goes indignant to the underworld; the identity of her killer was unknown to her, but she suffers an unworthy, undignified end in that such a lesser man was responsible for dispatch-
ing her (though with divine assistance, as in the case of Paris and Achilles).

Achilles is like Camilla; the word *decus* is used to describe him (12.612),
just as Turnus had used it of Camilla, the *decus Italiae*. Achilles had been the
hawk that pursued the lesser bird in his chase after Hector; Camilla was accorded the same simile—not Turnus—in her *aristeia*. In Turnus' admiration of
the warrior girl, there is a direct evocation of Achilles' admiration for Penthesilea, whom he fell in love with after death (to the taunts of Thersites, who died
for his insults). Ovid has a definite judgment about the fate of Achilles. At first
he speaks in language that strikes the audience as deprecatory; the great hero's
body is burned on the pyre, and Achilles is reduced to only so much ash, a quantity that would barely fill an urn. Ovid continues:

at vivit totum quae gloria compleat orbem.
haec illi mensura viro respondet, et hac est
par sibi Pelides nec inania Tartara sentit. (12.617-619)

But it lives, his glory that fills the world.
This measure responds to that man, and in this
the son of Peleus is equal to himself and does not feel empty Tartarus.

At first, we do not know the subject of *vivit*; we might expect it to be Achilles. Instead, it is his glory, which is undying and great enough to measure up to the reality of the man. At Homer, *Odyssey* 11.465 ff., Odysseus had an encounter with the shade of Achilles, where he commented that the great hero must, after all, be the lord of the dead. Achilles famously responded that he would rather be the poor hireling of another than rule over the shades. The passage is not an explicit disavowal of the hero's choice to embrace an early death as the price for eternal fame, but it is a powerful comment on the fate of the dead, even those who know undying glory after their mortal sojourn. At the end of the *Iliad*, Achilles' anger had been quelled by the powerful reconciliation of his rage in Priam's presence, as he granted the burial of Hector and the fit obsequies for the Trojan prince whose body he desecrated.

In Ovid, there is no such peace for Achilles. Instead, Ovid immediately proceeds from his detail about the eternal fame of Achilles to mention of his famous shield:

ipse etiam, ut, cuius fuerit, cognoscere posses,
bella movet clypeus, deque armis arma feruntur. (12.620-621)

That very thing truly, in order that, whose it was, you may be able to recognize,
it stirred wars, the shield, and concerning arms arms are borne.

The passage wonderfully delays the noun; *clypeus*, the shield, is held in suspense. The shield was Achilles', and so, Ovid asserts, it should not surprise us that it causes wars. There is no peace *per se* for Achilles, because in Ovid's world the Homeric saga only leads on to the Virgilian; Homer's Iliadic theme was the wrath of Achilles, but in Ovid's larger vision, Achilles' anger is still not quelled. It leads to more suffering and strife, in this case, arms are borne for arms. The repeated *arma* once again, as before, serves as an effective anaphora to introduce the themes of the forthcoming *Aeneid*, and as we now learn, also the *Odyssey*.

The audience had no sense of whether Ovid would devote much attention to that greatest of the *nostoi*, the returns from Troy; now he announces that he will describe the contest between Ajax and Odysseus for the arms of Achilles. In a sense, the *Iliad* is being reborn, since the contest reminds us of the judgment of Paris that had started the war. Agamemnon is smarter than Paris; he will not make the decision, but, as the closing lines of this book announce, he will defer the judgment of the arms to the entire assembly of Greeks.

The audience is made aware, then, that as the next book opens Ovid will concern himself with the judgment for the arms of Achilles. Given Ovid's past practice we have no idea whether or not he will quickly dispense with his great subject and move on to other affairs of the period after the fall of Troy (for now history is advancing rapidly, as we prepare to begin the last fifth of the epic).

Book 13 of the *Metamorphoses* is significantly longer in comparison to its predecessor; it is, in fact, the longest book of the poem, in deliberate contrast to 12, the briefest. We have suggested that Ovid purposefully shortened his Troy account to contrast with Homer's lengthy poem; in a sense Book 13 is so long because it raises issues that deal not only with the aftermath of Ovid's *Iliad*, but also with his *Odyssey* and *Aeneid*. Book 14 will crown that epic narrative with a conclusion of the narrative of events proper to the *Aeneid*.

And so the "middle" of the three books will be the longest, and more than a third of it will be devoted to the debate between Ajax and Odysseus over the fate of Achilles' arms; Ovid will be in no rush to hurry through the opposing arguments of Ajax and Odysseus for control of the heroic mantle the dead Achilles had left behind as a gauntlet. Through the contest over a divinely wrought shield, we shall learn much about Ovid's views on the Homeric and Virgilian world of heroes, and the application of those lessons to the Augustan present. In Ajax, we shall also learn something about the death of a heroic world, while in Odysseus the falsehood theme that has so captivated our poet will come to its fullest exposition.

And so now we shall sit with the chieftains of the Greeks, as the ghost who would not speak to Odysseus in hell delivers a speech that proves more eloquent than Homer's silence.

Notes

1. Book 12 has not received much separate attention; as for Book 11, we await Reed's commentary in the Lorenzo Valla series, besides Tissol's completion of Anderson. Bömer's XII-XIII appeared in 1982. J. Huyck's 1991 Harvard dissertation is a commentary on *Met.* 12.612-13.398, the *armorum iudicium*. See further Zumwalt, N., "*Fama subversa*: Theme and Structure in Ovid, *Metamorphoses* 12," in *CSCA* 10 (1977), pp. 209-222, and Ellsworth, J. D., "Ovid's *Iliad* (*Metamorphoses* 12.1-13.622), in *Prudentia* 12 (1980), pp. 23-29 (which also examines Ovid's account of Aeneas' journey to Hesperia). Zumwalt sees extensive evidence of what we have called the "falsehood theme" throughout the narrative of Ovid's *Iliad*, signaled by the appearance of Fama, who is just as likely, of course, to tell lies as the truth. Although it does not concern itself with the *Metamorphoses per se*, a good introduction to an important part of the concern of this book is Putnam, Michael C. J., "Troy in Latin Literature," in *The New England Classical Journal* 34.3 (2007), pp. 195-205.

2. Cf. *Iliad* 2.303 ff.

3. *A.* 5.84-93 (where see Williams' Oxford edition).

4. For a different analysis of the opening of this book, note Musgrove, Margaret Worsham, "Change of Perspective in Ovid, *Metamorphoses* 12.11-23," in *The American Journal of Philology* 118.2 (1997), pp. 267-283.

5. See further Euripides' *Iphigenia in Tauris* (where Platnauer's commentary is the most convenient for English speakers); the story of Iphigenia's salvation is as old as Hesiod (*Eoeae* fr. 71 Merkelbach-West).

6. Ovid was the main influence for Chaucer's description of the same house; the Ovidian ecphrasis is actually among the briefer and least developed of his great personifications (cf. Invidia, Fames, Somnus, the three major ones). See further Delany, S., "Chaucer's *House of Fame* and the *Ovide moralisé*," in *Comparative Literature* 20 (1968), pp. 254-264.

7. See further Fordyce, and Horsfall ad loc. Virgil never records the fate of Messapus, who does not appear in extant literature outside the *Aeneid*.

8. Bull-fighting is not well attested at Rome (see further Bömer, and Hill); Pliny mentions it at *Historia Naturalis* 8.182.

9. See further *Iliad* 2.688-691, with Kirk ad loc.

10. The name is also reminiscent of Patroclus' father Menoetius; elsewhere I have argued that if there are affinities between Palinurus (whom Ovid had evoked in the second half of *M.* 11) and Patroclus, then in the story of the helmsman Menoetes, lost overboard like Palinurus, there may be a hint that Palinurus has affinities with Pallas, the Patroclus of the *Aeneid*—a complicated web of associations that provides Virgil's epic with tight cohesion. Virgil's Menoetes also connects to Misenus, the "doublet" of Palinurus who is lost in the sixth *Aeneid*.

11. It is probably a coincidence that Ovid calls Aulis "fishy" (11.10)—the only place in extant literature where the locale has that epithet—before recalling the story of the poor fisherman from Lerna. But the coincidence is rather striking, and may serve as good evidence of the highly allusive level of close reading that Ovid practiced with his Virgilian predecessor.

12. And, like his immortal parallel Juno, his anger is ultimately rewarded.

13. On the whole matter see further Murgatroyd, Paul, "Ovid's Achilles and Cycnus," in *Latomus* 67.4 (2008), pp. 931-939.

14. For excellent commentary on all three of the Ovidian Cycnuses, see further Barchiesi ad 2.367. We might also note that apparently all the heavenly discussion on Olympus about the gods being able to perform certain boons for themselves and others is now forgotten; Neptune will be able to secure his nephew Apollo's aid in killing Achilles, with no difficulty—just as Jupiter and Apollo are able to effect the death of Camilla with no questions of what is or is not fated to stand in their way.

15. As we have noted, the story is very old; Ovid and Virgil before him borrowed from the extensive coverage of the basic outline of the myth in previous literature.

16. 8. 305.

17. *Iliad* 1.250-252.

18. Note Diodorus Siculus 4.12.3-7 and 4.70.304, the latter with mention of the nuptials as locus for a battle.

19. And, as Virgil makes clear at *A*. 6.89, Turnus is the new Achilles. Aeneas and he will sometimes shift back and forth between the Achilles and Hector parts in the second half of the *Aeneid*, but ultimately it is Turnus who plays the new Achilles. Virgil and Ovid show the death that Homer's *Iliad* only prophesies.

20. Of course we also think of Homer's Achilles and the loss of Briseis.

21. So also the battle of the suitors in Ithaca, once Odysseus comes home to his wife Penelope.

22. This is, in fact, arguably the goriest death thus far in the poem, as Celadon's nose is thrust into his throat by the force of the blow, and his eyes are nearly gouged out.

23. Orion, for example, is a *Centaur* in the Hesiodic *Shield* (186). Ovid may be having fun with the idea of Rumor and its reliability; the aged Nestor, too, may be expected to have a few slips here and there from faulty memory.

24. See further my notes on the battle in Cepheus' hall, on 5.38.

25. Anchemolus, Virgil notes, had dared to defile the bed of his stepmother. For the whole matter see further Harrison ad loc.

26. On this passage see further Horsfall ad loc. See also *A*. 7.209 (with Horsfall), 9.10 (with Hardie), and 10.719 (with Harrison).

27. We may just be supposed to imagine the pastoral life of the early Italians in the vanquisher of this equine slayer of Corythus.

28. The suppression of almost all mention of Hercules' exploits in Nestor's story is thus foreshadowed here, for those with a good memory of the events at Evander's Pallanteum.

29. See further Hill ad 12.308 for discussion of the chronological order of the stories in Ovid's epic.

30. Note also the Phorbas at 5.74-78, during the *Perseid*.

31. For a good account of the significance of Fama in *Metamorphoses* 12 and beyond, note Tissol's aforementioned article on the "House of Fame," in the *Brill Companion*, pp. 305-335.

32. Ovid may also have in mind the key part played by Camilla and the equestrian combat in the threatened destruction of the Trojans in *A*. 11, so serious a threat, in fact, that both Jupiter and Apollo feel the need to respond to the peril.

33. Individual readers will have to judge for themselves whether they agree with Brooks Otis' influential view that "the epic battle is on the whole tedious and otiose." I might note that Otis misreads the Cyllaros and Hipponome story and seems to think that the latter is human: "the delicate manners of the Centaur Cyllarus (who had a human

PRIAM, UNKNOWING . . .

365

spouse and dressed up for her." (*op. cit.*, p. 283).

34. For the possibility that Ovid modeled his Caeneus/Caenis after a lost elegiac poem on Teiresias, note Gärtner, Thomas, "Die Geschlechtsmetamorphose der ovidischen Caenis und ihre hellenistischer Hintergrund," in *Latomus* 66.4 (2007), pp. 891-899.

35. See further her "Caeneus and Dido," in *Transactions of the American Philological Association* 110 (1980), pp. 315-325.

36. West does well to point out that Dido can never be both a good ruler and a good lover at the same time; it is as if she can only fulfill one function, never both simultaneously.

37. *Iliad* 22.139-142. In Quintus of Smyrna, Penthesilea is a dove in the face of Achilles the hawk (vid. *Posthomerica* 1.529-572); in Virgil, Camilla is the Achillean accipiter.

38. Ovid thereby "gets his way," as it were, in nodding to Virgil as well as making a point about his view of Caeneus' ultimate fate; note, too, that Ovid does not say that it is untrue that Caeneus ended up in Tartarus (so Virgil), only that Mopsus and Nestor saw the new (and unique) bird. The uniqueness of the bird is also highlighted by the fact the hero/ine's name means "new" in Greek.

39. In my notes on the passage in *Madness Unchained*, I observed that the hemistich at 702 seems rather pointless, and that the whole passage, with its doublet avian similes, may well have lacked the *ultima manus*, especially since the comparison between Messapus' men and swans seemed pointless. While the half-line still strikes me as evidence of lack of revision (though Ovid may well have noticed it and been inspired by the passage), I now think that the fact that Messapus was invulnerable to fire and sword made Virgil think of the Cycnus of cyclic epic, which occasioned the mention of the swans. The fact that Messapus is fighting on the same side as Turnus (as one of his principal commanders in fact), and that Turnus is equated by Virgil with Cycnus' traditional opponent Achilles, should not disturb us; linkages such as these need not be pressed in every case to the breaking point.

40. For a very different view, note Otis, *op. cit.*, pp. 281 ff.: "But Ovid's Trojan section has, nonetheless, no resemblance to Virgil's."

41. The story is utterly unknown outside Ovid.

42. See further Hill ad loc.

43. The Clytius and Cydon scene is the only one in the *Aeneid* where two lovers are described together in combat, since the Nisus/Euryalus epyllion depicts a night raid, an altogether different sort of thing.

44. See further Hill ad loc.

45. There may be a slight hint of a connection between Ovid's narrative and Virgil's in the sense that the Centaurs, like the Trojans in the *Aeneid*, are especially hateful to Juno on account of their father Ixion, who was traditionally tied to a burning wheel for all time in the afterlife as punishment for his crazed attempt to rape Hera.

46. A nice touch; Camilla had shunned the *domestic* works of Minerva, spinning and life at the loom, while her example of valorous death spurs the women of Italy to give up their prayers to Minerva and engage in warfare, the works of the battle goddess, by hurling down weapons on the enemy soldiers below the walls of the capital.

47. So Homer (*Iliad* 2.653 ff.; Tlepolemus was from Rhodes).

48. Elsewhere I have posited a possible connection between Camilla and the Harpies (if not also the Sirens); the bird image applies here too, given the avian nature of those monstrous women. In Caenis' avian fate we may also see an evocation of the phoenix.

49. Note Pseudo-Apollodorus 1.9 for the bare bones mythographic treatment.

50. The subject of the cyclic *Aethiopis*, along with the deeds of Memnon, the son of the Dawn.

Chapter XIII

The Leaders Sat

Book 13 is the longest book in the epic, in studied contrast to its exceedingly short predecessor.[1] Ovid has already announced the subject of the *armorum iudicium*, though given his past practice the audience has no clear sense of whether the debate between Ajax and Odysseus will be dispensed with briefly or at great length.[2] Book 12 devoted much attention to the story of Caeneus, who in Virgil was a barely sketched (however memorable) underworld denizen; Book 13 opens with a commentary on another Virgilian underworld scene, itself based on a Homeric antecedent. Homer's Odysseus saw the ghost of Ajax in the underworld (*Odyssey* 11.543-551); Ajax refused to speak to his onetime co-combatant and rival for Achilles' arms. In Virgil, the great Carthaginian queen Dido similarly departed away from Aeneas in silence; the two famous suicides both refused to speak to the person who could most justly be blamed for their respective situations.

The debate over the arms of Achilles is known to Homer, then, though it was of course the proper subject of other cyclic epics, the *Aethiopis* and the *Ilias Parva*. Tragedy also dealt with the story; Aeschylus composed a play or plays on the theme, and both Pacuvius and Accius had treatments of the same material. In a sense, the rhetorical contest between Ajax and Odysseus really started during the embassy to Achilles in *Iliad* 9, where Ajax's succinct address to Achilles was received better than Odysseus' longer speech, which Achilles dismissed with obvious feelings of contempt for the man who thinks one thing, but says another.

Ajax was famous for his sevenfold shield; as Ovid notes this characteristic accoutrement of the mighty warrior (13.2), we are reminded of Turnus, who had a similar shield Aeneas pierced with his spear before the final scene of the *Aeneid* (*A.* 12.925). Fittingly enough, Ajax's first claim to valor is how he drove back the Trojans when they tried to fire the ships; the reference to the events of *Iliad* 15-16 is designed to show how after Achilles, Ajax is the greatest of Greek warriors.[3]

Ajax sets up a dichotomy between himself and Odysseus; Ajax is the man of deeds, while his opponent is a man of words. This note of self-deprecation in speaking ability is designed to alert the audience to the fact that Odysseus may be more persuasive in his rhetorical skills, but in the matter of actual physical accomplishments, Ajax is by far the superior warrior.

The first half of Virgil's *Aeneid* is modeled after Homer's *Odyssey*; Aeneas is the new Odysseus, heading west on a journey home (though a very different sort of home from Odysseus' Ithaca). Virgil reverses the order of the Homeric epics; his *Odyssey* comes first, as preface to the violent, martial struggle of his Italian *Iliad*. Virgil explicitly says that his *Iliad* is the *maius opus*, the greater work; it is difficult not to see a judgment here on the importance of the *Iliad* over the *Odyssey*. There is also a subtle commentary on Aeneas, whose homecoming *precedes* his war; Odysseus fought for ten years at Troy and spent ten years trying to return home, but in the end he was successful, and his miniature *Iliad* with the suitors in a dining hall was over very quickly. The *Odyssey* ends with peace and stability in the home.

But Odysseus was a problematic figure for the ancients, a trickster and an often downright unscrupulous hero. There was no question of his prowess in battle, and certainly not of his rhetorical abilities, but the use of those talents was sometimes the subject of serious question. The *Ilias Parva* knows a version of the capture of the Palladium from the Trojan camp where Odysseus tried to stab Diomedes in the back so he could take all the credit for the deed.

Odysseus is a dire foe of the Trojans, and his image is, on the whole, less than positive for Aeneas' exiled Trojan band in the first movement of the *Aeneid*. Elsewhere, I have argued that at the crucial juncture in *Aeneid* 11 where the Trojans conceive a plan to have a cavalry feint cover an infantry march under Aeneas' direction over difficult terrain to attempt a surprise attack on the Latin capital, Aeneas' Trojans break the arranged burial truce that had been set up in the aftermath of Pallas' death.[4] If correct—and Virgil certainly leaves the matter open for speculation—then Aeneas does more than simply follow the Odyssean model for the first half of the epic: he rather learns something of the unscrupulous lessons of his Greek epic pattern.

Ajax notes that his valorous deeds were all performed in the light of day, whereas Odysseus prefers the cover of night for his implicitly questionable activities (13.13-15). The Trojans—though not Aeneas—had authorized the night expedition of Nisus and Euryalus, modeled on the *Doloneia* of Odysseus and Diomedes in *Iliad* 10; Virgil's Trojans acquire characteristics of their Greek conquerors.

Ajax employs the same rhetorical device we have heard from others in both Ovid and Virgil: Odysseus has gained glory simply from competing with such a hero as Ajax (13.17-20). Again, the "Ajax" in Virgil is *Dido*, as we learn from her powerful underworld scene. Like the Ajax of cyclic epic and tragedy, Dido committed suicide rather than face a world she could not tolerate. In a nice touch, Virgil's Dido did something exactly like the goddess Minerva, Odysseus' traditional patroness and practical fairy godmother:

illa solo fixos oculos aversa tenebat. (*A.* 6.469)

That one, turned away, held her eyes fixed on the ground.

The context is Dido's silent response to Aeneas' underworld address; Dido exactly replicates what Virgil said Minerva had done to the Trojan women in ignoring their appeal for help (*A.* 1.482 *diva solo fixos oculos aversa tenebat*). That scene had been depicted as one of the images in Dido's own temple to Juno in Carthage; the picture has come to life for Aeneas. The women of the Latin capital also pray to Minerva, in *Aeneid* 11, as Aeneas' Trojans set in motion their plan to capture Latinus' city by force; the goddess sends them Camilla, she who had forsaken the domestic arts of Minerva but was a master of the martial.

Dido = Ajax for Virgil because Aeneas = Odysseus and, in the context of an underworld sojourn, if there has to be someone who is hostile to Aeneas, Dido is the obvious candidate.[5] On another level, the gender divide helps to show in relief how Dido straddles the lines between masculine and feminine (so also Caeneus/Caenis). The Odysseus image also shows that in Dido's view, Aeneas has somehow tricked her; she represents the sort of blunt honesty we associate with Ajax. The Ajax comparison also shows the future military prestige of Carthage, Rome's great enemy, though ultimately defeated (like Ajax).

But Ovid's debate between Ajax and Odysseus owes the most not to Homer or the Virgilian evocation of Ajax's ghostly meeting with his *quondam* opponent, but rather the great Latin war council in *Aeneid* 11. That debate centered on the conflict between Drances and Turnus. In that contest of rhetorical ability, there was no clear winner. The debate took place during the burial truce that had been agreed upon after both sides had suffered serious losses (though probably the Latins had had the worst of it). Drances challenged Turnus and essentially argued that his young enemy was a coward, a man unwilling to face Aeneas alone and end the war with single combat. Turnus refuted the charges of his glib opponent, but the whole debate was interrupted by the word that the Trojans had resumed military operations—again, either we must imagine that the Latins had collectively forgotten when the truce was set to expire, or we must concede that the possibility at least exists that the Trojans violated the truce and began the plan we later learn about from scouts who report to Turnus that Aeneas intends a secret assault on the city under the cover of a frontal attack by cavalry forces. It is as if *Odysseus* wins the debate in Latinus' court: Aeneas' *trickery* resolves the Latin war council.

The debate in the Latin capital began with the report of the emissaries that had been sent to secure an alliance with Diomedes (now in retirement in southern Italy). Diomedes had refused any aid; King Latinus follows the report with a proposal that some concessions be made to the Trojans, though, significantly, he makes no mention of Lavinia. When Drances then rises to speak, Virgil notes that he was of noble lineage on his mother's side, but uncertain on his father's (*genus incertum*). Where Latinus had omitted mention of Lavinia, Drances makes her the centerpiece of his argument: if Turnus is not willing to settle with Aeneas, he should fight alone and spare the rest of the Latins any further burdens. Turnus responds that he is more than willing to face Aeneas, even if he should play the part of Achilles or excel his epic forbear, wearing arms that, like Achilles', were made by Vulcan (*A.* 11.438-440).

If Ovid's account of the death of Achilles at the end of Book 12 was meant to evoke Virgil's account of the death of Camilla, then the beginning of Book 13, with its reminiscence of the debate between Drances and Turnus, means that we are moving back in time, as it were—the great Latin war council occurred right before Camilla's *aristeia* and eventual death. We are moving back, as we prepare to examine the Odysseus image that had been abandoned by Virgil, since his *Odyssey* was not sequel but preface to his *Iliad.* Since Ovid's universal history has a forward chronological sweep, the movement of his narrative from *Iliad* to *Odyssey* to *Aeneid* must proceed apace, though he pervasively wraps his linear progress in a Homeric and Virgilian tissue.

Ovid's Ajax relates that he has family connections to Aeneas, whereas Odysseus is the son of Sisyphus, another notorious trickster.[6] More damningly, Ajax reminds the assembly that Odysseus had feigned madness to avoid coming to Troy in the first place (13.34 ff.), a reference to the famous story where Palamedes uncovered Odysseus' draft dodging by putting the infant Telemachus in the way of Odysseus' plow as he tried to sow salt into his fields to fool the Greeks into thinking he was insane. The cyclic *Cypria* would have detailed that episode, which painted Odysseus in a negative light even before he set sail for Troy; it makes for another obvious weapon in Ajax's arsenal.[7]

The story of Philoctetes also allows for reflection on one of Odysseus' less admirable moments; this tale too was part of the *Cypria.* Philoctetes was abandoned on Lemnos on the recommendation of Odysseus because of the unbearable stench from a seemingly incurable snakebite on Philoctetes' leg.[8] The story is best known to us from Sophocles' tragedy, where Odysseus shows himself as a corruptor of Achilles' son Neoptolemus as they prepare to set off to acquire Philoctetes' bow, which the Greeks learn is essential for the fall of Troy. In Ajax's speech, Philoctetes is, at present, lost on Lemnos with the weapons the Greeks will soon need if they are to win the war. Philoctetes, at least, is still alive—Odysseus made sure that Palamedes would be executed as part of a plot to avenge that hero's discovery of Odysseus' fakery (13.55 ff.).

We have already met Nestor as the eloquent storyteller of Book 12; Ovid's Ajax now remembers another Homeric incident, where Odysseus abandoned Nestor to likely death.[9] Nestor had been wounded by Paris and was being pressed hard by Hector, when Diomedes rushed to try to help him; Diomedes called for assistance from Odysseus, who was already fleeing away to the safety of the Greek ships. The Homeric passage is admittedly vexed.[10] Some have noted that Homer says Odysseus was "like a coward," that is, not a coward *per se*, just like one (I have never found this argument convincing), and that Homer may not be saying that Odysseus did not listen to Diomedes, but rather that Odysseus simply did not hear him. Hopkinson has noted that Diomedes is usually a notoriously loud hero—he of the great war cry and all that—and so it is unlikely Homer means to say that Odysseus was having hearing problems in the din of battle. I would suggest that Homer is indeed showing Odysseus in a negative light, and that the debate that has gone on since antiquity on this passage should be won by the "Ajax" side: Odysseus abandoned Nestor. Ovid's Ajax calls on Diomedes as witness—not a good strategy were the story not true. And, significantly, Odysseus does not try to refute the charges.

The gods love reversals of fortune; Odysseus, Ajax recalls, soon found himself in a similar mess (13.70 ff.).[11] As Hopkinson notes, in that Homeric incident, there is no hint of Odyssean cowardice—but that is not, after all, Ajax's point. Ajax is concerned with noting that *he* helped a comrade in arms, unlike Odysseus. In Homer, Menelaus called for help to save Odysseus, and Ajax responded to the call and provided cover while Menelaus saved Odysseus. Ajax adds details that are not in Homer; his Odysseus is fearful in the face of impending death. There is no good reason to imagine that Homer would not have agreed with this characterization, even if Ajax is clearly making his case in a way that paints his own actions in as favorable as light as possible, in contrast to his present opponent.

Interestingly, Ajax ends his reminiscence of the scene with a detail that is certainly not in Homer and that should give us pause:

at postquam eripui, cui standi vulnera vires
non dederant, nullo tardatus vulnere fugit. (13.80-81)

But after I snatched him away, he whom wounds had
not granted the power to stand, slowed by no wound, he fled.

Homer has no hint whatsoever that Odysseus' wounds were faked, and a reader of Homer would have no justification for assuming that was the situation all along. We are forced to conclude either that Ajax is lying, or that this fakery actually happened. The fact that Odysseus feigned madness to escape fighting at Troy makes Ajax's case more credible.

Ajax next recalls how he once laid Hector low with a huge boulder.[12] In that passage, the Greeks rushed in to finish what Ajax had started, but they were unable to kill Hector, since the Trojans covered him. Ajax moves from the recollection of that incident to a more heroic example of his battle prowess: he once agreed to single combat with Hector.[13] The duel was famously inconclusive; dusk fell and the heroes agreed to a truce, though the combat was never resumed. Odysseus was one of the contestants who had vied for the position of Greek champion; the lot fell to Ajax. The fact that Ajax could not be defeated by Hector redounds to his glory, of course, though it is just as important to note that unlike Achilles, Ajax could not kill him in single combat.

Lastly, Ajax recalls the great episode at the ships from *Iliad* 15. Here, he did indeed defend the Greek fleet, though eventually Hector broke his spear and he was forced to retreat, which is where the Greeks lost one ship. Patroclus, meanwhile, donned the arms of Achilles and went forth into battle; the Trojans fell back in the face of the would-be Achilles.

Ajax has recalled multiple episodes from the *Iliad* in the span of less than a hundred lines. The war at Troy is not over yet, though Achilles is dead and it is clearly in its final stages. Book 12 was an *Iliad* in miniature, retold through the "ancient history" of the Battle of the Lapiths and the Centaurs. Much of the overlay on Ovid's narrative came not from Homer, but rather from Homer's successor and Ovid's predecessor, Virgil and *his Iliad*. Now, in *words but not deeds*, the *Iliad* is being brought back to life in clear focus. Book 12 was a book of action; Book 13 is a book of words. Book 12 was a book for an Ajax; Book 13 is for an Odysseus. Similarly, in the great debate in the Latin war council, it was Turnus who refuted Drances and was a man of words; *Camilla* took the lead in active combat, while Turnus was relegated to waiting in ambush for Aeneas' infantry assault.

Right before Ajax makes the astonishing and rather arrogant claim that the arms seek him more than he seeks the arms—so great, after all, is his glory (13.95-97), Ajax recalls his performance before the ships. His deeds there were certainly heroic and worthy of praise, but it was *Patroclus* who put on the arms of Achilles and rushed forth to check the Trojan assault. Ajax is demanding the arms that the young hero Patroclus donned as he rode off to his eventual doom at the hands of Hector. It does not seem to have occurred to Ajax that he is recalling the day another man put on the very arms he is now claiming cry out for him. Similarly, Camilla—another Patroclus figure in the *Aeneid*, like Aeneas' young friend Pallas—rides off to fight and stay the Trojan assault, while Turnus—like Homer's Achilles with Pallas, and like Ajax—retreats into the shadows. If Turnus' debate with Drances has affinities with Ajax's with Odysseus in Ovid, then certainly the point can be extended: Turnus is like Ajax not just in the debate, but also in the matter of how he stood by while *his* Patroclus, Camilla, rushed off to the front lines.

And, again, we should note that we are moving backwards in time in Ovid's manipulation of his Virgilian source material: Achilles' death at the end of Book 12 = Camilla's, and now we return to the debate that preceded it. We are moving ever closer to a consideration of Odysseus, the great *survivor* of the war at Troy and the difficult aftermath of the returns.

Ovid's Ajax has already noted that Odysseus prefers the cover of night for his operations, and now he directly evokes the spirit of the failed night mission in the *Aeneid*, Virgil's answer to Homer's Doloneia. Ajax observes (13.105-106) that Odysseus' own helmet will betray him as he furtively carries out his nocturnal missions. This is a reference to the gleam from the metal of a stolen helmet that betrayed Euryalus and led to his death along with his loyal friend and lover. Odysseus is like a Trojan; the evocation also gains contemptuous force by the reminiscence of the pair of young lovers. Hopkinson notes that besides the Virgilian echo, there may be a nod here to the cyclic tradition that Diomedes was only saved from Odysseus' murderous intentions on the night they went to steal the Palladium by the glint of the sword's blade in the moonlight as it was raised to dispatch him.

Ajax ends his speech with a powerful address:

arma viri fortis medios mittantur in hostes:
inde iubete peti et referentem ornate relatis. (13.121-122)

Let the arms of the strong man be sent to the enemy:
thence order that they be sought, and adorn the one who brings them back with
that which he brought back.

As the commentators have noted, the custom is one familiar from early Roman history.[14] But most significantly, Ajax echoes the very opening words of the *Aeneid, arma virumque*, where the man is the new Odysseus, Aeneas. Here, the man is not Odysseus, but Achilles, the man whose *arma* have occasioned the present debate, and whose Homeric wrath was reborn in the *arma* of the first line of the *Aeneid* that evokes the wrath that is soon to be identified by Virgil as Juno's seemingly unquenchable rage. Interestingly, if we take the first line of the *Aeneid* and its evocation of Odysseus (= Aeneas in Virgil's first six books) alongside the Sibyl's declaration in the underworld that "another Achilles" will be born in Latium (= Turnus), then we have an equation where the *arma* of *Aeneid* 1 = Turnus', and the wrath they represent (= the mortal version of Juno's divine anger) is the greater theme, the *Iliad* that is superior to the *Odyssey* (hence the *arma* are noted first, then the *virum*, even though the *virum* will be described first—the lesser theme as prolegomenon to the greater).[15] Hence the importance of Turnus' words in the war council about Aeneas' either playacting or excelling Aeneas.[16]

Ovid's Odysseus now responds to Ajax (13.123 ff.). His first point is acknowledgment of the common sentiment: would that Achilles himself were still alive. He then implicitly calls Ajax a liar, by delineating his own divine ancestry from Jupiter and, tellingly, Mercury: himself a trickster god (140 ff.).

But Odysseus' main point is that everything Achilles did is, essentially, Odysseus' own doing: 13.171 *ergo opera illius mea sunt.* Odysseus tells the story of how Thetis, fearful for her son's life, disguised him as a girl on Scyros; Odysseus was able to uncover the trick by offering the girls a variety of gifts, one of which was a warrior's arms. Achilles made straight for the weapons, and Odysseus sent him off to war in much the same way as Palamedes detected Odysseus' feigned madness. The difference, of course, is that Odysseus' trickery was his own, not his divine mother's; further, it is unlikely that Odysseus would credit Palamedes with all that the Ithacan managed to do at Troy—at least before Palamedes himself suffered execution because of his part in sending Odysseus to fight in the first place. It is a somewhat subjective matter to judge a speech, but Odysseus' argument seems bombastic; Ajax, after all, focused on his own deeds and what Odysseus had not done, while Odysseus has made his opening argument a celebration not of his deeds *per se*, but of Achilles'; Odysseus was the facilitator, not the doer, of all the great exploits that culminated in Hector's death (178 *per me iacet inclitus Hector*).

Next, Odysseus moves to an even grander level: not only did he bring Achilles to the war, and thus won credit for everything that hero ever did (at least the heroic accomplishments), but he also deserves praise for the fact that the Greeks even made it to Troy, since at Aulis, it was Odysseus who persuaded Agamemnon to proceed with the sacrifice of Iphigenia, and Odysseus who went to secure the girl from her mother with the false promise that she would marry Achilles (13.181-195). From a Roman point of view, the breakdown of the father's love would be a particularly questionable exploit, though Odysseus' appeal to the common good might well be appealing. The argument is a good example of the ambiguous nature of part of Odysseus' speech; he makes valid points, though his penchant for trickery lies beneath the surface and is readily employed in manipulative efforts to secure his will—even if that will is also the people's.

Elsewhere, I have argued that the Trojans break the truce in *Aeneid* 11. If so, that is the first example of trickery and deceit from Aeneas as Trojan leader. Throughout the so-called Odyssean *Aeneid*, we see no such Odyssean deception or falsehood from Aeneas. Certainly Dido thinks that Aeneas is perfidious, but there is nothing of the "trickster" figure in Virgil's Aeneas in the first half of his epic.

In short, Aeneas is supposed to be Odysseus as the *Aeneid* opens, and yet, since Turnus is destined to be Achilles (as we learn on the very cusp of the Iliadic *Aeneid*), it is as if Aeneas does not win the *arma* of Achilles—unlike the Odysseus of cyclic epic, this Odysseus will not win the arms.[17] To be sure, Aeneas is sometimes akin to Achilles, and will be modeled after Achilles on several occasions—not least of which in the awarding of his own divine arms, newly crafted with appropriate scenes from Roman history in the future tense—but in the end, when he slays Turnus, he will be an unredeemed Achilles, an Achilles without the last movements of Homer's *Iliad* to cure his rage.

Odysseus also tried to reason with the Trojans alongside Menelaus when he approached their leaders about the return of Helen (13.196-204). This was, of course, a failed mission to the Trojan *curia*—it does not exactly bolster confidence in Odysseus' case.[18] Odysseus proceeds to describe how he spent the nine years when the Trojans were mostly penned up within the city's walls and not willing to engage in open combat; he was a useful man in those quiet, tediously frustrating days, while men like Ajax who know only about the heat of battle had nothing to do (at least in Odysseus' appraisal). So for the vast majority of the war's decade, Odysseus indicates, he was a major part of the Greek's ultimate success, while his opponent did nothing.

Odysseus next recalls the beginning of *Iliad* 2, where Agamemnon was punished by Zeus for his bad treatment of Achilles by a baleful dream. The dream told him that the gods had decided on Troy's immediate fall. Rather foolishly, Agamemnon decided to test Greek morale by telling them all was lost and he wanted to go home. The Greeks rush at the chance; Athena inspires Odysseus to prevent the departure, and the great orator proceeds to restore the lost Achaean morale. Ajax had spoken of an Odyssean flight; now Odysseus returns the favor by noting that Ajax had been one of the Greeks who fled away to his ships when Agamemnon announced the impending departure (13.223-224). This episode is not in Homer, which may indicate unfairness on Odysseus' part, though Homer does imply that all the Greeks ran, with the sole exception of Odysseus (admittedly, under Pallas' oversight). Because Odysseus was able to restore Greek morale and call back the flight of the warriors to the ships, he can take credit for anything Ajax subsequently did (and, implicitly, for anything any of the Greeks did).[19]

Odysseus also praises himself for his close friendship with Diomedes (13.238 ff.). Turnus' allies had sought the help of Diomedes, who refused to assist; he knew what divine forces protected Aeneas. In that refusal to help the Latins there is also something of the tradition of close loyalty between Odysseus and Diomedes, despite the fact that, as we have seen, the story was current that Odysseus had tried to murder the man he here would have us believe is his closest friend. Odysseus recalls the night raid, the Doloneia; he implicitly criticizes Ajax, who had fought Hector in single combat merely because he drew the lucky lot. Diomedes had picked Odysseus, so it was not exactly an act of extraordinary bravery to go on the mission. Odysseus does tell one clear lie in this scene: he claims to have killed Dolon (244-245 *Phrygia de gente Dolona / interimo*), though at *Iliad* 10.446-457, it was *Diomedes* who did the deed. Clearly Odysseus' rhetoric has impressed the audience, since no one objects to what is, in effect, an Odyssean deception so as to link his deeds with those of Diomedes— this is, in fact, the main point of Odysseus' entire speech. *Everything glorious that someone else did was made possible in some way by Odysseus.* Nor is Odysseus content with the one lie; he also claims that he killed the Thracian king Rhesus on the same fateful night, whereas for Homer it was again Diomedes who slew the monarch.

Odysseus proceeds to detail his victories over various Trojans; interestingly, he begins with Sarpedon's Lycian ranks, though in Homer it was not Odysseus' destiny to slay Sarpedon, and so Athena sent him against the Lycian rank and file.[20] Sarpedon, of course, is the son of Zeus whom the supreme god uses as an example of how he did not spare his own son in battle in his consolatory words to Hercules, who is upset over the impending death of his beloved Pallas.[21] Sarpedon was fated to die, though not at the moment in *Iliad* 5 when Odysseus was ready to dispatch him; Odysseus cannot countermand fate, and Athena sends him against other warriors—as if to protect him from trying to do that which would challenge the dictates of fate. But it is also interesting that Odysseus begins his catalogue with the name of a hero he did not actually kill, which rather undercuts the hero's glory. Odysseus concludes his dramatic recitation with an equally theatrical revelation of his scars, noting in contrast that Ajax has none.[22]

Metamorphoses 13.258 is the only line in the epic that is directly copied from Virgil (*Aeneid* 9.767), where Turnus, alone in the Trojan camp, slaughters various victims. The line is a translation of Homer, *Iliad* 5.678, where it describes exactly what Odysseus is boasting of here at the assembly; in the context of *A.* 9, the point is that in the absence of Aeneas, Turnus assumes the heroic mantle of both Achilles and Odysseus—he is at the zenith of his *aristeia*. Philip Hardie has noted ad loc. that Ovid "corrects" Virgil here; I think the point is that Odysseus is reasserting his Homeric victories after the Virgilian appropriation of them to Turnus to underscore how the Rutulian had taken over the "total hero," as it were, in Aeneas' absence.

The strongest part of Odysseus' argument is probably where he asserts that Ajax was not alone in defending the Greek fleet from Trojan fire, but that Patroclus was a main bulwark of the defense (13.268 ff.). But immediately thereafter, Odysseus utters one of the more interesting of his lies. He claims that in the drawing of lots for single combat with Hector, Ajax was ninth. In Homer, the two Ajaxes held the third and fourth places—and Odysseus was ninth.[23] The Latin (*nonus in officio et praelatus munere sortis*) can be taken to mean that Ajax was the last to come forward, though that is a stretch (*pace* Hopkinson)— the easier way to take the passage is that Odysseus has simply engaged in mendacity yet again. Are we to imagine that no one remembered these stories, and that no one was willing to challenge Odysseus? Was such the power of his eloquence that lies craftily proffered could seduce the ears of the assembly?[24]

Odysseus had opened his speech with words of praise for Achilles, and now he describes how he defended the body by holding off the Trojans who sought to despoil it (13.280 ff.). Here, too, the tradition was that Odysseus held off the Trojans while *Ajax* carried away the body (so the *Aethiopis*).[25] The point would again seem to be that Odysseus is responsible for everything that was done in the war, since he brought Achilles to Troy and helped the Greek fleet escape Aulis; similarly, since he shielded Ajax, he was really the one who carried off the body. There are those who will believe such things, if they repeat them or hear them often enough.

Ovid then has Odysseus insult Ajax in a brilliant reference to Virgil. Odysseus notes that he deserves the arms because he can understand what is carved on them; Ajax knows nothing about astronomy and the images on the shield. This is a powerful reminiscence of the very last lines of *Aeneid* 8, where Aeneas assumes *his* shield, decorated as it is with the images of the future history of Rome. Virgil says that he assumed the shield, though unknowing of what it depicted; he rejoiced in the image—essentially, in the pretty pictures, we might say—but he did not understand what he saw. The Ovidian Odysseus is equating Ajax with the Virgilian Aeneas, who, after all, is supposed to be the new *Odysseus*.

Hopkinson calls it "outrageous" that Odysseus should now argue that yes, he tried to avoid service at Troy, but his situation was identical to Achilles'—

Thetis held back the one, Penelope the other. This is a nearly complete misrepresentation of reality; Thetis knew her son would die, while nowhere else in extant sources does *Penelope* have anything to do with Odysseus' fakery.[26] The outrage is followed by Odysseus' defense for his dealings with Palamedes (if I was guilty, so were you) and Philoctetes (since now we need his bow to capture Troy, if my services are not required, let Ajax go in my place and try to talk to him).

We have observed that the debate between Ajax and Odysseus was inspired in part by Virgil's Latin war council debate between Turnus and Drances. In the climax of that speech, Turnus had announced that he "devoted his soul" (*A.* 11.442) to the Latin assembly and his father-in-law Latinus (a presumptuous anticipation of reality). Some have seen in this gesture an allusion to the ancient Roman tradition of *devotio*; others have seen no such thing in Turnus' action, or, if anything, a perversion of the Roman custom. Ovid's Odysseus says that even if Philoctetes should curse him, still he could go to win his arms for the common good of the Greeks: 13.329-330 *licet exsecrere meumque / devoveas sine fine caput*.[27] The word is not common; it will recur in an interesting context soon enough. Its appearance here is a signal that we are in the midst of a recollection of the Virgilian debate, in the manner of Ovid's subtly allusive style.

Odysseus notes that other heroes could well claim the arms of Achilles (this is one of the weaker sections of his speech); he notes, significantly, that he has intelligence and concern for the future—13.363 *tu vires sine mente geris, mihi cura futuri*. This is a reference, ultimately, to the fact that Odysseus is the subject of a lengthy epic about life *after* Troy, the world that Ajax does not understand and does not wish to inhabit. Odysseus has his eye to the future, to the return from Troy; the war at Troy is not for him the sum total of his life or the total extent of his purpose.

The climax of Odysseus' speech comes when he urges that the Greeks either give him the arms of Achilles, or give them to the statue of Minerva, the Palladium he had helped retrieve from Troy (13.381 *et ostendit signum fatale Minervae*). The speech thus ends on a note of divine reverence; if you do not wish to give the arms to the hero, then give them to the goddess. Minerva was a great protector and patroness of Odysseus; there is no hint of arrogant blasphemy toward the goddess, who was, after all, defending the Greek cause and helping in the fight against the Trojans.[28]

Are the Greeks supposed to feel that awarding the arms to Ajax would be an affront to Minerva's apparent favorite? In any case, as the audience already knows, Odysseus wins the weapons: 13.383 *fortisque viri tulit arma disertus*. The eloquent man took the arms of the strong one. The phrase is wonderfully ambiguous; does it mean that Odysseus won the arms of Achilles, or of Ajax? Clearly the triumph here is of speaking over deeds; *facundia* won the arms (382-383), Ovid notes. Subtly, the poet shows where his sympathy lies.

Ajax commits suicide (13.384 ff.). There is no mention in Ovid of the madness that drove the hero against the flocks; no mitigation is given for his heroism, though anger is his motivator (385 *unam non sustinet iram*). The fact that the sword Ajax uses was one given by Hector (as Sophocles is at pains to remind us in his play) emphasizes how even the greatest Trojan warrior had more respect for Ajax than his own fellow Greek. The blood itself expels the sword from the fatal wound and stains the ground with purple (that baleful color); a flower is born from the gore, which bears the same letters (αι) as the hyacinth of the eponymous *eromenos* of Apollo (394-398). Here the letters mark his name, there, the god's lament.

Ovid did not invent this connection of the "hyacinth" with the suicide of Ajax.[29] The fact of the preexisting tradition of a metamorphosis in association with the death made it difficult for Ovid not to mention the botanical detail.

Odysseus must go to Lemnos to win back Philoctetes' arms for the Greeks (13.399 ff.). Ovid uses an elaborate epic periphrasis to identify Lemnos as the island that was famous for the behavior of its infamous women. In the story,[30] the women of Lemnos did not honor Aphrodite and were cursed with a foul odor. Their husbands sought other women; in anger, the Lemnian women slaughtered their spouses and fathers. Only Hypsipyle refused; she saved her father Thoas. When the Argonauts landed at Lemnos, Jason had intercourse with her; she bore him two sons.[31]

This story provides an interesting counterpoint to the Hyacinthus reference. Orpheus sang of boys loved by the gods (= Hyacinthus), and of women possessed by irrational passions. The elaborate allusion to the Lemnian women is a direct reference to the Orphic song of the Cerastae and the Propoetides, the two tales of women in Cyprus punished for wrongdoing (cf. also the Venusian connections, etc.). Ovid has neatly introduced references to the two main themes of Orphic song, and in order to make sense of the allusions, they must be taken together. We are, in a sense, seeing a rebirth of what Orpheus had sung, a quiet rousing of the same melody that introduced the great conclusion of the poem's second third, the second of its three acts.

Odysseus secures the great bow and arrows, and Troy falls (13.401 ff.).[32] Priam dies; Cassandra is abducted along with other Trojan women. Astyanax is hurled from the walls. All of this was material found in the *Ilias Parva* and the *Iliupersis*; *Aeneid* 2 (and 3) looms large too, for the audience. Hecuba is the last Trojan woman to board the Greek vessels for life in captivity; she brings Hector's ashes—a detail, as the commentators note, that is not found elsewhere, and which has special resonance for readers of *Aeneid* 3 and the Helenus-Andromache scene: in Ovid's conception, Hector has his Trojan tomb, his ashes with Hecuba, and, presumably, the cenotaph in Buthrotum—a wonderful reminder of the scattered Trojan leavings of the Greeks.

The scene is somewhat parallel to the Trojan exiles' departure after the fall of their city; Ovid immediately mentions the death of Polydorus in Thrace, just as Virgil opened *A.* 3 with the same story (13.429-438). In Ovid the body is thrown in the sea as in Euripides' *Hecuba*, where the youth "was stabbed and left between shore and waves" (Horsfall ad *A.* 3.13-68); in Euripides, Hecuba eventually buries the body. The Greeks stop briefly at Troy, waiting for the weather to improve; the scene is reminiscent of the beginning of the Trojan War narrative, at Aulis: a virgin must be sacrificed so ships may sail. Achilles' ghost appears, demanding honor; besides the extensive tragic (Euripidean) reminiscences—mostly of Polydorus' ghost—there is a reworking here of the beginning of *A*. 3 (note we are now in the *Odyssean* half of Ovid's recollection of Virgil's epic), where the ghost of Polydorus spoke to the Trojans.

Ovid's scene of Polyxena's noble death is deeply indebted to Euripides; it is also a testament to the pitiful condition of the Trojan women we meet in *A*. 3, scattered exiles who, in Aeneas' eyes, are at least now fortunate in that they have a home (and, in Andromache's case, that she has reverted to a Trojan spouse, Helenus). Polyxena offers an alternate to Aeneas' thoughts; she wants nothing to do with survival as a slave, but prefers death—and an unsullied, free death (her repetition of *libera* is especially poignant in a Roman context).

Ovid now commences a lengthy section on the fate of not only Polyxena, but also Hecuba; in a sense, these women distantly echo Virgil's Lavinia and Amata. Lavinia was betrothed to Aeneas, who, in the final scene of the *Aeneid* was like Achilles slaying Hector; Turnus gave over Lavinia—*tua est Lavinia coniunx*.[33] Amata, for her part, committed suicide rather than see Aeneas' victory; like Aeneas/Achilles, she was also overcome with madness. And, in the last book of the *Aeneid*, Aeneas even sought to put into effect a plan to storm the Latin capital where, of course, his future wife resided. Significantly, when Hecuba fondles the corpse of Polyxena, Ovid notes that the girl's soul was *fortis*—13.488 *quae corpus complexa animae tam fortis inane*—a perfect match for the *fortis viri* that was Achilles. There is no question that in some perverse sense, she is Achilles' perfect match—though no author dared imagine them together in the underworld.[34]

The first half of Book 13 also offers room for some future hero to improve a less than praiseworthy set of heroic models. Ovid's Odysseus does not impress us with his mendacious rhetoric, and Achilles has become a cruel ghost who demands the blood of a virgin. The *Aeneid* ends with Aeneas definitively becoming Achilles—the wrath of Juno is transferred to Aeneas. As we have observed, we are left in the last lines of Virgil's epic with an Aeneas who is an unredeemed Achilles—the *Aeneid* shows a regression, a decline, from the moral highpoint of the end of Homer's *Iliad*. Ovid, here, leaves us with his last mention of Achilles, and it has affinities with Virgil's vision: the hero as bloodthirsty savage.

As in Euripides, so in Ovid the washing of Polyxena's corpse in preparation for burial is the locus for Hecuba's discovery of the death of her son Polydorus—Ovid is yet again under the strong influence of Greek tragedy. Once she learns of Polydorus' murder, Ovid compares her to a lioness out for blood when its cub has been stolen (13.547-553). The image is borrowed from Homer's description of *Achilles* as he mourns the death of Patroclus and plots revenge on Hector.[35] Hecuba has become a living Achilles now, mad with rage and lust for vengeance. The wrath of Achilles—reborn in the demand for Polyxena's slaughter—has been transferred to Hecuba. The perpetuation of this madness, the transference of it from godlike mortal to goddess in Virgil and, here, from godlike mortal to noble queen, is a major theme of both Virgil's and Ovid's reading of Homer.

Euripides' *Hecuba* details the revenge; in the tragedy, Agamemnon actually assists Hecuba, since he sympathizes with her cause and is angry with Polymestor for his murderous duplicity. There is something in Ovid's description of Polymestor's fate that is reminiscent of another Thracian horror scene, the revenge of Procne and Philomela on Tereus—appropriately enough, so late in the epic, Ovid recalls the supreme story of madness and horror from the earlier movements of the work. The war at Troy has had shockwaves of savagery that now extend to the lonely spot where Hecuba—as if she were some raving Bacchant—has called together serving women to help her destroy Polymestor.

Hecuba proceeds to gouge out his eyes (13.561 ff.). In Euripides, the women help her and they use hairpins; in Ovid, she works alone and with her bare hands. Before Polymestor's Thracians can respond effectively, she is transformed into a dog, a barking horror that has given the location its name—*Cynossema*, the Sign of the Dog.[36]

Ovid offers a coda to Hecuba's metamorphosis that has not been much appreciated:

illius Troasque suos hostesque Pelasgos,
illius fortuna deos quoque moverat omnes,
sic omnes, ut et ipsa Iovis coniunxque sororque
eventus Hecaben meruisse negaverit illos. (13.572-575)

The fortune of that woman moved her own Trojans
and the enemy Pelasgians; it also moved all the gods,
so all, as even the very spouse and sister of Jupiter
denied that Hecuba had merited that end.

There is no explanation for Hecuba's transformation; her own rage seems to have expressed itself in canine metamorphosis. Juno, the inveterate enemy of the Trojans, here has her moment of reconciliation that echoes the great surrender of her madness toward the end of the *Aeneid*. Here she softens in her attitude regarding Trojans; Hecuba did not deserve her fate. Hecuba's madness is reminiscent of the supreme wrath of Juno, manifested in the actions of the Fury Allecto and her victim, Lavinia's mother Amata; here, the angry goddess lets her passion cool as she pities a mother whose actions she can understand. It is an Ovidian nod to the climactic scene in the divine machinery of the *Aeneid*, and a sign of forward progress in Ovid's epic after the terrible evocation of Thracian savagery that Hecuba's gouging of Polymestor's eyes had occasioned.

The Trojan saga would seem to be nearing its close, but Ovid is not finished with the theme—he transitions to Aurora, the divine mother of Memnon, who

mourns for her son, another victim of Achilles (13.576-622).[37] Aurora is overcome with grief that her son has died; she begs some solace from Jupiter. The
supreme god agrees. For what happens here, Ovid is our earliest surviving
source; he describes how the ashes from Memnon's pyre begin to thicken and
take on shape: a bird is fashioned from the smoky mess. Then other birds appear, countless sisters of the first.[38] The birds soon divide into two groups and
engage in combat with each other; they fall down to earth as funeral offerings
(615 *inferiae*) for Memnon. Every year, Ovid notes, they repeat the same ritual.
It is as if they were gladiators at a Roman funeral.[39]

As the commentators have noted, Aurora's lengthy supplication of Jupiter is
clearly modeled on Thetis' invocation of Zeus in *Iliad* 1, where the marine goddess begs that Zeus may do honor to Achilles by aiding the Trojans and thereby
showing the Greeks how much they need the hero they dishonored. So, on the
one level, the transition from Hecuba and the grief of the Trojan women to
Aurora and her lament for Memnon is a rebirth of the *Iliad* (Hopkinson speculates that the cyclic *Aethiopis* had a lament similar to the Iliadic one).

But why does Ovid move from Hecuba's tragedy to an extended sequence
on Aurora and the origin of the warring birds of Memnon? I would suggest that
the answer lies in the sympathy of Juno for Hecuba, which echoes the reconciliation of that goddess at the end of *A.* 12. That reconciliation set up the final
revelation in the *Aeneid* regarding the fate of Rome: the city would be Italian,
not Trojan. After recalling that key passage from Virgil, Ovid proceeds to describe what amounts to an etiology for an eminently Roman practice, a custom
borrowed from Etruscan funeral rites, the gladiatorial combats at Roman obsequies. The birds also engage in what is essentially a yearly renewal of civil strife
(they rose, after all, from the same ashes); we see here another etiology for the
origin of the Roman civil wars. And, as others have noted, Aurora's "pious
tears" (13.621-622 *pias . . . lacrimas*) set the stage for Ovid's imminent introduction of Aeneas, who in Virgil is the inheritor of Juno's madness.

Non tamen—the fates did not, nevertheless, allow for Troy's expectation to
be overturned together with her walls (13.623-624 *non tamen eversam Troiae
cum moenibus esse / spem quoque fata sinunt*). The expectation of Troy is
Rome, and Ovid now quietly introduces Aeneas, who, as at the end of *Aeneid* 2,
is carrying his household gods and his father out of Troy. Aeneas is obliquely
introduced as the *Cythereius heros*, the "Cytherean hero," setting a Venusian
stamp on him from the first. Besides the Penates and his father, he has his son
Ascanius; he sets out from Antandros, the Trojan port. Ovid briefly nods to the
episode at the beginning of *Aeneid* 3: Aeneas stops in Thrace, where Polydorus
had been murdered. He then swiftly arrives at Delos (630-631).

Virgil had described this landfall in the third *Aeneid*; the Trojans land at Delos and are received by King Anius.[40] Ovid notes the two tree stumps that were
said to be the trees Latona had gripped when she was in labor with the divine
twins; Virgil had not mentioned this, but it is appropriate for Ovid's narrative,
since in Book 6 he had described Latona's troubles in pregnancy. In Virgil, the

Trojans receive an oracle from Apollo that they should seek their ancient home; Anchises interprets this as Crete, and the Trojans quickly depart from Delos.[41]

Niobe had been rendered bereft of her children; King Anius, too, has suffered losses in this regard. Anchises notes that he thought Anius had a boy and four girls—where are they now? The story that lurks here is vexed, and, as often, Ovid's account is the earliest extant continuous version.[42] Anius' daughters had the gift to make endless supplies of wine, grain, and oil. In some versions, Agamemnon came to Delos and demanded their aid in the expedition against Troy; Anius outfitted the Greeks with enough supplies for nine years. In other accounts—including Ovid's—the king and his daughters resisted, and they were eventually pursued to the point that they had to invoke divine aid. Bacchus transformed them into doves—Venus' sacred bird.

Usually there were three daughters, with names that evoked their talents (Wine, Grain, Oil); in Ovid there are four, and they are left unnamed. As Hopkinson notes, there was a tradition of a fourth daughter, Launa, who had the gift of prophecy and was taken by Aeneas from Delos to Italy (according to some Aeneas raped her). Launa eventually gave her name to Aeneas' first settlement, *Lavinium*. Ovid conveniently nods to the tradition, without getting trapped in the morass it would cause him, by having four daughters—but they are all transformed into birds. Ovid thus implicitly denies the veracity of the report that Launa was taken by Aeneas to Italy (either willingly or by force).

According to custom, gifts are exchanged (13.675 ff.). Aeneas receives a drinking bowl that is decorated with a detailed picture. The cup was originally brought to Delos by one Therses from Boeotia, a figure who is otherwise unknown to us. There is a city with seven gates, a traditional description for Thebes, but also a nod to Rome's seven hills. Here Ovid recalls his earlier epic cycle on Thebes, the centerpiece of the early movements of the *Metamorphoses*, where Cadmus' exile from his Phoenician home presaged the westward journey of the Trojans in search of a new home. The city is in mourning; funerals and pyres are all arranged before its seven gates, and women—both mortal and quasi-divine nymphs—lament with disheveled hair.

The cause of the lament is not martial strife (though we might be tempted to see a foreshadowing of the forthcoming war in Latium), but rather the suicide of the daughters of Orion. The story is obscure; it survives only in Antoninus Liberalis, who credits it to Nicander and the lyric poet Corinna. Boeotia was overcome by pestilence; an oracle reported that the only way to save the locale was by the self-sacrifice of the daughters of Orion, who proceeded to commit suicide: the gods of the underworld demanded the deaths. According to the oracle, two virgins were required; no Theban girl was willing to give up her life, and the daughters of Orion responded with the admittedly logical observation that if they failed to commit suicide, they would eventually die of the plague anyway. Hades and Persephone were so impressed with the girls that they changed them into comets, and a sanctuary was set up in their honor, with yearly rites.

Ovid's version is slightly different; he has twin youths emerge from the ashes of the girls' funeral pyres, youths who are named the *Coroni*. In the absence of further extant testimonia, it is uncertain whether the change from the account in Antoninus Liberalis is an Ovidian invention or a version borrowed from Corinna or some other author, a problem that makes elucidation of the metamorphosis more difficult.[43] The passage is vexed; most manuscripts call the youths not *Coroni* but *Coronae*; *Coroni* is obviously easier, but it has less manuscript authority.[44] Most critics have argued that the picture on the drinking cup is related to the situation of Anius' own daughters, who were lost like those of Orion; others have added that there is a parallel between Orion's daughters and the Memniades. But none of this, however true, is satisfactory for why this illustration should grace the Delian king's gift for Aeneas.

Some help may come from a detail preserved in Antoninus Liberalis. He notes that the daughters were reared by their mother after Artemis had taken away the hunter Orion to be her companion (which would eventually engender jealousy in her brother Apollo). Athena taught Orion's daughters weaving, while Aphrodite bestowed loveliness upon them. We have an odd situation here, then: a virgin goddess of domestic and martial arts instructs the girls in household duties, while the goddess of beauty sees to their appearance (there may be a hint that she instructs them in the use of her wiles). Artemis, the virgin goddess *par excellence*, meanwhile relaxes her usual *de facto* ban on men (excepting her divine brother) and consorts with the girls' father. Somehow, all of this causes irritation; Apollo is apparently the source of the plague,[45] and his oracle says that the gods of the lower world must be appeased—they are the deities who eventually "reward" the girls with transformation into comets, which in Ovid's version becomes a birth from their ashes of young men who are called the *Coroni* or *Coronae*, who lead the procession in honor of their mother's ashes (13.699 *et cineri materno ducere pompam*).[46]

Ovid also deals with Orion-lore at *Fasti* 5.493-544, where Neptune, Jupiter, and Mercury visit the humble Boeotian lodging of one Hyrieus. The kind hospitality the old man offers is rewarded by the gift of a son, Orion; he becomes a mighty hunter and a defender of Latona. He boasts one day that he can subdue any beast, and the earth sends a giant scorpion. The scorpion attacks Latona; Orion throws himself in its path and is killed in sacrificial death. Latona rewards her savior with a catasterism.[47]

Ovid here disagrees with Hesiod, who says that Orion was the son of Poseidon and Euryale. Further, at *Odyssey* 5.118 ff., Calypso complains about the gods and mentions that when Eos took Orion for herself (cf. Ovid's recent mention of Aurora and Memnon), Artemis slew Orion (in apparent jealousy and anger that he abandoned her service for another). Another version[48] has Orion killed because he tried to rape Diana.

The story of Hyrieus is a doublet of Baucis and Philemon, except that Hyrieus is a widower and prays not to remain forever with his wife—he in fact explicitly says that he is not asking to be a husband, but a father (5.530 *nec coniunx et pater esse volo*). Hyrieus wants a son, and the son he is granted is killed—like the daughters of Anius, whose wife is also absent from the narrative—in an act of self-sacrifice.[49]

What we have, then, between the two Ovidian narratives—as ever, it is impossible to know for sure which has precedence—is a tale of self-sacrifice, both from the father, Orion, and his daughters. The daughters have inherited the selflessness of the father; the *Metamorphoses* narrative complements the *Fasti* passage.[50] Orion died to save Latona; his daughters die to save Delos, the island sacred to the great goddess and her divine offspring. It is a powerful narrative to hand over to Aeneas (and, by implication, Ascanius). It is a call to self-sacrifice and heroic nobility, and can be compared with the advice Anchises bestows on his son in Virgil's underworld—a very different lesson indeed.

Significantly, while Ovid does not specify how many daughters Orion had, he does note that there were *two* youths who emerged from the virgin ashes (13.697-698 *geminos . . . iuvenes*). These two youths, the *Coronae*, symbols of self-sacrifice, may just represent Pallas and Camilla, which fits neatly with both the gender confusion and Camilla's presence in the masculine world of war.

Ovid quickly notes the tradition of the abortive Trojan landing in Crete, but with minimal detail; Virgil had already described the failed sojourn. In both poets there is a storm after Crete; likewise both accounts note the stopover at the Strophades (13.709-710) and the Harpies, though in Virgil a baleful prophecy is given by Celaeno, and in Ovid, Aello. Aello is Greek for "storm wind," and the Harpies were the personifications of the storm winds, so there is perhaps a learned nod to the etymology and no other significance behind the change of name.

Other brief geographical descriptions follow, as in Virgil; most notably, Odysseus' country of Ithaca is identified as the kingdom of the liar (13.712 *regnum fallacies Ulixis*), a change from Virgil's "savage" Odysseus (*A.* 273 *saevi*). As the commentators have observed, the Ovidian epithet better accords with the debate from earlier in the book; it offers a powerful but subtle comment on Ovid's appraisal of the hero. Ovid mentions Ambracia, a place omitted in Virgil; given his general theme of metamorphosis, it is not surprising that he alludes to an obscure story of how the divine twins Castor and Pollux, and Hercules, contested possession of the island. The judge awarded the land to Hercules, and Apollo petrified him in punishment.[51] Similarly, a brief metamorphosis is told of the children of the Molossian king: they were besieged by robbers who were trying to burn down their house; Jupiter saved them by transforming them into birds.[52] Actium is mentioned, though briefly; Virgil also does not spend much time in *Aeneid* 3 on the site (though more than Ovid), since he reserves a grand treatment of the battle for Aeneas' shield.

Corcyra, the legendary home of the Phaeaecians, also receives a brief Ovidian mention that imitates Virgil's (equally) short allusion; Ovid is here employing rapid narrative as Aeneas' Trojans land at Buthrotum in Epirus (13.719 ff.). Not surprisingly, Ovid rushes over this section, mentioning the prophecies of Helenus but attempting nothing like Virgil's treatment of the Trojan visit to the miniature Troy set up by exiles in this remote locale. The Trojans finally arrive in Sicily, where they land at Zancle, near the twin horrors of Scylla and Charybdis.

Virgil's Helenus warned of the need to avoid those (Homeric) pests; in Virgil, Aeneas reaches Drepanum, where, at the end of *Aeneid* 3, Anchises dies. Hopkinson notes that in both Virgil and Ovid, "curiously," the Trojans land at a place named for a word for "sickle" (Zancle = Sicilian or Ligurian, Drepanum = Greek), a word with appropriate associations for the death of Anchises.[53]

Virgil does not spend much time on any Scylla or Charybdis lore; Ovid makes much of Scylla. For Virgil (*Eclogue* 6.74-77), Scylla the daughter of Minos and Scylla the sea monster are the same; Ovid does not tell us in the *Metamorphoses* whether or not they are one woman (cf. the "two" Atalantas), though the fact that his Scylla underwent an avian metamorphosis would seem to point to a different creature here.[54] Still, the appearance of the same name does make us recall the former Scylla, even if the two accounts are difficult if not impossible to reconcile. Further, Ovid was no doubt influenced by the fact that in the Virgilian song of Silenus, which the poet mined for so much of his *Metamorphoses*, the two Scyllas are one and the same woman. *This* Scylla is the daughter of Crataeis (13.749; so also *Odyssey* 12.124-125); Hesiod says Scylla was the daughter of Hecate.[55]

Ovid prepares to digress to Scylla lore: she was once a beautiful girl, sought by many lovers, but she rejected all of them, for unspecified reasons. She spent her time with the nymphs of the sea, charming them with stories of her rejected lovers. One of the nymphs, Galatea, observes that Scylla has the luxury of rejecting suitors without fear; in Galatea's case, rejection was harder—she was loved by the Cyclops Polyphemus.[56]

In the *Aeneid*, at this point the Trojans meet Achaemenides, the Odyssean "survivor" of the Cyclopean horror who was left behind to face an uncertain fate; at first reading we might think that Ovid is here substituting other Cylcopean lore for that episode, but in fact we shall meet Achaemenides in due course, in the next book. Myers has argued that the insertion of a long series of love stories here corresponds to Virgil's Aeneas-Dido episode.[57] The problem with that attractive interpretation is why Ovid would insert the long episode before Achaemenides, a story he does not omit, though in Ovid's version, Achaemenides is taken on board Aeneas' fleet without mention, only to appear later, in Italy, when another former Odyssean meets and recognizes him.

Galatea begins her story of woe (13.750 ff.).[58] She was loved by Acis, a youth of sixteen who was the son of Faunus (a Roman sylvan deity) and a river nymph. The Cyclops, however, also pursued her; she hated the one as much as she loved the other. At first the scene is fairly comic; Polyphemus for once worries about his appearance, and he foregoes his savage ways, since all he cares about is the pursuit of Galatea; he has no time for the distraction of harassing ships unfortunate enough to sail his way. The Acis story, we must note, is not found in literature before Ovid; the presence of the name in Theocritus (1.69) as a river does not prove the preexistence of a story.

What follows in Galatea's recollection (13.798-869) is an extended imitation of both Theocritus and Virgil; as much for its sheer length as anything else, it has been taken as a burlesque parody of the work of those august predecessors.[59] If Myers is correct that the extended set of love stories is meant to evoke the Aeneas-Dido romance, then Ovid's narrative must be offering some commentary on the whole digression from Aeneas' journey to Rome; if there is parody and mockery, it is of the decision Aeneas made to stay with Dido in Carthage. But parallels between the two do not work well and cannot be pushed too far on any level of detail.[60]

Dido fell in love with Aeneas under the influence of Venus and Cupid; she was not entirely responsible for her own actions, even if one is not particularly surprised to find that she developed strong feelings for the Trojan hero. The complicated and elaborate Galatea-Polyphemus-Acis triangle is completely different; it will be balanced by the Glaucus-Scylla-Circe story that will take us into Book 14. Both sets of stories are about romantic rivals; in the Aeneas-Dido tale, the only rivals to speak of are the suitors Dido has forsaken in Carthage (cf. the many suitors of Scylla); Iarbas is most prominent among these, and he prays to Jupiter to intervene in the Carthaginian romance.

Ovid's Polyphemus finds Galatea and Acis in each other's embrace (13.870 ff.). Galatea flees—hardly a model of self-sacrifice, we might note—and Acis is killed by a huge boulder the Cyclops throws. The boulder only grazes the youth, but the graze is enough to kill him. There is something here of the Venus-Adonis narrative from the end of *Metamorphoses* 10 (note, also, the presence of the "second" Atalanta there, and the "second" Scylla here); the goddess is ineffectual in saving her lover.[61]

Galatea is not without power, however, and she now works a remarkable metamorphosis (13.885-897). Blood trickles from under the stone; we might expect a floral metamorphosis, though the audience knows that Acis is a Sicilian river. The blood begins to turn color; it becomes clear step by step, first like a stream that has been flooded by early (i.e., spring) rains, and then beautifully translucent. The rock splits open, and from the rock a reed emerges, and then waters rush forth and—the climax of the transformation—a new river god emerges, a new Acis, now transformed from youthful lover to youthful god.

The coterie of sea nymphs departs; Scylla, for her part, does not go in the deep water, but stays close to shore, sometimes wandering the sand naked, and at other times seeking a secluded pool to bathe. The sea god Glaucus sees her, himself but recently a mortal (13.904 ff.). This story is largely unknown before Ovid, though Aeschylus wrote a play on the subject of Glaucus' transformation; Cicero apparently exercised his poetic talents on the theme.[62]

Glaucus is a merman, with the body of a mortal man and the tail of a fish. He pursues Scylla, who flees in fear; she knows not whether he is a man or a monster. He tries to persuade her in every way he knows how to accept his love; she flees to a promontory (where, presumably, a marine god cannot follow her).

Glaucus leans against the rock and makes his appeal yet again, this time explaining something of his identity (apparently for the first time). He is now a powerful god of the sea, though once he was a mortal, and, indeed, a humble fisherman. He describes a virginal field, a place where no animals ever graze and no bees ever gather flowers (13.928 *non apis inde tulit conlectos sedula flores*). Glaucus uses the beautiful, isolated locale as a suitable ground for counting his fish; as he puts them in order and inspects the day's catch, he is amazed at how they start to come to life—the grass seems to have restorative properties. Glaucus proceeds to test his theory that the grass might be magical; he proceeds to eat some grass—thus becoming, we might note, the first person to eat the virgin pastureland.

Glaucus has a sudden passion for the water; like the rejuvenated fish, he dives into the sea. The marine deities welcome him, and they beg Ocean and Tethys to purify him by taking away his mortal parts (13.949 ff.):

> . . . ego lustror ab illis,
> et purgante nefas noviens mihi carmine dicto
> pectora fluminibus iubeor supponere centum (13.951-953)

> . . . *I am purified by them,*
> *and with a spell having been sung to me nine times that purifies me of my evil,*
> *I am ordered to submerge myself in a hundred rivers*

Glaucus does not have to worry about undertaking some massive trip; the rivers suddenly appear as soon as Ocean and Tethys announce the watery imperative. They pour themselves all over Glaucus, removing the *nefas* that is apparently his mortal life. This is Orphism: the body must be purified and purged in order to prepare for a new life. Here, the new life is nothing less than divinity. Glaucus cannot really explain what happened:

> hactenus acta tibi possum memoranda referre,
> hactenus haec memini, nec mens mea cetera sensit. (13.956-957)

> *Thus far I am able to tell you the things that happened that must be recalled,*
> *thus far do I remember these things, but my mind did not feel the rest.*

Glaucus remembers the waters of a hundred rivers cascading over his body; when he recovers his senses (958 *quae postquam rediit*), he is a sea god, a merman with a fin-bearing tail (963 *pinnigero . . . pisce*).

Glaucus, like Polyphemus with Galatea, is madly in love with Scylla; he cares not for his magical transformation and apparent immortality as a new god, if Scylla continues to reject him. Scylla, however, is silent and does nothing but run away—she abandons the god (13.966-967 *reliquit / Scylla deum*).

The ending of this book is among the most terrifying in Latin poetry:

... furit ille inritatusque repulsa
prodigiosa petit Titanidos atria Circes. (13.967-968)

... He was maddened, and, enraged by the rejection,
he sought the prodigy-filled courtyard of Circe.

Glaucus will seek the aid of the witch Circe, to enlist the aid of the sorceress in trying to win the heart of Scylla. The results, as the audience might anticipate, will be disastrous.

Some summary considerations can be offered here on a densely packed book. I would suggest that we begin by recalling that Ovid is interested in retelling not one or two but three epics: Homer's *Iliad* and *Odyssey*, and Virgil's *Aeneid*. He weaves the three together, not following a strict chronology, and making his own narrative a tissue of allusions to the other three works (this is especially the case when he manipulates his Virgilian source material, itself an *Odyssey* followed by an *Iliad*).

Virgil considered his *Iliad* the greater work than his *Odyssey*, and I believe Ovid agreed with that appraisal.[63] The first part of Book 13 is concerned with events that are broadly linked to the *Iliad* (and to the events at Troy immediately after the fall, events that are not part of the tradition of the *nostoi* or returns). This narrative fills the book from lines 1 through 622, where the narrative of the Memnonides ends. Thus fully two-thirds of the book's enormous length is devoted to what could be called Iliadic themes (more than Odyssean, despite Odysseus' central part in the judgment of the arms). It takes two-thirds of the book's length before Troy's fall is "complete," as it were.

Then, Ovid commences his *Aeneid* (13.623 ff.).[64] He begins with a direct evocation of the events described in Virgil right after the city's fall and the beginning of the long voyage westward, with Polydorus and all that. His narrative is pure imitation of Virgil, with practically no dissension from his epic predecessor's account of the early wanderings of the Trojan exiles.

The significant exception to this retelling of Virgil comes on Delos, the island of the divine twins who hold such significance to the Augustan regime. There, Ovid details a gift of a drinking bowl that King Anius presented to *Aeneas* (not Anchises, we might note, despite his preeminence while he lives). That drinking bowl shows the story of the self-sacrifice of the daughters of Orion. The story of their sacrifice relates to the story Ovid tells in his *Fasti* of the self-sacrifice of their heroic hunter-father, who gave his life trying to defend the mother of the divine twins.

The daughters of Orion die for the people of Delos, but from them two young men are born, youths who are crowned with glory, as it were (the *Coronae*). I wonder if we are meant to see in this portent—especially given the version of the story where the daughters were changed into comets—something of the famous comet portent of 44 B.C., which was taken as a sign of the apotheosis of Caesar. That comet will figure in the last movements of Ovid's epic, to be sure, but I wonder if it is part of the great evocation of the drinking bowl's artwork. As we have noted, it may also portend the self-sacrifice of Pallas and Camilla, who die as virtual protomartyrs for Italy. In any case, it offers an *exemplum* for Aeneas and Ascanius as Roman progenitors. In the gender change from the daughters to the youths, youths who remain *Coronae*—a significant shift that has apparently bothered readers of the poem since medieval scribes tried to turn *Coronas* into *Coronos*—we see something of the symbolism of Caeneus/Caenis, that woman who became a man while retaining feminine characteristics. Virgil's Camilla likely lurks behind all of this gender shifting.

But after the digression on the drinking bowl—a brief expansion that, in Hopkinson's memorable phrase, fills in the "interstices" of Virgil—Ovid resumes a narrative that follows Virgil's account more or less closely (however briefly). It is only when we arrive in Sicily that the story changes more dramatically. At this point, we would expect to hear of Achaemenides and the death of Anchises. Instead, we get a lengthy set of stories loosely connected to the horror occasioned by Scylla and Charybdis.

The stories are twofold: Scylla was once a maiden who was pursued by many; she ended up hearing from Galatea about *her* problem with Polyphemus. Scylla is now pursued by Glaucus; as the book ends, we know that trouble looms on the horizon, since the rejected Glaucus intends to approach the sorceress Circe for help. In the end, as Ovid will soon make clear, *Circe* loves Glaucus, and so rather than helping Glaucus woo Scylla, she will be responsible for turning Scylla into a loathsome monster.

This entire digression is essentially a reminiscence of the *Odyssey*, inserted, appropriately enough, into a retelling of Virgil's Odyssean *Aeneid*, so that it becomes an *Odyssey* within an *Odyssey*. In it there is nothing of Odysseus *per se*; we do not hear of him after his victory in the contest for Achilles' arms. It is not a retelling of Homer's *Odyssey*, but rather an extended recollection of some of the *amatory* themes of that poem, in which the amatory themes become the centerpiece of the epic (an amatory reading of Homer, in which Ovid shows that he considers the *Odyssey* to be a fundamentally amatory epic). This is, after all, how Virgil read the *Iliad*, when he declared that Erato would be his patroness in the second *Aeneid*, and when he highlighted that the amatory theme was central to his *Iliad*. For Ovid, the poet of amours, the application to the *Odyssey* was irresistible; Virgil himself had done the same thing in making the Dido and Aeneas episode so central to his version of the *Odyssey*. So Ovid's long digressions on Scylla-Galatea-Polyphemus-Glaucus-Circe is not so much a response to Virgil's Aeneas and Dido, but to the desire to make the *Odyssey* a clearly amatory epic, one where love is the governing principle.

Odysseus rejected Calypso, and he rejected Circe. He defeated the Cyclops Polyphemus, outwitting him in a supreme display of his versatile arts. In *Metamorphoses* 13, the rejections come from Galatea and Scylla; they respectively turn down the amorous advances of Polyphemus and Glaucus. Both are monstrous suitors, despite the obvious fact that the marine god Glaucus is more appealing than the Cyclops. Galatea is in love with another, Acis; Scylla, for her part, seems intent on rejecting *all* suitors. There is no hint that she would succumb to anyone. Glaucus will soon enough reject Circe (in imitation of Odysseus).

Scylla rejects all suitors, and Galatea tells her a story about Polyphemus' pursuit of her, and her own rejection of a monster. Galatea's story is a cautionary tale, and in this it mirrors Venus' story to Adonis about not pursuing lions: that sequence ended in the death of Adonis, just as Galatea's story ends in Acis' death (though he finds redemption as a river god, not a flower).

Essentially, Ovid is providing an *Odyssean* counterpart to his *Iliadic* lore: the Venus-Adonis sequence contained the cautionary story of Atalanta, which recalled the very center of the *Metamorphoses* and its story of Meleager and Atalanta.[65] That, in turn, recalled the cautionary story told by Phoenix to Achilles in the great embassy of *Iliad* 9. Since the *Iliad* is greater than the *Odyssey* (at least in the apparent estimation of Virgil and Ovid), the cautionary story about Meleager appears at the very midpoint of the epic, and then, at the close of the epic's second third, we get the "conclusion" of the Meleager-Atalanta sequence, in Venus' cautionary tale to Adonis. The lesson to Meleager, as we have already discussed, was related to Virgil's Turnus and his fatal infatuation with Camilla. The point was *not* to give in to love. Similarly, the point of the Atalanta and Hippomenes story that Venus used as a cautionary tale to her lover Adonis was that Atalanta was better off not married, and that Hippomenes' lust for Atalanta led to his undoing.

In the *Iliadic* tales of caution, then, the point is that passion is bad; erotic love, not to mention what we moderns might call infatuation or lust, leads to doom. That was how Jupiter ensured the destruction of Turnus' best hopes for winning the war in Italy; Ovid's Meleager was similarly destroyed in *Metamorphoses* 8 because of his infatuation with the Camilla-like Atalanta, who was herself destroyed in *Metamorphoses* 10 very much in the manner of Virgil's Camilla—distracted by gold.

In the *Odyssean* tales of caution, the point is to surrender to love. The "first" Scylla, the daughter of Minos, loved only one, and she loved him irrationally—Scylla of Nisus loved Minos so much that she was willing to sacrifice her own father to have her lover. This is the sort of erotic irrationality that Ovid discusses in the stories of Meleager and Atalanta; no wonder that Scylla's story appears at the head of the same book that contains the key story of the Calydonian boar hunt and Meleager's lust for a huntress. The "second" Scylla is unlike the first in that she will have no suitor; many pursue her, but she rejects them all. She is not a Diana-like huntress; she is not a new Camilla-like figure or forest denizen. Instead—as appropriate for Ovid's *Odyssey*—she is a marine creature, a dweller of the watery haunts near the shore—since she is not, after all, a marine goddess, and so she cannot venture too far out into the deep in the manner of Galatea (and, for that matter, her suitor Glaucus).

Scylla will have no one. Galatea provides an unintentionally cautionary response. She notes that not everyone is fortunate in having suitors that are easily repelled; she had to face the horror of being pursued by the monstrous Cyclops Polyphemus, whose amorous advances led directly to the death of her beloved Acis. Galatea did not intend her speech as a warning against any particular course of action; for if so, what then would be Galatea's point? Should she have given in to Polyphemus? No, but her tale remains a warning to those who might grow too smug or complacent; one never knows what sort of suitor might emerge. The answer, quickly enough, is Glaucus. Glaucus is a problematic figure; we might understand why Scylla does not want this merman, but she is attracted to the water, and here a very god of the sea, the obvious recipient of significant divine favor, has pursued her. She rejects him, ultimately to her doom. He is no monstrous Polyphemus, and unlike Galatea, Scylla has no Acis who might be holding her back from yielding to the half-man, half-fish.

This is, after all, the amatory point of Homer's *Odyssey*, which is about the dangers of rejection of love (Calypso, Circe), and the ultimate reward of fidelity (Penelope). Significantly, Acis—the victim of the Cyclops' savagery—is rewarded by Galatea—who is rather like Circe, though benevolent in every way—Acis receives transformation into a god, an extraordinary boon of the sort we usually associate with Jupiter and Hercules.

And there is more to Ovid's complex game. Glaucus has been purged of his mortality, he is, rather like Acis, a new god. Acis went through a quick transformation: he was painfully massacred by a boulder, and a goddess at once turned him into a river god. There is no question of how Acis was changed; he was altered at once by divine machinery. How different is the case of Glaucus, who was changed after he plucked blades of grass—exactly like Aeneas with the Golden Bough, and in reminiscence, too, of Persephone with her pomegranate seeds in the underworld. He is purged of his mortality in a process of cleansing of his *nefas*, which can be nothing other than his mortal nature. Where else is one's humanity called an unspeakable thing, a veritable crime? For the Orphics, that is exactly what the mortal shell ultimately might well be termed. Ovid's story of Glaucus is a resurgence of Orphic doctrine.

But Glaucus does not go into the ethereal fire; instead, he becomes a very traditional sort of sea god, and one with an impeccably old mythological pedigree in previous sources. It seems likely that Ovid invented the story of the transformation, though of course we cannot be sure in the absence of evidence to the contrary, and the appeal from silence must always be treated with suspicion. What we can state with assurance is that in Ovid's conception, the Orphic process of rebirth has been presented as resulting in not a reborn soul *per se*, but a very traditional sort of god. The Orphics would not countenance the idea that their process of renewal through purgatory and rebirth would result in a mythological marine god. The idea would be abhorrent to them. But this is, after all, Ovid's *Odyssey, the epic of falsehood*. Odysseus the liar has been replaced by the false story of Glaucus' transformation: it could never have happened, and so it did not, except in the lies of Ovid's verse. Orphism is still a lie; there is no rebirth and renewal according to the manner of the songs of Orpheus—and the key to understanding the lie is appreciating the impossible result of the renewal in the case of Glaucus, fisherman to sea god—a transformation that would be unthinkable to any devotee of Orphic philosophy. And we should note that in Virgil (*A*. 6.36), Glaucus is the father of *Deiphobe*, the Cumaean Sibyl, thus further cementing his connection to the milieu of Virgil's underworld.

The lie about Glaucus' purgation allows Ovid's *Odyssey*, with its cautionary story of Scylla and Glaucus, to have the same sort of Orphic conclusion that the cautionary story of Atalanta and Hippomenes had; the tale of Venus to Adonis in *Metamorphoses* 10, after all, was followed immediately by the death of Orpheus as Ovid began the last third of his epic. As we have seen, in both the aftermath of the second third of the epic and here, Orphism has been dismissed as impossible—though Ovid has much more to say on the whole matter, as he responds to the great highpoint of the center of Virgil's *Aeneid* and its concerns with the ultimate fate of the soul.

The point of Ovid's *Odyssey*, then, is how to pursue the right love, the proper love—and that makes a wonderful counterpoint to Virgil's Aeneas and Dido. In this sense, Myers' thesis may well be right that the extended sequence on love is a response to Virgil's great consideration of the same theme; certainly the point in *Aeneid* 4 is that Aeneas must pursue his true love, a woman he has not yet met—in marked contrast to the situation his epic predecessor Odysseus faces. Indeed, the death of Creusa makes it quite impossible, in an important sense, for Aeneas to be able to be a true Odysseus. The true Odysseus must have a wife for whom he longs, a wife to whom he intends to return. Without one, Aeneas is chasing after heroic shadows. In a nice touch, Aeneas can of course have no part in any of the digressions Ovid is now immersed in—an Ovidian response to how Aeneas is absent from significant portions of Virgil's epic.

For now, then, as Book 13 closes, Ovid provides a terrifying image: the sorceress Circe. She was a key figure in Homer's *Odyssey*, of course, and as Ovid's *Odyssey* straddles books, buried within his *Aeneid*, she will now take center stage. She appears at the beginning of Virgil's *Iliad*, at the opening of *Aeneid* 7, as Aeneas just passes by her haunts and escapes her spell. But her place in the *Aeneid* is much more significant than as just a geographical marker for those checking the mythological details along the route of a famous sea voyage. She is, in fact, the figure who looms over the transition of Virgil's epic from an *Odyssey* to an *Iliad*, and the figure who looms over Ovid's transition, across book lines, from what is unmistakably an *Odyssey*, devoid of any Trojan presence, back into an *Aeneid*—albeit an *Aeneid* that will still have to cover some Odyssean ground, though quite briefly indeed. With Glaucus, the marine god who acquired immortality but not much good sense, we shall now travel to the lair of Circe, who, like Diana, is a mistress of animals. We shall catch a glimpse of what Aeneas was spared, as we learn more about the power of transformation, and as Ovid reflects on why Circe is the goddess who must open a book about the birth of Rome, just as Circe presides over the book in which Virgil unfolds the coming of the Trojans to the promised land of Italy. With Ovid, we shall see how a witch could be a symbol of the lupine nourishment of a nascent Rome.

Notes

1. Philip Hardie is preparing a commentary on Books 13-15 for the Fondazione Lorenzo Valla series. Cambridge University Press has also begun a series of *Metamorphoses* commentaries; the first volume to appear was Neil Hopkinson's 2000 edition of Book 13, which is at present the finest available overall guide, with interests both philological and literary. There is a still useful 1899 London commentary by Simmons on Books 13-14. Note also Stitz, M., *Ovids und Vergils Aeneis: Interpretationen Met. 13, 623-14, 608*, Freiburg, 1962, and Lamacchia, R., "Ovidio interprete di Virgilio," in *Maia* 12 (1960), pp. 310-330.

2. Throughout this book, I refer to the Ovidian hero *Ulixes* as Odysseus, not Ulysses (let alone Ulixes) for the sake of convenience in frequent cross-referencing between Greek and Latin sources. I do not apologize for using Ajax instead of Aias.

3. Ajax had stood against the entire Trojan army at one point in the attempted firing of the fleet, and eventually had to give way at the cost of one ship. Odysseus, for his part, was not involved because he had been wounded; the whole episode is an obvious arrow for Ajax's quiver.

4. See further my 2005 *Maia* article, "Trickery and Deceit in *Aeneid* XI," and the relevant commentary in *Madness Unchained* and my *Aeneid XI*.

5. And she is *inimica*, personally hateful, to Aeneas (*A.* 6.472).

6. A famous slander against Odysseus: his mother Anticleia had a sexual relationship with Sisyphus before she married Laertes.

7. Odysseus contrived the death of Palamedes later in vengeance for the unmasking of his feigned madness.

8. Lemnos was a fitting drop-off point for Philoctetes given that the island was the early home of Hephaestus, himself something of an exile from the Olympians because of his physical defects.

9. *Iliad* 8.80-98, where see Kirk.

10. See further especially Hopkinson ad loc.

11. The episode is at Homer, *Iliad* 11.411-488.

12. *Iliad* 14.409-432.

13. *Iliad* 7.66-310.

14. See Hopkinson ad loc. for the parallel passages.

15. And, too, Ovid may be manipulating these Virgilian issues in his lengthy account of the debate for Achilles' arms—the *Aeneid* is about the Odyssean man struggling to become the Achillean, though he is not aware of the transformation.

16. *Aeneid* 11.438-440, where the crucial verb *praestare* either means to pretend or to excel.

17. Hence the point of the closing remarks of Ajax about tossing forth the *arma viri fortis* among the enemy; in the end, in Virgil's conception it will be Turnus who in some sense wins the arms, not Odysseus.

18. The Trojans have a *curia* because one day Troy will be a point of origin for the future Rome; further, Antenor is presented as a reasonable Trojan because he will one day enjoy a successful settlement in Italy.

19. The needlessly controversial line 13.230 says that Agamemnon called the Greeks back, not Odysseus; Odysseus was then responsible for the morale-boosting

speeches. Hopkinson well points out that Odysseus is responding to the presence of Agamemnon in the audience, and is being deliberately deferential to the leader of the expedition; further, Ovid's narrative overall makes clear that it was Odysseus (at least in his own mind) who was the responsible party for the quelling of the army's desire to return home without having conquered Troy.

20. *Iliad* 5.671-676.

21. *Aeneid* 10.469-472.

22. As the commentators note, the point here may be the rather obscure tradition that Ajax was invulnerable, either to everyone save himself, or on every part of his body save his side. Of course Odysseus would then be alluding to a story that makes Ajax very much like Achilles.

23. *Iliad* 7.162-168.

24. See Hill ad 13.279, and Hopkinson, for further points of difference from Homer.

25. If the later prose epitome can be believed.

26. Odysseus' point is that he did not want to leave his wife, though he makes Penelope the active force in the detention (13.301 *me pia detinuit coniunx, pia mater Achillem*); the repeated emphasis on *pietas* is also striking in light of how Odysseus had talked about his violation of *pietas* in persuading Agamemnon to forget he was a parent to Iphigenia.

27. See further my notes ad loc.; I have argued there and in *Madness Unchained* that Turnus does indeed perform a solemn *devotio* as a prototype of a Republican hero.

28. In contrast to the Minerva of the *Aeneid*, who—while depicted in her traditional function in the first half of the poem, where the fall of Troy is the centerpiece of Book 2, appears quite differently in the penultimate book of the epic, where she is invoked by the women of Latium and, in effect, sends Camilla to help them—a mirror image of the goddess in terms of martial deeds, though not domestic. The part Minerva plays in the second half of the epic is subtle, but it is signaled from the start by her presence in the Camilla pendant to *Aeneid* 7, where first we learn of how the Volscian shunned the works of the loom and preferred battle—one half of Minerva, we might say, not the whole goddess.

29. For the sources (Euphorian, etc.), as well as the relevant botany, see Hopkinson ad loc.

30. Pseudo-Apollodorus 1.9.17 is a convenient summary.

31. Note Ovid's *Heroides* 6, Hysipyle to Jason.

32. Lines 13.404-407 are usually omitted as the marginal notations of a scribe that were eventually incorporated into the text.

33. *Aeneid* 12.937.

34. Hopkinson notes the parallel between Amata's words to the dead Polyxena— 13.523 *funeribus dotabere, regia virgo*—and Juno's words about Lavinia—*Aeneid* 7.318 *sanguine Troiano et Rutulo dotabere, virgo*, further cementing the connection between the two heroic war prizes.

35. *Iliad* 18.318-322.

36. Euripides knows about the metamorphosis (*Hecuba* 1260-1274).

37. Book 2 of Quintus Smyrnaeus' *Posthomerica* is concerned with Memnon.

38. Again, the Latin for "bird" is feminine; there is no reason to read much into the gender of these avian creatures.

39. Ovid's language (note 13.619 *parentali . . . voce*) evokes the February rites of the Parentalia, for which see *Fasti* 2.533-568. The text of 13.619 is vexed; some manuscripts read *more* for *voce*, and still others *morte*; Heinsius conjectured *Marte* (!), and Slater *caede* (on the strength of *Amores* 1.13.3-4).

40. On *Aeneid* 3 see Horsfall, and Williams' Oxford edition.

41. Significantly, Anchises mentions the Cretan origins of the Magna Mater, thus forming a contrast between the Delian haunts of the divine twins who hold such prominence for the Augustan regime, and Cybele, the prototypical Trojan-related deity, a more problematic figure for Rome.

42. Hopkinson's introduction, pp. 29 ff., offers a convenient summary of the evidence.

43. See further Hopkinson, and Papathomopoulos on the Antoninus Liberalis passage; another problem is that the attribution of the story to Nicander and Corinna may be interpolated. Hopkinson agrees that the attributions are "probably correct," but the whole matter only increases the uncertainty about interpretation.

44. Anderson, and Tarrant, print the feminine; Hopkinson prefers the masculine.

45. See further Hopkinson, *op. cit.*, p. 33.

46. The story is vaguely reminiscent of the tale told at the end of the Pseudo-Virgilian *Aetna* about the rescue of parents from fire by pious children; the author of that poem may have had Ovid in mind.

47. For good commentary see Schilling ad loc.

48. Cf. Hyginus, *De Astronomia* 2.34.2; Horace knows this version (c. 3.4.71 ff., where see Nisbet and Rudd).

49. There may be a parallel between the self-sacrifice of the daughters of Orion and the wicked actions of the Danaids, whose murder of their husband decorates Pallas' fateful sword-belt in *Aeneid* 10, thereby contrasting the action of "good" women and "bad."

50. The *Metamorphoses* narrative does not make clear whether or not Orion is already dead.

51. Antoninus Liberalis 4, the only other extant version.

52. Antoninus Liberalis 14, again, the only other account we have.

53. And note 13.930 *falciferae . . . manus*, of the sickle-bearing hands that do not touch Glaucus' meadow.

54. At *Ars Amatoria* 1.331-332 and *Fasti* 4.500 he considers them as one.

55. Fr. 262 Merkelbach-West.

56. Hopkinson has a convenient summary of the antecedent lore (*op. cit.*, pp. 35 ff.). Besides the famous story in *Odyssey* 9 of Polyphemus and his blinding, there are the two Theocritean idylls (6 and 11), the former depicting Galatea in pursuit of the Cyclops, the latter a song of Polyphemus to his would-be love. The Sicilian poet Philoxenus composed a lost lyric poem about the love c. 400 B.C. Virgil's *Eclogues*, in imitation of Theocritus, also deal with the lore. Note also the helpful material in Glenn, J., "Virgil's Polyphemus," in *Greece & Rome* 19 (1972), pp. 47-59.

57. Myers, *Ovid's Cosmos*, pp. 101 ff.

58. Lully composed a *pastorale-héroïque* on the love of Acis and Galatea; Handel also set the same story to music.

59. Note Griffin, A. H. F., "Unrequited Love: Polyphemus and Galatea in Ovid's *Metamorphoses*," in *Greece & Rome* 30 (1983), pp. 190-197, and Farrell, Joseph, "Dialogue of Genres in Ovid's 'Lovesong of Polyphemus' (*Metamorphoses* 13.719-897," in *The American Journal of Philology* 113 (1992), pp. 235-268.

60. In this section of the *Metamorphoses* there may also be a deliberate echoing of Virgil's *Eclogues* and his *Georgics*; the nymph assembly has much in common with the gathering to hear the stories of Cyrene in *Georgics* 4.

61. And note the name similarity between *Acis* and *Adonis*.

62. Note Hyginus, *Fabulae* 199, clearly based on Ovid.

63. I remain unconvinced of efforts to downplay the clear twofold division of the *Aeneid*; despite other valid arrangements of the books, the main division for Virgil is between Books 1-6 on the one hand and 7-12 on the other.

64. Note Galinsky, G. K., "L'*Eneide* di Ovidio (*Met.* XIII 623-XIV 608): ed il carattere delle *Metamorfosi*," in *Maia* 28 (1976), pp. 3-18, and Ellsworth, J.D., "Ovid's *Aeneid* Reconsidered (*Met.* 13.623-14.608)," in *Vergilius* 32 (1986), pp. 27-32.

65. The story is formally an explanation for why lions are hateful to Venus, though the larger point is why Venus has urged Adonis not to hunt after large game.

Chapter XIV

And Now Etna . . .

Book 14 of Ovid's epic is a direct continuation of its predecessor.[1] The marine god Glaucus has decided to approach the witch Circe about successfully wooing Scylla, who has rejected him along with all other suitors.

The book opens with an elaborate geographical description of how Glaucus made the journey from Sicily to Italy, from the land of Mount Etna (i.e., the gigantomachy) to the "promised land" of the western coast of central Italy and Latium, the dwelling of the sorceress Circe. Neither Ovid nor Virgil was responsible for locating Circe in this western locale; the tradition was old and well established.[2] In some sense, the journey of Glaucus represents the history of the world from the coming of the Olympian order to the founding of Rome (the city that symbolizes the same sort of governing principle embodied in Jupiter's accession).

In Virgil, the second half of the *Aeneid*, the *maius opus*, commences with the death of Aeneas' nurse Caieta.[3] After her burial at the site that bears her name as a lasting memorial, the Trojans just skirt the shores of Circe's island of Aeaea, and they make a safe nocturnal transit past the dangerous coast only because of Neptune's aid (*A.* 7.10-24).

Circe presides in some sense over the second half of the *Aeneid*; she is the figure at the beginning of the Iliadic *Aeneid*. She is a goddess of transformations, and so on one level she is a fitting patroness for the change from a Virgilian *Odyssey* to a Virgilian *Iliad*. Elsewhere, I have raised the speculation that her appearance at the beginning of *Aeneid* 7, linked with Camilla's at the end of the same book, offers a deliberate connection between the goddess who can transform men into wolves (*A.* 7.18 *saevire ac formae magnorum ululare leporum*) and the Volscian warrior who may well be lycanthropic.[4]

In Virgil, Circe marks the transition from *Odyssey* to *Iliad*; she represents the point where Aeneas would ideally make the transition from being a new Odysseus to becoming a new Achilles. As we have seen, there are serious problems with equating Aeneas with either Homeric hero, especially after the Sibyl's announcement in the underworld that a new Achilles would be born in Italy—an admittedly ambiguous prophecy that looks forward both to the new Achilles of Turnus and the end of the poem, where Aeneas will be rendered the mad Achilles of the moment of Hector's death—unredeemed and heroically incomplete, if

399

you will, in light of the end of Homer's *Iliad* with its reconciliation of the hero's wrath.

Ovid's Circe appears at the book transition from the first part of Ovid's *Aeneid* to the second part, in direct imitation of Virgil's use of Circe as the marker of the transition from the first to the second half of his epic. The difference, of course, is that for Virgil the Odyssean material is already finished by the time Circe appears (she bids farewell to it), while in Ovid we are not entirely finished with the account of Aeneas' Odyssean journey to Italy.[5]

The fact that Virgil has Circe preside over the beginning of his epic's second half, as a transitional figure as he proceeds to his *maius opus*, must have appealed deeply to Ovid, since Circe is, before all else, a goddess of metamorphoses. There are many transformations in the second half of the *Aeneid*, among them the shifting alignments of Virgil's heroes with their Homeric antecedents.

Ovid's Circe is also another Medea, though those who approached the Colchian witch sought new life, not help in love (that was her private concern with Jason). Glaucus wants amatory assistance, and it is not entirely clear why Circe would be a suitable place for him to go. He claims that he understands the power of magic herbs because of his own experience of them (14.14-15), though of course he had no reason to think that those herbs were Circe's doing. Recourse to magic was a common ploy for hapless lovers in erotic elegy, though Ovid had already noted that if herbs could help in matters of the heart, then Circe would have won Odysseus.[6] Dido, of course, famously resorted to magic in her madness over Aeneas; part of Ovid's point here is that if Glaucus knew his literature, he would understand that spells do not work in erotic pursuits.

Circe is amenable to helping Glaucus, though not in the way the sea god intends (14.25). At *Circe*, Ovid begins—the same strong beginning that Virgil uses three times to describe Dido, *at regina*, at the openings of each of the sections of the Carthaginian queen's three-act tragedy. Circe, Ovid says, is prone to the flames of love, either because of her natural disposition, or (the weighted alternative) because Venus made her so, angry at how often Circe's solar father reported *les affairs d'amour*. Virgil put Circe at the beginning of *Aeneid* 7 because of the erotic theme of his *Iliad*; in the *Odyssey*, she represented exactly the sort of lustful temptation that Odysseus is supposed to avoid in his quest for reunion with his beloved wife.

Ovid presents Venus, the mother of Aeneas, as angry and vengeful in the matter of Circe's father's activities. In the *Aeneid*, we associate Juno with angry vengeance; here, Ovid reverses the Virgilian goddesses and makes Venus the immortal with a grudge—and a grudge that returns us, however briefly, to the world of the early *Metamorphoses*, with its repeated emphasis on divine peccadilloes.[7] Circe is a victim of Venus; she wastes no time in telling Glaucus that he should have been the one to be pursued, and she makes a coy promise:

. . . si spem dederis, mihi crede, rogaberis ultro. (14.31)

. . . If you give hope, believe me, you will be sought spontaneously.

If Glaucus were to be sought spontaneously, then there should be no need for a protasis to establish a condition for the seeking; Circe has already sought Glaucus spontaneously, and so there is no need for the conditional sentence. Circe is being flirtatious, and looking for some confirmation from the god that he will yield to her advances.

Circe asks that Glaucus "avenge" both Scylla and herself.[8] Glaucus refuses, and, in striking contrast to Polyphemus with Galatea, and Glaucus himself with Scylla, Circe does not try to persuade him. She makes no attempt to change his mind, no blandishing words of appeal. She might as well now be Virgil's Juno with Allecto; she is intent on destruction. She begins to mix her herbs and chant her spells; Hecate is involved (14.44), a nod to the tradition that Scylla was her daughter. Circe dons a blue-green cloak because of the association of Glaucus, and Scylla for that matter, with the sea. She proceeds on her way to Rhegium, opposite the coast of Zancle (46 ff.). She skims over the surface of the water in exactly the same manner as Ovid described the swift running of Atalanta and Hippomenes, a passage that was inspired by Virgil's similar description of Camilla's swiftness from the end of *Aeneid* 7. The description is characteristic of divinity,[9] but Camilla, Atalanta, and Hippomenes are not divine; Ovid's point is to remind us of Virgil's Circe and her connection with Camilla in the frame of *Aeneid* 7.

Scylla takes her rest in a lovely pool at the very hottest part of the day, the noon hour that marks the zenith of the sun's power—and also of Circe's power, given her descent from the Titan. Circe arrives at the waters of the pool before Scylla, and poisons them with both her potions and her spells, which she chants twenty-seven times (14.58 *ter noviens*) in magic ritual. There is something here of the curse that Hermaphroditus, the son of Venus and Mercury, invoked over the waters of the pool where he was assaulted by Salmacis; Circe gives the waters the same sort of power as the grass Glaucus had found in another *locus amoenus*, though these waters cause transformation into something terribly monstrous.

Scylla arrives at the pool; the transformation happens with breathtaking speed. She submerges herself up to the waist in the water, and soon sees that her lower body has been changed into a mass of barking dogs (14.59 ff.). This is a reversal of Salmacis' situation, in that Scylla had rejected all male advances, while Salmacis had been the exact opposite of the Diana-like nymph she was supposed to be; Salmacis was lustful in the case of Hermaphroditus, while Scylla was positively virginal in her shunning of all suitors. In some sources, Scylla was noted as a symbol of excessively libidinous behavior;[10] her transformation here can be seen as a punishment for her previous lifestyle. What is interesting in this is that Ovid had raised the possibility that Venus had, in effect, punished Circe for the sun's tattletale behavior; here, through Circe's magic arts, Scylla is punished and transformed into a symbol of lust, even if her present condition does not allow her to make any amorous advances (unlike Circe). No one will try to woo Scylla now, and Scylla herself can woo no one. Again, the lesson of the *Odyssey* is to choose the correct passion, the right love at the right time.

Scylla has a maw that is like Cerberus' (14.65 *Cerbereos rictus*); she is some underworld horror now, though perhaps not as fearsome as Homer's monster with six mouths, where each gaping maw has three rows of teeth.[11] If Circe thought that by this transformation she would win Glaucus, she was quite wrong; the sea god flees her and weeps at the sight of his beloved Scylla—he will have nothing to do with her either now. Scylla, for her part, first attacks Odysseus' companions; she would have attacked the Trojans, too, Ovid says, had she not been transformed into a rock, albeit a rock that sailors still fear (72-74). This is the first mention in extant literature of such a transformation, with no explanation given for how or why it happened. It may just reflect an appropriate end for a girl who had hardened her heart to all suitors. Galatea had rejected Polyphemus, but she accepted Acis; Scylla had preferred no one, and now she is a rock that is still full of danger for those would sail too close to its hidden perils.

In Virgil, Helenus warned the Trojans about the dangers from Scylla and Charybdis.[12] Helenus reports that on the Italian side of the Straits of Messina, Scylla lurks in a cave's hidden recesses, with a girl's face and lovely upper body, but the lower body of a sea monster, with the tails of dolphins and wolves decorating her stomach. Aeneas is instructed to avoid both Scylla's monstrous form and the whirlpool that is Charybdis, and indeed both dangers are successfully evaded, though there is no hint in Virgil's account that Scylla is now some rock—quite the opposite. At *Aeneid* 1.200-201, there is a reference to how the Trojans approached the "deeply sounding crags" (*penitusque sonantis / scopulos*) of Scylla, where the crags are probably meant to resound with the baying hounds of Scylla.[13]

Leaving aside questions of the unfinished state of the *Aeneid* and its lack of the poet's *ultima manus*, we can offer some salient observations.[14] Virgil makes a distinction between the dangers of Scylla and Charybdis, which Helenus warns about, and the Sirens and Circe, who are not part of any prophetic admonition, but who are, nonetheless, successfully evaded. Neptune seems to be the one responsible for both evasions: Virgil is explicit at *Aeneid* 7.23 that Neptune enabled the Trojan fleet to make it past Circe rapidly enough to avoid peril, while at the end of *Aeneid* 5, Neptune seems to be in control of the ships as they make it past the noisy rocks where the Sirens dwell.[15] Helenus, we should note, need not be aware of any petrifaction of Scylla at the time when he offered advice to Aeneas; the transformation may not yet have occurred.

Ovid could not be briefer in his description of subsequent events from the *Aeneid*. The Trojans are forced to make a sojourn in Carthage; we are barely aware there is a storm (14.77 *Libycas vento referuntur ad oras*). Dido falls in love with Aeneas almost as quickly as she commits suicide. Aeneas and his men travel to Sicily, where King Acestes receives them and honors are paid at the grave of Anchises (whose death had not previously been mentioned). Some have seen a tone in these quickly moving lines of hostility to Aeneas and favor for Dido, as if the whole affair of *Aeneid* 4 is presented here only from Dido's side, and with anger against Aeneas (cf. Ovid's own *Heroides* 7, Dido to Aeneas). But there is nothing in this exceedingly short section that causes any more or less sympathy for Dido than what is found in abundance in Virgil; Ovid is hurrying on now, aware that he must touch on every major event from the journey of the Trojans to Italy, but without having any reason to linger too long on what Virgil had already covered to Ovid's satisfaction. Aeneas departs Sicily in the ships that Junonian Iris almost burned (85); the Sirens are mentioned, and, significantly, the loss of Palinurus (87-88).

Palinurus is thrown overboard in Virgil by Sleep; later Aeneas learns that the helmsman successfully made it to the shores of Italy, only to be murdered by hostile natives. We have seen how Ovid was deeply influenced by the Palinurus story, and the fact that Palinurus makes an appearance even in such a brief compass as this present passage is testament to Ovid's appreciation for the Virgilian story. In Virgil the Sirens are passed *after* Palinurus is lost; he is, however, easily enough interpreted as a sacrifice to their rocky crags. Ovid seems to have understood this interpretation, since for him Palinurus' loss comes right after the Sirens' haunt is passed; he is an offering to appease them.

For a few lines, then, Ovid almost exactly follows Virgil; he then inserts a strange little interlude: the Trojans coast along by the barren hill of Pithecusae (14.89 ff.). Here, Ovid says, Jupiter—the "father of the gods" (91 *deum genitor*) sent the Cercopians, transforming them into monkeys. Jupiter was angry over their deceitful ways:

... fraudem et periuria quondam
Cercopum exosus gentisque admissa dolosae (14.91-92)

  ... once upon a time thoroughly hateful of the fraud and
  crimes of the treacherous race of the Cercopians

Pliny the Elder dismissed the etymology of the name "Pithecusae" from a "multitude of monkeys," though clearly the animal metamorphosis was more appealing to Ovid.[16] The story is obscure; Ovid is the earliest surviving attestation. The Cercopes were the subject of a comic poem credited to Homer; the simian transformation was meant to make the Cercopes objects of mockery (both Greeks and Romans seem to have found monkeys and apes especially funny).[17] All the liars and cheats can do now is make raucous shrieks and noises that do not deceive, but rather elicit mockery.

This is the farewell, in a sense, to the falsehood theme; the liars have been duly punished. While the Odyssean part of the *Aeneid* is not yet over, it is rapidly drawing to a close; in the fate of the Cercopes we cannot help but think of the deceptive Odysseus from the contest with Ajax, and also, perhaps, the image of Aeneas as a deceiver (at least if we can accept Dido's judgment). For Ovid, the end of the *Odyssey* represents the end of falsehood. The *Odyssey* is a poem about knowledge regarding the right time for love and the right object for one's love; there may well be a hint in Homer's vision that the deceitful are the best suited for this sort of correct approach to matters of the heart.

The monkeys, further, remind us of Circe and animal transformations lurking just off the Italian coast.

Ovid lingers over the Sirens—the Trojans pass Parthenope (14.101-102), which was said to have been named after one of the Sirens whose body was washed up on its shores. The mention of the Siren is deliberate; after Parthenope, Ovid's Trojans pass the site of the *tumulus* of Misenus. Misenus was the Trojan trumpeter who was foolish enough to try to engage in a music competition with Triton.[18] Misenus is a doublet of Palinurus in Virgil; as Palinurus presages the death of Pallas, so Misenus—whose death is mentioned near the beginning of Aeneas' underworld book—presages the loss of Marcellus that occurs at its end. Aeneas cannot travel to the underworld until he finds and buries a lost companion; he—and the audience—might well imagine that *Palinurus* is the unburied friend, when, fortunately, Aeneas and Achates stumble upon Misenus' body.[19]

It would seem that in Ovid's conception, Misenus is already dead. Strabo knows a version in which Misenus is a companion of Odysseus.[20] The Latin is ambiguous; 14.102-103 *laeva de parte canori / Aeolidae tumulum* could just as well look forward to the trumpeter's burial spot, and it is likely that Ovid's language offers a learned nod to the alternate views that Misenus is either one of Odysseus' men or one of Aeneas'.

Aeneas finally arrives at Cumae and meets the Sibyl.[21] The Sibyl praises Aeneas' *pietas* (14.109) and other fine qualities; she announces that he will, indeed, receive his desired transit to the underworld. Ovid is moving quickly here, and his Sibyl is decidedly "nicer" than Virgil's—though still raving (107 *furibunda*). Interestingly, the Sibyl announces that Aeneas will see the *simulacrum* of his father: 112 *simulacraque cara parentis*. The word is a virtual technical term for Epicurean philosophy to describe the image that emanates from something; Virgil does not use it to describe the shade of Anchises in the underworld.[22] Here, Ovid puts a definite Lucretian stamp on the underworld; I have argued elsewhere that Virgil's underworld offers a Lucretian conclusion—in Virgil's conception, the riddle of the Gates of Sleep is solved by understanding that both the traditional Homeric and the more novel Orphic. Pythagorean, Neoplatonic conceptions of rebirth and regeneration are all false in light of Lucretius. Here, Ovid offers a clue that he is moving in the same direction as his poetic predecessor, towards a Lucretian vision of the afterlife.

At this point, Ovid describes the famous Virgilian Golden Bough:

... dixit et auro

fulgentem ramum silva Iunonis Avernae
monstravit iussitque suo divellere trunco. (113-115)

> . . . *she spoke, and she showed him*
> *the shining branch in the forest of Avernal Juno,*
> *and she ordered him to rip it off from its trunk.*

Ovid's passage is a splendid reading of Virgil's original.[23]

In Virgil, the Sibyl announced that the Bough must be located and must be "plucked" (*carpe*), if the hero were meant to make a successful transit to the underworld. In the actual event, the Bough was located by the helpful aid of Venus' doves, and Aeneas did not "pluck" the Bough, but rather broke it off rather forcefully in his eagerness (*avidusque refringit*). The Bough hesitated (*cunctantem*), not because Aeneas was somehow not fated to travel to the infernal regions, but because he had not followed the Sibyl's instructions. In Ovid's version, the Sibyl tells Aeneas to tear the Bough away violently (*divellere* is a quite strong word); Aeneas obeys (14.116 *paruit*).[24] And, besides, there is no need for help from Venus in Ovid; the Sibyl shows Aeneas the necessary offering for Persephone.

The mention of the Bough, the gift for Persephone, and the Lucretian *simulacrum* of Anchises all prepare us for the eschatological movements of the dramatic end of Ovid's poem, which is fast approaching. Ovid's account of the Bough is an acknowledgment of the point of Virgil's narrative about Aeneas' actions in light of the Sibyl's commands.[25] Ovid's Aeneas is told to do exactly what he *did do* in Virgil, though in contravention of the Sibyl's command there. It is a marvelous example of Ovid's close reading of his source (since the Bough was most probably adapted by Ovid solely from the *Aeneid*).

Virgil's Sibyl told Aeneas that the descent to Avernus is easy; the return is hard.[26] In Virgil's narrative, Anchises sends Aeneas and the Sibyl to the upper world through the Ivory Gate of false dreams. There is brisk, indeed rapid narrative, and no mention of a difficult trip; there is also no precise localization of the Gates. Ovid's narrative is more faithful to *Aeneid* 6.125-129; Ovid's Aeneas has a more extensive return transit from the underworld than Virgil's. Aeneas and the Sibyl converse on the journey to the upper air; Aeneas is full of understandable thanks. Where is Venus in all of this? She was not involved in the finding of the Bough—Ovid's Sibyl did that. I suspect that some of this is an Ovidian acknowledgment that Venus is excluded, and significantly, from the final divine reconciliation in *Aeneid* 12. She has no place in that climactic revelation about Rome's future, and so Ovid omits mention of her in the key passage about the Bough.

Aeneas vows a temple to the Sibyl (14.128). As Austin notes ad *A.* 6.71, the famous Sybilline books were kept under the temple of Jupiter on the Capitoline; after that temple burned in 83 B.C., a new collection was created for the rebuilt temple. Augustus removed them and put them in his temple to *Apollo* on the

Palatine, which was dedicated in 28 B.C. In accord with this, we might note that Ovid's Sibyl denies that she is a goddess and tells Aeneas not to think a mortal head worthy of divine honor (130-131 *nec sacri turis honore / humanum dignare caput*). The Sibyl reveals that she could have had eternal life, had she lost her virginity to Apollo.

In wooing her, Apollo promised any gift she requested; the Sibyl admits she was foolish in asking that her years be equal to those of the particles of sand in a nearby pile. Apollo granted the boon, and offered eternal youth if she would yield to him; she refused and decided to remain a virgin, though now a terribly old and wretched creature, since she has the same problem Aurora's Tithonus endures: she cannot die anytime soon. The story may well be Ovid's own; it survives in no earlier source.

The commentators have noted the balance between Apollo's failed relationship with Daphne from Book 1, and this failed relationship with the Sibyl—the two would-be Apollonian unions have many parallels and many differences. While the balance is effective—both Daphne and the Sibyl present a permanent, lasting source of honorable association for Apollo with the laurel and his eventual custody of the Sibylline books—I would not push the connection too far. Thematically, the Sibyl is another example of a woman who fails to understand the right choices to make regarding *les affairs d'amour*. The Sibyl played something of a game with Apollo: why did she ask for any boon in the first place, if she intended to keep her virginity? She admits her foolishness in not asking for youth. Apollo noticed her omission, and offered youth in exchange for her yielding to his advances; her refusal, however honorable, led to her accursed thousand years of life. She is a parallel to Scylla in some sense—and here Ovid makes effective use of the similarity between the names *Sibylla* and *Scylla*. We are still, after all, in Ovid's *Odyssey*—and the Sibyl is the last example of a woman who did not know the timely and correct choices to make in love.

Aeneas and the Sibyl emerge from an evocation of Virgil's *Odyssey* to, we might expect, an *Iliad*, as the Trojans now come to the shores that, as Ovid notes, do not yet bear Aeneas' nurse's name (14.157). The poet now reveals a surprise. As the *nondum* at line 157 announces, Ovid is not ready to embark on a retelling of the Iliadic *Aeneid*. He had earlier interrupted his *Odyssey*-within-an-*Aeneid* to digress on themes of love, and now he shall balance that with a similar interruption, an interruption that keeps us firmly grounded in an Odyssean world. Two "living" monsters occasion these Odyssean digressions: Scylla and the Cyclops (the Sirens and Circe also make healthy appearances in the narrative of Ovid's *Odyssey*-within-an-*Aeneid*.

In Virgil, there was a progression from Caieta to Circe; in Ovid, we move from Circe to Caieta to Circe to Caieta—a neat chiastic balance. As Ovid's Trojans arrive at Caieta's shores, they meet "Neritean Macareus," a former comrade of Odysseus—a doublet of Virgil's Achaemenides. Virgil's Odyssean castaway was probably an invention of the poet; similarly, there is no previous trace of Macareus. "Achaemenides" and "Macareus" are opposites: the first name signifies grief or woe, the second, blessing. Virgil's Achaemenides is a doublet of Sinon, the lying Greek; in a sense Achaemenides "lies," since according to Homer (*Odyssey* 9.424 ff.), Odysseus made sure all his men escaped before he left Polyphemus' cave.[27] Macareus cannot believe that he has met Achaemenides after so long; the "new" Trojan proceeds to describe his adventures with the Cyclops (14.167 ff.).

We have met Achaemenides before, in Virgil; similarly, Scylla was mentioned by the Mantuan, though briefly. In both cases, Ovid uses Virgil as a point of departure for a new twist in his retelling of his two epic sources. We saw that in the first lengthy digression, on the loves of Scylla *et al.*, Ovid was balancing the message of the Meleager story on caution in passion with an Odyssean lesson about caution regarding when *not* to avoid erotic love. Circe was a key figure in that digressive narrative, and she was the linkage for Virgil between the Odyssean and Iliadic halves of his epic.

But after the digression, as we have noted, Ovid still had ground to cover in his *Odyssey*. And so now, just before he commences his *Iliad* in Italy, it is fitting that he should reintroduce Circe. He does this by retelling the Achaemenides story, though Macareus—like Achaemenides a castaway from Odysseus' Ithaca—is indeed the man of blessing. For he will symbolize the *Italian* future, not the Trojan past.[28]

Achaemenides' Ovidian story is longer than his account in Virgil, though of course he can now relate it in safety and security, not in terror of being imminently devoured. After his tale is finished, he invites Macareus to report what he as yet does not know: what happened to the Ithacans after they left the Cyclops' cave. He briefly details the misadventure with the winds of Aeolus (14.223-232) and the terrible encounter with the cannibalistic Laestrygonians (233-242). Macareus is now ready to embark on his (and Ovid's main point): Circe, whom he of course urges Aeneas to avoid at all costs (247).

Macareus follows Homer very exactly; in both accounts twenty-two men set out to reconnoiter Circe's haunts. The scene is quite reminiscent of Homer's (and Virgil's) description of the many animal forms in the witch's home; soon enough the Greek party meets the sorceress herself. The Nereids and nymphs who accompany Circe do not spin (14.264-265); this detail is a change from Homer and Virgil, who both mention Circe's weaving: Ovid's point is to recall *Camilla*, from the end of *Aeneid* 7, who is explicitly described as shunning the Minervan works of the loom (in contrast to Circe from the beginning of the book). Circe offers them a meal in accord with the usual dictates of hospitality; the Nereids and nymphs, of course, have been playing with organizing Circe's herbs and ingredients for her potions, and the food is poisoned. Soon enough, the transformation begins to take effect; all except Eurylochus (as in Homer) are changed into swine (not mentioned in Homer until this scene, while in Virgil, interestingly, there is a mention of swine when Aeneas' men sail past Circe's island).[29]

The narrative continues its brisk pace; Odysseus comes to the witch's lair armed with instructions from Mercury and the special "moly" that will serve as protection against harm. Circe is foiled; Odysseus makes his threat to kill her with his drawn sword. In Homer, Odysseus agrees to sleep with Circe after she promises not to do any further harm; in Ovid, it is almost as if Odysseus agrees to marry the sorceress, with the demand that the safety of his companions be his wedding gift (14.297-298 *thalamoque receptus / coniugii dotem sociorum corpora poscit*). The Greeks end up spending a year with Circe, a long—and arguably quite unnecessary—delay in Odysseus' homecoming voyage.

The year Odysseus spends with Circe was reworked by Virgil in Aeneas' yearlong dalliance with Dido. In Ovid's account, the year provides ample opportunity for stories, and Macareus relates but one of the tales that Circe's handmaidens sang. Macareus is explicit: Odysseus was off alone with Circe (indulging in their love, we can be sure), when one of the servants told a tale about "Picus," the woodpecker.[30]

The servant shows Macareus a marble statue of a young man who has a woodpecker on his head. Here, with the story of Picus, Ovid abandons any direct recollection of Homer and transitions to the material of *Aeneid* 7.[31] In the palace of King Latinus in Latium, there are statues carved from cedar of the royal ancestors; among them is Latinus' ancestor Picus (Latinus' father was Faunus, his mother the nymph Marica—at least in Virgil). We have already noted some of the earlier Greek traditions about Circe; one of them placed her firmly in Italy and made her the mother of Latinus.[32] Circe is at the beginning of *Aeneid* 7 because of this tradition that made her Latinus' mother (by Odysseus)—as the putative mother of Latinus, she presides over the Italian *Iliad* and is, in an important sense, a mother of Rome. Picus was a figure from Italian folklore and religion; at *Fasti* 3.259 ff., Ovid describes how Picus and Faunus once lent aid to King Numa. The woodpecker was a bird sacred to Mars and connected to augury.[33]

The story begins: Picus was a son of Saturn, and exceptionally good at horsemanship (a Virgilian detail, appropriate in connection to the eventual fateful cavalry battle in which Camilla dominates). Picus was somewhere between 12 and 19 years of age when the story begins (the nymph gives the date by an elaborate, though imprecise, epic periphrasis that utilizes the date of the Olympic Games—a splendid anachronism of uncertain import).[34]

Picus is sought by many female suitors from among all the dryads and nymphs; the stage is thus set for another tale of love, once again involving Circe (cf. Glaucus-Scylla-Circe). Besides these Circean triangles, there was also the Galatea-Acis-Polyphemus triangle, for a total of three love triangles involving nine people, with Circe counted twice. Scylla forsook all suitors; Acis and now Picus—note the similar names, and the neat frame these two lovers make with Scylla in the middle—both loved but one girl. In Picus' case, the girl is the nymph Canens (otherwise quite unknown), who is identified as the daughter of the great Roman god Janus and the nymph Venilia, elsewhere most famous as Turnus' mother. Janus may be a Roman god, but he is *Ionian* in origin (14.334

Ionio . . . Iano).[35] Ovid is concerned (perhaps more so than Virgil) with the reconciliation of the Greek and the Italian (Virgil is somewhat more preoccupied
with the assimilation of Trojans and Italians).

Canens—with an obvious etymology of her name from the Latin *canere*,
"to sing," is like Orpheus: she has remarkable powers of song, and can charm
both stones and beasts.

For those who remember the *Aeneid*, the story is inviting trouble; at *A.*
7.189-191), Virgil notes that Picus was changed into a bird by Circe: *Picus,
equum domitor, quem capta cupidine coniunx / aurea percussum virga versum-
que venenis / fecit avem Circe sparsitque coloribus alas.* The passage is notoriously vexed by the word *coniunx*—Circe was not Picus' wife *per se*. But neither
was Odysseus her husband, yet Ovid called their union a *coniugium*. Some
commentators think the Virgilian passage is a deliberate echo of the tradition
whereby Circe was Latinus' mother *(fortasse recte)*; I would suggest that Ovid's
decision to call the relationship between Odysseus and Circe a *coniugium*, besides recalling Dido's inappropriate judgment that her relationship with Aeneas
was a marriage, is an example of the same sort of allusive nod to other traditions.

We can guess the direction of Macareus' story: Circe will be jealous of
Canens. Picus goes out to hunt; he wears a (baleful) purple cloak with a golden
brooch (14.345); we might compare Aeneas and Dido on their fateful hunt, or
Camilla in her purple and gold finery. Picus is hunting in the same area where
Circe decides to look for magic herbs; the goddess sees him and at once falls in
love with him (her libidinous nature has already been well established). Picus is
hurrying off with his horses and companions; Circe cannot approach him, but
she has trust in the efficacy of her magic. Circe creates a phantom boar that lures
the unsuspecting hunter into a dense area of the forest where his horse cannot
tread.

Circe recites her magic charms; the area grows dark and Picus' companions
are lost in the mists. She finally has her chance to approach the youth; she announces, as she did to Glaucus, a direct invitation: she wants to marry him, she
offers him the sun god as a father-in-law (14.372 ff.). Glaucus is Picus' model;
he flatly rejects the sorceress, noting that he already loves another, and he practically invites trouble, it might seem, by saying that as long as Canens is safe
and secure, he will remain loyal to her.

Glaucus had pursued Circe for help in winning Scylla (who would have
nothing to do with him); Picus was pursued by Circe, and his beloved, Canens,
loved him with a mutual affection. *Unlike* the situation with Glaucus, this time
Circe tries again and again (14.382 *retemptatis precibus*); nothing works.[36] Circe
punishes not Canens, but *Picus*—he is changed into a woodpecker, an angry bird
that strikes at wood in its indignation, and a bird that still retains the dark purple
and gold colors of its accoutrements.

The mist lifts, and Picus' companions come searching for him (14.397 ff.).
They find Circe and learn of what has happened; they bravely prepare to attack

her. As if she were Medea, or even Bacchus in a full mode of vengeance, she makes the whole forest suddenly become a place of horror, with the howling of animals and the sudden growth of dense trees. She transforms all of the assembly into wild beasts.

The companions learned the truth (to their doom); Canens has no idea what has happened, and she spends six nights and days hunting for her lost love. Finally, at the Tiber, Canens sinks down in grief; she eventually wastes away and is transformed into water, melting into thin air. According to Macareus, the story is remembered by the ancient Italian Muses, the *Camenae*, who call the place of the liquefaction "Canens" after the name of the lost nymph.

Macareus notes that he heard many other stories during the long year at Circe's court, but that in the end, when everyone else left, he stayed behind—afraid as he was to face any further danger. Thus at last ends Ovid's account of an *Odyssey*-within-an-*Aeneid*.

Dido and Aeneas had hunted amid purple and gold; Camilla wore purple and gold at the end of *Aeneid* 7, when she came as the leader of the Volscian contingents in the catalogue of Italian heroes. The hunt was baleful for Dido and Aeneas; coming to war was problematic for Camilla. In the case of Picus, if the lesson is that one must learn when to accept a certain love (as with Glaucus, and Scylla), then the point must be that infidelity is sometimes necessary (Picus should have been unfaithful to Canens with Circe), which seems unlikely—though the hard lesson remains, sometimes rejection of love carries a heavy price; in this case, Picus becomes a woodpecker.

Ovid is finally ready to "begin" his Iliadic *Aeneid*, with a return to Caieta to finish his chiastic arrangement of Circe-Caieta-Circe-Caieta. At this final conclusion of Ovid's Odyssean *Aeneid* (which has been intertwined with an *Odyssey*), we can make some observations on the poet's purpose.

We have observed that Ovid began his *Aeneid* in Book 13, in the aftermath of the fall of Troy, with a narrative that remained faithful to Virgil until the approach to Scylla. There, Ovid digressed on two major stories (really a story within a story, after one of his favorite devices). Scylla was desired by many; she rejected them all; Galatea told a story about Polyphemus and Acis; Scylla was pursued by Glaucus, whom she rejected to her ultimate peril, once he fled to Circe for help and the witch became enamored of her supplicant. The one story, then, is the Glaucus-Scylla-Circe triangle; the story within it is the Polyphemus-Acis-Galatea affair (with a neat contrast of two men and one woman instead of one man and two women).

All of this, we have argued, was Ovid's reflection on Homer's *Odyssey*, with the lesson of the hazards of trying to guess when not to love and when to surrender to it. This lesson contrasted with the case of Meleager, where the point was *not* to give in to passion. Here, not giving in proves just as perilous as surrender.

Having finished this contrasting point, Ovid resumed his *Aeneid*. He advanced this time as far as Caieta, where we expected a transition to his Iliadic

Aeneid and the war Aeneas and his Trojans faced in Italy. In Virgil, after Caieta was introduced (if only to give her name to a shore), Circe was bypassed—she marked the transition, the transformation, from one world to another. Very shortly after arriving in that new world, the Trojans entered the palace of Latinus, where, not surprisingly, his ancestor Picus was carved in cedar, with a brief allusion to a love affair with Circe that is, perhaps, quickly forgotten.

But in Ovid, there is a surprise, quite unexpected. *Before* we commence an Ovidian version of the Iliadic *Aeneid*, there is another digression, just as was occasioned before by Scylla. This digression is occasioned by the discovery of a Greek, Macareus—a blessed man—who recognizes another Greek, Achaemenides—a man of woe, who, as in Virgil, gets a chance to recite his baleful tale (with an admittedly happy ending). Macareus proceeds to tell Achaemenides the story of what happened to Odysseus and his men *after* the Cyclops—after the "old" material, in other words, that we have already heard. Some of the story is also "old" material from Homer's *Odyssey*, material that had no place for either brief mention or extended narrative in Virgil's *Aeneid* (e.g., the Laestrygonians, Circe). But the mention of the famous witch occasions a strange story, a tale that explains what Virgil had described only in brief and highly allusive lines about a *wooden* statue of cedar in Latinus' palace. This time, the story is occasioned by a *marble* (14.313 *marmareo*) statue in Circe's palace: the statue of the Latin ancestor Picus.

Macareus' story of Picus offers a third love triangle. This time we have Picus-Canens-Circe (man, beloved, rival), where before we had Glaucus-Scylla-Circe. In the story within that story, we had Acis-Galatea-Polyphemus. Some have seen a connection in these triangles to the great Virgilian triangle of Aeneas-Lavinia-Turnus. That yields interesting connections to the (one) Ovidian story with two men and one woman; it is attractive to connect *Acis* and *Aeneas*, and the watery ends of both men (Acis the river, and the strange tradition of Aeneas' loss in the Numicus). And some might find an appealing comparison between the *contemptor Iovis* Polyphemus and Turnus. The big problem, of course, is that Turnus does not kill Aeneas; quite the opposite. But there are enough parallels to give pause.

The other two Ovidian triangles, however, do not fit the Virgilian. But there is also Aeneas-Dido-Lavinia, and there is Turnus-Camilla-Lavinia. No one, of course, rejects Lavinia, though Aeneas and Turnus have their respective infatuations with Dido and Camilla. But the comparisons do not work out very well here either.

And, further, there is also Turnus-*Juturna*-Lavinia, which does yield interesting comparison to Picus-Canens-Circe; the same end more or less befalls Juturna and Canens (a watery fate)—Turnus' desire for Lavinia tore him from his sister. And Venilia is the mother of both Canens *and* Turnus-Juturna. But it is hard to find a good parallel for Glaucus-Scylla-Circe in Virgil's *Aeneid*. While I think that the Canens-Juturna parallel was deliberate, I do not think there is any intentional linkage of all three triangles to Virgil's narrative. Ovid's point in evoking the Juturna lore would be to end his *Odyssey* with an evocation of the end of Virgil's *Iliad*, a neat reversal of his poetic model. But there is more than just skillful reworking of an original.

I would suggest that the key comes instead with where the Picus-Canens-Circe story appears in Ovid: right on the cusp of his Iliadic *Aeneid*, right before Caieta—*right where in Virgil we find the Gates of Sleep.* The key here is how the *wood* of Virgil's Picus statue has become the *marble* of Ovid's.[37] These correspond to the horn and ivory of the Gates. In Virgil, Picus is Latinus' ancestor, and is last in the miniature catalogue of Italian ancestors at the beginning of *Aeneid* 7, just as Camilla will be last in the catalogue of Italian heroes at the book's end.[38] Both Picus and Camilla are masters of horsemanship.

In Virgil, Picus is depicted (in cedar wood) in ritual vesture as an augur; he is like some priest in liturgical vesture (*Aeneid* 7.187-188 *ipse Quirinali lituo parvaque sedebat / succinctus trabea laevaque ancile gerebat*). But, Virgil then adds, he was the one who was turned into a bird by his wife, Circe. In Ovid, Picus is depicted (in marble) as a handsome young man with a woodpecker on top of his head.

Virgil says that Latinus was the son of Faunus and Marica, and that Picus was Faunus' father.[39] As we have seen, though, the tradition was vexed. At *Aeneid* 12.164, the sun is Latinus' *avus*, thus implying Circe is his mother (though *avus* can simply mean "ancestor"). Ovid also says that Faunus is Latinus' father (14.449).

I suspect that the point of Ovid's story is to evoke the Virgilian Gates of Sleep, in this case through the evocation of the *two* statues of Picus: the Virgilian one of cedar wood (the religious augur and father of Faunus), which corresponds to the Gate of Horn, and the Ovidian one of marble (the young man with the woodpecker), which corresponds to the Gate of Ivory. But Ovid is silent about Faunus' parentage, either here or in the section of the *Fasti* where Picus and Faunus assist Numa as rustic deities. I suspect that the point of the marble statue is its anachronism—from an *Italian* perspective, but not a Greek. As we have seen, Ovid is concerned in this section with the molding of Greeks and Italians into one (in contrast to Virgil's preoccupation with the union of Trojans and Italians, where some Greeks are seen as unexpected allies of the Trojans and little more). In response to Virgil's concern with Trojans, Ovid is concerned with Greeks; the marble statue, with none of the Roman accoutrements of Virgil's cedar image, is a *Greek* statue, in a story told by a fortunate *Greek*. This is false in light of the final ethnic disposition of Rome. No room in either Virgil or Ovid, then, for a *Greek* world that might dream of *Odysseus* as the father of Latinus; no, at the very end of his *Odyssey*, the idealized marble statue of Picus, some sort of Greek hero, is dismissed as being a false dream.[40]

With that brilliant comment on his predecessor, Ovid is finally ready to commence his *Iliad* in Italy, his Iliadic *Aeneid*. Caieta is buried, and in a *marble* tomb (14.442 *marmoreo . . . tumulo*), a splendid comment in the aftermath of the lengthy digression occasioned by the marble statue of Picus. With Caieta, both

Circe and the Greeks are put to rest. The cables are loosened from the *grassy* mound (445 *herboso*), where the adjective refers to the magic herbs that have worked such transformations. Circe's shores are known for treachery (446 *insidias*) and infamy (*infamatae . . . deae*); this is where Odysseus had found a fitting match—a Camilla, if you will, instead of a Lavinia. But Odysseus gave up Circe (a key lesson in the *Odyssey*); Turnus knew not when to surrender his passion for Camilla.[41]

Rome is essentially now reached: the Tiber, the home of Latinus, the son of Faunus, and his daughter (14.447-449). The inhabitants of Latium are ferocious (*gente feroci*); Turnus rages for his promised marriage (*pactaque furit pro coniuge Turnus*). Ovid, thus, follows Livy in agreeing that Lavinia had been promised to Turnus. Virgil never explicitly says this, though it can be argued the implication is there.[42] The search for allies on both sides is briefly detailed, with mention of the Arcadian Evander (*Aeneid* 8); Ovid now digresses again from the path of his Virgilian predecessor, and moves to Diomedes in southern Italy.

In Virgil, the embassy to Diomedes that is sent out in Book 8 does not return until Book 11. We have noted that there are affinities between the debate over the arms of Achilles and the Latin war council in *Aeneid* 11; the Diomedes episode Ovid now undertakes is also based on material from that key book of Virgil's epic, the book where the main themes of the poet's reworking of the *Iliad* are outlined in careful relief. Turnus' emissary Venulus learns that Diomedes cannot help him, saying that he does not wish to expose himself or his father-in-law Daunus to harm, and, besides, he has no forces to send.[43] Diomedes briefly recalls the sufferings the Greeks faced after leaving Troy; this is material familiar from the Virgilian model. Minerva killed the Lesser Ajax—a famous image that Juno uses as an example of how other divinities seem able to do as they wish with enemies—but the goddess of weaving and war also saves Diomedes from harm. Venus, in contrast, is furious with Diomedes because of the famous Homeric episode where he nearly kills Aeneas and succeeds in wounding the goddess.[44] Minerva in some ways presides over much of the action of Virgil's *Aeneid* 11; in Ovid, she is a patroness of Diomedes—an eminently Italian goddess, we might note—in opposition to Venus.

Diomedes and his men are more or less like Aeneas and his Trojans, with a substitution of Venus for Juno in the part of wrathful goddess. Diomedes' men are weary from the goddess' constant harassment; one of them, Acmon, scorns her power and insults her (14.484 ff.). Virgil tells the story of what happened next; most of Diomedes' men were transformed into birds. The passage must have proven irresistible to Ovid in adapting his *Aeneid* source material.[45] The bird is famously unidentified in either Ovid or Virgil, though Ovid notes that they were very much like swans in their white color—appropriate given the association of swans with Venus. The passage is not unduly extended, and, as we have noted, the story had obvious appeal for the poet of transformations.

Ovid has more or less conflated two Virgilian scenes, the departure of the embassy in *A.* 8 and its return (with story) in *A.* 11. Ovid maintains the Virgilian division, however, by inserting a brief tale between Venulus' departure from Diomedes and his return to Turnus (14.527 ff.). The obscure story of what happened near a cave Venulus passes on his way back to Turnus is not in Virgil; Antoninus Liberalis (31) has it, crediting the lore to Nicander. In Antoninus, Messapian shepherds once challenged local nymphs to a singing contest; once defeated, the shepherds were turned into trees. In Ovid, an Apulian shepherd scares off some nymphs; they run in fright but soon resume their dancing. The shepherd then mocks them boorishly; he is finally transformed into a wild olive tree, an *oleaster* (525), which still retains the bitterness of its origin. The story somewhat balances the tale of the monkey-like Cercopians (91 ff. above). But there is more at play than mere ring composition.

The *oleaster* is key to the last movements of the *Aeneid*. At *Aeneid* 12.766 ff., during the combat of Aeneas and Turnus, Virgil mentions an oleaster that was sacred to Faunus. Saved from a shipwreck, the tree had become a place for Laurentine votive offerings. The Trojans wanted an open plain, and so they removed it—a definite sacrilege. Aeneas' spear stuck in the stump of the tree. Aeneas—his wounded leg still hurting him, even after Venus' magical cure (a testimony to how serious the wound was)—tries to pull out the spear. Turnus prays to Faunus and Terra to hold the spear fast. While Aeneas tries in vain to retrieve his spear—for the *Italian* gods listened to Turnus—his sister Juturna gives her brother his sword (in his rush he had mistakenly taken the sword of his charioteer Metiscus). Venus is enraged that Turnus should have his sword, and so she tears the spear out of the tree to help her son. The combat resumes. It is at this point in the Virgilian narrative that the great divine colloquy between Juno and Jupiter takes place on Olympus.

The Virgilian scene is of tremendous significance in appreciating the final movements of the epic. The Trojans have desecrated a tree sacred to a native Italian woodland god. In something of a reversal from the situation with the Bough, Aeneas cannot retrieve his spear—Venus must help him, and only after she is enraged that Turnus should have his own sword back. The whole episode serves as precursor to the revelation that Troy will be Italian, not Trojan. Venus "wins" in that Aeneas retrieves his spear—and this is the goddess' last appearance in the *Aeneid*—but she loses in the much larger contest unfolding on Olympus. Faunus and Juturna battle Venus; the result on earth is inconclusive, but decisive in heaven.

Here, then, after the *defeat* of Turnus in the embassy to Diomedes—the man who once almost killed Aeneas and who wounded Venus will not help the Rutulians—we have the bitter origin of the *oleaster*. It is bitter because Turnus is bitter; he is indignant at the injustice of his situation. Neither he nor Aeneas is privy to the divine discussion about the ethnic disposition of the future Rome.

The embassy returns with the news of Diomedes' refusal, and the *Aeneid* narrative resumes (14.527 ff.). Battle rages, but Ovid turns at once to an episode from Virgil's *A. 9*: the transformation of Aeneas' ships into sea creatures.[46] Once again, the metamorphosis tale from his predecessor must have been irre-

AND NOW ETNA ...

sistible; but there are other considerations. The episode from *Aeneid* 9 has been criticized by some as an absurdly fantastic account clumsily inserted into Virgil's war narrative. Cybele complains to Jupiter that her sacred pine trees should not be destroyed by Turnus' fire; Jupiter consents to letting the ships be transformed into mermaids. The episode is a powerful sign of the forces arrayed against Turnus and the fundamentally "unfair" nature of the fight he faces; the conversation between Cybele and Jupiter also contrasts with that in *Aeneid* 12 between Juno and Jupiter, where the subject matter is rather more serious. In Virgil, Turnus knows he can win against the Trojans, absent divine favor; he sees the transformation of the ships in part as a sign that his job is easier now— the Trojans now have no vessels with which to escape his grasp.

In Ovid's account, Jupiter plays no part in the nautical metamorphosis. Cybele herself handles the problem of Turnus' firebrands; she saves her sacred trees from destruction (14.536 ff.). As with the birds of Diomedes, the transformation of Aeneas' ships is a sign of the favor of a mother goddess (Venus, Cybele) against those who would harm her own—Diomedes' men are associated with his attack on Venus and her son, not to mention the blasphemy of Acmon; Cybele preserves her ships against another impious foe who would do them harm. Ovid moves at once to the rest of the *Aeneid*, and makes an interesting comment on the nature of divinity:

> . . . habetque deos pars utraque, quodque deorum est
> instar, habent animos . . . (14.568-569)

> . . . and each faction has its gods, and, that is of the value
> of the gods, they have courage . . .

Each side has its own patron deities; these are easy to identify as one moves through the pages of Virgil. Each side also has *animi*, "courage." *Instar* is a difficult word to translate precisely. It can mean that the *animi* = the likeness or resemblance of the gods; when the heroes possess *animi*, they are god-like. It can also mean that the *animi* are just as good as gods; each man makes a god for himself out of his courage and valor. *Animi* can also carry an astonishing range of meanings, from the rational spirit to violent passion. Ovid's highly significant verses—regrettably understudied—offer a marvelous example of the rich capability of Latin to say a dozen things with elegant economy and wonderful ambiguity. Further, there is just a hint—but a noteworthy one—of impiety here, of a world without need for gods, or of a world that lacks them altogether. No god, after all, motivated Aeneas to kill Turnus, and no god motivated Turnus to persist in his fight against Aeneas to the very end.

Ovid next offers an interesting comment on the end of the *Aeneid*:

> . . . nec iam dotalia regna,
> nec sceptrum soceri, nec te, Lavinia virgo,
> sed vicisse petunt deponendique pudore

bella gerunt . . . (14.569-572)

> . . . and now not the dowered kingdoms,
> not the scepter of the father-in-law, nor you, virgin Lavinia,
> do they seek, but to have conquered, and they wage war
> out of shame of giving up . . .

This passage, too, has not received much attention. We saw in the battle in Phineus' dining hall in Book 5 that Perseus and his combatants were dehumanized by the experience of war; this is a theme that certainly recurs in Virgil's battle books. The climax of the ascending tricolon here, however, is Lavinia: she had been the erotic cause of the war in Italy, though by the end of Aeneid 12, there is little focus on her, even after Turnus announces that Lavinia is now Aeneas'—part of this, to be sure, is the emotional resonance of Aeneas with Dido and Turnus with Camilla—Lavinia is rather lost in the shadows, and she remains a hauntingly silent figure.[47]

Turnus dies, and his hometown of Ardea is burned (14.573). The story seems to be Ovid's invention; it may have been inspired by the idea Aeneas conceives in Aeneid 12 to set fire to Latinus' capital (which has Lavinia in it, of course). From the ashes of Ardea a bird arises, the heron—in Latin, ardea. Virgil knows the bird association too;[48] he may derive the name of the town from arduus, however, "hard" or "difficult." The heron was associated with augury. As the commentators note, this metamorphosis somewhat balances the appearance of the warring birds from the ashes of Memnon's pyre (M. 13.604-619), which came after the fall of Troy. But the parallels are not exact. The passage is also vexed by textual problems at 14.574-575, where we have quam postquam barbarus ignis, of fire burning Ardea, against quem postquam barbarus ensis, of Aeneas killing Turnus. Ensis is the reading of the primary manuscripts, and offers a powerful commentary on Aeneas' killing of Turnus—barbarus fits very well with the final reconciliation of Jupiter and Juno in Aeneid 12.[49] Barbarus has bothered some; Ovid is, after all, Virgil's "best reader"—as many (especially Jim O'Hara) have well noted—and he understood the point of the end of the Aeneid. Trojan savagery is well illustrated in his version of how Ardea must now burn (ardere come to life); his point of how both sides fought for victory alone, out of shame of surrender, is relevant here—Ardea was also a cult site of Juno.[50] Barbarus ensis is a stunning confirmation of Ovid's reading of the end of the Aeneid—and barbarus ignis does not offer much solace to those bothered by the implications of the reading.

In the closing movement of the Aeneid, Virgil unfolded the future ethnic realities in Rome. Juno was happy with this turn of events, and left her husband and brother's presence in rejoicing. But Jupiter did announce to his wife that Aeneas would become a god (A. 12.794-795); he had made the same prediction to Venus in Book 1. Virgil thus leaves no doubt that in his vision, Aeneas will be deified. Livy was not so sure; at Ab Urbe Condita 1.2.6[51] he observes that

Aeneas lies buried: *situs est, quemcumque eum dici ius fasque est, super Numicum flumen: Iovem indigetem appellant.* At Dionysius of Halicarnassus 1.64.5, we read that the Latins built a hero shrine to Aeneas, but that some people said it was built by Aeneas to honor Anchises—the tradition is vexed. Virgil follows the tradition that Aeneas would rule in Latium for three years (*Aeneid* 1.259-260); the story went that Aeneas was eventually killed in a subsequent battle against the Rutulians, near the River Numicus—Virgil does not allude in any explicit way to this somewhat bleak outcome of the Trojan's wanderings. Aeneas was then worshipped near Lavinium as a sort of local god.

Ovid says that after Ardea burned, all the gods were compelled to give up their wrath—even Juno—by the virtue of Aeneas: 14.581-582 *iamque deos omnes ipsamque Aeneia virtus / Iunonem veteres finire coegerat iras.* The question of when Juno gave up her wrath is somewhat vexed; Virgil makes it quite clear that the goddess is reconciled at the end of *Aeneid* 12—some, however, have seen that reconciliation as rather limited, especially given the goddess' anti-Roman part in the Punic Wars. Servius (ad *A.* 1.20 and 281) preserves evidence that Ennius had a scene of Junonian reconciliation in the *Annales*, where the goddess was appeased sometime during the Second Punic War.[52] What is clear is that Virgil places the reconciliation in Aeneas' lifetime, Ennius, apparently, in the third century—and Horace (c. 3.3) associates it with the death of Romulus.[53]

In Ovid, the *virtus* of Aeneas compelled Juno to give up her wrath.[54] The passage would seem to contradict Virgil, or at the very least offer a different emphasis. As we shall see, in Ovid's vision the quelling is but temporary, and so the contradiction is noteworthy as a signpost of sorts: Juno's wrath is not finished.

We are now, ostensibly, at the end of Ovid's *Aeneid.* Fittingly, Ovid begins the next movement of his epic with Venus approaching Jupiter; the scene is modeled on the great conversation between the divine father and daughter in *Aeneid* 1. Venus wants to win immortality for her son (14.585 ff.). Venus "canvasses" the gods (*ambierat*); as the commentators have noted, the word is from the language of political contests, and is not favorable. The point here is not parody of the epic tradition, but criticism of Aeneas and Venus, whose mother is now reduced to the level of political boss, despite all Aeneas' *virtus* and Juno's alleged reconciliation—indeed, if Juno and "all the gods" are now free from wrath, why the need for *ambire*? Juno, of course, assents to the request; she had already heard that Aeneas was destined to become a god. Ovid's real game here is to have fun with the progression from Jupiter's conversation with his wife in *Aeneid* 12 to his discussion here with this daughter in *Metamorphoses* 14; if Venus had read the *Aeneid's* closing book, she would know that Aeneas would become a god—let alone if she remembered the Jovian speech of *Aeneid* 1.

Ovid now details a purgation of Aeneas' mortal body that echoes rather closely the purification of Glaucus before his transformation into a sea creature (14.600-604). Aeneas is at the Numicus—Ovid avoids all mention of the details of a second war with the Rutulians and hastens to Venus' orders to the river—

the waters are to cleanse Aeneas and purge the Stoic hero of his mortality. The purgation, of course, is also a cleansing from Aeneas' Trojan roots; he becomes *Indiges*, a notoriously obscure title that defies definitive definition. It is the term Virgil has Jupiter use at *Aeneid* 12.794 to describe Aeneas' divine fate; the Trojan exile has become a prototype of a native Italian god. But, as with the death of Romulus, Roman tradition countenanced different views on Aeneas' fate. "The cult of Aeneas never reached Rome, although the legend did."[55] Part of the problem, of course, was the conflict between the dueling stories of Romulus and Aeneas regarding the foundation of Rome; the Aeneas story is the later of the two traditions, and reflects a *Greek* view of Rome's origins (cf. our earlier consideration of the significance of Picus' marble statue).

Ovid continues with a wonderful comment on all of these themes:

> inde sub Ascanii dicione binominis Alba
> resque Latina fuit. (14.609-610)

> *Then, under the power of Ascanius of the double name was*
> *Alba and the Latin state.*

Virgil had spoken of three centuries of Alban kings (one must fill the chronology between 1184 B.C. and 753 B.C. somehow, after all); the ruler list commences with Virgil's son Ascanius. *Binominis* is loaded with meaning; it relates to Greeks + Latins, Trojans + Latins, Ascanius' two names (Iulus, etc.)—even the tradition that Ascanius was not Creusa's son, but Lavinia's—a nice way to suppress still further the Trojan origins.[56] In Virgil, Alba Longa was founded by Ascanius thirty years after Aeneas founded Lavinium. But the tradition was vexed, as was that of the next king, Silvius. In Virgil, he is Lavinia's son, born after Aeneas died (*Aeneid* 6.763-766); Ovid does not take a position on the parentage, though in the *Fasti* (4.41-42), Silvius is the son of Ascanius. Other kings follow; notable among them is Tiberinus, who, drowned in the famous river, lends it his name (14.614-616). Virgil has a different story—more accurately, Virgil's *Evander* (*Aeneid* 8.330-332)—where the river derives its name from an Etruscan named Thybris. Ovid may well nod to that tradition (hence 615 *Tusci . . . fluminis*), but he uses not the name Evander would prefer, but the name that appears in Roman cult, *Tiberinus*.

The Alban king Remulus imitated lightning, and so lightning fittingly killed him (14.617-618); he is reminiscent of Virgil's Numanus Remulus, the braggart who was slain by Ascanius (with Apollo's assistance), though lending his name to a storied line in early Rome.[57] Ovid continues his list of kings through Proca (cf. Virgil, *Aeneid* 6.767 *Procas*). But then, with no announcement, Ovid digresses to his great story of Pomona and Vertumnus.[58]

The Pomona and Vertumnus epyllion comes right before the story of the Alban kings reaches its climactic point on the path to Romulus. The story has tremendous significance that cannot be exaggerated: it is the first post-*Aeneid* story in Ovid's epic. The mention of the "Tuscan river" leads to a prototypical Etruscan god, the god Varro called the *deus princeps Etruriae*, Vortumnus (note the spelling).[59] The god's story in Propertius' elegy—the first extant appearance of the deity—is about change, specifically the change that Rome embraces as it gains power over foreign entities and absorbs them—this is, after all, the main theme of metamorphosis Ovid is now concerned with his description of Rome's foundations and immediate precursors. Ovid starts with Pomona, a Latin hamadryad who is not some forest denizen or necessarily virginal huntress, but rather an expert gardener. Pomona—her name bearing obvious connections to fruit— appears nowhere else and may be the poet's invention; first fruits were put in the hands of the statue of Vortumnus on the edge of the forum.[60] Pomona is Latin, but she is a hamadryad; she is a hybrid creature, like so many in Rome's earliest history. She is Greek and Latin, and, as we have noted, Ovid's main concern now is the melding of the Greek and the Latin—it is, in fact, one of the main themes of his poetry.[61]

It is as if we are back in the world of the earliest books of the epic, in a world that is reminiscent of Diana's woods, yet so very different. Pomona is a forest creature, a hamadryad, but she is also domesticated in her garden expertise. She does not like the forest (14.626-627 *non silvas illa nec amnes, / rus amat*). She is no huntress; instead of a javelin, she has a curved pruning hook to cut back overgrowth. It is as if Ovid is evoking the world of Virgil's *Georgics* (he had already covered the *Aeneid* and much of the *Eclogues*, especially in his Polyphemus and Galatea interlude). She is a preeminent gardener: 634 *hic amor, hoc studium*—a direct quote from *Aeneid* 11.739, the passage where Jupiter stirs up Tarchon in the wake of Camilla's *aristeia* and the Etruscan leader upbraids his men for being given over to luxury (a common stereotype regarding the Etruscans).

Pomona is no huntress, no forest denizen, but she is a virgin (14.634 *Veneris quoque nulla cupido est*). In the woods, she might be easy prey to rape, like so many nymphs from earlier in Ovid's long epic—conveniently, gardens allow for locked gates and no easy ingress. Pomona is wooed; the satyrs desire her, as do Silenus and the Pans, not to mention the phallic Priapus. The garden god is no guardian of Pomona's virgin preserve; he is excluded because he would rape the gardener. Vertumnus also loves the orchard nymph. The god is mentioned without any sort of introduction or preface; he simply appears as the last and worthiest in the catalogue of Pomona's lovers, but a failure nonetheless—she will have nothing to do with him. The theme of Ovid's *Odyssey*—knowing when to succumb to love—would seem to be at play here too.

Vertumnus tries disguise after disguise to win Pomona; he is at least happy that he has frequent chances to gaze on her beauty (14.653 *ut caperet spectatae gaudia formae*). Finally, he disguises himself as an old woman. Quite significantly, he wears a *mitra* (654), a headdress that was associated with the East and the world that would have no place in the final ethnic disposition of Rome.[62]

Vertumnus makes an appeal that is indebted to Catullus: a tree without a vine is only good for its leaves; a vine without a tree will languish on the ground. Pomona has not learned the example of the very plants, trees, and vines she tends; she should yield to love. Helen would not have more suitors; neither would Hippodamia or Penelope—Vertumnus has clearly read the *Metamorphoses*, since he knows that Ovid had used the drama of the combat of the Lapiths and the Centaurs at the wedding of Pirithous and Hippodamia as a paradigm for his *Iliad*.[63] The old woman makes the case for herself—Vertumnus is the lover Pomona should accept. He has the power to transform himself into anything, and he will perform any task the hamadryad requires; he also loves gardening, and will be a suitable partner for her. Vertumnus has Etruscan origins, and he is wearing a rather Phrygian sort of headdress, very un-Roman in its effeminate connotations (cf. Iarbas' taunts about Aeneas' appearance). Vertumnus warns Pomona that Venus and Nemesis (14.694 *Rhamnusidis*, the Rhamnusian goddess) cannot tolerate those who would be too stubborn about love.

Here, Venus returns to the narrative, and not surprisingly given the theme of love.[64] The disguised Vertumnus will tell a story that is designed to be a cautionary fable on the theme of not being overly difficult in matters of the heart; the same theme we have known so well from the *Odyssey* here returns (and the allusive mention of Penelope at 14.671 helps to announce the return of the theme). The story is that of Iphis and Anaxerete, which (we should not be surprised) is essentially unknown outside Ovid.[65]

The tale is said to be well known in Cyprus, which is Venus' sacred island. Anaxerete was a girl of Teucer's line—she is descended from Ajax's half-brother, who was said to have founded a new Salamis in Cyprus. She is an eminently Greek girl, of heroic origins and proud lineage. Iphis is a youth of humble background; his ethnicity is not specified here, though the earlier Iphis in the poem was Cretan (*M.* 9). Anaxerete rejects the youth despite all his blandishments; among other comparisons, she is harder than iron tempered by Noric fire (the simile may in part be inspired by Ovid's evocation of the *Georgics* and a desire to recall the great plague at Noricum).

Iphis is overcome with grief at Anaxerete's repeated rebuffs; he resolves to kill himself. Significantly, he tells Anaxerete that she has won, and that she may celebrate a triumph now:

> . . . laetos molire triumphos
> et Paeana voca nitidaque incingere lauru! (14.719-720)

> . . . *accomplish your happy triumphs*
> *and call on the Paean, and bind your head with gleaming laurel!*

The triumph imagery is Roman, and eminently so; the mention of the Paean, however, is Greek: *Paean* was a cult title for Apollo in his capacity as a god of medicine. The laurel, of course, reminds us of Apollo and Daphne.

There will be no triumph, of course; the only procession will be Iphis' requiem. The key to the story rests in Iphis' description of the mingled (and anachronistic) Roman-Greek triumph. Anaxerete is Greek, but she is asked to participate in a Roman triumph. Iphis is also Greek (perhaps Cretan); he is of low birth, Anaxerete of a royal line. She will have nothing to do with him, and she suffers the consequences of her arrogant *hauteur*.

Iphis makes threats and promises of haunting and expresses hopes for vengeful gods; he hangs himself outside Anaxerete's door, and, apparently, his feet knock on the door in a ghoulish play on the tradition of the *exclusus amator*.[66] He is carried away in a funeral procession; Anaxerete hears the mourners pass by, and she comes to the window—driven on already by an avenging god (14.750 *iam deus ultor agebat*). She is transformed into stone, in bodily imitation of her emotions toward Iphis' love. Vertumnus adds "evidence" and weight to his story—the statue is still kept in Salamis, and there is a temple to Venus, the disguised lover adds, with a statue of the Gazer (760-761 *Prospicientis*). The mention of this cult site is obscure;[67] Venus was clearly involved in some way in the whole business (as she is in the similar story in Antoninus Liberalis).

Vertumnus, the Etruscan, has sought admission into Pomona's garden. Like Iphis with Anaxarete, he is reasonably close in connection to Pomona, though different enough to occasion some question. The story is a cautionary one for Rome, which must accept foreign elements; they must be absorbed even at the price of what change they might bring. Vertumnus finally throws off his disguise; he appears like the sun out of the clouds. Interestingly, Pomona is given no chance to respond before he doffs his disguise; he prepares to rape her (14.770 *vimque parat*). But the orchard goddess is smitten by his appearance, by his *figura* (770), and she submits: *et mutua vulnera sensit*. The coda offers a magnificent closing to the whole matter of change: Rome has learned the lesson, the nascent city that is so soon to be born under Romulus; Pomona, the goddess of the first fruits, will make her offerings to Vertumnus and live with him, struck by the same wound of love in mutual union. Pomona has learned the lesson of when to submit, and she has learned the lesson of assimilation—she has opened the door of the garden, as Rome would admit Etruria.

It is no accident that the founding of Rome follows immediately on this exemplary story. As Myers notes ad 14.772, "the Alban king list recommences . . . as if it had not been interrupted." The story of Pomona and Vertumnus operates almost as a dream sequence, a divine interlude that explains that has happened in the mystical background to Roman history. The story Ovid now tells is highly compressed and another good example of his rapid style. Numitor had been the rightful Alban king; his younger brother Amulius robbed him of the crown. Numitor's son was murdered while his daughter, Ilia or Rhea Silvia, was famously compelled to be a Vestal Virgin. Mars raped her, and Amulius tried to destroy the babies Romulus and Remus. The she-wolf saved the founding twins, who eventually slew Amulius and restored the crown to their grandfather Numitor. They then embarked on the founding of their own city, Rome; the subsequent death of Remus was always a matter for learned debate.

Ennius thought Romulus and Remus were Aeneas' grandsons.[68] Most scholars think Amulius and Numitor were simply tacked on to the end of the list of Alban kings once a reconciliation had to be effected between the earlier Romulan tradition of Rome's founding and the Aeneas lore. The whole business of reconciling the Greek tradition with its filled-in chronology of the Alban kings and the preexisting Romulus story is a metaphor for the reconciliation of the diverse elements in Roman culture; the Pomona and Vertumnus story, a cautionary fable on the need to accept change as much as love, is a symbol of that reconciliation, and is thus deliberately placed before the "last kings" appear, figures from preexisting lore now appended to a convenient list of Alban monarchs so as to fill out a chronology.

Rome is founded at last:

> . . . festisque Palilibus urbis
> moenia conduntur . . . (14.774-775)

> . . . and on the festive days of the Palilia
> the walls of the city are founded . . .

The date is 21 April; the feast day the Palilia.[69] The solemnity was a shepherd's purification holiday; Ovid describes the whole business at *Fasti* 4.721-862 (where see Fantham). In these quiet verses, after so much reconciliation in the wake of savage violence and conflict, Virgil's *tanta moles* is finally realized in Ovidian verse.

The rejoicing that accompanies the great birth of the new city is exceedingly short-lived. Titus Tatius and the Sabines at once launch a war (14.775, within the same line as the founding of Rome's walls). The famous treachery of Tarpeia, itself, like Vertumnus, the subject of a Propertian elegy (c. 4.4), is briefly described. Tarpeia was said to have admitted Tatius and his Sabines to the Capitolium; the story is old, though with variants—Propertius, not surprisingly, has Tarpeia motivated by love, not greed, as if she were another Scylla with Nisus. After mentioning her betrayal of Rome, Ovid describes how the men of Cures, the famous Sabine town, came on in the manner of wolves, silent and predatory (778 *inde sati Curibus tacitorum more luporum*). They test the gates that Romulus had locked; this comes as a bit of a surprise, since one might well imagine that Tarpeia had handled letting them inside. Instead, they are now depicted as approaching another gate, this one locked. At this point, Juno—the goddess who was allegedly reconciled to Rome—makes her reappearance in Ovid's epic. She silently unlocks the gate for the Sabines (781-782).

Only Venus realizes that her archenemy has opened the gate. She knows it, but Ovid says that a god may not undo the actions of another, and so open the gate must stay. But Venus does what she can; she asks the assistance of Ausonian nymphs (eminently Italian) who hold a place near Janus' temple. They open their waters for the goddess. They place sulfur underneath the waters, and burning pitch (14.791-792 *lurida subponunt fecundo sulphura fonti / incenduntque cavas fumante bitumine venas*). The resulting smoke and smell blocks the gate rather effectively; Juno's work was for naught since the Romans now have a chance to rise from slumber and fight. Soon the whole area is covered with dead Sabines and Romans. The scene is impious; the Romans and Sabines are related by marriage, after all, and the *inpius ensis* (802) has slaughtered brothers in Rome's first civil war (at least according to Ovid's narrative). Once the whole business is finished, however, the Romans and the Sabines agree to peace and to a shared rule between Romulus and Tatius. Once again, assimilation is the point and central theme; Rome must admit the Sabines, and even share power with them (at least for now). Juno, for her part, is the god of the Roman future in that she *unlocks the gate*: certainly the Sabines must not be allowed to conquer the sleeping Romans and slaughter them; they must lose, in a sense, though they also win—there are dead on both sides, and the battle results not in a clear victory for either party, but in a shared rule. Juno is forward looking; she is reconciled to Rome after all, though not, perhaps, in the manner Venus or the audience had expected.

Tatius dies quickly in Ovid's narrative; there is nothing of the tradition that he was killed after some breakdown in relations between his people and those of Lavinium. Romulus is now the *sole* ruler of both Romans and Sabines (there is just a hint of the dual consuls in the joint rule of Romulus and Tatius). Soon enough, Mars decides that the time has come for his son's apotheosis, and he makes an appeal to his father Jupiter. Here, as with so much else in early Roman mytho-history, the matter is vexed. The two traditions were essentially these: either Romulus was taken up to heaven as a god, or he was murdered by senators who were angered at his increasingly autocratic tendencies. In poetry, it seems that the last episode in Book 1 of Ennius' *Annales* was the deification of Romulus; he may well have been the inventor of the tradition. As with Aeneas, so with Romulus the end is shadowy and obscure. Ovid deals with the apotheosis both here and at *Fasti* 2.475-512, where the whole business of the murder is dismissed as a falsehood.

Res Romana valet, Mars says (14.809), and Rome's power is no longer dependent on one man (*nec praeside pendet ab uno*)—an interesting comment in the context of the Augustan Age, as we shall see. We have been used to speeches back and forth between Jupiter and his daughter and wife; appropriately, at this key moment in early Roman history, we see a rare speech from the war god who sired Rome's progenitor. Mars reminds Jupiter of the promises he made at a council of the gods; Ovid's Mars is asking Jupiter and the audience to remember their Ennius. Jupiter, of course, agrees to the apotheosis, and Mars prepares to descend to earth in his chariot and take up his son.

The god finds Romulus on the Palatine, where he is giving laws:

reddentemque suo iam (*or* non?) regia iura Quiriti
abstulit Iliaden . . . (14.823-824)

as he was giving royal laws now (or *not royal laws?*) *to his Quirites,*
[Mars] *stole away the son of Ilia* . . .

The textual problem is serious here; *non* is almost certainly the correct reading, which would have Ovid depicting Romulus as giving laws that are not regal to his *Quirites*: the Sabine element alive and well.[70] *Non* is the *difficilior lectio* here, and must be right; the point is that Romulus is not a king. Roman power may depend now on one man, Mars had said to Jupiter, but the one man is also not a king. Again, in an Augustan context the word has great significance— Romulus' partner Tatius is dead, he is giving laws alone—but he is *not* a monarch.

Romulus ascends with his father, and his mortal part vanishes, not by some watery purification like Glaucus or Aeneas, but in an appropriately martial way (and note that Romulus, unlike Aeneas, rises heavenward)—his mortal body disappears like a leaden bullet that vanishes in the air, now melted away, once shot from a sling (14.824-826). The simile is *Lucretian* (cf. *De Rerum Natura* 6.177-179 and 306-308), and deliberately so: we are moving towards an Augustan, and a Lucretian world.

In a brilliant display of the unity of his poem, Ovid links the present passage to an much earlier one, *M.* 2.726-729, where *the same simile* described Mercury's passion for *Herse.* And now, right upon the apotheosis of Romulus, Ovid introduces his wife *Hersilie.*[71] Livy (*Ab Urbe Condita* 1.11.2) calls her a Sabine and Romulus' wife; the story of her apotheosis may be unique to Ovid. Hersilie is overcome with grief over the loss of her husband (there may be just a hint here of the tradition that he was murdered). Juno sends Iris—and how fitting that Juno is involved in this key passage, given Hersilie is Sabine—and the whole scene rather rehabilitates Juno for those troubled by her apparent rancor against the Romans in the manner of playing with locks. Juno's Iris is to invite Hersilie to come to the Quirinal, to a grove on the hill (14.836 *duce me lucum pete*). Iris is to note that there is a temple there to the *king of Rome* (837 *templum Romani regis*), which has bothered commentators after the *non regia iura*—but Romulus is now Quirinus, not his mortal, non-regal self, which melted away like airborne lead.

The goddess of the rainbow obeys, and makes her approach to the Sabine Hersilie (14.838 ff.). Hersilie is suitably modest as she follows Iris to the Quirinal. A star descends from heaven; Hersilie's hair bursts into flame. Quirinus receives her into heaven, and she is joined to him as a goddess—*Hora Quirini.*[72] Her hair bursts into flame just as Virgil's Lavinia, Iulus, and Augustus all have the same fiery locks.

As in the twelfth *Aeneid*, so here Juno has her surprise: the Sabine Hersilie will be deified too, and she will join Romulus in nuptial bliss as a new pair of eminently Roman divinities, Quirinus and his companion, the Hora Quirini. To describe the transformation of Romulus from mortal, non-regal lawgiver to divine king, Ovid deliberately—and subversively—uses a Lucretian simile, a simile Lucretius uses twice in fact, in a wonderful acknowledgement of the haunting presence that the Epicurean poet exercises over Ovid's whole epic of transformation: there is no Quirinus, no Hora Quirini, and the glorious vision of Roman-Sabine apotheosis is, after all, a beautiful lie.

But we are very close now to the end, and the evocation of Lucretius as the lynchpin of the divine union and nuptial apotheosis of Romulus and Hersilie opens the door for the poet's last book. Therein we shall gaze on Rome's future, as Ovid unfolds the most important of his transformations, and prepares for the stunning vision of his own personal challenge to the confident self-assurance of Horace, as well as the laughing ghost of Lucretius.

Notes

1. Best now for commentary is the 2009 Cambridge "green and yellow" of K. Sara Myers.

2. *Theogony* 1011-1016, where see West; in Virgil, Circe's abode is localized half-way between the Tiber's mouth and Cumae. See further Myers ad 14.9-10, and Horsfall on the opening of *Aeneid* 7.

3. Caieta is balanced by Camilla at the book's end.

4. See further my "Chiastic Doom in the *Aeneid*," *Latomus* (2009).

5. The reason for this is mostly structural; Ovid would have been hard pressed to de-tail the fall of Troy, only then to move on to a dual return, describing Odysseus' wander-ings as well as Aeneas'.

6. *Ars Amatoria* 2.103-104.

7. On this important theme see further Myers ad 14.27.

8. 14.36 *ulciscere*; note Myers, and Bömer, for this key word, which can mean both to take vengeance on and to give someone their just desserts. But it is a very strong word (cf. 13.546, of Hecuba's decision to avenge Polydorus, indicative of Circe's maddened state of love).

9. Note Myers ad 14.49-50.

10. Note Myers ad 14.59-67.

11. *Odyssey* 12.90—sometimes Homer is more excessive in his descriptions than Ovid. Note also Austin ad *A.* 6.286, of the "Scyllas" at the entrance to the underworld.

12. *Aeneid* 3.416-432; 684-686.

13. Though this is not certain; see further Austin ad loc.

14. On the whole vexed question of Ovid's retelling of Virgil's third *Aeneid*, note Casali, Sergio, "Correcting Aeneas' Voyage: Ovid's Commentary on *Aeneid* 3," in *Transactions of the American Philological Association* 137 (2007), pp. 181-210,

15. I have speculated elsewhere that Neptune causes the sound of water crashing on the rocks so as to drown out the Sirens' voices; note *A.* 5.867 *tum rauca adsiduo longe sale saxa sonabant*. For a full discussion of the whole problem see my forthcoming *Princeps ante omnis* article in the 2011 *Latomus*, as well as *Chiastic Doom*.

16. *Historia Naturalis* 3.6.82; he notes that the real etymology was from the multi-tude of pottery factories in the locale.

17. See further Bömer, and Myers, ad loc.

18. *A.* 6.162 ff., where see Austin.

19. Which, in a marvelous Virgilian trick, leaves the Palinurus question unre-solved—for we know that he, too, was not buried. Apparently Misenus' body *must* be buried, while Palinurus' can be ignored. Cf. Marcellus (especially his grand Augustan tomb). Pallas, of course, will receive a solemn requiem at the beginning of *A.* 11; Palinu-rus is never buried.

20. 1.2.18. Myers does not address the possible discrepancy.

21. Note Bömer, F., "Aeneas landet bei Cumae: zu Verg. *Aen.* VI.2 und Ovid *Met.* XIV.102 ff.," in *Gymnasium* 93 (1986), pp. 97-101.

22. *OLD* 4c.

23. Here, as throughout, I expect the reader to be familiar with my arguments on the Bough from *Madness Unchained*.

24. *Carpere*, as we have seen, is a notoriously vague word; in a nice touch, Ovid uses it to describe not the Sibyl's instructions regarding the Bough, but rather Aeneas'

taking his leave of the underworld: 14.122 *dumque iter horrendum per opaca crepuscula carpit.*

25. And we might note that in neither Virgil nor Ovid does Aeneas find the Bough on his own.

26. *Aeneid* 6.125-129.

27. Virgil has two characters in the *Aeneid* who are identified only by patronymic: Achaemenides, and a victim of Camilla, the lying Aunides. The presence of the characters' deceptive qualities is announced by their lack of direct name, as if they were concealing some secret. The deceptive Achaemenides is a substitute for Odysseus, himself notoriously fallacious.

28. Hence Achaemenides makes lavish praise of Aeneas before starting his story: he is firmly a man of Aeneas now (and understandably so).

29. Also bears, which has occasioned much critical comment; on this ursine matter see Horsfall, and Myers.

30. On this complex figure see Mackay, T. S., "Three Poets Observe Picus," in *The American Journal of Philology* 96 (1975), pp. 272-275.

31. For the whole episode see Fordyce, and Horsfall ad loc.

32. Hesiod, *Theogony* 1011-1013, where see West.

33. See Myers ad 14.308-434.

34. 14.324-325 *nec adhuc spectasse per annos / quinquennem poterat Graia quarter Elide pugnam*; Courtney is probably right (*apud* Myers) that the reference underscores Picus' love of equestrian pursuits.

35. The text has caused problems because of the failure to accept (or understand) Janus' Greek origins.

36. The point is to underscore how with Glaucus, he had approached her first; here, she sees Picus and approaches him. The Italian hunter may also just be more attractive to her than the marine god.

37. Virgil's Gate of Horn (Latin *corneus*) is an adjectival rendering of Homer (and Plato's) κέρας, "horn" (Homer does not specify which animal horn is meant); this *corneus* is rare, though classical. But there is also *corneus* = "of cornel-wood," also Virgilian (and with no difference in any vowel quantities), and the two words clearly echo each other.

38. I would suggest that a parallel possibly exists between both of them as victims of metamorphosis: the avian Picus and the lupine Camilla.

39. On the whole matter see Rosivach, V., "The Genealogy of Latinus and the Palace of Picus," in *Classical Quarterly* 30 (1980), pp. 140-152, and Moorton, R., "The Genealogy of Latinus in Vergil's *Aeneid*," in *Transactions of the American Philological Association* 118 (1988), pp. 253-259.

40. Achaemenides, the man of woe, found peace; Macareus, the man of blessing, also knew peace, though not, perhaps, exactly what he expected—there is great significance in the fact that he refused to go on with his fellow Greeks.

41. Cf. Aeneas with Dido. Of course, divine intervention helps.

42. A comprehensive study of *coniugium* in Augustan poetry is a *desideratum*. Virgil significantly makes Circe the *coniunx* of Picus, and of course there are Dido-Aeneas and Turnus-Lavinia.

43. For Diomedes and Daunus, note Antoninus Liberalis 37.

44. *Iliad* 5.297-349.

45. Lycophron has an account of the avian metamorphosis (*Alexandra* 594-611); there are some fragmentary testimonia as well.

46. See Hardie ad loc.

47. On Virgil's Lavinia, with reference to other appearances of the character in literature, see my *"Laviniaque venit litora*: Blushes, Bees, and Virgil's Lavinia," in *Maia* (2008).

48. *A.* 7.411-413, where see Fordyce, and Horsfall.

49. And the force of *barbarus* works well whether we prefer *ensis* or *ignis* here. Heinsius did not like this; he misguidedly conjectured *Dardanus*. Tarrant prints *ignis*, but notes the reading *ensis* may well be right (*"fortasse recte"*).

50. It was a mere bywater by the late Republic and essentially a ghost town in the Augustan Age; see further Myers ad 14.573-580.

51. See further Ogilvie's extensive notes here.

52. Note Skutsch ad *Annales* 8.15-16.

53. See Nisbet and Rudd ad loc.

54. See Myers ad 14.581-582 for the possibility that in Aeneas' *virtus* we are supposed to see an emphasis on a *Stoic* hero, which would fit very nicely indeed with our reading of Ovid's movement towards an Epicurean ending for his epic. In the poet's last book, we shall come to see how the threefold arrangement of his epic is a response to the triple division of Horace's odes, and that in contrast to his lyric predecessor, Ovid was, however unwillingly, compelled to surrender to Lucretius' dark vision.

55. Ogilvie ad Livy, *Ab Urbe Condita* 1.1.10.

56. Livy, *Ab Urbe Condita* 1.3.2, where see Ogilvie; note Myers ad 14.609.

57. For the story note Dionysius of Halicarnassus 1.71.3, and *Fasti* 4.50, with Fantham's notes.

58. On this lore see Littlefield, D., "Pomona and Vertumnus: A Fruition of History in Ovid's *Metamorphoses,*" in *Arion* 4 (1965), pp. 465-473, Gentilcore, R., "The Landscape of Desire: The Tale of Pomona and Vertumnus in Ovid's *Metamorphoses,*" in *Phoenix* 49 (1995), pp. 110-120, Johnson, W. R., "Vertumnus in Love," in *Classical Philology* 92 (1997), pp. 367-375, Lindheim, S., "I am Dressed, Therefore I am? Vertumnus in Propertius 4.2 and in *Metamorphoses* 14.622-771," in *Ramus* 27 (1998), pp. 27-38, and Jones, P., "Aversion Reversed: Ovid's Pomona and her Roman Models," in *The Classical World* 94 (2001), pp. 361-376. On the Propertian elegy note especially Hutchinson ad loc.

59. Varro, *De Lingua Latina* 5.46.

60. Note Skutsch ad Ennius, *Annales* frs. 116-118, on the *flamen Pomonalis*, instituted by Numa; see further Myers ad 14.622-771.

61. Myers ad 14.623-624 points out that hamadryads are exceedingly rare in Latin poetry, occurring only ten times from Catullus 61 to Statius' *Silvae* 1; she wonders if they have association with Gallus' verse. In the *Met.*, Myers notes that only Callisto, Syrinx, and Pomona are of this class, though I would not push any connections too far.

62. Cf. Propertius c. 4.2.31 *mitra*, which has inspired Ovid here.

63. The text of 14.671 is vexed, and offers one of the more interesting examples of textual problems in the epic. *Nec coniunx timidi aut audacis Ulixis* has presented problems; *audacis* may be fine to describe Odysseus, but *timidi?* Some prefer to read *nimium tardantis*, which does not quite work in my view; Tarrant does not offer a solution (nor Anderson). See further Possanza, M., "Penelope in Ovid's *Metamorphoses* 14.671," in *The American Journal of Philology* 123 (2002), pp. 89-94. I would suggest that the manuscripts are correct, and that the text must stand: Odysseus was a maze of contradictions, among them his timidity and his audacity. When Glaucus rejected Circe, his beloved Scylla was punished. When Picus rejected Circe in favor of Canens, he was

changed into a woodpecker. Odysseus knew when to give in to love, even when it meant infidelity; unlike Glaucus and Picus, he surrendered himself to Circe, and for a long year, like Aeneas with Dido. This means that he was *fallax* to his wife, as suits his character; he was duplicitous and thus his infidelity should not come as a surprise. But he was also *timidus* in that he feared the retribution of Circe: this makes sense in light of Ovid's narrative, where Odysseus is contrasted with the two men who refuse to accede to the goddess' bed. This is the wonderful paradox; Odysseus was wise to have an affair with Circe, though this does not make him faithful to his wife (quite the opposite), and it does mean that he is less brave—for all his daring (*audacis*)—than Glaucus and Picus. There may also be a hint of his preferred nocturnal exploits, though, as we saw in the debate for the arms, he would assert that night raids carry more danger.

64. Note Myers' especially good remarks on this reappearance ad 14.694.

65. The story at Antoninus Liberalis 39 of Arceophon and Arsinoe is a similar exploration of the theme. The story is there attributed to Hermesianax. No connection seems to exist between the Iphis/Anaxerete story and that of Iphis and Ianthe from earlier in the epic.

66. 14.739 *aperire iubentem*, Shackleton Bailey's brilliant conjecture for *et multa timentem*.

67. See Bömer, and Myers, ad loc.; an attestation in Plutarch of a statue of a "peeking" woman in Cyprus is the only other evidence.

68. See Skutsch ad *Annales* 1.39, and Myers ad 14.772-775.

69. See the commentators ad loc. for the controversy over the spelling (Palilia *vs.* Parilia) and resulting etymologies.

70. See Myers ad 14.823 for the folk etymology and relevant notes.

71. See Myers ad 14.830-831 for the spelling of the name (Greek *vs.* Latin), where the use of a Greek spelling by Ovid, if textually sound, may emphasize the same theme we have noted before—the assimilation of foreign elements. Ovid may also want to underscore the connection to Herse in the second book of the poem, since she balances Hersilie in this second-to-last book.

72. Note Skutsch ad Ennius, *Annales* 1.99-100.

Chapter XV

Meanwhile There is Sought . . .

In a marvelous display of the unity of his epic, near the end of Book 14 Ovid introduced a simile borrowed from Lucretius to describe the apotheosis of the Roman progenitor Romulus, just as near the end of Book 2 he had used the very same Lucretian image, in a quite different context. Mercury's love for Herse has been transformed into Romulus' for Hersilie; as the penultimate book of the epic ended, we were left with the glorious vision of the new god Quirinus and his wife, the Hora Quirini, now enthroned in heaven—but with the celebration tainted, as it were, with a Lucretian simile to keep our flights of fancy grounded in Epicurean realities.

Book 14 ends with no indication of what will follow. The poem's last book opens at once with a wonderful evocation of two major themes borrowed from Virgil, themes that are the heart of the Augustan Ovid's philosophical and political concerns.[1] The first theme follows quite naturally from the deification of Romulus:

> quaeritur interea qui tantae pondera molis
> sustineat tantoque queat succedere regi. (15.1-2)

> *There is sought, meanwhile, who could hold up the weight of*
> *such a mass, and who could succeed so great a king.*

Ovid could not be plainer in his language; this is the succession theme, one of the most pressing questions for the Augustan regime. In the quest for Romulus' successor, the anxiety in the Augustan realm over who would replace the *princeps* is foreshadowed. *Molis* echoes the opening of Virgil's *Aeneid*; Rome has been founded, and at tremendous effort; who can sustain its burden? The theme of the *pondera*, the weight of Rome, had also been a concern of Ovid's, especially in the image of the Titan Atlas sustaining the globe—heavier once, for example, Hercules was deified. The end of the *Metamorphoses* rings back to the beginning of the *Aeneid*.

Numa is chosen as the next Roman king; we might note that in 15.2 *regi*, Ovid makes clear that we are now in the regal period, which, as we saw at the end of Book 14, Ovid seems to link to the apotheosis of Romulus: surely the

431

successors of a god ought to be kings.² Numa is a Sabine, but he is not content with knowledge of Sabine lore. Here Ovid introduces his second major theme:

> . . . animo maiora capaci
> concipit et, quae sit rerum natura, requirit. (15.5-6)

> . . . *in his capacious mind, he conceives*
> *greater things, and he asks what is the nature of things.*

In the wake of his Lucretian simile, Ovid makes explicit his great Epicurean theme: Numa seeks to know about the nature of the universe. Numa is in search of a *De Rerum Natura.*

In order to pursue his philosophical goals, Numa leaves his fatherland and Cures (15.7 *patria Curibusque relictis*), an interesting phrase that allows us to read *patria* as Rome and Cures as a separate place—though Numa is, after all, Sabine and we might want to take the expression as a hendiadys for Sabine territory. I would suggest instead that Numa, the Sabine king, is imagined now as eminently Roman, and Rome is his *patria.* Numa travels to the "city of Herculean hospitality," Croton in the far south of Italy.³ Numa wants to know who founded a Greek city in Italy, and he is told by an aged local of how Hercules enjoyed the hospitality of Croton and predicted that one day Croton's descendants would have a city on the spot. Here we see more of the theme of assimilation; Numa, the Sabine who is now Rome's king, the monarch of a combined Roman-Sabine kingdom, is curious about the Greeks of southern Italy.

The old man continues to tell Numa of how one Myscelus, from Argos, was warned in a dream by Hercules that he must travel to Croton; the problem was that the death penalty applied to anyone who tried to change his country voluntarily.⁴ Diodorus Siculus (8.17) mentions this Myscelus in his universal history; there he is a Greek who consults the Delphic oracle about the birth of children. He is told to travel to Croton in that account too. Ovid's Myscelus hesitates, but a second Herculean dream persuades him to leave; he is caught and prosecuted (15.30 ff.). He is certain to be condemned and executed, when he prays to Hercules; the god secures his release, and Myscelus is soon on his way to the toe of Italy. After he arrives safely, he visits the tomb of Croton and founds a city nearby.

All of this, as the learned audience would come to realize as these prefatory matters unfold, is prelude to the appearance of Pythagoras. Ovid did not invent the idea that Numa learned of the teachings of the great philosopher from Samos. Livy knows of the tradition;⁵ he notes that some held that Numa had learned his beliefs from Pythagoras. Livy dismisses the whole idea on chronological grounds: Numa is usually dated to 715-673 B.C., whereas Pythagoras lived c. 530 B.C. Livy is contemptuous of the notion that there was any connection; he asks how Pythagoras' teachings could ever have reached the Sabines, given problems of language and geography. Pythagoras, the old man tells Numa, had fled Samos because of hatred of tyranny and had settled in Croton, where he began to teach.[6]

Croton was associated with composers of Orphic poems;[7] the relationship between the Orphics and the Pythagoreans—if indeed they are to be considered separate entities—is difficult if not impossible to disentangle. Neither Orphics nor Pythagoreans ate meat, and this major theme of vegetarianism will be the old man's first concern in his disquisition to Numa; it will, in fact, ring his discourse and serve as its main topic. Pythagaros, the old Crotonian says, taught about the causes of things and what nature is (15.68 *et rerum causas, et, quid natura, docebat*); Lucretius lurks here, of course: the Pythagoreans were interested in rational causes for things and scientific explanations, mathematics and the like (in contrast to the Orphics, who we might call more mythological in their interests). But rationality aside, the Pythagoreans, like the Orphics, believed in the purification of the soul and very un-Epicurean things indeed. The Pythagoreans were motivated by the same concerns as the Epicureans; the conclusions they reached were very different indeed.

With vegetarianism, Pythagoras suffers his first defeat; he was learned, the old man notes (15.73-74 *ora . . . docta*), but he was not believed (*sed non et credita*) in the manner of abstaining from meat. The idea was that abstinence from flesh was a sign of the Golden Age, when men did not bury another's viscera in their own innards (88 *heu quantum scelus est in viscera viscera condi*). There is an interesting textual problem that vexes Ovid's passage where he has the old man tell Numa about the end of vegetarianism:

> . . . postquam non utilis auctor
> victibus invidit, quisquis fuit ille, deorum
> corporeasque dapes avidum demersit in alvum (15.103-105)

> . . . *after a not useful author*
> *envied the food, whoever he was, of the gods*
> *and sent bodily feasts down into a greedy belly*

Deorum has occasioned controversy; at 127-129, Ovid notes that men implicated the gods in their sin by claiming the immortals loved sacrificial offerings.[8] The genitive has been variously emended; *leonum* is popular, also *ferorum*; Heinsius preferred *priorum*.[9] I think the point is not sacrificial offerings, but rather the fact that Saturn—despite his patronage of the Golden Age—was also a devourer of his children (albeit an unsuccessful one). That does not explain the plural, but it seems difficult to believe that the Pythagoreans were unaware of the fact that the god of the Golden Age also practiced a form of cannibalism.

Ovid is using one of his favorite devices here, as he has an old man speak to Numa the words of Pythagaros; the long digression on why meat should never be consumed is reminiscent of Lucretius' history of primitive humanity in *De Rerum Natura* 5.[10] Man learned the gift of agriculture (we recall Ceres and Triptolemus from the end of *Metamorphoses* 5); soon thereafter, man started killing the very animals that aided him in farming. While vegetarianism was a key feature of Pythagorean dogma, the length to which the old man devotes attention to the master's teaching has something of the effect of parody: we have moved from the glorious scene of Romulus and Hersilie, enthroned in heaven, to asking what sheep did to merit slaughter, given they provide us with lovely wool and sweet milk.[11] Numa had gone to learn about the nature of things; he has thus far learned why he should eat grass instead of goats. And, as Virgil did in the sixth *Aeneid*, Ovid uses distinctly Lucretian language, with echoes of the Epicurean philosopher, to undercut what the old man reports of Pythagoras' teaching. The audience knows of a very different sort of philosophy, expressed in similar language.

And, of course, there is the fact that meat must be avoided because a man's soul might be housed in an animal's flesh as part of the process of purification and rebirth into new bodies (this is something of what the Glaucus story in Book 13 is mocking). Animals may become men, provided that they were originally men at some point in the long chain of renewals and the pursuit of the ultimate attainment of a definitively purified state (cf. the Stoic desire to rise up into the ethereal fire, and the *Herculean* (= Stoic) stamp with which the Croton episode began).

We now see more clearly why Ovid's epic is so concerned with transformations of humans into animals. The fables of mythology about the metamorphoses occasioned by the gods for all manner of offenses—and, quite often, for no apparent offense at all—merely reflect what the Orphics taught; men can be reborn as animals, and so in the animals we see, there may well be a man lurking—therefore, one should abstain from eating its flesh lest one become a Tereus or some Laestrygonian cannibal.[12] In retrospect, after almost fifteen books of change, so many of them involving animals, we see how Ovid has prepared for this lengthy speech on why animals must be spared from human tables. Trees and plants are acceptable, of course: whenever anyone tried to violate a sacred tree where some nymph might dwell, there was usually a warning; from Daphne to Dryope, trees are held in special reverence—at least certain trees. Small wonder that when Erysichthon chopped down a sacred arbor, he was punished with undying hunger. And no Orphic or Pythagorean, after all, taught that a man could ever be reborn as a plant. Certain trees are sacred and easily enough avoided by pious men (poor Dryope notwithstanding). But any common animal might be a reborn human, and so the devout Pythagorean will avoid consumption of its flesh. Quietly and subtly, Ovid reveals a major theme that he has been aiming at throughout his epic: the frequent animal metamorphoses from throughout the poem are now given a Pythagorean relief.

Animals are our fellow co-workers, Pythagoras emphasizes, and when you consume their flesh, you consume your own fellow laborers (15.141-142 *cumque boum dabitis caesorum memora palato, / mandere vos vestros scite et sentite colonos*). The point—which Ovid repeats in his reported discourse—is that the servant animal may well hold a soul that was once human.

A god inspires me, Pythagoras is imagined to say (15.143 *deus ora movet*), and so the philosopher will open Delphic secrets: Apollo was, after all, a patron god of the Pythagoreans (reconciled with the Bacchus of Orphic cosmogony). This patronage was not the invention of Ovid or the Augustans, but could not be denied; if suppressed, the tradition lurked too powerfully to be forgotten by a learned audience. Pythagoras' language could not be more Lucretian, and, for that matter, more evocative of the great revelation of future Roman history at the end of the sixth *Aeneid*:

> . . . iuvat ire per alta
> astra, iuvat terris et inerti sede relicta
> nube vehi validique umeris insistere Atlantis
> palantesque homines passim et rationis egentes
> despectare procul trepidosque obitumque timentes
> sic exhortari seriemque evolvere fati. (15.147-152)

> . . . *it is pleasing to go through the high*
> *stars, it is pleasing, with the lands and the inert seat having been left behind*
> *to be carried on a cloud and to stand on the shoulders of strong Atlas*
> *and to look down from a distance on men wandering everywhere below*
>   *aimlessly and*
> *lacking reason, nervous as they fear death, and*
> *thus to exhort them and to unfold the series of fate.*

Lucretian language, then, announces a most un-Lucretian song, just as Virgil did in his underworld book, where Orphic and Pythagorean teachings were most useful in having Anchises describe to Aeneas the future Rome: souls would be reborn into other bodies, and those new bodies would be the great luminaries of Rome's destiny. The history lesson is accurate; from the vantage point of Augustan Rome, all of Virgil's vision was undeniably true. But the mechanism by which Anchises reported the future to his son in Elysium was false in light of Lucretian poetics and philosophy.

All philosophical systems have their origin, I would argue, in explaining away the fear of death, and Pythagoras takes that fear as the starting point for the theory of metempsychosis, or the transmigration of souls.[13] This was not the way in which Anchises introduced the same material to Aeneas, since the audience was quite different; Aeneas wondered, in fact, why anyone would want to live twice and experience rebirth. The Homeric hero, after all, often considers blessed the one who died in battle and did not live to experience the horrors encountered on the long and perilous return. The body does not suffer any further pain after death, Pythagoras says (of course the new body the soul inhabits can, but that is not the philosopher's point)—the soul is immortal. Pythagoras announces that he himself has experienced this reincarnation; he was Panthoüs' son Euphorbus, slain by Menelaus at Troy.[14] Euphorbus had been the first to wound Patroclus; the story of his reincarnation is not new to Ovid, but can be paralleled at, e.g., Horace c. 1.28.10-13.[15] Pythagoras was said to have been many people in past lives; the philosopher claims that he has even seen a shield he once owned (in his life as Euphorbus) in a temple of Juno at Argos (15.163-164), another tradition Ovid borrowed.[16]

Lucretius taught that the atoms cannot die, though their fortuitous combinations do perish, and with that perishing comes the death of what was before. Pythagoras sounds like Heraclitus as he announces that all things flow (15.178 *cuncta fluunt*, an exact translation of Heraclitus' famous dictum), that time itself is like a river in motion—nothing persists (177 *nihil est toto quod perstet in orbe*). This is in direct contravention of Lucretius' beliefs about the permanent nature of the atoms; for Pythagoras, the only constant is constant change.

Pythagoras further underscores how nature changes with an odd set of astronomical comparisons. The heavens do not look the same, he notes, when it is midnight and when it is noon; the sun does not have the same color at dawn as at its zenith. Diana, too, has her changing phases (15.186-198). Indeed, the sun and moon and the celestial array are always in motion, but they do return to their original phases and forms. Ovid's Pythagoras (as reported by the old man to Numa, we should remember) uses the events in heaven as introduction to the four seasons, which he links to the ages of man's life (199-213). This is all borrowed from Pythagorean teaching, at least as reported in our admittedly scanty sources.[17]

The speech continues in the Lucretian didactic style, and in a section that is rather full of commonplaces that an Epicurean would not much mind; a man is born and grows and eventually ages, and in his dotage he laments the weakness of his body. Milon groans over the fact that his body is no longer powerful as it once was; Helen wonders how she could ever have been snatched away twice by lustful suitors (15.229-232).[18] The mention of Helen in a section on the passage of time may echo Lucretius' similar mention of Helen's abduction in his explanation of temporal phenomena (*De Rerum Natura* 1.473 ff.).[19]

At this point, Pythagoras' speech directly attacks Lucretian philosophy:

haec quoque non perstant, quae nos elementa vocamus,
quasque vices peragant, animos adhibete: docebo. (15.237-238).

These things also do not persist, which we call elements;
and to what changes they undergo, apply your minds: I shall teach you.

Here Ovid's Pythagoras begins his disquisition on Empedocles' four elements.[20] The lines criticize the Epicurean view of the permanence of the atoms, the *elementa* of nature; also, we might note that the phrase *animos adhibete: docebo* is taken verbatim from *Aeneid* 11.315, where it introduces Latinus' remarks at the great Latin war council (which Ovid had evoked often in recent movements of his epic). In that speech, Latinus offers to bestow land on the Trojans in Latium and make peace; Turnus, of course, will not be satisfied with the concessions, and Latinus does not address the key issue of Lavinia's marriage. The echo of the Virgilian passage is deliberate and no accident; the context is also intentionally evoked. By putting the words of the frail and ineffectual Latin monarch into Pythagoras' mouth as he prepares to attack Epicureanism by the celebration of Empedoclean doctrines, Ovid undercuts his philosopher. He is like the soon to be silenced Latinus, weakly and ineffectively making an address at the Latin war council during a burial truce.

Pythagoras outlines the four elements of earth, water, fire and air (15.239 ff.). These four elements are the source of everything in nature. The theme is not maintained for very long, and with nothing of the scientific precision we would expect if this were didactic epic. Ovid's Pythagoras instead moves on quickly to a summary of the idea that all things are always being made new, and that nothing stays the same. Ovid calls Nature the *Novatrix*, the woman who makes things new; this word, appropriately enough, may be his own invention. The fate of the atoms, the *elementa*, is what Lucretius would be most troubled by in the views expressed in this section. And *novatrix* neatly rings back to 1.1 *in nova*.

The discourse continues in much the same vein; all things change, so that land that was once water is changed in turn, and the ages pass from gold to iron (15.259 ff.).[21] In a brilliant touch, Ovid's Pythagoras mentions the Lycus, the great river that disappears underground for a while and then reappears, as an example of how things seem to appear and vanish as a sign of constant flux.[22] Lycaon, of course, was the first man punished in Book 1 of the epic, and the river's appearance (Lycus = "wolf") here forms a neat ring with the werewolf from the poem's first book (just as Herse-Hersilie linked Books 2 and 14); Lycaon became Lycus, as it were, when he was transformed from man into wolf (an example, Ovid's Pythagoras would say, of how nothing stays the same). Here, "Lycus" the river introduces a miniature catalogue of rivers that do not retain either their appearance or their qualities; there is something here of an echo of the catalogue of rivers that went to mourn with Peneus, Daphne's father, in Book 1—another nice linkage between the beginning and end of the epic.

Lands that were once islands are noted next, along with other geographical metamorphoses. Leucas, once continuous with the shore but now washed by waves, is among the more notable sites mentioned, given its significance to the Augustan regime and the battle at Actium (15.290-291). The commentators note an anachronism in that Ovid's Pythagoras mentions the loss of Helice under the waves caused by an earthquake;[23] this occurred in 373 B.C. and could not have been known to Pythagoras—another deliberate sign, I would argue, of the falsehood of the discourse which, like Virgil's Anchises' speech in the underworld of *Aeneid* 6, tells the truth in its enumeration of the future heroes of Rome, though according to an impossible philosophical system.

And there is a mountain near Troezen (15.296-306), where the ground swells because the force of the winds was once trapped in the earth, and the earth's tumescence is like that of a bladder one swells by breath, or the similar swelling of a goat's skin. Here, the ridiculousness of the comparison helps to undercut the argument. The argument has also become repetitive; Pythagoras announces, though, that a few more examples will suffice (308 *pauca super referam*). Here, two cases are given that are borrowed from Lucretius: the spring of Jupiter Ammon, and the fountain of Jupiter at Dodona.[24] In Ovid as in Lucretius, the two phenomena are listed one after the other (cf. *De Rerum Natura* 6.848-878, and 879-905).[25]

The Lucretian language, then, continues, though to a very different end from what the Epicureans would approve; Pythagoras notes that some waters can change not only one's body, but also one's mind—among them the waters of Salmacis' spring, where it is as if Ovid's Pythagoras is citing Ovid as a source for his doctrines. The waters near Clitor in Arcadia make one desire water instead of wine, either because there is some power in the water that is in opposition to wine (15.324 *seu vis est in aqua calido contraria vino*), or because of the story the locals tell, namely that the seer Melampus once cured the madness of the daughters of Amythaon and had them wash in the spring—thus infecting the waters with their fury (325-328). The point is similar to that of Pythagorean purgation and cleansing, and reminds us of the story of Midas with his quasi-Golden Bough that announced his own purifying bathing in the waters of the Pactolus, which stained that river with gold. In another Lucretian nod,[26] Ovid's Pythagoras notes that Etna was not always active, and will someday cease to erupt (15.340 ff.).

As the long discourse continues, then, the audience does well consider to the similar address of Anchises to Aeneas in Virgil's underworld—with the realization that the two speeches are quite different indeed. The address the old man relates to King Numa is slightly over four hundred lines, and we are well advanced through it, but there has been little on the transmigration of souls: metempsychosis and the process of the purification of the human soul after death, with its rebirth into new bodies. Instead, we have been treated to a lengthy disquisition in decidedly Lucretian language, most of the content of which would upset the Epicurean, while some of it would please (or at least not raise any objections). The address of Anchises to his son in Virgil also had Lucretian language, while the content was decidedly anti-Epicurean. But Ovid's Pythagoras began his talk with a warning about eating meat, the main point of which was, you might be committing cannibalism if there were some reborn human in your stew. That led to a repetitive and belabored point that all things change (the connection being, if you die and are reborn as a pig, you have changed your form). The principal objection an Epicurean would make to the whole business is the avowed belief that even the *elementa* of nature change—Lucretius would say that such an admission is nothing less than the beginning of the destruction of nature.

Ovid's Pythagoras says that there is a report that if you dip yourself nine times in the pool of Minerva somewhere in Hyperborean Pallene, you will sprout feathers (15.356-369); the ludicrous tale is not vouched for by Pythagoras (*haud equidem credo*), but he does note that there are women in Scythia who sprinkle their bodies and have the same result. At times Ovid is channeling Lucretius, at times Herodotus; here, a lengthy scientific section on Etna that just possibly makes one forget the nonsense about not eating animal meat lest you consume a fellow human is abandoned, and the fantastic returns: there are people who grow feathers because of a certain spring.

Pythagoras' speech continues, with an interesting shift:

sive fides rebus tamen est addenda probatis,
nonne vides . . . (15.361-362)

But if faith must nevertheless be given to things that have been tested,
do you not see . . .

Pythagoras goes on to note how we see small animals emerge from putrefying corpses.[27] Nobody, after all, has seen a Scythian sprout wings, let alone some denizen of Hyperborean Pallene (wherever that is imagined to be); here we have an example that can be verified from science, even if the mechanism for the apparent spontaneous generation is not entirely understood. Bees cannot be generated from the corpses of animals, though many ancients believed it to be the case, ignorant as they were of the biology involved. Buried horses do not give birth to stinging wasps (15.368), but white cocoons on trees do indeed give birth to butterflies (372-374). In this short section, after the unbelievable case of the waters that cause feather eruptions, Ovid's Pythagoras reports phenomena that do seem to take place, even if the reasons behind the "transformations" are not scientifically explicated to modern satisfaction. The apparent spontaneous generation of wasps from the bodies of horses and of scorpions from crabs can be paralleled in other sources;[28] these are not peculiarly Pythagorean beliefs, and they do not necessarily lend particular credence to the argument that the soul migrates from one body to another. These *exempla* are, rather, proofs of how things change—but the unavoidable conclusion one reaches is that it is as if a soul jumps from one body to another, as in the dead warhorse giving birth to vicious wasps.

At *De Rerum Natura* 2.865 ff., Lucretius argues that atoms have no sensation. The extant remains of Epicurus do not address this issue; the commentators speculate that Lucretius may have been eager to avoid attributing any sort of feeling to the atoms, since then death would have to be feared. But life, nonetheless, arises from these insensible things, Lucretius argues, just as we see spontaneous generation of worms, for example, from putrid manure (2.871-872). Ovid's Pythagoras is using the language of Lucretius, and, in some cases, the content would not be objectionable to an Epicurean: Lucretius had no problem asserting that living worms arose from insensible dung. But the Pythagorean view that the *elementa* themselves can undergo change would be repugnant to Lucretius and, further, the point of the whole discourse is supposed to be metempsychosis. We are still waiting for more information on that fundamental point of Pythagorean philosophy.

The quasi-scientific discourse continues; the peacock is born from an egg, as are doves and the eagle (15.385-388). Here, Ovid's Pythagoras touches on an etiology from Book 1 of the epic, from Ovid's story of Io's guardian Argus and how Mercury had subdued him, and how Juno had fixed his many eyes on the tail of her sacred bird. Pythagoras' story is more scientifically plausible, except that of course it is no story: who could believe a bird is born from an egg, unless you concede that all things change? This is no better or satisfactory an explanation than to say that a goddess created a new bird to remember her deceased favorite; Pythagoras is merely using example after example in a rambling speech to defend the notion of constant change and perpetual metamorphosis—the stuff of a *carmen perpetuum* on transformation, we might think.

Transmigration of souls requires two bodies, two receptacles for the immortal entity to make its move; there is one bird, Pythagoras says, that does not owe its life to another creature: the phoenix (15.391 ff.). Herodotus told the story of this magical bird (2.73) in a famous passage where the historian, as so often, expresses skepticism. The story is essentially the same in both Herodotus and Ovid. The phoenix lives for five centuries. After that long span of life, it retreats to a beautiful nest that is bathed in myrrh and sweet smells. It dies, and a new bird rises from the old by spontaneous generation. The new bird carries the dead father to the temple of the sun god. The child-bird is *pius* (405) as it carries its burden; we might think of Aeneas fleeing the city of Troy with his admittedly living father, and the arrival of Aeneas at the temple of Apollo in Cumae, before he visits his father's shade in the lower world.

The phoenix is an exception to the idea that souls migrate from one body to another, it would seem. It is also what Ovid's Pythagoras would call a "novelty" (15.408 *si tamen est aliquid mirae novitatis in istis*). Pythagoras uses the phoenix as an introduction to a strange, brief catalogue of other novelties. There is the hyena, which is sometimes a male, sometimes a female. The commentators note that this is the first appearance of the hyena in Latin literature; Pliny the Elder notes that some think the animal changes its sex in alternate years.[29] Even Aristotle did not believe this.[30] The chameleon changes its colors; the urine of lynxes hardens into little stones. Again, both of these phenomena—the one true, the other false—can be paralleled in Pliny and, no doubt, in sources now lost to us.

The phoenix may be a novelty of sorts, but the point of the phoenix's birth was supposed to be that there is one bird that does not take its body from another. That key difference between the phoenix and what preceded it in Pythagoras' long list of apparent types of the transmigration of souls is not highlighted in what follows in the description of this rare bird. Instead, the emphasis shifts to the *novelty* of the bird; there is nothing else like it. Then, in turn, Pythagoras prepares to conclude his speech by noting that he could spend the entire day (he nearly has) outlining all the things that have changed into new forms.

The phoenix changes into a new form, but without the aid of another—it repairs itself. Ovid's Pythagoras does not say that the phoenix is the only creature in the world that does this, rather that it is the only bird (15.392 *una est quae reparet seque ipsa reseminet ales*). The implication may be there that this is the only creature to be found in nature that has this ability; certainly Pythagoras does not mention any other with the same trait. The phoenix not only creates itself anew from itself, but also exhibits admirable *pietas* towards its father. And its father's corpse is conveyed to the temple of the sun—a sort of happy change from the great journey of the sun god's son Phaethon from earlier in the epic, which ended in such disaster both for him and the world. And, just possibly, we may see Apollo in the sun, and, in the phoenix, an image of nothing less than Rome.

Times change, too; Pythagoras had already noted this commonplace, but now he recalls how Troy was once great and is now a ruin (15.420-425). Lines 426-430 have been condemned by some, following Heinsius; they detail how Sparta, Mycenae, Thebes and Athens have also all fallen. The lines have been criticized for anachronism and repetitiveness; the first charge is perhaps valid, while the second could be leveled at many other sections in Pythagoras' disquisition.[31] Here, the passage reads much better without them, as Pythagoras moves on to detail the rising power of Rome:

> nunc quoque Dardaniam fama est consurgere Romam,
> Apenninigenae quae proxima Thybridis undis
> mole sub ingenti rerum fundamina ponit:
> haec igitur formam crescendo mutat et olim
> immensi caput orbis erit . . . (15.431-435)

> *Now also the story is that Dardanian Rome is rising,*
> *which, next to the waters of the Tiber that was born from the Apennines*
> *is placing the foundations of things under a huge mass;*
> *this therefore by growing is changing its form, and one day*
> *will be the head of the immense world*

Pythagoras himself (436 *quantumque recordor*) remembers that Helenus had consoled Aeneas with the prophecy that so long as the son of the god (*nate dea*) was safe, Troy would not entirely fall.

Here, we have the beginning of the closest that Ovid's Pythagoras will come to a direct evocation of the content of Anchises' speech to his son Aeneas in Elysium. Rome is *Dardanian* here because in Virgil Anchises had begun his announcement of Rome's future with the *Dardaniam prolem* (A. 6.756). In Virgil, Anchises spoke of "what glory would follow the Dardanian offspring" (*Dardaniam prolem quae deinde sequatur gloria*), and what grandchildren would remain from the Italian race (*qui maneant Itala de gente nepotes*), a wonderful introduction to the glorious souls (*illustris animas*) that mark the history of Rome. The phraseology in Virgil is significant in that Anchises announces the *Italians* who are going to follow the Dardanian offspring (= Aeneas, most notably, and his son Ascanius, etc.). The glory that is Rome will come from Italy, not Troy; Anchises does not announce the future details of the reconciliation of Juno (which he would not have known), but he only sees Italian souls rising up, as it were, to new life—there is no rebirth, we might note, for Aeneas and Ascanius (or Anchises) in the future Rome. None of those three major figures are shown, because the souls that Anchises reveals are the ones waiting for new bodies—they are not the reincarnations of the great triad from Troy. For Pythagoras, Rome is Dardanian because it sprang from Dardanus' seed, Aeneas—it is also Dardanian because Pythagoras has come to southern Italy, and he is a Greek: he is rather ignorant of the Italians, and speaks like a Greek, with the Greek view of the birth of Rome from Aeneas, not Romulus. Thus there is no mention of Romulus in any of Pythagoras' survey of the rising growth of Rome, its change from the fall of Troy to being the new city that will be the mistress of the world. Pythagoras' discourse is firmly fixed in the world of a glorious Trojan renascence—though, as we shall see, he does make mention of a "son of Iulus" (15.447 *natus Iuli*), whose identity is left deliberately vague. Virgil's *Anchises*, we might note, was a Trojan exile—he would have little knowledge indeed of Rome—and yet he details a very Roman future, to be sure, to his son in Elysium. But unlike Pythagoras, Anchises was dead, and thus privy to more than the philosopher at Croton. This reality does serve to undercut Pythagoras' reliability as a witness. He remembers Helenus' predictions to Aeneas; in fact, that is his main source of information about the future rebirth of Troy as Rome. But his memory is not perfect, and his knowledge not complete; as he observes— 436 *quantumque recordor* is significant.

The origin of the prediction about Aeneas' future fame is ultimately the important passage at Homer, *Iliad* 20.293 ff., where Poseidon saves Aeneas from death at the hands of Achilles, noting that Aeneas is doomed—and would die absent divine intervention—since he listened to Apollo, who indeed told Aeneas not to give in to Achilles' threats. The Homeric passage is at the heart of the Virgilian sequence in *Aeneid* 9 where Phoebus Apollo urges Ascanius to *desist* from fighting; Aeneas' son will kill the braggart Numanus Remulus, but he will not be risked in further combat—the succession motif is too important to the Virgilian program. Apollo, the central god to the Augustan regime, is blamed by Poseidon in Homer for sending Aeneas to certain death; Poseidon laments that Aeneas listened to the god and is thus in need of help. Part of the Homeric point is that Aeneas should not display cowardly behavior; he clearly has the favor of the gods, and Apollo does not apparently actively wish the death of the son of Aphrodite—after all, Poseidon is able to rescue him without much fanfare, and without so much as a word to Apollo. Indeed, Homer's Apollo seems to be calling Aeneas to a heroic future indeed.

Everything changes, Pythagoras sang; the small become the great, and the great fall, as Troy once did. All of this long sequence of summation of metamorphosis began because Pythagoras enjoined his listeners not to eat meat. Otis and others have dismissed the vegetarian frame as merely that, a frame; as we shall soon see, Ovid will return to the meatless theme quickly enough, as Pythagoras' speech draws to its close. We should not eat meat because we might be consuming a friend or relative, perhaps even a great worthy from the past, now reborn in animal form. The seemingly ludicrous frame cannot be divorced from the contents it conceals. And the manner of the discourse is pointedly Lucretian, in imitation of Virgil's sixth *Aeneid* and the speech of Anchises to his son. But that speech was not in the least concerned with one's diet, and that discourse had far more to say about transmigration. Though Pythagoras was never named (Orpheus was), we learned more about metempsychosis in *Aeneid* 6 than we have in *Metamorphoses* 15.

Pythagoras does not explain how he remembers that Helenus made any predictions to Aeneas when Troy fell; we might even want to quibble and note that Helenus' great prediction in the *Aeneid* came at Buthrotum, not at the moment of Troy's fall. Here, too, the discourse is somewhat suspect, as signaled by the important *quantum recordor*. But the content—like that of Anchises' speech to Aeneas in Virgil's Elysium—is beyond reproach.

Numa traveled to southern Italy—we might recall Venulus' approach to Diomedes to seek Greek aid for Turnus against Aeneas—in order to learn of the nature of things. He went in search of a Lucretian song, and he has found one, though much of the content would greatly displease the Epicurean poet. In Book 13, Glaucus was purified by all the waters of the world and changed into a sea god; the episode evoked the process of rebirth through purgation that was a major part of Orphic and Pythagorean lore. But Ovid's Pythagoras has not exactly done justice to the tenets of his philosophy. Through almost four hundred lines now, the great bulk of his speech, he has unfolded a dogma of change—unobjectionable to Pythagoreans, to be sure—but he has omitted any sustained mention of the key tenet of his doctrine: *katharsis* or purification. This was central to Anchises' discourse to Aeneas; it is nearly absent from Ovid's Pythagoras. Here, instead, we have a Pythagoras who speaks in Lucretian language and avoids mention of purgation. In what amounts to a brilliant *tour de force*, after the great announcement of Lucretius' arrival, as it were, in the leaden pellet simile from the end of Book 14—where it is perhaps not fanciful to imagine that Ovid envisages Lucretius literally being shot into his narrative—the Augustan poet has introduced a Pythagoras who does not do justice, indeed perhaps harm, to his philosophy's cause. If there is sustained mockery and parody in the *Metamorphoses*, it may well be here, as Numa listens to four hundred lines that ultimately, we should not forget, begin and end with heartfelt explanations for why we should avoid eating meat.[32]

Ovid's Pythagoras recalls that Helenus had predicted to Aeneas that there would be a new home for the Trojans in a friendlier land (15.443 *externum patria contingat amicius arvum*), and that while other descendants would make the new city powerful, it would be a son of Iulus who would make Rome the mistress of the nations:

sed dominam rerum de sanguine natus Iuli
efficiet . . . (15.446-447)

*But one born from the blood of Iulus will make her
the mistress of things . . .*

Virgil has a passage in *Aeneid* 1 that is of ambiguous intepretation: Julius Caesar
or Augustus Caesar (*A.* 1.286-290). In the underworld vision from *Aeneid* 6,
Anchises mentions both Julius and Augustus explicitly. Here, in imitation of the
famous ambiguity from *Aeneid* 1, Ovid leaves it unclear who will make Rome
the world's master. This son of Iulus is destined for divinity, like Romulus; he is
just possibly meant to be none other than Romulus, though saying that Romulus
was born from Iulus' blood is perhaps difficult to justify. Pythagoras, mindful of
his own Trojan connection as the reincarnation of Euphorbus—rejoices in the
future glory of Rome, and notes that he is happy that the Greeks conquered
Troy, since it has led to the foundation of Rome: 451-452 *cognataque moenia
laetor / crescere et utiliter Phrygibus vicisse Pelasgos*).[33]

Even Ovid's Pythagoras is aware that he has gone on for some time, in a
speech that has filled almost half the book. He returns now to his main theme:
vegetarianism. The last lines of Pythagoras' address are devoted to the same
theme as the beginning; those who slaughter animals for food are only beginning
the path to greater crimes, murder and the like. Wool is permitted for clothing,
as he noted from the outset; again, there may be a bit of intentional humor here,
since, as we have noted, the use of wool was also problematic for some who
followed the sort of tenets we find expounded here. Pythagoras is clear; we are
not merely bodies, but also winged souls (15.457 *volucres animae*), and we can
fly into the bodies of wild animals—again, if you eat some cow or bird, you
might be consuming a relative or friend, no differently than if you were served
some banquet of Thyestes (462).[34] Again, it is as if the terrible myths of Lycaon,
Tereus, and the like have served as prelude to this lengthy injunction against
carnivores.

Numa returns from his visit to Croton; he is asked to assume the reins of the
state (15.481 *populi Latialis habenas*). He has a nymph for a wife, and the *Camenae* are his leaders (*ducibusque Camenis*). The question of who the Camenae
were in origin is much vexed; the matter was a subject of debate in antiquity.[35]
Some derived the name from *carmen* and considered the *Camenae* to be prophetic nymphs; they may have originally been the patron goddesses of springs
(some have tried even to connect "Numa" with the Numicus/Numicius and
make him a sort of water deity). Numa was a Sabine, though, it should be noted,
his name is also an Etruscan *praenomen*; we cannot be sure if the original name
was eventually rendered into Etruscan and then Latin. At a very early date, the
tradition developed that Numa was a priest-king, in contrast to the warrior Romulus; Numa brought Rome the great origins of its religious practice (15.483 *sac-
rificos docuit ritus*).[36] The whole *rapport* between Numa and Pythagoras, in

origin a Greek story, eventually became popular in Rome.[37] But, as we have noted, eventually the chronological problems became well known; there is a highly instructive story that in 181 B.C. a chest was discovered on the Janiculum that contained twelve books ascribed to Numa, with Pythagorean philosophy; the praetor Quintus Petilius ordered them destroyed.

In Ovid's rapid narrative, Numa dies and is greatly mourned; his wife Egeria—as yet unnamed—runs off in lament and finds herself in the dense forests of Aricia, where she stumbles upon the rites of Orestean Diana (15.485 ff.).[38] Here begins one of Ovid's most significant sequences, a passage that merits close study as key to much of the poet's program.

The cult of Diana at Aricia was originally administered by Latin communities; Rome was dominated by the Etruscans and was not one of the towns in question.[39] In Livy (*Ab Urbe Condita* 1.45.1), it is the Latin Servius Tullius who establishes a temple of Diana on the Aventine around 540 B.C. Significantly, in Livy the Latins assist the Romans in the erection of the temple, in admission of the fact that Rome was the capital: *ea erat confessio caput rerum Romam esse*. This is directly echoed in Ovid's language about Rome as mistress of the world; the cult of Diana on the Aventine was perhaps meant to establish Rome as a political power of greater weight than the Latin confederation at Aricia.[40]

In Ovid's narrative, the nymph intrudes on the rites and is quickly told by the "Thesean hero" (15.492) to stop her lament; he advises her that she can be calmed by hearing of the woes of others, and that while he wishes he did not have material for grief, his tale of trouble can console her. The Thesean hero is Hippolytus; he will tell the famous story of his death and rebirth.

At Virgil, *Aeneid* 7.761 ff., "Virbius" had been one of the heroes in the catalogue of Turnus' allies. In Virgil's account, Virbius was sent by his mother, Aricia, from the area around the groves of Egeria. Hippolytus was killed by Phaedra's wicked arts; the herbs of Asclepius and prayers of Diana restored him to life. But Jupiter was indignant that anyone should return from the dead— 7.770 *tum pater omnipotens aliquem indignatus ab umbris*. The phrase links to Virgil's description of both the death of *Camilla* and that of Turnus (they share the same death line with its famous *indignata sub umbras*, of their souls going to the lower world).[41] Asclepius is killed, but Trivia—Diana in her underworld manifestation as Hecate—gave the reborn Hippolytus to the nymph Egeria in the shady groves of Aricia. He lived a quiet life there, a Diana-like sylvan denizen, and was named *Virbius*—the Twice Man. He has a son, also named Virbius, with the nymph Aricia; that son is one of Turnus' allies (he is never mentioned in the *Aeneid* after the catalogue).[42] This younger Virbius is not mentioned elsewhere, and raises problems given "Hippolytus'" famous celibacy.[43]

Hippolytus-Virbius begins to tell his story to Egeria (15.497 ff.). He admits that it is difficult to believe, but he is the very son of Theseus, the stepson of Phaedra; if "Virbius" were in origin some local god of Latium, a deity who was imagined by creative thinkers to be Hippolytus himself, brought back to life, then the statement has special import. The story he tells is well known from Euripides' tragic treatment;[44] Seneca would also develop his own version of the drama (*Phaedra*). Hippolytus' horses are soon spooked by a great sea creature, some horned bull that rises from the water; the story of his death was used as explanation for the prohibition on horses from Diana's precinct, and may account for the great equestrian battle in *Aeneid* 11, where Camilla is a master equestrian but ultimately destroyed during a cavalry engagement.

Hippolytus describes his injuries to Egeria in gory detail; he asks if the nymph can possibly compare her sorrows to his (15.530-531 *num potes aut audes cladi conponere nostrae, nympha, tuam*). Hippolytus travels to the underworld, and life would not have been restored to him had Asclepius not worked his magic; Dis was indignant at the reversal of the natural order (535 *Dite indignante*), a neat response to the Virgilian passage about the indignant Jupiter who punished Apollo's son for restoring Hippolytus to life. Hippolytus says that he bathed his lacerated corpse in the waters of Phlegethon, which is the underworld river of fire; we might be tempted to see some sort of Stoic purgation, the *katharsis* of which Pythagoras had not spoken to Numa. It is not clear what happened to Hippolytus in Ovid's vision right after life was restored; Diana, the poet has Hippolytus relate, made her favorite older (539 *addidit aetatem*) and left no part of him recognizable (539-540 *nec cognoscenda reliquit / ora mihi*). This passage relates to how Hippolytus made the gory observation to Egeria that there was no part of his savaged body that could be recognized (528-529 *nullasque in corpore partes, / num potes aut audes cladi componere nostrae*). The implication is that Asclepius' action restored Hippolytus to life with his original (pre-accident) appearance.[45]

The story of Ovid's Hippolytus accords with the brief vignette from Virgil's *Aeneid* 7. Egeria, Ovid notes, was not consoled by the story; her grief over Numa was too great. Diana eventually pitied her and transformed the weeping woman into a spring. The nymphs are amazed at the goddess' power and the metamorphosis; Hippolytus-Virbius too is stunned. He is stunned, in fact, no less than as when some Etruscan ploughman saw a glob of earth begin to move and eventually take on human shape and became the Etruscan soothsayer Tages, who was responsible for teaching the Etruscans the art of prognostication.[46] Virbius is no less amazed than was Romulus, when he saw his spear suddenly erupting in leaves, transformed from a spear into a hardy tree.[47] And he is no less amazed than was Cipus, when he looked at himself in the water and saw horns spring from his head. This obscure story is found in fuller form in Valerius Maximus (5.6.3), where the praetor Genucius Cipus was leaving Rome when he began to sprout horns.[48] The answer was given to him that if he returned to Rome, he would be made king. He thus decided never to return to the city, rather than let Rome experience a king.

The three stories, briefly told in Ovid's allusive style, are of great significance, especially after the Hippolytus episode. The Hippolytus episode is shrouded in the political machinations of a Rome under Etruscan domination and the eventual ousting of the Etruscan element. The Diana cult at Aricia was not served by Rome because it was a Latin religious league, and Rome was then Etruscan. Eventually, the establishment of the Diana cult on the Aventine was as much motivated by political considerations as by religious sentiment. In Ovid's narrative, once Cipus sees the horns, he consults an Etruscan soothsayer—cf. the Tages story—and is told how he could be king of the Latin citadel (15.582 *Latiae . . . arces*). It is interesting (and perhaps not to be pushed too far) that the Etruscan soothsayer urges Cipus to accede to the kingship, hailing him as monarch; there may be a hint here of the Etruscan domination of Rome in the regal period. Romulus' story comes between the creation of the Etruscan art of prognostication and the chance of this praetor to become king; Romulus had been a lawgiver of what were probably *non regia iura*; his kingship came only after he became the deified Quirinus.[49] Rome, we might note, is in Ovid's vision almost implicitly a Republic from the earliest times; Ovid does not detail the coming of the Republic or the transition from a monarchy to the system of the annual consuls, but his language and presentation offer a definitely anti-regal view of early Roman history.

The scene Ovid paints is redolent with the spirit of the old Republic (15.590 ff.). Cipus calls an assembly of the Roman senate and alerts them to the presence of one who will make himself king unless he is driven into exile. Cipus says that this would-be monarch would have burst into the city of his own accord, had "we not stood in his way" (599 *sed nos obstitimus*). The phrase can be taken as poetic plural for singular, but it also refers to *we* as in, the senatorial body. Cipus calls for exile or even death: 599-602 *vos urbe virum prohibete, Quirites, / vel, si dignus erit, gravibus vincite catenis / aut finite metum fatalis morte tyranni.*[50] In a marvelous touch, Ovid's Cipus veils his head with laurel, sacred to Apollo and associated with both peace and victory.

The murmur that arises in the senate is as when the east wind—*trux*, just as Cipus' face was *trucem* as he averted his gaze from the walls of Rome (15.586, 603)—moves through a pine grove, or as when the sound of waves is heard from afar. The crow asks who the horn-bearing destined king might be; Cipus announces his identity and moves to remove his laurel, while, significantly, the people try to stop him—610 *populo prohibente*. The scene is reminiscent of Julius Caesar with Mark Antony and the famous attempt of the latter to crown his master king as a test of popular favor. The crowd of senators here does not want to imagine that Cipus must be driven away or even killed; he is clearly a champion of the Republic, a force against monarchy. The senate cannot stand to see Cipus dishonored, and so they replace the laurel on his head—a significant gesture of respect and honor—and they give him rural honor, allowing him as much land as could be plowed by a yoke of oxen in a single day. The horns that marked the presence of one who might be king are engraved on bronze pillars at the gates of Rome, as a permanent memorial of the episode.

The Cipus episode comes between the Hippolytus sequence and what amounts to its conclusion in some sense, namely the coming of Asclepius into the Roman pantheon (15.622). The Hippolytus story has its ultimate origins for

Ovid in the account of how Coronis, the ill-fated lover of Apollo, was the mother of the healer; in the matter of Hippolytus, Apollo's son helped his aunt Diana in restoring her favorite to life. The resurrection of Hippolytus connects to the issues we have seen surrounding what is fated or destined, and how the gods can work their will on behalf of favorites. This theme is also at the heart of the microcosmic drama of the eleventh *Aeneid*, and indeed the *Aeneid* as a whole. In the case of Hippolytus, Diana was able to save her favorite; Horace (c. 4.7) disagreed, however, with Virgil and Ovid. Virgil's Hippolytus has a son, Virbius, which is hardly in accord with Hippolytus' virginal purity; as we have noted, this may foreshadow the destructive influence of romantic attraction in the case of Turnus' feelings for Camilla.[51] Diana is able to save Hippolytus, but she cannot save Camilla (she can only see to it that Camilla is avenged, and that her body will be safe from despoiling). But the problem remains: if Hippolytus-Virbius could be saved, why not Camilla? And what does the end of Horace c. 4.7 add to the debate, where we read *infernis neque enim tenebris Diana pudicum / liberat Hippolytum, / nec Lethaea valet Theseus abrumpere caro / vincula Pirithoo* (25-28)?[52] Essentially, how did Virgil and Ovid read the Hellenizing attempt to link the local god Virbius with the Artemis legend?

At this point, Ovid announces the beginning of a great new theme; he invites the Muses to open Helicon as he prepares for the last movements of his long epic:

> Pandite nunc, Musae, praesentia numina vatum,
> (scitis enim, nec vos fallit spatiosa vetustas),
> unde Coroniden circumflua Thybridis alti
> insula Romuleae sacris adiecerit urbis. (15.622-625)

> *Open now, o Muses, the present divine powers of bards,*
> *(for you know, and spacious age does not deceive you),*
> *when the island washed round by the deep Tiber*
> *added the son of Coronis to the sacred things of Romulus' city.*

Ovid did not invoke the Muses *per se*, but all the gods in the brief proem to his *carmen perpetuum*; here he calls upon the maidens of Helicon to bless his song. The tale will be that of how the healer of Hippolytus, the son of the great god of the Augustan regime Apollo, came to have his cult brought to Rome.[53] But here, Asclepius, is, perhaps significantly, identified as the *son of Coronis*, and we may recall the *Coronae* (feminine noun, male entities) that arose from the ashes of the daughters of Orion (13.698), the daughters of the seven-gated *Thebes* (cf. the seven hills of Rome), the daughters who had given their lives in self-sacrifice.

Asclepius lost his life to save Diana's favorite; now the Muses will sing of how Apollo's son came to Rome as a god. Apollo had entrusted Asclepius to Chiron the centaur (cf. Achilles).[54] The centaur's daughter Ocyroe had predicted the death of Asclepius (because of indignant gods), and how the slain son of a god would himself become a god; now we see its fulfillment (and the neat association of Asclepius with the equine Chiron is an attractive balance to the equine Hippolytus). Now, Ovid will tell of how the son of Apollo was made a god in Rome—a fitting deity for a regime that celebrated Apollo as its patron.

Dira lues (15.626)—as in the sixth and final book of Lucretius' epic, which detailed the plague at Athens, so in Ovid the last book will have a plague, and now so close to the end. The plague is not Ovid's invention.[55] The Latins were falling victim to the devastation of the pestilence, and they sought the advice of the Delphic oracle. Apollo's cult site is filled with the presence of the god, and makes its response (637 ff.). The oracle reveals that the Latins need not have come so far for aid; they have a closer divinity that can help, the son of the god. They travel to Epidauros, the city opposite Athens that was famous for a temple to Asclepius, and they beg the Greek elders there to give them the succor of the god. The Epidaurians are conflicted; some do not think that assistance can be denied—which is of course not the same thing as saying that help should be offered, let alone willingly—while others do not want to surrender the god's power to the Latins. Night approached without resolution of the debate (651 ff.). In a dream, Asclepius appeared to one of the Romans in all his divine glory. The god has his snake emblem on his caduceus; he announces that he will transform himself into a snake, but of course a much larger and more impressive one than the present serpent. He will assume the form and size of a snake that befits the divine presence. The assembly of Greeks still does not know what to do; they gather and ask for divine assistance in resolving the dilemma. Suddenly, the huge snake appears and strikes fear in the hearts of all (675 *territa turba pavet*). The priest announces the god's presence and begs that he might help those who are gathered in his presence; the Romans—here the sons of *Aeneas* (682 *Aeneadae*)—make their prayers along with the Greeks. The snake prepares to wind his way to the Ausonian ship (693 *in Ausonia . . . rate*), a nice touch—the Latins are the sons of Aeneas, but the ship is eminently Italian; the sons of Aeneas (695 *Aeneadae*) rejoice that the god has blessed their ship with his presence and his *weight*—another mention of that commonplace of how the gods have bulk beyond mortal expectation. The Roman ship departs; it is crowned with garlands (696 *coronatae . . . navis*), a neat detail given that the god is the son of *Coronis*.

The ship makes its return to Rome from Greece (15.697 ff.). The trip is described at some leisure—on the sixth day, the boat reaches Italy, and Ovid indulges in a lengthy catalogue of all the places the ship skirts before it finally arrives at Antium (modern Anzio), where the snake disembarks and enters a temple of Apollo (722).[56] The reason for the stopover is a storm; the seas were calm when the ship set out, but rough weather forced a delay at Antium. Soon enough the journey recommences, and the snake-god arrives at the Tiber. Rome is now imagined as the head of the world: 736 *iamque caput rerum, Romanam intraverat urbem*. The god takes up his abode on the island in the middle of the Tiber, and without further ado puts an end to the Latin plague.

Lucretius' plague, of course, ended the poem abruptly and with such sud-

450

CHAPTER XV

denness that some have wondered if the poem is unfinished. The Athenians have so many dead that there is wrangling over the funeral pyres. Ovid had already described a great plague, at Aegina, and there is no repetition here of the epic stereotype of a mighty plague description. Instead, the whole matter is ended with Ovidian rapidity after an equally Ovidian digression over geography. The god must, after all, take possession in a sense of all Italy. Asclepius is a foreign cult, though he is a son of Apollo (and he is no Cybele, after all)—but *Caesar* is a god in his own city: 15.746 *Caesar in urbe sua deus est.* At this point, we have had a stirring denunciation of kingship and the celebration of the accession of a god who was martyred, in effect, because he saved the favorite of Diana—he violated the natural order, and now, in another violation of that order, he ends the plague that had caused so much doom in Latium.

There is also a neat association between the presence of Io near the end of Book 1, where Jupiter's amour was ultimately transformed into the goddess Isis, and the enthronement of Asclepius in Book 15. We have moved from an Egyptian paramour, as it were, to the savior of Diana's favorite—another mark of Diana's victory, which Ovid celebrates in the Hippolytus lore of this book.

Caesar's appearance comes with a suddenness that equals the speed with which the plague is quelled. For Ovid, there was no interest in detailing the history of Rome from c. 291 B.C. to the death of Caesar. Ovid announces the famous comet of 44 B.C., which according to Suetonius was seen the July after the assassination.[57] Ovid is also quick in detailing why Caesar deserves this honor—it was not because of his own great accomplishments, but rather because of whose father he was—the great announcement of the glory of Augustus: 15.750-751 *neque enim de Caesaris actis / ullum maius opus, quam quod pater exstitit huius.* Ovid details how Caesar subdued the Britons and conquered Egypt (a reference to the Alexandrian War in 48-47 B.C.), not to mention the Numidians that had sided with Pompey and suffered the loss of their king, Juba, who committed suicide after the Battle of Thapsus in 46 B.C., and Mithridates of Pontus, who was defeated at Zela in 47 B.C.—all of this is not so much in comparison to the fatherhood of the one who would be the guardian of the world:

... quo praeside rerum
humano generi, superi, favistis abunde (15.758-779)

... *with whom as guardian of affairs,*
the human race, o immortals, have you favored abundantly

Someone such as this, Ovid notes, could not have been born from mortal seed, and so Caesar must be made a god (761 *ille deus faciendus erat*). This seemingly glorious fact is a source of great stress for Venus, however, because she sees the conspiracy forming to kill Julius. Here there is a marvelous Ovidian interpretation of the events of 44 B.C.; the conspirators had to kill Julius Caesar, because by their dagger strikes he would be made a god, and, after all, his son could not possibly have been born to merely mortal seed. Ovid does not deny the great accomplishments of Caesar—all of which, we might note, are *foreign* triumphs—but the greatest was the question of whose father he was. He was a man of peace (cf. 746 ff.) as well as of war; this refers mostly to his accomplishment as the father of the future Augustus—Ovid's long catalogue of his achievements in foreign conquest do not list any domestic glories, and the only accomplishment outside of foreign war for which he is praised is the fatherhood of Augustus.[58]

And, now, he must die; the main reason for his deification is so that *Augustus* can have a divine ancestor. Venus is disturbed by the threat to her descendant, the last living link to Iulus, she notes: 15.767 *quod de Dardanio solum mihi restat Iulo*. The sentiment is highly significant; Julius is the father of the future Augustus, and yet he is the last link to Aeneas' son Iulus—Augustus was adopted, after all, and in the accession of Augustus to power we see, perhaps, the last vestige of Troy pass away—Iulus' descendants are gone, the Dardanian line extinguished. Here, at the end of Ovid's epic, we see the Venus who did not appear at the end of the *Aeneid*. There she did not hear the news that would have filled her with anger; she did not learn of the final ethnic disposition of Rome. Here, she learns of the plan to make Caesar a god—which should fill her with delight—but she is pained to hear of his assassination. Venus outlines her claim to anger; she is here a reincarnation of the Juno Virgil depicted at the beginning of his *Aeneid*: we have come fully around to *Venus* as the aggrieved goddess, as she complains about the wound she suffered from Diomedes, and about the fall of Troy, and the forced exile of her son Aeneas—even how he had to visit the underworld, which is a particularly odd thing for the goddess to complain about: 772 *sedesque intrare silentum*. There Aeneas had seen his father and learned of the glorious future of such as Julius Caesar, but here Venus views the whole business as part of why she should complain. This is a reference to the goddess' appearance with her uncle Neptune at the end of Book 5, where she begged for safe passage on the way to Italy; she did not mention the underworld trip there, which she did assist with in having her sacred birds guide the way to the Golden Bough—but otherwise the goddess had nothing to do with the great *katabasis* her son undertook. Ovid here closes a great ring with the first *Aeneid*.

I would suggest that here we see Venus' recognition of what she was not privy to in the last movements of the *Aeneid*, where Virgil unfolded his surprise ending regarding Troy. The underworld vision, too, is part of the point: there Augustus was presented, and here Augustus is the ostensible reason for the assassination of Julius. Julius must die so a god can be conveniently furnished for Augustus. Venus's defeat in these matters—implied strongly by Virgil's omission of the goddess from the final scenes of the *Aeneid*—is also signaled by the accession of Asclepius to divinity in Rome. Asclepius died so that Diana's favorite might live. Asclepius was mysteriously restored to life, but he had given up his own self in sacrificial offering, as it were, so that Hippolytus might be reborn. Diana is now on the Aventine, and Hippolytus-Virbius is safely ensconced where he cannot be found and face retribution for his resurrection. Diana and Venus are presented in opposition throughout the *Aeneid*, and here, Diana has seen her benefactor enthroned as a god, while the last scion of Iulus must die. He will, of course, be made a god—the *divus Iulius* that was heralded by the comet of 44 B.C.—but that comet was a wonderful element of Octavian's propaganda, designed, after all, to give divinity to his adopted line.

In Ovid's depiction of Venus there is also something of the capricious goddess who thinks only of the immediate present; she does not stop to seek solace in the fact that her beloved Julius will become a god, only that he is to be stabbed by the conspirators. As for Brutus and Cassius and the rest, they have been neatly turned into agents of Octavian's glory; their blades will bring divinity to his adopted father. It is a marvelously ambiguous comment on what happened on the Ides of March; it allows for both positive and negative interpretations of the deed. Lucan was perhaps inspired by this passage, when he began his *Pharsalia* with the observation that all that Rome has suffered was worth the cost, if it meant that Nero would come to rule.

Venus' laments move the gods; but it is all in vain (15.779-780 *talia nequiquam toto Venus anxia caelo / verba iacit*). She has suffered a defeat, in marked commentary on the divine machinery of the end of Virgil's *Aeneid*. The decision, we learn, is one of fate; the iron decrees of the old sisters cannot be violated, Ovid notes (781 *ferrea non possunt veterum decreta sororum*). All that can be done is to give signs of the coming woe, portents that cry out the news of the impending catastrophe Venus will suffer. Here Ovid is imitating Virgil, *Georgics* 1.466-488, where the same sort of catalogue of Caesarian portents is given; Ovid is traveling well-known ground here, but with a rather novel explanation for why the heavens should scream their grief. The coming assassination is called a *nefas* (785), that strongest of words; the strength of the label befits the power of the great goddess of the Trojans, the mother of Aeneas, who here suffers the loss of her "other" son. In Virgil she had worked feverishly to help her son Aeneas; here she loses her other son, Julius, and the last of her Julian line. It is the embodiment of why Juno was rejoicing at the end of the *Aeneid*; it is the fulfillment of the final ethnic disposition of Rome that was foretold there, in Virgil's hexameters, so long before Rome had even been founded.

The portents are without efficacy; they cannot stop the coming death (15.799 ff.). The swords are drawn, and the scene is set for the final destruction of Troy. Ovid may well have had in his mind the proposed plan of Caesar to restore the capital to Troy; whether the idea was ever taken seriously or not, in Ovid's narrative, this assassination is depicted as the final death of the Trojan state. Ovid notes that the only place in the city that could suffice for the crime was the *curia* (802), another marvelously ambiguous word. Taken most generally, it would simply refer to the Roman senate, and indeed Caesar did die in the senate's presence, though not, of course, in the *Curia Hostilia*, which had been in disuse since the Clodian disturbances in 52 B.C. The senate was instead using a *curia* in the area of Pompey's theater, outside the *pomerium*; Ovid's point about suitability can be taken as referring to the fact that Caesar's assassination was vengeance, in a sense, for the death of Pompey—Pompey's ghost seen as presiding over the assassination of the man who had defeated him—but also there is the strong odor of Republican sentiment. The man should die in the senate, precisely because he tried to usurp the prerogatives of senatorial authority by dictatorship and would-be monarchy. He is the anti-Cipus; he has a use, though—death so that he may be a convenient god to adorn the family tree of his adopted son (who, presumably, is and will be wiser than his storied father).

There is also a hint here of the tradition that Romulus was murdered because he was becoming too despotic.

Venus tries to intervene (15.803 ff.). She tries to wrap Caesar in the same mist that had once been used to save Paris and Aeneas.[59] Here we have an evocation of Juno and Juturna, trying in vain to save their Rutulian hero, Turnus; the tables have been turned. The gods (Jupiter, we should say) were indignant that Hippolytus should be brought back to life, just as Turnus and Camilla were indignant that they had to suffer death. But the indignation of Jupiter failed in the matter of Hippolytus; he may hide, but he was resurrected, and his savior is now an honored god on the island in the Tiber. Now Venus will fail where Diana succeeded: no mist will save Julius from his bloody end.

Jupiter had met with his beloved daughter Venus in the first book of the *Aeneid*, and she had left his presence happy and rejoicing. Now, the father and daughter have another meeting together. Jupiter outlines that nothing can destroy the decrees of fate; this is the same Jovian view that is expressed again and again in the pages of both Virgil and Ovid. Nothing can countermand the dictates of the three sisters; if something *does* happen, even if it seems to be contrary to fate, it must instead be acknowledged as fated indeed. One of the points would then be the limits of knowledge, both for mortals and for at least some of the gods. Your knowledge may also be incomplete, as was the case with Venus in her first meeting with Jupiter in the *Aeneid* (Jupiter may well also have had incomplete knowledge there too, if he was unaware of what would eventually happen for Troy and Italy in the new Rome). There is also a hint of the idea that some things cannot be changed, while others can; Rome must be founded, for example, but it need not be Trojan. Juno's anger achieved that much, and here we see the fruits of her productive rage. Conveniently, we can then say the whole thing was fated from the beginning and we simply did not know. In that ignorance can be born both free will (or at least the image of free will, since we do not know what our predetermined fate is) and the illusion of self-determination.

And the decrees of the fates are kept in a *tabularia* (15.810)—a very Roman concept indeed, the office for public records. Again, the point at stake here is the ethnicity of Rome, the fulfillment of the end of the *Aeneid*.

Anchises had met with his son Aeneas at the end of the sixth *Aeneid*, and there he had unfolded the future course of Roman history—the past in the future tense, if you will, from the perspective of Virgil's Augustan audience. Now Jupiter will do the same thing for Venus. This speech neatly rings the speech of Jupiter to Venus at *Aeneid* 1.257-296, thus sealing the two epics in a mighty circuit: Ovid's *Metamorphoses* as sequel to and commentary on Virgil's *Aeneid*. The greatest and most encompassing of rings will now be closed.

Anchises' speech was cloaked in the mechanism of Orphic and Pythagorean mystic philosophies of rebirth and renewal through purgation. Jupiter's speech is based on the immutable decrees of fate.

Caesar is finished, Jupiter announces; he has lived for his allotted years (15.816-817 *hic sua conplevit, pro quo, Cytherea, laboras, / tempora, perfectis, quos terrae debuit, annis*). Venus will see to it that he is a god, and his son will also become a god—this is only natural for one whose father is divine. The son will avenge the murder of his father—*pietas* makes that demand, after all, even if the conspirators are acting for the better of Octavian, so that the youth may have a divine father. Die they must, and Jupiter will be the ally of the son in slaying those who slew his father. Mutina will seek peace under his auspices. The reference is to the events of 43 B.C., when Mark Antony faced the combined forces of the two consuls, Hirtius and Pansa, who died in the year Ovid was born. Antony was defeated, and despite the consuls' death, Octavian triumphed and thereby became consul himself. Pharsalia will feel the power of Octavian, Jupiter notes (823 *Pharsalia sentiet illum*), and the Emathian plains will once again be wet with slaughter. This is a reference to 42 B.C. and the events at Philippi. This is the passage, I would argue, that most inspired Lucan in the composition of his great epic. These are the lines that move us from Ovid's epic to Lucan's; the Neronian poet saw himself as the third in a triad of Roman epicists—and he would be the poet of madness triumphant. Sextus Pompey, the son of Pompey the Great, will be defeated; this is a reference to the events of 36 B.C., when Octavian (more accurately, Agrippa) finally defeated Sextus in a naval battle.

Cleopatra will also fall (here Ovid is also inspired by the shield of Aeneas from *Aeneid* 8); she is the *coniunx* of Antony, Ovid notes, but she trusted too much in the marriage and will fall nonetheless. The appellation is interesting given that Antony and Cleopatra were not legally married in the eyes of Roman law; Antony is here imagined as little more than a foreign despot, married to an Eastern barbarian and threatening the peace and security of Rome. Cleopatra had boasted, Ovid says, that Rome would serve Canopus, an island at the Tiber's mouth; there is a nice juxtaposition here of Canopus with the Tiber island where Diana's helper Asclepius, the son of Apollo, now rules.[60]

Octavian will also be a man of peace; he will give laws (cf. Romulus) to his people as a most just legislator (15.833 *iustissimus auctor*). And he will have a son, the fulfillment of the dream of the Augustan succession. In A.D. 4, Tiberius was formally adopted as the son and heir of Augustus, and these lines look forward to his accession. We have come very far, of course, from Virgil's account of the death of Marcellus at the end of *Aeneid* 6; in A.D. 4 and at the time of Ovid's composition of these lines there was an answer to the problem Virgil faced at the close of his underworld vision, though the answer might not have pleased Augustus.

Jupiter closes his speech with an imperative to Venus; she is to snatch up the soul of her slaughtered son and oversee his deification, his apotheosis (15.840 ff.). Venus takes the soul from the body, and, as she carries it heavenward, she feels it begin to heat up and take on light. She did not allow the soul to be dissolved into the air (845-846 *nec in aera solvi / passa recentem animam*). This was, after all, what Lucretius said was the fate of the soul (cf. *De Rerum Natura* 3.576-579, with Kenney's notes). No, there can be nothing of that Lucretian fate for Caesar, since he will be made a god, so that Octavian may have a divine father and be a god in turn himself. The star rises higher than the moon (848 *luna volat altius illa*), an interesting remark given the rivalry between Diana and Venus; certainly here we see Venus in triumph, as she takes her son to the heavens. Ovid then announces an interesting twist, though one that fits in with what he has already revealed about the reason for this apotheosis: the star (Caesar) gleamed, and, seeing the deeds of his son (Octavian), it confessed them to be greater than his own, and rejoiced to be conquered by that one (850-851 *stella micat natique videns bene facta fatetur / esse suis maiora et vinci gaudet ab illo*). Caesar may now be a god, but he is defeated by his *mortal* son. Octavian is destined to be a god himself, but he is not one yet; the passage is a wonderful deflation of Julius and a reminder that, after all, his deification was merely a device to allow the *greater* one, Octavian, to be a god in turn. Diana's Hippolytus was able to be saved and so, it would seem, was Venus' Julius.

Octavian does not allow his own deeds to be set above those of his father (15.852 ff.). But *fama*, Ovid says, is "free" (*libera*) and disobeys Octavian/Augustus in this one regard. For Ovid, this is the natural order; so Atreus yielded to Agamemnon, and Aegeus to Theseus. Achilles was greater than Peleus. Saturn is less than Jupiter. Jupiter may have the ethereal realms (858-859 *Iuppiter arces / temperat*), and the kingdoms of the three-formed world (*mundi regna triformis*), but Augustus has the *terra* (860 *terra sub Augusto est*).

The division deserves comment; it is strange and not altogether clear. The "kingdoms of the three-formed world" would seem to mean the earth, the sky, and the water; Jupiter has sway over all. What, then, is the portion for Augustus? We might also note now the interesting comment Ovid makes about Augustus' own deification at 15.838-839, where the text is vexed: *nec nisi cum senior Pylios aequaverit annos, / aetherias sedes cognataque sidera tanget*. This text, printed by Tarrant, has Heinsius' conjecture *Pylios* for the manuscript *similes* (*patrios* has weakly attested support). Housman conjectured *meritis*, which is best—the point being that Augustus will die when his future years equaled his merits. If we were to read *Pylios* with Heinsius, we would have to imagine that Augustus cannot become a god unless he equals Nestor's years. The sentiment is the commonplace that we do not wish the swift end of the beloved leader (cf. Venus' grief over Caesar's assassination), but there is no need to inject Nestor into this passage. Still, the textual problems reveal the difficulty of these lines, and the significance they bear for Ovid's Augustan program.

But what of the division of the *mundus* for Jupiter and the *terra* for Augustus? The point would seem to be that the three-formed world must be the sky, the sea, and the *lower world*, with no place for the earth. This does not, however, accord with the division Ovid himself outlined at the very beginning of the epic, at 1.5 *ante mare et terras et, quod tegit omnia caelum*. This passage is not exactly a technical division of the *mundus per se*, but we might want to find a neat ring between the beginning and the end of the epic. Jupiter is the supreme god; his rule surpasses that of Neptune and Hades, who might admittedly be displeased at hearing Jupiter described as in charge of their realms. Ovid says that both Jupiter and Augustus are "father and ruler" (15.860 *pater est et rector uterque*). In any case, Ovid now makes more explicit the call that the day be later than our age when Augustus might ascend to heaven; in 868 *nostro serior aevo* there is a direct echo of Horace, c. 1.2 *serus in caelum redeas*. Jupiter and Augustus are directly equated; both of them *temper* (859 *temperat*, 869 *temperat*) their respective realms, Jupiter the ethereal seats, etc., and Augustus the head of the world (*caput*). The evocation of the beginning of Horace's odes is deliberate: it prepares for Ovid's surprise for his attentive readers: the end of the epic will be a response to the end of the three books of Horace's odes. Virgil had his surprise near the end of the *Aeneid* in the reconciliation of Juno, and Ovid is now preparing for his own twist.

Rome is the climax of Ovid's universal history, because for once in the chronology of his epic there is a truly global capital, a mistress for the world. Where Virgil's epic was the poem of Rome, Ovid's has been the poem of the world, with Rome as its high point.

At the end of Book 14, between the description of the apotheosis of Romulus and the subsequent deification of his wife Hersilie, Ovid subversively introduced Lucretius by means of a simile he repeated from his second book, a sort of Lucretian frame that called into question the veracity of the whole matter of apotheosis and deification. The end of Book 15 has another divine metamorphosis, as Caesar is transformed into a comet. That metamorphosis is explicitly designed to provide Octavian with a divine father and a godly ancestry. When Venus was commissioned by Jupiter to guide the soul of Caesar to his new heavenly seat, the language was vaguely anti-Lucretian: Lucretius, after all, would have nothing of this sort of deification, and yet here it was—admittedly, a contrivance so Octavian could himself one day become a god. And there was a wife, a *sancta coniunx* (836), who would have to be Livia (though with interesting family associations in terms of children)—here we see a balance between Romulus and Hersilie (and, as we have seen, some find an echo of Livia in Ovid's Hersilie). We have another divine couple, then (she is *sancta* because we can imagine she will also be honored some day as the divine consort). But if Romulus could not really be deified, if we could shoot a Lucretian pellet into that metamorphosis to deflate its pretensions of immortality, can we not do the same for Caesar and Augustus?

Yes, of course, and quietly we may smile and do just that. But Ovid has another game to play, a final trick for his readers, a surprise that he saves for the very end of his epic, the place where we see that a poem so bound by *tempora* can *perhaps* still fulfill the dream of a *carmen perpetuum*. In the *temper*ing action of Jupiter and Augustus, there is but the faintest echo of the *tempora*, the chronological boundaries that weigh upon the poet's vision and constrain him. Virgil could not extend his vision in the underworld past a certain point out of ignorance of the future; Ovid can say there is a son for Augustus because Tiberius was adopted in A.D. 4, but he, too, cannot go past his own times.

In Virgil's *Aeneid*, there is only one passage where the epic poet gives voice to the idea that his poem might have lasting power. At 9.446-449, he says that Nisus and Euryalus will be famous as long as Rome holds sway; if, that is, his songs have any power (*si quid mea carmina possunt*). This is not a statement about the eternal, enduring strength of his work, but a protasis to a condition: Nisus and Euryalus will have the fame, if—and the *si* is important—Virgil's poem has any power.

But in 23 B.C., Virgil's contemporary Horace—who called Virgil one half of his soul, *dimidium animae meae*—concluded his great three books of odes with a stunning declaration of the poet's enduring power, c. 3.30, *Exegi monumentum*. It is to the lyric bard *Horace*, not the epic poets Virgil or Lucretius *per se*, that Ovid now turns. He declares that he has completed his work—*opus exegi*, in imitation of Horace—and it is a work that Jupiter's anger will not destroy. This is Homer and the world of Homeric divine wrath, and it will not harm his achievement. Fire and the sword will not destroy it (and twice before Ovid noted that fire and the sword yielded before Aeneas and his sons as Troy burned). The passage of time that consumes all will not destroy it (15.872 *nec edax abolere vetustas*)—no Lucretian destruction of the slow and steady sort that we remember from the close of the second book of the *De Rerum Natura*.

The day will come when Ovid's *body* will die, and the space of an uncertain age will finish him. But his better part—*parte tamen meliore mei*—will be borne above the stars: 875-876 *super alta perennis / astra ferar*. The first person singulars should be followed. In Horace, there was *exegi*—which Ovid copies. Then there was *moriar*—the poet would not wholly die. Then there were *crescam* and *dicar*—the poet would grow in fame and be spoken of. *But*, as in Virgil, there is a *caveat*: Horace will be famous so long as the pontifex climbs the Capitol with the silent virgin (cf. Virgil's *dum domus Aeneae Capitoli immobile saxum / accolet imperiumque pater Romanus habebit* with Horace's *dum Capitolium / scandet cum tacita virgine pontifex*).

In Ovid, after *exegi*, there is *ferar*—the poet will be taken above the stars, he will be a new god, in some sense. And he will be *read*—*legar*, not Horace's *dicar*—wherever Roman power extends (*quaque patet domitis Romana potentia terris*). Venus took the soul of her descendant Julius Caesar from his body as he ascended to the stars; someone will presumably do the same for the poet. As we shall soon see, Ovid is making what we might call a *vatis praesagium*, a bard's

presentiment.
At the end, rather quietly, Ovid notes:

... perque omnia saecula fama,
siquid habent veri vatum praesagia, vivam. (15.878-879)

... and through all the ages in fame,
if the presentiments of the bards have anything of truth, I shall live.

The three first person singular verbs (*exegi, ferar, legar*), two of them passive as in Horace, are here crowned with the poem's stunning last word, the active assertion of his enduring life: *vivam* (cf. Horace's *crescam*). And, this time, there is a strong *caveat*: the poet will live, *if the presentiments of the bards have anything of truth*, if the poet's predictions ring true. On that important protasis depends the eternal life of the poet. Like Horace before him—indeed more assertively than Horace—Ovid announces his future fame. He has finished his work—none could deny this. He will be borne above the stars—exactly like Caesar, we might note. Like Caesar, he will lose his body and ascend with whatever we might say is his *melior pars*—perhaps his *anima*.

But what are the *vatum praesagia*? Did someone predict Ovid's undying fame? *Fama*, as we have seen, can be a problematic word in Ovid—rumor is often true, though it carries negative connotations and can be a loaded word. Are the *vatum praesagia* true? Do they carry something of truth? (*si quid . . . veri*). *If* they do, then the poet will live—not only his work, we might note, *but he himself as well*—even if without a body, he will survive. We can say he will live in his work, but, as in Horace, the point is the first person singular and the poet's own immortality—he has already asserted the endurance of his work, and now he speaks of himself. He will live on—Lucretius be damned—in his better part. In this, too, the poem will be a *carmen perpetuum*, though not another line could be added to its measure of verses—it will endure in part because its author endures; how could the work of a god disappear? Or, if you prefer, the work is so great that in its continued survival—it will be read wherever Roman power extends (15.877-878)—the poet will live. The poet has uttered a presentiment, and if it proves true, then his immortality is assured.

There is a separation between the craft and the craftsman. The work will live. As for the poet, his body will die (15.873-874). But his *melior pars*, his "better part," will be carried above the stars, and his name will be eternal (875-876). The *melior pars* is presumably his soul, or just possibly his work. He will live (the emphatic *vivam*), *but only if the vatum praesagia are true*. If not, then he will not live. Ovid has tempered Horace's declaration from c. 3.30; Ovid's triple work ends with a protasis that offers a direct response to Horace, who was himself a *vates*.

The poet will be immortal. Like Caesar, he will, in effect, become a god—*if you believe that sort of thing*. If you do not, then you agree with the haunting groan of Lucretius, which laments that death is the end, and the poet's hope-filled *vivam* is, in the end, but a vain dream. If the *vatum praesagia* of the poet's protasis do not speak the truth, then the apodosis cannot be realized, and *vivam* does not ring true.

The poet's last *praesagium* is that his work will be immortal, that it will conquer the realm of death, and that he too will live. If the poet's *praesagia* are false—and there is reason to believe they often are—then there is no endurance for the poet, and the future indicative *vivam* does not come to fruition (indeed, the end of Ovid's own *Amores* 3.12 seems to present the *vatum praesagia* as problematically trustworthy). Ovid here returns, at the very end, to the falsehood theme once again, a theme that is linked to the reports of *fama*. There is an echo here too of the Virgilian Gates of Sleep and the notion of truth and its opposite.[61] Virgil had barely hinted at the idea of personal immortality through the enduring quality of one's work; Horace had asserted it more boldly, and Ovid responds to that bold declaration. *Ovid divides his poem into three parts in imitation of Horace's threefold division of the odes.* Horace's c. 3.30 made a firm declara-tion of the poet's immortality: he will not wholly die, even if his fame (*dicar*) is linked to Rome's power (he was wrong, as it turns out, since his fame has sur-passed Rome's temporal dominion). The triple division of Ovid's poem offers reflections on the nature of the afterlife and the fate of the soul that, we learn only at the close of Book 15, are ultimately read in light of Horace's great decla-ration at the end of the odes.

Ovid closes his epic, then, with a poignant reply to Horace, a surprise for the close reader. The *carmen perpetuum* can be read as a triumphant paean to Augustan Rome and the great poet's achievement. And, Ovid has solemnly de-clared, the work will live for all time—a *carmen perpetuum* in the truest sense. The work will live, just as Augustus will be a god. Ovid has larger concerns than whether or not Augustus should be criticized; he realized that the *princeps*—whom he chose to call the *praeses* and the *pater* and *rector*—had at least brought peace and order to Rome after seemingly interminable civil strife, and, just possibly, had also secured his succession in the person of Tiberius. Ovid's concerns were more philosophical in the end than political. And the bleak vision of Lucretius mars these last lines of the epic, and infuses them with its haunting sorrow.

The end of the *Metamorphoses* offers a quiet correction, not to say gentle rebuke, to Horace's fond wish; the Roman phoenix may not be forever reborn after all. The end of Horace's *carmina* offered eternal life through poetic achievement. Ovid, however hopeful, is less certain of eternal endurance. The specter of Lucretius broods over Ovid's epic *Metamorphoses*, just as it did for Virgil's *Aeneid*, infecting the poet's heartfelt hope with a haunting tinge of pain-ful reality.

Notes

1. There is no separate commentary as yet on this key book; on the speech of Pythagaros see the important article of Hardie, Philip, "The Speech of Pythagaros in Ovid, *Metamorphoses* 15: Empedoclean Epos," in *The Classical Quarterly* 45.1 (1995), pp. 204-214, Swanson, R. A., "Ovid's Pythagorean Essay," in *The Classical Journal* 54 (1958), pp. 21-24, and Galinsky, G. K., "The Speech of Pythagaros at Ovid, *Metamorphoses* 15.78-478," in Cairns, F., ed., *Papers of the Leeds International Latin Seminar 10*, ARCA: Classical and Medieval Texts 38, 1998, pp. 313-336. On the book's close note especially Segal, C., "Myth and Philosophy in the *Metamorphoses*: Ovid's Augustanism and the Augustan Conclusion of Book XV," in *The American Journal of Philology* 90 (1969), pp. 257-292. Also of interest is Curran, L.C., "Transformation and Anti-Augustanism in Ovid's *Metamorphoses*," in *Arethusa* 3 (1972), pp. 71-91. There is still much of use in the classic article of Saint-Denis, E. de, "La genie d'Ovide d'après le livre XV des *Métamorphoses*," in *Revue des études latines* 18 (1940), pp. 111-140.

2. For a convenient study of Ovid's intertextual depiction of Numa in the *Fasti*, see Littlewood, R. Joy, "*Imperii pignora certa*: The Role of Numa in Ovid's *Fasti*," in Herbert-Brown, Geraldine, ed., *Ovid's Fasti: Historical Readings at Its Bimillennium*, Oxford, 2002, pp. 175-197.

3. For the connection of Hercules to the place, note Diodorus Siculus 4.24.7.

4. On the name of this character note Robertson, Noel, *Religion and Reconciliation in Greek Cities: The Sacred Laws of Selinus and Cyrene*, Oxford, 2010, pp. 132-133. For the reduction of Numa's status by Ovid's narrative technique, see Janan, Micaela, *Reflections in a Serpent's Eye: Thebes in Ovid's* Metamorphoses, Oxford, 2009, p. 72.

5. *Ab Urbe Condita* 1.18.2-3, where see Ogilvie.

6. Convenient summary of the evidence for Pythagaros at Croton can be found in Kirk, Raven, and Schofield's *Presocratic Philosophers*, pp. 225 ff.

7. Guthrie, *op. cit.*, pp. 216 ff., has a useful survey.

8. Anderson has no serious problem with *deorum*, which he does not obelize and which he suggests may refer to sacrifices (*pace* the evidence of 127-129, where see Hill).

9. Tarrant obelizes *deorum* and offers no new conjecture.

10. On Lucretius' description of primitive man, best is Campbell's Oxford commentary; note also Monica Gale's exemplary Aris & Phillips student edition.

11. At Herodotus 2.81, it is noted that the Egyptians do not take wool into their temples or consent to be buried in it, since the Orphic and Pythagorean teachings do not countenance such use of sheep fur. Ovid's Pythagoras will also mention wool near the end of his speech, at 15.471 *horriferum contra Borean ovis arma ministret*, where he will make a final appeal against the eating of meat and note that one should restrict oneself to, *inter alia*, the use of wool for protective clothing against the cold blasts of Boreas.

12. Cf. Ovid's pathetic description of the sacrificial animal that sees the knife rising to slaughter it at the altar, and fears for its life—the implication being that it has human sense (15.132-135).

13. Convenient introduction and commentary to Lucretius, *De Rerum Natura* 3 can be found in Kenney's Cambridge green and yellow edition.

14. Homer, *Iliad* 16.806 ff.

15. The Archytas Ode, on which see Nisbet and Hubbard.

16. Pausanias 2.17.3 mentions the shield.

17. See Börner here; Diogenes Laertius 8.10 has the Pythagorean division of a man's life into twenty year blocks.

18. Milon of Croton was a famous athlete; the commentators note Cicero, *De Senectute* 9.27 for the lament of his old age.

19. The reference to Helen's two abductions most probably = Paris and Menelaus, though it is possible the tradition of Theseus' abduction is meant (Herodotus 9.73).

20. The chronology is problematic, since Empedocles was not born until some four decades after Pythagoras may have come to Croton. See further Hill 15.237-258, who notes the testimony of Simplicius on Aristotle's *Physics* (25.19) that Empedocles was an "emulator" of Pythagoras.

21. There is another interesting possible textual crux at 15.271-2 *clausit, et antiquis tam multa tremoribus orbis / flumina prosiliunt aut excaecata residunt,* where some have questioned the point about the antiquity of earthquakes ("*vix sanum,*" says Tarrant of the text here). I am inclined to think that the age-old reality of earthquakes is part of Ovid's Pythagoras' point; the novel workings of nature are not so very novel after all.

22. Herodotus 7.30.

23. See Strabo 1.3.8 and 8.7.2 ff.

24. See further Börner, and Hill, ad loc.; for the Ammonian spring, note Herodotus 4.181, and for the Dodonian, Pliny the Elder, *Historia Naturalis* 2.106.228.

25. With Bailey's notes.

26. *De Rerum Natura* 6.639-702, with Bailey.

27. 15.364 is notoriously corrupt, though the meaning is clear. *i quoque delectos* is probably correct; see here Tarrant's apparatus and Börner ad loc.

28. Hill ad loc. has convenient testimonia.

29. *Historia Naturalis* 8.44.105, where see Beagon.

30. *Historia Animalium* 6.32.

31. Tarrant brackets them; Anderson, who on the whole dislikes cutting lines, does not. It is not entirely clear why someone would have interpolated these lines, even given the similar passage at Virgil, *Aeneid* 1.283-285; the mention of "Oedipus' Thebes" is attractive since otherwise Oedipus is mentioned nowhere else in the epic, and Ovid does enjoy inserting at least a brief mention of every major and most minor myths.

32. We should also not forget that the legend of a meeting between Numa and Pythagoras had been roundly mocked by a number of Romans and Greeks (Cicero, Dionysius of Halicarnassus); see further Cameron, Alan, *Greek Mythography in the Roman World*, Cambridge, 2004, pp. 275-276.

33. A pagan version of *o felix culpa.*

34. Another good example of how Ovid likes to mention stories briefly, even if he does not describe them in his epic at length.

35. Cf. Varro, *De Lingua Latina* 7.28.

36. There is a certain humor in this fact, given the Pythagorean prescription against meat consumption.

37. See Ogilvie ad Livy, *Ab Urbe Condita* 1.18-21.

38. *Orestean* Diana because of the legend that Orestes set up the image of Diana at Aricia after he fled from Tauris.

39. On all aspects of the cult see now Green, C., *Roman Religion and the Cult of Diana at Aricia*, Cambridge, 2006.

40. Some of this history may lie behind Virgil's Camilla narrative, with the death of

Diana's forest denizen.

41. Virgil thus connects the death and rebirth of Hippolytus with the death of the Diana-like Camilla, who is proxy to Turnus. Jupiter, of course, is the central figure behind the death of Camilla and the effect it has on Turnus, which leads to his losing the best chance he would have to destroy Aeneas.

42. On this lore see Fordyce, and Horsfall, ad *A.* 7.761 ff.; cf. Pfeiffer on Callimachus, fr. 190, and *Fasti* 3.263 ff. and 6.737 ff. (with Littlewood).

43. I would speculate that there may be a deliberate connection in Virgil's (invented) story between the romantic feelings Turnus may have for Camilla, feelings that result in his emotional reaction to her death, and the implicit account here that Hippolytus-Virbius had a relationship with Aricia that led to the birth of a warrior; in any case, Virgil clearly connects the deaths of Hippolytus-Virbius, Camilla, and Turnus, with the figure of Jupiter looming over all; Jupiter was indignant that Hippolytus was resurrected, and his indignation is eventually transferred to the souls of Camilla and Turnus, indignant at their fates (in which Jupiter played no small part).

44. Where see the full commentary of Barrett.

45. Ovid omits any mention here of Jupiter's punishment of Asclepius; he will return to Apollo's son soon enough.

46. For a critical view of the veracity of the story, note Cicero, *De Divinatione* 23.50-51.

47. The story is known to Plutarch, *Vita Romuli* 20.5.

48. See also Pliny the Elder, *Historia Naturalis* 11.37.45.

49. The *Fasti* opens with Quirinus giving the *iura* of the calendar to Rome (1.37-38). At *Fasti* 2.492, Romulus is also imagined as giving laws to the Quirites when he is taken up to heaven: *forte tuis illic, Romule, iura dabas.* At *Fasti* 3.62, both Romulus and Remus are depicted as lawgivers to farmers and herdsmen: *Iliadae fratres iura petita dabant.*

50. *Fatalis* here has connotations both of how Cipus was destined to be king, and of how he would be a bringer of death to his people—loss of liberty and slavery (15.597 *si Romam intrarit, famularia iura daturum*).

51. And cf. Ovid's Meleager and Atalanta, and his Atalanta and Hippomenes.

52. Housman lavished praise on this ode, as Gilbert Highet recalls in his *Classical Tradition.*

53. Note Valerius Maximus 1.8.2; the cult arrived in 291 B.C. and was fixed on the Tiber island.

54. Once again, with Ovid's (and, to a far greater extent, Virgil's) trick of using the first and last letters of a name to draw associations.

55. See Bömer, and Hill, ad loc.

56. This temple is not otherwise known.

57. *Divus Iulius* 88; note the usual sources: Virgil, *Eclogues* 9.47 (with Coleman, and Clausen), Propertius c. 4.6.59 (with Hutchinson).

58. Caesar is mentioned in less than flattering terms at *Fasti* 3.202 *tum primum generis intulit arma socer*, where Ovid notes the episode of the Sabine women as the first time a father-in-law broke arms against his daughter's husband. But very different is the reference to Caesar's assassination Ovid makes in the *Fasti* for the Ides of March, where Vesta complains that her priest (Caesar as *pontifex maximus*) was slain by impious hands, and that Octavian will be practicing *pietas* to avenge his father: 3.709-710 *hoc opus, haec pietas, haec prima elementa fuerunt / Caesaris, ulcisci iusta per arma patrem*, where the

elementa bring a Lucretian air to the whole matter of Octavian's rise to power: it is as if Aeneas earned his reputation to *pietas* by carrying Anchises out of the burning wreck of Troy, and Octavian will earn his by avenging the death of his father. Ovid's depiction of the assassination is very different in the *Fasti* and in the *Metamorphoses*; it is as if the two works were consciously designed to offer two different views of the murder. Ovid is clear about the just fates of the assassins: 3.705-707 *at quicumque nefas ausi, prohibente deorum / numine, polluerant pontificale caput, / morte iacent merita.*

59. *Iliad* 3.340-380, where Paris is saved from Menelaus by Venus' timely intervention, and *Iliad* 5.297-310, where Aeneas is similarly saved from Diomedes.

60. On Antony and Cleopatra the literature is enormous; for the basic history see now Adrian Goldsworthy's exemplary monograph (Yale, 2010), and Pelling on the main surviving source, Plutarch's *Antony.*

61. Lucretius, too, is a *vates*, though it is difficult to imagine Ovid saying that if Lucretius' *praesagia* are true, than the poet will live, given that Lucretius made no predictions about immortality. Ovid's main concern at the end of the end of his epic, his surprise for the attentive reader, is to offer response to Horace's three-part masterpiece within the context of what had always been a sequel and response to Virgil's *Aeneid*; the poet who considered Virgil to be one-half of his soul has been, in some sense, Ovid's concern together with Virgil all along.

The end of the *Metamorphoses* offers a marvelous Ovidian ambiguity. Horace made an unabashed declaration of his immortality; Ovid prevaricates. He does not call Horace a liar or say that Horace is wrong. Virgil, too, was not explicit about his eschatological views. But Ovid's protasis about the *vates* is telling; it is a response to Horace's work that also nicely blurs the genre lines between epic and other poetic forms: Ovid's epic is seen to be modeled after not only Virgil's *Aeneid* but also Horace's *Odes*; in the evocation of Horace c. 3.30 at the end of *Metamorphoses* 15, Ovid leaves the audience with more memory of Horace than Virgil. We cannot be sure of the precedence of c. 3.30 and Virgil's *Aeneid* 9 passage about Nisus and Euryalus; the two passages have affinities. Whether Virgil's passage preceded Horace's or *vice versa*, Horace's declaration of immorality goes far beyond anything in Virgil. Ovid, in the wake of both Virgil and Horace, tempers Horace's unqualified declaration of how the poet will not wholly die through his poetic achievement. Ovid's *vivam* can be read as being in fundamental agreement with Horace. His qualifier about the veracity of the *vatum praesagia* is a bit of Lucretian subversion that Virgil would have appreciated.

And, in the final analysis, the end of Horace c. 4.7 may indicate that Horace himself knew better than to expect immortality, perhaps even through literary creation, though I suspect Ovid was more skeptical about the whole business than Horace; the Augustan world had already changed significantly in the course of only a few years. Ovid's phoenix is a symbol of the idealized Augustan succession, always self-perpetuating and forever reborn in the image of Aeneas' pious conveyance of his aged father. Tiberius, Caligula, Claudius and Nero would be the Julio-Claudian children of the Roman phoenix.

Select Bibliography

This select bibliography contains an annotated (also selectively) guide to books on Ovid (including dissertations, bibliographies, collections of papers, and translations). Relevant articles are cited in the endnotes to the individual chapters of this volume and are not listed here.

Adams, Ethan T. *Gods and Humans in Ovid's Metamorphoses: Constructions of Identity and the Politics of Status.* Dissertation, Washington, 2003.

Ahl, F. *Die Parenthese in Ovids Metamorphosen und ihre dichterische Function.* (Spudasmata 7.) Hildesheim, 1964.

———. *Metaformations: Soundplay and Wordplay in Ovid and Other Classical Poets.* Ithaca, NY: Cornell University Press, 1985.

Anderson, William S. *Ovid's Metamorphoses: Books 6-10.* Norman: University of Oklahoma Press, 1972.

The first of a very useful set of (hitherto unfinished) volumes that provide the editor's Teubner text (minus the apparatus) and fairly detailed notes that are especially good on the preexisting traditions for Ovid's myths. Garth Tissol is preparing the concluding volume of the set, on Books 11-15.

———. *Ovidius: Metamorphoses.* Leipzig: Bibliotheca Teubneriana, 1977.

———. *Ovid's Metamorphoses: Books 1-5.* Norman: University of Oklahoma Press, 1997.

Andrae, J. *Von Kosmos zum Chaos: Ovids Metamorphosen und Vergils Aeneis.* Trier, 2003.

Arnaud, D. L. *Aspects of Wit and Humor in Ovid's Metamorphoses.* Dissertation, Stanford, 1968.

Avery, M. M. *The Use of Direct Speech in Ovid's Metamorphoses.* Dissertation, Chicago, 1937.

Barchiesi, A. *Il poeta e il principe: Ovidio e il discorso augusteo.* Rome-Bari, 1994. (translated as *The Poet and the Prince: Ovid and Augustan Discourse*, Berkeley and Los Angeles: University of California Press, 1997).

Barchiesi, A., Hardie, P., and Hinds, S., eds. *Ovidian Transformations: Essays on the Metamorphoses and Its Reception*. Cambridge: Cambridge Philological Society, 1999.

Barchiesi, A., ed. *Ovidio Metamorfosi, Volume I (Libri I-II)*. Milano: Fondazione Lorenzo Valla, Arnoldo Mondadori Editore, 2005 (2nd edition 2008).

The first volume of a new Italian edition of the epic, with translation by Ludovica Koch and an extensive introduction by the late Charles Segal. The virtues of this splendid initiative cannot be stated too highly. I have noted the other volumes in this series (published and forthcoming) in the appropriate places in the commentary.

Barkan, L. *The Gods Made Flesh: Metamorphoses and the Pursuit of Paganism*. New Haven, CT: Yale University Press, 1986.

Barnard, M. E. *The Myth of Apollo and Daphne from Ovid to Quevedo: Love, Agon, and the Grotesque*. Durham, NC: Duke University Press, 1987.

Barsby, J. A. *Ovid* (Greece and Rome New Surveys in the Classics 12). Oxford: Clarendon Press, 1978.

Bartolomé, H. *Ovid und die antike Kunst*. Leipzig: Noske, 1935.

Bate, Jonathan. *Shakespeare and Ovid*. Oxford: Clarendon Press, 1993.

Binns, J. W., ed. *Ovid*. London: Routledge, 1973.

A superb collection of valuable essays.

de Boer, Cornelius, ed. *Ovide moralisé* (5 vols.). Amsterdam: Koninklijke Akademie van Wetenschappen, 1915-1938. (The set has been conveniently reprinted by Sändig Reprint Verlag: Vaduz, 2009).

———. *Chrétien de Troyes: Philomena, conte raconté d'après Ovide*. Paris: Geuthner, 1909.

Boillat, M. *Les Métamorphoses d'Ovide: Thèmes majeurs et problèmes de composition*. Berne-Frankfort-am-Main, 1976.

Bömer, F. *P. Ovidius Naso Metamorphosen: Kommentar I-III*. Heidelberg, 1968.

The first volume of the "standard" commentary on the entire poem, a monumental achievement that dwarfs the size of the author's previous edition of the *Fasti*. Bömer provides exhaustive parallel passages and especially helpful notes on Ovidian language and meter; there is little if any literary criticism.

———. *P. Ovidius Naso Metamorphosen: Kommentar IV-V*. Heidelberg, 1976.

———. *P. Ovidius Naso Metamorphosen: Kommentar VI-VII*. Heidelberg, 1976.

————. *P. Ovidius Naso Metamorphosen: Kommentar VIII-IX*. Heidelberg, 1977.

————. *P. Ovidius Naso Metamorphosen: Kommentar X-XI*. Heidelberg, 1980.

————. *P. Ovidius Naso Metamorphosen: Kommentar XII-XIII*. Heidelberg, 1982.

————. *P. Ovidius Naso Metamorphosen: Kommentar XIV-XV*. Heidelberg, 1986.

Boyd, B. W. *Brill's Companion to Ovid*. Leiden: Brill, 2002.

Branciforti, Francesco, ed. *Piramus et Tisbé*. Florence: Olschki, 1959.

Brown, Sarah Annes. *The Metamorphosis of Ovid: From Chaucer to Ted Hughes*. New York: St. Martin's Press, 1999.

Buccino, C. *Le opere d'arte nelle Metamorfosi di Ovidio*. Napoli, 1913.

Castiglioni, L. *Studi intorno alle fonti e alla composizione delle Metamorfosi di Ovidio*. Pisa, 1906 (reprinted Rome, 1964).

Cormier, Raymond, ed. and trans. *Three Ovidian Tales of Love (Piramus et Tisbé, Narcisus et Dané, and Philomena et Procné)*. New York: Garland, 1986.

Coulson, F. T. *The "Vulgate" Commentary on Ovid's Metamorphoses: The Creation Myth and the Story of Orpheus*. (Toronto Medieval Latin Texts 20.) Toronto, 1991.

Crump, M. *The Epyllion from Theocritus to Ovid*. Oxford: Blackwell, 1931.

Davis, G. *The Death of Procris: "Amor" and the Hunt in Ovid's Metamorphoses*. Rome: Edizioni dell'Ateneo, 1983.

Deferrari, R. J., Barry, M. I., and McGuire, M. R. P. *A Concordance of Ovid*. Washington, DC: Catholic University of America Press, 1939.

Döpp, S. *Virgilischer Einfluß im Werk Ovids*. Munich, 1968.

Dowdall, L. D. *Ovid's Metamorphoses, Book I*. Cambridge, 1892.

Due, Otto Steen. *Changing Forms: Studies in the Metamorphoses of Ovid*. Copenhagen: Museum Tusculanum Press, 1974.

Ehwald, R. *P. Ovidius Naso: Metamorphoses*. Leipzig: Bibliotheca Teubneriana, 1915.

Elliott, A. G. "Ovid's *Metamorphoses*: A Bibliography 1968-1978." *Classical World* 73 (1979), pp. 385-412.

Engels, Joseph. *Etudes sur l'Ovide moralisé*. Groningen: Wolters, 1945.

Fantham, Elaine. *Ovid's Metamorphoses*. (Oxford Approaches to Classical Literature.) Oxford, 2004.

Feeney, D.C. *The Gods in Epic: Poets and Critics of the Classical Tradition.* Oxford: Clarendon Press, 1991.

Feldherr, A. *Playing Gods: Ovid's Metamorphoses and the Politics of Fiction.* Princeton, NJ: Princeton University Press, 2010.

Forbes, P. *Metamorphosis in Greek Myths.* Oxford: Clarendon Press, 1990.

Fränkel, H. *Ovid: A Poet Between Two Worlds.* Berkeley: University of California Press, 1945.

Frécaut, J.-M. *L'Esprit et l'humour chez Ovid.* Grenoble, 1972.

Fyler, J.M. *Chaucer and Ovid.* New Haven, CT: Yale University Press, 1979.

Galinsky, G. Karl. *Ovid's Metamorphoses: An Introduction to the Basic Aspects.* Berkeley and Los Angeles: University of California Press, 1975.

Gantz, Timothy. *Early Greek Myth* (2 vols.). Baltimore: Johns Hopkins University Press, 1993.

A very helpful set of books on the mythological background of many of the stories told in the epic: this is one of the best first references for exploring a particular Ovidian myth.

Gieseking, K. *Die Rahmenererzählung in Ovids Metamorphosen.* Dissertation Tübingen, 1964.

Guthmüller, H.-B. *Beobachtungen zum Aufbau der Metamorphosen Ovids* Dissertation, Marburg, 1964.

Hardie, P. R. *The Epic Successors of Virgil: A Study in the Dynamics of Tradition.* Cambridge: Cambridge University Press, 1993.

———, ed. *The Cambridge Companion to Ovid.* Cambridge: Cambridge University Press, 2002.

———. *Ovid's Poetics of Illusion.* Cambridge University Press, 2002.

Haupt, M., and Ehwald, R., eds. *Metamorphosen.* (2 vols., revised by von Albrecht, M.), Dublin-Zurich: Weidmann, 1966.

A still quite valuable German commentary on the entire epic, which has retained its usefulness even after the appearance of Bömer et al.

Henderson, A. A. R. *Ovid: Metamorphoses III.* Bristol: Bristol Classical Press, 1979.

Herescu, N. I., ed. *Ovidiana: Recherches sur Ovide.* Paris: Wetteren, 1958.

Hershkowitz, D. *Madness in Epic: Reading Insanity from Homer to Statius*. Oxford, 1998.

Hill, D. E. *Ovid: Metamorphoses I-IV*. Warminster: Aris & Phillips Ltd., 1985.

The first of a set of four volumes that provide a complete text, translation, and commentary on the poem. The notes are quite brief and suffer from the series constraint of being coded to lemmata from the translation, not the Latin; the work sometimes displays an unnecessary dogmatism against rival views.

———. *Ovid: Metamorphoses V-VIII*. Warminster: Aris & Phillips Ltd., 1992 (with corrections, 1997).

———. *Ovid: Metamorphoses IX-XII*. Warminster: Aris & Phillips Ltd., 1999.

———. *Ovid: Metamorphoses XIII-XV and Indexes*. Warminster: Aris & Phillips Ltd., 2000.

Hinds, Stephen. *The Metamorphosis of Persephone: Ovid and the Self-Conscious Muse*. Cambridge: Cambridge University Press, 1987.

———. *Allusion and Intertext: Dynamics of Appropriation in Roman Poetry*. Cambridge: Cambridge University Press, 1998.

Hollis, A. S. *Ovid Metamorphoses VIII*. Oxford: Clarendon Press, 1970.

A very useful commentary, with excellent coverage of the Hellenistic antecedents of Ovid's poem.

Hopkinson, Neil, ed. *Ovid: Metamorphoses Book XIII*. Cambridge: Cambridge University Press, 2001.

The first of (at present) two Cambridge "green and yellows," with extensive introduction and solid notes.

Holzberg, N. *Ovid: Dichter und Werk*. Munich, 1997 (translated as *Ovid: The Poet and his Work*). Ithaca, NY: Cornell University Press, 2002.

The best general introduction to Ovid now available.

Keith, A. *The Play of Fictions: Studies in Ovid's Metamorphoses Book 2*. Ann Arbor: University of Michigan Press, 1992.

———. *Engendering Rome: Women in Latin Epic*. Cambridge: Cambridge University Press, 2000.

Kienast, D. *Augustus: Prinzeps und Monarch*. Darmstadt, 1982.

Klimmer, W. *Die Anordnung des Stoffes in den ersten vier Büchern der Metamorphosen*. Dissertation, Erlangen, 1932.

Knox, P. E. *Ovid's Metamorphoses and the Traditions of Augustan Poetry*. (Cambridge Philological Society Supplementary Volume 11.) Cambridge, 1986.

————, ed. *Oxford Readings in Ovid*. Oxford: Oxford University Press, 2006.

————, ed. *A Companion to Ovid*. Malden, MA: Wiley-Blackwell, 2009.

Kubusch, K. *Aurea saecula: Mythos und Geschichte. Untersuchungen eines Motivs in der antiken Literatur bis Ovid*. Frankfort-am-Main, 1986.

Lafaye, G. *Les Métamorphoses d'Ovide et leurs modèles grecs*. Paris, 1904 (reprinted Hildesheim, 1971).

————. *Ovide: Les Métamorphoses* (3 vols). Paris: Les Belles Lettres, 1925-1930.

The text is now out of date, but Lafaye's translation is excellent and often a helpful guide to explicating the Latin.

Lee, A. G. *Ovidi Metamorphoseon, Liber I*. Cambridge: Cambridge University Press, 1953.

An edition with text (no apparatus, but a critical appendix that discusses numerous textual problems fully), commentary, and a good introduction, which was conceived as a replacement for Dowdall for the use of schools, but which contains much that is useful for readers of all levels.

Little, D. A. *The Structural Character of Ovid's Metamorphoses*. Dissertation, Texas-Austin, 1972.

Ludwig, W. *Struktur und Einheit der Metamorphosen Ovids*. Berlin, 1965.

Mack, S. *Ovid*. New Haven, CT: Yale University Press, 1988.

A useful introduction for the general reader by a distinguished Ovidian.

Martindale, C., ed. *Ovid Renewed: Ovidian Influences on Literature and Art from the Middle Ages to the Renaissance*. Cambridge: Cambridge University Press, 1990.

————. *Redeeming the Text: Latin Poetry and the Hermeneutics of Reception*. Cambridge: Cambridge University Press, 1993.

Martini, E. *Einleitung zu Ovid*. Prague, 1933 (reprinted Darmstadt, 1970).

Melville, A. D., trans. *Ovid Metamorphoses*. Oxford: Oxford University Press, 1986.

The best English translation, with exemplary notes by E. J. Kenney. In general, Ovid has been better served than Virgil by English translators.

Miller, Frank Justus. *Ovid Metamorphoses* (2 vols). Cambridge, MA, and London: Harvard University Press, 1916 (3rd edition revised by G. P. Goold, 1977).

The convenient Loeb edition of the poem, revised well by George Goold (then series editor) in light of some recent scholarship, though preceding both Anderson and Tarrant.

Moore-Blunt, J. J. *A Commentary on Ovid, Metamorphoses II.* Vithoorn, 1977.

Munari, F. *Catalogue of the Mss. of Ovid's Metamorphoses.* (Bulletin of the Institute of Classical Studies, Supplement 4.) London, 1957.

————. *Ovid im Mittelalter.* Artemis, 1960.

Murphy, G. M. H. *Ovid Metamorphoses Book XI.* Oxford: Oxford University Press, 1972.

Bristol has reprinted this brief commentary, which is aimed at students more than advanced scholars, though with useful material even for the more experienced.

Myers, K. Sara. *Ovid's Causes: Cosmogony and Aetiology in the Metamorphoses.* Ann Arbor: University of Michigan Press, 1994.

————, ed. *Ovid: Metamorphoses Book XIV.* Cambridge: Cambridge University Press, 2009.

Otis, Brooks. *Ovid as an Epic Poet.* Cambridge: Cambridge University Press, 1966 (second edition, 1970).

Papathomopoulos, M. *Antoninus Liberalis: Les Métamorphoses.* Paris: Les Belles Lettres, 1968.

Proosdig, van, B. A. *P. Ovidii Nasonis Metamorphoseon Libri I-XV, Textus et Commentarius.* Leiden: Brill, 1951.

Rand, Edward Kennard. *Ovid and his Influence.* New York: Cooper Square Publishers, 1963.

Rhode, A. *De Ovidi arte epica.* Dissertation, Berlin, 1929.

Salzman-Mitchell, Patricia B. *A Web of Fantasies: Gaze, Image and Gender in Ovid's Metamorphoses.* Columbus: Ohio State University Press, 2005.

Schmidt, E. A. *Ovids poetische Menschenwelt: die Metamorphosen als Metaphor und Symphonie.* (Sitzungsberichte der Heidelberger Akademie der Wissenschaften, Philosiphisch-historische Klasse 2.) Heidelberg, 1991.

Schmitzer, U. *Zeitgeschichte in Ovids Metamorphosen.* (Beiträge zur Altertumskunde 4). Stuttgart, 1990.

Schnuchel, K. *Ovidius qua parte Metamorphoseon libri composuerit.* Dissertation, Greif-swald, 1922.

Segal, C. P. *Landscape in Ovid's Metamorphoses: A Study in the Transformations of a Literary Symbol.* (Hermes Einzelschriften 23.) Wiesbaden, 1969.

Siegel, J. F. *Child-Feast and Revenge: Ovid and the Myth of Procne, Philomela, and Tereus.* Dissertation, Rutgers, 1994.

Solodow, Joseph B. *The World of Ovid's Metamorphoses.* Chapel Hill and London: University of North Carolina Press, 1988.

     A marvelous study of the epic, with chapters on structure, narration, mythology, art, and Ovid's response to the *Aeneid.*

Spahlinger, L. *Ars latet arte sua: Untersuchungen zur Poetologie in den* Metamorphosen *Ovids.* Stuttgart, 1996.

Stitz, M. *Ovid und Vergils Aeneis.* Dissertation, Freiburg, 1962.

Syme, Sir Ronald. *History in Ovid.* Oxford: Clarendon Press, 1978.

Tarrant, Richard J., ed. *P. Ovidi Nasonis Metamorphoses.* Oxford, 2004.

Thiry-Stassin, Martine, and Tyssens, Madeline, eds. *Narcisse, conte ovidien français du XIIe siècle.* Paris: Les Belles Lettres, 1976.

Tissol, Garth. *Narrative Style in Ovid's Metamorphoses and the Influence of Callima-chus.* Berkeley and London: University of California Press, 1988.

―――. *The Face of Nature: Wit, Narrative, and Cosmic Origins in Ovid's Metamor-phoses.* Princeton, NJ: Princeton University Press, 1997.

Viarre, Simone. *L'image et la pensée dans les "Métamorphoses" d'Ovide.* Paris, 1964.

Vinge, Louise. *The Narcissus Theme in Western European Literature Up to the Early 19th Century.* Lund: Gleerup, 1968.

Wheeler, Stephen M. *A Discourse of Wonders: Audience and Performance in Ovid's Metamorphoses.* Philadelphia: University of Pennsylvania Press, 1999.

―――. *Narrative Dynamics in Ovid's Metamorphoses.* Tübingen: Narr, 2000.

White, P. *Promised Verse: Poets in the Society of Augustan Rome.* Cambridge, MA: Harvard University Press, 1993.

Wilkinson, L. P. *Ovid Recalled.* Cambridge: Cambridge University Press, 1955.

     Bristol has recently reprinted this basic guide to Ovid's vast *Nachleben.*

Wimmel, W. *Kallimachos in Rom.* Wiesbaden, 1960.

Ziolkowski, Theodore, ed. *Ovid and the Moderns.* Ithaca, NY: Cornell University Press, 2005.

Index

About the Author

Lee Fratantuono finished degrees in classics at Holy Cross, Boston College, and Fordham University, where he studied under Robert Carrubba and Seth Benardete. His dissertation was a thesis commentary on Book 11 of Virgil's *Aeneid* (published later as *A Commentary on Virgil, Aeneid XI* in the Collection Latomus, Brussels, 2009), and he specializes in Latin poetry, especially epic, lyric, and elegiac. He is associate professor of classics and William Francis Whitlock Professor of Latin at Ohio Wesleyan University, where he also serves as advisor to the Delta Upsilon chapter of the Delta Delta Delta sorority and the Equestrian Club. He has also taught classics at the University of Dallas. Besides Greek, Latin, and classics in translation, he has offered tutorials in Old French, Old Norse, and the films of Ingmar Bergman and Eric Rohmer. Outside of academia, he is a collector of and dealer in the postage stamps and coinage of Monaco and the former French colonies in Africa. He is the author of (*inter alia*) the 2007 Lexington Books monograph, *Madness Unchained: A Reading of Virgil's Aeneid*, some twenty articles on Latin poetry, and more than a hundred entries in the forthcoming Wiley-Blackwell *Virgil Encyclopedia*, edited by Richard Thomas and Jan Ziolkowski of Harvard University. His next major project is a commentary on Book 5 of the *Aeneid*, along with a volume on Lucan's *Pharsalia*. He is also working on collaborative projects with Stephen Maddux of the University of Dallas on Peter the Lombard and on Tacitus with Mary McHugh of Gustavus Adolphus College. He resides in Delaware, Ohio.